"Seventy-five years after his death in the ruins of Berlin, Adolf Hitler remains an enigma, in large part because we still rely largely uncritically on sources produced by Hitler and his entourage. Mikael Nilsson's magnificently researched and brilliantly argued *Hitler Redux: The Incredible History of Hitler's So-Called Table Talks* brings us much closer to understanding Hitler. By dissecting how Hitler's 'Table Talks' were compromised and revealing *The Testament of Adolf Hitler* to be a cover forgery, Nilsson manages to unmask Hitler."

— *Thomas Weber, University of Aberdeen, UK*

"Nilsson's book provides historical research at its best. Grounded in exhaustive study of primary sources he paints a gripping picture of how historiography for far too long followed misleading narratives. His fascinating findings provide lessons for historians and the wider public how to apply critical rationality and shrewd analysis of documents. It's a feast of enlightenment."

— *Magnus Brechtken, University of Munich, Germany*

"In a series of hard-hitting and well-researched articles, Mikael Nilsson has shown that Hitler's fabled 'Table-talk' and 'Political Testament' cannot be used as direct evidence of what he actually said. His work is essential reading for anyone wishing to understand the challenges which his biographers face."

— *Brendan Simms, University of Cambridge, UK*

"Mikael Nilsson provides an unsparing but long-overdue critique of one of the touchstone sources of Hitler scholarship. Future biographers will be well-served to read Nilsson's meticulously researched analysis before turning to Hitler's table talk conversations and monologues. Hitler Redux is fascinating, sobering, enlightening."

— *Timothy W. Ryback, Director of the Institute for Historical Justice and Reconciliation in Paris, France*

HITLER REDUX

After Hitler's death, several posthumous books were published which purported to be the verbatim words of the Nazi leader – two of the most important of these documents were *Hitler's Table Talk* and *The Testament of Adolf Hitler*. This ground-breaking book provides the first in-depth analysis and critical study of these works and their history, provenance, translation, reception, and usage.

Based on research in public and private archives in four countries, the book shows when, why, where, how, by, and for whom the table talks were written; how reliable the texts are; and how historians should approach and use them. It reveals the crucial role of the mysterious Swiss Nazi Francois Genoud, as well as some very poor judgement from several famous historians in giving these dubious sources more credibility than they deserved. The book sets the record straight regarding the nature of these volumes as historical sources – proving inter alia *The Testament* to be a clever forgery – and aims to establish a new consensus on their meaning and impact on historical research into Hitler and the Third Reich.

This path-breaking historical investigation will be of considerable interest to all researchers and historians of the Nazi era.

Mikael Nilsson is a currently unaffiliated Swedish historian who has written and published extensively on the Cold War and on Hitler's table talks. Previously he has been a researcher and teacher of history and military history at the Royal Institute of Technology, the Swedish National Defense College, Stockholm University, and Uppsala University. His research interests have mainly been related to Swedish–American military technological collaboration and US propaganda activities in Scandinavia during the Cold War, as well as Hitler, National Socialism, and Nazi Germany in general.

Routledge Studies in Fascism and the Far Right

Series editors

Nigel Copsey, Teesside University, UK and Graham Macklin, Center for Research on Extremism (C-REX), University of Oslo, Norway.

This new book series focuses upon fascist, far right and right-wing politics primarily within a historical context but also drawing on insights from other disciplinary perspectives. Its scope also includes radical-right populism, cultural manifestations of the far right and points of convergence and exchange with the mainstream and traditional right.

Titles include:

Hitler Redux
The Incredible History of Hitler's So-Called Table Talks
Mikael Nilsson

Researching the Far Right
Theory, Method and Practice
Edited by Stephen D. Ashe, Joel Busher, Graham Macklin and Aaron Winter

The Rise of the Dutch New Right
An Intellectual History of the Rightward Shift in Dutch Politics
Merijn Oudenampsen

Anti-fascism in a Global Perspective
Transnational Networks, Exile Communities and Radical Internationalism
Edited by Kasper Braskén, Nigel Copsey and David Featherstone

For more information about this series, please visit: www.routledge.com/Routledge-Studies-in-Fascism-and-the-Far-Right/book-series/FFR

HITLER REDUX

The Incredible History of Hitler's So-Called Table Talks

Mikael Nilsson

Routledge
Taylor & Francis Group

LONDON AND NEW YORK

First published 2021
by Routledge
2 Park Square, Milton Park, Abingdon, Oxon OX14 4RN

and by Routledge
52 Vanderbilt Avenue, New York, NY 10017

Routledge is an imprint of the Taylor & Francis Group, an informa business

British Library Cataloguing-in-Publication Data
A catalogue record for this book is available from the British Library

Library of Congress Cataloging-in-Publication Data
Names: Nilsson, Mikael, 1976- author.
Title: Hitler redux : the incredible history of Hitler's so-called table talks /
    Mikael Nilsson.
Description: London, UK ; New York, NY : Routledge/Taylor &
    Francis Group, 2020. | Series: Fascism and the far right | Includes
    bibliographical references and index.
Identifiers: LCCN 2020004885 (print) | LCCN 2020004886 (ebook) |
    ISBN 9780367353056 (hardback) | ISBN 9780367353063 (paperback) |
    ISBN 9780429330582 (ebook)
Subjects: LCSH: Hitler, Adolf, 1889-1945—Authorship.
Classification: LCC DD247.H5 N56 2020 (print) | LCC DD247.H5
    (ebook) | DDC 943.086092—dc23
LC record available at https://lccn.loc.gov/2020004885
LC ebook record available at https://lccn.loc.gov/2020004886

ISBN: 978-0-367-35305-6 (hbk)
ISBN: 978-0-367-35306-3 (pbk)
ISBN: 978-0-429-33058-2 (ebk)

Typeset in Bembo
by Apex CoVantage, LLC

CONTENTS

Preface   x
  The "official" history of the table talks x
  The various published editions xi
  Short biographies of the table talk authors xii
Acknowledgements   xvii
List of abbreviations   xx

1   The table talks: how were they made and how have
    historians used them?   1
    Introduction 1
    Troubling finds indeed 2
    The stenography myth 5
    Wolfram Pyta's analysis of the table talks 7
    Other scholars engage with the table talks 14
    *The case of Rainer Zitelmann: a source-critical debacle and notes
       on bad methodologies* 18
    More recent examples of uncritical usage of the table talks 23
    The table talks vs. Mein Kampf: *is there really a difference?* 26
    Conclusion 46

2   A scholarly scandal: the publication of Henry Picker's
    Hitlers Tischgespräche in 1951   58
    The Quick *affair* 75
    Ritter and his odd source-critical thinking 85
    Albert Speer on Tischgespräche: *a reliable witness?* 87

Critique against Tischgespräche *90*
Bormann's note attached to the Bormann–Vermerke *91*
More confusion regarding the table talks 93
The mystery of the Bormann note facsimile 95
The 1963 second edition of Picker's Tischgespräche *98*
Conclusion 103

3   François genoud and his table talk manuscript   112
Genoud battles Picker and the IfZ 112
*The first court case: who should own the copyright to the table
   talk notes? 125*
How did Picker get hold of Heim's notes? 131
The second court case: Picker sues Genoud 133
The myth of the unsuspecting Hitler 137
*When did Genoud actually acquire the table talk
   manuscript? 144*
Theodore Schmitz: Catholic priest and Stasi *agent 150*
*Rudolfo Siviero (the "007 of art") and Edilio Rusconi: the
   sources of Genoud's documents? 155*
Conclusion 160

4   The Heim proof pages: how a revolutionary discovery and
     its implications went unnoticed   172
*How Heim's proof pages were found: the CCP gallery assistant
   Joseph Ehrnsberger 172*
Mau goes to the United States 173
Editorial changes in Picker's text 176
Some examples of the differences 181
How many copies of the table talks were originally made? 190
Evaluating Heim's proof pages 194
Significant changes made in the proof pages 204
Odd similarities between Genoud and Picker 211
Conclusion 220

5   The publication of *Hitler's Table Talk* and the role of Hugh
     Trevor-Roper   230
Introduction 230
Meeting Genoud 232
Lost, and added, in translation 236
*Trevor-Roper's questionable handling of Genoud and his
   documents 258*

Trevor-Roper and the second edition of Table Talk
  from 1973 267
Conclusion 270

6 *The Testament of Adolf Hitler:* the last table talk or a
    clever forgery?   279
    Introduction 279
    The beginnings: a new text of questionable provenance 281
    Trevor-Roper re-discovers that The Testament *was translated
      from the French 293*
    Continuing doubts and the exposure of more lies 297
    *More indications of fraud: analysis from the internal
      evidence 301*
    The best textual evidence of forgery 311
    A German text is finally published 321
    An odd postscript 326
    Conclusions 327

7 Werner Jochmann and the *Monologe im Führerhauptquartier*
    edition: the publication of Genoud's "original" manuscript   340
    Introduction 340
    In the beginning was the word 340
    An incomplete source-critical evaluation 344
    An odd find in Jochmann's archive 352
    The table talks on trial again 355
    The aftermath 363
    The Enigma re-print of Table Talk: *a bizarre affair 364*
    Conclusions 377

8 Conclusions   384

Bibliography and sources   *389*
Appendix   *401*
Index   *410*

PREFACE

What kind of sources are Hitler's so-called table talks? When I first asked myself this seemingly simple question back in 2013, I certainly did not expect the answer to be as complicated as it turned out to be. I also did not expect that there was no real answer available in the existing literature. Surely, many historians had looked into this matter a long time ago, considering that the first edition of the table talks was published already in 1951. The reality was actually another thing. It turned out that there was in fact no thorough scholarly examination of these sources. The first peer-reviewed article on the subject was published as late as 2003.[1] My initial investigations grew into a three-year research project at Uppsala University, Sweden, financed by the Swedish National Bank Centennial Fund (Riksbankens Jubileumsfond, RJ) between 2015 and 2018. The result of this project, some of which has previously been published in different form in three articles in peer-reviewed journals, is what is presented in this book.[2]

This book asks, and answers, a series of questions. When, where, and by whom were the table talks produced? How did they get to be published, and what did the translation process look like? Perhaps most pertinently: *Why* were they written down? Who published them and under what circumstances? How did they survive the war? Are they reliable? Are they even genuine? This book will sort out these vexing problems and show why historians in fact cannot trust what is in them without having corroborated the information with independent sources. While much information about the history of the table talks was scant and uncertain, it became obvious that much was in fact available to the historian who bothered to actually check the facts.

The "official" history of the table talks

There are several versions of the table talks' history. According to one wide-spread version these sources record Hitler's unguarded statement in front of a small circle of confidants in various military Führer headquarters (FHQ) from the beginning of the invasion of the Soviet Union in the summer of 1941 until late 1944, faithfully jotted down by two stenographers,[3] Heinrich Heim and Henry Picker, on the orders of *Reichsleiter* Martin Bormann.[4] A few notes were made by Martin Bormann himself, as well as a Hans Müller (although Müller is almost always forgotten). Hitler is usually claimed to have been totally unaware of the fact that notes were being made, hence the reason that one can supposedly trust that he was speaking freely. Picker, however, claimed that Hitler *did* know that notes were being taken and that he even read parts of Picker's notes and gave his permission for Picker to publish them after the War.

The various published editions

Henry Picker was the first to publish his version called *Tischgespräche im Führerhauptquartier 1941–1942* (henceforth: *Tischgespräche*) in 1951. It contained his own notes as well as some of Heim's. *Tischgespräche* was thematically arranged by its editor, historian Gerhard Ritter, and published by Athenäum Verlag in cooperation with the *Institut für Zeitgeschichte* (IfZ) in Munich.[5] A second edition with the same title was published in 1963, this time chronologically arranged and edited by historian Percy Ernst Schramm.[6] In 1952 the Swiss Nazi sympathizer, banker, and financer of international terrorism François Genoud[7] published the first volume of *Libres propos sur la guerre et la paix* (henceforth: *Libres propos*); the second volume followed in 1954. This was based on another manuscript, the so-called *Bormann-Vermerke*, acquired by Genoud after the war. This consisted mostly of Heim's notes but also of notes by Picker, Bormann, and Müller.[8] In 1953 all of the notes in Genoud's possession were published in English as *Hitler's Table Talk 1941–1944* (henceforth: *Table Talk*) introduced by, and with the help of, British historian Hugh R. Trevor-Roper.[9] Genoud also published a single-volume edition in Italian in 1954.[10] Finally, a German edition with the title *Monologe im Führerhauptquartier 1941–1944* (henceforth: *Monologe*) and edited by historian Werner Jochmann was published in 1980. This edition does not contain Picker's notes due to a copyright conflict.[11]

Then we have *The Testament of Adolf Hitler*, a text that has already been questioned by critical scholars.[12] This text is said to be a continuation of the first table talk notes, supposedly taken down in Hitler's bunker in Berlin in February and April 1945. This text was also published by Genoud, first in French in 1959[13] and then in English and German in 1961 and 1981, respectively, all with the active collaboration of Trevor-Roper.

How easy it is to get the details surrounding all of these texts and editions mixed up is accidentally illustrated by John Lukacs in his book *The Hitler of History* where he writes:

> There are various editions of his "Table monologues." The first is by the stenographer Henry Picker (first ed. Bonn, 1951; English translation . . ., 1953). . . . More extensive are the records of Heinrich Heim in *Adolf Hitler: Monologe im Führerhauptquartier 1941–1944*, ed. Werner Jochmann,

Hamburg, 1980. . . . Finally, the so-called Bormann Notes (stenographer unknown), seemingly authentic (though that has been questioned) and very interesting because they focus on the last months of Hitler's life: The Dictator's Last Thoughts. They were carried by Bormann's wife first to Italy, then transmitted by an Italian to Hitler's respectful admirer, the Swiss François Genoud; published as *Libres propos sur la Guerre et la Paix, . . .*, 1952; and *The Testament of Adolf Hitler . . .*, 1959.[14]

There are many inaccuracies in this short paragraph. First, Picker was not a stenographer; in fact, he never ever stated that he was. Second, the English translation is not a translation of Picker's book, but purportedly of the manuscript that Genoud had, although in reality it is a translation of Genoud's highly corrupted French edition. Third, the "Bormann Notes" that Lukacs refers to consist not only of Heim's notes, and who is hence not unknown, but also of Picker's, as well as some by Bormann and Müller. The authors of that manuscript are thus not at all unknown. They are the same as for the one edited by Jochmann, which Lukacs falsely ascribes to only Heim. Fourth, the story about Italy has to do with the manuscript used by Jochmann and not the manuscript that became *The Testament of Adolf Hitler*. Fifth, it is only *The Testament of Adolf Hitler* that purportedly is from the last months of Hitler's life. Sixth, it is only the authenticity of that text that has been questioned. A seventh point is that Genoud's *Libres propos* is not from the same manuscript as *The Testament of Adolf Hitler*, and the story behind how Genoud got the latter text is completely different and does not include the route via Italy at all. The eighth mistake in this short paragraph, although it is just a minor detail, is that *The Testament of Adolf Hitler* was published in 1961. One could even add a ninth point, namely that *Libres propos* was published in two volumes in 1952 and 1954.

Genoud's manuscript is lost and so is Picker's original manuscript. However, at *Bundesarchiv* in Koblenz I found a typed manuscript that was the basis for the second edition of *Tischgespräche*. The closest we get to Heim's original notes are about 40 proof pages dated January 1942 that were initially stored at the Library of Congress in Washington, D.C. (since then returned to *Bundesarchiv* in Berlin, Germany; see chapter 4).[15]

Short biographies of the table talk authors

Heinrich Heim (15 June 1900–26 June 1988) was a lawyer who became a member of the NSDAP in 1920 after meeting Hitler in August. In 1923 he left the party but re-joined the NSDAP again in 1931. He did not re-join the party in 1925 because he thought he could be more useful to the NSDAP if he was not a visible member. He was too young to serve in First World War, but he was a member of the infamous *Freikorps Epp* from 1919 to 1923, one of the most brutal of the "white" paramilitary formations that committed the absolute majority of the illegal executions of suspected communists after the crushing of the Soviet republic (*Räterrepublik*) in Munich in May 1919. In August 1933 he started working for Rudolf Heß at the

NSDAP headquarters (HQ) in Munich. Heim had known Heß since 1920, when they had met at the university in Munich. In 1936 he became a member of the civilian branch of the SS (*Allgemeine SS*), and in 1943 he was granted the honorary rank of SS *Standartenführer*. He was also a holder of the honorary SS *Totenkopfring*. From 1940 to mid-1941 Heim was Heß's adjutant, and after Heß's flight to England on 10 May 1941 he became adjutant to the new Head of the Party Chancellery, *Reichsleiter* Martin Bormann. Heim was a committed Nazi and a convinced anti-Semite. During 1943–1945 Heim worked with legal issues related to the planned Nazi reorganization of Europe at the Department of International Law (*Staatsrechtlichen Abteilung*) at the party HQ. The Americans finally arrested him in Munich on 11 May 1945.[16] Thanks to witnesses who insisted on his wonderful character and that Heim had not really been a convinced Nazi, he managed to avoid a prison sentence.[17]

Henry Picker (6 February 1912–2 May 1988) was also a lawyer, with a *doctor juris* degree. It is certainly very ironic that Bormann should choose two lawyers as his adjutants, considering how much Hitler despised lawyers. Picker's father (1876–1952) was a merchant and a senator in the city of Wilhelmshaven and was an early member of the NSDAP. In this way he had rather good connections to Hitler, and the latter is even reported to have stayed at Picker's father's house when visiting Wilhemshaven. While studying law at Marburg (he also studied at universities in Berlin and Kiel) Picker was a member of the *Corps Teutonia*, and he joined the NSDAP on 1 April 1930 when he was just 18 years old. Picker's dissertation had the ambition to make a considerable contribution to the re-birth of a Germanic-Aryan concept of law.[18]

In the spring of 1940, he began working at the party HQ in Munich, and in March 1942 Picker replaced Heim at the FHQ. In August he returned to the Nazi state bureaucracy again before he, apparently disappointed with the NSDAP, served in the *Wehrmacht* from mid-1943 until the end of the war (although it is uncertain if ever saw any action at the front – no such evidence exists). In a striking similarity to what was said about Heim after the war, Picker was claimed to have helped political dissidents, uttered critical statements about the regime, and so on.[19]

Picker later stated that the notes he had taken with him from the FHQ had been buried by his wife in a compost heap at her father's house. There they supposedly lay until August 1946. Even though Picker did not have the typical National Socialist (NS) career, he has been described as being the "prototype of the NS elite: young, dynamic, intelligent, and dedicated." He also displayed a typical attitude during the denazification trial against him. Not only did he characterize his arrest as "persecution", but he also compared his internment at the *Esterwegen* camp from 28 May 1945 to being put into a concentration camp (KZ). He never served any prison time. He never showed any signs of remorse or of having realized that he had in fact contributed to the survival of the criminal NS regime, and he remained a convinced supporter of Hitler and an anti-Semite after the war. While the editions of *Tischgespräche* from 1951 and 1963 had been introduced by a critical apparatus by acclaimed historians, Picker opted for removing this introduction from 1976 onwards. He would later tell the readers of *Tischgespräche* that the Jews had declared war on Germany in September 1939, that the Holocaust had been performed mostly by foreign (Austrian and Eastern European) anti-Semites, and so on. Not least, Picker used to tell people that "Anyone who, like me, knew the Führer personally can consider themselves lucky."[20]

Hans Müller was a lawyer born in 1906 who had been a member of the SA since November 1933 and became a member of the NSDAP on 1 May 1937. In late July 1940 Müller was transferred to the office of the *Riechskommissar* for the occupied territory of the Netherlands until he was called back to Munich in the spring of 1941 to work at the legal department of the NSDAP HQ. Müller denied having been Bormann's assistant in his statement to the court after the war, claiming it was a case of mistaken identity. The court had evidence to prove otherwise, however, including an early interrogation with Müller where he confessed to having worked for Bormann. But since several witnesses testified (though not under oath) on his behalf that he had been an unpolitical person who always had put his sense of justice over politics, he, too, avoided prison time.[21]

Notes

1 Carrier, Richard, "Hitler's Table Talk: Troubling Finds" in *German Studies Review*, Vol. 26, No. 3 (October 2003), pp. 561–576.
2 Nilsson, Mikael, "Hugh Trevor-Roper and the English Editions of *Hitler's Table Talk* and *Testament*" in *Journal of Contemporary History*, Vol. 51, No. 4 (2016), pp. 788–812; "Constructing a Pseudo-Hitler? The Question of the Authenticity of *Hitlers politisches Testament*" in *European Review of History – Revue Européenne d'historie*, published online 15 November 2018; "Hitler redivivus: '*Hitlers Tischgespräche* und *Monologe im Führerhauptquartier*' – eine kritische Untersuchung" in *Vierteljahrshefte für Zeitgeschichte*, No. 67 (January 2019), pp. 105–145.
3 The myth has been so successfully established that even the description of the content in Heim's papers at the Institut für Zeitgeschichte (IfZ) in Munich states that Heim was "stenographer of Adolf Hitler's so-called table talks." See: Vol. 1; "Archive description", p. 1; IfZ, Munich; ED 416 (Heinrich Heim).
4 Martin Bormann (17 June 1900–2 May 1945) joined a paramilitary *Freikorps* in 1922, and on 17 March 1924 he was sentenced to one year in prison as an accomplice to Rudolf Höß, the later Auschwitz commander, in the murder of schoolteacher Walther Kadow in May 1923. He joined the NSDAP 2 May 1927. In July 1933 he was transferred and became chief of staff at the office of the Deputy Führer, Rudolf Heß. On 10 October the same year Hitler promoted Bormann to *Reichsleiter*, the highest party rank within the NSDAP. He joined the SS in 1937. After Heß's flight to England on 10 May 1941 Bormann took over Heß's duties as dead of the *Parteikanzlei* (the position of Deputy Führer, and the office of *Stellvertreter der Führer*, was abolished at this time so this title was never tranferred to Bormann). For Hitler's decisions, see: Domarus, Max (ed.), *Hitler. Reden und Proklamationen 1932–1945. Kommentiert von einem deutschen Zeitgenossen* (Band 1–4) (henceforth: *HRP*) Band II/4 (München: Süddeutscher Verlag, 1965), pp. 1716–1717, 1721–1722. On 8 May 1943 Bormann reached the highest rung of his career when he became secretary to the Führer.
5 *Hitlers Tischgespräche im Führerhauptquartier 1941–1942. Im Auftrage des Deutschen Instituts für Zeitgeschichte der nationalsozialistischen Zeit geordnet, eingeleitet und veröffentlicht von Gerhard Ritter, Professor der Geschichte a. d. Universität Freiburg* (Bonn: Athenäum-Verlag, 1951).

6 *Hitlers Tischgespräche im Führerhauptquartier 1941–1942. Neu herausgegeben von Percy Ernst Schramm in Zusammenarbeit mit Andreas Hillgruber und Martin Vogt* (Stuttgart: Seewald Verlag, 1963). Several editions have been published since then.

7 For more on Genoud, see: Péan, Pierre, *L'extrémiste: François Genoud de Hitler à Carlos* (Paris: Fayard, 1996); Laske, Karl, *Ein Leben zwischen Hitler und Carlos: François Genoud* (Zürich: Limmat, 1996); Winkler, Willi, *Der Schattenmann. Von Goebbels zu Carlos: Das gewissenlose Leben des François Genoud* (Berlin: Rowohlt, 2011).

8 *Libres propos sur la Guerre et la Paix. Recueillis sur l'ordre de Martin Bormann. Préface de Robert d'Harcourt de l'Academie française. Version française de François Genoud*, Vol. I (Paris: Flammarion, 1952); *Libres propos sur la Guerre et la Paix. Recueillis sur l'ordre de Martin Bormann. Préface de Robert d'Harcourt de l'Academie française. Version française de François Genoud*, Vol. II (Paris: Flammarion, 1954).

9 *Hitler's Table Talk 1941–1944. With an Introductory Essay on The Mind of Adolf Hitler by H. R. Trevor-Roper* (London: Weidenfeld and Nicolson, 1953) An American edition was published the same year under the title: *Hitler's Secret Conversations 1941–1944. With an Introductory Essay on The Mind of Adolf Hitler by H. R. Trevor – Roper* (New York: Farrar, Straus and Young, 1953). The American edition was printed with a somewhat smaller typeface grade and was thus much shorter than the English edition; 597 pages compared to 746. Despite this the American edition is actually a bit thicker than its English counterpart due to the fact that it was printed on thicker paper.

10 *Conversazioni segreti. Ordinate e annotate da Martin Bormann durante il periode più dramatico della Seconda Guerra Mondiale (5 luglio 1941–30 novembre 1944).*

11 *Monologe im Führerhauptquartier 1941–1944. Die Aufzeichnungen Heinrich Heims herausgegeben von Werner Jochmann* (Hamburg: Albrecht Knaus Verlag, 1980).

12 See e.g. Kershaw, Ian, *Hitler 1936–45: Nemesis* (London: Allen Lane, 2000), pp. 1024–1025.

13 *Le testament politique de Hitler. Notes receuillies par Martin Bormann. Commentaires de André François-Poncet; version française et présentation de François Genoud* (Paris: Fayard, 1959); *The Testament of Adolf Hitler: The Hitler – Bormann Documents, February – April 1945.* Edited by François Genoud; with an Introduction by Hugh R. Trevor-Roper; Translated from the German by R. H. Stevens (London: Cassell, 1961); *Hitlers politisches Testament. Die Bormann Diktate vom Februar und April 1945. Mit einem Essay von Hugh R. Trevor-Roper und einem Nachwort von André François-Poncet* (Hamburg: Albrecht Knaus Verlag, 1981).

14 Lukacs, John, *The Hitler of History* (New York: Vintage Books, 1997), pp. 47–48.

15 "Hitlers Tischgespräche im Führerhauptquartier"; BABL; Partei-Kanzlei der NSDAP; NS6/819.

16 Handwritten statement by Heim, 19 February 1947; Questionnaire "Camp 74, Ausweiskarte Nr. 12796", 9 February 1946, p. 1; questionnaire "Headquarters 1st INF DIV Civilian Interment Camp NO 22", 13 June 1947, p. 1; notes "CI Detachment Civilian Interment Enclosure No. 47 APO 154 U.S. Army" for Heinrich Heim (No. 12796), 2 November 1946; questionnaire for the "Ministerium für politische Befreiung Würtemberg-Baden", 16 April 1947, p. 2; "Auskunftserteilung an den Ausschuss der politischen Parteien München", 28 August 1947; see also undated questionnaire signed by Heim; "Erklärung in eigener Sache für die Spruchkammer X in München" signed by Heim, 19 November 1948, p. 1; Staatsarchiv München (henceforth: StAM); SpkA K 659: Heim, Heinrich. Copies of the StAM documents have been provided to me by Professor Wolfram Pyta in Stuttgart, and I extend my deep gratitude to him for having shared his personal archival material with me. See also: Letter from Heim to Karen Kuykendall, 25 October 1975, p. 9; University of Arizona Library, Special Collections (henceforth: UALSC); Papers of Karen Kuykendall, MS 243 (henceforth: PKK MS 243); Series II: Interviews and Correspondence, 1971–1978 (Series II); Box 2, Folder 5; Ullrich, Volker, *Adolf Hitler. Biographie. Die Jahre des Aufstiegs* (Frankfurt am Main, 2013), pp. 123, 867. For the information about *Freikorps Epp*, see: Weber, Thomas, *Wie Adolf Hitler zum Nazi wurde. Vom unpolitischen Soldaten zum Autor von "Mein Kampf"* (Berlin: Propyläen, 2016), p. 315.

17 Sentence from the *Berufskammer* in Munich, 14 July 1949, p. 2; StAM; SpkA K 659: Heim, Heinrich.

18 Delblanco, Werner, "'Wer wie ich den Führer persönlich kennt, kann das Glück ermessen. . .' Ein biographischer Abriss und ein Skandalon" in Bernd Kasten, Matthias Manke and Johann Peter Wurm (eds.), *Leder ist Brot. Beiträge zur norddeutschen Landes- und Archivgeschichte. Festschrift für Andreas Röpcke* (Schwerin: Thomas Helms Verlag, 2011), pp. 296–297. A copy of this chapter was provided to me by Professor Wolfram Pyta in Stuttgart, and I extend my deep gratitude to him for having shared his personal archival material with me.

19 Ibid., pp. 297–299, 302.

20 Ibid., pp. 299–306.

21 Letter from Lauerbach to Helm, 29 August 1941; "Ausführliches Gesamturteil", 16 September 1941; Letter from Nadler to Müller, 6 October 1941; Bundesarchiv, Lichterfelde-Berlin (henceforth: BABL); BD6/PK, Müller, Hans. See also: Copy of an interrogation with Müller, 8 October 1947, p. 3; Declaration for the public prosecutor in Munich, 16 November 1948; "Ermittlung über: MUELLER, Hans" from the Spruchkammer in Munich, undated 1948; "Aussagen den Betroffenen" in Protocol from Munich Spruchkammer 16 March 1949, pp. 1–6; "Eidesstattliche Erklärung" by Friedrich Schmidt, 22 November 1948, pp. 1–2; "Eidesstattliche Erklärung" by Franz Antishofer, 22 July 1948; "Eidesstattliche Erklärung" by Friedrich Wimmer, 5 June 1947; Testimony by Ilona Arnold, 28 February 1949, pp. 3–4; StAM; SpkA K 1207: Müller, Hans. See also: Letter from Müller to Dr. Brandt, 24 February 1945; Nationalsozialismus, Holocaust, Widerstand und Exil 1933–1945. Online-Datenbank. De Gruyter. 14.11.2011. Dokument-ID: APK-008305. Originally published in: *Akten der Partei-Kanzlei der NSDAP. Rekonstruktion eines verlorengegangenen Bestandes, Band I. Hrsg. vom Institut für Zeitgeschichte. Bearb. von Helmut Heiber unter Mitw. von Hildegard von Kotze, Gerhard Weiher, Ingo Arndt und Carla Mojto [u.a.]* (Oldenburg: K.G. Saur, 1983), p. 1035. I want to thank Professor Wolfram Pyta for having shared a copy of this document with me.

ACKNOWLEDGEMENTS

This book would not have been possible to write were it not for the extremely kind and helpful assistance of so many people and institutions. Writing a book is in many ways a very lonely business, and yet one can never claim sole credit for anything that one accomplishes in life. I will obviously not be able to mention all of these people by name, since I frankly do not know the name of, for example, every archivist who has helped me find documents. Nonetheless, I have done my best to remember and mention everybody who was instrumental for this book to be written. Needless to say, all eventual mistakes remain my own.

One of the most important people in this respect is Professor Wolfram Pyta who not only took time to meet with me to discuss the table talks but who (via his kind secretary) very generously also gave me copies of thousands of pages of documents that he had found in various archives. Without your amazing help I could not have started my research project, much less finish it, with anything close to the sense of completeness that I now have. The acting director of the Institut für Zeitgeschichte (IfZ) in Munich, Magnus Brechtken, has assisted me in so many ways and has patiently and kindly answered all my many emails. You took the time to meet an unknown historian from Sweden, and you always treated me with the utmost respect. Without the expert evaluation of my initial research proposal to Riksbankens Jubileumsfond (RJ) by Professor Thomas Weber, this book would never have been written. Thank you, Thomas, for believing in my idea and for assisting me so kindly over the years. I also want to thank the anonymous reviewer who also recommended that I should get funding for the project, as well as the people at RJ that decided to award me the research grant. I also want to extend my deepest gratitude to historian Richard Carrier, who gave the impetus to this project by his initial investigations into the table talks and who gave me access to email correspondence and copies of documents.

My dear friend and former thesis advisor, Niklas Stenlås at Uppsala University, has been an enormous support during this research project. You have been so patient and kind and listened to me talk for hours on end about Hitler's table talks, and you have always asked the right kind of critical questions whenever I have presented a hypothetical explanation for the evidence. Without your encouragement this book would not be a reality. Furthermore, I want to thank the following people: Margaret Hunt (for your reading of and comments on parts of this manuscript), Marco Wyss (who has listened to all my ramblings about the table talks so patiently and always come with helpful advice), Lars M. Andersson (for all the great conversations and support), Iva Lucic (who kindly assisted with translation issues and friendly advice), Timothy Ryback (who answered my questions regarding Hitler's private library), the late Pierre Péan (who gave me access to a large part of François Genoud's private correspondence), Willi Winkler (for replying to my email queries), Professor Ursula Büttner (for giving me access to Werner Jochmann's papers), Professor Richard Steigmann-Gall, Research Manager Britta Lövgren at RJ (for all the kind assistance), Roger Griffin, and Mirella Kraska. A general thanks also goes to Thomas Schütte, Tim Blanning, Cathryn Steele, Eva Stensköld, the late Jürgen Zarusky, Deuker Bendix, Sir Ian Kershaw, David Olusoga, Richard Pearson, Christopher Read, Despina Stratigakos, Deborah Lipstadt, Don Guttenplan, Niclas Vent, Gerhard L. Weinberg, Othmar Plöckinger, Tobias Svanelid, Louis E. Schmier, Eberhard Jäckel, Gina Thomas, the late Robert Miller at Enigma Books, Jil Sörensen at *Der Spiegel*, Claudia Vidoni at Knaus-Verlag, David Irving, Klaus Lankheit, Klaus von Schirach, and Anna Lindblom at Editions-Fayard.

My warmest thanks also goes out to the curator of Museo Casa Rodolfo Siviero in Florence, Attilio Tori; archivist Sven Schneidereit at the *Bundesarchiv* Berlin-Lichterfelde; archivist Virginia Lewick at the Franklin D. Roosevelt Presidential Library in New York; the manuscript reference librarian at the Manuscript Division at the Library of Congress, Patrick Kerwin; the archivists at Hugh Trevor-Roper's archive at Christ Church College, Oxford University, Blair Worden, Janet McMullin, and Judith Curthoys; archivist Gotthard Klein at *Dioezesanarchiv* in Berlin; archivist Kurt G. F. Helfrich at the Gallery Archives at the National Gallery of Art in Washington, D.C.; Wolfgang Henninger at *Niedersächsisches Landesarchiv* in Oldenburg; archivist Roland Böhlen at the Swiss Red Cross in Berne, Switzerland; Werner Jochmann's daughter Renate Miron; and Genoud's lawyer Cordula Schacht. I also want to thank all the other archivists at *Bundesarchiv* in Koblenz and Berlin-Lichterfelde at the IfZ in Munich who have assisted me in some way along the way but whom I do not know the name of. The librarians at Uppsala University and the Royal Swedish National Library (Kungliga biblioteket) in Stockholm deserve to be mentioned here because they have always been very helpful with the many books I borrowed and ordered. All the administrators and colleagues at the Department of History at Uppsala University also deserve to be mentioned. Moreover, I want to thank my Routledge editor, Craig Fowlie, who consistently believed in this book, as well as editorial assistant Jessica Holmes. I also want to give a special "thank you" to Cambridge Professor Brendan Simms for trusting me to read through (and comment on) the manuscript for his *Hitler: Only the World Was Enough* and who incorporated my research findings in his book.

I owe so much gratitude to my family and friends who have also supported me during my research for this book; you all know who you are!

Stockholm, 16 January 2020

ABBREVIATIONS

BBC	British Broadcasting Corporation
BRD/FRG	Bundesrepublik Deutschland/Federal Republic of Germany (West Germany)
BVP	Bayerische Volkspartei – the Bavarian People's Party
CEO	Chief Executive Officer
CCP	Central Collecting Point – the US collection point for stolen art in Munich
DAP	Deutsche Arbeiterpartei – German Workers' Party (the NSDAP's original name)
DDR/GDR	Deutsche Demokratische Republik/German Democratic Republic (East Germany)
DM	Deutschmarks – the currency in West Germany
FHQ	Führer Headquarters – Hitler's wartime headquarters
HICOG	High Commissioner for Germany – the head of the American occupation authorities
HQ	Headquarters
HRP	Hitler. Reden und Proklamationen 1932–1945 – Hitler's speeches and proclamations edited by Max Domarus
IfZ	Institut für Zeitgeschichte – Institute for Contemporary History in Munich
LoC	Library of Congress in Washington, D.C.
MfS	Ministerium für Staatssicherheit (Stasi) – the East German security police
MS	Manuscript
NS	NS National Socialism/National Socialist
NSDAP	Nationalsozialistische Deutsche Arbeiterpartei – German National Socialist Workers' Party

OKH	Oberkommando des Heeres
OKW	Oberkommando der Wehrmacht
POW	Prisoner of War
RAF	Rote Armeefraktion – Red Army Faction – extreme-Left terror group in West Germany
RM	Reichsmark – the currency of Nazi Germany
RSA	Hitler. Reden, Schriften, Anordnungen 1924–1933 – Hitler's speeches and writings collected and published by the IfZ
SA	Hitler. Sämtliche Aufzeichnungen 1905–1924 – Hitler's collected writings and speeches edited by Eberhard Jäckel
SA	Sturmabteilung – the Nazi brown shirt storm troopers
SS	Schutzstaffeln – Hitler's personal security force
TBJG	Tagebücher Joseph Goebbels – Goebbels' diaries

1

THE TABLE TALKS

How were they made and how have historians used them?

Introduction

It would not be an exaggeration to say that thus far most historians cite the table talks without including any source-critical reflections. It is the purpose of this book to show why we need to have a different attitude towards these sources and that they can no longer be treated as a primary source containing Hitler's own formulations. This is not a minor problem or one that we can disregard. The reason is that quotes do an important thing to our mind; in fact, it changes our whole attitude towards the sentence that we are reading. When reading words inside quotation marks, our brains automatically assume that what we are reading is a faithful representation of the words uttered (or written). Indeed, it is even difficult to remain critical even *if* the author includes a cautionary note in connection with the quote. And even if professional historians *may* be able to keep a clear head through all of that, our books are often read by the interested lay public who are not, in most cases, trained by years of socialization and immersion in the trade to keep the source-critical aspects in their mind at all times. The quotes then take on a life of their own.

Some historians have already noticed that the English translation is flawed. The poor English translation was commented on already in 1953 in a review of *Table Talk* in *International Affairs* where it was said that it was "not impeccably translated". The reviewer must obviously have compared it to Picker's *Tischgespräche*.[1] Nonetheless, e.g. Richard J. Evans uses *Table Talk* in his Third Reich trilogy even though he himself had criticized David Irving for relying on the English translation of these notes once the German "original" (i.e. *Monologe*) had become available in 1980, citing Irving's own admission that the German text was "completely different from the published English translation." Evans's conclusion was that "obviously the passages that he had used from the 1953 translation now had to be checked against the German original and amended if necessary."[2] As we shall see, this completely ignores the main issue regarding these sources, namely that the German versions simply cannot be trusted to purvey Hitler's words unfiltered.

It is therefore hard to understand why Evans would quote from the English translation himself, when he cites other German titles frequently in his books, and uncritically use *Table Talk* at one point to direct the reader to Hitler's thoughts regarding Julius Streicher and the newspaper *Der Stürmer* and frequently when it comes to describing Hitler's aims with the war in the East.[3] In *The Third Reich at War* he even includes a short history of the table monologues based on Hugh Trevor-Roper's introductory essay in the *Table Talk*. He states that Hitler agreed to have a notetaker present, i.e. Heim, who then is supposed to have dictated the full text, on the basis of these notes, to a stenographer after which they were handed to Martin Bormann, who then corrected them and filed them. Evans also writes that these notes were intended for publication after the war.[4] The latter is perhaps a misinterpretation of Trevor-Roper writing that Bormann wanted the Führer's words preserved for the future because Trevor-Roper does not say that the notes were to be published later on.[5] Trevor-Roper based his story exclusively on Genoud, of course, and almost all of it contradicts Heim's own statements. Moreover, Trevor-Roper does not mention the name of the fourth notetaker, i.e. Hans Müller. Indeed, it is as if he has no idea who that was even though it ought to have been well known to Genoud, since he had the original notes.

Interestingly, Evans includes *Monologe* in the bibliography in *The Third Reich at War* but I have been unable to find an actual reference to this book in the text. All quotes and references instead seem to be from the highly flawed English translation (for more about this, see Chapter 5). There is one exception though. In *The Third Reich in Power* Evans cites Picker's *Tischgespräche* regarding Hitler's views on Alfred Rosenberg's book *Der Mythos des 20. Jahrhunderts*. However, he cites Hitler as speaking in the first person, which is not how Picker has it in his book (where he talks about Hitler's statements in the third person).[6] Evans never uses the Koeppen notes.

Troubling finds indeed

It was not until very recently that a serious effort at investigating the various editions and translations in a critical manner was published. In an article from 2003 in *German Studies Review* the American historian Richard C. Carrier compared the English, French, and German editions and concluded that historians have a lot of source-critical work to do before we can use either of the German versions as an authoritative source to Hitler's utterances.[7] The result of Carrier's comparison of the various editions was anything but consoling. He showed that Genoud had added utterances on a number of occasions which often made Hitler seem more critical of Christianity than in the German versions, and he also proved that Trevor-Roper's English version was at least partly translated from Genoud's French version.[8] As we saw in the introduction, Genoud's *Libres propos* was divided into two volumes published in 1952 and 1954, respectively. Both of these volumes are exceedingly rare, but the second one is even harder to find than the first. When Carrier did his comparative investigation, he only had access to the first volume (he actually did not even know about the second one), which meant that he could not know that all of *Table Talk* had been translated from the French. I have discovered that this odd translation practice was stipulated in the contract with the publisher of *Table Talk* Weidenfeld & Nicolson (see Chapter 5).

Many years later, Trevor-Roper would claim that he actually *did* know that his book was translated from the French and not from the German original all along. According to him, the publisher had hired the translator (Trevor-Roper uses the singular form as if he was not aware that there were two translators) without him knowing about it, and he supposedly discovered that the translation was made from the French because of a word that appeared to say that Hitler was "confused" about something, and Hitler was never confused about anything, Trevor-Roper claimed. Then, he says, he checked the translation against the German original that "was a little more available" at that time (it is not said *when* this happened so we do not know if Trevor-Roper was referring to *Tischgespräche* or *Monologe* here) and discovered the whole thing. The translator was only allowed to use the French version, he said.[9] Trevor-Roper's own correspondence shows that this later version of events is not correct (see Chapter 5).

On the Internet you can find loads of websites that quote from the English version of *Table Talk* when referencing Hitler's hatred towards the Catholic Church and towards established Christianity, but even bona fide scholars cite it. For example, Jonathan Glover quotes it in his book *Humanity: A Moral History of the Twentieth Century*, where he quotes Hitler as saying:

> I shall never come to terms with the Christian lie. . . . Our epoch will certainly see the end of the disease of Christianity. It will last another hundred years, two hundred years perhaps. My regret will have been that I couldn't, like whoever the prophet was, behold the promised land from afar.[10]

This is from a note in *Table Talk* dated 27 February 1942. The problem with it is that it has been tampered with by Genoud and contains phrases that are not in the German texts. Changes were not only made to the French text, however. Picker made many changes in his text too. For example, *Tischgespräche* from 1951 does not contain the first phrase in the example taken from Glover earlier, i.e. "Personally, I could never accept such a lie" (*Ich persönlich werde mich einer solchen Lüge niemals fügen*), but it has been inserted back into the text in the 1963 edition (see Chapter 2).[11] Note that the word "Christian" is not in the German text; that, too, was inserted by Genoud. The note from 27 February 1942 is problematic also in other ways:

> *I admit that one cannot impose one's will by force*, but I have a horror of people who enjoy inflicting sufferings on others' bodies and tyranny upon others'

> souls. Our epoch will certainly see the end of the disease of Christianity. It will last another hundred years, two hundred years perhaps. My regret will have been that I couldn't, like whoever the prophet was, behold the promised land from afar.[12] [Italics added.]

This agrees exactly with the French translation, except for a mistranslation of the italicized phrase (which does not make sense), a mistake that could only have been made by someone translating a French text. The Italian edition from 1954 follows the French too, which proves that this version was also translated from the French.[13] In French this italicized phrase reads as follows: "J'admets qu'on *ne* puisse s'imposer *que* par la force."[14] But the translators of *Table Talk* misunderstood the French grammar in the phrase "ne . . . que", which does *not* mean "not" (as the word "ne" alone would do), but instead "only" or in this case "except by". The meaning of the sentences is thus the exact opposite of that which *Table Talk* has rendered it as, namely that it is not possible to impose one's will on someone else *except by* force.[15] This makes perfect sense. Any analysis of Hitler's mind based on the English translation will in this case be entirely mistaken. Moreover, the phrase calling Christianity a disease is not present in the German versions. It is an interpolation by Genoud.[16] The German text also contains a sentence (italicized) that is not included in either *Libres propos* or *Table Talk*:

> I have never found any pleasure in tormenting others, even though I know that it is not possible to endure in the world without violence. *Only he who fights the fiercest for his life will be granted life. The law of life states: Defend yourself!* The time in which we are living is the beginning of the end of this thing. It can go on for yet 100 or 200 years. I am saddened that I, like Moses, can only see the Promised Land from a distance.[17] [Italics added.]

Without the preceding context, it is impossible to understand that Hitler is talking about Christianity here, and it is as if Genoud decided to clarify that to the reader. The sentence after the italicized one is also quite different in all other translations. Note that in the German version Hitler is said to have mentioned Moses by name, while in the English (and Italian, since they both follow the French) this has been changed into "whoever the prophet was." Even more importantly, the meaning of the sentence has been changed completely. The English version says that Hitler was sorry he "couldn't" view the Promised Land from afar, while the German states that he was sorry he "can only" view it from afar. The difference may be subtle but yet significant. The whole point, it seems, is to play down Hitler's references to the Hebrew Bible and his use of Jewish and Christian metaphors.

Ground-breaking though his investigation was (or perhaps because of it), Carrier did get a few things wrong in his article. Carrier's evaluation of the two German texts was unambiguous; Picker's *Tischgespräche* was the one that best agreed with the original text followed by Jochmann's *Monologe*. The reason, Carrier thought, was that Picker's version was published closer to the events that it describes, that

Picker was a witness to the monologues, and that he himself wrote the steno-graphic originals. From a source-critical point of view, those were seemingly justified conclusions. That, together with Picker's statement that Hitler read some of his notes, sealed the deal for Carrier. But Carrier should have been more critical of his sources here. Picker indeed states in his preface to *Tischgespräche* in 1951 that Hitler approved several of his notes as corresponding with what he had said.[18] But we cannot simply trust Picker on this; much of what he says can be shown to be untrue. Picker did not write stenography, and he actually made changes to the text before publication in 1951 (hence, it did not matter that it was published closer to the events). Moreover, Hitler never read and approved any of his notes (see Chapter 2). Nonetheless, Carrier deserves credit and praise for having initiated the critical dissection of the table talks.

The stenography myth

If the table talk notes were not a stenographic record of Hitler's statements, how then did this idea become established truth? In fact, this is not very strange at all because this myth accompanied the notes already from the very beginning. It was, of course, also alluring to think that this source related Hitler's words exactly as he spoke them. It turns out that the book dust jacket (*Bauchbinde*) attached to the first edition of *Tischgespräche* stated: "Stenographic notes by Dr. Henry Picker."[19] It thus not only claimed that Heim's notes were stenographic, but Picker's too. This was probably a marketing stunt by the publisher because no such claim is ever made in the book title or in the book itself. The claim was seized upon by Genoud, however, who used this as evidence *against* Picker when he contested Picker's copyright in a Düsseldorf court in 1952 (see Chapter 2).[20]

No wonder then that the newspapers reporting about the notes in the early 1950s repeated this as a fact over and over again. Genoud was, of course, more than happy to play along, since it suited his purposes. For example, when Genoud was interviewed by a German journalist from the Munich newspaper *Abendzeitung* during the second copyright trial in Paris in the summer of 1952 (Picker had counter-sued the publisher of *Libres propos* for copyright infringement), he said that Bormann's wife had managed to flee with all of her husband's writings and that it "was a matter of stenographic notes of all of Hitler's conversations." Heim and Picker had made their notes using stenography, claimed Genoud, on Bormann's orders, and they had then made copies of these notes without permission.[21] Genoud's statement that Heim had taken a copy of his notes with him too, just as Picker had, was, of course, completely untrue.

These false details were repeated on the covers of the various editions of *Table Talk*, as it was marketed and spread to a credulous public. The cover of the American edition *Hitler's Secret Conversations*, for example, touted the lie that "Martin Bormann, persuaded Hitler to let these talks be taken down by a discrete team of shorthand writers." It even said that "Hitler intended to use these notes as source material for the books he planned to write." This was all taken out of thin air, and how this idea could be squared with the idea that the notes recorded "the private, off-the-record" Hitler is not clear. The publisher claimed that the notes were "indisputably authentic" and "a mirror of [Hitler's] mind" and sprinkled the inner flaps with words such as "terrible" and "diabolical." In addition, it was claimed that this was indeed "the only authentic text."[22] This claim would later be repeated by Werner Jochmann in *Monologe*.

Picker also had no qualms of lying as long as it served his purposes. In Paris he stated in court that Bormann, on Picker's suggestion no less, had decided in 1944 to combine Picker's and Heim's notes and to have them published together.[23] This was an obvious lie. All of these falsehoods contributed to the spread of the stenography myth, and both Picker and Heim are called stenographers in most newspaper articles from that time it seems.[24] One article in German written by Trevor-Roper even says that:

> Every single one of Hitler's words was recorded by stenography on Martin Bormann's orders. Dr. Heinrich Picker, who copied the stenographic notes from 1942 with a typewriter, managed to save copies of them from the collapse.[25]

Not much in that sentence is correct, and all of it is probably based on Genoud. At one point, however, even the IfZ seems to have been convinced that the notes were recorded using stenography. In an internal memorandum (written in late March or early April 1952) it is stated regarding the complete manuscript for *Tischgespräche* given to the IfZ by Picker that it was "the transcription of the stenographic notes of Hitler's table talks."[26] Picker was thus telling the IfZ the same lie.

Some additional information can be gained from the German journal *Klüter Blätter* from December 1981. In it, the publication of Jochmann's book is reviewed, and the main part of the article consists of an interview that the BBC did with Heim on 14 September 1953. Heim stated that he thought that Genoud's manuscript was most likely genuine, although he admitted simultaneously that he really did not know for sure. He had no copies of his notes of his own, and Genoud had only let him see photocopy negatives of a few pages. Despite this, and despite that he had not really read the translations in either *Libres propos* or *Table Talk* carefully at all, he stated (mistakenly) that the quality of the translations was good. However, Heim added that he thought he remembered that he had made a large number of notes that did not appear in either the French or the English editions, a fact he also stated to John Toland in 1971. Moreover, he stated that the pages he did get to see contained paginations that neither he nor Bormann had put on them.[27] This is, of course, of *huge* significance for the discussion regarding what kind of manuscript Genoud actually had. The question is also what notes that had been excluded and by whom? In a crucial sentence in the manuscript for the 1953 BBC interview Heim wrote:

> If you adhere to the explanation in the preface, then you will believe that what you have before you is the utterances of Hitler's words, witnessed by

Martin Bormann and me, which even if it was not the purpose of the trans-mission, then at least uttered with the knowledge that they were recorded in order to find their way into the ears of an audience that was wider than the group of listeners that it was [immediately] directed to. The truth be told, Hitler's words as recorded by me were spoken freely in a much broader sense than François Genoud claims in his initial statement in "Libres propos": Hit-ler did *not* know about my notes![28] [Word in square brackets added by me for clarification.]

Heim would, with one notable exception (see Chapter 3), never stray from his insistence that Hitler never knew that Heim was making notes for Bormann. This does not mean that we have to take Heim at his word. As will become apparent throughout this book, it is highly unlikely that Hitler did not understand that what he said was being recorded in some form by the various people present. Indeed, that may have been the whole purpose of him making these statements in the first place, i.e. as an intricate part of his ruling strategy of hinting to his underlings what he wished for them to do. Without access to taped recordings of Hitler's original statements there is no way to conclusively determine which manuscript records his words the best.

Wolfram Pyta's analysis of the table talks

The only scholar to discuss the table talks' source critically and at length in a Hit-ler biography is Stuttgart University Professor of Modern History Wolfram Pyta. In the introduction to his book *Hitler. Der Künstler als Politiker und Feldherr* Pyta provides a long and initiated analysis based on many new sources. There are some things in this analysis worth addressing though. Before I proceed, however, I wish to state that the reason why I appear to be singling out Pyta is that he is the only one who has written on the topic at any length.[29] It is obvious that Pyta really thinks that Heim's notes are an amazing gift to historians, and they seem to have been very important for him and the argument that he puts forth in his book. For example, he accepts Heim's claim that the notes were made without Hitler's knowledge, and he states that the chroniclers, by writing Hitler's words down, have taken the spoken word and, like the legendary King Midas, turned it into "the gold of the historian" preserved in permanent textual form. The table talks were created immediately during the conversation and record either the spirit or exact wording of Hitler's utterances, he writes.[30] He also claims that the notes give the reader a unique access to "the complete Hitler."[31]

Pyta thus perpetuates many of the myths surrounding these sources. He states that these sources, which he calls "tea conversations" (*Teegespräche*), have a unique value as historical sources and that Hitler is speaking completely without constraints in a small circle of personal confidants with the conviction that his confidential statements would not be recorded (Pyta bases this entirely on Hitler's former sec-retary Christa Schroeder). He claims that what Hitler says about his childhood and his experiences during the First World War contradicts the quasi-dogmatic tale regarding his early life in *Mein Kampf*, without providing any evidence of this. Pyta again and again stresses that the participants in these conversations were absolutely and unquestionably loyal to Hitler and would never betray his trust.[32] This is a strange assertion because the existence of the table talk notes proves that this argument is wrong.

The argument is all the more strange considering that Pyta himself details how Hitler from the early summer of 1942 allowed Colonel (*Oberst*) Walter Scherff from the Military History Department of the Army High Command (*Oberkommando der Wehrmacht*) (henceforth OKW) to follow him around and write down everything concerning not only Hitler's military activities but also topics of a more general political character. The purpose of this was to chronicle and to re-write this history in an imaginative literary way so as to emphasize Hitler's military genius. Internally, at the FHQ, Scherff's chronicle was called "Hitler's Secret Main Log" (*Das geheime Hauptbuch Hitlers*), and it was planned to be published after the war.[33] Regarding the military situation talks (*Lagebesprechungen*) that were taken down by stenographers, Pyta states that they were a way for Hitler to performatively display his genius as commander of the German armed forces and that the people present during these performances formed a faithfully subordinate audience and that was absolutely necessary to Hitler. According to Wilhelm Heinrich Scheidt, who later replaced Scherff, Hitler wished to both affect and impress his audience.[34]

Why should we then accept the claim that in the case of the table talks Hitler had absolutely no knowledge of them being made, and even expressly prohibited notes to be made? On the contrary, Hitler was making sure to constantly surround himself with people who recorded his utterances. Therefore, it is very reasonable to assume that Hitler was in fact readily aware that Bormann, Heim, Picker, Müller, Engel, Werner Koeppen (Alfred Rosenberg's representative at the FHQ), and many of the others present were indeed going to write down what he was talking about. This was an essential part of how Hitler ruled, and it was the whole point of what Ian Kershaw has called "working towards the Führer."

Pyta states regarding the nightly discussions that Hitler could talk freely because he did not have to fear a breach of confidence, since in these (and other comparable) situations there was a strict rule that said that no participant could make notes.[35] This does not fit well with any of the most trustworthy sources we have access to, and it is contradictory because it implies that Hitler knew that notes were being made at other times. Even Werner Jochmann refutes the idea of the free and unguarded Hitler when he says:

> He never forgot, even during his monologues in the Führer headquarters, the required caution regarding his intentions and plans. Not even in the smallest circle did he betray any secrets, or make any doubts or uncertainties known. . . . Heim's notes confirm Hitler's great self-discipline, but also his distrustful wariness.[36]

This does not only stand in complete opposition to what Pyta claims about this source, but it also demands some serious reflection on Jochmann's part regarding how these facts affect *Monologe* as a historical source document. These are, unfortunately, not forthcoming in Jochmann's introduction. The problem is an intricate one indeed, since we are not privy to Hitler's thoughts and cannot look inside his mind to see how well the themes recorded in *Monologe* and *Tischgespräche* correspond to what Hitler really thought on a certain subject. All that we as historians can do, and this is really the only thing we *should* do, is to treat these sources as recollections on the part of those who wrote them down. Once historians realize that there is nothing special about the table conversations with regard to how accurately they portray Hitler's statements or how honest Hitler was, the mythical aura that has surrounded them for so long can finally be done away with.

But even without Jochmann's refutation, Pyta's assertions do not seem entirely plausible. Because flying in the face of these assurances is the fact that we are faced with a situation where many of the participants not only made notes afterwards but claim that they made certain notes *during* some of the conversations in question (albeit not the nightly ones). Pyta himself points this out when he, based on Jochmann, explains that Martin Bormann wished to have his boss' "holy words" put on paper for him to use in his political struggle within the Nazi bureaucracy. He thus ordered his adjutant Heim to take diligent notes.[37] Apparently then, Hitler's strict orders were not respected by anyone, and Hitler seems to have been so extraordinarily absent-minded that he never once noticed Heim – or Picker or anyone else – jotting down supporting words. That everyone would have managed to keep these notes a secret from Hitler, also after Bormann sent them around in his policy-making activities, is simply not believable. Peter Longerich seems to share this view and has suggested that Hitler was probably informed about the fact that notes had been made at least on the occasions when Bormann used them explicitly.[38]

Pyta also repeats one of the most central myths about these sources, namely that they were noted down using stenography. This implies, of course, that they are extremely reliable and provide an *ad verbatim* record of what Hitler said. Pyta writes that Bormann ordered Heim to:

> discretely make stenographic notes during lunch and dinner, on the basis of which Heim the next day dictated the most important content of the statements to Bormann's secretary. During the "Teegesprächen" Heim could not make any notes to support his memory. Therefore, he imprinted Hitler's utterances during the nightly hours in himself, only to dictate to the secretary a few hours later and in this way put it on paper.[39]

That Heim produced a very faithful and accurate record is also implied elsewhere in the book.[40] There is a problem here. Paradoxically, Pyta claims that the records of the nightly monologues are even more faithfully preserved than the notes from the daytime utterances because here there were even fewer hours between Heim "imprinting" (*prägte*) – this is Pyta's own word because Heim never uses it, and it is a rhetorical way of giving this memory process a greater sense of exactness – Hitler's words onto his brain and the dictation to the secretary. But stenographic notes *have* to be more exact than notes made from memory after the events they record.

The period between writing and dictation is not relevant in this case. Neither does Pyta consider the fact that our memory becomes worse, not better, when we are tired. It is simply not reasonable to assume that Heim would have a better ability to recollect statements uttered at 3 or 4 a.m. after a whole day of activities and after no sleep during the night.

Moreover, the fact that Hitler's utterances were dictated to Bormann's secretaries only adds to the absurdity of claiming that Hitler did not know that his words were being put on paper. As will become obvious later in this book, the evidence for knowledge of Bormann's note-making among the Nazi hierarchy was so extensive that we are faced with a situation where the claim is being made that Hitler himself was almost the only person who did *not* know about this. This is an obviously untenable idea and cannot be accepted by historians any longer. Pyta himself refers to the consternation caused by Bormann's notes, and his usage of them in his political machinations, at Rosenberg's *Ostministerium* in Berlin.[41] Peter Longerich, too, subscribes to this idea, but gives no source for it, pointing out that it seems as if Bormann could make direct use of this "Treasure trove of citations" (*Zitatenschatz*) only on rather few occasions and that he mostly had to refer to the more vaguely formulated "will of the Führer."[42] Bormann made many such notes that did not make it into Genoud's manuscript. For example, he made one dated 26 January 1943. This note relates Hitler's utterances about Christianity, making parallels between Christianity and communism, and Bormann has him saying that Christianity was hostile to progress; that it was the downfall of the Roman Empire; that it contained communist tendencies; as well as calling the Christian missionaries in the Germanic territories "Political Commissars."[43] This note is basically exactly like the last entry in Genoud's manuscript from 30 November 1944, which Longerich also mentions in his book.[44] Certainly, this must have meant that Hitler understood that his conversations were being recorded by Bormann.

Heim never (according to his own statements) made anything remotely close to a complete stenographic record of what Hitler said. Instead, he could at most take only occasional supporting notes (*Stichworte* in German) from the dinner and evening conversations. Pyta is right, however, when he states that Heim could not take any notes at all during the nightly *Teegespräche*, but he exaggerates the proximity in time between the conversations and the point when the content was dictated to a secretary (see Chapter 4).

Cognitive science and neuroscience have shown that human memory, even short-term memory, is highly unreliable. Consciously recalling a memory, what is called explicit memory by cognitive scientists, is not like pulling out a file from a file cabinet. It is a creative process whereby the brain builds upon what is thought to be only a core memory, which is then elaborated upon (unconsciously) by the brain in order to produce the final memory that is recalled. Nobel Prize winner Eric R. Kandel writes:

> For all of us, explicit memory makes it possible to leap across space and time and conjure up events and emotional states that have vanished into the past

yet somehow continue to live on in our minds. But recalling a memory epi-
sodically – no matter how important the memory – is not like simply turning
to a photograph in an album. Recall of memory is a creative process. What
the brain stores is thought to be only a core memory. Upon recall, this core
memory is then elaborated upon and reconstructed, with subtractions, additions, elaborations, and distortions.[45]

Moreover, it is not even the case that events enter our brains unfiltered or undis-
torted, even from the outset. Neuroscience has shown that sensations coming into
the brain via our sensory organs (eyes, ears, and so on) are immediately filtered
through several layers in the brain. It is not even one single sensation that the brain
receives, but millions of signals from our sensory nerves that lie between reality and
our perception of it. These signals are then first broken down and decoded by the
brain, and only after this process are the signals put together in order to form a, for
us, subjectively intact image or experience. Kandel writes:

> the belief that our perceptions are precise and direct is an illusion – a per-
> ceptual illusion. The brain does not simply take the raw data that it receives
> through the senses and reproduce it faithfully. Instead, each sensory system
> first analyzes and deconstructs, then restructures the raw, incoming informa-
> tion according to its own built-in connections and rules. . . . The sensory
> systems are hypothesis generators. We confront the world neither directly
> nor precisely. . . . "*Sensation is an abstraction, not a replication, of the real world.*"[46]

One of the most powerful factors in perception and memory is selective attention.
Since the brain's capacity to process information is much more limited than the
sensory organs' ability to gather information about our surrounding environment,
some selection has to be made by the brain. Attention is what acts as the filter that
cuts short the endless stream of input from the sensory nervous system. This means
that in every moment we focus on some part of reality and, more or less, exclude
the rest of the world entirely. Human ability to focus on more than one thing at a
time is extremely limited because of this fact.[47]

Modern memory research has established that memories are not stored in one
piece in one place in the brain, but in various parts of the brain. The memories are
then reassembled as they are retrieved and presented to the conscious mind. Daniel
L. Schacter writes:

> memories are stored as patterns of activation across numerous units and con-
> nections that are involved with the storage of many different memories.
> Because memories are necessarily superimposed on one another, the output
> that a connectionist model produces as a "memory" of a particular event
> always contains some influence from other memories; that is, to a greater
> or lesser degree, the output of a connectionist model reflects a composite
> construction of individual underlying representations.[48]

This should be enough to allay any illusions about the reliability of human memory within the historical community. Yet the advances of cognitive science and neuroscience have not really been acknowledged and used by historians in the process of evaluating historical sources. Among the traditional source-critical criteria, it is only the factor of time that really seems to encapsulate the realization that memory is a fallible and changing thing. However, this criterium does not consider that even memories of events that happened very recently are subject to the processes described by Kandel. The distortion of events begins already *before* the memory is physically formed and stored in the brain's malleable network of neurons.

In the specific case of studies of Hitler and National Socialism, historians really have to begin to ponder the consequences of what neuroscience has taught us about how human memory and perception work and what this means for the reliability on the table talks (as well as all other sources of the same kind). The fact that science introduces a huge degree of uncertainty regarding the reliability of our sources cannot be used as an argument not to accept the findings of neuroscience and apply them appropriately to the field of history. Historians simply have to bite the scientific bullet here; at least if our effort to be multi-disciplinary in our approach to our subject is going to be worth anything.

When, for example, Heim is repeatedly described as "reliable", "this reliable chronicler", and even "an especially reliable notetaker of Hitler's conversations", we have to understand that this is not an objective description of Heim.[49] This is to hugely overstate Heim's reliability as a witness and to effectively make it almost impossible to question Heim's statements and his notes. Nothing warrants the statement that Heim's memory was any more reliable than any other person's memory. The trustworthiness and reliability of Heim's memory and his text are only asserted by Pyta; they are never proven or based on good evidence. Despite the fact that Pyta has had access to a potentially important source of material, namely Heim's personal papers that are kept "privately" somewhere in Germany by a person whose name he does not disclose, he does not use this material to lay a concrete foundation for his case.[50] One has to assume that there was not much in there to build on.

At the same time, however, Pyta contradicts himself outright because elsewhere he claims that Hitler actually gave Bormann permission to have a chronicler present (except from at the nightly talks, to which Picker did not have access) and to write down "Hitler's semi-official utterances during midday and evening."[51] However, we are not provided with any evidence or argument for what the difference in content between these notes and those made during the night actually is. This also readily undermines Pyta's prior arguments about the incredible value of Heim's purportedly stenographic notes from precisely these meals. If we are to follow the logic of what is being presented here, we have to draw the following conclusions: 1) the value of Heim's notes from midday and evening are lessened by the utterances being half-official and 2) the value of the notes from the nightly utterances are lessened by them being made entirely from memory.

Hitler tolerated, Pyta writes, that the liaison officers at the FHQ held his utterances at table in such high regard that they sent reports to their superiors.[52] This statement contradicts what he has previously said about Hitler having forbidden notes to be made and him not knowing that notes were made. How this is compatible with the idea that Hitler would not have spoken freely if his words were written down is not addressed. We are also told, based entirely on Picker's *Tischgespräche* this time, that "Hitler appreciated that Bormann made his words into his own, in an almost slave-like manner as if they were divine statements, and let him be."[53] But Bormann was not the one writing most of the utterances in *Monologe* or *Tischgespräche* down; his adjutants did, so this argument is not a valid one.

Pyta is entirely correct that the table talks are nevertheless unique. As he writes: "There is no comparable cohesive text corpus" that portrays Hitler's statements during the war.[54] Moreover, even though Pyta makes a serious effort to evaluate these sources and come to terms with them and what they represent, he nonetheless lists them, as well as the hugely problematic *Hitlers politisches Testament* (for more on this, see Chapter 6), as "printed sources."[55] Pyta is of course not alone in treating the table talks in this way. In fact, the new critical edition of *Mein Kampf* lists both *Monologe* and *Tischgespräche* under the heading "Source volumes and document collections." Hitler is even listed as the author of *Monologe*, an honour not extended to *Tischgespräche*, indicating the tendency to view this collection of notes as in some way more authoritative.[56]

This is a generally troublesome tendency, one which seems to be a common trait shared by most historians who distinguish between secondary literature and printed primary sources in their bibliographies, namely that they often lump the table talks together with real primary sources of Hitler's words such as his speeches and, perhaps most unfortunate, *Mein Kampf*. But while *Mein Kampf* as a source has been thoroughly dissected, scrutinized, and criticized by scholars so that every historian today knows that *Mein Kampf* is an unreliable source to quote in many respects (not least when it comes to biographical details of Hitler's life and ideological development),[57] the same awareness is simply not present when it comes to quotations from the table talks. Instead they are cited as if they were equivalent to *Mein Kampf* or Hitler's speeches, i.e. in the sense of them being Hitler's own words.

Pyta does not include any critical evaluation of *Hitlers politisches Testament* even though this collection of documents, in contrast to those contained in *Tischgespräche* and *Monologe*, actually *has* been seriously questioned, and their authenticity greatly doubted, by historians before (see Chapter 6). He does not reference or comment on, e.g. Ian Kershaw's refusal to use this source. Instead, Pyta writes about *Hitlers politisches Testament*:

> Several of Hitler's conversations up until the collapse in April 1945 were written down, faithful to content, so that the historian has access to a rich trove of pregnant sources if he is looking for a basis for Hitler's unaltered views.[58]

He then goes on to cite this source uncritically in the book.[59] We are never told what his grounds are for assuming it is authentic in the face of all indications to the contrary or why the statements are to be considered "true to content" and as "unaltered views." In fact, those very statements fly in the face of almost everything we know about this text. But despite these criticisms of mine, just the fact that Pyta is the only historian to attempt a critical evaluation of these sources, even though the result is far from convincing or perfect, must be considered a major positive contribution to the field. These are discussions and evaluations that ought to be included in every Hitler biography and every other book that uses them. This has not been the case so far, and this is a real weakness for the reliability of our historical knowledge of Hitler, National Socialism, and the Third Reich.

Other scholars engage with the table talks

The table talks were used from early on after they had become available to scholars and always without a critical discussion concerning what kind of sources they were. Alan Bullock, for example, in the revised edition of his famous biography *Hitler: A Study in Tyranny* made use of quotes not only from Picker's *Tischgespräche* and *Table Talk* but also the *The Testament*, all of which he listed under "Writings and Speeches of Adolf Hitler" in his bibliography together with *Mein Kampf*. *Table Talk* is thus treated as if it contained Hitler's own words *ad verbatim* and is cited quite extensively at times, as is *The Testament* towards the end of the book.[60] At one point Bullock simply notes that "another version has been published by one of the reporters, Dr Henry Picker . . ." without discussing the matter any further.[61]

Needless to say, the latter remark and the extensive quotes from *Table Talk* are not in the original edition of Bullock's book from 1952, because by then *Table Talk* had not yet been published. At that time *Tischgespräche* was the only version available to Bullock, and he did not make nearly as frequent use of it as he later would do of *Table Talk*. In the 1952 edition, Bullock says, in the two of only four times that *Tischgespräche* is referred to, that on the one hand the "extravagant conversations recorded by Hermann Rauschning for the period 1932–1934, and by Dr. Henry Picker at the Fuehrer's H.Q. for the period 1941–1942, reveal Hitler in another favourite role, that of visionary and prophet", and on the other hand the "Hitler of the *Tischgespräche* indeed reveals nothing new; it is the same harsh and uncouth figure already familiar from the pages of *Mein Kampf* or the earliest of his speeches."[62] Surely, these two statements seem a little bit hard to square with one another. In this original version of the text Bullock listed *Tischgespräche* under the heading "Nazi Sources."[63] But apparently the English translation made Bullock drastically change his mind. Not only did he cite it extensively and frequently; he also now considered it to "give a vivid impression of Hitler's mood at the peak of his fantastic career."[64]

One is tempted, then, to conclude from this that Bullock had perhaps not read *Tischgespräche* all that thoroughly, since the *Table Talk* made a so much bigger impact on him. Indeed, *Tischgespräche* was completely uninteresting to him, and this fact taken together with the quite different treatment of *Table Talk* may actually say a lot about the major importance of the translation of these texts into English for Anglo-American historians more generally. It is not enough to explain this difference in treatment and evaluation by referring to the fact that *Table Talk* stemmed from a different manuscript and included more notes. The difference in content is simply not big enough to warrant such a conclusion. Moreover, what Bullock writes in the preface to the revised edition testifies to this fact as well; he wrote that he "should like to mention . . . Professor Trevor-Roper whose essay on *The Mind of Adolf Hitler* convinced me that Hitler's table talk would repay careful re-reading."[65] Bullock thus was unaware of the fact that *Table Talk* was translated from a different manuscript than Picker's *Tischgespräche*. At the same time he acknowledged that the passing of time and the new available sources had forced a "change of perspective", although he had found "no reason to alter substantially the picture" he had originally painted of Hitler.[66] Ironically, then, Bullock still contended in the epilogue, as he had in the original edition from 1952, that Hitler's "twelve years' dictatorship was barren of all ideas save one – the further extension of his own power and that of the nation with which he had identified himself." The only "theme" of the Nazi revolution was, Bullock contended, "domination, dressed up as the doctrine of race" and "a vindictive destructiveness, Rauschning's *Revolution des Nihilismus*."[67] Such were the limitations of Bullock's understanding of National Socialism and of Hitler.

Joachim Fest, on the other hand, used the table monologues extensively, and his Hitler biography is probably the most extreme example of reliance on these sources in the entire Hitler literature catalogue (although Rainer Zitelmann is not far behind; see later). But considering that Fest's biography has been greatly celebrated and still enjoys an influential position in the research about Hitler, this fact is all the more interesting and worthy of bringing up. What is odd about Fest, and this separates him from all other Hitler biographers as far as I have been able to ascertain, is that he cites not only *Tischgespräche* and *Table Talk* (*Monologe* had not been published when Fest wrote his book) but also *Libres propos* and *Le Testament Politique de Hitler*, as if *Table Talk* and *Libres propos* were two different sources. At times he refers to both *Table Talk* and *Tischgespräche* even though Picker's notes are being quoted in both books. True, Fest often refers to several other sources pointing towards the same conclusion, but many times he cites only one version of the table talks directly and in isolation. Nowhere in Fest's work is there a critical discussion regarding these sources either.[68]

William Carr treated both *The Testament* and *Tischgespräche* as "printed primary sources" in his *Hitler: A Study in Personality and Politics*, albeit he only cites them on a few occasions. In the bibliography he added that Picker's book was the "most reliable version", which of course, at that time, was certainly a reasonable conclusion considering that it was the only German version available.[69] However, Carr should still have been able to realize that these texts could not be treated as primary sources in this context. They had obviously gone through enough editing that they ought to have been used much more carefully.

Ian Kershaw used *Tischgespräche, Monologe,* and Koeppen's notes in his Hitler biography, and although he does include a critical discussion of *The Testament* he does not apparently see any problems in quoting and referring to these other sets of notes. Kershaw, too, forgets to mention Hans Müller as one of the contributors to *Monologe* (although that may have been a consequence of the title of Jochmann's book, which mentions only Heim).[70] On one occasion Kershaw does note that the "translation in *Hitler's Table Talk* 97–8 is incomplete and, as often, somewhat too loosely rendered."[71] However, he does not include any discussion on how reliable the table talks are when it comes to representing Hitler's words.[72] Kershaw tends to use Koeppen's notes and *Monologe* interchangeably where they do not overlap, but never to compare these notes and discuss their differences and the possible meanings and implications of these. Not even on dates where there is such an overlap is this opportunity taken advantage of.[73] Thus the critical discussion regarding how accurately Heim and the other scribes remembered Hitler's words does not even get started (for such a discussion, see Chapter 8).

Even an otherwise extremely diligent, cautious, and source-critical historian as Anton Joachimsthaler cites *Monologe* (and on one occasion also *Tischgespräche*) without any critical comment.[74] Joachimsthaler's will to simply accept everything that *Monologe* states is truly remarkable. It is as if *Monologe* is thought of as a corrective to any other source when in reality it must be independently corroborated at every turn. Another historian who uncritically cites both *Monologe* and *Tischgespräche* extensively is Brigitte Hamann in her *Hitlers Wien*. It is certainly indicative of the way in which historians have viewed these sources that Hamann otherwise includes very insightful critical discussions about other sources to Hitler's early history and views.[75] Sometimes these sources are used to support really important arguments indeed. For example, Eberhard Jäckel, while arguing that Hitler ordered the Holocaust, cites *Table Talk* and Hitler as saying that "he was doing humanity a service by exterminating this pest."[76] *Table Talk* does state: "By exterminating this pest, we shall do humanity a service of which our soldiers can have no idea." But this translation is not necessarily an accurate representation of Heim's version as published in *Monologe*, which says in German:

> Wenn wir diese Pest ausrotten, so vollbringen wir eine Tat für die Menschheit, von deren Bedeutung sich unsere Männer draußen noch gar keine Vorstellung machen können.[77]

Note that the German word "*wenn*" is an ambiguous conjunction and could mean 1) "if" and 2) "when/that/as/as soon as." The problem is that meaning 2) basically only applies when it appears inside a sentence. If meaning 2) was what was intended here, it would have been much more natural to use the adverb "*wann*", which unambiguously means "when." When the word *wenn* appears at the beginning of a sentence it usually has meaning 1) and the sentence thus becomes a hypothetical. Thus, the quoted phrase rather means:

> *If* we exterminate this pest [*then*] we complete a deed for humanity, the importance of which our men out there cannot even imagine. [Italics added.]

It is hard to understand how Jäckel could make this mistake because *Monologe* was available to him when he wrote his book. We must also ask ourselves who the word "pest" refers to in this case. Jäckel clearly argues it refers to the Jews, but is that really the case? The context of this passage rather suggests that it refers to the detrimental effects upon culture by Bolshevism (the Jews are mentioned but are not the main topic of the preceding paragraphs); i.e. it is Bolshevism, to which the Jews were of course intrinsically tied in Hitler's mind, that the term "pest" refers to. The timing of this utterance also strengthens this interpretation, i.e. Germany had recently invaded the Soviet Union. This context changes the implication of what is said completely, and it can no longer be interpreted as a clear-cut admission of the Holocaust. Jäckel also cites the oft-questioned *Hitlers politisches Testament* to the effect that the world would be eternally grateful to the Nazis for having eradicated the Jews in Germany and Central Europe.[78] It goes without saying that it is hugely important whether Hitler actually said these things, if *Hitlers politisches Testament* is a forgery, or, even if he stated something to this effect, what words he used.

In his *The Hitler of History* John Lukacs uses Werner Koeppen's notes for the most part and, a bit surprisingly, *The Testament* without any critical commentary. He also includes *Monologe* in his "Bibliographical Note", although he does not seem to quote it in the text.[79] Another biography that makes extensive use of *Tisch-gespräche* is Werner Maser's *Adolf Hitler. Legende, Mythos, Wirklichkeit* from 1971. The book is filled with quotes and references from, and to, these sources. Yet there is no source-critical discussion of them. Because he was writing before the publication of Jochmann's *Monologe* he is relying upon Picker's book (specifically the second printing, published in 1965, of the second edition, first published in 1963). Why the first edition of 1951 is not used is unclear. It appears that Maser figured that the two are identical, but they are not (the second edition actually contains material and changes to the text that are not in the one edited by Gerhard Ritter). Maser does not reflect upon, or let the reader know, why we should assume that Hitler is more honest in the table monologues than in, say, *Mein Kampf*. Nevertheless, Maser treated *Tischgespräche* as "literature" in his bibliography. On the other hand, he lists *The Bormann Letters* there too, so it is unclear what this placing of *Tischgespräche* means from a source-critical perspective.[80] Maser even uses Genoud's first volume of *Libres propos* at one point.[81] Here it should be noted that Maser's abilities as a historian have been shown by many to be doubtful at best, and outright fraudulent at worst. His biography is littered with statements that are untrue and most probably the result of fabrications on Maser's part. Maser's edited source volume *Hitlers Briefe und Notizen* has also been shown to be filled with inaccuracies, misreadings, etc.[82] In short, Maser's books cannot be trusted at all.

John Toland used both *Hitler's Secret Conversations* (the American edition of *Table Talk*) and *The Testament* completely uncritically. Towards the end of his book he quotes frequently from the latter source without any problematization. Toland states:

> A final mark of honor came to Bormann early in February [1945, M.N.]. The Führer began dictating to him a political testament. If the Reich *did* fall – and Hitler still entertained the faint hope of some miracle – he wanted

to record for history how closely he had come to achieving his magnificent dream. It was typical that he wanted the last word. And so on February 4, with the Bolsheviks at the gates of Berlin, the indefatigable Bormann began jotting down the Führer's final explanation to history of what went wrong.[83] [Italics in original.]

Most of this is completely taken out of thin air, or rather, a staging of the claims made about the source, decorated with some dramatic details intended to put the reader in the right mood. Toland could not really have gotten this from Heim because although he thought these notes were authentic, he did not think they were the result of dictations. It is well-written prose, but it is not a good description of the true nature of things. Thus, it is not good historical science.

Picker is depicted as having been a stenographer also by Ralph Giordano in the preface to Rochus Misch's book *Der letzte Zeuge*. Picker is called Hitler's "court stenographer" (*Liebstenographen*), and it is claimed that he recorded Hitler's monologues word for word. Giordano does this not in order to argue for the authenticity or good quality of *Tischgespräche*, but in order to completely annihilate Picker's character. Picker, writes Giordano, appears in *Tischgespräche* to be "a spiritual lackey and an unteachable apologist" for Hitler.[84] Incidentally, this is true.

The case of Rainer Zitelmann: a source-critical debacle and notes on bad methodologies

In 1987 Rainer Zitelmann published his book *Hitler. Selbstverständnis eines Revolutionärs*. He does include a critical discussion of the table monologues, along with Rauschning and some other similar sources, but his discussion is flawed and the criteria according to which he decides to accept a statement in his sources as genuine are too inexact. For example, he starts off with a quote from *Hitlers politisches Testament*.[85] Zitelmann writes that in order to support his arguments concerning Hitler's views, he uses many similar quotations from various types of sources.[86] This is a common and well-established method used by historians. But Zitelmann states the following regarding sources such as Rauschning and Otto Wagener's memoirs:

> The notes by Hitler's conversation partners, primarily Hermann Rauschning's and Otto Wagener's, will be used with all the necessary reservations toward these sources: we have only drawn on these "unreliable" sources where they can be supported by other "reliable" or at least seamlessly be inserted in the resulting full image based on the analysis of other sources.[87]

This method, however, even though it is commonly applied by historians, has serious flaws. First, if a source is so problematic that it always has to be supported by other, more reliable sources then what is gained by using it? Would it not then be better to simply use only the more reliable sources? Second, what does Zitelmann mean when he says "all the necessary reservations"? He never explains this in any detail, rendering the assurance meaningless. Thirdy, this qualification must in turn be qualified with regard to context and usage; we cannot simply accept it as a valid general rule. We must, for example, be sure that the less reliable source is not simply borrowing from another more reliable source, so that we in fact do not have to do with two independent sources at all. This can often be difficult to determine. Hitler's views remained constant during his political career, and thus his views on many topics were very easy to estimate for anyone writing a book about him and claiming to have had conversations on certain subjects with him.

It is quite obvious that this kind of reasoning is too uncertain to be taken seriously as a source-critical method, since Zitelmann uses not only Rauschning and *Hitlers politisches Testament*, which we know are highly questionable – and most probably forgeries – but he also uses the so-called "Hitler-Breiting Gespräche", or *Ohne Maske* (which is the real title of this book),[88] and applies the same reasoning to this source. He does this even though these conversations were shown to be forgeries several years before Zitelmann published his book. This is what Zitelmann writes about the Hitler–Breiting conversations in his book:

> Regarding the Breiting-conversations, whose authenticity have been doubted (e.g. *Der Spiegel* 37/1972, p. 64 f.) the following can be noted: That some of the utterances ascribed to Hitler by Breiting are not authentic is clear. But since it nonetheless seems certain that Hitler and Breiting spoke to each other in 1931, and many parts of the Breiting-version agree to an astoundingly high degree with Hitler's opinions as stated elsewhere, is it reasonable to assume that Breiting made up opinions that he added to those that Hitler really did utter to him, and which he faithfully purveyed, just as is the case with Rauschning and Wagener. In the present study, then, these sources will be used with the same reservations as are the conversations reproduced by Rauschning and Wagener.[89]

Zitelmann makes several mistakes here. First, he assumes that it is Breiting's own notes that he is using. Second, he assumes that because the statements contained in them correspond to an "astoundingly high degree" with what Hitler says in other sources, they are therefore genuine (he never explains why that should be astounding if they are forgeries – rather the opposite is true, since a good forger will do his (or her) best to look as much as the original as possible). As it turned out, the reason for this astoundingly high degree of correspondence was indeed that it had been based upon other genuine sources. Third, he uses the source even though he knows that its authenticity has been questioned, without being able to conclusively prove that it is genuine. For instance, Zitelmann refers to the Breiting source when arguing that Hitler had stated that the raw materials were unevenly distributed in the world and that this injustice would be mended in the future. He then writes that this seemed genuine to him, since Hitler spoke of the raw material problem in two speeches in the summer of 1931.[90] Moreover, when speaking about Hitler's true attitude towards communism, which differed from the official propaganda view in that it contained an amount of admiration, he quotes from *Ohne Maske* saying that the historian has to rely on these kinds of sources in order to get at Hitler's true views (at the same time pointing out the "surprising" fact that Rauschning, Wagener, and Breiting agree on this matter independently of each other).[91] While this kind of reasoning may seem perfectly sound and legitimate, it clearly is *not*, since Zitelmann was wrong concerning the authenticity of the sources he was using. His source-critical reasoning was hence worth absolutely nothing at all. The reason for this was simply that his method for evaluating his sources was seriously flawed. Rauschning, Wagener, and Breiting may have been independent of each other, in the sense that none of them were based upon the other, but they were most likely *not* independent in the sense that the forged statements they contain were likely based on some of the same sources.

The fact that Zitelmann refers to an issue of *Der Spiegel* from 1972 when noting that the authenticity of Breiting had been questioned is perhaps the most astounding of all. The reason is that this article has not just questioned part of the source he is using but had reported that Hans Mommsen and Fritz Tobias had unequivocally declared the whole thing to be a forgery. *Der Spiegel* in fact wrote:

> Two history detectives have discovered that West Germany's historians and journalists have fallen for a manipulation of contemporary history; the protocol from two secret Adolf Hitler interviews – published as key documents on National Socialist conquest policy in 1968 – are not authentic.[92]

Zitelmann uses the Hitler–Breiting conversations anyway, and without any serious attempt to counter Mommsen's and Tobias's claims. The forgery had indeed been conclusively proven by the time Zitelmann published his book in 1987.[93] This had probably been pointed out to Zitelmann who in the second edition of his book acknowledged that it was indeed a forgery.[94] Indeed, as the journalist Karl-Heinz Janßen pointed out, it was one of the most brazen falsifications of history in the twentieth century.[95] Zitelmann's methodology gets even more confused and questionable when he, towards the end of his book, discusses when Hitler came to the conclusion that Stalin was essentially pursuing a nationalist and anti-Semitic policy. He notes that if Breiting can be trusted, even though it could not be considered a completely trustworthy source, then Hitler had come to this conclusion by June 1931 at the latest. Zitelmann then quotes extensively from *Ohne Maske*, only to then also quote Goebbel's diary that shows that Hitler had not yet reached a position on this matter even by 1937.[96]

It had been claimed by the journalist Edouard Calic, who also acted as editor of the book *Ohne Maske*, that the book contained the stenographic record of two long open-hearted and private conversations between Hitler and the editor-in-chief of the newspaper *Leipziger Neuesten Nachrichten*, Richard Breiting, that ostensibly had taken place in May and June 1931 (but not published until 1968). Calic said that Breiting had been allowed to make the notes on the precondition that none of it was to be published. One of the more sensational pieces of information in this book was that the *Reichstag* fire had been set by the Nazis themselves. However, Breiting had only met Hitler once – not in the spring/summer of 1931, but in the fall that year, and Hitler had not revealed his plans to the editor. Neither had Breiting made any stenographic notes during the conversation (no notes at all were made at the time), nor had there been a second meeting. Calic had simply contrived the conversations, perhaps based upon some notes made by Breiting *after* his meeting with Hitler.[97] The conspiracy theory that the *Reichstag* fire was set by the Nazis has been slow to die, however.[98] Sven Felix Kellerhoff, who goes through every aspect of the case in his book *The Reichstag Fire*, has recently conclusively proven it to be false.[99]

Zitelmann uses both *Monologe* and *Tischgespräche*, but also Koeppen's notes, and quotes these sources frequently, which he describes as containing statements that Hitler made "relatively free of tactical and propandistic considerations."[100] But this is not based on a thorough investigation into the nature of these sources. Zitelmann on one occasion refers to both *Monologe* and Koeppen's notes, while saying nothing about the fact that the quoted passage reads differently in Koeppen's version than in Heim's.[101] At one point, Zitelmann, after a short discussion about the authenticity of Rauschning's *Gespräche mit Hitler*, uses *Hitlers politisches Testament* to support a passage from Rauschning's book.[102] For Zitelmann, the reliability of Heim's, Picker's, and Koeppen's notes is simply a non-issue.

This is quite problematic considering that, as has already been mentioned, the authenticity of Rauschning has been doubted on good grounds and that, for all we know, it may even be that Rauschning is the source for the statement in *Hitlers politisches Testament*. The way Zitelmann treats these notes, and the way he evaluates them, becomes obvious when one notices that not only *Monologe* and *Tischgespräche* but also *Hitlers politisches Testament* and Rauschning's *Gespräche mit Hitler* are considered by him to be "printed sources", even though he could have placed these under e.g. "contemporary works" where one can find Rauschning's *Die Revolution des Nihilismus*. Thus, he chooses to place these texts in the same category as e.g. Hitler's printed speeches, printed documents from the *Reichskanzlei*, and Goebbel's diaries.[103] Once again this is a sign that historians tend to treat the table monologues and *Mein Kampf* as the same kind of source. When one quotes Goebbel's diary one actually quotes the propaganda minister's own words as he wrote or dictated them, while in the case of *Monologe* and *Tischgespräche* the best we can say is that they are Hitler's words re-constructed, mostly from memory – i.e. they show a Hitler redux.

It is worth reflecting upon this for a moment because it does indeed tell us something about the lack of critical acumen with which Rauschning, Breiting, and the table talks have been treated by even highly serious and otherwise very knowledgeable historians. Even by the time Zitelmann published his book, i.e. in 1987, enough evidence had been presented for historians to feel less than comfortable in deciding to quote Rauschning. In 1972 Theodor Schieder published his evaluation of *Gespräche mit Hitler* in which he concluded not only that much of the content, which portrayed Hitler as a man with not only a plan but one laid out according to his ideological convictions, contradicted the whole thesis of Rauschning's *Revolution des Nihilismus* but also that it could not be used as a source to Hitler's utterances, since it mixed subjective and objective elements to such a degree that it was impossible to tell the one from the other. Nonetheless, Schieder still considered it a valuable source because of its purported insights into Hitler's character.[104] That, too, was a mistaken assumption. Zitelmann is of course aware of Schieder's book, and even refers to it when arguing for the authenticity of another Rauschning quote he uses.[105] But as if this was not enough, there was also the devastating book from 1984 by Wolfgang Hänel *Hermann Rauschings "Gespräche mit Hitler": Eine Geschichtsfälschung* to take into consideration. Hänel's verdict was brutal, as he claimed to have proven that Rauschning had concocted the conversations entirely – he had simply made them up.[106] Apparently, Rauschning himself realized what the result of Hänel's book would be and stated that Hänel would "expose" him.[107]

Ian Kershaw drew the only reasonable consequence from all of this and states unequivocally in the preface to his Hitler biography: "I have on no single occasion cited Hermann Rauschning's *Hitler speaks*, a work now regarded to have so little authenticity that it is best to disregard it altogether."[108] This is of course the only way we as historians can treat a source like this, since the methodology that assumes that similar statements appearing in several sources means that the one before us is reliable is clearly insufficient and very often leads us down the garden path. Bad methodology gives us bad history. Rauschning, just like Calic's Hitler–Breiting conversations, ought to be discarded altogether.

This only goes to show that even serious historians have trouble letting go of sources that they have used and come to like, not to a small degree because they confirm deeply held beliefs about Hitler. This seems to be an especially common phenomenon with regard to so-called "witnesses to history" (*Zeitzeugen*), another such case being Albert Speer, who managed to claim more or less total control over how his role in the Third Reich was interpreted, i.e. as an unwitting technocrat (whose only fault was to be so feeble-minded as to not understand what was really going on), even despite multiple scholars having proven that he lied and forged his stories in such a way that his biographers (journalists and historians alike) had in fact been propagating clever Nazi propaganda myths.[109]

Zitelmann uses the table monologues when, e.g. documenting Hitler's problem with authorities and cites this source extensively when Hitler purportedly said that he had questioned his school teacher's lessons about the Bible by confronting him with facts from natural science class.[110] But he also uses it to confirm that Hitler had become aware of social and political issues during his time in Vienna.[111] Zitelmann also repeats several other myths regarding Hitler's life that have since been proven to be false, such as him being a convinced anti-Semite already during his years in Vienna and the claim that Hitler was a brave soldier. The latter was based on the fact that Hitler received two Iron Crosses during his time in the army.[112] These myths, all based on Hitler's own version of events, have been questioned and disproven by Thomas Weber in the book *Hitler's First War*, and before him by Anton Joachimsthaler in *Hitlers Weg begann in München*. Weber and Joachimsthaler point to the fact that we have no contemporary evidence of Hitler having uttered any anti-Semitic remarks before 1919 and explains the Iron Crosses by showing that this honour was awarded to Hitler partly because of his connections to the officers of his regiment (to which he as a regimental headquarter dispatch runner stood close to and admired) and not because of bravery in the field. The latter was a propaganda myth fostered by the NSDAP after the war.[113]

Nota bene that this is not to say that Zitelmann's statements were not reasonable in the light of the then available evidence, but the point is to underline just how much of what historians have considered to be facts about Hitler in reality have turned out to be cleverly devised Nazi propaganda. On the other hand, these conclusions were always based on questionable sources, e.g. Hitler himself, that should perhaps have aroused a certain amount of suspicion even when no evidence to the contrary was present.

Here one can point out that *Monologe* also spreads lies and half-truths about Hitler's activities during the First World War. For example, Heim records a statement saying that Hitler did not wear his Iron Cross 1st Class during the war because he had seen the way in which it was given to people who did not deserve it (which is ironic considering several witnesses said exactly the same about Hitler having been given the honour). He then apparently went on to claim that a Jew by the name of Gutmann, whom he accused of being a coward, had worn his Iron Cross 1st Class and that this was a scandal and very upsetting to Hitler.[114] Hugo Gutmann was, as it happens, the officer who had recommended Hitler for the Iron Cross. But the interesting thing about this statement is that it gives the impression that Hitler had made a very conscious, and conscientious, decision not to wear his Iron Cross during the war. However, as Anton Joachimsthaler has pointed out, considering that Hitler did not receive this decoration until 4 August 1918, he would only have had just over a month to wear it anyway, because on 14 October he was exposed to a British mustard gas attack and removed from the war for good.[115]

Since we cannot expect that Hitler, or anyone else, would have worn an Iron Cross 1st Class while operating as a dispatch runner for his regiment, the text must be referring to occasions when he was on leave. The only such opportunities would have been between 23 and 30 August, when Hitler was in Nuremberg, and between 10 and 28 September, when he was on leave in Berlin. Note that Hitler was on leave a lot during this period, a fact that may indicate war fatigue on his part. But the story is most likely entirely fictional anyway considering that Hitler's hatred for Jews cannot be established at this point in time. There would therefore have been no reason for Hitler to disrespect Gutmann. Heim is thus recording no fewer than two lies in this short paragraph.

More recent examples of uncritical usage of the table talks

Another case when the table talks have been used frequently is when it comes to Hitler's reading habits. Timothy W. Ryback quotes *Monologe* extensively in his book *Hitler's Private Library*, and here he also perpetuates the myth of the notes having been made using stenography, going as far as to mistakenly work this assertion into the title of Jochmann's book.[116] Ryback even claims that Picker's *Tischgespräche* was written down with the use of stenography.[117] Ambrus Miskolczy, too, cites Picker (here Hitler's monologues are called "roundtable") although less often than Ryback.[118] These quotations are always made in order to support an argument about Hitler's character, habits, or remarks on various topics.

Another recent Hitler biography that lists the 1976 edition of *Tischgespräche* as well as *Monologe* under "printed sources", even though there is a section called "memoirs", is *Adolf Hitler. Die Jahre des Aufstiegs* and *Die Jahre des Untergangs* by Volker Ullrich. Not only that, but Ullrich even states Hitler as the author of *Monologe*.[119] As one can expect from this evaluation, Ullrich cites both *Monologe* and *Tischgespräche* throughout his books. He does not, however, include a source-critical discussion about them. Since he refers to source-critical problems with other sources, such as Rasuchning's books and Goebbels' diaries, one has to conclude from the absence of such a discussion with regard to *Tischgespräche* and *Monologe* that Ullrich does not consider there to be any such issues. This is, of course, a problem considering that the aim of Ullrich's book is to shed light on "Hitler's personality" and Hitler's private life.[120] The French historian Johann Chapoutot extensively cites both *Monologe* and *Tischgespräche* without including any source-critical discussion in his books on Nazi ideology. He also uses *Hitlers politisches Testament* and Rauschning's *Gespräche mit Hitler.*[121]

One of the few contemporary scholars to make use of *Table Talk* is Timothy Snyder in his *Black Earth*. A number of quotes from *Table Talk* are included in the first chapter of the book, and on most occasions the English edition actually gives a reasonably fair translation of the German contained in *Monologe*. However, in one case we find a quote that comes from a phrase that is not in *Monologe* at all. Snyder states that Hitler had said that the author Karl May "had opened his 'eyes to the world.'"[122] In *Table Talk* it indeed does say:

> It would be nice if his work were re-published. I owe him my first notions of geography, *and the fact that he opened my eyes to the world.*[123] [Italics added.]

The latter part of the sentence is only to be found in the first volume of *Libres propos*:

> J'amerais qu'on rèèditât son œvre. Je lui dois mes premières notions de géographie *et d'avoir ouvert les yeux sur le monde.*[124] [Italics added.]
>
> [Translation] I would like it if his works were re-published. I owe him my first notions of geography and to have opened my eyes to the world.

In *Monologe*, on the other hand, this phrase is not present:

> Ich würde den Karl May wieder erscheinen lassen, meine ersten geographischen Kenntnisse gehen darauf zurück![125]
>
> [Translation] I would re-publish Karl May; my first geographic knowledge draws upon it!

Genoud had fabricated the italicized part of the sentence that Snyder is quoting. It is also obvious that the implication of the first sentence in *Table Talk* and *Libres propos* is a bit different compared to the German text. To be fair, Snyder's argumentation does not stand or fall on this particular quote, but the fact that forged passages get cited by important scholars in the field is certainly disturbing anyhow. The main source-critical point is also another, namely that the table talks are not *ad verbatim* sources of Hitler's own words.

At another point he quotes one of Picker's notes in *Table Talk* that is consequentially not present in *Monologe*. Snyder writes that Hitler said that "a single loudspeaker in each village would 'give them plenty of opportunities to dance, and the villagers will be grateful to us.'"[126] In *Tischgespräche* this part reads like this:

> Und wenn die Leute viel tanzen könnten, so werde auch das nach unseren Erfahrungen in der Systemzeit allgemein begrüßt werden.[127]

In English this translates into:

> And if the people can dance a lot, then that will – according to our experiences during the time of the Weimar Republic – also be generally appreciated.

The phrase "the villagers will be grateful to us" is another one of Genoud's inventions, which has no real counterpart in the German text. It comes from *Libres propos*, Vol. II (1954), which says:

> If the people there are given the opportunity to dance a lot, they will be grateful to us.[128]

Snyder also quotes a longer paragraph from *Table Talk* that is worth comparing to the German text as published in *Monologe*, because here we find, again, slight differences in meaning.

Comparison between *Table Talk/Black Earth*, **Libres propos, and** *Monologe*[129]

Table Talk /Black Earth	Libres propos	Monologe	My translation
It is inconceivable that a higher people should painfully exist on a soil too narrow for it, whilst amorphous masses, which contribute nothing to civilization, occupy infinite tracts of a soil that is one of the richest in the world.	Il et inconcevable qu'on people supérieur subsite avec peine sur un sol trop étroit pendant que des masses amorphes, qui n'apportent rien à la civilization, occupant sur des étendues infinies un sol qui est l'un des plus riches de la terre.	Widersinnig ist es, daß ein hochstehendes Volk auf knappen Raum sich kaum ernähren kann, während die niedrigstehende russische Masse, die der Kultur nichts nützt, in unendlichen Räumen einen Boden innehat, der zum besten der Erde gehört.	It is absurd that a high-standing people almost cannot feed itself on limited space, whilst the lower-standing Russian mass, which does not benefit culture, possess a territory within infinite spaces that is among the best on earth.

The significant differences in meaning in these quotes are a result of *Table Talk* having been translated from *Libres propos*. This version, with its peculiar phrases, is to a large extent a creation by Genoud. Note also that the French "*inconcevable*", which means "inconceivable", is rather different compared to the German word "*widersinnig*", which means "absurd". Observe, again, that these comparisons are made only to show that the English translation cannot be trusted to give an accurate image of what the German text, which it is said to be based on, says. In a study that argues to get at the heart of Hitler's ideology, it cannot be at all unimportant what words Hitler actually used. Indeed, the whole analysis hinges on the assumption that this is indeed what Hitler said, because it makes no sense whatsoever to quote it as things that Hitler said otherwise. It would at least have made more sense to use the German text and make translations from it, since there is nothing authoritative about the English translation in *Table Talk*. It is also always a good idea to include the original wording, at least in a footnote.

What is perhaps an even graver mistake is the uncritical way in which *Table Talk* is used, and Snyder indeed treats it as if it was an *ad verbatim* record of Hitler's words; he repeatedly writes using phrases such as "said Hitler", "he stated", or "thought Hitler" when quoting this source.[130] On one occasion he even writes "wrote Hitler" when citing *Table Talk*, although this must be a mistake.[131] This is also why he, in his bibliography, has chosen to put it under the heading "Published Hitler Primary Sources."[132] *Table Talk* is by no means a "Hitler primary source." It is a poor translation of a poor translation, one filled with inaccuracies and completely fictitious additions courtesy of Genoud. In fact, not even the German texts are primary sources in the sense that, for example, *Mein Kampf* and *Hitlers zweites Buch* are (which Snyder includes under the same heading, although he uses the English translations of these). They are a secondary source with regard to Hitler's statements, based on the recollections of those who heard him speak. They are thus primary sources in the same sense that Goebbels's diaries, or any other such retroactive recollection of what Hitler said, are primary sources.

The table talks vs. *Mein Kampf*: is there really a difference?

As we have seen, there is a conception among most historians that the Hitler in the table talks is more honest and forthcoming than the one we meet elsewhere, for example, in *Mein Kampf*. Certainly, this is something that would have to be the case for any argument regarding the credibility of *Monologe* and *Tischgespräche* to hold water, since if Hitler is not more candid and truthful in the table talks, there is no reason at all for historians to trust them any more than they trust *Mein Kampf*. However, no one has actually systematically compared the table talks to *Mein Kampf* in order to see if this assumption is correct. The question is: are the table talks really are more reliable than *Mein Kampf*?

The answer seems to be: "no." I will illustrate this point with a few examples. In *Tischgespräche* Hitler tells his audience how the international press paid for his exorbitant bills at the Berlin Hotel Kaiserhof during the so-called *Kampfzeit*. According to Picker, Hitler said that these bills reached *Reichsmarks* (RM) 10,000 per week, and the interviews and articles granted to the foreign press had often brought in $2,000 to 3,000 each.[133] This, however, is a blatant lie. First, the bills for the hotel were nowhere near that high. In fact, one bill from September 1931, including seven rooms for three days (including all meals), was for RM 650.86. This was still a sum that meant that Hitler was spending more money on his hotel bills per day than an average German worker made in a month.[134] It is very likely that the sums for the interviews that Hitler is recorded as having mentioned are also false. In order for us to understand why Hitler would want to lie about this, we need to remember that already by 1930 Hitler had become a rich man from the sales of *Mein Kampf*. That year in his tax returns he stated an income from the sales of his book to the amount of RM 45,472, and for 1931 and 1932 this sum was RM 40,780 and RM 62,340, respectively.[135] The fact that Hitler gained considerable income from *Mein Kampf* – and used it to pay for galleries and museums in cities like Linz and for the FHQs – is mentioned by Picker. The amount of money is not stated, however.[136]

In the fall of 1930 the NSDAP and Hitler had also gained an important source of income in the industrialist Fritz Thyssen, who gave the party a credit of RM 300,000, which, among other things, helped pay for the purchase of Palais Barlow in Munich, which was to become the NSDAP party HQ – the so-called *Braune Haus*. Goebbels records in his diary in mid-April 1932 that a couple of generous donors had provided RM 100,000 for the party's election campaign. Hitler's life of luxury in the *Hotel Kaiserhof* had actually been exposed in 1932, much to his chagrin of course, by the left-wing Liberal newspaper *Welt am Montag* that published a bill from March that year. The extant bills from 1931 and 1932 show that Hitler paid between RM 606 and RM 829 over four days for himself and his entourage of three to four people. For five days between April and May 1932 he paid RM 837. The NSDAP declared that the bill published by *Welt am Montag* was a forgery, and Hitler, who took great care to spread the image of himself as a man who led a minimal existence, went on to claim in public speeches that he, in contrast to the leaders of the other parties, had no need of luxury and that he lived as "the bird in the woods."[137]

Goebbels lies about the article in *Welt am Montag* in his diary on 1 April 1932 and states that the "*Judenpresse*" had published a forged *Kaiserhof* bill.[138] He goes on to say that the article was nothing but "slander."[139] Naturally, it is totally implausible to assume that Goebbels did not know about the costs of Hitler's stays at *Hotel Kaiserhof*. The explanation for this lie is that this part of Goebbels's diary was intended for publication. The text from the diary entries were later published *ad verbatim* in 1935 in the propaganda book *Vom Kaiserhof zur Reichskanzlei*.[140] The claim in *Tischgespräche* that the international press paid for the *Hotel Kaiserhof* bills is simply not true.

Now the fact that Hitler kept the truth hidden also from those present at the FHQ shows that he was not at all more open, candid, or truthful in this setting. If Hitler refrained from being honest even about his income during the later years of the *Kampfzeit* to his entourage in the FHQ, then why are we supposed to believe that he spoke more freely on other matters? On the other hand, one could of course argue that since Hitler was actually acknowledging that the hotel bills had been quite high, he was being more open than he probably would have been in public. Even so, the fact remains that he is still not telling the truth regarding how these bills were paid for. It is of course still ironic that Hitler mentioned a sum more than twice as high as that which had been publicized by *Welt am Montag*, which the Nazis had then claimed to be a forgery. This also suggests that Hitler's memory was not always reliable.

There is not a lot about Hitler's childhood in the table talks, which means that a comparison between these sources and *Mein Kampf* is not a straightforward one. But the things that do appear in the former sources do not differ significantly from what is stated in the latter. In fact, the editors of the critical edition of *Mein Kampf* refer offhandedly to these parallels on occasion. For instance, the same art historic stereotypes regarding gifted artists (going back to the 1500s, but immensely popular during the romanticism in the late 1800s) – i.e. how their talent and wish to become artists are obvious already in childhood but still not acknowledged by family, schools, or society at large – as expressed in *Mein Kampf* also appear in *Tischgespräche*. The editors of *Mein Kampf* uncritically accept *Tischgespräche*'s claim that Hitler's father had taken him to the central customs office in Linz when Hitler was 13 years old in order to convince him to give up his artistic dreams and instead become a customs officer like his father.[141] Without any independent evidence to back this claim up, historians should not accept it.

The parts in *Monologe* that relate to Hitler's school years portray him as a clever boy who always stood up to, and questioned, authority. Heim's notes portray a Hitler that constantly drove his teachers mad with his informed obstinacy, often pointing out the contradictions between the religion and science education.[142] This is most certainly not a correct description of Hitler's time in school. While it is very seldom clear what specific time Hitler is talking about in these notes, we know from other evidence that Hitler did relatively well until his move in fourth grade to the *Realschule* in Linz in 1900 and later in Steyr. After this point his grades dropped dramatically. However, that the reason for this drop was that he opined against his teachers is not something that is supported by the available independent evidence. None of his teachers seem to have remembered any such thing.[143]

In December 1923, one of Hitler's former teachers, Eduard Huemer (who was Hitler's teacher in German and French from 1901 to 1904, or from first to third grade), would recall him as being talented but also lazy, dull, obstinate, and ill-tempered; a boy who often reacted with "poorly disguised recalcitrance" when confronted with his teacher's demands.[144] The latter conforms well to what Hitler states in *Mein Kampf*, namely that he was "rather difficult to handle" and that, once his grades started to get worse, he learned only what he found interesting but sabotaged everything else. Hitler does not mention the kind of debating with his teachers that appears in the table talks, however. Instead, he says that he debated his classmates.[145]

What appears in Heim's notes thus seems to be an elaboration, and embellishment, of what is in *Mein Kampf.* Hence, we cannot accept the stories contained in the table talks as portraying what really happened. Dirk Bavendamm has pointed out that Hitler's father was dead since 3 January 1903, so any reference to the poor results being a protest against his father's will after that point cannot be correct. Moreover, although Bavendamm does not make this point, Hitler did not really do well in the subjects he claimed to be most interested in either, i.e. geography and history, in which he managed to finally lift his grades only one point from a 4 to a 3. Hitler seems to have been able to learn anything only once he had a Damocles sword hanging over him.[146]

The historian has to apply some additional source-critical acumen here. Huemer was in fact acting as a character witness for Hitler during his trial in Munich in 1923–1924. Hitler's former teacher had been approached by the defence and asked to write a statement, and Huemer did just that. In fact, it is Huemer's investigation and judgement that are the source for most of the information about Hitler's school years (except for the grade reports that are extant). Huemer's comments about Hitler's character cited earlier also come from this statement, dated 12 December 1923.[147] This is before Hitler started writing *Mein Kampf,* which means that it is not at all implausible to imagine that it is actually Huemer's statements that influenced what Hitler later wrote in his autobiography.

Moreover, Huemer is actually very lenient towards Hitler with regard to his behaviour during his school years, and it is quite obvious that he did not wish to harm Hitler by painting a too negative image of his accused former student. What Huemer stated regarding Hitler's character as a child could easily fit into a larger argument as to why Hitler had participated in a revolution attempt and why he behaved as he did during the trial. But at the same time Huemer said that the school years often did not say very much about how people would later turn out, and he expressed his sincere hope that Hitler would be able to turn his life around and accomplish honourable and great things once he was granted the "elbow room" to do so.[148]

The description of how Hitler in Vienna in 1908 had surprised the people at the architecture university when he told them that he had no prior formal education in the field, and how his wish to enter the architecture school had failed because he did not have a middle-school degree (*Abitur*), and thus could not attend the Construction School (*Bauschule*) at the Technical University in Vienna, are basically identical in *Monologe* and *Mein Kampf,* even down to specific details. In *Mein Kampf* Hitler wrote that his talents were "obviously" (*ersichtlich*) in the field of architecture, and in *Monologe* Heim writes that the professor told Hitler that he had to have had some prior training because he obviously had a talent for architecture (*ersichtlich Talent für Architektur*).[149]

Hitler's views upon history education in the schools are the same in both *Mein Kampf* and in Heim's notes as published in *Tischgespräche* and *Monologe.* In both sources he states that history education should not be a matter of forcing children to learn names of kings and dates of battles and so on. Instead, good history education was supposed to teach the reasons for why things had happened and give the pupil the tools of analysing and understanding the contemporary world.[150] We see the same attitude towards the education of the German youth in *Tischgespräche* as in *Mein Kampf* as well.[151] Let us also not be fooled by the apparently modern and reasonable views on history education that Hitler is expressing here. Hitler was absolutely not interested in any objective analysis of history; in reality he was only interested in matters that confirmed his racist and nationalist worldviews. The views expressed are identical, most often down to the smallest details.

Comparison between views on education in *Mein Kampf* and *Monologe*[152]

Mein Kampf	*Monologe*
Es soll eben ein scharfer Unterschied bestehen zwischen allgemeiner Bildung und besonderem Fachwissen.[153]	Die Schulbildung soll nur ein allgemeines wissen geben, auf das man dann spezielle Wissen aufbaut. [. . .]
[Translation:] *There will continue to be a sharp difference between general knowledge and specific specialized knowledge.*	[Translation:] *The school education shall only give a general knowledge, upon which one then will build up specialized knowledge.*
Erstens soll das jugendliche Gehirn in allgemeinen nicht mit Dingen belastet werden, [. . .] und daher auch wieder vergißt. [Italics in original.][154]	Das Gehirn kann das gar nicht alles aufnehmen, es gibt nur eines: daß man wieder abstößt!
[Translation:] *First, the young brain ought in general not be burdened with matters, [. . .] and then also immediately forgotten.*	[Translation:] *The brain can absolutely not absorb all of this; one can only do one thing: keep rejecting it.*
Der Hauptwert liegt im Erkennen der großen Entwicklungslinien.[155]	Das Gemeinsame muß man in wenigen großen Zügen sehen!
[Translation:] *The main value lies in acknowledging the big lines of development.*	[Translation:] *The commonalities must be seen in a few big strokes.*
Es ist zum Beispiel nicht einzusehen, warum Millionen von Menschen im Laufe der Jahre zwei oder drei fremde Sprachen lernen müssen [. . .].[156]	Es hat doch gar keinen Sinn, jedem Kind in einer Mittelschule zwei Sprachen beizubringen!
[Translation:] *It is, for example, not clear why millions of people must learn two or three foreign languages over the years.*	[Translation:] *There is absolutely no point in teaching two languages to every child in a middle school.*
[. . .] *die es fünfundneunzig Prozent nicht braucht [. . .].*[157] [Italics in original.]	Fünfundneunzig Prozent brauchen das doch gar nicht!

Mein Kampf	Monologe
[Translation:] [. . .] *ninety-five percent of which there is no use for.*	[Translation:] *Ninety-five percent of it there is no use for!*
[. . .] Mathematik, Physik, Chemie usw. [. . .] gefärlich ist es aber auch, wenn die allgemeine Bildung einer Nation immer aussließlicher darauf eingestellt wird.[158]	Was braucht ein Junge, der Musik üben will, Geometrie, Chemie, Physik?
[Translation:] *Mathematics, Physics, Chemistry and so on [. . .] it is also bad if the general education of a nation is steered towards these to an ever larger degree.*	[Translation:] *What use has an adolescent who's going to practice music, for Geometry, Chemistry, Physics?*

The idea that 95 percent of what people learned in school is later forgotten is present in both sources; it is only the context that is changed. Also present is the idea of the general uselessness of the natural sciences (two of three being exactly the same in both sources). Here, too, the table talks add nothing to our knowledge of Hitler. It is almost as if Heim's text was modelled on *Mein Kampf*, and, in a way, it probably was because Hitler was simply purporting the same information that he had written in his biographical epos.

In *Mein Kampf* Hitler also writes about what he considered the correct way to read books, which in his view was a selective reading. One should not read a book "letter by letter" or from start to finish, but instead find that which serves one's purposes and commit this to memory. The same view is expressed in *Tischgespräche*, where Picker writes that Hitler would first look at the end of a book, then read a few sentences in the middle, and only once he had in this way formed a positive opinion of the book would he read it in its entirety.[159] In *Mein Kampf* Hitler expresses sympathy towards Social Democracy for having contributed to the fall of the Habsburg monarchy through its struggle for democratic elections. This is repeated in Heim's notes in *Monologe*.[160] Oddly, Longerich claims that *Monologe* gives another view on Social Democracy than *Mein Kampf* does.[161]

Another theme from *Mein Kampf* that is repeated almost *ad verbatim* in *Monologe* is that a government only has the right to rule as long as it serves the interest of the *Volk*. In *Monologe* we read:

> A regime has a right to exist only if, and as long as, its quest for power serves the development of the power embedded in the people.[162]

This corresponds to the following passage in *Mein Kampf*:

> that a state authority only has the right . . . if it conforms to the interests of a people.[163]

In the same note by Heim, Hitler also states, in connection with a discussion about the failure of Schönerer's *Alldeutschen* movement, that a leader, in order to succeed, "needs the faith that is only to be found in the people" (*braucht den Glauben, der sich nur in der Masse findet*).[164] This, too, comes straight out of *Mein Kampf*, where he wrote about the "the winning of the masses" (*der gewinnung der Massen*) and of the latter's "almost religious faith" (*fast religiöse Glaube*).[165] The fact that Hitler both in *Mein Kampf* and *Monologe* brings these points up in connection with a discussion about Schönerer and the Habsburg monarchy makes it obvious that what we see in *Monologe* is nothing but a regurgitation of Hitler's arguments in *Mein Kampf*.

In *Monologe* Heim writes that Hitler talked about how difficult a time he had had in Vienna, and how he sometimes had not had a warm meal in months at a time, and how he then had "lived on milk and dry bread."[166] In *Mein Kampf* Hitler writes that while working at a construction site, he "drank my bottle of milk and ate my piece of bread."[167] Note that it is very probable that Hitler made up the whole story about having worked in construction in Vienna, because we have no other sources that can confirm this.[168] In *Mein Kampf*, however, the bread and milk are not made into evidence of Hitler's poor circumstances.

Hitler's views in *Mein Kampf* of the mayor of Vienna (1897–1910), Karl Lueger, and the Christian Social Party (*Christlichsoziale Partei*) are the same in *Monologe*. Hitler writes that he had been hostile towards both Lueger and his party on his arrival in Vienna. However, after a while he came to adore Lueger, and by the time he wrote *Mein Kampf* he thought that Lueger was the greatest "German" mayor of all time.[169] He also writes that his sympathies were totally on the side of the "All-German Movement" when he arrived in Vienna[170] According to Heim, Hitler stated regarding Lueger that he was a fanatical enemy of him when he came to Vienna; as a Schönerian he was a firm opponent of the Christian Social Party. Heim also writes that Hitler thought that Lueger was the most genial mayor to have ever lived.[171]

What do all of the similarities between *Mein Kampf* and Heim's and Picker's notes mean then? One could argue that they actually confirm the reliability of the table talks. However, the point of contention here is not whether Heim and Picker purvey views that Hitler did not hold. Considering that Hitler held these views constantly from 1925 onwards, it would indeed be surprising if the table talks recorded anything that contradicted what is in *Mein Kampf*. The main point to make here is really that the table talks perpetuate the same lies that *Mein Kampf* does, and it is thus not at all a better source for Hitler's true thoughts or personality. This also conclusively proves that Hitler was no more honest in his table talks than he was in *Mein Kampf*.

Some scholars have rather uncritically accepted the idea that Hitler was already a follower of Georg Ritter von Schönerer when he came to Vienna. But when doing so they are relying exclusively on *Mein Kampf*, *Tischgespräche*, and *Monologe*. Ian Kershaw writes that Hitler "was plainly drawn in his Linz school – a hotbed of German nationalism – to the . . . Schönerer-style pan-German nationalism" and that he was an "avid supporter" of Schönerer's politics when he came to Vienna, although he never actively joined this movement. Volker Ullrich, too, states that Hitler brought the conviction of German cultural superiority with him to Vienna and that the young man idolized Schönerer. Ullrich adds that Hitler's statements regarding this part of his biography in *Mein Kampf* is "wholly trustworthy."[172] But it turns out that there are good reasons to doubt that part of Hitler's biography too.

Wolfram Pyta is more sceptical of this idea and argues, based on Dirk Baven-damm's *Der junge Hitler*, that Hitler's references to Schönerer in *Mein Kampf* were really just another way for Hitler to cover his tracks. Hitler's political preferences were not readily formed when he arrived in the Austrian capital in February 1908, he argues. Peter Longerich, too, seems to take this view. Even though he states that Hitler's claim in *Mein Kampf* to have been foremost a supporter of Schönerer is "wholly trustworthy", he specifically says that this was "during his Vienna years." Longerich thus does not seem to think that Hitler was a Schönerer supporter already in Linz, although he points out that the environment in Linz was fiercely German nationalist, and Hitler had probably acquired strong sentiments for the All-German movement before his arrival in Vienna. Two of Hitler's teachers in the *Realschule* in Linz were active in this movement, he points out. One of them, Leopold Poetsch (the other was supposedly Eduard Huemer), who taught Hitler geography and history, was even celebrated by Hitler in *Mein Kampf* as the one who awoke in him a sense of German nationalism. Longerich furthermore notes that Hitler's argumentation is so similar to that put forth by Schönerer and the *All-deutschen* that we must conclude that Hitler engaged with Schönerer's ideology in detail during his years in Vienna.[173] The latter actually implies that Longerich does not consider the 18-year-old Hitler to have been a "Schönerian" in February 1908.

The question thus still remains to what degree Hitler had actually read, and internalized, Schönerer's ideological tracts before his arrival in Vienna. It does not seem likely that he had, judging by the available evidence, because no sources can corroborate it. Rather, the opposite is true. Franz Jetzinger, in his book *Hitlers Jugend*, shows that Hitler's claim to have been a nationalist already in school is false; none of his classmates (or his teachers) remember anything like that.[174] Bavendamm has put forth a strong case for why historians ought not to accept the idea that Schönerer was a main source of inspiration for Hitler at this time. For example, he points out that since Hitler in *Mein Kampf* stresses that he had not yet any idea about anti-Semitism when he first arrived in Vienna, Hitler cannot have been as much of a "Schönerian" as he later claimed. The reason is that Schönerer was a dyed-in-the-wool anti-Semite. A "Schönerian" that was not an anti-Semite was a contradiction in terms, Bavendamm points out. Instead, Hitler's claim in *Mein Kampf* was most likely an effort to gain the trust and support of the German national conserva-tive voters.[175] It probably is significant also that Heim mistakenly thought that the movement was called *Altdeutsch*, meaning "old German" instead of "all German" and that this was not caught in any of the proofreadings.[176] In *Table Talk* this has been translated, or transformed rather, into "Germans of the old school." This is a direct translation of Genoud's French "Ces Allemands de la vieille école", which means that Genoud had not caught Heim's mistake either.[177] This is reasonably a sure sign that Hitler did not talk about Schönerer a lot and that Schönerer had not been very significant for his ideological development. If he had, Heim would certainly have known what the movement was called because he would have heard Hitler talk about it many times before.

Now it is time to look at a very enlightening passage from *Monologe*, a paragraph that perhaps better than any other illustrates just how unreliable the table talks are. Heim dates his note to 21 September 1941, and the key part relates a "memory" from Hitler's childhood regarding the Russo-Japanese War and reads:

> The Czechs will be most impacted by the collapse of Bolshevism. They have no doubt always looked to "Mother Russia" with silent hope. When during the time of the Russo-Japanese War the news of Russia's defeat [or: collapse] came in, [then] the Czech boys in my class cried while the rest of us celebrated. From this time dates my feelings for Japan.[178] [Words in square brackets added by me.]

Interestingly enough, Hitler writes about the Russo-Japanese War in *Mein Kampf*, too. However, there he makes no mention of the reactions of his non-existing Czech classmates:

> The Russo-Japanese War already made me considerably more mature, and also more attentive. I had, more out of national grounds, already taken sides there and then quickly put myself on the Japanese side when we differed in our views. In the defeat of the Russians I also saw the defeat of the Austrian Slavs.[179]

The fact that the Czech boys' despair is not mentioned in *Mein Kampf* should make us pause. Stories tend to be become less reliable over time, not the other way around, and therefore any added details at a later point must be regarded with suspicion. It is also perhaps important that in *Mein Kampf* Hitler gives the impression that it was he alone who took the side of the Japanese, not a collective of German-speaking pupils, although we certainly have reasons to doubt that even this is true. In this version of the story it seems to be other so-called German children that rooted for Russia. In fact, this conclusion is supported by the first record of Hitler telling the story in public, which comes from 1937 when he told the Japanese Prince Chichibu Yasuhito during the latter's visit to Berlin that he as a school boy had rooted for Japan in contrast to many of his fellow students. He then supposedly jumped with joy when the news about the Japanese victory at Tsushima arrived.[180]

An important fact to address in this context is, as Peter Longerich has pointed out, that the contention that there were a lot of Czech boys in Hitler's class is a figment of the latter's imagination. In reality, in 1903 there were only two pupils in Hitler's entire school that had Czech as their native language. Instead, we have to interpret this passage as a sign of the anti-Czech sentiments that Hitler carried with him, and then embellished, during his life, argues Longerich.[181] It is very likely that Hitler's impressions of a struggle between German and Czech elements were based on his later re-interpretation of his time in Vienna, which by 1900 had 350,000 to 500,000 Czech-speaking inhabitants (out of a total population of about 2 million). In *Mein Kampf* Hitler expressed his hatred of the multi-ethnic city and its, according to him, disgusting mixture of Jews, Poles, Hungarians, Czechs, Ruthenians, Serbs, Croatians, and so on. He considered all of this the embodiment of the sin against the blood, he wrote.[182] Note, however, that this cannot be an accurate description of Hitler's views while he was living in Vienna, as Hitler did not become a racist and an anti-Semite until he returned to Munich after the First World War.[183] Also, it certainly cannot be without importance that Maria Zakreys, the woman who Hitler had rented a furnished apartment from on Stumpergasse 31 during his second visit to Vienna in the fall of 1907 and that he and his friend Kubizek lived in from February to July 1908, was Czech.[184] Why would Hitler rent an apartment from a Czech woman if he hated Czechs with such passion?

There was, however, a small Czech population in Linz, as Franz Jetzinger has shown, but there were no great conflicts or tensions between the two ethnic groups in the years when Hitler lived there.[185] Now, granted, Longerich's and Jetzinger's statements about the number of Czech students are referring to Hitler's school in Linz, while Hitler went to school in Steyr during most of the Russo-Japanese War. Should we assume that there were many more Czechs in Steyr, a smaller town located about 30 km south of Linz and thus twice as far from the Czech border? Moreover, Upper Austria, which is where both Linz and Steyr are located, consisted of 99.7 percent ethnic Germans according to a census made in 1910. It turns out that there actually was a sizeable Czech colony in Steyr at this time due to the fact that a munitions factory there employed many Czechs. However, this population of Czech workers (probably mostly male) does not automatically translate into lots of Czech boys in Hitler's class at the time.[186] It is thus simply not plausible to assume that there were a lot of Czech pupils (or even that there were any at all) in Hitler's class in Steyr.

However, the real and final blow to this passage seems to be dealt by the historical timeline. The Russo-Japanese War began on 8 February 1904; Port Arthur capitulated on 2 January 1905; the battle of Tsushima took place on 27–28 May 1905; Russia accepted defeat on 5 September that year. Hitler went to school in Linz in third grade (1903–1904), but then in September 1904, when he was 15, moved to Steyr. However, as Jetzinger shows, Hitler left school already at the end of June 1905.[187] This means that Hitler was no longer in school when the news about Russia's final defeat came in, i.e. in September 1905. The statement, taken from *Monologe*, that he and his German-speaking classmates celebrated at this point simply cannot be true.

Hitler's version could be made to make more sense if we assume that he is talking about the victory at Tsushima in May 1905, as he would then still have been in school. In this context it is important to point out that Werner Koeppen's

notes from 21 September 1941 actually have Hitler mentioning Tsushima during this conversation. The relevant part of Koeppen's edited and proofed (typed)
version reads:

> The Führer then came to speak about childhood memories and labelled the
> Czechs as fanatical supporters of pan-Slavism. During his school time during
> the Russo-Japanese War his Czech classmates always had their sympathies on
> the Russian side, while the Germans on the other hand were on the Japanese
> side. Tsushima [!] was considered a big loss by all Slavs.[188]

Let us be clear about the fact that Koeppen's notes were also written down sometime after the conversation had taken place – the day after at the earliest – but it is
likely that the final version of the notes was typed up even later than that. There
was a process of proofreading, as in the case with Heim's notes, and since we do
not have access to the original notes and the changes made during the proofreading process, we cannot be absolutely sure that Koeppen is more reliable in this case.
However, both *Mein Kampf* and *Monologe* do seem to make more sense if we assume
that Hitler talked about the *final* defeat and collapse of Russia in the war, not about
its defeat in one (albeit important) battle. In fact, Koeppen seems to imply that
Tsushima was brought up as an example of Russia's many battle losses during the
war, since he is clearly talking about the Czech classmates' sympathies over a longer
period of time. It is certainly an interesting question why Heim did not include the
Tsushima comment. Did he forget it? Or did he not consider it important enough
to include it?

What thus seems to have happened here is that what is recorded in *Monologe*
is an embellished version of what Hitler wrote in *Mein Kampf*. At some point
Hitler must have decided to add the story about there being several Czech boys
in his class. Perhaps this was the first time that he ever told this story in this way.
No matter when or why Hitler added this to the version told in *Mein Kampf*, it is
not true. The idea of tensions between Czechs and Germans in Linz and Steyr is
also a product of Hitler's imagination. But the anti-Czech motif, and the idea that
the Habsburg monarchs were slowly but steadily making Austria "Slavic" or even
"Czech", is also a recurring theme in many places in *Mein Kampf*.[189] There was of
course no real basis for this view either, but the idea was founded upon the effort
of the Habsburgs, before 1914, to effectively try to put the various ethnic groups
within the empire on equal footing, as well as on a critique of Archduke Franz Ferdinand's marriage to Duchess Sophie, who came from Czech nobility. Yet another
reason for the conflict between Czechs and Germans in Austria had been a decree
from 1897 that had made it obligatory for all government officials in Bohemia to
be able to speak both German and Czech.[190]

Yet another fact that strongly speaks against this passage being about something that actually happened in Hitler's childhood is that, as Thomas Weber has
shown, Hitler became an anti-Slavic racist only very late in his ideological and
political career. During the early 1920s he in fact argued for an alliance between

anti-Bolshevik Russia and Germany as a way to put Germany on equal footing with Germany's real enemies: Britain and the United States. Hitler during the same time kept ideologues and friends around him – such as Alfred Rosenberg and Max Erwin von Scheudner-Richter – that at that time openly expressed pro-Slavic views. Rosenberg, for example, wrote in Dietrich Eckart's paper *Auf gut Deutsch* on 21 February 1921 that the Russians and the Germans were the finest and most noble peoples in Europe. Weber writes that even as late as 1921 "He did not display any apparent anti-Slavic sentiments. . .; his racism still took a rather selective form." It was not until he, while at the Landsberg prison writing *Mein Kampf*, came to include the concept of *Lebensraum* that his view of Russia and the Slavs shifted to murderous racism and colonialist annihilation. The key transition point seems to have been Lenin's death in 1924 after which time Hitler no longer believed that an alliance between Russia and Germany was possible.[191]

Are we then supposed to believe that Hitler had been a Slav-hating racist as a child only to later lose these sentiments before finally *again* becoming an anti-Slavic racist? No, it seems much more likely that Hitler had never been prejudiced against Russia and the Slavs before re-evaluating his ideological tenets while writing *Mein Kampf*. The story of how his Czech classmates reacted negatively to the news about Russia's defeat as it appears in *Monologe* and Koeppen's notes is clearly an elaboration of the legend presented in *Mein Kampf* almost 20 years earlier. In *Mein Kampf* Hitler used this story to position himself against Russia and to execute the ideological turnabout with respect to Russia that he felt the need to do.

Hitler then briefly goes on to describe his time in Munich, before the war, which he states was the happiest and most fulfilling time in his life.[192] This is repeated in *Monologe*, but then regarding the period *after* the war, where Heim has him saying that it was the best time that he could remember.[193] The table talks does not add anything new in terms of Hitler's views on the so-called survival of the fittest as God's law for all life on earth, as expressed in *Mein Kampf*. This includes his idea of the right of the "stronger" people to colonize the land of other "weaker" people. These were matters that were dealt with also in Hitler's unpublished second book.[194]

In *Monologe* Hitler states that he became a politician against his will and if another leader had been available, he would have become an artist or philosopher instead.[195] This is a theme that also traces its roots back to *Mein Kampf*, where he wrote that when he joined the army he wanted nothing to do with politics. He hated every politician, he says, but he could not help but take a position on the pressing issues that the German nation was now faced with. Finally, once the news of Germany's defeat and capitulation had reached him at the hospital in Pasewalk, Hitler claimed to have decided to become a politician.[196] This myth has been uncritically repeated by several authors, e.g. Fest.[197] This was a narrative that Hitler had invented years before he started writing *Mein Kampf*, and it appears in his statements in 1923 during, and in connection with, his trial.[198]

The fact that this lie is repeated in the table talks is of course significant, but the fact that it is repeated in one of Heim's nightly notes, i.e. one of those that so many historians have asserted are the most reliable, private, and intimate, is even more remarkable. The fact that Hitler lies to his small private entourage shows us that there is absolutely no reason for us to accept the portrayal of Hitler's character as it comes across in the nightly conversations recorded in *Monologe*. The fabricated biographical details were so central to the persona that Hitler projected before his followers that he would not let anyone look behind the façade and see the reality of his early life. In that sense there was no "real" Hitler to be revealed during those nightly conversations; he had become the propaganda image.

Another interesting subject to investigate in this context is what Hitler states about his wartime experiences. Do the table talks add any new, and more reliable, information about this period in Hitler's life, or do they simply perpetuate themes already published in *Mein Kampf*? Heim writes that Hitler stated that he went into the war in a state of "purest idealism", but that the mass death was a wake-up call that made him realize that life is a "continuous horrific struggle."[199] This certainly maps very well to Hitler's narrative in *Mein Kampf* and brings us no new knowledge.[200] When Hitler in *Monologe* says that the war was the only time in his life "in which I had no worries", then this is just a restating of what he wrote in *Mein Kampf* where he (no doubt falsely) claimed that it was "the most unforgettable and greatest time in my earthly life."[201] Note that Hitler by now has contradicted himself no fewer than three times and declared that the happiest time in his life was before, during, and after the war.[202] The use of superlatives was part and parcel of the idealized self-image of Nazi propaganda, and Hitler used this phrase, as well as the opposite – such as "hardest decision" – several times in *Mein Kampf*.[203] Thus whenever we encounter these types of formulations, we know that we are not dealing with a true statement about events.

Hitler mentions the first time he saw the river Rhein, as his regiment was riding the train towards the front in both *Mein Kampf* and *Monologe*, and although the details vary a bit the pathetic sentimentality of the narrative is the same.[204] There are also a couple of places in *Monologe* where Hitler talks about the importance of humour among the troops and about having laughed a lot with his comrades – especially in the early days of the war. He also mentions that the war experience either hardened one's character or made one a coward. This is simply a development of what is in *Mein Kampf* where Hitler wrote that in the early days of the war, he took part in the enormous rejoicing and laughing, but that he after a while became calm and decisive.[205] Sure, the reason for why these stories are the same in both sources could of course be that they are true; however, these stories bear all the hallmark traits of being idealized propaganda tales.

In this context it is also worth bringing up a glaring contradiction between the table talks and *Mein Kampf*, one that has not been acknowledged before even though scholars have certainly made use of the version entailed in *Monologe*. It concerns a comment about the mass slaughter warfare at Verdun. Pyta writes – based upon notes made by the chief of staff of Hans Guderian's tank group, Kurt Freiherr von Liebenstein, dated 21 December 1941 – that Hitler regarded the decisions of the generals at Somme and Verdun to have been a positive expression of the will to stand one's ground. He absolutely did not view this mass killing of hundreds of thousands of people as a consequence of madness (*Starrsinn*), writes Pyta.[206] However, Heim records Hitler on 13 October 1941 as having said that the offensive at Verdun was "an act of madness" (*eine Wahnsinnstat gewesen*). Apparently, Hitler also said that the commanders on both sides should have been court-martialled. Since then the attitude had changed, Heim continues, and one day such misdeeds would not be dealt with so lightly.[207] It is a complete contradiction.

So, which is it? Did Hitler think the generals' actions at Verdun was madness or recommendable? We cannot be expected to believe that Hitler changed his mind over a period of little more than two months. Pyta does not notice this contradiction, and the source he uses fits easily into the larger point he wants to make, namely that this was why Hitler issued a halt order to the forces outside Moscow on 17 December 1941 instead of allowing a tactical retreat.[208] Hitler does not describe Verdun in *Mein Kampf*, but he does mention the battle at the Somme, in which he took part and was wounded (although he greatly embellished his role in the battle). He describes the "material slaughter" (*Materialschlachten*) that more resembled hell than war. He does mention how the German forces stood their ground, but there is no condemnation of the generals here.[209] Pyta's argument makes no sense on the hypothesis that Hitler is telling the truth in *Monologe*, since that contradicts the argument he makes in his book.

We now have to ask: which source is more reliable? Once again, we are dealing with one of Heim's notes made during a nightly conversation, which Pyta and many others have argued are the most reliable. Could the reason for the discrepancies be that the statements in *Monologe* have been redacted, perhaps in case the notes were to be published after the war? There are other examples that show that Hitler was not being honest about decisions on military matters in *Monologe*. Hitler is there also portrayed as saying, also on 13 October 1941, that he recently had stopped an attack that would have brought the German forces only four kilometres further forward, because it was not worth the sacrifice in manpower.[210] Heim's note is suspicious simply because it does not conform well with the facts.

Hitler issued War Directive No. 37 on 10 October, but that had to do with a reorganization of the German forces in the Arctic area of northern Norway, Finland, and Murmansk, so that cannot be what Heim is referring to. However, if it is this directive that Heim is referring to then Hitler's stated reason for issuing it has nothing to do with reality, because the motives for putting a halt to forward operations in the Arctic was to prepare for winter warfare. Since the mass of the Soviet army had been destroyed on the central part of the front, the directive stated, there was no longer any need to tie them down through offensive operations. The German forces in Finland had neither the required strength nor the time to seize Murmansk and cut the Murmansk railway before the end of the year. Preparations were to be made to start offensive operations against these areas later during the winter and during early 1942.[211] Obviously, it was not a mere four kilometres that was being talked about here.

The German forces were still experiencing large success, despite the onset of bad weather in October, and the military situation reports in Goebbels's diary speak only of forward movement. Nowhere is there any mention of Hitler having issued an order to halt operations on the Eastern Front during the week preceding 13 October; German forces were constantly closing encirclements around the Soviet forces.[212] The only exception is a mentioning of hard resistance around Orel on 7 October, where Goebbels notes that this is not a problem, since a further push forward in this area was not planned anyway.[213] Nothing is said about Hitler having acted against an attack, however, and Werner Koeppen's description of the military situation between 6 and 9 October does not mention any such thing either. In Koeppen's report Guderian is stated to simply having pushed forward past Orel on 6 October.[214] Hitler did issue a War Directive to abandon the offensive on 8 December, however. But this directive still contained orders for offensive action; e.g. Sevastopol was to be seized, as was the lower Don area, and the isolation of Leningrad was to be secured. Moreover, the transition to defensive warfare was motivated by the great difficulties encountered due to the harsh winter conditions.[215]

The only reasonable conclusion that can be drawn from this state of affairs is that Heim's notes, once again, have been shown to be inherently unreliable. But how can this inaccurate version of events be explained? It is not really likely that Heim could have so massively misunderstood what was said. One plausible explanation is that he remembered wrong. This was, after all, said during the night and he could thus not make any notes to support his memory. Yet another plausible explanation is that this note was made only after a longer time had passed and that it is simply made up. Since we do not know what Genoud's original document for this note looked like, it is impossible to answer this question with any certainty. What is clear, however, is that the text in *Table Talk* and *Libres propos* is rather different and that at the very least Genoud took great liberties when translating the text into French.[216]

There are, indeed, several passages about his wartime experiences in the table talks that contain information not in *Mein Kampf*; e.g. the narrative about Hitler's dog Foxl and some rather prosaic references to various experiences during this period.[217] But the question of how useful this information is for historians is debatable. Since most of it cannot be corroborated by independent evidence, we are in no position to judge the veracity of the information, and thus historians cannot accept it as true due to the general unreliability of both *Mein Kampf* and *Monologe*. There is nothing that really gives us any insight into Hitler's personality, other than the fact that he consistently told falsehoods regarding his own personal history.

For example, it is not very likely that Hitler carried the five volumes of Schopenhauer's collected works with him during the war, as Müller records in a note from 19 May 1944.[218] This seems unlikely to be true for several reasons, although Hitler had told a group of generals and officers at the Platterhof Hotel in Berchtesgaden the same thing on 26 May that same year.[219] A five-volume edition was published by Insel Verlag in Leipzig in 1920, and it just so happens that Hitler got the 1920 five-volume edition of Schopenhauer's collected works delivered to the prison in Landsberg on 4 December 1923.[220] Obviously, Hitler did not have Schopenhauer's collected works already. Granted, he could of course have lost them at some point during or soon after the war. But it was hardly neither feasible nor practical to carry five books around during the war. Where did he keep them? Note, however, that we have several sources that tell a similar, but not identical, story. Hans Frank writes in his memoirs that Hitler (not clear when) told him that he carried a well-read paperback (*Reclam-bändchen*) copy of *Welt als Wille und Vorstellung* with him during the later war years.[221] Otto Dietrich claims in his memoirs that Hitler told him that he had carried "an abbreviated edition of Schopenhauer's collected works" with him in the field.[222] Julius Schaub also corroborates that Hitler told a similar story and says in his memoirs that Hitler had carried an abbreviated edition of Schopenhauer with him during the war.[223] This does not prove that the story is true, only that Hitler told some version of it to several people.

Hitler's idealizing and exaggerated statements about his ability to capture his audience with his speaking talent during his early days in Munich after the war are also present in both sources. In *Mein Kampf* Hitler states that he "nationalized" thousands of soldiers in this way, and in *Monologe* he mentions how in 1919 he made "flaming patriots" out of a battalion of soldiers in Passau.[224] We have absolutely no reason to think that either is true; rather, both statements are likely to be huge hyperbole, if not complete falsehoods. There is in fact no corroborating evidence of Hitler holding any such speeches among the troops during this period.[225] Hitler held no speeches in Passau during 1919 (he does not seem to have left Munich at all that year); in fact, his first speech in Passau appears to have taken place on 17 June 1923 when he addressed an NSDAP crowd there.[226]

In the table talks Hitler is also frequently depicted as criticizing every effort of the Church to meddle in politics, expressing the idea that organized religion (Christianity in particular) cannot be done away with until a viable alternative ideology is in place and the view that the Church could only lose a conflict with science. These views were developed and present already in *Mein Kampf*, and thus contain essentially nothing new at all.[227] What the table talks do add to what we find in *Mein Kampf*, however, is the strong criticism of Christianity and Christian dogma. We see the same in other independent sources, too, such as Werner Koeppen's notes and Rosenberg's and Goebbels's diaries, so we can be sure that he expressed such views, although the exact formulations are impossible to nail down exactly.

A striking example is the connection that is made in the table talks between Christianity and Judeo-Bolshevism and the characterization of Christianity as being nothing but communism or Bolshevism (the differences between these ideologies were never acknowledged by Hitler) or (in one instance) a precursor to Bolshevism; *Monologe* gives different versions of this view. At one point (a note dated 17 February 1942) Heim writes that Hitler used the term "Judenchristentum", and Christianity is even said not to be a true religion, which stands in total contrast to Hitler's view in *Mein Kampf* where the Jews are generally portrayed as the enemies of Christianity, which is there absolutely seen as a true religion.[228] The contradiction can be resolved once we remember that Hitler stated in *Mein Kampf* that the Jews were only a people and not a religious group and that they even lacked the idealism (i.e. the spiritual and mental capacity) to have a religion in the first place and to form a religious community.[229] In this instance the parts in *Mein Kampf* and Heim's notes are extremely similar.[230]

Once Hitler came to hold the view that Christianity was in fact a Jewish creation, then it logically followed that the Christianity preached by the established churches could not be a real religion either, since the Jews could not create such a thing. It could be that the resistance that Hitler and the Nazi regime met from some of the Christian churches, both real and imagined, during the latter half of the 1930s (e.g. Pope Pius XI's encyclical *Mit brennender Sorge*, read in German churches 21 March 1937, which was seen as a great provocation by Hitler), brought about this change in Hitler's view.[231] Hitler had in fact uttered a critique against the church for its "humane" attitude with regard to eugenics in the second volume of *Mein Kampf*.[232] The question of when Hitler first made the connection between Christianity and the Jews in the matter that is resembling that in the table talks is impossible to answer conclusively, simply because we do not possess the sources that we need for this undertaking. However, we do have some leads in the sources that exist. These points were raised by Hitler in numerous speeches throughout the early 1920s.[233] These early speeches bear a resemblance to what is in the table talks, but it seems to be an early stage in a process of formation of these thoughts – the seeds, stalk, and leaves are here, but not the full blossom. At this time, Hitler did not claim that Christianity was communism in another form, and he also clearly still considered Christianity itself to be something other than a Jewish invention. The Jews, according to Hitler's view in August 1920, used Christianity as a means to an end, but by stressing that the Jew could not become truly Christian, Hitler clearly still associated Christianity with something positive, i.e. as something that was separate from the negative traits ascribed to the Jews.[234]

There is, however, a consistent distinction made in the table talk notes in this context, namely that it was Paul who had corrupted the original teachings of Jesus, a view also expressed in Eckart's book *Der Bolshevismus von Moses bis Lenin* from 1924. But the Hitler in the table talks and *Mein Kampf* both celebrate Jesus as a hero and as a fighter against the Jews and their purported materialism and deification of money etc. Jesus is considered to be not of Jewish but of Aryan descent.[235] Another consistency in this context is Hitler's condemnation of atheism. The disapproval of atheism is repeated also in Hitler's second book.[236] Hitler's condemnation of political religion, i.e. parties that used Christianity for their political purposes (such as the Zentrum and BVP) in *Mein Kampf* is also kept intact throughout the table talks (and also all other sources).[237]

I do not believe, as many historians do, that Hitler's implicit and explicit references to the Bible and to Christianity in *Mein Kampf* was intended as nothing more than a propaganda trick. In that case we should reasonably expect his confessions to Christianity to be much more frequent and much more in alignment with mainstream Christian beliefs. That would surely be a much better strategy if the goal were to gain Christian followers. The fact that we do not see this should tell us that Hitler was probably expressing views that were his own. He kept presenting his *völkisch*-inspired and rather unorthodox interpretations, and *Mein Kampf* is certainly not in any way written to be a crowd-pleaser within Christian circles. Yet another reason that there may have been some sort of radicalization in his views of the Church could be that as he came to power in January 1933, he for the first time got to experience the Church's political power against him and the NSDAP in earnest.

This view of Christianity and Jesus was absolutely not Hitler's own creation. It had a long history within the right-wing racist nationalist movement and was in a sense a natural outgrowth of the racial ideas that took form during the 1800s. It was only a matter of time before this would influence the theological discussions within Christianity. Racializing Christianity was not a difficult thing to do, as Susannah Heschel has shown, because of the theological anti-Semitism already prevalent in the religion for many centuries. Ernest Renan, a French Catholic linguistics and religion scholar, was the one to provide this movement with the language necessary to complete the racial transformation of Jesus from a Jew into a Galilean Aryan. Hitler's views cannot only be traced to Renan, however. This view was taken over by Hitler's idol, Houston Stewart Chamberlain, in his *Grundlagen des neunzehnten Jahrhunderts* (1899). Hitler did not share Chamberlain's view of the apostle Paul, however, whom Chamberlain considered to be a pagan who brought Hellenistic influences into Christianity. Hitler's idea of Paul as a Jew who had corrupted Jesus's original teachings was inherited instead from the German philologist Paul Lagarde. Many German theologians picked up these ideas and elaborated upon them during the early 1900s, and the Aryan Jesus was used to justify racist violence and murder of other "races" even before Hitler became chancellor of Germany. A new Christian ethics, based on racism with the Aryan Jesus as its foundation, was thus created. In these circles the German defeat in First World War was seen as a crucifixion of Germany; a view that Hitler explicitly alluded to in *Mein Kampf* when he spoke of the need, and his struggle, for "the revival" and "resurgence of the German nation." All of this led to a movement within German theology and Christianity to root out all the Jewish influences in the New Testament.[238]

Several famous theologians were involved in this effort, and it was the central idea behind the pro-Nazi organization within the German Protestant church called *Deutsche Christen*.[239] From Rosenberg's diary we know that Hitler was aware of Lagarde's hypotheses, because Rosenberg talked about this with Hitler on 13 December 1941. The next day Rosenberg wrote in his diary that he had also told Hitler that Chamberlain's effort to save Paul's reputation was incomprehensible to him. According to the diary, Hitler affirmed that this was an error in Chamberlain's thinking: "Yes, that was Chamberlain's mistake."[240] Interestingly, Heim recorded this statement in his notes as well, and here the problematic nature of *Monologe* and Heim's notes generally becomes apparent. First, according to Heim, Hitler said "H. St. Chamberlain's mistake was to believe in Christianity as a spiritual world", which gives the distinct impression that it was Hitler, *not* Rosenberg, who brought up Chamberlain during the conversation. Second, Heim renders the part about Chamberlain almost unintelligible, since he excludes the context in which the statements were made and he states that Hitler said that Chamberlain's error was to be a believing Christian. That is to completely corrupt what was most likely said – Rosenberg actually appears to be a much more trustworthy witness here, since his notes make more sense in context than Heim's do. Lagarde is not mentioned by Heim, and neither is the fact that this was a conversation initiated and driven by Rosenberg.[241]

Naturally, the table talks record Hitler speaking about the Jews, a theme that is also one of the most central ones in *Mein Kampf*. Although the table talks touch on many issues that are not brought up in *Mein Kampf*, it is still the same ideas about race that underpin the statements recorded in the former.[242] Much of the basis for this is already evident in Hitler's famous response letter, dated on 16 September 1919, to a question about the Social Democratic government's attitude towards the Jews posed to him by one of the participants at the DAP on 12 September, the first DAP meeting that Hitler ever attended, a man named Adolf Gemlich. This is the first evidence we have of his anti-Semitism.[243] These are the same views that Hitler then put forth in *Mein Kampf* in chapter 11 entitled "Volk und Rasse."[244] The table talks thus add nothing new to our knowledge of Hitler's ideological underpinnings in this respect either.

Another piece of information in *Monologe* that contains false information is when Heim has Hitler, on 17 February 1942, talking about the German writer of books for children about the Wild West, Karl May (essentially a James Fennimore Cooper copy-cat), whose books *Monologe* states that Hitler read in the moonlight during his childhood. Heim writes that the first May book that Hitler read was one called *Der Ritt durch die Wüste* (The ride through the desert).[245] Dirk Bavendamm has pointed out that there is no May book with the title *Der Ritt durch die Wüste* and points out that May is never mentioned in either *Mein Kampf* or *Tischgespräche*. May's first book *Durch Wüste und Harem* (1892) was published as *Durch die Wüste* in 1895, which must be what Heim is referring to. Thus, Heim is either mistaken regarding the title of the book or Hitler was perhaps not as familiar with May's books as he claimed he was. Bavendamm argues that the several post-war eyewitness accounts may simply be reiterations of a questionable newspaper article from *Sonntag-Morgen-Post* 23 April 1933.[246] Interestingly, the British journalist Ward Price wrote in 1937 that Hitler "finds relief from responsibilities in stories of adventure. Karl May . . . whose books, like *Through the Desert*, are popular with German boys, is one of his favorites." The source for this was supposedly "his closest friends."[247] This book was about travel through the desert in Tunisia, not about the Wild West.

However, we know that Hitler spoke about Karl May from other independent sources. Koeppen records something similar on 5 October 1941.[248] Jetzinger shows that Hitler's former teacher, Eduard Huemer, stated already in December 1923 that Hitler appeared to have been influenced by May's stories about American Indians during his school years.[249] This has been picked up by many Hitler biographers,[250] and Pyta has several references to May in his book in which he argues that Hitler got much of his "territorial discourse" (*Raumdiskurs*) from his reading of May and that he took certain images of the geography and peoples of the "Wild West" and applied it to the wide open spaces of Russia.[251] What is at question is how much Hitler was really inspired by May, and for this we have much less secure knowledge. Koeppen's and Heim's reports are essentially identical, but contain no real details, which seems to imply that this was nothing more than one of Hitler's highly formalized anecdotes. Traudl Junge never mentions Karl May in her memoirs, and neither does Rosenberg in his diaries. Volker Ullrich, however, refers to an instance on 20 December 1936 when Goebbels states in his diary that Hitler was talking about Karl May and that he both loved May as a person and loved to read his books.[252] Christa Schroeder mentions Hitler talking about May, and says that he had claimed to have learned that it was a sign of courage to not show emotions when in pain, from reading May's books.[253]

However, the editors of the critical *Mein Kampf* edition stress that Karl May experts have shown that Hitler's understanding of America was not taken from May and underline that the passages about America in *Mein Kampf* have no relation to May's books.[254] Bavendamm, too, underlines this point, namely that certain ideological aspects in May's books were in stark contrast to National Socialist values, but still argues that Hitler was inspired in other ways.[255]

According to Heim's notes, Hitler stated on 27 February 1942 that he had refused to attend church on 21 March 1933.[256] This is only half correct. The Nazi leadership visited two churches on this day, which saw the opening of the new *Reichstag* celebrated in the *Garnisonskirche* in Potsdam. The day began with a service in the evangelical Nikolai-church, and also in the Catholic *Pfarrkirche*. It was only the latter one that Hitler did not attend, choosing instead to visit the graves of Nazi members.[257]

These findings can mean one of two things: 1) either Hitler had so internalized his false narrative from *Mein Kampf* that he actually thought that he was speaking the truth (perhaps he did already in 1924) or 2) Hitler was careful enough never to let his tongue slip when talking to his entourage in the FHQs. Perhaps the most plausible answer is that we are seeing a combination of these two alternatives in the table talks, filtered through those witnesses who wrote it down. The way in which Hitler and other top Nazis had internalized other false narratives, such as the anti-Semitic idea of Jewish world domination (and the even more bizarre idea that it was the Jews that had started the war), certainly suggests that this is a clear possibility. What is also an interesting question is to what degree *Mein Kampf* actually influenced the content in the table talks. Did Heim or Picker, or perhaps Bormann, ever take recourse to Hitler's book in order to make the two agree? It is actually not at all unlikely that some of the agreement between *Monologe* and *Mein Kampf* may have come about due to the proofreading and editing process (more about this later). Note that these are problems that are stacked on top of the more general problem with these sources, i.e. that they are reconstructions of Hitler's words made from memory after the events that they describe.

Conclusion

This chapter had three main objectives: 1) to show how the table talk notes were made, 2) to show how the table talks have been used by historians thus far, and 3) to illustrate if and how the content of the table talks differ from the content of other sources. The first objective is important if we wish to understand what kind of sources the table talks actually are. It has been shown that these notes were made almost exclusively from memory after the conversations they describe had taken place. They present the historian with a subjective selection of statements, utterances, and topics that the note takers in conjunction with Bormann considered important enough to put on paper and which could be remembered by the time they were written down.

The second objective is central if one wants to understand why a study such as the one in this book is necessary at all. Only by illustrating how these sources have been used can we come to a clear understanding of how they have impacted on the research, and thus also our understanding of, Hitler. The table talks are some of the most central and frequently used sources in the field. Basically, *all* historians since 1951 onwards writing about Hitler, National Socialism, or Nazi Germany have used them to a lesser or greater extent. Most historians have also used these sources entirely uncritically, citing from them as if they contained Hitler's own words. This is a serious mistake, and this practice has to stop. Instead, it should be replaced by a much more mindful and critical approach. The table talks should never be quoted as if they contained Hitler's own statements in the same way as his speeches or his writings, and they should be evaluated with the same level of scepticism as these other sources.

We have also seen that the table talks essentially do not contain anything new that radically changes our understanding of Hitler compared to other sources such as, for example, *Mein Kampf*. Some of the same themes and lies that we find in the latter are included in the former. This shows that what we find in the table talks is not really a more intimate and private Hitler. This result should be important in order to make historians rethink the almost sacred reverence with which they have so far approached these sources. The table talks are therefore no more reliable or worthy of citation than any other notes and memoranda, such as Werner Koeppen's, that were made at the same time and in the same way, i.e. not by the use of stenography.

Notes

1 Wiskemann, Elizabeth, "Hitler's Table Talk 1941–1944" in *International Affairs (Royal Institute of International Affairs 1944 –)* , Vol. 29, No. 4 (October 1953), pp. 493–494.
2 Evans, Richard J., *Lying About Hitler: History, Holocaust, and the David Irving Trial* (New York: Basic Books, 2001), pp. 74–75.
3 Evans, R. J., *The Coming of the Third Reich: How the Nazis Destroyed Democracy and Seized Power in Germany* (London: Penguin Books, 2004), pp. 189, 498; Evans, Richard J., *The Third Reich at War 1939– 1945* (London: Penguin Books, 2010), pp. 171–172, 175, 784–785.

4 Evans, R. J., *The Third Reich at War . . .,* pp. 170, 784.

5 *Hitler's Table Talk. . .* (1953), p. xii.

6 Evans, R. J., *The Third Reich in Power* (London: Penguin Books, 2006), p. 250. For Picker, see: *Hitlers Tischgespräche. . .* (1951), p. 275.

7 Carrier, R., "Hitler's Table Talk . . .", pp. 561–576.

8 Ibid.

9 Rosenbaum, Ron, *Explaining Hitler: The Search for the Origins of His Evil* (London: Papermac, 1999), p. 74.

10 Glover, Jonathan, *Humanity: A Moral History of the Twentieth Century* (London: Jonathan Cape, 1999), p. 355. See also: Carrier, R., "Hitler's Table Talk . . .", pp. 565–566.

11 *Hitlers Tischgespräche. . .* (1951), p. 353; *Hitlers Tischgespräche. . .* (1963), p. 186. See also: See also: Carrier, R., "Hitler's Table Talk . . .", p. 570.

12 *Hitler's Table Talk. . .* (1953), p. 343. This is also included in Glover and remarked on by Carrier: See also: Carrier, R., "Hitler's Table Talk . . .", pp. 561–576.

13 *Conversazioni segrete . . .,* p. 367.

14 *Libres Propos. . .* (Vol. I, 1952), p. 332. The key words have been italicized.

15 This mistake was first discovered by Carrier, see: Carrier, R., "Hitler's Table Talk . . .", p. 568.

16 *Libres propos. . .* (Vol. I, 1952), p. 332.

17 *Hitlers Tischgespräche. . .* (1951), p. 353; *Monologe . . .,* p. 303.

18 *Hitlers Tischgespräche. . .* (1951), pp. 33–34.

19 Copy of Genoud's complaint before the court in Düsseldorf, 18 March 1952, p. 3; Instiut für Zeitgeschichte, Munich (henceforth: IfZ); ID 103/19; Korrespondenz G. Genoud presented this *Bauchbinde* as evidence.

20 Ibid., p. 4.

21 "Millionen-Streit um Hitlers Tischgespräche" in *Abendzeitung,* 3 July 1952.

22 *Hitler's Secret Conversations. . .* (1953), see text on the inner flaps and the front- and back-side of the cover.

23 "Teure Tischgespräche" in *Die Welt* 2 July 1952. The same was reported by *Le Monde* ("La publication en France de Propos familiers de Hitler donne naissance à un procès de propriété littéraire au cours duquel risqué d'être évoquée la disparition de Martin Bormann" in *Le Monde* 2 July 1952) in an article littered with incorrect information.

24 See e.g. "Prozeß um Hitlers 'Tischgespräche'" in *Westfälisches Volksblatt,* 13 August 1952.

25 Trevor-Roper, Hugh, "Paula Hitler fordert ihr Erbe. Großer Streit um den persönlichen Nachlaß des braunen Diktators" in *Westfalen-Post* 18 October 1952.

26 "Aktenvermerk", undated (late March or early April) 1952, pp. 1–3; IfZ; ID 103/202.

27 Franz-Willing, Georg, "Hitlers Tischgespräche" in *Klüter Blätter. Monatshefte für Kultur und Zeitgeschichte,* Jahrgang 32, December 1981, Heft 12, pp. 22–24. See also: Toland, John, *Adolf Hitler* (New York: Doubleday & Company, 1976), p. 682. This is obviously the article referred to by Pyta, although he mistakenly states the year as 1980 (Pyta, Wolfram, *Hitler. Der Künstler als Politiker und Feldherr. Eine Herrschaftsanalyse* (München: Siedler, 2015), p. 666).

28 Manuscript for Heim's recorded statement to the BBC, 14 September 1953, p. 5; Werner Jochmann Nachlaß (in the hands of Professor Ursula Büttner, Hamburg) (henceforth: WJN); Binder: Schriftwechsel: A – K 1977.

29 I have huge respect for Professor Pyta's work, and he has assisted me immensely in my research for this book, including giving me access to many documents that I would probably never have discovered otherwise. However, since it is my conviction that the available evidence in this case does not support Pyta's conclusions, I have to bring these points up in this chapter.

30 Pyta, W., *Hitler . . .,* pp. 31–36; for the quotes, see: p. 31.

31 Ibid., p. 34. The idea that Hitler did not know about the notes being made is also, based on Heim, uncritically reproduced by Jochmann: *Monologe . . .,* p. 16. This myth will be criticized and thoroughly debunked later in this book.

32 Pyta, W., *Hitler . . .*, p. 32. Pyta notes that the conversations that took place during lunch and dinner (*Mittags- und Abendstafel*) included people that were far less close to Hitler than those present at the nightly *Teegespräche* and that these discussions mostly concerned military matters (ibid., pp. 32–33). These are statements that simply cannot be sustained by the evidence. Heim and Picker did not note military matters at all (in contrast to Werner Koeppen, as will become evident), and neither *Tischgespräche* nor *Monologe* supports Pyta's claims in this regard. In fact, no qualitative difference between the various notes can be discerned based on when the statements they record were uttered. Jochmann notes that Heim left all military matters out because he did not have enough knowledge about this field (*Monologe . . .*, p. 14).

33 Pyta, W., *Hitler . . .*, pp. 313–333.

34 Ibid., p. 331.

35 Ibid., p. 33.

36 *Monologe . . .*, p. 22.

37 Pyta, W., *Hitler . . .*, p. 33.

38 Longerich, Peter, *Hitlers Stellvertreter: Führung der Partei und Kontrolle des Staatsapparates durch den Stab Heß und die Partei-Kanzlei Bormann* (München: K. G. Saur Verlag, 1992), p. 161.

39 Pyta, W., *Hitler . . .*, p. 33.

40 Ibid., p. 34.

41 Ibid., p. 667.

42 Longerich, P., *Hitlers . . .*, p. 161.

43 Ibid., p. 254. Longerich has dated this note to 1944, but that seems to be wrong, see:"Vorlagen für Reichsleiter Bormann", Christentum – Vermerk Bormanns über eine Unterhaltung bei Hitler, 26 Jan. 1943; Bundesarchiv, Berlin-Lichterfelde (henceforth: BABL); NS 6; Vol. 166.

44 Ibid., p. 255.

45 Kandel, Eric R., *In Search of Memory: The Emergent New Science of the Mind* (New York: W. W. Norton & Company, 2007), p. 281.

46 Ibid., p. 302.

47 Ibid., p. 311.

48 Schacter, Daniel L., "Memory Distortion: History and Current Status" in Daniel L. Schacter (ed.), *Memory Distortion: How Minds, Brains, and Societies Reconstruct the Past* (Cambridge, Ma: Harvard University Press, 1995), p. 24.

49 Pyta, W., *Hitler . . .*, p. 33.

50 Ibid., pp. 33, 666.

51 Ibid., p. 35.

52 Ibid., pp. 35–36.

53 Ibid., p. 36.

54 Ibid., p. 34.

55 Ibid., pp. 825–827. He does this even though he also has a section called "Erinnerungen und zeitgenössisches Schrifttum" (ibid., p. 829).

56 *Hitler, Mein Kampf. Eine kritische Edition, Band II. Herausgegeben von Christian Hartmann, Thomas Vordermayer, Othmar Plöckinger, Roman Töppel* (München: Institut für Zeitgeschichte, 2016), pp. 1770–1771 [henceforth: Hitler, Mein Kampf . . . (Band II)].

57 A first brief outline of Hitler's fake biography appears in a letter he wrote to an unknown person on 29 November 1921; see: Jäckel, Eberhard and Kuhn, Axel (ed.), *Hitler. Sämtliche Aufzeichnungen 1905–1924* (Stuttgart: Deutsch Verlags-Anstalt, 1980) (henceforth: *SA*), pp. 525–527 (Document 325). This biography differs in some of the details compared to the one that appeared later in *Mein Kampf*. However, it shows that Hitler had already by that time started to erase his true past and begun the construction of the edifice of lies that he would erect in its place.

58 Pyta, W., *Hitler . . .*, p. 36.

59 Ibid., pp. 636, 643.

60 Bullock, Alan, *Hitler: A Study in Tyranny* (Harmondsworth: Penguin Books (Completely revised edition) 1962), pp. 27, 73, 79–80, 82–83, 134–135, 171, 248, 263, 337, 343, 357, 374, 388–390, 444, 591, 655–657, 670–673, 769–773; for the bibliography, see: p. 809. Most of Bullock's citations are from *Table Talk*.

61 Ibid., p. 655.

62 Bullock, A., *Hitler: A Study in Tyranny* (London: Odhams Press, 1952), pp. 342, 616. See also references on pp. 225, 406.

63 Ibid., p. 739.

64 Bullock, A., *Hitler. . .* (1962), pp. 655–656.

65 Ibid., pp. 14–15.

66 Ibid., p. 14.

67 Ibid., p. 804. See also: Bullock, A., *Hitler. . .* (1952), p. 736.

68 Fest, Joachim, *Hitler. Eine Biographie* (Berlin: Propyläen, 1973), passim.

69 Carr, William, *Hitler: A Study in Personality and Politics* (London: Edward Arnold, 1978), pp. 183–184.

70 Kershaw, I., *Hitler 1936–45 . . .*, especially chapter 9 pp. 393–457 cites frequently from *Monologe* and Koeppen's notes (and on occasion *Tischgespräche*); see for references e.g. pp. 944–945, 964–969; regarding his critical discussion, see: pp. 1024–1025. Kershaw mentions Heim, Picker, and Koppen as authors of the table talks but forgets Bormann and Müller.

71 Kershaw, Ian, *Hitler 1889–1936: Hubris* (London: Allen Lane, 1998), p. 632. This, however, leaves us with the incorrect impression that this part of the *Table Talk* was translated from the same German manuscript that was the basis for *Monologe*, which was *not* the case. Instead, this part was translated from Genoud's French *Libres propos*. The "loosely rendered" translation is thus often the work of Genoud and not of the translator working on *Table Talk*. More on this later on in this book.

72 Ibid., pp. 381, 711.

73 See e.g. Kershaw, I., *Hitler 1936–45 . . .*, see for references e.g. pp. 432–435.

74 Joachimsthaler, Anton, *Hitlers Weg begann in München 1913–1923* (München: Herbig, 2000), pp. 22, 25, 34–38, 40, 47, 52, 82, 97, 113, 115, 122–123, 127–128, 131–132, 140–141, 144, 149, 156, 163–164, 168–170, 177, 179, 183, 198, 204. Interestingly, Joachimsthaler most often lists Heinrich Heim as the author of this work (ibid., p. 324), except in one endnote where Hitler is stated as the author (ibid., p. 326). This is not entirely correct, since *Monologe* also contains notes made by Müller and Bormann.

75 Hamann, Brigitte, *Hitlers Wien. Lehrjahre eines Diktators* (München: Piper Verlag, 1996), passim, but especially pp. 125–168.

76 Jäckel, Eberhard, *Hitler in History* (Hanover, NH: University Press of New England, 1984), p. 48.

77 *Hitler's Table Talk 1941–1944. With an Introductory Essay on The Mind of Adolf Hitler by H. R. Trevor-Roper* (London: Weidenfeld & Nicolson, 1953), p. 79; *Monologe . . .*, p. 99.

78 Jäckel, Eberhard, *Hitler in History* (Hanover, NH: University Press of New England, 1984), p. 62.

79 Lukacs, J., *The Hitler of History*, pp. 68, 85, 89, 109, 123, 151, 155–156, 192.

80 Maser, Werner, *Adolf Hitler: Legende, Mythos, Wirklichkeit* (München: Bechtle Verlag (12th ed.) 1989), p. 646.

81 Ibid., pp. 183, 565. Maser seems to have forgotten to include the book in the bibliography.

82 Anton Joachimsthaler details this criticism in: Joachimsthaler, Anton, *Hitlers Weg begann in München 1913–1923* (München: Herbig, 2000), pp. 10–16, and passim.

83 Toland, John, *Adolf Hitler*, Vol. II (New York: Doubleday & Company, 1976), p. 958 (pp. 848–849 in the one-volume edition).

84 Misch, Rochus, *Der Letzte Zeuge. "Ich war Hitlers Telefonist, Kurier und Leibwächter". Mit einem Vorwort von Ralph Giordano* (München: Pendo Verlag, 2008), pp. 21–22.

85 Zitelmann, Rainer, *Hitler: Selbstverständnis eines Revolutionärs* (Hamburg: Berg, 1987), p. 1.
86 Ibid., p. 13.
87 Ibid.
88 Calic, Edouard, *Ohne Maske. Hitler – Breiting Geheimgespräche 1931* (Frankfurt: Societäts-Verlag, 1968).
89 Zitelmann, R., *Hitler: Selbstverständnis . . .*, p. 13.
90 Ibid., pp. 305–306.
91 Ibid., p. 431.
92 "Hitler-Dokumente. Frei erfunden" in *Der Spiegel* 37/1972, p. 62.
93 This had been shown in: Seebold, Gustav Hermann, "Die Hitler-Breiting-Geheimsepräche als historische Quelle" (Bochum: Master thesis, 1975). The newspaper *Die Zeit* had also published a series of articles on this subject collected in: Janßen, Karl-Heinz, "Geschichte aus der Dunkelkammer" *Sonderdruck* from *Die Zeit* 38–41/1979 (Hamburg, 1979).
94 For this point, see: Backes, Uwe, *Politischer Extremismus in demokratischen Verfassungsstaaten* (Wiesbaden: Springer Fachmedien, 1989), p. 62, *n*106.
95 Janßen, Karl-Heinz, "Geschichte aus der Dunkelkammer" *Sonderdruck* from *Die Zeit* 38–41/1979 (Hamburg, 1979), p. 17.
96 Zitelmann, R., *Hitler: Selbstverständnis . . .*, pp. 441–442.
97 For this, see: Janßen, K.-H., "Geschichte aus der Dunkelkammer". Zitelmann was far from the only historian to be fooled by Calic's forgery. For example, Calic managed to get the famous historian Golo Mann to write an enthusiastic foreword to his book. Mann even manages to state the falshood that the *Tischgespräche* were stenographed as well (Calic, E., *Ohne Maske . . .*, pp. 5–8). Calic also forged other documents, which he claimed proved that the Nazis themselves had started the Reichstag fire in 1933 (for this, see: von Hehl, Ulrich, "Die Kontroverse um die Reichstagsbrand" in *Vierteljahr für Zeitgeschichte* 36/1988, Heft 2, pp. 259–280). There are, thus, many parallels between how Calic managed to dupe historians and how Genoud did the same.
98 Hett, Benjamin Carter, *Burning the Reichstag: An Investigation into the Third Reich's Enduring Mystery* (Oxford: Oxford University Press, 2014).
99 Kellerhoff, Sven Felix, *The Reichstag Fire: The Case Against the Nazi Conspiracy* (Stroud: The History Press, 2016).
100 Zitelmann, R., *Hitler: Selbstverständnis . . .*, p. 14.
101 Ibid., pp. 25, 38, 41, 48, 154.
102 Ibid., p. 34. Zitelmann actually makes generous use of Rauschning in this book. There is another similar critical note on Rauschning (ibid., pp. 82–83), but in all other instances Zitelmann has no such discussion, either before or after these examples, and it is not at all clear why we are to trust Rauschning in most cases without a motivation when we are provided such motivations on these few occasions.
103 Ibid., pp. 469–470.
104 Schieder, Theodor, *Hermann Rauschnings "Gespräche mit Hitler" als Geschichtsquelle* (Opladen: Westdeutscher Verlag, 1972), p. 62. This is not the only weakness in Schieder's book. He seems also to be unable to see that the fact that several years went by between Rausching left Germany and the writing down of his conversations with Hitler is hugely problematic for the credibility of Rauschning's book (ibid., pp. 29–30).
105 Zitelmann, R., *Hitler: Selbstverständnis . . .*, pp. 82–83.
106 Hänel, Wolfgang, *Hermann Rauschnings "Gespräche mit Hitler": Eine Geschichtsfälschung* (Ingolstadt: Veröffentlichung der Zeitgeschichtlichen Forschungsstelle, 7. Band, 1984).
107 Malanowski, Wolfgang, "'Zitat, Zitat, Zitat und nichts weiter'" in *Der Spiegel* 37/1985, p. 99.
108 Kershaw, I., *Hitler: 1889–1936 . . .*, p. xiv.
109 For a good summary of this, see: Brechtken, Magnus, "'Ein Kriminalroman könnte nicht spannender erfunden werden' – Albert Speer und die Historiker" in M. Brechtken

(ed.), *Life Writing and Political Memoir – Lebenszeugnisse und Politische Memoiren* (Göttingen: V&R Unipress, 2012), pp. 35–78.

110 Zitelmann, R., *Adolf Hitler. Eine politische Biographie* (Göttingen: Muster-Schmidt Verlag, 1998), pp. 14–15.

111 Ibid., p. 18.

112 Ibid., pp. 19–21.

113 Weber, Thomas, *Hitler's First War* (Oxford: Oxford University Press: 2010); Joachimsthaler, A., *Hitlers Weg . . .,*.

114 *Monologe . . .*, p. 132.

115 Joachimsthaler, A., *Hitlers Weg . . .*, pp. 171–174. Interestingly, Hitler apparently stated to the director of the prison in Landsberg, Otto Leybold, who wrote this down on the front page of Hitler's prison act, that he had "gone through a whole series of battles and fights, always against France." He thus does not seem to have mentioned Britain. See: Fleischmann, Peter, *Hitler als Häftling in Landsberg am Lech 1923/24. Der Gefangenen-Personalakt Hitler nebst weiteren Quellen aus der Schutzhaft-, Untersuchungshaft-, und Festungshaftanstalt* (Neustadt: Verlag PH. C. W. Schmidt, 2015), p. 84.

116 Ryback, Timothy W., *Hitler' Private Library: The Books That Shaped His Life* (New York: Vintage Books, 2010), for the references see, pp. 269–272, 275, 279, 282, 284. Ryback also uses Rauschning uncritically.

117 Ibid., p. 282.

118 Miskolczy, Ambrus, *Hitler's Library* (Budapest: Central European University Press, 2003), pp. 40, 42, 60, 92, 124–126, 143. One more weakness in Ryback's book is that he does not refer to any of those scholars who had studied Hitler's private library before him, such as Miskolczy and also: Wallach, Jehuda L., "Adolf Hitlers Privatbibliothek" in *Zeitgeschichte*, No. 1–2 (1992); Phelps, Reginald H., "Die Hitler-Bibliothek" in *Deutsche Rundschau* (September 1954), pp. 923–31.

119 Ullrich, Volker, *Adolf Hitler. Biographie. Band I: Die Jahre des Aufstiegs 1889–1939* (Frankfurt am Main: S. Fischer Verlag, 2013), pp. 1040–1041; Ullrich, V., *Adolf Hitler. Biographie. Band II: Die Jahre des Untergangs* (Frankfurt am Main: S. Fischer, 2018), pp, 857–858.

120 For this, see: ibid., pp. 14–20, 840, 842; quote on p. 14.

121 Chapoutot, Johann, *La loi du sang. Penser et agir en nazi* (Paris Gallimard, 2014), passim; Chapoutot, J., *La révolution cuturelle nazie* (Paris: Gallimard, 2016), passim; Chapoutot, J., *Le nazisme et l'Antiquité* (Paris: Quadrige, 2016), passim.

122 Snyder, Timothy, *Black Earth: The Holocaust as History and Warning* (London: The Bodley Head, 2015), p. 15. See also: Fest, J., *Hitler . . .*, p. 1034.

123 *Hitler's Table Talk. . .* (1953), p. 316.

124 *Libres propos. . .* (Vol. I, 1952), p. 306.

125 *Monologe . . .*, p. 281.

126 Snyder, T., *Black Earth . . .*, p. 18.

127 *Hitlers Tischgespräche . . .* (1953), p. 73 (11 April 1942). Snyder is also taking this passage slightly out of context here. Picker's German text does not imply that the Germans should simply put up a loudspeaker in every village and play music through it. Instead, this is part of an argument to the effect that "it is much better to set up a radio loudspeaker in each village to tell people news and provide entertainment . . .", rather than offer them education (ibid.).

128 *Libres propos. . .* (Vol. II, 1954), p. 65.

129 *Hitler's Table Talk. . .* (1953), p. 38; Snyder, T., *Black Earth . . .*, p. 18; *Libres propos . . .* (Vol. I, 1952), pp. 38–39; *Monologe . . .*, p. 66. The exact same paragraph is also quoted by Richard J. Evans in: Evans, Richard J., *The Third Reich at War . . .*, p. 171.

130 Snyder, T., *Black Earth . . .*, pp. 8, 18.

131 Ibid., p. 6.

132 Ibid., p. 397.

133 *Hitlers Tischgespräche . . .* (1951), p. 437.

134 Kellerhof, Sven Felix, *"Mein Kampf". Die Karriere eines deutschen Buches* (Stuttgart: Klett-Cotta, 2015), p. 219.
135 Ibid., pp. 218–219.
136 *Hitlers Tischgespräche. . .* (1951), pp. 435–436.
137 Ullrich, V., *Adolf Hitler . . .*, pp. 277–278, 281, 339–340 (for more on Hitler's luxurious lifestyle, see also: pp. 449–453). See also: Goebbels, Joseph, *Die Tagebücher von Joseph Goebbels 1924–1945. Im Auftrag des Instituts für Zeitgeschichte und mit Unterstützung des Staatlichen Archivdienstes Rußlands. Herausgegeben von Elke Frölich. Band 1–4 & 1–15* (München: K.G. Saur 1987–1995) (henceforth: *TBJG*), I/2, p. 156 (15 April 1932). Goebbels also states that the NSDAP was able to spend RM 200,000 on propaganda in the spring of 1932, although he still complained that the Nazis had less funds available for propaganda than the other parties, see: ibid., p. 137 (6–7 March 1932).
138 *TBJG*, I/2, p. 149 (1 April 1932).
139 Ibid., p. 150 (2 April 1932).
140 Goebbels, J., *Vom Kaiserhof zur Reichskanzlei. Eine historische Darstellung in Tagebuchblättern (vom 1. Januar 1932 bis zum 1. Mai 1933)* (Munich: Zentralverlag der NSDAP, 1935), pp. 73–74.
141 *Hitler, Mein Kampf. Eine kritische Edition, Band I. Herausgegeben von Christian Hartmann, Thomas Vordermayer, Othmar Plöckinger, Roman Töppel* (München: Institut für Zeitgeschichte, 2016), pp. 106–107 **[7]** [henceforth: Hitler, Mein Kampf . . . (Band I)]; *Hitlers Tischgespräche. . .* (1951), pp. 363–364. See also: *Monologe . . .*, p. 115. A clarification regarding the page references to the critical edition of *Mein Kampf* is here in order. This work is arranged so that a page from *Mein Kampf* occurs only on odd page numbers, with critical commentaries on every even page (or spread). The ordinary page numbers refer to the pages in *Hitler, Mein Kampf* as such, while the page numbers in bold square brackets refer to the page numbers in the first edition of *Mein Kampf* as given in the critical volume.
142 *Monologe . . .*, pp. 103, 185–190, 312–313, 394; *Hitlers Tischgespräche. . .* (1951), p. 340.
143 Jetzinger, Franz, *Hitlers Jugend. Phantasien, Lügen – und die Wahrheit* (Wien: Europa Verlag, 1956), pp. 105–108.
144 Ibid., pp. 101–102, 304; Ullrich, V., *Adolf Hitler . . .*, p. 32. Hitler started first grade of the *Realschule* in the fall of 1900, when he was 11 years old. However, he had to repeat this class in 1901–1902.
145 *Hitler, Mein Kampf . . .*, pp. 99, 109 **[3, 8]**.
146 Bavendamm, Dirk, *Der junge Hitler. Korrekturen einer Biographie 1889–1914* (Graz: Ares Verlag, 2009), pp. 144–145. Bavendamm also correctly points out that Hitler's story is doubtful for other reasons too. Hitler claimed to have only been interested in subjects that he thought would be useful in his artistic pursuits, but what possible need would an aspiring artist have for history and geography?
147 Jetzinger, F., *Hitlers Jugend . . .*, pp. 100–106.
148 Ibid., p. 106.
149 *Hitler, Mein Kampf . . .* (Band I), p. 131 **[18]**; *Monologe . . .*, p. 115.
150 *Hitler, Mein Kampf . . .* (Band I), p. 115 **[11]**; *Monloge . . .*, p. 312; *Hitlers Tischgespräche. . .* (1951), p. 350. Note that the date on the note is mistakenly stated as 3 February, instead of the correct 3 March 1942 in the first edition of *Tischgespräche*.
151 *Hitlers Tischgespräche. . .* (1951), pp. 225–228, 284–288 (this note is dated 19 May in this edition, but 20 May in the 1963 edition), 350–351, 360–362, 367–369; *Monologe . . .*, pp. 311–313; *Hitler, Mein Kampf . . .* (Band II), pp. 1041–1109 **[41–75]**.
152 *Monologe . . .*, p. 312.
153 *Hitler, Mein Kampf . . .* (Band II), p. 1075 **[58]**.
154 Ibid., p. 1065 **[53]**.
155 Ibid., p. 1071 **[56]**.
156 Ibid., p. 1067 **[54]**.
157 Ibid., p. 1065 **[53]**.
158 Ibid., p. 1075 **[58]**.

159 *Hitler, Mein Kampf. . .* (Band I), pp. 165–169 **[34–36]**; *Hitlers Tischgespräche. . .* (1951), p. 385.
160 *Hitler, Mein Kampf. . .* (Band I), p. 171 **[37]**; *Monologe . . .*, p. 64. On the other hand, Heim also records a contradicting statement on 22 January 1942, according to which Hitler stated that the "introduction of general suffrage in Austria will necessarily lead to the collapse of the Germans" (*Durchführung des allgemeinen gleichen geheimen Wahlrechts mußte in Österreich zu einem Zusammenbruch der Deutschen führen*); see, *Monologe . . .*, p. 216.
161 Longerich, P., *Hitler . . .*, p. 61.
162 *Monologe . . .*, p. 64.
163 *Hitler, Mein Kampf. . .* (Band I), p. 303 **[98]**.
164 *Monologe . . .*, p. 65.
165 *Hitler, Mein Kampf. . .* (Band I), p. 317 **[105]**.
166 *Monologe . . .*, p. 317.
167 *Hitler, Mein Kampf. . .* (Band I), pp. 175 **[39]**.
168 Ibid., p. 176. This refers to the commentaries.
169 Ibid., p. 207 **[55]**.
170 Ibid., p. 309 **[101]**.
171 *Monologe . . .*, p. 153.
172 Kershaw, I., *Hitler: 1889–1936 . . .*, pp. 18, 36; Ullrich, V., *Adolf Hitler . . .*, pp. 48–49.
173 Pyta, W., *Hitler . . .*, pp. 118–119; Longerich, P., *Hitler . . .*, pp. 22–24, 35–38. Poetsch, however, was never willing to accept this responsibility and kept his distance from Hitler in the later years, while Huemer became an avid Hitler supporter. In the first edition of *Mein Kampf* Hitler mistakenly stated his teacher's name to be Ludwig Pötsch, see: *Hitler, Mein Kampf . . .* (Band I), p. 117 **[12]**. The same point is made in: Bavendamm, D., *Der junge Hitler . . .*, p. 136. Thus, he may not have been too important for Hitler after all. For Poetsch's letter to Hitler on 20 June 1929 and Hitler's reply on 2 July 1929, see: *Hitler. Reden, Schriften, Anordnungen. Februar 1925 bis Januar 1933* [14 volumes with different editors] (München: K.G. Saur, 1992–2003) (henceforth: *RSA*), Band III/2, p. 279 (Document 46).
174 Jetzinger, F., *Hitlers Jugend . . .*, pp. 105–111, 113.
175 Bavendamm, D., *Der junge Hitler . . .*, pp. 264–267, 279. This is a good logical point, although Bavendamm also uses Kubizek as evidence. Kubizek, however, cannot be trusted at all in this case. Kubizek at the same time says Hitler was a full-blown anti-Semite and hater of the clerics already in Vienna, and we know this is not true (Kubizek, August, *Adolf Hitler. Mein Jugendfreund* (Graz und Göttingen: Leopold Stocker Verlag, 1953), p. 298).
176 *Monologe . . .*, p. 65.
177 *Hitler's Table Talk . . .* (1953), p. 36; *Libres propos. . .* (Vol. I, 1952), p. 37.
178 *Monologe . . .*, p. 64.
179 *Hitler, Mein Kampf. . .* (Band I), p. 445 **[166]**. This statement actually seems to be contradicted (contradictions are rife in *Mein* Kampf) by Hitler's contention that the Habsburg rulers had been trying to turn their state into a Catholic-based Slavic state "as protection against Orthodox Russia" (ibid., p. 299 **[96]**).
180 For this, see: ibid., p. 446. The version of events as reported in both *Mein Kampf* and *Monologe* is uncritically accepted in: Hübner, Stefan, "Hitler und Ostasien. 1904 bis 1933. Die Entwicklung von Hitlers Japan- und Chinabild vom Russisch-Japanischen Krieg bis zur 'Machtergreifung'" in *OAG Notizen*, No. 9 (2009), pp. 23–24.
181 Longerich, P., *Hitler . . .*, p. 23. Longerich is here referring to a statement made by Hitler in a speech, where he said that he had grown up in an area that was torn by conflict over German language and culture. In the endnote he states that Hitler also made similar statements in *Monologe* but does not go into detail regarding this particular incident.
182 *Hitler, Mein Kampf . . .* (Band I), pp. 298, 365 **[129]**. The editors of the critical volume point out that the use of the word "Blutschande" in this context makes no sense at all

and shows that this was in fact pointed out already in 1925. The term is normally used for incestuous relationships, but Hitler, racist as he was, could not have seen Slavs and Jews as brothers and sisters. Thus, if he had been able to follow his own logic, he ought to have held the opposite view (ibid., p. 364).

183 Several historians have shown this, but it is dealt with in detail in: Weber, T., *Wie Adolf Hitler zum Nazi wurde . . .*, passim.

184 Bavendamm, D., *Der junge Hitler . . .*, p. 172.

185 Jetzinger, F., *Hitlers Jugend . . .*, pp. 119–120.

186 Email to the author from Dr. Klaus-Dieter Mulley at the *Institut für Geschichte der Gewerkschaften und AK, Kammer für Arbeiter und Angestellte für Wien*; Vienna, Austria; 18 January 2019. Mulley refers in the email to an article on the topic in *Pilsener Tageblatt* 18 April 1905, p. 2.

187 Jetzinger, F., *Hitlers Jugend . . .*, pp. 102–103, 304; *Hitler, Mein Kampf. . .* (Band I), pp. 108, 124, 445. These are references to the commentaries on these pages.

188 Koeppen, Werner, *Herbst 1941 im "Führerhauptquartier". Berichte Werner Koeppens an seinen Minister Alfred Rosenberg. Herausgegeben und kommentiert von Martin Vogt* (Koblenz: Materialen aus dem Bundesarchiv Heft 10, 2002), p. 37. For Koeppen's typed notes, see: "Reichsministerium für die desetzten Ostgebiete, Aufzeichnungen des persönlichen Referenten Rosenbergs, Dr. Koeppen, über Hitlers Tischgespräche 1941"; Bundesarchiv, Berlin-Lichterfeld (henceforth: BABL); R6–34a.

189 *Hitler, Mein Kampf. . .* (Band I), pp. 119 **[13]**, 171 **[37]**, 297–299 **[95–96]**, 333 **[113]**, 357 **[125]**.

190 Ibid., pp. 118, 330. These are references to the commentaries on these pages.

191 Weber, Thomas, *Becoming Hitler: The Making of a Nazi* (Oxford: Oxford University Press, 2018), pp. 217–223, 313–327; quote on p. 223.

192 *Hitler, Mein Kampf. . .* (Band I), p. 373 **[132]**.

193 *Monologe . . .*, p. 209.

194 *Hitler, Mein Kampf. . .* (Band I), pp. 383–439 **[138–164]**; *Monologe . . .*, p. 67; *Hitlers Tischgespräche. . .* (1951), pp. 227–228, 322–323; Hitler, Adolf, *Hitlers zweites Buch. Ein Dokument aus dem Jahr 1928. Eingeleitet und kommentiert von Gerhard L. Weinberg. Mit einem Geleitwort von Hans Rothfels* (Stuttgart: Deutsche Verlags-Anstalt, 1961), pp. 46–144.

195 *Monologe . . .*, p. 234. This statement is exactly mirrored by the claim that he also became a military leader against his will and that if another leader had been available, he would have become an architect instead (ibid., p. 101). This is another equally false claim in one of Heim's nightly notes.

196 *Hitler, Mein Kampf. . .* (Band I), pp. 467, 543, 557 **[175, 210, 217]**.

197 Fest, J., *Hitler . . .*, pp. 526–527.

198 *SA*, pp. 1055, 1062–1064 (Document 596 & 605).

199 *Monologe . . .*, p. 71.

200 *Hitler, Mein Kampf. . .* (Band I), pp. 453–457, 545 **[169–171, 211]**.

201 Ibid., p. 459 **[172]**; *Monologe . . .*, p. 79. In *Mein Kampf* Hitler actually remarks that the only "sorrow" he had during that time was the initial worry that his regiment would arrive at the front too late and thus miss the battle.

202 Volker Ullrich simply quotes *Monologe* without noticing the contradictions; see: Ullrich, V., *Adolf Hitler . . .*, (Vol. I), p. 110.

203 *Hitler, Mein Kampf. . .* (Band I), p. 593. See editors' comments on this page. For example, Hitler describes the decision of whether or not to join the DAP to have been the hardest in his life. Once he finally decided to join, he describes this as "the most decisive decision" (*der entscheidendste Entschluß*) in his life (ibid., p. 599 **[236]**).

204 *Hitler, Mein Kampf. . .* (Band I), p. 461 **[173]**; *Monologe . . .*, pp. 407–408.

205 *Hitler, Mein Kampf. . .* (Band I), p. 465 **[174]**; *Monologe . . .*, pp. 171, 295–296.

206 Pyta, W., *Hitler . . .*, p. 390. Pyta also makes the curious claim that Hitler had lived through the "alltäglichen Schützengrabenkrieg" on the Western Front for almost four

years (ibid., pp. 389–390). This is absolutely not true, as Thomas Weber has shown in *Hitler's First War* (Hitler spent most of his time in the army many kilometres behind the frontline), and Pyta has to be aware of this. It is a careless formulation indeed.

207 *Monologe . . .*, p. 80.

208 Pyta, W., *Hitler . . .*, pp. 388–390.

209 *Hitler, Mein Kampf. . .* (Band I), pp. 524–525 **[201]**. Hitler states that his regiment entered the battle in September 1916 and that he was wounded on 7 October. However, his regiment did not see any action until 7 October, and Hitler was most likely wounded in the left butt cheek two days before that.

210 *Monologe . . .*, p. 80.

211 "Weisung Nr. 37" in: Hubatsch, Walther (ed.), *Hitlers Weisungen für die Kriegsführung 1939–1945. Dokumente des Oberkommando des Wehrmacht* (München: Deutscher Taschenbuch Verlag, 1965), pp. 186–189. See also: Warlimont, W., *Im Hauptquartier . . .*, pp. 208–209.

212 *TBJG*, II/2, pp. 57–58, 64, 68–70, 74, 78–79, 84–85, 90–91, 97–98, 104, 109–110 (5 October – 14 October 1941).

213 Ibid., p. 74 (8 October 1941).

214 Koeppen, W., *Herbst 1941 im "Führerhauptquartier" . . .*, pp. 62, 66, 70. Koeppen was not in the FHQ between 9 and 16 October so there are no parallel notes from him for 13 October.

215 "Weisung Nr. 39" in: Hubatsch, W. (ed.), *Hitlers Weisungen . . .*, pp. 199–203.

216 *Hitler's Table Talk. . .* (1953), pp. 55–56; *Libres propos. . .* (Vol. I, 1952), pp. 56–57.

217 *Monologe . . .*, pp. 80, 132, 171–172, 219–220, 290, 324–325, 339.

218 Ibid., pp. 411. This note is dated 18 May in the French edition, but 16 May in the English: *Libres propos. . .* (Vol. II, 1954), p. 343; *Hitler's Table Talk. . .* (1953), p. 718. These differences are impossible to explain, but this is not the only time that different dates are given for one and the same note in the various editions.

219 Weikart, Richard, *Hitler's Religion: The Twisted Beliefs that Drove the Third Reich* (Washington, DC: Regnery History, 2016), pp. 18, 298 *n*7.

220 Fleischmann, P., *Hitler als Häftling . . .*, p. 89.

221 Frank, Hans, *Im Angesicht des Galgens. Deutung Hitlers und seiner Zeit auf Grund eigener Erlebnisse und Erkenntnisse* (München: Friedrich Alfred Beck Verlag, 1953), p. 40. See also: Weikart, R., *Hitler's Religion . . .*, pp. 18, 298 *n*7 who refers to the wrong page in Frank's book (p. 46).

222 Dietrich, Otto, *12 Jahre mit Hitler* (München: Isar Verlag, 1955), p. 92.

223 Rose, Olaf (ed.), *Julius Schaub – In Hitlers Schatten. Erinnerungen und Aufzeichnungen des persönlichen Adjutanten und Vertrauten Julius Schaub 1925–1945* (Stegen and Ammersee: Druffel & Vowinckel Verlag, 2005), p. 228.

224 *Hitler, Mein Kampf. . .* (Band I), p. 579 **[227]**; *Monologe . . .*, p. 295.

225 For the latter point, see: *Hitler, Mein Kampf. . .* (Band I), p. 578.

226 *SA*, pp. 84–99937.

227 *Hitler, Mein Kampf. . .* (Band I), pp. 699–703 **[282–284]**; *Monologe . . .*, pp. 66–67, 82–85, 104, 144, 150–152; *Hitlers Tischgespräche. . .* (1951), pp. 339–375.

228 *Monologe. . .* pp. 41, 96–99, 134–135, 279, 412–413; *Hitler, Mein Kampf. . .* (Band I), p. 799 **[325]**. See similar statements in: *TBJG*, I/3, p. 55 (23 February 1937).

229 *Hitler, Mein Kampf. . .* (Band I), pp. 781–799, **[318–325]**.

230 Ibid., pp. 427, 793–795 **[158, 323–324]**; *Monologe . . .*, p. 130.

231 The Nazi regime's relationship to the Christian churches was a complicated, and often conflicted, one; see: Longerich, P., *Hitler . . .*, pp. 423–433, 501–515, 520–523; Ullrich, V., *Adolf Hitler . . .*, (Vol. I), pp. 705–726. Longerich and Ullrich, and in fact all other Hitler biographies as well, give more or less the same view of National Socialism's confrontation with the Christian churches. This is a view that has not really incorporated most of the research done on this subject. This research has highlighted the fact that German Christians (including the churches) often willingly cooperated

with the Nazi government, and even sympathized expressly with Nazi ideology and found ways to make their Christian faith and Nazi politics function without conflict. This included many German priests who willingly served in the *Wehrmacht*, as well as famous theologians who worked hard to make National Socialism and Christianity compatible. For some of the more important works, see: Steigmann-Gall, Richard, *The Holy Reich: Nazi Conceptions of Christianity, 1919–1945* (Cambridge: Cambridge University Press, 2003); Spicer, Kevin P., *Hitler's Priests: Catholic Clergy and National Socialism* (DeKalb: Northern Illinois University Press, 2008); Bergen, Doris L., *Twisted Cross: The German Christian Movement in the Third Reich* (Chapel Hill: The University of North Carolina Press, 1996); Heschel, Susannah, *The Aryan Jesus: Christian Theologians and the Bible in Nazi Germany* (Princeton: Princeton University Press, 2008); Gutteridge, Richard, *Open Thy Mouth for the Dumb! The German Evangelical Church and the Jews, 1879–1950* (Oxford: Basil Blackwell, 1976); Hastings, Derek, *Catholicism & the Roots of Nazism: Religious Identity & National Socialism* (Oxford: Oxford University Press, 2010); Moritz, Stefan, *Grüß Gott und Heil Hitler: Katholische Kirche und Nationalsozialismus in Österreich* (Wien: Picus Verlag, 2002); Klee, Ernst, *"Die SA Jesu Christi". Die Kirche im Banne Hitlers* (Frankfurt am Main: Fischer Taschenbuch Verlag, 1989); von Preradovich, Nikolaus and Stingl, Josef, *"Gott segne den Führer". Die Kirchen im Dritten Reich. Eine Dokumentation von Bekenntnissen und Selbstzeugnissen* (Leoni am Starnberger See: Druffel-Verlag, 1985); Conley Nelson, David, *Moroni and the Swastika: Mormons in Nazi Germany* (Norman: University of Oklahoma Press, 2015); Missalla, Heinrich, *Für Gott, Führer und Vaterland. Die Verstrickung der katholischen Seelsorge in Hitlers Krieg* (Munich: Kösel, 1999); Faulkner Rossi, Lauren, *Wehrmacht Priests: Catholicism and the Nazi War of Annihalation* (Cambridge, MA: Harvard University Press, 2015).

232 *Hitler, Mein Kampf. . .* (Band II), p. 1029 **[35]**.

233 See: *SA*, pp. 273–274, 478, 488, 563, 572–573. For more background on this, see: "Hitlers 'gründlegende' Rede über den Antisemitismus" in *Vierteljahrshäfte für Zeitgeschichte*, 16. Jahrgang 1968, 4. Heft, Oktober, pp. 400–420; *SA*, pp. 191–192 (document 136). An odd thing connected to this is to be found in Werner Maser's *Hitlers Briefe und Notizen* from 1973. Includes supporting words for a speech that he dates to shortly before 20 February 1920 in which Hitler mentions "religion" as one of the ways in which the Jews brought about the destruction of the national power of a people. He also includes an undated draft for a work with the working title "Monumental history of mankind", which Werner Maser dates to shortly after the speech just mentioned (see: Maser, Werner, *Hitlers Briefe und Notizen. Sein Weltbild in handschriftlichen Dokumenten* (Düsseldorf: Econ Verlag, 1973), pp. 237, 290–297, 386). None of these notes appear in Jäckel/Kuhn's *SA*, which does not even list a speech on 20 February 1920.

234 "Hitlers 'gründlegende' Rede über den Antisemitismus" in *Vierteljahrshäfte für Zeitgeschichte*, 16. Jahrgang 1968, 4. Heft, Oktober, pp. 400–420; *SA*, pp. 191–192 (document 136).

235 *Hitler, Mein Kampf. . .* (Band I), p. 799 **[325]**; *Monologe . . .,* pp. 96–99, 105, 412–413. The fact that Hitler actually considered Jesus not to be Jewish is corroborated by Werner Koeppen's notes, see: Koeppen, W., *Herbst 1941 im "Führerhauptquartier" . . .,* pp. 92–93. Hitler gives the same view of Jesus in: *TBJG*, I/3, p. 55 (23 February 1937).

236 *Hitler, Mein Kampf. . .* (Band I), p. 799 **[325]**; *Monologe . . .,* pp. 40, 82, 105; Hitler, A., *Hitlers zweites Buch . . .,* pp. 88–89.

237 *Hitler, Mein Kampf. . .* (Band I), p. 895 **[366]**; *Monologe . . .,* pp. 83, 248, *Hitlers Tischgespräche . . .* (1951), pp. 355–357.

238 Heschel, S., *The Aryan Jesus . . .,* pp. 30, 33–37, 41–44, 48–55. See also: Kelley, Shawn, *Racializing Jesus: Race, Ideology and the Formation of Modern Biblical Scholarship* (London: Routledge, 2002); *Hitler, Mein Kampf. . .* (Band I), p. 896 **[353]**. The term for "resurrection" in German is *auferstehung*, a term not used by Hitler; however, the implication is still the same, namely the bringing back to life of a spiritually dead Germany.

239 Ericksen, Robert P., *Theologians under Hitler: Gerhard Kittel, Paul Althaus, and Emanuel Hirsch* (New Haven: Yale University Press, 1985); Bergen, D. L., *Twisted Cross . . .*, passim.

240 Rosenberg, A., *Alfred Rosenberg . . .*, pp. 415–416.

241 *Monologe . . .*, p. 151.

242 See for instance: *Hitlers Tischgespräche. . .* (1951), pp. 312–313; *Monologe . . .*, pp. 62–63, 148–149, 237–238.

243 Weber, T., *Wie Adolf Hitler . . .*, pp. 200–203; for the whole letter, see: Maser, W., *Hitlers Briefe und Notizen . . .*, pp. 223–226. Maser does not mention Gemlich and seems to think that it was Mayr who asked Hitler about this subject. Gemlich seems to have been a *Vertrauensmann* in the German army's *Gruppenkommando* in Munich (see commentary in: *Hitler, Mein Kampf. . .* (Band II), p. 1112). Hitler's anti-Semitism was apparently well developed already by this time, and the views he expresses are the same ideas that are later laid out in *Mein Kampf* (fully developed) and which Hitler kept until his death in the bunker in Berlin; however, this is the first evidence that we have of it.

244 *Hitler, Mein Kampf. . .* (Band I), pp. 743–759 **[302–308]**.

245 *Monologe . . .*, p. 281. Jochmann comments that Hitler had read all of May's books, but gives no source for this statement (ibid., p. 456).

246 Bavendamm, D., *Der junge Hitler . . .*, pp. 359–360. Bavendamm has not used Koeppen's notes, however, and does not seem aware of this source.

247 Price, Ward, *I Know These Dictators* (London: Harrap, 1937), p. 19.

248 Koeppen, W., *Herbst 1941 im "Führerhauptquartier" . . .*, p. 61.

249 Jetzinger, F., *Hitlers jugend . . .*, p. 106.

250 Fest, J., *Hitler . . .*, pp. 199, 615, 481, 1034 (Fest also exaggerates the number of May books that Hitler allegedly owned according to his sources); Toland, John, *Adolf Hitler* (single-volume edition 1976), pp. 13 (no source), 317 (based upon Egon Hanfstaengl's unpublished memoirs), 604 (interview with Manstein in the 1970s); Kershaw, I., *Hitler. . .* (Vol. I), pp. 15, 17, 387; Ullrich, V., *Adolf Hitler . . .*, (Vol. I), pp. 32, 142; Longerich cites another historian (also cited by Fest on p. 199) who remarks that Hitler's style of clothing during the *Kampfzeit* was reminiscent of Karl May: Longerich, P. *Hitler . . .*, p. 117. Albert Speer's *Spandauer Tagebücher* also brings up May as an important influence on Hitler (Speer, Albert, *Spandauer Tagebücher* (Berlin: Propyläen, 1975), p. 523), but this source can absolutely not be trusted considering that this text is largely fictitious with enormous differences between the drafts and the published text (see: BAK; N 1340 (Speer Nachlaß); Vols. 372, 376, 381, 431).

251 Pyta, W., *Hitler . . .*, pp. 288, 367, 373. Interestingly, Pyta never refers to *Monologe* in any of these instances. Instead, he refers to Koeppen in one endnote and to prior research in the two others.

252 Ullrich, V., *Adolf Hitler . . .*, (Vol. I), p. 845.

253 Schroeder, C., *Er war mein Chef . . .*, p. 63.

254 *Hitler, Mein Kampf. . .* (Band I), pp. 790–791 **[322]**.

255 Bavendamm, D., *Der junge Hitler . . .*, pp. 365–366, 369–370, 372–376. Pyta actually makes the point of May's image of America, too, but explains this by referring to Hitler's selective reading (Pyta, W., *Hitler . . .*, p. 373). Bavendamm nevertheless accepts the idea that Hitler got his first impressions of American geography from May (Bavendamm, D., *Der junge Hitler . . .*, p. 372). One of the major problems with Bavendamm's book is that he often builds his case on very unreliable sources, and his arguments are therefore in many places not believable.

256 *Monologe . . .*, p. 303.

257 *HRP* I/1, pp. 224–225 (21 March 1933).

2

A SCHOLARLY SCANDAL

The publication of Henry Picker's *Hitlers Tischgespräche* in 1951

The *Institut für Zeitgeschichte* (IfZ) had been formally established on 11 September 1950, after a long and arduous effort that had started back in 1947, when the suggestion for such an institute was first made. It was difficult to get funding for it because the state governments in Germany, with the exception of Bavaria, were not very keen on financing an institute devoted to the NS era. That the IfZ came to be established in Munich was, of course, not a coincidence, because the fact was that the records of the NSDAP that had been seized by the Americans and the British were deposited there, at the so-called Central Collecting Point (CCP) housed in the former *Führerbau*, or Führer Building (located next to, and attached to, the NSDAP Party HQ). Getting access to these documents proved to be much harder than what the Bavarian authorities had first thought, however. Resistance also came from the West German state archivists who were worried that the institute would become a rival institution. The matter was solved by making the IfZ so-called *Zentralnachweisstelle*, i.e. a central documentation office, which would house only copies of official documents, and, in addition, private papers, eyewitness documentation (*Zeitzeugnissquellen*), and transcripts of documents. The IfZ was also put in charge of locating Nazi documents around the world.[1]

The IfZ's part in the *Tischgespräche* affair began almost immediately after its formation. In late January 1951 historian Gerhard Ritter at the IfZ was contacted by the CEO of the Bonn-based publisher Athenäum Verlag, Dr. Paul W. Junker. The letter began in the following way:

> Honourable Professor!
> I come today with an offer to You: We have acquired a manuscript that contain notes from the speeches regarding a series of problems held by Hitler at dinner in the Führer headquarters. These notes were made by two

government clerks from the Department of the Interior on Hitler's orders, and it is an extremely interesting document regarding the history of National Socialism that is especially characteristic for Hitler's personality.[2]

We can see that Picker had obviously made several untrue statements regarding his manuscript to Junker. Either that or Junker had completely misunderstood Picker when he explained the history of the text. Apparently, Picker had told Junker that both he and Heim had made their notes, not only with Hitler's consent but on his orders (*Auftrag*). Apparently, then, at this time it seemed like a good idea to market this document as containing notes officially sanctioned by Hitler. That would later change, as we have already seen.

Junker was of the opinion that it was of utmost importance that this source be published immediately, but he realized that it would be a very delicate matter to do this so soon after the war. It would probably be impossible, he felt, unless the text was engaged with critically by a professional scholar. Junker told Ritter that he would be happy to meet him by the end of the week and present him with the manuscript and to ask Ritter to write a short introduction to the planned book. Ritter could only have a quick look at the text, however, since Junker had to return the manuscript to the "holder of the copyright" (Besitzer der Autorenrechte), i.e. Picker.[3] Ritter later explained that the manuscript itself was, according to Junker, the only in existence:

> apart from a copy that Dr. J has kept for himself (Dr. Junker's letter from 13.2). It was not a carbon copy, but a typed main document already set up as a print manuscript: spelling mistakes were corrected, a lot of linguistic improvements were added.[4]

Whether these changes had been made already in the FHQ or later on was unknown to Ritter at the time.[5] This must reasonably mean that the publisher had not made the changes.

Ritter accepted the offer more or less immediately, because in early February an "understanding" had been reached between them. Now the various problems regarding the necessary changes to the manuscript were to be discussed with Picker during the next couple of days. The agreement consisted of a number of points. First, Ritter would write an introduction, as well as make a historical–critical evaluation of the text. He had also expressed the wish to publish the book in cooperation with the IfZ. Picker's consent to the latter would of course have to be forthcoming first. Second, the title seems to have been already formulated by the publisher. Third, Ritter would receive 750 German Marks (*Deutschmark*, DM) for the job, as well as DM 150 for an assistant. The money had at this point been paid to Ritter, since the work on the edition had already begun. Fourth, it had been decided to arrange the text thematically, as Ritter had suggested, and minor comments would be added where such were deemed to be necessary.[6]

Ritter very soon noticed that Picker's text ended where the stenographic notes from Hitler's military conferences began. These records had been published in English translation the year before by Felix Gilbert under the title *Hitler Directs His War* (Oxford University Press). It would not be long before these were published in Germany, he thought, and therefore the publication of Picker's text was even more urgent. Ritter, however, was of the opinion that the manuscript could not be published without the removal of a number of "banalities", or without making changes to Picker's preface and afterword. The reason for the latter was that a certain amount of admiration for Hitler was readily apparent in Picker. This made it impossible for Ritter to allow his name to be associated with the book. He had no wish to draw more polemics to his person, and he did not want to put his name on a text that was so contradictory to his political convictions. Moreover, Ritter also felt that the summarizing titles next to each note were often mistaken or confusing. The text itself was better than Picker's own contributions, he thought. Ritter then asked Junker to inquire with General Karl-Heinrich Bodenschatz (Göring's liaison officer by Hitler) and Major Gerhard Engel (Hitler's army adjutant) and ask whether they could remember if Picker and Heim had really gotten Hitler's permission to record his words and if they had actually taken them down as Hitler spoke. He also wanted to know if they, from the examples that had been shown to them, considered the notes to be authentic and not in any way changed afterwards (*daß die Niederschrift in Ordnung und nicht etwa nachträglich umfrisiert ist*). He also suggested various other persons that might be able to confirm the correctness of Picker's notes.[7]

What is clear is that the work with the edition was therefore made in extreme haste. Already by 13 February, i.e. not even a month after he had first laid eyes on the text, Ritter had already sent his introduction to the publisher. Junker wished to come to an agreement with Picker on the final form of the publication during the next few days. It was estimated that only a few issues had to be worked out between Picker and Ritter before the manuscript could be made ready to print.[8] Ritter's suggestion to receive 0.5 percent of the sale price for the 11,000 to 20,000 first copies sold was accepted by Junker.[9] Ritter, however, found it hard to get along with Picker. He was also unhappy with the title suggestions, since it did not clearly enough state that the IfZ stood behind the publication, a fact that Ritter considered absolutely critical.[10] A few issues thus still remained to be solved before Ritter was satisfied. For example, a few pages were missing from the manuscript, and Junker had still not questioned either Bodenschatz or Engel.[11] By 21 February Ritter had made his suggested changes to the text and sent it to Junker, who had in turn presented it to Picker, and the latter was very happy with the work. The text was now ready to go to the printers; any further minor changes could be made on the print proofs, Junker thought.[12]

Picker accepted most of Ritter's suggested changes to his introduction and made some additions; however, Ritter was still not satisfied. He wished to see yet a few smaller improvements made. But more important for Ritter was that Picker, and he had told Picker this in person, never considered the moral aspects of the

Hitler regime. The only standard Picker judged Hitler by, said Ritter, was if he had been successful or not. This attitude was typical for the Fascist, according to Ritter; moral issues were considered to have nothing to do with politics.[13] There was indeed no need for "time and distance" (*Zeit und Abstandes*) in order to make a moral judgement about Hitler's regime, as Picker suggested in his introduction. Although Picker was naturally responsible for his own introduction, Ritter made it clear that he considered the apologetic attitude towards Hitler to taint the publication as such. Ritter would put Picker's introduction before the IfZ scientific council (*Beirat*) to see if the IfZ could accept it and in what form. Junker, on the other hand, suggested that the problem regarding the title should be solved by stating that Ritter had edited, introduced, and published the book, and instead of saying that he had been commissioned by the IfZ to do so, the title should say "In connection with the Institute" (*In Verbindung mit dem Institut*). He also suggested that the title should state "Recorded with Hitler's approval" (*Aufgezeichnet mit Genehmigung Hitlers*), which Ritter said that the IfZ *Beirat* would have to take some time to consider.[14] Junker's last suggestion indicates that at this stage the view was still that Picker's claim to have gotten Hitler's consent for recording his statements was taken seriously.

A few days later Junker got back to Ritter and could deliver the good news that Engel had visited the publisher and he could report:

> after having controlled the manuscript himself and, based on his own knowledge, confirmed that it is faultless. In particular, he considered the person Dr. Picker completely credible.[15]

Ritter obviously found this fact to be very important because he marked it in red. Bodenschatz would be soon presented with copies of the proofs, said Junker.[16] We can thus assume that it was the fact that Engel had, in Ritter's eyes, authenticated Picker's manuscript that made him accept it as authoritative as well. Perhaps this was even what made Ritter decide to sign the publishing contract with the Athenäum Verlag the very same day. The contract stipulated that Ritter was to be paid DM 1,000 for the first 10,000 copies, as well as an extra DM 0.10 per sold copy.[17] Let us pause and reflect upon this for a moment. Ritter's way of going about making sure that the manuscript was authentic was certainly a bit strange considering the fact that Ritter *knew* that Picker was still sympathetic to National Socialism and Hitler. Now another former Nazi and member of Hitler's closest entourage – and who was most likely still sympathetic to Hitler himself – considered Picker trustworthy. Why did Ritter take Engel's word for this? What is more important, of course, is that Engel's estimation of Picker's character was completely off the mark, which Ritter would soon get to experience first-hand.

It is furthermore not clear why Ritter thought that Engel, or anyone else for that matter, could authenticate a text that recorded statements that had been uttered almost a decade earlier and that Engel had not been privy to (except in a few cases). The most that Engel could do was to tell if the topics and overall views corresponded to his own memory of what he had heard Hitler say. This contributed little to the question of whether Picker's text had been edited in any way and how faithfully it relayed Hitler's words. This point was actually made most forcefully by historian Kurt Rheindorf in his very detailed, and very critical, dissection of *Tischgespräche*. Referring to the passage in Picker's introduction where he stated that many of the people who had heard Hitler speak in his FHQ were still alive and able to authenticate the notes, Rheindorf wrote scathingly:

> Such an appeal is a pure fraud! It is not the authenticity of the table talks, but the authenticity of Picker's portrayal of them, that has to be authenticated. In that sense, none of the crown witness referred to by Picker . . . is in a position to, after nine years, authenticate the wording of a "table talk" in the form that Picker purveys it.[18]

Rheindorf hits the nail on its head here. The main question was not, and still is not, if the table talks actually occurred – we know that they did – but rather whether, and how well, the notes from them actually give us Hitler's words. It seems as if Ritter's critical thinking did not reach that far, and he settled for taking Engel's and Picker's words for it. It was not that such insightful criticism was unthinkable in 1951; Rheindorf certainly managed to be critical in this respect. This would, as mentioned, turn out to be a mistake on Ritter's part. Ritter, too, was the object of much, and hard, criticism from Rheindorf, who wrote that the very fact that the IfZ was mentioned in the title implied that Picker's documents had been "strictly proven according to the basic principles of scientific source criticism" (*nach den Grundsätzen wissenschaftlicher Quellenkritik genau geprüft*), and he continued to criticize the fact that Ritter used the same argument as Picker regarding the reliability and ability of other "witnesses" to the table talks, who had been presented with "examples" (*Stichproben*) from the manuscript, to argue that the reliability of *Tischgespräche* had been thoroughly proven. Apparently, Ritter had no idea what "thoroughly proven" (*grundsätzlich bestätigt*) meant, Rheindorf scoffed. For something to have been "thoroughly proven" one had to do a lot more than simply present some eyewitnesses with a few document samples, Rheindorf correctly remarked. He also criticized Ritter's decision to arrange the text thematically, since it made it much more difficult for the reader to notice important points, such as Hitler's knowledge about the Holocaust, which would have been easier to follow and detect if the notes had been laid out chronologically.[19]

It is perhaps ironic that Rheindorf put forth a critique that was much better, and much more detailed, than any historian before or since has been able, or cared, to produce. His keen sense of logical mistakes, and important semantic decisions on Picker's part, led Rheindorf to highlight many passages in the former's introduction that surely deserved to be elaborated on and explained further. For example, he pointed out that Picker stated that he, on the one hand, had made most of the notes without an expressed wish from Bormann, but on the other hand, he stated that on one occasion Bormann gave him "a card with the for him typical order" (*eine Karte mit der für ihn typischen Weisung*) to dictate Hitler's utterances made during dinner. Now, Rheindorf noted, one can only receive a "typical" request to do something if such requests have been rather frequent in the past. Picker thus seemed to be, inadvertently as it were, betraying the fact that he had made many more, if not all, of his notes on Bormann's direct orders. Why would Picker choose to keep this information from the reader, Rheindorf perceptively asked?[20] Furthermore, Picker's statement that someone had given their "approval" (*Genehmigung*) to him, and Heim, to make the notes seemed contradictory. Obviously, he could not mean Hitler, because Picker at the same time claimed that Hitler knew nothing about him making his notes. So, who was he talking about? But then, again, Picker contradicts himself when he on the same page claims that Hitler had, on several occasions, "acknowledged" (*anerkannt*) that his notes presented a correct view of Hitler's statements. To whom had Hitler made this statement; was it to Picker or to someone else? Rheindorf found no satisfying answer in *Tischgespräche*.[21] The inconsistency between the initial assertion that the notes had been made with Hitler's approval and that Picker then argued that Hitler knew nothing at all about it does not seem to have appeared to either Ritter or the IfZ.

Rheindorf was acquainted with Hitler's former *Luftwaffe* adjutant, Nicolaus von Below, and he interviewed him on several occasions. According to von Below, Picker had been "a really peripheral character" (*wirklich eine Randfigur*) in the FHQ, one who, in contrast to Heim, did not know stenography. The former adjutant did not know why Picker was dismissed from his post at the FHQ in August 1942, but he noted that Bormann had a habit of often replacing his staff (including his secretaries), since he did not want anyone to gain a good understanding of his working methods.[22] Clearly, there were former Nazi officials who also did not like Picker, and von Below told Rheindorf about one such person that he had recently met who reportedly had stated that he would have had Picker shot had he known that the latter was to come to the FHQ. This had been said by a former colleague of Picker's at the offices of the National Youth Leadership (*Reichsjugendführung*).[23]

What follows in Rheindorf's interview notes is really interesting; von Below stated that Picker's mission had been the same as that of all the military adjutants at the FHQ, i.e.:

> Notes, and purveyance of these to the proper places, of occasional wishes or ordered uttered at the table. v.Below considered it wholly possible that Bormann had ordered Picker to record more, *in addition to this "mission" known to Hitler*. Bormann was a greedy man who always went out of his way to shine and be alert in front of Hitler. It is possible that Bormann also collected material about Hitler; he didn't know. [. . .] What Ritter published were not "records." When I asked v.Below if he could say that Picker's notes corresponded to reality and what he thought of it *on the basis of Hitler's long-standing knowledge of them*, v.Below said that he could not remember such individual conversations with the best will. It was just as it was in all the officers' messes in the world and you really couldn't say more. There was

talk about everything – not only about Hitler – and in a relaxed form. It is completely impossible to take statements out of such officers' mess conversations of individual people and then make of it what Ritter is doing now. In order to have a real picture, one would have to know exactly what the others had said about it, because it was by no means just monologues, as Picker claims.[24] [Italics added.]

What is notable about this interview is that von Below seems to confirm that Hitler was actually well aware of the fact that people made notes of what he said in order to report it back to their respective masters. He even says that this was the purpose for them being there in the first place. This does, indeed, sound much more plausible than the idea that Hitler had no idea of what was going on around him.

It is interesting to note that in von Below's memoirs from 1980 his memory of how the table talks were created had changed considerably. There he writes that the table talks were written down with the use of stenography at the table (*mitstenografiert*) by Heim and Picker. He also repeats the idea that Hitler had spoken very relaxed and free during these dinners.[25] Time had apparently allowed von Below to integrate the official myth of the table talks and make it his own. Apparently, von Below did not remember much about what Hitler talked about during these discussions either because he later on claims that he never heard Hitler make the aggressive kind of critique of the Church that Bormann did.[26] The table talks are full of these statements – and they are corroborated by other independent sources – so von Below is either remembering incorrectly or is purposefully lying about this matter.

Needless to say, perhaps, we ought to assume that von Below's earlier memories and judgements regarding these events should be considered more trustworthy than his memoirs written several decades later. We must also be careful enough to point out that since *Tischgespräche* contained a large number of Heim's notes, Rheindorf's and von Below's conclusions are equally damaging for the Heim notes, and thus also for *Monologe*. As we have seen, and as will become even more apparent later on, when we compare Heim's notes to those made by Alfred Rosenberg's representative at the FHQ, Werner Koeppen, the latter's notes often reflect the conversational aspect of these table talks much better than either *Tischgepräche* or *Monologe* do. Interestingly, however, Rheindorf does not seem to have been interested in Heim, and there is no sign of any contact between them in Rheindorf's papers at the *Bundesarchiv*.

Rheindorf's appreciation of Genoud, and his claims, was also rather low at this time. Genoud's claim to have the "authentic" documents was deemed by Rheindorf to be just another invention of the "memory industry" (*erinnerungs-Industrie*) that had appeared in Germany since the end of the war, and he compared it to the enormous amount of pieces of the "cross of Christ", with which one could now build a "respectable" forest. He had, however, asked his book dealer to alert him whenever Genoud's blockbuster (*knüller*), "My

Führer Speaks" (*Mein Führer spricht*) landed in his store and was presented to the astounded or distraught contemporary audiences in Germany. Even better, he thought, would the publication of the letters between Gerda and Martin Bormann be.[27] But von Below, on the other hand, looked forward to Genoud's table talk publication with some excitement. However, he considered the letters between Martin and Gerda Bormann "somewhat dubious" (*etwas zweifelhaft*), because, as he told Rheindorf:

> I never thought that these two had written so many letters to each other. In general, they would limit themselves to the telephone.[28]

This information is interesting because it shows that both von Below and Rheindorf must have spoken to Genoud and knew which documents he had and what he was planning on publishing. The title of Genoud's coming book is also an important clue; *Mein Führer spricht* was obviously the title of a planned German edition of the *Bormann-Vermerke*. Apparently, it was even planned to come out in Germany very soon. But for some reason Genoud decided to publish a French translation under the title *Libres propos* instead. Genoud clearly planned on publishing the Bormann letters in German as well, but he later changed his mind regarding this too. *Libres propos* would eventually be published in English in 1953, and the Bormann letters too in 1954. A German edition of Genoud's table talk manuscript would be published in 1980, but a German edition of the Bormann letters has still not seen the light of day.

Tischgespräche had turned out to be somewhat of a disappointment to von Below apparently, and he was of the firm opinion that it gave "a completely false image" (*ein völlig falsches Bild*) of the conversations and of Hitler's words. It was lacking many things that Picker [and, reasonably, Heim too, M.N.] either had not heard, or had not written down, or that had been left out of the book by Picker and Ritter, he thought. On the other hand, it contained matter, although he did not go into any details on this, that looked:

> like various phrases that, at the very least, appear strange to me, and from this one may conclude that they have moved a lot around in the original.[29]

Thus, von Below felt that *Tischgespräche* gave a thoroughly false picture of Hitler, not because the statement themselves were necessarily giving a false representation of Hitler's views, but because the text seemed to have pulled together bits and pieces of statements and placed them out of context so as to give an impression that he felt did not correspond to his memory of either the manner or the situation of how Hitler uttered his views. It does not seem as if von Below was referring to the way in which *Tischgespräche* had been edited by Ritter; rather it was a general impression of the text he gave expression to. Once again, we must note that this judgement is equally valid also for Heim's notes and thus, by necessity, also for *Monologe*.

Furthermore, von Below clarified where various people sat at the dinner table in the FHQs. He stressed that Picker always sat at a side table (*Nebentisch*), which stood about 2 metres from the far-right corner (and towards the door) of the long dinner table, towards the door, where all the main Nazi dignitaries sat. Hitler sat in the middle of the 6- to 7-metre long and about 1-metre wide, table, with his back against the windows, which were on the left side of the room (seen from the door). Picker's table could thus be seen by Hitler simply turning his head slightly to the right towards the door. Directly across from Hitler sat Keitel, and on the right and left side of him, respectively, sat Bormann and Bodenschatz. To Hitler's left sat Jodl, and to the right sat either Sepp Dietrich or a guest. Rheindorf received a detailed sketch of the layout of the dinner room at the *Wolfschanze* and the placement of everyone present. Next to Jodl sat Puma, and then von Below, and next to him, at the far end, sat Engel. What is perhaps the most interesting about this image is that Heim is not mentioned at all, even though he was there much longer than Picker.[30] From this sketch it is clear that some of the notes included in *Tischgespräche* – which expressly mentions Heinz Lorenz, Gabriel (Keitel's adjutant), and Richard Schulze (Hitler's ordinance officer [*Ordonnanzoffizier*]) – were the result of conversations that Picker had with the men at the side table, because von Below places Picker together with these three.[31]

The room at *Wolfschanze* was very cramped (*sehr eng*) and had bad acoustics, according to von Below. The dinner room at *Werwolf* at Winniza was much bigger, and so had good acoustics; however, the people at the side table could not hear the conversation taking place at the main table as well in *Werwolf* anyway due to the large distances involved, von Below stated. The placements at the tables were the same also in *Werwolf*. He took care to add that, regardless of the acoustics, one could hear statements in the dinner room in *Wolfschanze* really well from anywhere in the room when (and only when) one person spoke. Conversations were much more difficult to make out, and the same was apparently true for *Werwolf*.[32] Considering that von Below had claimed that it was not really a matter of monologues, but of conversations, it follows that we should expect it to be a bit difficult to be able to follow what was being said, and definitely to make precise and accurate notes from these occasions. The exception would be if only one person spoke and the others were quiet. However, it still seems rather implausible to assume that Hitler (or anyone else) could not see what was going on at the side table. Surely, the view would perhaps be a bit obscured by the people sitting opposite to Hitler; however, that depends entirely on the precise angles involved. It could just as well have been that Hitler had a clear line of sight towards the side table where Picker and Heim were sitting. According to von Below's sketch, Picker would have been sitting with his back towards Hitler, which could then mean that he could perhaps make notes without being seen. However, if that would mean that Picker (and Heim) was the only person in the room *not* looking at Hitler as he spoke, then that in itself would be suspect, and perhaps even impossible to do other than for a very short while (which is, of course, perhaps all you would need if you were writing down supporting words; it would, however, make the person taking the notes much less "unobtrusive", since they would be turning around repeatedly in their chair).

Be that as it may, this point is perhaps moot anyway, since we have already seen that Hitler was most likely aware of the fact that several of those present would write down what he was saying. It is only of real importance if what Heim and Picker later claimed was actually true, i.e. that Hitler had strictly forbidden notes to be made and that he therefore had no idea that they were making them. But that claim is, quite obviously, false. This is proven conclusively by von Below's statements to Rheindorf, which show us that it was indeed the task of many of those present to note what Hitler was saying and to report these statements to their bosses for them to turn Hitler's utterances into policies and orders.

Another thing that speaks for Hitler knowing full well that his words were being taken down on paper, as well as the untruth in statements to the effect that Hitler disliked when the things he said during these monologues were written down, is an interview that the Hitler biographer John Toland made with one of Hitler's two favourite architects, Hermann Giesler. According to Giesler, Bormann would take out a small piece of paper each time Hitler said something that interested him and make quick notes, which he then used as a basis for his *Vermerke*. Hitler must have known about this, since Giesler states that Hitler used to make jokes about Bormann's handwriting.[33] Interestingly, this version of events is corroborated by Werner Koeppen, who, in an interview with Lew Besymenski in the early 1970s, testified to the same fact. This is how Besymenski puts it:

> If Hitler was reminded of anything at the beginning of lunch or asked for anything, no one suspected that Bormann would already have the answer at the end of the meal (he then quickly used to write a note on a paper napkin and send the adjutant to obtain the information). He developed a special mastery in picking up on the thoughts expressed by the leader. In his famous table conversations, the Führer uttered unusual strings of words. No sooner had Hitler expressed some thoughts than Bormann formulated it as an instruction or order a few hours later. It goes without saying that in this way Bormann alone determined the choice and formulation. He knew everything that happened in the Reich Chancellery and lumbered between all.[34]

Here Koeppen also explicitly points to Bormann's role as an arbiter who was central to the process of deciding what should be preserved and in what form. The obvious implication of this, of course, is that Hitler was well accustomed to having Bormann occasionally making notes at the table while he was talking. There is no reason to think that Hitler would not also approve of a person working for Bormann making the notes, as long as this person did not make their presence and activity too obvious. It is also equally obvious that when Koeppen says that "no one" suspected that Bormann did this he is, first, exaggerating and, second, not including Hitler in that category.

Returning to Ritter, Picker, and Athenäum Verlag before the actual publication of the book, the problematic matter for Ritter, with regard to keeping a critical distance to the text was that Picker was allowed to express views on what went into Ritter's introduction. The publisher was well aware of the fact that Picker was still a convinced National Socialist, but Junker was of the opinion that with Ritter's introduction, the impression on the reader would be one of discouragement. In the end of February, Junker wrote to him and stated that Picker had been presented with Ritter's edited introduction and he had a number of points that he felt could be changed. Junker sent these suggestions along, stating that it was of course up to Ritter to judge, in the end, how he wished to formulate his introduction. Ritter told Junker that he would look at Picker's suggested changes and consider them carefully, and, in the cases that he found it acceptable, make changes to the proofs.[35]

In the second week of March Ritter had presented offprints of his own and Picker's introductions to the IfZ *Beirat*, held at the Department of the President in Bonn (*Bundespräsidialamt*) that was presided over by the president (*Bundespräsident*) himself. The IfZ had at that meeting, on Ritter's suggestion, decided to acknowledge the book as being commissioned by the IfZ, and Ritter was pleased with this decision. The main problem, according to Ritter, was now presented by the necessity to somehow make the two introductions align better with each other. He pointed out to Picker that the latter's introduction was not, as had been agreed to with Athenäum, simply a statement about how the document had been created. Ritter had tried his best to meet Picker's wishes concerning changes in his introduction, he said. He brought up the issue of describing Hitler's invasion of the Soviet Union as a "Crusade" (*Kreuzzug*), a term which he could not decide upon whether or not to accept until he had seen the specific places in the text. Ritter also mentioned that Picker had previously agreed to make some changes to his text, but he had now received word from Athenäum that Picker opposed making any further changes to his introduction. Ritter told Picker that he would be most grateful if the latter nonetheless would consider making yet some minor changes to the text.[36]

Picker was of course happy, and considered it a great success, that Ritter had managed to get the IfZ to back the publication. This lent his book much more authority and made it acceptable to the German public. He then launched into an apologetic effort to show that he had always stood up for what was right, as well as for humanism, during his service under Hitler. He also mentioned that his interest in history went back to his school days [perhaps unwittingly mirroring Hitler, M.N.]. Picker was glad that Ritter wanted to look into the issue of Hitler's "*Kreuzzug*" against the Soviet Union, and remarked:

> because I even blame myself for not having recorded Hitler's statements of this nature more often; he was more or less obsessed by this "crusade" idea.[37]

The production of the proofs for the book then took much longer than planned, and by late March Ritter had still not received them. Meanwhile, however, Junker had been visited by the former *Reichspresschef* (Press Chief of the Reich), Otto

Dietrich, who apparently "corroborated the fact of the table talk notes" (*die Tat-sache der Niederschrift der Tischgespräche bestätigte*). Dietrich remembered Heim very well, according to Junker, and Picker only vaguely.[38] From Ritter's perspective, then, the text had now been authenticated by no fewer than three people who had been present during the conversations that *Tischgespräche* was said to record. It is thus no wonder if he perhaps felt comfortable in expressing a high amount of confidence in Picker's manuscript. Still, though, one could certainly wonder what it actually meant when Junker stated that Dietrich had confirmed "the fact" of the text. Moreover, Dietrich's statement also corroborates the fact that Heim's and Picker's roles and activities in the FHQ must have been well-known to everyone in Hitler's entourage, and thus by implication to Hitler himself as well. Dietrich obviously knew that Heim and Picker had produced notes of Hitler's utterances; that fact is what he corroborated, *not* the specific content in *Tischgespräche*.

The irony of all of this was that at the same time Junker brought up a problem in the text that had apparently been discussed already. It concerned the only place in the manuscript where Hjalmar Schacht – the former head of the National Bank (*Reichsbankspräsident*) in the Third Reich – was mentioned, where Hitler was said to have spoken about an elaborate scheme, attributed to Schacht, whereby Germany was to sell stock abroad in order to fill its foreign exchange coffers. Apparently, this had sounded strange to Ritter who had then asked Junker to find someone who could confirm or deny this information. Junker had done so, and the expert's answer was that this did not sound very plausible. Junker thus suggested to Ritter that this part of the text should be taken out, since it appeared that Hitler had misunderstood the whole matter.[39] That would of course have been to give the readers the wrong impression of Hitler's character. About two weeks later Ritter asked Junker to send him the text for this note so that he could use it in his "negotiations" with Schacht.[40] This part was not taken out after all, but appeared in *Tischgespräche* together with a footnote explaining that Schacht had been asked about this matter and had categorically denied that any such discussions had ever been held with Hitler.[41] Junker's reaction is of course very interesting in that it did not seem to occur to him that it might have been Picker, and not Hitler, who had misunderstood something.

It must therefore be considered deplorable that Schramm did not include this footnote in the second edition of *Tischgespräche*.[42] Picker also made changes to the text in the manuscript that Schramm used, e.g. the final sentence of the note dated 22 April 1942 reads differently in the two versions. In the first edition we find:

> By the way, Schacht is the only one who writes to him: "Dear Mr. Hitler" instead of "My Führer" and "with the best greeting, your devoted Schacht" instead of "Heil Hitler" or "with German greeting".[43]

In Schramm's edition this part looks like this:

> By the way, Schacht is the only one who writes to him: "Dear Mr. Hitler" instead of "My Führer" and "with the best greeting (your devoted Schacht)"

instead **[of the usual]** "Heil Hitler" or "**[W]**ith German greeting".[44] [Bold text was added by hand to the manuscript and was then printed in *Tischgespräche*.]

The point here is not whether the meaning of the text has changed. It really has not. Rather, the point is that Picker did not mind making changes to the text some 21 years later. This testifies to the literary character of the text, and it also shows that Schramm accepted such manipulations without protest, and without making the reader aware that such manipulations had been made.

In early April 1951, Ritter received the first proofs of the text. The suggested main title for the book was at this point the rather awkward "Hitler's Table Talk Written Down in the Führer Headquarters" (*Hitlers Tischgespräche aufgezeichnet im Führerhauptquartier*), a suggestion that Picker had concurred to.[45] Ritter would later suggest that the word "*aufgezeichnet*" be removed, which was something that Junker felt was a very good idea.[46] At this stage Picker had made suggestions for more changes in the text, which the publisher had agreed to, apparently without realizing that these changes were clearly not made because the original manuscript demanded it. These were changes that Picker made for cosmetic reasons.[47] Picker made small changes to every proof, it seems;[48] it was certainly a process that denoted the literary character of the text. The consequences for the authenticity of the text seem to have escaped everyone involved.

It is perhaps worth mentioning again that the issue of even small changes in the text could have potentially huge effects on a close analysis of Hitler's ideology. If we are really interested in what Hitler was thinking on a specific matter, then it could mean a world of difference depending upon which word he uses in a certain context. The absolute majority of these problems are hidden from us, however, because they concern choices made by Picker (and Heim, as well as the other authors) that are now inaccessible to us. As historians we can only see the traces left behind, but these form only the tip of the iceberg. In reality, we have absolutely no way of determining if Hitler actually used a certain phrase or not. Thus, even if we assume that the *Tischgespräche* and *Monologe* portray the themes and basic arguments correctly, we can never hope to recover Hitler's words as they were once spoken at the FHQ. Words matter, and the fact that historians keep quoting these sources extensively should make us care even more about this fact.

The proofreading process turned into a nightmare for Ritter as the publisher and Picker, without asking Ritter, changed the numbering system of the notes in the text. This meant that Ritter now had to re-make the whole numbering according to his own preferences again. At this point Ritter had also made the questionable decision not to allow the expression "*Kreuzzug*", i.e. Crusade, when describing Hitler's attack on the Soviet Union. Instead he had reformulated this idea in his introduction, since, as he wrote: " 'Struggle against the Bolshevist danger' is really not a crusade"). He had also noticed what he considered to an imbalance between Heim's and Picker's notes. Ritter thought that Heim's notes were "much more defective . . . that those of Mr. Picker" and they were sometimes not intelligible unless some words were inserted here and there.[49] Unfortunately, though, Ritter does not go into any details regarding this matter. Apparently, also, the term "Crusade" was not deemed appropriate on moral grounds by Ritter, and it is likely that his own Christian faith was the reason for him feeling uneasy with Hitler's war being connected to a central theme in Christian history.

Ritter was not happy with many of the headings that Picker had inserted at various places in the text, and he had therefore taken the liberty of changing those he felt needed correction. However, this was not popular with the publisher and Picker. Junker asked Ritter not to make any more such changes and reminded him that he had already agreed to let them stand as they were. In order not to lose any more time the publisher would disregard Ritter's suggested changes.[50] Ritter did not accept this without a fight. It was his prerogative as editor, of course, in conference with Picker, to decide the final form of the text himself, he told Junker. His changes had been purely factual, and he had made them so that the headings should correspond as well as possible with the text. Political opinion was out of the question, and Picker thus had no basis for opposing the changes, Ritter stated. He also stressed that he had at no point agreed to simply accept Picker's suggested headings. If that was to be the case, then the publisher might as well take on the editorial responsibilities. He had really tried to be attentive to the wishes of Athenäum and Picker, he said, but it would be absolutely impossible to accept an editorial process where every little edition would have to be double-checked in order to get Picker's approval. That would mean that Picker was given editorial rights, which Ritter was firmly against. At the end of the day, he stated, he was himself responsible for the editorial work.[51] It is clear, then, that Ritter was prepared to take a stand for what he considered to be the correct manner in which to go about producing a book of this kind. Unfortunately, for Ritter, however, he was not able to get his way in this case either.

Junker explained to Ritter that Picker, as the "author" of the text, had a copyright to it, and this was a completely different matter than when other historical texts were concerned, which often lacked a living author who could claim the rights to the text. The publisher actually thought that Ritter's suggestions were better than Picker's; however, there was really nothing that they could do about it now that Picker had proven unwilling to agree to the changes suggested by Ritter. If it would make Ritter feel better, the publisher could agree to letting him include a remark to this effect at the end of the book, i.e. a note stating that the headings stemmed from Picker and not from Ritter.[52] This is the background to Ritter's note called "Regarding the edition" (*Zur Einrichtung der Ausgabe*) at the end of *Tischgespräche* where it says that Picker was the one responsible for the formulations in the text.[53] At the same time, Ritter stated that the text corresponded "in every detail" with Picker's "notes as well as those of *Minesterialrat* Heim"[54] How Ritter could write this even though the proofing process had entailed a large number of changes to the text by Picker, and even though Ritter had noted that Heim's text often was hard to understand if one did not insert certain words (whether this was done or not is not known). In any case, what Ritter wrote in his endnote was not completely true.

Picker also wished to remove a reference to Heim, which Ritter had included, because Heim was certainly still alive.[55] This led Ritter to change the reference, but he still considered such a reference necessary, since, as he wrote:

> since the text, as Heim's text so often is, as it now stands can only be understood with difficulty. There must be a misunderstanding here. Mr. Heim has obviously only made short notes and did not make them like Mr. Picker, who always worked them out in full immediately after dinner.[56]

What this "reference" was is unknown, since this is not detailed in any of the letters. However, in Ritter's endnote in *Tischgespräche* there is a remark that makes the reader aware regarding Heim's notes that "the shortness of these notes often makes the understanding [of them] difficult; sometimes one could also suspect some sort of a misunderstanding."[57] Considering that the word "misunderstanding" is used in both Ritter's letter and in the endnote we can assume that this is what Picker wished to have removed from the preface, but that Ritter put in at the end of the book instead.

Ritter was forced to accept Picker's headings, since he had the law on his side in this case, although he still thought it was odd. He had written to Picker to ask him not to oppose any possible future changes to the headings. The matter was one of making the book readable, argued Ritter, and that was certainly in the interest of both Athenäum and Picker.[58] The publisher expressed its satisfaction with the fact that Ritter now had agreed to let Picker's headings stand as they were and stated that even though they agreed that Ritter's suggestions were better, they could not force Picker to accept any changes. This was obviously a matter of great importance to Picker. But the publisher stressed that Picker was very adamant that his proof changes were to be duly considered, and since Ritter had kept Picker's suggested changes for himself, the publisher could not check whether Ritter had chosen not to oblige Picker's wishes. He was thus asked to send these proofs to Athenäum so that they could check and see for themselves.[59]

The cooperation between Ritter and Athenäum had now reached an unprecedented low, and a real crisis of confidence had set in. Ritter desperately tried to retain some independence and professional responsibility by threatening to withdraw from the project entirely if his wishes were not respected in some critical areas. He was extremely upset and could not help but feel offended (*gegränkt*) by Ahtenäum's wish to double-check his proof corrections. He felt that this symbolized an enormous degree of a lack of confidence in him as editor of the book. The publisher, probably on Picker's instigation, had apparently fought him on almost every footnote, and he considered it impossible to agree to an elimination of them altogether. He would not budge with regard to the footnote about Schacht (and yet another one), he stated; Schacht had now responded to him and he included his reply in the letter to Athenäum. In a critical sentence Ritter wrote that Schacht had said that:

> if all the notes of Hitler's conversations are as impossible as those sent to him, then he could only insistently recommend against publication.[60]

Thus, if these footnotes were also stricken from the manuscript, Ritter said, he would not only withdraw himself from the publication but he would also see to it that the IfZ would not cooperate with the publisher either. He now asked Athenäum to consider his ultimatum.[61]

The solution to this whole mess, which was finally resolved over the telephone, was to collect Ritter's comments to the text at the end of the book. Athenäum had spoken to Picker and had tried to convey to him that the changes suggested by Ritter had been made in order to better the text. It was the hope of the publisher that this matter had now finally been cleared up.[62] Athenäum asked Ritter to understand that it had not been the publisher's intent to question his authority by asking him to send them Picker's proof changes. All of this stemmed from Picker and his "wholly irrational anxiety" not to be considered the real author of the manuscript, it was said. Picker was extremely keen on guarding his copyright. At the same time, Junker sent Ritter yet more of Picker's proof changes, even though he understood that Ritter must be tired of proofreading by now. The collaboration, and negotiations, with Picker had been difficult for the publisher too, Ritter was assured, and the publisher begged Ritter to understand this situation.[63]

In view of these explanatory remarks on the part of the publishers, Ritter could only thank Athenäum for their, although only partly successful, negotiations with Picker. Ritter took care to make clear, however, that Picker's claim to have a veto on what Ritter wrote in his endnote to the book (expressed in a letter to Athenäum) could not be accepted; he, and he alone, would be responsible for his own text, Ritter said.[64] Nonetheless, the problems continued, and it was Ritter's corrective footnote concerning Schacht that caused Picker to object. The latter wished to have Ritter's last sentence in the footnote removed. The publisher hoped that Ritter would be kind enough to agree to this demand.[65] Ritter could, of course, not agree to any such meddling by Picker in his footnote. He pointed out that he, as editor, was indeed also "politically" responsible for the project, and he considered it impossible to take this task lightly, not least because of his obligations towards the IfZ. He understood that Athenäum was having a hard time in dealing with Picker, but he could not yield any ground on this particular point, and he had already retreated on other matters. A line had to be drawn somewhere.[66] He could, however, agree to change the passage to read as follows:

> Since the financial actions in foreign countries mentioned by Hitler have to be considered 'completely impossible', also according to the financial experts we have asked, it is not evident what to make of the (for Hitler characteristic) claim.[67]

The work on the book had thus not only been made in great haste, it is also obvious from the correspondence between Ritter and Athenäum that he did not really have access to Picker's original manuscript during the proofreading process. This is of course problematic from a source-critical point of view. However, Ritter does not seem to have had any such objections to this way of going about things. On the other hand, Ritter certainly did not have an easy time dealing with Picker and

Athenäum, and it is clear from the archival record that he did his best to try and uphold at least some scientific rigour. He obviously had principles that he would not compromise on, and he repeatedly threatened the publisher to walk away from the project unless his demands were met. It is thus perhaps not only a little unfair to criticize Ritter for not having included a critical commentary to the text and for having "naïvely" and "thoughtlessly" presented the text to the reader, as Nicolas Berg has done. According to Berg, Ritter repeated many of the themes in Picker's preface and thereby made matters even worse.[68] Ritter did make several mistakes, and there were many questions that he should have asked that he did not ask, but he at the same time fought hard to get at least some critical reflections into the book.

Ritter was constantly under pressure from the publisher (and Picker) to forego as much of the critical apparatus as possible. Junker wrote to him in the beginning of May and complained about the many delays that had plagued the publication process. The book was now planned to be launched in June; any later would simply not be possible, Junker stated. He brought up the high prices of paper, the lack of any more credits from the bank, etc. On a more positive note Junker brought up the fact that re-prints from the book would be published in the newspapers over the coming weeks, and Dr Hermann Mau[69] from the IfZ had arranged for two appearances on the radio in early June. But the Schacht issue kept causing problems for the publisher, and thus also for Ritter. Junker said that Ritter's suggested change to the passage in question had not yet been presented to Picker, who was away on business. Junker said that he understood how taxing the whole affair with Picker had been for Ritter but explained that they were dealing with "a remarkably unique, almost pathological symptom." He then asked Ritter, once again, to heed to Picker's wishes and to let the disputed passage be moved to the endnote.[70] Finally, and in a rather disrespectful tone, he asked Ritter:

> I beg You to not make our work even more difficult at this last moment by [being] unyielding on one issue, which decidedly is not of great importance for the work in its totality.[71]

Junker followed this up by reminding Ritter that the publisher had originally only asked him to write an introduction to the book and that he had taken it upon himself to enlarge his workload.[72] This was certainly a bit unfair to Ritter, a professional historian, who had been clear all along that he intended to treat the text critically.

Needless to say, Ritter was taken aback by Junker's letter. He understood that the many delays had put pressure on Athenäum but added that he had absolutely not contributed to these delays in any way. On the contrary, he told Junker, he had worked with extreme haste during the whole proofing process; no proofs had been with him for more than one or two days before being sent back to the publisher, and he challenged Junker to find another historian in Germany who worked with such haste and punctuality. In his view, he had delivered a text ready to print already in the middle of February, and all delays were entirely either Picker's or the Athenäum's own fault. The accusation that he had taken upon himself more than had originally been agreed to was not something that he would even try to justify by commenting upon, Ritter wrote scathingly, but he pointed out that he had repeatedly offered to step aside.[73] Then, in a passage that in hindsight sounds almost prophetic, Ritter wrote:

> I fear: that this very cautious edition, lacking commentary, will be misused by politically by extreme right-wing groups, such as the Remer Party. My critical comments, which have been stuffed away at the end of the book, will not be considered. These kinds of considerations have recently also been expressed by Dr. Mau, and the political responsibility towards the German Institute rests in the end upon me.[74]

This shows that Ritter was almost too well aware of the fact that any political blow-back from the publication of *Tischgespräche* would tarnish only his own reputation; the IfZ had, in a way, washed its hands of him.

He also pointed to a major mistake in the text, namely when Hitler supposedly spoke about Hindenburg concurring to Hitler's decision to re-militarize the Rhineland in 1936, even though Hindenburg had died in 1934.[75] Once again, though, Ritter does not seem to have considered the possibility that the mistake was perhaps Picker's. Ritter added that Picker could not object to the new version of the Schacht passage, and thus this matter could, finally, be considered over.[76] However, this judgement would prove just as illusory as the ones preceding it. Picker, it turned out, would *not* accept Ritter's changed Schacht passage, since he deemed it to be a subjective decision on Ritter's part. Because of this the publisher asked Ritter, again, to drop the passage.[77] Ritter's refusal to accept any blame for the delays seems to have had the intended effect. A week later Junker wrote to tell Ritter that the publisher had contemplated his letter from 16 May, and he wished to say that everyone at Athenäum understood very clearly that it was thanks to Ritter's hurried work pace that the book would be published at all, and he acknowledged that they could have found no other university scholar who could have done a similar job.[78]

The *Quick* affair

Ritter had marketed the project to the IfZ with the argument that *Tischgespräche* would help the IfZ to get noticed and put it on the map. That certainly turned out to be true, as parts of the book were serialized in the German illustrated magazine *Quick*. But the book did not generate the kind of attention that the IfZ had wished, nor the kind that Ritter had intended. In short, the book caused a huge scandal.[79] Mau was in Washington, D.C. when the *Quick* affair exploded in Germany in June 1951 (for more on his visit to the United States, see Chapter 4). Ritter claimed that he had had no idea about the fact that parts of the book would be published in *Quick* or that parts of his preface, including his name, would be made public in this sensationalist way. He had not taken part in the publication, nor had he been asked about it. If he had known about it, he would have had doubts as to what a publication in such a "popular" organ as *Quick* could result in, even though he never expected such an outcry. The article itself, however, was basically innocent, he wrote to Mau. He hoped the whole thing would soon be laid to rest, and he had in the meantime demanded that Athenäum-Verlag should stop any further publication of *Tischgespräche* in *Quick*. His experience with the publisher was not all that good, he said, but he hoped that the buzz over the *Quick* publication would be good news for the book in the long run. However, Ritter found out, before sending his letter to Mau, that the publication in *Quick* would continue. Ritter said that he would have never taken part in the publication of *Tischgespräche* and never attached the IfZ's name to it had he known beforehand that such large parts of the book would be serialized in the magazine.[80]

Genoud's biographer, Willy Winkler, has suggested that the decision to publish bits in this magazine was made by the IfZ and that things were made worse by the fact that the man chosen to select the bits for *Quick* was Hans Georg von Studnitz, a former member of NSDAP who had worked at the Press Department in Joachim von Ribbentrop's Foreign Ministry. He writes that the IfZ even paid for Picker's travel costs in association with the publication in *Quick*.[81] However, this is incorrect. According to a letter from the Athenäum-Verlag to Mau in September 1951, the IfZ had had nothing to do with the *Quick* episode. It was instead Picker who chose the passages that were to be published, together with a representative of *Quick*. Picker had told *Quick* that Engel and Bodenschatz, as partakers at the dinners in the FHQ, had testified to their authenticity. In addition, it had been concluded that "new finds in the United States and Switzerland" proved "that the documents are authentic."[82] The latter must have referred to Heim's proof pages, found by Mau in July (see Chapter 4), and to Genoud's manuscript, which had been brought to the IfZ's attention since the publication of *Tischgespräche*. This conclusion was of course only valid in so far as it related to the documents themselves, *not*, however, regarding the credibility of the content of those documents.

However, it turns out that Ritter was perhaps not entirely honest with Mau when he told him he had had no idea about the publication in *Quick*. Because the fact is that Junker had told Ritter all of this in a letter to him on 23 May:

> At this time I would like to tell You that the magazine QUICK will serialize parts of the book, which they will begin on 6 June, whereby they will also make use of Your preface.[83]

Considering that Ritter would later emphatically deny having had any knowledge of the publication in *Quick*, this passage is rather damning to say the least. This does not mean that his effort to defend himself in this way is not understandable; however, it was not a good match to reality. At the time, Ritter apparently thought nothing of it and simply accepted it.[84] Neither can the argument be made that Ritter had perhaps not seen this passage, which was indeed inserted rather offhandedly, because Ritter acknowledged not only that he had read this particular part of Junker's letter well but also that he well understood the possible problematic consequences of such a publication. In a letter to Junker dated 31 May he stated that some of the content in the book appeared to him to be only embarrassing banalities and gossip:

> in the vein of the "illustrated" with whose help the book will now be presented to the world – all of these are experiences that more and more make me regret that I attached my and the German Institute's names to this publication.[85]

It thus seems as if Ritter had already realized in which direction the whole affair was going, and there is indeed a sense of dejection and lethargic abjection about it all. One wonders, of course, why Ritter could not amass the strength to actually put his foot down, or even withdraw from the project completely. Perhaps the idea of being the historian to edit these talks was simply too alluring to him.

Unsurprisingly, Junker and his colleagues at Athenäum did not share Ritter's gloomy view of the planned publication in *Quick*. This would surely be good for the book, they thought, because through this magazine the book could reach a section of the German public that was not as interested in the scientific side of it as in the political and human (*politische und menschliche*) side. They also claimed to have taken care to publish nothing tacky or sensational, but only material that would preserve the book's dignity.[86] Ironically, Ritter would actually agree with the last statement once he saw the material in *Quick*, As things turned out, however, they could not have been more off the mark.

All of this would soon lead to a very strange blame game regarding who was actually responsible for what turned out to be a disastrous decision. Just a few days after *Quick* had published the first *Tischgespräche* issue Ritter began to hear, from various directions, "doubts, complaints, shaking of heads, and accusations" over the fact that he had lent his name, as well as that of the IfZ, to a magazine like that. Ritter had also thought that the book should be promoted in an illustrated magazine, but he nevertheless now felt that a publication in *Quick*, which was a "sensationalist" magazine, seemed to him to contradict the aim of presenting it in a strictly factual manner. The publication had, due to the reactions to it, obviously defeated its purpose, even though the content of *Quick*'s publication was above reproach in this particular case, he thought. Then Ritter made quite an outrageous claim; he stated that the "publication in 'Quick' took place without my prior consent." Now, how on earth could Ritter state such a claim when Junker had in fact informed him just a few weeks earlier? Well, according to Ritter this had been done in a manner that was unsatisfactory. He told Athenäum that "You informed me about this on 23 May; that is, at a point when everything was already arranged and the first publication was immediately forthcoming."[87] Ritter thus tried to claim that he had been against the publication all along. This was a half-truth at best; all he had done was to express certain apprehensions, but he never protested it. This was an obvious afterthought and an effort to rationalize what had turned out to be a bad choice on his part. We have little reason to assume that Ritter would have thought twice about it if the publication had not caused a stir.

Athenäum now began to backpaddle as well. It was pointed out that *Quick* was one of the biggest illustrated magazines in Germany with a circulation of over 700,000 copies. However, the final decisions on what to publish had been made between Picker, *Quick*, and the IfZ. The publisher thus tried to wash its hands of the whole thing. Junker did not think that this would adversely affect the publication of *Tischgespräche*, which was to follow, and neither did it damage the credibility of the book, they argued.[88] But the scandal only grew, and four days later Ritter wrote to Junker and told him straight up that the publication in *Quick* had had "a completely disastrous political effect"; the regional and national governments had reacted very negatively. The Bavarian radio had told Ritter that it had received urgent visits from the Americans, with whom Mau had previously discussed the publicity issues, and had therefore not gone through with the planned broadcasts. According to the radio representative, matters had come to this point only because of the fact that *Quick* had been chosen as the first venue for publication. The consequences for the IfZ would surely be severe, since it now had even the West German Chancellor (*Bundeskanzler*) and the president (*Bundespräsident*) against it. Ritter asked Junker to tell him exactly what Dr Mau had known about the publication, because to Ritter he had only stated that he had heard that this publication was planned – nothing more.[89]

Junker did not know specifically which Americans Mau had spoken to before he went to the United States; it was simply known that had done so. Mau would certainly be able to clear this thing up once he got back, Junker thought, "since even the *Quick* publication did not occur without the approval of the interested American institutions."[90] The Americans had thus been duly briefed beforehand, Junker claimed; however, now that the whole thing had exploded, all of those involved were trying to save face and would have nothing to do with the decision to publish the table talks in *Quick*. Junker continued by stating that it did seem as if the publication in *Quick*, to the greatest of sorrows of the publisher, had caused a certain sense of "dejection" (*Verstimmung*) in Germany. This was something that Athenäum had not anticipated. Junker thought it was strange because, as far as he was concerned, *Quick* had not only presented the text in a "completely dignified way", but the chosen material was also not of such a nature that ought to cause political misunderstandings or to really justify the strong reactions. But, he continued, at Athenäum they were convinced that this would not last for long and that the whole matter would soon be forgotten by the public. Furthermore, the book itself would soon be out, and discussions would then turn to that instead.[91] It is not entirely clear whether Junker was actually this naïve or if he was trying to make Ritter worry less about the consequences; perhaps it was a bit of both.

Ritter did not buy Junker's effort to make him feel better though. He pointed out that this publication had done exactly what he had tried to avoid all through the editorial process. The *Quick* publication had divided the text into small bits of "'spicy' details", and it had given the examples headings like "'letting the skirts fall'" and "'women and Hitler.'" The latter was the kind of heading that Ritter had taken a stand against in the book; now it instead appeared like this. This was not a serious way to present the matter, he argued. Moreover, the bigger and serious magazines such as *Gegenwart* had begun to utter criticism against the publication too. Ritter considered it of utmost importance that any further publications in *Quick* be stopped immediately before any more damage could be done. This was the only way to save the reputation of the book, he said.[92] But Ritter's hopes were, again, expressed in vain. It was not possible to stop the coming publications in *Quick*, Junker told him, because Athenäum was bound by contract and *Quick* had the lawful right to six issues. However, the publisher urged Ritter not to overestimate the implications of this publication.[93]

This was the background to Ritter's explanatory, and self-exonerating, letter to Mau presented earlier. Mau replied that he, too, hoped that the controversy would soon die away and said that when he had mentioned *Tischgespräche* to the Americans the only wish expressed by them had been that commentary should be included in a future second edition.[94] Dr Dieter Sattler from the *Bayerischer Rundfunk* contacted Ritter in early September, after he had read *Tischgespräche*, and stated that while he thought it was important that the public should get access to Hitler's statements, he thought that the publication in *Quick* had been less than optimal for a number of reasons. First, Sattler thought that it was a mistake to publish the book without proper commentaries by Ritter, because there were so many things contained in it that were impossible for the readers to judge if what was said was correct or not. Second, he wondered if it had not been better to keep the text in chronological order, instead of breaking it up thematically. Furthermore, he thought that the headings that preceded every note gave Hitler's utterances "a certain weight that they, judging from the quality of what was said, did not have." Third, he pointed to some rather embarrassing mistakes in the text, such as the fact that Wagner's grandchild was not named Wahnfried, which was the name of Wagner's house in Bayreuth, but Wieland. Nevertheless, Sattler considered the decision to publish the book to be correct "since we must insist on a naked portrayal of the truth."[95]

In his reply to Sattler, Ritter stated that he had struggled with the headings to the notes but that he had only been partly successful against the oddities of Picker. He had early on remarked upon the mistake regarding Wagner's grandchild, he said, but since Picker had insisted on keeping "Wahnfried" in the book, he had assumed that the mistake must have been Hitler's.[96] This mistake was corrected in the second edition.

Ritter continued his effort at damage control by writing articles in several newspapers as well as appearing in the Stuttgart-based radio channel *Süddeutsche Rundfunk*. Needless to say, he did not appreciate Junker's effort to place some of the blame for the critique in his lap. He pointed out that this critique would never have come about in the first place:

> if Mr. Picker's subtitles, some of which were rather unfortunate, had not overemphasized the weight of Hitler's statements, and if the publisher had followed my proposal to provide an overview with which one could reconstruct

the original context of the talks. I was convinced of this by the debate about the book that took place in Marburg on the Historians' Day. It has had a particularly unfortunate effect that the critical comments I had given had, at the request of Mr. Picker, been thrown out of the text and banished to the last page of the book in fine-print.[97]

It is certainly not possible to argue that Ritter accepted any part of the blame for what had happened. It must surely be the case, however, that in the back of his mind he knew by now that it was a huge mistake to agree to take part in the publication of *Tischgespräche* under the given circumstances. A part of him must have wished that he had parted ways with Athenäum and Picker long before the book was published, and long before the first re-prints appeared in *Quick*.

Ritter continued by telling Junker that in the meanwhile Heim, whom he described as being an acquaintance of the former SA *Gruppenführer* Julius Schaub, had presented himself to the IfZ. Ritter stated:

Some of his [Heim's] manuscripts, which have remained unknown to Mr. Picker, have also now surfaced in the United States, where Dr. Mau has partially taken transcript. In a new edition, they would have to be included in a new edition, in my opinion. In your letter, you don't go into it at all, why not?[98]

The fact that the book was not expected to have sold out until the end of the year implied to him quite clearly that the book was now a commercial disappointment. Could it not have something to do with the high price set on the book, he asked rhetorically. Many people had read what had been printed in *Quick* and felt quite satisfied with that; it was not necessary to purchase the book. If a second edition was to be produced later on, Ritter stated five examples of things that had to be done to it: 1) errors and mistakes should be corrected; 2) the form of the subtitle should be checked; 3) the critical remarks to the text should be placed in their proper places; 4) the index should be enlarged; and 5) the newly discovered texts should be included.[99]

Ritter had to give a detailed account of the whole affair to the IfZ in late October. In it he repeated that he had had no knowledge of the publication in *Quick* and the extent it would have beforehand, even though, as we have seen, he had been duly informed about all of this by Junker in late May. It is difficult to believe that Ritter did not know that he was not telling the truth in this case. Moreover, he stated that he had wished to include more footnotes in *Tischgespräche* so that he could have made comments about outrageous statements made by Hitler and to correct mistakes. Picker, however, would have none of it. Otherwise, Picker had had no major viewpoints on how he treated the text, said Ritter. Picker was solely responsible for the text itself, except for the thematic structure, pagination, and chapter headlines, which Ritter had arranged.[100]

Ritter still defended the decision not to have critical commentaries in the book. A historian who tried to correct a historical person like that would be the laughingstock of the world, he thought. The words of the dead were forever the same, but the critique of the living changed constantly. Such a thing had no place in a source book, said Ritter.[101] The reason for why Ritter downplayed the difficulties he had encountered during his work on *Tischgespräche*, and why he did not mention the fact that he had failed in convincing Athenäum and Picker to include a critical commentary, something that he had clearly stated was a disappointment to him, was most likely that if he had detailed this to the IfZ *Beirat* he would no doubt have had to confront the question of why he did not stand his ground or why, if all else failed, had not walked away from the project.

But Mau (as was Junker) was wrong in assuming that the controversy would blow over quickly. In fact, it caused him, and the IfZ, great difficulties with the Americans. The British also joined the choir. The British Foreign Office complained about the whole affair to Bernard Noble, the head of the Historical Office of the U.S. State Department, who, apparently, felt forced to agree that the publication of *Tischgespräche* did not seem very appropriate so early after the IfZ's founding. Noble had expressed the Americans' surprise and embarrassment to Mau while he was still in Washington, and Mau had, according to Noble, stated that he, too, regretted the whole matter. The British High Commissioner's office in Germany even produced a report on the issue that unjustly accused Mau of being a convinced Nazi sympathizer. *Tischgespräche*, the report concluded, had basically no scientific value, which threatened only to stimulate a renewed interest for the Hitler regime among the German population. The scandal surrounding the publication also led to the IfZ being refused access to the Berlin Document Centre in 1952 by none other than Mau's former supporter within the organization of the High Commissioner for Germany (HICOG), Shepard Stone.[102] This was a later development, however, most likely induced by the British reaction, because when Mau was still in Washington, on 11 July, Stone had told him that the Americans considered the *Quick* incident to be over. According to Stone, it was felt that *Quick* had handled the text in such a way as to allay the American fears that it might be exploited "in a sensational manner."[103] At that time, however, no one really had any idea yet of how much consternation the publication of *Tischgespräche* would cause in Germany.

Mau then handled the matter very clumsily upon his return to Germany. He had, most likely through Noble, received some offhanded remarks regarding the content of the policy paper on the confiscated German documents that was underway while in the United States, and from these remarks he had concluded, correctly, that Washington was not ruling out the possibility of returning all the captured documents to the Germans. Mau, understandably, was happy and surprised to hear this, and jotted this down in his travel journal. So far, so good; but Mau then went several steps further and included this information as being a fact in his report from his journey and even mentioned Noble by name, saying that the latter had officially informed Mau of this decision. Mau then distributed this report widely, and it was published in both the *Frankfurter Allgemeine Zeitung* and the *Süddeutsche Zeitung*. But by that time the policy paper was about to go into the final round of consultations in Washington. The result was that Noble, and the State Department, was embarrassed, and the Departmental Records Branch (DRB) officially stated that Mau was wrong. Noble let Mau know what he felt regarding this issue, and as a consequence Mau revised this particular passage and sent the new version of the report out again. This was to no avail, of course – the damage had already been done. It took Noble a long time to regain his trust for the Germans at the IfZ, and the next IfZ historian was not allowed to travel to the United States until 1954. The publication of *Tischgespräche* had raised several warning flags among American historians regarding the direction in which contemporary history, as a subject, was heading in Germany, and the prospect of getting the German documents returned seemed more distant than ever before for German historians after this crisis.[104]

In a letter to State Secretary (*Staatssekretär*) Erich Wende that Mau had written while in Washington it became clear that Mau had never negotiated the *Quick* publication with the Americans. However, it had been negotiated with *Quick* by Picker, at which point Mau had been present, and Mau had given his approval to the mentioning of the IfZ based on having seen the first paragraph of the future article, in which a part of Ritter's introduction had been mentioned. From this Mau had simply assumed that Ritter had acquiesced to the publication and could not imagine that Ritter, as he put it, had not even been asked about it. Ritter had also considered it necessary to go on the offensive in the magazine *Gegenwart* to defend himself.[105] Picker, on the other hand, was of another opinion. According to him, as related to Ritter by Junker, Mau had negotiated the publication in *Quick* with an American by the name of Stone, although Junker was not sure who this was.[106] Junker also confirmed that Mau had been involved in the discussions with *Quick* and then launched the absurd claim that Athenäum had had no knowledge at all about what would be included in the first *Quick* issue; they had not seen it. Therefore, Athenäum had also not had any reason to ask for Ritter's permission to re-print a small part of his introduction in the illustrated magazine. Junker could certainly understand that Ritter considered his work with *Tischgespräche* one of the most unpleasant experiences in his life as an author; in fact, Junker insisted that he and Athenäum shared this view. However, the guilt for this should not be laid at either Ritter's or Athenäum's door; the fault was entirely "Dr. Picker's stubborn character", Junker stated.[107] As we shall see, Junker was not being honest with Ritter.

Picker claimed that the negotiation regarding the introduction had been handled by Mau, and it had been a matter of verbal agreement. Athenäum had in fact checked Picker's statements with representatives of *Quick*, who had confirmed this. Athenäum did, in the light of this, not feel obligated to undertake further negotiations with Ritter and were truly surprised to see such a large part of Ritter's introduction included in the second part of *Quick*'s serialization.[108] Ritter foresaw that the next meeting of the IfZ *Beirat* would be a very unpleasant experience where massive critique would be levelled against him and the book. What really seems to have frustrated Ritter at this point was that much of the criticism that had been uttered, even in the Office of the Chancellor (*Bundeskanzler-Amt*), concerned issues that he had tried so hard, but ultimately to no avail, to change.[109] This must truly have been a very bitter pill to swallow for Ritter.

In preparation for the discussion of the publication in *Quick* by the IfZ *Beirat* Athenäum tried to rally support from other members of the latter. In late September Junker wrote to Professor Erich Kaufmann to explain the situation to him, since it was deemed important to have allies on the *Beirat*. Junker complained that in the media it had been stated that the IfZ had had nothing whatsoever to do with the *Quick* publication, but this was not true. Junker now stated facts that show he had been lying to Ritter. Athenäum had indeed handled the negotiations with the magazine regarding re-printing rights, Junker wrote, but the IfZ had certainly been involved in the process too. Junker then quoted from the contract with *Quick* in order to prove his point:

> The selection of the publicized part of the book and its introduction was made by the Martens-Verlag [the publisher of Quick, M.N.] with the cooperation, and on the advice, of Dr. Picker. Regarding the title, the introductory texts, the selection from the introduction of Professor Ritter and the preface by Dr. Picker was made according to an agreement between Martens-Verlag and Dr. Mau from the German Institute for Contemporary History [IfZ] in Munich, whereby the decision is left to the Martens-Verlag.[110]

Junker followed this up with yet another quote, this time from a letter from *Quick* to Athenäum from mid-May where it was stated that:

> The coordination with Mr. Mau that You mention in § 1 has already been made so that the addition at the end of the paragraph in § 1 cannot lead to any further problems.[111]

It thus seems as if Mau, and thereby the IfZ, had been much more involved in the *Quick* deal than Mau wished to admit once this affair had exploded in the face of the IfZ.

But the one who got into the worst trouble due to the publication was not Mau, but Ritter, who up until then had been one of the most respected historians in Germany. One of many critics to go through the roof was Hanna Arendt. By choosing to publish the text without a critical footnote apparatus, and by thus letting Hitler speak unopposed, the book was seen as a neo-Nazi tract that risked being used for dark political objectives. The critique came all the way from Bonn, with Chancellor Konrad Adenauer himself and had several other big political names, such as the Bavarian Minister President Hans Ehard, behind it. This critique was delivered in public for everyone to see. Ritter, too, had expressed such fears during the work on the edition, and it is difficult to understand why he chose to publish it as he did anyway. In the end though, Ritter felt that his purpose with the book, namely, to show how ridiculous Hitler's ramblings were, had been reached.[112]

Ritter made the point that it was he, not Picker, who had had to shoulder the critique in the public domain because he had put his name to the book as a sign of the serious nature of it. He also complained (again) that he had not understood just how much from the book would appear in *Quick*. When Junker had informed him that parts would be re-printed in the newspapers and in *Quick* he had, he claimed, inferred that only a few shorter passages would be published, and he had thus had no chance to acquiesce to the deal made between *Quick* and Athenäum. He also noted that according to the contract between the publisher and *Quick* Mau was made partly responsible while at the same time the final decision regarding what would be published had been placed in the hands of *Quick*. It was Ritter's opinion that no publication should have been allowed to be made apart from the pieces from his introduction, and neither Junker, Picker, Mau, nor *Quick* should have had the right to decide without conferring with him first, since he was, in the eyes of the public, the person responsible for the publication of *Tischgespräche*.[113]

Athenäum, on the other hand, tried to argue that every party involved had been duped by *Quick*.[114] That was not a view that was shared by Mau, however. He, too, felt deceived by Athenäum and did not feel that he had been properly informed about the contractual agreement between the publisher and *Quick*. The last part of the contract gave *Quick* in practice the sole right to decide which parts of the text it would re-print but did not extend any real rights corresponding to the responsibilities that Mau, in the name of the IfZ, had accepted by consenting to the publication in *Quick*.[115] Athenäum wrote to the IfZ *Beirat* in early November with the purpose of explaining the circumstances behind the *Quick* publication. According to Athenäum, Picker had met with representatives of *Quick* and the IfZ in May 1951; before this point no publication in *Quick* had been contemplated by Picker. The latter permissioned Athenäum to negotiate with *Quick* on his behalf, and at the same time he insisted on a paragraph in the contract to the effect that *Quick* should have to confer (*abzustimmen*) concerning the publication with Mau. According to Athenäum, *Quick*'s publishing company Martens-Verlag had added this paragraph and inserted the phrase that gave them the right to make the final decision. Athenäum had then protested against this and got the response that this addition was now superfluous, since the coordination had already taken place. Therefore, Athenäum was forced to assume that all the details had been discussed and cleared with Mau. Apparently, though, there had been further negotiations between *Quick* and Mau. The publisher now asked the IfZ in what way the content of the *Quick* publication was "irrelevant or even politically offensive?" The risk, brought forth by many critics, that Hitler-friendly consequences would result from the publication, had now been shown to be without merit.[116] In a sense, Athenäum had a point here: considering the massive critique the book received, it was hard to argue that it had given rise to Hitler apologetics.

Athenäum also told Ritter that the first meeting between Picker and Mau on this subject had taken place without the knowledge of the publisher. The whole misunderstanding had resulted from the fact that Athenäum thought that Mau and Picker had understood, and respected, their consultation paragraph.[117] This was, of course, entirely novel to Ritter, and the fact that the initiative had not come from Athenäum was to him a very important piece of information. However, since the *Beirat* had had its meeting the day before, and since Ritter was himself not present at this discussion, there was nothing that he could do about the matter anyway.[118] Despite Ritter's best efforts to defend himself against the various accusations, by November 1951 he was forced out of the IfZ, despite having tried to ride out the storm and hold on to his seat on its advisory board.[119]

In fact, according to the current deputy director of the IfZ, Magnus Brechtken, there was more to this story than met the eye. Ritter became a victim of a power struggle within the IfZ, as he was trying to gain control of the institution and determine its course for the future. Ritter's leading opponent inside the IfZ was Karl Buchheim, and their differences in religion played an important role in this affair. Buchheim, who was a Catholic, wished for the IfZ to be an institute in the Liberal Catholic tradition of northern Germany whereas Ritter, a Protestant, was more for the Prussian ideal of adhering to state policy. The scandal surrounding *Tischgespräche*, in which the publication in *Quick* was an important part, then sealed Ritter's fate.[120] It also seems as if the IfZ, in forcing Ritter to leave his post, hoped to rid itself of the bad publicity almost instantly, as if Ritter was somehow entirely to blame after all. Things did not work out that way, however, and Mau noted with apprehension that the IfZ remained tainted by this "questionable publication" even after Ritter had left, and the publication of *Tischgespräche* caused great damage also to Mau's visit to the United States.[121]

Ritter and his odd source-critical thinking

Willy Winkler has correctly noted that Ritter did seem to have uncritically accepted Picker's claim that the text conveyed Hitler's thoughts and words as they were uttered. So, in this sense it truly was a source-critical disaster. In his preface to *Tischgespräche* he wrote that this was a "historical document" that he took to show "how it really is" (*wie es eigentlich gewesen ist*: a quote from the German nineteenth-century historian Leopold von Rancke). As Ritter correctly remarked that *Mein Kampf* was a piece of propaganda, he implicitly admitted that he did not consider the *Tischgespräche* to be the same. At the same time, according to Ritter, Picker's text was "a meticulously planned, very comprehensive self-witness" by Hitler of his ideas and aims at the peak of his power.[122] Ritter writes that Bormann may very well have had political motives for assuring that Hitler's words were put down in writing, and parts of the notes that had "an official character" to them (only about three occasions as far as Picker claimed to remember) had been shown to, and approved by, Hitler. There could thus be no doubt about their authenticity, according to Ritter. Moreover, Ritter states that "we", which reasonably must mean the IfZ, had presented excerpts to some of the people present at some of the monologues, and these persons had confirmed that they were a correct reproduction of the Führer's words. The question was, Ritter asked, whether the monologues actually showed the true Hitler or not.[123]

At the same time, Ritter concludes that the *Tischgespräche* was not uttered to a group of people that were "closest" to Hitler, at least not before August 1942, and neither is the Hitler in the text one who speaks "freely" (*zwanglos*), with a few exceptions mostly concerning private matters. This obviously contradicted his conclusion that *Tischgespräche* showed the truth as it really was. Ritter went on to state that Hitler was not speaking without intentions, because he knew that the most important utterances were written down "Wort for Wort", i.e. word for word. He thus portrayed himself as he wishes to be seen, not by the public or by the masses, Ritter adds, but by those who were present and, not least, by history.[124] This statement is odd because it seems to imply that Picker had the opportunity to write down *ad verbatim* all that Hitler said on an important matter. The only way to do that would be via stenography, but as we already know Picker could not write stenography.

The judgment that the notes accurately reproduced Hitler's words because Hitler himself approved some of them is astoundingly naïve and entirely dependent upon Picker's version of events. Ritter concluded:

> History therefore has every reason to take these notes very seriously. Hitler is here consciously standing on the stage, in the stage lights of history. He sings, as it were – that is how the impression can be summarized – the heroic anthem of his own glory: a Wagnerian heroic tenor.[125]

How this could then be considered less propagandistic than *Mein Kampf* is unclear. From what Ritter writes, it seems that there could not be a less cunningly thought-out way to purvey to the future an image that was exactly what Hitler wanted "history" to see. Equally uncritical is Ritter when it comes to the roots of Hitler's fanaticism, which Ritter claimed could best be viewed in the notes containing Hitler's critical remarks about Christianity.[126] Here Ritter seems just as spellbound by Hitler's words as his followers were.

The reason for this is easy to understand when we consider Ritter's background in the Protestant *Bekennende Kirche* (which was in theological opposition, although not necessarily in political-ideological opposition, to the thoroughly nazified group of Protestant churches known as *Deutsche Christen*), as a believing historian of religion, who was critical of Nazism's wish to affect Christian theology, and who by the end of the war eventually ended up in prison.[127] Naturally, Hitler's lack of belief in Ritter's interpretation of Christianity would seem to him to be the root of all the bad things that Hitler did. It did not occur to him that millions of believing Christians followed Hitler and acted on his ideology and that Hitler's purported anti-Christian ideology cannot possibly explain that. This is leaving the issue of whether Hitler actually uttered those exact words or not aside. Ritter then gives his reader what can only be described as an apologetic argument for why a belief in God is the only moral guarantor in the world, as if no Nazi held sincere Christian beliefs or moral convictions). He even quotes Bismarck and Moltke (who both had brought war on Germany) when doing this, pointing out that in contrast to these God-fearing men, Hitler's worldview had a long way to go.[128]

This was not a serious historian writing anymore, but a Christian apologetic who tried to explain National Socialism's success, and destructive nature, by pointing out that Hitler was not a "true" God-fearing Christian. However, not even Ritter could claim that Hitler was an atheist; Hitler did indeed believe in a higher power, a creating force of the universe, and he points out that Hitler's belief in the so-called *Vorsehung*, or Providence, was the content of the often talked about "belief in God" (*Gottgläubigkeit*) of Hitler and his entourage. He even calls it a religion and states that from this worldview follows no hinders or tempering of the will. For Ritter this is so important that he spends three pages trying to convince the reader of the importance of Hitler's lack of Ritter's own Christian beliefs.[129]

The question here must also be what Picker's own attitude towards Christianity was. Was he a believer himself, or did he share Hitler's views? These factors naturally affect Picker's ability to, always after the fact, reconstruct Hitler's statements correctly. It may therefore be relevant in this context that Picker published a book, written with the assistance of the Vatican Library librarian Graf Giuseppe Newlin, about Pope John XXIII in 1963. This does indeed point toward him at least having "found" Catholicism at some point (perhaps after the war).[130] Whether or not Picker was biased against Hitler's anti-Catholic statements also during the war is not clear.

Albert Speer on *Tischgespräche*: a reliable witness?

Albert Speer mentions Picker's *Tischgespräche* in his best-selling *Spandauer Tagebücher* from 1975. Speer appears to give us a review of *Tischgespräche* by someone who knew Hitler intimately for many years and who was present at many of the conversations recorded by Heim and Picker. In a note dated 24 March 1960 Speer claims that he received a copy of *Tischgespräche*, and his review amounts to nothing less than a massive dismissal of this source as largely untrue to its subject matter. The language in *Tischgespräche* had been so edited that Hitler was completely unrecognizable, and it gave a flawed view of the Führer. The Hitler that one was presented with in Picker's book was too eloquent and kept to the subject too well. Furthermore, Hitler would never have expressed himself freely in the type of company that he was in when providing the material for *Tischgespräche*, it says. This included Picker himself who, according to Speer, always looked out of place. But at the same time, the content in *Tischgespräche* was correct in another sense, namely that all the themes were subjects that Speer had heard Hitler speak about in one way or another. In this way a correct text could give an incorrect impression.[131]

But there is ample reason for us not to trust what is written in *Spandauer Tagebücher*. This is because it is not certain who the true author of the *Tischgespräche* passage in *Spandauer Tagebücher* actually is. This passage was not included in many of the draft versions of the manuscript for Speer's book, and it is doubtful that

Speer himself wrote the part about *Tischgespräche* that is in the printed version of the book. More likely, it is Joachim Fest who is the originator, and author, of the opinions about *Tischgespräche* that we find in *Spandauer Tagebücher*.[132] One draft version, which must have been produced rather late because it is a photocopy of a typed text with proof corrections made to it, has no entry for the date in question, i.e. 24 March 1960. Instead it goes directly from 19 March, the date before 24 March in *Spandauer Tagebücher*, to 11 April 1960, the date after 24 March in the published version. Furthermore, the text for the entries is a lot longer than in the final version, and long sections of the text have been marked with a red pen and the notation "Fe" for Fest.[133] This most likely signifies the parts written by Fest.

The date "24 March" appears for the first time in a volume containing "Notes on each chapter in the manuscript" where it simply says: "The pair of wild doves have returned from their winter holiday in Morocco."[134] This remark does not appear in the published version of the book. In the same document there are three short notes dated 4 April 1960, which is a date that also does not appear in *Spandauer Tagebücher*. One of these reads: "Schirach is being more and more friendly to me."[135] This sentence has been transferred to 11 April in the edited proof manuscript, where it says: "Schirach is friendlier to me."[136] This, too, is not in the published version of the book. In a handwritten version of the manuscript, which reasonably must be earlier than the other two versions, we find that text dated to 24 March 1960 has been dated to 11 April in one of the later versions, and none of it is present in *Spandauer Tagebücher*.[137]

Then, suddenly, *Tischgespräche* and the date 24 March 1960 makes its appearance in a draft manuscript. But this text is entirely different than what ended up in *Spandauer Tagebücher*:

> The good thing about reading Tischgespräche: A number of Hitler's expressions are coming back to me. Should I make a new effort? Can I meet the responsibility, to retroactively write down his utterances just as I began to do some years ago? They are still, word for word, fresh in my memory.[138]

This is indeed the exact opposite to what is in *Spandauer Tagebücher*, which proves conclusively that what is in the final book has very little, if anything, to do with reality. This means that the published version of the 24 March note is a late creation, and one that bears no similarity to the only mentioning of Picker's book that is in any of the many draft manuscripts.

What we can be absolutely sure of is that Speer never wrote a diary entry about Picker and the *Tischgespräche* on 24 March 1960 (or anywhere near it). It seems likely that this "event" was not created until Speer and Fest were working on the *Spandauer Tagebücher* together in the early 1970s. Thus, we cannot trust the draft version of this entry to be more reliable than the later version – both could be entirely fictional. Because of this fact, it is also very doubtful that Speer received a copy of Picker's book in March 1960, as it says in his book. Since Speer obviously did not write it down until much later, he cannot be expected to remember exactly when he read *Tischgespräche* more than a decade earlier. Speer, and the *Spandauer Tagebücher*, in short, simply cannot be trusted at all. The content has been worked over so many times that very little of any genuine reflections from the time in the Spandau prison is long gone.

That said, however, the draft entry, which was later removed and completely re-written, was written by Speer, although it is not likely to stem from Speer's time in Spandau. It is not possible to say with any certainty when it was actually written. What speaks for Speer being the author is the much less embroidered language in it. Moreover, it speaks of Speer working on a collection of Hitler's utterances. This obviously never came to anything, and this is probably why it was not included in the final version of the book. It also expresses a certain admiration for Hitler, since Speer wonders to himself if he will be able to "meet the responsibility" of writing down Hitler's words. In this entry he can still remember Hitler's statements "word for word", while in the *Spandauer Tagebücher* it says that Picker's book did not correctly portray the way Hitler constantly started a sentence only to stop and then start again. This is obviously a bit contradictory because how could Speer possibly remember such confused speech word for word?

A comparison between Speer's notes from his many conversations with Hitler (*Führerbesprechungen*) during the war, which can be found in Speer's *Nachlaß* in Koblenz, offers no confirmation of the themes in either Picker or Heim. In fact, Speer has notes that parallel Picker's first two notes, i.e. 21 and 22 March 1942. But the treatment of Russian POWs, which is the topic of Speer's text, is not mentioned by Picker.[139] Another fact that should be mentioned is that the long note by Picker dated 23 June is paralleled by 14 pages of notes made by Speer from a *Führerbesprechung* held that day (one page of these notes is missing). Unfortunately, there is no parallel in the content of the notes. While Picker's text deals with problems related to the supply of agricultural products, Speer's text deals almost exclusively with issues relating to military production.[140] Speer relates a discussion on the preparation for gas warfare held on 8 July 1942, which is not mentioned by Picker.[141] The same is true for such a discussion on 25 July that does not appear in *Tischgespräche*, and one on 12 August that is not in *Monologe*.[142] Speer also relates a discussion about the treatment of POWs that is not related by Heim in *Monologe*. There is a discussion about winter clothing in both Heim's and Speer's notes, but the content is entirely different. While Hitler, according to Heim, spoke about how he used to wear shorts during winter and that the *SS-Standarte Hochland* would only wear shorts in the future, Speer states that Hitler had agreed to provide better winter clothes for the POWs so that their work performance would improve.[143] None of the other (many) matters noted down by Speer appear in *Monologe*.[144] Although *Monologe* confirms that Speer was a guest at the *Werwolf* on 7 September 1942 the points mentioned in Speer's notes are not included in Heim's text.[145] This does not mean that Heim's notes are fraudulent, but it is certainly a bit disturbing that the content does not overlap at any point.

Critique against *Tischgespräche*

Regarding the reliability of Picker's text, the editor of the second edition (1963), Percy Ernst Schramm, writes in his preface that mistakes inadvertently had found their way into the text and that many difficult factors affected the outcome. Hitler's wish not to have notes taken, his confused manner of speaking, and the fact that Picker had to re-create Hitler's words from his notes all contributed to this. None-theless, Schramm maintains that Picker's text is as accurate as anyone could demand under these circumstances.[146] That, of course, was neither helpful nor true.

The German journalist Willi Winkler has contributed many interesting and important details to this case in his biography of Genoud entitled *Der Schat-tenmann*. He does not hold back when he criticizes *Tischgepräche* from 1951. He states that scientifically it was a disaster; the authenticity had never been checked, much had obviously been re-formulated *ante facto*, words and phrases have been added, etc. Winkler writes that the IfZ distanced itself from Picker's edition even before Genoud had published his French version, admitting that Genoud's manuscript was the best. The reason for this, according to Winkler, was that they were afraid to lose contact with Genoud because they wanted his material.[147] On the other hand, Winkler does not really hold Genoud's manu-script to be too reliable either, even though he is never as tough on that text as he is on Picker's. This is odd in a way, considering that Genoud's original notes are missing, while at least one version of Picker's text exists at *Bundesarchiv* in Koblenz, Germany.

But reviewers of *Tischgespräche* were not always correct in their critique. One of them noted that Picker mentioned Hitler's notably large and blue eyes. But Hitler, the reviewer stated, had brown eyes. Nazi propaganda had thus found its way into Picker text.[148] However, Hitler *did* have piercing blue eyes. This is confirmed by many witnesses, including Hitler's friend from childhood and adolescence, August Kubizek.[149] The reviewer was thus mistaken. Winkler's book has flaws too; flaws that seem strange when considering the information that is available regarding the creation of *Tischgespräche*. For example, Winkler states that Picker used ste-nography, which we know is not true. Winkler also lets on that Heim and Picker wrote down every word that the Führer uttered, but that is, as we have seen, not true either. Neither Heim nor Picker ever claimed anything like that. Heim even said in his interview with the BBC in 1953 that any entry from nightly sessions (and that is a large part of his notes) was something that Hitler had said in a small room in the Führer bunker that served as Hitler's office, around a round table, and where only very few people were invited. These circumstances meant that Heim could not make any notes at all as the monologues unfolded. This is what he said to the BBC:

> When I know explain that not a single word from these nightly utterances could be recorded by me, while Hitler babbled on – all that was dictated to one of the Reichsleiter's secretaries, [who used] a typewriter, from memory the next day.[150]

The statement is a bit confused, which is natural, since it is a verbatim record of Heim's words. People speak very differently than they write and that is why spoken language often looks very strange in writing. What Heim said was that he could not get down one single word on paper from the nightly sessions until the day after when he dictated all of it from memory to one of Bormann's secretaries. It is obvious that fidelity suffers from this practice. Naturally, Heim would have had no possibility to remember correctly even half of what Hitler had said (and Hitler could talk for hours on end) – nobody has that good a memory. Heim stated:

> I make an effort to record the word as it was spoken, but you don't find every word spoken in this context here, and it's also not possible for me to convey that which I deliver as it was, as if it had been recorded mechanically or by a stenographer.[151]

From a source-critical perspective, the historians must look at these notes with an even greater degree of scepticism than the rest of the entries. The repetitious nature of the monologues, i.e. the fact that the same subject comes up again and again, is actually commented upon by Christa Schroeder, one of Hitler's private secretaries, as being a more or less conscious choice on Hitler's part. Supposedly this was a way for Hitler to memorize certain things that he had read; *Gehirngymnastik*, or brain gymnastics, Schroeder called it.[152] Too much should thus perhaps not be made of the content of Hitler's statements in the table talks.

Nonetheless, but perhaps less surprising, Heim did not feel that he had in any way lessened the value of his notes as sources to Hitler's words – not even the slightest. He insisted that he had not put anything down on paper that he was not absolutely sure of. Furthermore, Bormann had acted as a regulatory party and infallible witness by reading the notes and correcting what he felt was wrong. As the facsimile in the beginning of *Table Talk* (and *Monologe*) shows, said Heim, Bormann had taken it upon himself to check his notes and make necessary changes as he saw fit. If no additions were made, it meant that Heim had gotten everything exactly right. The possibility that Heim knew approximately what Bormann would want to see in the notes did not occur to Heim.[153] This is, of course, not to say that the notes necessarily always gave a correct version of Hitler's utterances before Bormann's changes either. The fact of the matter is that we cannot know this, and this is why the table monologues have to be treated so carefully by historians.

Bormann's note attached to the *Bormann-Vermerke*

Let us look a bit closer at Bormann's note. In *Libres propos* it is said that Bormann wrote it after all the notes had been completed (which must mean not earlier than 30 November 1944, since this is the last entry in *Monologe* and *Table Talk*), Genoud wrote:

> At the head of the complete document he wrote with his own hand: "Please keep, with the utmost care, these notes of capital interest for the future."[154]

Trevor-Roper copied this in his introductory essay to the *Table Talk* entitled "The Mind of Adolf Hitler."[155] There is only one problem with this nice story: it cannot be true. The reason is that Bormann's note is dated 20 October – the year being unknown. Confusion grows when one finds that Jochmann dates this note to 1941. The complete note reads:

> Please preserve these, in the future very valuable, records well. Finally, I have now got Heim to make detailed notes as the basis for these records. Every not so precise notation will be corrected once more [yet again; a second time] by me.[156]

The fact that Bormann wrote "finally" must mean that the note was written not long after Heim started making notes. Jochmann even says that Bormann wrote the note for the party headquarters in Munich but without telling us where he got this information.[157] He does not tell his readers why he adds this particular year, although it makes more sense than the Genoud/Trevor-Roper version. To write that he had "finally" convinced Heim to make notes makes no sense if he wrote it in the end of 1944. Furthermore, there is no entry anywhere near the date 20 October in either 1942 or 1943. The closest entry can actually be found in 1941 when one note was made of a conversation taking place the night between 19 and 20 October. The source that Jochmann used when reaching his conclusion must have been Heim's manuscript for his BBC recording in 1953 where we find:

> in addition there was Martin Bormann's order: as is apparent in the introductory facsimile of Bormann's handwritten note in "Table Talk" from 20.X.1941, the Reichsleiter had taken the right to insert his own diverging recollections, if any, into my notes.[158]

Genoud's dating is thus complete nonsense. If Jochmann is correct in stating that the note was intended for the party HQ in Munich, then this means that it was likely originally attached to only a few notes made before 20 October 1941. The note also makes no sense if Bormann intended to keep the notes himself. No, it *only* seems to make good sense if Bormann gave these notes to someone (perhaps at the NSDAP HQ) who did not understand the value of them. This could not have been his wife, who surely would have understood the value of these notes anyway. The note would also not have been formulated in this way if Bormann did not expect to see them again (and have control over them) for a longer period of time. Bormann's true motive for writing it may likely never be known.

There is also an interesting difference between the two facsimiles: in HTR's book the Bormann note contains the holes for a binder, four in the left margin and two, strangely enough, to the right parallel to Bormann's signature. These do not appear in Jochmann's book. The reason for these differences is unknown. It could be that these were simply covered up when replicated in *Monologe*.

More confusion regarding the table talks

Let's now turn our attention back to Picker's text. Winkler also quotes some information from an article in *Der Spiegel* from 1966 regarding the notes, and he states that Hitler's will to hold long monologues became worse the closer the Allies came to Berlin. In the end they were supposed to have filled no fewer than 110,000 pages.[159] This was a sensational statement to say the least, and it immediately made me curious about Winkler's source. It corresponds very poorly with Jochmann's *Monologe* where the number of entries *decreases* considerably the closer to 1945 we get. In short, it goes against everything we know about *Tischgespräche* and *Monologe*. That does not automatically mean that it is wrong, but it does call for a good check of the sources.

And in fact, it turns out that the article in *Der Spiegel* contains several things that ought to have made Winkler question the veracity of the article. Among other things it says that historians should be happy about Hitler's love of putting all his words down on paper and make sure it made it into the protocols. Yes, according to *Der Spiegel*, Hitler supposedly was the one who had almost everything he said noted down, and refers specifically to Picker's book from 1951.[160] *Der Spiegel* does indeed make a connection between Hitler's love for stenography and his monologues in *Tischgespräche*, no doubt about that, but then the article shifts focus. The massive amounts of stenographic notes that are mentioned had to do with Hitler's military briefings with his officers regarding Germany's strategic position, *not* the table talks. That was why Hitler talked more and more the closer to the end one goes; the situation was getting worse and there was more to discuss with the officers of his staff. A number of the stenographers that took part are also mentioned, and Heim or Picker is not mentioned here. Some of these notes had been published, the article stated, in 1962 with the title *Hitlers Lagebesprechungen*.[161]

It could be added that Heim supports *Der Spiegel*'s version in one of the interviews that was made with him in 1952. Heim stated that his own and Picker's position was completely different from the stenographers that worked for Hitler and who were present at his *Lagebesprechungen* jotting down every word that was said.[162] There are even more dubious representations of the facts in Winkler's book regarding Picker's *Tischgespräche*. He states, as I showed earlier, that the IfZ *ante facto* admitted to the poor editorial work, as he calls it, in Picker's edition. The source for this information is an anniversary book edited by Horst Möller and published to celebrate the IfZ's fiftieth anniversary.[163] But Möller in fact writes quite the opposite of what Winkler would have him say, i.e. that Ritter not only took care to evaluate the text according to all the source-critical aspects, but also that the differences that later were shown to exist between Picker's and Genoud's texts did not give rise to any doubts about Picker whatsoever; that Picker's editing of the text did not in any way give the text any kind of political slant; and, finally, that the overall impression (and thereby also its authenticity) did not change at all. At the same time, however, he does state that a certain amount of carelessness on Picker's part had been noted by the time of publication in 1951.[164] Winkler's statement that the IfZ never gave one thought to source-critical issues is thus not supported by his own source.

At one point Winkler says that Picker has put the term "Iron Curtain" in Hitler's mouth when speaking about the Soviet Union and refers to an entry dated 2 August 1941 (i.e. five years before Churchill's famous speech in Fulton, Missouri, in 1946) in Hitler's headquarters *Wolfsschanze*.[165] Winkler does this in order to illustrate the striking unreliability of Picker's text. There are two problems with this, however. First, Picker does not put this phrase in Hitler's mouth. What Winkler is obviously referring to is the headline that Ritter formulated, which reads: "An Iron Curtain?" (*Eisener Vorhang?*).[166] Second, Churchill was *not* the first to use the term "iron curtain." It was actually a Nazi slogan, and it had been used by Goebbels in an editorial in *Das Reich* at least as early as February 1945.[167] The phrase itself goes back to even further to the First World War.

In his afterword to the 1963 edition Picker reports a lot about Bormann's style and working methods that, if true, would even further diminish the credibility of both *Tischgespräche* and *Monologe*. Picker claims that it was he himself who had approached Bormann and asked if the latter wanted him to continue taking notes just like Heim had done. Picker had, he says, by accident seen some of Heim's notes. According to Picker, Bormann was not crazy about the idea at first, but then came to accept it. One of Heim's notes where Hitler spoke about the Church, religion, and science had apparently leaked and been picked up by the foreign press, something that, according to Picker, had deeply upset Hitler. After that, Bormann supposedly did not wish to assume the role of either "contracting authority" (*Auftraggeber*) or responsible party for the notes being made. Nonetheless, Bormann told him, after much hesitancy, and after Heim had been sent away on another mission, that he needed someone to collect the Führer's utterances, and Picker got the job.[168] We have no way to know if this is correct, so we cannot rely on it.

Picker then also claims that Hitler had indeed initially been unaware of Heim's jotting – that is until one of Hitler's underlings had shown him one of the notes, which was supposedly full of inaccuracies due to the fact that it had been made completely out of memory, and thus related Hitler's words incorrectly. Hitler had become upset and had apparently given Bormann a verbal scolding. Hitler wanted his private sphere to be respected. That clearly did not discourage Bormann, but it explains why he from that moment on wished to have complete control over the notes being made, Picker states. However, it was not very often that Bormann ordered him to take notes, Picker claims, i.e. we are meant to believe that Picker did most of them on his own initiative. He himself thought that it might have been about five to ten occasions during Picker's short time at the headquarters.[169] What Picker says about Heim is likely false and intended to simply undermine *Table Talk*. Interestingly, he here inadvertently admits that Heim did not use stenography.

But what about when he says that Bormann had asked him to take notes on only five or ten occasions? At first, this may strike the reader as obviously false because Genoud's manuscript contains 100 of Picker's notes between 24 March and 29 July 1942 (notes 174–274 in *Table Talk*).[170] It is hard to imagine that Picker delivered so many notes to Bormann without having been asked to do so. Picker even stated in the 1963 edition that Heim had told him that Bormann had asked him too to only make "'a few memoranda' for the Party Chancellery."[171] Surely this must be fiction too. Rather surprisingly, however, Picker's version of events is sort of corroborated by none other than Heim himself in an interview with John Toland in 1971:

> Shortly after their arrival to Wolfschantze [sic], Bormann had suggested almost offhandedly to Heinrich Heim, his adjutant, that he surreptitiously note down what the Chief said. . . . Bormann instructed his adjutant to rely on his memory. But Heim wanted more accurate results and on his own initiative he began making copious notes. . . . Bormann was taken aback but he gave Heim tacit approval to continue taking notes.[172]

Both Heim and Picker thus say that they took the initiative to make either more, or more voluminous, notes than expressly ordered and that Bormann simply accepted *fait accompli* in a sense. Note that Heim is not corroborating Picker's claim that Bormann only told him to make notes on a few occasions. However, Heim and Picker both seem to have gone further than instructed, although for very different reasons. Even so, the claim that Heim made more notes because he wanted "more accurate results" does not ring true. It does not appear in any of the interview notes in Toland's archive and was probably invented by Toland to lend the table talks more credibility.

The mystery of the Bormann note facsimile

Picker states that Bormann was primarily interested in notes concerning questions that he himself thought to be the most pertinent: Jews, *Volk*, and Church-related issues. On a few occasions, Picker says, Bormann had also written something down himself (in fact, Bormann made a lot of notes over the years, although these were not included in Genoud's manuscript). One such note was dated at the end of November 1944 and dealt with Jews and Christianity.[173] What Picker is talking about is the last entry in *Table Talk/Monologe*. By 1963 Picker had read *Table Talk* and he of course knew that this entry appeared at the end of it. He also knew that Bormann had written it because it was included as a facsimile in *Table Talk* and at the top it says "Bo" for Bormann. It is indeed worth quoting a part of the entry:

> During a tea conversation yesterday evening, the Führer said e.g.: Jesus was certainly not a Jew. [. . .] Jesus fought against the pernicious materialism of his time and thus against the Jews. [. . .] Saul-Paul cleverly falsified the Chris-tian idea: From the challenge against the deification of money, from the chal-lenge against Jewish selfishness, Jewish materialism became the supporting idea of the infatuated, the slaves, the oppressed, the ones in money and goods against the ruling class, against the superior race, "against the oppressors"!

> Paul's religion, and the Christianity represented from then on, was nothing more than communism![174]

These views correspond well to things that Hitler said at other times as corroborated by independent sources. Even so there is really no way of knowing whether this particular conversation took place in reality or if Bormann wrote down things Hitler had said at other times. This was the view of Jesus held by the *Deutsche Christen*.[175] It was also the view expressed by the Catholic apocalyptic thinker and writer Franz Schrönghamer-Heimdal (an early member of the NSDAP) in early 1920 in a series of articles entitled "Was Jesus a Jew?" in the *Völkischer Beobachter*. Nothing had been added to Schrönghamer's ideas in what Hitler expresses in Bormann's note.[176] Dietrich Eckart's book *Der Bolschewismus von Moses bis Lenin* from 1924 has Hitler saying basically the same thing as well.[177] Note that the dialogue in Eckart's book is fictitious. Nonetheless, we know from Hitler's speeches from the early 1920s that he expressed similar views, and it is likely that Eckart was an important influence for him on this topic. Eckart's book illustrates the point that forged sources often contain true opinions.

But what is a bit problematic is that there seems to be too many "originals" of this note. There appear to be at least three versions of it. One appears as a facsimile in *Table Talk*.[178] A second copy of this note can be found in *Bundesarchiv* in Berlin.[179] A third copy I received in the form of a photocopied negative from Genoud's lawyer and guardian of his estate, Frau Cordula Schacht (the daughter of Hitler's former *Reichsbank* chief, Hjalmar Schacht). The note found in *Bundesarchiv* has a handwritten notation in the top right corner saying that it had been sent to a "Party comrade" (*Pg.*, i.e. *Parteigenosse*) at the NSDAP Main Archive (*Hauptarchiv*). It also contains Bormann's signature and the date "30.11."[180] Both the handwriting and the signature are missing on the two other copies. There are some similarities between the *Bundesarchiv* copy and the Schacht copy, however. Interestingly, both of them have the same two handwritten changes to the text on the second page (not displayed in *Table Talk*, which only shows the upper half of the first page). These two copies were thus produced together and then proofread and corrected at the same time. These two copies are very much alike, but they are not entirely identical. The most interesting difference is of course that Bormann's signature is missing on the Schacht copy. This is a bit odd because we have been told that *all* the notes in Genoud's manuscript were signed either by Bormann, Picker, or Heim. Here we are thus confronted with an example of the contrary. The signed copy is instead located in *Bundesarchiv*. The Schacht copy also contains page numbers in the top right corner: 1,044 and 1,045. Trevor-Roper states in the preface to *Table Talk* that the manuscript that Genoud had was exactly 1,045 pages long.[181]

The reader may reasonably suspect that the facsimile in *Table Talk* and the copy I received from Schacht is in fact the same document. However, it turns out that they are actually slightly different. For example, the facsimile in *Table Talk* does not have the same space between the heading lines as the copy I received from Schacht (see the photograph), which has identical spaces to the one at *Bundesarchiv*. In fact, it lacks space between the lines completely. Also, the first page of both the Schacht copy and the one located at *Bundesarchiv* has the number "2" on it. This certainly seems to imply that there was at one point a title page attached to them. It seems, thus, that no fewer than three copies of this particular note managed to survive the ravages of war and history. That is certainly an amazing coincidence. Not least because Genoud managed to get his hands on two of them – none of which is present in original form today. It has been suggested to me that it is just the reproduction of the note in *Table Talk* that has changed the spaces between the lines in order to fit the facsimile in under Bormann's handwritten note, which is reproduced on the same page. This does seem plausible when one looks at the version in the first edition of *Table Talk* where the facsimile is of a poorer quality than in the second edition from 1973. But in the 1973 edition we can actually see diagonal lines in the paper that have not been broken, which would most likely have happened if the spaces had been tampered with (see the photograph).[182]

Picker states that the notes Bormann made were from memory, and since they were intended to satisfy his political agenda "he edited them in a shameless manner, and may also have dictated parts intending a sharper formulation."[183] We do not have to, and should not, take Picker's word for this. But Bormann himself says as much in the facsimile where he wrote that any entry that did not correspond to his memory was edited by him.[184] Picker's statement is also backed up by Peter Longerich's research that shows that this was precisely what Bormann did in several cases so that Hitler's words would better serve his own purposes.[185] Longerich also shows that as Bormann became increasingly confident that he knew Hitler's mind, he started to state Hitler's position on various matters without even consulting Hitler first.[186]

If there ever was a National Socialist who hated Christianity it was Bormann. Joseph Wulf writes in his biography of Bormann that while he took on the Jewish and Slavic questions with a bureaucratic and almost mechanistic attitude, he had the ambition of being the party's foremost ideologist when it came to Christianity. In his hatred of Christianity, he went far beyond both Hitler and Goebbels, Wulf states. Already long before he became Heß's replacement on this post he had engaged in this ferocious battle through, at the time, rather harmless written statements, but while Hitler envisioned a compromise with the churches, at least for the foreseeable future, this was not possible in Bormann's universe. Wulf remarks that Hitler far from always supported Bormann in his battle against the churches, not the least during the war when Bormann regarded the German Catholic Church to be an inner enemy that it was just as important to fight as the external ones.[187] Jochen von Lang argues that Bormann always tried to move Hitler in a more anti-Christian direction. He provides the example of Bishop Alois Hudal's book – in which the bishop tried to harmonize Catholicism and Nazism – which Franz von Papen gave to Hitler with the hope that it should be published in Germany to illustrate this point. He writes that von Papen had only just convinced Hitler to allow this when Bormann intervened and turned Hitler against the idea, according to von Papen himself. He also gives examples of several other witnesses that have testified to the fact that they were convinced that Bormann pursued his anti-Christian crusade behind Hitler's back. Hitler was more pragmatic and considered every priest who was with him to be a friend.[188] Nonetheless, on 19 August 1942 Bormann recorded that the aim in Ukraine was to preserve Christianity there in order to use it as a "means of distraction" (*Ablenkungsmittel*) for the population.[189] If we do not understand this vital difference between Hitler and Bormann, it becomes very hard to evaluate the utterances such as the one in the last entry in *Monologe* in a correct manner.

The 1963 second edition of Picker's *Tischgespräche*

What we as historians are quoting when we quote the table talks – no matter which version – is thus not Hitler, per se, but at best a re-construction based on something that he said. The spirit may be Hitler's, but the words to a large extent are most often not. Moreover, we have no way of knowing when his words have been remembered or recorded verbatim, since we have no access to either the original notes or tape recordings of the statements.

The judgement regarding Heim's notes by the editor of the second edition of Picker's book, Percy Ernst Schramm, is not better than Trevor-Roper's about Picker. He also perpetuates untruths about how the notes were made. Schramm writes that Heim's stenographic notes went via Bormann's desk where they were heavily edited with the latter's internal party-political motives in mind. That way they deserve no trust whatsoever, says Schramm. We now know, however, that Schramm's work is a complete bungle. He is entirely uncritical towards his source, and towards Picker.[190] Other scholars have noticed this too. Nicolas Berg notes that Schramm's introduction does not represent a step forward in terms of scientific analysis compared to Ritter's introduction. What dominated in Schramm's text was the traditional "'Hitlerism'", one of "demonization and pathologizing". The Holocaust was mentioned only once, and Schramm even managed to diminish Hitler's anti-Semitism by calling it a psychological "tic" that made him appear like a person from the Middle Ages that saw the Devil all around him. The many editorial comments to the text gave it a veil of scientific rigor, but it did not really deliver.[191] Instead of taking sides in the conflict between Genoud and Picker, historians should have engaged in a critical study of the history and nature of the *Tischgespräche*.

The 1963 edition was different in several ways compared to the one published in 1951. One major difference was that the notes were now published in chronological order. A major problem is also that the second edition contains several entries and parts that are not present in Ritter's edition. Some of these also show clear signs of being literary products, perhaps created after the 1951 edition. This becomes clear by a comparison between the published text and the manuscript that it was based on, henceforth called *Ms. 63*. I found this manuscript at *Bundesarchiv* in Koblenz, Germany, and it is quite unique because it is the only known surviving manuscript for any of the table talk editions that we currently have access to. No historian has previously analysed it.

For instance, there is a short note dated 2 May 1942, which is said to record a conversation taking place on the train from the *Berghof* to the *Wolfsschanze* during which Hitler apparently was speaking about the centrality of the *Berghof* in his reign. In *Ms. 63* we see the following:

> I introduced myself to Ribbentrop a[**A**]t the Berghof [**I also introduced myself to Minister Ribbentrop.**][192] [Underlined text has been stricken out in *Ms. 63*; bold text in square brackets are handwritten additions.]

In the 1963 edition of *Tischgespräche* we find the following text:

> At the Berghof I also introduced myself to Minister Ribbentrop.[193]

Picker had thus first typed this text up and then reformulated the sentence later on. The fact that Picker re-wrote this sentence in *Ms. 63* actually proves it is fiction. This is also clearly false, since Hitler met Ribbentrop, who was made Foreign Minister on 4 February 1938, in Berlin in 1932. Picker is clearly making this statement up while putting together the manuscript for the second edition of *Tischgespräche*. It is perhaps symptomatic that Schramm notes that this entry does not appear in *Table Talk* but forgets to mention that it was missing from the first edition of *Tischgespräche* as well.[194] Once again, and as is also the case with Heim's notes, it is not Hitler's words that we are quoting when we quote *Tischgespräche*. While Schramm states that it was a record of a conversation "on the train, Berghof – Wolfsschanze" the *Ms. 63* only says "on the train."[195]

Yet another such example we find in a note dated 6 May 1942 in Ritter's volume, but 7 May in Schramm's edition and in *Table Talk*. In the 1951 edition, the last paragraph reads:

> *As Lorenz showed me, every OKW report of Hitler is personally corrected by hand. Apparently, Hitler considers the perfecting of the Wehrmacht reports so decisive because he thinks that even the smallest little trifles can become big and decisive by multiplication.*[196] [Italics in original.]

But in the *Ms. 63* Picker changes this paragraph so that it reads:

> As Lorenz showed me, every OKW report of Hitler is personally corrected by hand. [**Hitler considers**] the perfecting of the Wehrmacht reports is so crucial because [– **as he says** –] even the smallest little trifles can become large and crucial due to the multiplication.[197] [Bold text in square brackets indicate handwritten changes; text stricken through has been stricken out.]

This, including the handwritten changes, then appears in the 1963 edition of *Tischgespräche*.

Note that this paragraph, which is Picker's own reflection written into the text, does not appear in *Table Talk*.[198] The changes made in *Ms. 63* also transform the text from Picker's own reflection upon, or analysis of, Hitler's habit of combing through OKW reports into something that Hitler himself said. The idea that Lorenz showed Picker every OKW report seems farfetched and probably never happened. There are also two introductory sentences in this 7 May note in *Tischgespräche* where it says that Hitler ate dinner alone with the Italian General Gariboldi (commander of the Italian 8th Army) and that he was very pleased with the smoked sturgeon. These are not present in *Table Talk* or in the 1951 edition of *Tischgespräche*. In a footnote Schramm takes note of the fact that it is not present in *Table Talk*, but again forgets to mention that it is missing in *Tischgespräche* too.[199]

There are other examples where Picker's redactional changes were much more thoroughgoing than this. For instance, in the note dated 19 May 1942 we see a striking difference in wording.

Comparison between *Tischgespräche* (1951), *Tischgespräche* (1963), and *Ms. 63*[200]

Tischgespräche (1951)	*Ms. 63*	*Tischgespräche (1963)*
Ribbentrop presented Hitler with a memorandum of a meeting between him (Ribbentrop) and the Japanese ambassador Oshima, in which he told the Japanese of a solution to the Indian problem by holding out the prospect of German troops appearing ante portas from the northwest and north from across Persia and Afghanistan.	Finally, they talked about cannibalism among the partisans and in Leningrad, where about 15.000 people a week are now going to die. I followed Ribbentrop's statement with skepticism; at Hewel's [place] I had recently read a memorandum of a conversation between him (Ribbentrop) and the Japanese ambassador Oshima, in which he told the Japanese of a solution to the Indian problem by holding out the prospect of German troops appearing ante portas from the northwest and north from across Persia and Afghanistan. "Fraudster or fanatic?" I think even Hewel is honestly doubting his [Ribbentrop's] abilities.	Finally, they talked about cannibalism among the partisans and in Leningrad, where about 15.000 people a week are now going to die. I followed Ribbentrop's statement with skepticism; at Hewel's [place] I had recently read a memorandum of a conversation between him (Ribbentrop) and the Japanese ambassador Oshima, in which he told the Japanese of a solution to the Indian problem by holding out the prospect of German troops appearing ante portas from the northwest and north from across Persia and Afghanistan. "Fraudster or fanatic?" I think even Hewel is honestly doubting his [Ribbentrop's] abilities.

Source: Text in square brackets added by me for clarity. My translation.

The process of creating this note, which once again includes Picker's own reflections in the text, can clearly be followed here. The part about cannibalism is not included in the 1951 edition. More odd, however, is it that in the 1951 edition it was stated that Ribbentrop had presented the memorandum of his conversation with Oshima to Hitler on this day, but in the 1963 edition this was turned into a situation where Picker had read this memorandum while visiting Hewel at some earlier time. The changes made to *Ms. 63* appear in Schramm's version without so much as a comment about the great differences between the versions.

Another such case concerns a part about the death of *Gauleiter* Carl Röver that is not included in Ritter's edition (or in *Table Talk*) but that does appear in Schramm's edition.

Comparison between *Tischgespräche* (1963) and *Ms. 63, 22 May 1942*[201]

Ms. 63	Tischgespräche (1963)
Despite this shock, however, Hitler is so much master of himself that before lunch he greeted ~~and~~ [**us**] in the reception hall with customary – albeit perhaps somewhat mask-looking – kindness, each with handshake.	Despite this shock, however, Hitler is so much master of himself that before lunch he greeted us in the reception hall with customary – albeit perhaps somewhat mask-looking – kindness, each with handshake.

Source: Bold text in square brackets is a handwritten addition; text stricken through has been stricken out.

The question of why this was not included in *Tischgespräche* in 1951 is never answered by Schramm. We have to assume that it is a later creation. This obviously does not mean that it does not reflect something that Hitler said, but it makes it all the more suspect. We really do need a scholarly commented volume that brings together all the various versions of the table talks.

There is a case to be made that Picker on several occasions edited the text of *Ms. 63* back to a wording that was more in line with how it first looked. The evidence is that when the two editions differ, the 1963 edition agrees with the version published in *Table Talk*. For example, on 5 July 1942 Hitler is talking about the annual Passion Play at Obergammau and the importance of letting it continue because it could teach future generations of Germans a lot about the Jewish menace. The 1951 edition says:

> It is one of the most important tasks to save Germany's coming generations from the same political fate (as the German one from 1918 to 1933) and therefore to keep the awareness of the racial dangers alive in them. For this reason alone, it is essential that the Obergammau Festival [Passion Play, M.N.] be preserved. For hardly ever was the Jewish danger to the ancient Roman Empire illustrated as vividly as in the depiction of Pontius Pilate at these Festivals; this one appears like a Roman so racially and intellectually superior that he looks like a rock in the midst of the pre-Asian swarm and throng. In recognizing the tremendous importance of these festivals for the enlightenment of all coming generations, he [Hitler, M.N.] is an absolute Christian.[202]

Now, in Schramm's 1963 edition this passage reads:

> It is one of *our* most important tasks to save *our* coming generations from the same political fate as the German one from 1918 to 1933 and therefore to keep the awareness of the *Jewish* danger alive in them. For this reason alone, it is essential that the Obergammau Festival [Passion Play, M.N.] be preserved. For hardly ever was the Jewish danger to the ancient Roman Empire illustrated as vividly as in the depiction of Pontius Pilate at these Festivals; this one appears like a Roman so racially and intellectually superior that he looks like a rock in the midst of the *Jewish* swarm and throng. In recognizing the tremendous importance of these festivals for the enlightenment of all coming generations, he [Hitler, M.N.] is an absolute Christian.[203] [Italics added.]

We see here that Picker had left only one mentioning of the word "Jewish menace" in the text in 1951. This tones the anti-Semitism of the passage down a bit. Now, we know that the wording in the 1963 edition was how it originally read because in *Table Talk* we find:

> One of our most important tasks will be to save future generations from a similar political fate and to maintain for ever watchful in them a knowledge of the menace of Jewry. For this reason alone it is vital that the Passion Play be continued at Obergammau; for never has the menace of Jewry been so convincingly portrayed as in this presentation of what happened in the times of the Romans. There one sees in Pontius Pilate a Roman racially and intellectually so superior, that he stands out like a firm, clean rock in the middle of the whole muck and mire of Jewry.[204]

The first thing we need to notice is that the last part in *Tischgespräche*, the one about Hitler being a true Christian in the sense that he wanted this anti-Semitic lesson to be taught to the German youth, does not appear in *Table Talk*. One could therefore assume that Picker has made this part up. But it turns out that this is not the case this time, because this statement in fact does appear in *Libres propos*:

> In recognizing the importance of this spectacle, and by encouraging it, who can say that I do not act irreproachably Christian![205]

This tells us that this sentence was present in the version of the note that Picker turned over to Bormann in 1942. This was then left out of *Table Talk* for some unknown reason.

What we do know is that *Tischgespräche* was heavily redacted before it was first published in 1951, much more so than Ritter let the reader know. It could of course be that Ritter did not know the full extent of the editing done by Picker and therefore could not have told his readers about it even if he had wanted to. The changes in *Ms. 63*, which then appear in the revised version of *Tischgespräche* from

1963, have sometimes taken the text closer to the "original" and sometimes distanced it from said original. This means that historians have to be even more careful when citing *Tischgespräche*, as it is far from obvious what they are actually quoting.

Conclusion

In this chapter I have investigated the publication of *Tischgespräche* and pointed out a number of source-critical problems with this text and its history. *Tischgespräche* was very controversial from the outset, and both the IfZ and Gerhard Ritter faced a lot of criticism for having agreed to publish it. The book was thought by many critics to be a glorification of Hitler, and the choice to publish it without real critical commentary was obviously a mistake. On the other hand, one almost has to have some sympathy for Ritter who tried to make the best of an impossible situation. Picker simply refused to have his text riddled with critical commentaries. Things did not become easier for Ritter when the German magazine *Quick* serialized parts of the table talks. The IfZ board was irate because of this and demanded that Ritter explain how he could allow this to happen. Ritter claimed that he had not been informed about this publication beforehand, but that was in fact not true.

This is also the first time that Picker's manuscript for the second edition of *Tischgespräche* from 1963, the *Ms. 63*, has been analysed. I have shown that Picker made a large number of changes to the text compared to the version published in 1951. The changes are, on the one hand, minor, but on the other hand major in their implications. They show that Picker did not shy away from putting words in Hitler's mouth even long after the events and statements that his notes record. The fact that the editor of the volume, Percy Ernst Schramm, did not think it necessary to elaborate and comment upon these changes and what they meant for the overall credibility and authenticity of the text also testifies to the lack of source-critical acumen that historians in general have displayed when citing or referring to *Tischgespräche*.

Notes

1 Eckert, Astrid M., *The Struggle for the Files: The Western Allies and the Return of the German Archives after the Second World War* (Cambridge: Cambridge University Press, 2012), pp. 335–336.
2 Letter from Dr. Junker at the Athenäum Verlag to Ritter, 22 January 1951; BAK; N 1166; Vol. 364.
3 Ibid.
4 Report by Ritter "Mein Anteil an der Publikation von 'Hitlers Tischgesprächen'", 18 November 1951, p. 2; IfZ; ID 101/1; Korrespondenz Hermann Mau 1950–1952 A – Z.
5 Ibid.
6 Letter from Junker to Ritter, 6 February 1951, p. 1; BAK; N 1166; Vol. 364.
7 Letter from Ritter to Junker, 9 February 1951, pp. 1–2; BAK; N 1166; Vol. 364.
8 Letter from Junker to Ritter, 13 February 1951, p. 1; BAK; N 1166; Vol. 364.
9 Ibid., p. 2.

10 Letter from Ritter to Junker, 19 February 1951; BAK; N 1166; Vol. 364.
11 letter from Ritter to Junker, 20 February 1951; BAK; N 1166; Vol. 364.
12 Letter from Junker to Ritter, 21 February 1951, p. 1; BAK; N 1166; Vol. 364.
13 This was a flawed interpretation, however. Fascists certainly live by a strict moral code. It is just that these morals are often quite different from what the rest of us normally consider morality. This fact has often led to the mistaken assumption that Fascism is a nihilist philosophy. What Ritter was seeing in Picker was rather the effect of Picker not being able to criticize morality that he fundamentally agreed with, and instead he inserted token criticism of Hitler because he understood that he could not do without expressing any criticism at all.
14 Letter from Junker to Ritter, 21 February 1951, p. 2; letter from Ritter to Junker, 22 February 1951, p. 1; BAK; N 1166; Vol. 364.
15 Letter from Junker to Ritter, 27 February 1951; BAK; N 1166; Vol. 364.
16 Ibid.
17 Signed copy of the contract, 27 February 1951; BAK; N 1166; Vol. 374a.
18 Notes regarding *Hitlers Tischgespräche*, 27 September 1951; BAK; N 263 (Nachlaß Rheindorf); Vol. 380; Document 178. It is not clear what the purpose of Rheindorf's critique against Picker was. His manuscript was never published. I want to thank Professor Wolfram Pyta for sharing his copies of Rheindorf's papers with me.
19 Ibid., Document 184–185, 188. For Ritter's statements here criticized by Rheindorf, see: *Hitlers Tischgespräche. . .* (1951), p. 12.
20 Ibid., Document 175–176; *Hitler Tischgespräche. . .* (1951), p. 215.
21 Ibid., Document 176–177; *Hitlers Tischgespräche. . .* (1951), p. 33.
22 Notes from interview with von Below 16 October 1951; BAK; N 263; Vol. 192; Document 8.
23 Ibid.
24 Ibid., Document 9.
25 von Below, Nicolaus, *Als Hitlers Adjutant 1937–45* (Mainz: v. Hase & Koehler Verlag, 1980), p. 282.
26 Ibid., pp. 416–417
27 Letter from Rheindorf to von Below, 25 October 1951; letter from Rheindorf to von Below, 26 January 1952; BAK; N 263; Vol. 192; Document 19 and 48.
28 Letter from von Below to Rheindorf, 21 November 1951, p. 1; BAK; N 263; Vol. 192; Document 24 (although there may be some mistake in this numbering).
29 Ibid., p. 2. He also added that he found the book tedious (*langweilig*).
30 Ibid., Document 47; sketch of the room with table placements made by von Below. This description of peoples' places at the table is the same at that which von Below includes in his memoirs (von Below, N., *Als Hitlers Adjutant . . .*, pp. 282–283).
31 See, for example: *Hitlers Tischgespräche . . .* (1951), pp. 75, 142.
32 Letter from von Below to Rheindorf, 13 January 1952; BAK; N 263; Vol. 192; Document 44–45. Why von Below bothered to tell Rheindorf about the acoustics in the room under these circumstances is hard to understand. In a small room you can still hear what is being said even if it has bad acoustics, and since speech in the bigger room with the good acoustics could only be properly heard under the same circumstances as in the smaller room, the point seems lost.
33 Franklin D. Roosevelt Presidential Library (FDRPL): John Toland Papers (JTP); Box 44; "Giesler, Hermann", transcript, interview, John Toland with Giesler, 5 October 1971, p. 35. I thank Professor Thomas Weber for having sent this part of the interview to me. According to the transcript Giesler said: "Hitler made a remark at the table, and Bormann right away got out his little slips of paper and made his little notes, which nobody could read except himself. Hitler often joked about Bormann's writing – he said he drew mountains and peaks." However, I have chosen not to use this quote in the text, because when Toland donated his material to the FDRL, he did so with express instructions that the transcripts should not be cited by scholars. Toland regarded the

transcript as "working notes" only and "not the authoritative texts of the taped interviews." Researchers should thus use the tapes and make their own transcripts. The latter "must not be quoted or cited as the authoritative texts of the taped interviews" read the instructions on the first page of the Finding Aid to "John Toland Papers" at the FDRL. Toland later (in 1999) let these restrictions fall, and these transcripts are now free for all to use and cite as they wish (FDRPL; JTP; "Findin Aid: John Toland Papers, 1962–1983"). This decision makes one wonder: Why is it suddenly OK to cite something as authoritative when they clearly are not? Nothing had changed to make them a better transcript, and less of working notes, than they were before.

34 Besymenski, Lew, *Die letzten Notizen von Martin Bormann. Ein Dokument und seine Verfasser* (Stuttgart: Deutsche Verlags-Anstalt, 1974), p. 45.
35 Letter from Junker to Ritter, 27 February 1951, pp. 1–2; letter from Ritter to Junker, 1 March 1951; BAK; N 1166; Vol. 364.
36 Letter from Ritter to Picker, 13 March 1951, p. 1; BAK; N 1166; Vol. 364.
37 Letter from Picker to Ritter, 14 March 1951, pp. 1–2; BAK; N 1166; Vol. 364.
38 Letter from Junker to Ritter, 27 March 1951; BAK; N 1166; Vol. 364.
39 Ibid.
40 Letter from Ritter to Junker, 12 April 1951; BAK; N 1166; Vol. 364.
41 *Hitlers Tischgespräche. . .* (1951), pp. 143–145.
42 *Hitlers Tischgespräche. . .* (1963), pp. 285–287.
43 *Hitlers Tischgespräche. . .* (1951), p. 145. "Übrigens schreibt Schacht als einziger an ihn: 'Sehr geehrter Herr Hitler' statt 'Mein Führer' und 'mit bestem Gruß Ihr ergebener Schacht' statt 'Heil Hitler' oder 'mit deutschem Gruß'."
44 *Hitlers Tischgespräche. . .* (1963), p. 287; Document 216 (22 April 1942); BAK; N 1128; Vol. 31. „Übrigens schreibt Schacht als einziger an ihn: "Sehr geehrter Herr Hitler" statt "Mein Führer" und "mit bestem Gruß (Ihr ergebener Schacht)" statt **[des sonst allgemein üblichen]** "Heil Hitler" oder "**[M]**it deutschem Gruß"."
45 Letter from Junker to Ritter, 2 April 1951; BAK; N 1166; Vol. 364.
46 Letter from Junker to Ritter, 11 April 1951, p. 1; BAK; N 1166; Vol. 364.
47 Letter from Junker to Ritter, 4 April 1951, p. 1; BAK; N 1166; Vol. 364.
48 Letter from Ritter to Athenäum Verlag, 13 April 1951; BAK; N 1166; Vol. 364.
49 Letter from Ritter to Junker, 10 April 1951, pp. 1–2; BAK; N 1166; Vol. 364.
50 Letter from Junker to Ritter, 11 April 1951, p. 2; BAK; N 1166; Vol. 364.
51 Letter from Ritter to Athenäum Verlag, 13 April 1951; BAK; N 1166; Vol. 364.
52 Ibid., p. 1. This letter crossed Ritter's letter from the same date.
53 *Hitlers Tischgespräche. . .* (1951), p. 453.
54 Ibid.
55 Letter from Athenäum Verlag to Ritter, 13 April 1951, p. 2; BAK; N 1166; Vol. 364.
56 Letter from Ritter to Athenäum Verlag, 16 April 1951, p. 2; BAK; N 1166; Vol. 364.
57 *Hitlers Tischgespräche . . .* (1951), p. 454.
58 Letter from Ritter to Athenäum Verlag, 16 April 1951, p. 1; BAK; N 1166; Vol. 364.
59 Letter from Athenäum Verlag to Ritter, 18 April 1951, pp. 1–2; BAK; N 1166; Vol. 364.
60 Letter from Ritter to Athenäum Verlag, 19 April 1951; BAK; N 1166; Vol. 364.
61 Ibid.
62 Letter from Athenäum Verlag to Ritter, 20 April 1951, pp. 1–2; BAK; N 1166; Vol. 364.
63 Letter from Athenäum Verlag to Ritter, 23 April 1951, pp. 1–3; BAK; N 1166; Vol. 364.
64 Letter from Ritter to Junker, 24 April 1951; BAK; N 1166; Vol. 364.
65 Letter from Gerhard Reutern to Ritter, 30 April 1951; BAK; N 1166; Vol. 364. See also: *Hitlers Tischgespräche . . .* (1951), p. 145.
66 Letter from Ritter to Reutern, 3 May 1951, p. 1; BAK; N 1166; Vol. 364.
67 Ibid.
68 Berg, Nicolas, *Der Holocaust und die westdeutschen Historiker. Erforschung und Erinnerung* (Göttingen: Wallstein Verlag, 2003), pp. 331–333.

69 Hermann Mau (1913–1952) was a German historian who had survived the war by "assuming the role in 1933 of the unpolitical individual", according to himself. He was not a member of the NSDAP, nor was he sympathetic to the Nazi cause, but he was not part of the resistance against Hitler either. The little political background that he did have was in having been involved in the CDU East, in a group at Leipzig University, for which he was punished with one month in prison. After this he fled to the West and settled down in Munich, where he soon got a teaching position in modern history at the University of Munich. He became the director of the IfZ on 1 February 1951 and was, apparently, "the ideal compromise candidate in such a highly politicized position." However, his time at the IfZ was cut short when he died in a car crash on 25 October 1952 (Eckert, A. M., *The Struggle for the Files. . .*).

70 Letter from Junker to Ritter, 8 May 1951, pp. 1–2; BAK; N 1166; Vol. 364.

71 Ibid., p. 2.

72 Ibid.

73 Letter from Ritter to Junker, 16 May 1951, p. 1; BAK; N 1166; Vol. 364.

74 Ibid., pp. 1–2.
   The "Remer Party" mentioned by Ritter was the German Socialist Reich Party (*Sozialistische Reichspartei Deautschland*) established on 2 October 1949 in Hameln, and it was led by Otto Ernst Remer. It was a West German party adhering to the Straßer wing of the NSDAP. It was dissolved on 12 September 1952 and finally banned on 23 October that year.

75 Letter from Ritter to Junker, 16 May 1951, p.2, BAK; N 1166; Vol. 364. See also: *Hitlers Tischgespräche . . .* (1951), pp. 432–433. Ritter addresses this in a footnote in his endnote, where he also points out that Franz von Papen, who is also mentioned by Hitler in this context, was no longer a minister in 1936; see: *Hitlers Tischgespräche. . .* (1951), p. 454.

76 Letter from Ritter to Junker, 16 May 1951, p. 2; BAK; N 1166; Vol. 364.

77 Letter from Ahtnëäum Verlag to Ritter, 16 May 1951; BAK; N 1166; Vol. 364. This letter obviously reached Ritter only after he had sent his letter to Athenäum the same day.

78 Letter from Junker to Ritter, 23 May 1951, p. 1; BAK; N 1166; Vol. 364.

79 Eckert, A. M., *The Struggle for the Files . . .*, p. 340.

80 Letter from Ritter to Mau, 26 June 1951, pp. 1–2; IfZ; ID 101/1; Korrespondenz Hermann Mau 1950–1952 A – Z.

81 Winkler, W., *Der Schattenmann . . .*, p. 77. For the same point, see: Corneließen, Christoph, *Gerhard Ritter: Geschichtswissenschaft und Politik im 20. Jahrhundert* (Düsseldorf: Droste Verlag, 2001), pp. 538–545; Eckert, A. M., *The Struggle for the Files . . .*, p. 340.

82 Letter from Athenäum-Verlag to Mau, 26 September 1951 (see attached letter from Athenäum-Verlag to Prof. Dr. Erich Kaufmann, 26 September 1951), pp. 1–2; IfZ; ID 101/2. See also: Letter from Mau to *Quick*, 31 May 1951. The passages from *Tischgespräche* was published in *Quick* No. 21 and 23.

83 Letter from Junker to Ritter, 23 May 1951, p. 1; BAK; N 1166; Vol. 364.

84 Letter from Ritter to Junker, 25 May 1951; BAK; N 1166; Vol. 364.

85 Letter from Ritter to Junker, 31 May 1951, p. 2; BAK; N 1166; Vol. 364.

86 Letter from Athenäum Verlag to Ritter, 4 June 1951; BAK; N 1166; Vol. 364.

87 Letter from Ritter to Athenäum Verlag, 11 June 1951; BAK; N 1166; Vol. 364.

88 Letter from Athenäum Verlag to Ritter, 15 June 1951, p. 1; BAK; N 1166; Vol. 364.

89 Letter from Ritter to Junker, 19 June 1951; BAK; N 1166; Vol. 364.

90 Letter from Junker to Ritter, 20 June 1951, p. 1; BAK; N 1166; Vol. 364.

91 Ibid., pp. 1–2.

92 Letter from Ritter to Junker, 21 June 1951; BAK; N 1166; Vol. 364.

93 Letter from Junker to Ritter, 22 June 1951; BAK; N 1166; Vol. 364.

94 Letter from Mau to Ritter, 22 July 1951, p. 1; IfZ; ID 101/1; Korrespondenz Hermann Mau 1950–1952 A – Z.

95 Letter from Sattler to Ritter, 4 September 1951, pp. 1–2; BAK; N 1166; Vol. 364.

96 Letter from Ritter to Sattler, 9 September 1951; BAK; N 1166; Vol. 364.
97 Letter from Ritter to Junker, 25 September 1951, p. 1; BAK; N 1166; Vol. 364.
98 Ibid.
99 Ibid., pp. 1–2.
100 Report by Ritter, 22 October 1951, pp. 1, 12; IfZ; ID 101/1; Korrespondenz Hermann Mau 1950–1952 A – Z.
101 Ibid., p. 13.
102 Eckert, A. M., *The Struggle for the Files . . .*, pp. 340–341.
103 Letter from Frederick H. Burkhardt (HICOG) to Dr. Wende (State Secretary, Bundesminister des Innern), 11 July 1951; IfZ; ID 101/5; Korrespondenz Hermann Mau: Bundesministerium 1951.
104 Eckert, A. M., *The Struggle for the Files . . .*, pp. 342–343, 352.
105 Letter from Ritter to Junker, 25 June 1951; BAK; N 1166; Vol. 364.
106 This must have been Shepard Stone, director of the Public Affairs Division at HICOG.
107 Letter from Junker to Ritter, 28 June 1951, pp. 1–2; BAK; N 1166; Vol. 364.
108 Letter from Athenäum Verlag to Ritter, 6 August 1951, p. 1; BAK; N 1166; Vol. 364.
109 Letter from Ritter to Junker, 8 September 1951; BAK; N 1166; Vol. 364.
110 Letter from Junker to Professor Dr. Erich Kaufmann, 26 September 1951, p. 1; letter from Athenäum Verlag to Ritter, 26 September 1951; BAK; N 1166; Vol. 364.
111 Bundesarchiv, Koblenz; N 1166; Vol. 364; letter from Junker to Professor Dr. Erich Kaufmann, 26 September 1951, p. 1.
112 Cornelißen, C., *Gerhard Ritter . . .*, pp. 538–545. See also: Eckert, A. M., *The Struggle for the Files . . .*, p. 340. Interestingly, *Quick* was the first magazine to be published in Germany after the war (starting in 1948), and Hitler's former secretary, Traudl Junge, worked for *Quick*'s editorial staff as its chief secretary for many years (it is unclear if she was working there at the time Picker's notes were published).
113 Letter from Ritter to Junker, 2 October 1951, pp. 1–2; BAK; N 1166; Vol. 365.
114 Letter from Reutern to Ritter, 2 October 1951; BAK; N 1166; Vol. 365.
115 Letter from Mau to Athenäum Verlag, 17 October 1951, p. 1; BAK; N 1166; Vol. 365.
116 Letter from Athenäum Verlag to the IfZ, 2 November 1951; BAK; N 1166; Vol. 365.
117 Letter from Athenäum Verlag to Ritter, 2 November 1951, p. 1; BAK; N 1166; Vol. 365.
118 Letter from Ritter to Athenäum Verlag, 6 November 1951; BAK; N 1166; Vol. 365.
119 Eckert, A. M., *The Struggle for the Files . . .*, p. 340.
120 Conversation with Magnus Brechtken, Deputy Director of the IfZ, on 23 April 2015.
121 Eckert, A. M., *The Struggle for the Files . . .*, p. 340.
122 *Hitlers Tischgespräche. . .* (1951), p. 11.
123 Ibid., p. 12. See also: *Hitlers Tischgespräche. . .* (1963), p. 510.
124 *Hitlers Tischgespräche. . .* (1951), pp. 12–14.
125 Ibid., p. 14.
126 Ibid., p. 15.
127 For this and more, see: Cornelißen, C., *Gerhard Ritter. . ..*
128 *Hitlers Tischgespräche. . .* (1951), p. 15.
129 Ibid., pp. 15–17.
130 Picker, Henry, *Johannes XXIII: Der Papst der christlichen Einheit und des 2. vaticanischen Konzils* (Kettweg: Blick und Bild, 1963).
131 Speer, Albert, *Spandauer Tagebücher* (Berlin: Propyläen, 1975), pp. 520–522.
132 Magnus Brechtken, who has studied Speer's relationship with Fest and the publisher Siedler in great detail, agrees with this conclusion. In an email to me he writes that this "is exactly the general impression which comes through when one analyses Speer's life and his influence on historiography after 1945. It is also correct that the Siedler and Fest where highly influential in shaping the style, the formulations and the general contents of what Speer produced in his memoirs and in the Spandau diaries. I read the note you mention in the Spandau diary and it very much sounds like Fest." Email

to the author, 20 September 2016. For Brechtken's own analysis of the relationship between Speer, Fest, Siedler, and the role of German historians in perpetuating Speer's tall tales, see: Brechtken, Magnus, "'Ein Kriminalroman könnte nicht spannender erfunden werden' – Albert Speer und die Historiker" in M. Brechtken (ed.), *Life Writing and Political Memoir – Lebenszeugnisse und Politische Memoiren* (as of yet unpublished *Sonderdruck*), pp. 35–78; Brechtken, M., *Albert Speer. Eine deutsche Karriere* (Munich: Siedler, 2017), pp. 293–576.

133 Proof draft for *Spandauer Tagebücher* "Kap. 14", pp. 22–24; BAK; N 1340; Vol. 368. It is not clear if this means that Fest wrote these sections or if Fest recommended the marked parts be removed.

134 "Anmerkungen" to note in chapter 14 dated 24 March 1960, p. 12; BAK; N 1340; Vol. 372. The description of the content is taken from the *Findbuch* located in the reading room at *Bundesarchiv*, Koblenz.

135 Ibid. "Schirach behandelt mich wieder freundlicher."

136 Proof draft for *Spandauer Tagebücher* "Kap. 14", p. 24; BAK; N 1340; Vol. 368. "Schirach behandelt mich freundlicher."

137 Handwritten manuscript for *Spandauer Tagebücher*, see entry dated 24 March 1960; BAK; N 1340; Vol. 431. "Kürzungen Kapitel 13–17; Kapitel 14", p. 267 + 16 (the odd paginating in original); BAK; N 1340; Vol. 381.

138 "Kürzungen Kapitel 13–17; Kapitel 14", p. 267 + 15 (the odd page numbers in original); BAK; N 1340; Vol. 381. While the entry for 11 April 1960 in *Spandauer Tagebücher* is only a short sentence, the note in this manuscript is several paragraphs long (see: ibid., p. 267 + 16).

139 *Hitlers Tischgespräche.* . . (1951), pp. 133, 384; *Hitlers Tischgespräche.* . . (1963), pp. 196–197; "Auszüge aus den Besprechungspunkten aus der Führer-Besprechung am 21. und 22. März 1942"; BAK; N 1340; Vol. 218.

140 *Hitlers Tischgespräche.* . . (1951), pp. 167–171, 250; "Führerbesprechungen 1941, 1942"; "Besprechungspunkte aus der Führerbesprechung vom 23.6.1942", pp. 1–14; BAK; N 1340; Vol. 235.

141 *Hitlers Tischgespräche.* . . (1951), p. 450; "Führerbesprechungen 1941, 1942"; "Kampfgas. Auszüge aus den Führerbesprechungen", p. 1; BAK; N 1340; Vol. 235.

142 *Hitlers Tischgespräche.* . . (1951), p. 122; *Monologe* . . ., pp. 338–341; "Führerbesprechungen 1941, 1942"; "Kampfgas. Auszüge aus den Führerbesprechungen", p. 1; BAK; N 1340; Vol. 235.

143 *Monologe* . . ., pp. 338–341; "Führerbesprechungen 1941, 1942"; "10.11/12.8.42 Punkt 69"; BAK; N 1340; Vol. 235.

144 *Monologe* . . ., pp. 338–341; "Führerbesprechungen 1941, 1942"; "Auszug aus Dok. 124. Fuehrerbesprechung am 10/12.8.1942", pp. 1–3; "Aus Führerprotokoll vom 10. – 12.8.1942 Punkt 36 (Munitionsherstellung in der Ukraine. Quelle: R 3/1505, fol. 45–46)", pp. 1–2; BAK; N 1340; Vol. 235.

145 *Monologe* . . ., pp. 394–395; "Führerbesprechungen 1941, 1942"; "Auszug aus Dok. 124. Führerbesprechung am 7./9.1942, Punkt 24", "7./9.9.42"; BAK; N 1340; Vol. 235.

146 *Hitlers Tischgespräche.* . . (1963), p. 10.

147 Winkler, W., *Der Schattenmann* . . ., pp. 76–78. It must be said that Winkler's references for all this information are entirely lacking, even though what he writes is largely correct. The only statement I have not been able to corroborate in the IfZ archive is what is said in the last sentence. Before Winkler published his biography, another one had been published in French: Péan, P., *L'extrémiste.* . .. As we shall see, this book is far more reliable than Winkler's.

148 Wareing, E. B., "Hitlers Tischgespräche im Führerhauptquartier 1941–2. By Henry Picker; Gerard Ritter" in *International Affairs (Royal Institute of International Affairs 1944 –)*, Vol. 28, No. 2 (April 1952), p. 226. For the blue eyes passage, see Picker's foreword: *Hitlers Tischgespräche.* . . (1951), p. 35. Wareing notes, just like Speer does, that *Tischgespräche* cannot be used as a source to Hitler's "true" views, since present at these monologues were people that were not part of the inner circle (e.g. Picker himself) (ibid.).

149 Kubizek, A., *Adolf Hitler . . .*, p. 275.
150 Franz-Willing, G., "Hitlers Tischgespräche", p. 26. See also: Werner Jochmann Nachlaß (in the hands of Professor Ursula Büttner, Hamburg); Binder: Schriftwechsel: A – K 1977; Manuscript for Heim's recorded statement to the BBC, 14 September 1953, p. 6.
151 Manuscript for Heim's recorded statement to the BBC, 14 September 1953, p. 7; WJN; Binder: Schriftwechsel: A – K 1977.
152 Zoller, Albert, *Hitler privat. Erlebnisbericht seiner Geheimsekretärin* (Düsseldorf: Droste Verlag, 1949), p. 40. Schroeder expands on this topic in an even more fanciful way in: Schroeder, Christa, *Er war mein Chef. Aus dem Nachlaß der Sekretärin von Adolf Hitler. Herausgegeben von Anton Joachimsthaler* (München: Herbig, 1985), p. 271. Schroeder devotes a short chapter in her memoirs to Zoller's book, which she says was published without her having the possibility of proofreading and that contained changes made by Zoller to her original statements. Zoller also put matters in her mouth that she had no knowledge of, she claimed. According to Schroeder, it was Zoller's book, and its reception by historians that made her decide to break her silence and to use her stenographic notes made during captivity after the war, which had formed the basis for Zoller's book, to try and correct the record (ibid., pp. 18–24).
153 Franz-Willing, G., "Hitlers Tischgespräche", p. 26.
154 *Libres propos. . .* (Vol. I, 1952), p. xxviii.
155 *Hitler's Table Talk. . .* (1953), p. xii.
156 *Monologe . . .,* see facsimile before title page, as well as: p. 8.
157 Ibid. This is repeated in: Ullrich, V., *Adolf Hitler. . .* (Vol. II), p. 225.
158 Manuscript for Heim's recorded statement to the BBC, 14 September 1953, p. 8; WJN; Binder: Schriftwechsel: A – K 1977.
159 Winkler, W., *Der Schattenmann . . .,* p. 74.
160 "Hitler-Dokumente: Vom Wege ab" in *Der Spiegel*, 3/1966, 10/1 1966, p. 30. The article is available online: http://wissen.spiegel.de/wissen/image/show.html?did=46 265276&aref=image036/2006/03/08/cqsp196603030-P2P-031.pdf&thumb=false, accessed: 2013–10–25.
161 "Hitler-Dokumente: Vom Wege ab" in *Der Spiegel*, 3/1966, 10/1 1966, p. 31.
162 Typed transcript of a conversation between Heim and Dr. Freiherr von Siegler 1 July 1952, p. 2; www.ifz-muenchen.de/archiv/zs/zs-0243_1.pdf, accessed: 2013–08–10.
163 Winkler, W., *Der Schattenmann . . .,* pp. 76–77.
164 Möller, Horst, "Das Institut für Zeitgeschichte und die Entwicklung der Zeitgeschichtsschreibung in Deutschland" in Horst Möller (ed.), och Udo Wengst, *50 Jahre Institut für Zeitgeschichte. Eine Bilanz* (München: Institut für Zeitgeschichte, 1999), pp. 35, 38, 40. Möller also calls Ritter one of the most important, most productive, and versatile Germans during the twentieth century, who wrote a lot on i.e. church and religious history (ibid., p. 37). For more on Ritter, see: Cornelißen, C., *Gerhard Ritter. . ..*
165 Winkler, W., *Der Schattenmann . . .,* p. 320 *n*23.
166 *Hitlers Tischgespräche. . .* (1951), p. 43.
167 Jones, Michael, *After Hitler: The Last Days of the Second World War in Europe* (London: John Murray, 2015), p. 99.
168 *Hitlers Tischgespräche. . .* (1963), pp. 506–507. I have not been able to confirm Picker's claim regarding the leaked note and publication of it in the foreign press.
169 *Hitlers Tischgespräche. . .* (1963), pp. 508–509.
170 *Hitler's Table Talk. . .* (1953), pp. 362–603.
171 *Hitlers Tischgespräche. . .* (1963), p. 509.
172 Toland, J., *Adolf Hitler* (Vol. II), pp. 780–782 (p. 682 in the one-volume edition).
173 *Hitlers Tischgespräche. . .* (1963), p. 509.
174 *Monologe . . .,* pp. 412–413. Other people have also noted this view. Volker Ullrich cites a collection of notes he calls "Hitler's Attitude to Religion" (*Hitlers Einstellung zur Religion*) where one of Hitler's physicians, Hanskarl von Hasselbach, writes (translated

from German): "'As a Galilean, Christ was of Aryan descent, and apart from his etic values he was also to be admired as a brilliant leader of the people in the struggle against power and the attacks of the demoralized Pharisees.'"; quoted in: Ullrich, Volker, *Adolf Hitler . . .*, p. 1014. Hasselbach stated this is an interview with Schramm made while Hasselbach was in a U.S. prisoner of war camp in 1945, see: Bundesarchiv, Koblenz; N 1128; Vol. 35; "Henry Picker Hitlers Tischgespräche im Führerhauptquartier 1941–1942. Percy Ernst Schramm und Andreas Hillgruber (Manuskripte der Neuausgabe)"; "Hitlers Einstellung zum Christentum" by Professor Dr. von Hasselbach, 26 September 1945, p. 1–2. Note that Ullrich has gotten the title of the document wrong.

175 For more about this, see: Hastings, D., *Catholicism & the Roots of Nazism . . .*, pp. 53–57, 60, 63, 66–67, 71, 123, 128, 191; Steigmann-Gall, R., *The Holy Reich . . .*, pp. 29–41. See also: Kelley, S., *Racializing Jesus. . .*; Heschel, S., *The Aryan Jesus. . . .*

176 Hastings, D., *Catholicism & the Roots of Nazism . . .*, pp. 56–57.

177 Eckart, Dietrich, *Der Bolschewismus von Moses bis Lenin. Zweigespräch zwischen Adolf Hitler und mir* (München: Franz Eher Verlag, 1924), pp. 44, 57.

178 *Hitler's Table Talk. . .* (1953), see facsimile before title page.

179 "Führergespräch vom 29.11.1944. Niederschrift von Martin Bormann vom 30.11.1944"; BABL; NS6–133.

180 Unfortunately, I am unable to read the entire name of this person as the handwriting is a bit messy.

181 *Hitler's Table Talk. . .* (1953), p. xiii.

182 *Hitler's Table Talk. . .* (1973), see facsimile before title page.

183 *Hitlers Tischgespräche. . .* (1963), p. 509.

184 *Monologe . . .*, see facsimile before title page; *Hitler's Table Talk. . .* (1953), see facsimile before the title page.

185 Longerich, P., *Hitlers . . .*, pp. 162–165.

186 Ibid., pp. 165–167.

187 Wulf, Joseph, *Martin Bormann – Hitlers Schatten* (Gütersloh: Sigbert Mohn Verlag, 1962), pp. 82, 105–106, 108.

188 von Lang, Jochen, *Der Sekretär: Der Mann der Hitler beherrschte* (Unter Mitarbeit von Claus Sibyll) (Stuttgart: Deutsche Verlags-Anstalt, 1977), pp. 135–136, 138–139. It is not clear why one would choose to support a statement about Bormann on Speer, not only because he is generally unreliable but also because there are much better sources for this than Speer.

189 Besymenski, L., *Die letzten Notizen . . .*, p. 76. This document, which also contained much on the inhumane treatment of Slavs generally, was used as evidence in the IMT against Alfred Rosenberg, who had received a copy of the memorandum; see: Gilbert, Gustave M., *Nürnberger Tagebuch. Gespräche der Angeklagten mit dem Gerichtspsychologen* (Frankfurt am Main: Fischer Taschenbuch Verlag (15th ed.), 2010 (first published in 1962), p. 264.

190 *Hitlers Tischgespräche. . .* (1963), pp. 9–10.

191 Berg, N., *Der Holocaust und die westdeutschen Historiker. . . .*, pp. 507–508.

192 Document 240 (2 May 1942); BAK; N 1128; Vol. 31. "Ribbentrop stellte ich mich i[I] m Berghof vor **[hatte ich mich auch Minister Ribbentrop vorzustellen.]**"

193 *Hitlers Tischgespräche. . .* (1963), p. 305. "Im Berghof hatte ich mich auch Minister Ribbentrop vorzustellen."

194 Ibid., pp. 304–306.

195 Ibid.; Document 240 (2 May 1942); BAK; N 1128; Vol. 31. "Im Zuge Berghof – Wolfsschanze" "Im Zuge."

196 *Hitlers Tischgespräche. . .* (1951), p. 149. *"Wie Lorenz mir Zeigte, wird jeder OKW-Bericht von Hitler persönlich handschriftlich korrigiert. Offenbar hält Hitler das Durchfielen der Wehrmachtsberichte deshalb für so entscheidend, weil er meint, daß selbst kleinste Kleinigkeiten durch die Multiplikation groß und von entscheidender Bedeutung werden können."*

197 Document 259 (7 May 1942); BAK; N 1128; Vol. 31. *Hitlers Tischgespräche. . .* (1963), p. 319. "Wie Lorenz mir Zeigte, wird jeder OKW-Bericht von Hitler persönlich

handschriftlich korrigiert. **[Hitler hält]** das Durchfielen der Wehrmachtsberichte deshalb für so entscheidend, weil **[– wie er sagt –]** selbst kleinste Kleinigkeiten durch die Multiplikation groß und von entscheidender Bedeutung werden können."

198 *Hitler's Table Talk. . .* (1953), p. 466.

199 *Hitlers Tischgespräche. . .* (1963), p. 318; *Hitlers Tischgespräche. . .* (1951), p. 148.

200 Ibid., p. 89; *Hitlers Tischgespräche. . .* (1963), p. 355; Document 42 (19 May 1942); BAK; N 1128; Vol. 32.

201 *Hitlers Tischgespräche. . .* (1963), pp. 372–373; Document 64 (22 May 1942); BAK; N 1128; Vol. 32. Note that the part about Röver in this note is longer than this; I only include the passage containing hand-written changes in *Ms. 63.*

202 *Hitlers Tischgespräche. . .* (1951), pp. 314–315.

203 *Hitlers Tischgespräche. . .* (1963), p. 443.

204 *Hitler's Table Talk. . .* (1953), p. 563. *Tischgespräche*, of course, does not mention anything about the Passion Play; this instead comes from the French edition.

205 *Libres propos. . .* (Vol. II, 1954), p. 198. It also appears in the Italian translation; see: *Conversazioni segrete . . .,* p. 599. Although there it is phrased as a question.

3

FRANÇOIS GENOUD AND HIS TABLE TALK MANUSCRIPT

Genoud battles Picker and the IfZ

The earliest preserved correspondence between the IfZ and Genoud is dated 29 May 1951. In this letter Professor Dr Karl Buchheim of the Historical-Political Department of the IfZ wrote to tell Genoud that they had heard that he was in the possession of the correspondence between Martin Bormann and his wife Gerda. The IfZ was interested in buying these letters from Genoud if they turned out to be authentic and if the IfZ was allowed to somehow estimate their value.[1] In his reply Genoud assured Buchheim that he was in the possession of these documents and included two photocopies of letters stating that these documents were very important to the writing of NS history, since Bormann was the "truest" (*echteste*) Nazi, only second to the Führer himself.[2] The photocopies closed the deal for the IfZ, and Buchheim told Genoud that the IfZ was very interested in acquiring them. Buchheim was not sure, however, that the IfZ could afford them. All depended upon how much Genoud wanted for them. The IfZ was even interested in buying just photocopies if Genoud did not want to sell the originals. It just so happened that Buchheim would come to Switzerland and Lausanne in August and he would very much appreciate if he could then visit Genoud and see the original documents for himself. Buchheim also stated that had been told of the existence of these letters by a colleague, who he did not name, in Hamburg.[3] As it turned out, Genoud was quite positive towards the meeting with Buchheim.[4]

Shortly after this initial correspondence Genoud was made aware of the publication of *Tischgespräche* under the auspices of the IfZ, probably through the serialization in *Quick* that had begun on 6 June. He now wrote in French (for some reason) and stated that he was in possession of Bormanns *Nachlaß*, which contained a large number of texts and that the utterances of the Führer were among these. At this point it is obvious that Genoud had not yet read *Tischgespräche* because he asked the

IfZ to send him two copies of the book so that he could compare that text to his own. If it would turn out to be the same text, Genoud said that he expressed his strongest reservations against any publication without the permission of the representative of the rights of Bormann's estate, i.e. Genoud himself. He wished that the IfZ would contact him immediately regarding this matter; otherwise, he would not hesitate to start a procedure against any translation of the text and against any publisher that the IfZ might have entered into agreement with, although he hoped it would not have to come to that.[5] However, Buchheim was in Switzerland at that point and could not reply to Genoud's threats of a lawsuit.[6] A secretary at the IfZ, Erna Waltz, did send a letter to Buchheim in Switzerland telling him, on behalf of Dr Mau, about Genoud's statements.[7]

After having received this letter Buchheim made an appointment with Genoud and saw him in Lausanne. They spoke for over two hours about the matter at hand. Genoud had acquired the rights to Bormann's *Nachlaß* from Theodor Schmitz, a Catholic priest who was the legal guardian (*Vormünder*) of Bormann's children. This *Nachlaß* also contained notes by Picker and Heim from the period 5 July 1941 to 7 September 1942 "seemingly somewhat more complete than the ones from Picker that have been published."[8] This means that Genoud only showed Buchheim the part of his manuscript that overlapped with Picker's book. Note that there are reasons to doubt Genoud's story, because according to a statement that Schmitz made to the East German security service, *Ministerium für Staatssicherheit* (MfS), or *Stasi*, on 16 January 1969 Schmitz had threatened that he would sue Genoud in court if the latter publicized the Bormann letters, since he regarded these letters to be the property of the Bormann children. According to the *Stasi* report from the debriefing with Schmitz, Genoud then stated that he had counted on such a process and that this would be the best kind of promotion for the planned publication. This had convinced Schmitz that it would be better not to sue Genoud, and instead the two had agreed that the Bormann children were to get a share of the revenue of *The Bormann Letters* (the decision to publicize the letters in English was, according to Schmitz, also a compromise agreed to by Genoud because Schmitz had stated that he did not want the letters to be made public at all). Apparently, the children subsequently received 1,500 West German marks (he also claimed that his attorney in West Berlin had the receipt for this payment).[9] This would seem to indicate that Schmitz had not, at least not at that point (i.e. in 1952), signed over any rights to Genoud.

In the introduction to the book *The Bormann Letters* in 1954 Trevor-Roper gave an even more detailed description of these events. There he wrote that Gerda Bormann, together with her nine children, fled to Wolkenstein in the Grödnertal in South Tyrol on either 25 or 26 April 1945, where she then lived in hiding under an assumed name for several weeks. By the summer, however, her failing health led her to declare herself "to an American headquarters in Bolzano" in northern Italy. She then spent some time in a hospital there before returning to Wolkenstein, but, being terminally ill with "cancer of the bowels", she soon found herself in a Prisoners of War Hospital in Merano where she died on 22 March 1946.

Trevor-Roper states that he bases this narrative on "a statement" by the Catholic priest, Theodor Schmitz, who visited her frequently in the hospital and who became the guardian of the Bormann children after her death.[10] Trevor-Roper had not himself talked to Schmitz, whom we will meet again later on in this book. He based this on a copy of a letter from Schmitz to Genoud.[11] Notice also that there are slight differences between the two versions. For example, Mrs. Bormann is said to have died on the 23rd in one version, while she died on the 22nd in the other; the Italian army hospital has turned into a Prisoners of War Hospital, and so on.[12]

Schmitz studied to be a priest in Rome and graduated on 26 October 1941.[13] In 1942 he became a chaplain at St Clara in Berlin-Neukölln, a position that he kept until he was called into wartime service as "Medical Officer" (*Sanitäter*) in Italy. At some point after the Allied invasion of Italy he was captured as a prisoner of war (POW) by the British and remained in British custody until 1946. During his POW period he served as a camp priest (*Lagerpfarrer*) in Bolzano and as a hospital priest (*Lazarettpfarrer*) in Merano.[14] It was there he happened to meet Gerda Bormann. According to Bormann's son, Martin Bormann, he, his siblings, and their mother had met up with Martin Bormann's brother, Albert Bormann, on 8 May 1945 in Saalbach, Austria. They stayed with a farmer in the mountains, who allegedly had no idea of who they were, until early August.[15] Schmitz had, with the assistance of the bishop of Brixen/Bressanone, in accordance with Gerda Bormann's wishes, put the children with the Catholic family of Dr Kiener in Pustertal in the South Tyrol in 1950.[16]

Trevor-Roper then goes on to give the reader even further details, although this time without stating the source for them. Before Mrs. Bormann's death, he writes, she "had taken care to dispose of her archives", which contained not only the letters but also the text published as *Hitler's Table Talk* in 1953. She had given these documents, via the *Gauleiter* of the Tyrol, Franz Hofer, to the Waffen-SS General Karl Wolff (the predecessor of Hermann Fegelein as Himmler's liaison to Hitler), who as the commander of the SS forces in Italy had been instrumental in negotiating the surrender of the German forces in Italy to British Field-Marshal Harold Alexander. Wolff then supposedly passed the papers on to "an Italian intermediary" before they ended up in Genoud's possession. Genoud then "proceeded to acquire the copyright from the Bormann family."[17] Reasonably, the only source that could have provided Trevor-Roper with this information was Genoud. On the other hand, in Genoud's introduction to the same book it says that:

> This exchange of letters between Bormann and his wife from [sic] part of a larger collection of documents – the secret archives which were in Bormann's keeping at Obersalzberg, and which he entrusted to his wife during his absence. She took them with her when she fled to the Tyrol, and it was somehow found possible to preserve them when the end of the war came in May 1945. *I received them directly from the people who saved them.* . . . It is also unnecessary for me to vouch for the authenticity of the archives, as it is no longer in doubt.[18] [Italics added.]

Genoud is thus very secretive about where he got the documents, and from this statement, coupled with what Trevor-Roper writes, one could easily get the impression that Genoud got the documents from either Wolff or Gerda Bormann herself. But the part about Wolff and the transmission of the Bormann *Nachlaß* was in fact *not* contained in Schmitz's letter. This information was inserted into Trevor-Roper's introduction at a very late stage in the production process, in early December 1953 to be more exact, and where it had originated is unknown.[19] It must have come from Genoud, however.

There is in fact a document in which Genoud mentions Hofer in question, and it is a protocol from when Genoud was being questioned by the Swiss state police in February 1952. In this document Genoud declared that he found out about the Bormann letters as well as the table talk notes in late 1948. The source for this information was an Italian friend of Genoud's whose name he did not wish to disclose. Genoud said that he was sceptical with regard to the authenticity of these documents, but undertook a trip to Italy in the summer of 1949, at which point he supposedly verified that the documents were in fact authentic. But according to Genoud it was just not one individual that he negotiated the sale with. Rather, it was a group of personalities in the world of arts and letters. The main character among them was allegedly a high functionary within the Italian Ministry of Education and Fine Arts in Rome (Rodolfo Siviero is implied here, although he was employed by the Italian Ministry of Foreign Affairs, M.N.; more on Siviero later). Once again Genoud did not wish to state this person's name. The whole thing was very hush-hush, according to Genoud, because none of these men wished to be known to be in the centre of this affair. As a cover for the deal with Genoud they apparently took on the name of a fictional publishing firm, and Genoud, on his part, stated that he acted on behalf of the firm *Agence Littéraire Générale S.A.* in Tangiers, Morocco. Then in January 1950 he supposedly came in possession of the Bormann letters. Genoud refused to state the sum that he had paid for the documents, but he said that an American editor had helped him gather the amount of money necessary to make the purchase. At the time of the interview, Genoud stated that one part of this document was kept in Switzerland and one part in Italy. Regarding how the Italians (Siviero and Edilio Rusconi, M.N.) had come by these historic documents, Genoud gave two versions. According to one of them, it was a German officer [Wolff?, M.N.] who had provided the Italians with the documents, and according to the other it was an American officer who had found the documents by chance in Austria who had sold the documents to the Italians. Genoud also stated that he had acquired the right to publish the material by signing contracts with Schmitz, as the representative of the Bormann children, and with a lawyer by the name of Alfred Seidl in Munich (more on the dealings between Genoud and Seidl later), who was the representative of Hitler's sister Paula.[20]

There is no independent verification of any of Genoud's statements available to us, i.e. nothing to confirm that either Hofer or Wolff was involved in the process whereby Genoud came into possession of either the paintings or the Bormann

Nachlaß. Jochen von Lang's book about Wolff says nothing about this, even though it in great detail, albeit without proper footnotes and reference system, reports on Wolff's activities during the last months of the war. It seems likely that he would have found out about this if Wolff had been involved. We cannot be absolutely sure of this of course, but it is hard to see why Wolff would choose to hide this information from Lang when he was apparently so open about much more important matters than that, or why the latter would not include this information in his book, especially since Lang does refer to both the *Tischgespräche* and Heim, whom Wolff had become acquainted with at the *Wolfschanze* FHQ, at one point.[21] However, it is perhaps of interest to note that Alfred Seidl had for a while been Wolff's lawyer (and he had also represented several other top Nazis during the International Military Tribunal in Nuremberg) during his trial where he was sentenced to 15 years imprisonment for assisting in the murder of 300,000 Jews.[22]

On the other hand, Karl Laske states that Wolff told a journalist of the Austrian news magazine *Profil* in 1985 that Genoud was an important contact during the war, since he could move about freely. He also claims that several witnesses had confirmed that Genoud had had an important role in the organizing of the escape of many Nazis after the war. But in Laske's version of events it seems that Hofer (whom he only mentions once) has been replaced by Dr Helmut von Hummel.[23] Martin Bormann, i.e. the oldest son of Martin and Gerda Bormann, had met von Hummel after the war. In a letter to Schmitz he talked warmly of him and said that perhaps von Hummel had saved him and his siblings from, as he called it, "the 'Goebbels' solution'" (*die "Goebbels'sche Lösung"*), thus indicating that his father may have suggested that Gerda should kill herself and the children rather than be taken prisoners.[24] According to Laske, Wolff claimed to know Genoud personally, but it is very hard to know how to evaluate this information. It is true that Wolff was crossing the border to Switzerland many times during the last months of the war, as he was negotiating with the American representative, Allen W. Dulles. It was also in Switzerland that Wolff's family was transported into safety. But no historian has ever mentioned Genoud, or any Swiss citizen, taking part in this process.[25] Considering that Wolff lied about many other matters, it is not at all unlikely that he was feeding the journalist in 1985 something that was not true. We do not know enough about the interview to tell for sure what may have been going on. Perhaps Wolff was simply picking up on a leading question from the journalist about Genoud's possible role. Genoud was not at all unknown at this time, and Wolff certainly did not have anything against spreading myths about his, or other Nazis', role during the war.

However, Genoud was never entirely consistent, and there are slight differences in his various stories about the origins of the documents. We can therefore not trust that Genoud is telling the truth in any of these sources. In one document from the Swiss state police dated July 1957 the American officer has vanished from the story and it is simply said that Genoud acquired the documents from either a German officer or a group of Italians in 1952.[26] Yet another version was told by a Dr Horst Weber of Zürich in a letter to Federal Lawyer (*Bundesanwalt*) Professor Dr Lüthi in

Berne. Weber had received the information from a representative of the IfZ, Walter Strauß, a state secretary at the Federal Ministry of Justice (*Bundesjustizministerium*) in Bonn. The story had thus travelled several steps already before it reached Weber, which is perhaps why it contains certain things we know for a fact are wrong. For example, Genoud is said to have been a French national living in Switzerland. According to the story told by Strauß, Bormann [sic] had travelled towards South Tirol in April 1945 with five chests (*Kisten*) filled with documents. The documents had then been handed over to the Gauleiter in Innsbrück, Austria, Hofer, who then apparently lost them, and the content had then likely been plundered. However, sometime later the material appeared in the hands of an American officer who had sold them to the *Agence Littèraire Gènèrale S.A.* in Tangiers. Genoud had, according to Strauß, acted as a representative for this publishing house in this purchase. Strauß stated that Genoud seemed trustworthy, but that he at the same time appeared to know more than he let on. Genoud had, on behalf of the publisher in Tangiers, contacted him regarding the publishing rights in September 1950, and an agreement was reached on the matter in 1951. It was the IfZ that, for political reasons, was opposed to a publication of the letters in German as long as the Bormann children were not of age.[27] Thus, we have two sources stating that Genoud had acted as a representative of *Agence Littèraire Gènèrale S.A.* in this purchase, although both sources had gotten their information from Genoud in the first place.

The story of the chests filled with material, however, seems to be confirmed by no other than Mrs. Bormann's priest, Theodor Schmitz, who in 1954 sent a letter to Genoud in which he attested to the fact that Genoud had the right to "safeguard" Bormann's archive on behalf of the heirs. To this material, wrote Schmitz, "belong, in particular, documents and other objects that were in the boxes that Mrs. Bormann sent to South Tyrol for custody in April 1945."[28] Note, however, that Schmitz never implicates either Hofer or Wolff as having been links in the chain that eventually brought these goods into Genoud's hands. Now, it is certainly possible that Schmitz is simply reiterating information that he got from Genoud that he was perhaps asked to confirm, but what makes this information a lot more plausible is the fact that Schmitz had spent time with Mrs. Bormann in Merano before she died. He was thus in an excellent position to know if she had sent these chests for safekeeping or not. Strauß's story seems far too detailed and elaborate for him to have misunderstood it all, and while he could easily have gotten the fact about Bormann travelling along with the chests wrong, the part about *Gauleiter* Hofer in Innsbrück and the American officer cannot reasonably be explained away like that. This information must ultimately stem from Genoud.

Genoud repeated his threat to block all publication of Picker's book abroad, since it had been published without taking Bormann's rights into consideration, and he planned to make his version the authoritative one by publicizing them via a publisher of his own choice.[29] Buchheim stated that he had seen the original letters between Martin and Gerda Bormann and that he was bringing with him "transcripts by Genoud of most of Bormann's letters, and a small part of the replies from his wife" back to Munich. Genoud intended to publish the letters and he seemed prepared to sell the originals to the IfZ, although he had not yet stated a price.[30] Buchheim also brought with him a photocopy of an authorization (*Voll-macht*) signed by Schmitz granting Genoud the right to publish Bormann's documents.[31] However, if Genoud had an authorization signed by Schmitz already in August 1951 then Schmitz's statement that he threatened to sue Genoud in 1952 makes absolutely no sense. Reasonably, Genoud is the person who has the most reason to lie in this case. Could the document shown to Buchheim have been a forgery? It is possible, although it cannot be confirmed.

In mid-August Genoud's lawyer, André Paschoud, wrote to Athenäum-Verlag to tell them that their book was entirely without right and that Genoud would take legal action against any translation of *Tischgespräche*. Interestingly, by implication, he left out the German version already published. Paschoud wrote, however, that his client assumed that the publisher had acted in good faith and that the matter could be solved without going to court.[32] In September Buchheim wrote to Genoud to tell him that the matter concerning the Bormann letters would be dealt with discretely at a meeting at the IfZ in the beginning of October.[33] Perhaps Genoud wanted to discuss an eventual publication of the Bormann letters with the IfZ, but nothing apparently became of this effort, and the letters were instead published by Weidenfeld and Nicholson in 1954.

Unavoidably, Picker soon became involved in this affair. Picker met with Genoud on three occasions in Godesberg but was unable to offer Genoud anything else than a part of the revenue from a second edition of *Tischgespräche* containing the documents that were missing in the first edition. This was apparently unacceptable to Genoud (and to the other interested parties, as he put it) and therefore he had telephoned Athenäum-Verlag and told them that a compromise with Picker was impossible. Since the publisher had announced its intention to publish the book in translation, Genoud said he would do his best to prevent such a publication. He could not understand how a serious publisher would want to go on publishing Picker's incomplete book when it had been made known to them that he (Genoud) was the one in possession of the original documents. Genoud proposed a deal to the effect that the publisher would forego all rights abroad in exchange for Genoud waiting a while before publishing his book in German so that the first edition of *Tischgespräche* could be sold out. Only Genoud would negotiate with foreign publishers, he stated confidently, and he would grant Athenäum-Verlag the option to act as publisher for his book in German. The ball was now in the hands of Athenäum-Verlag, Genoud wrote, but he feared that their dealing in this matter had made a compromise impossible.[34]

Genoud then wrote to Dr Mau at the IfZ in the end of October to tell him – referring to their meeting – that it had been a pleasure to get to know him in person. He then also gave some examples of where Picker's text differed from the original. He wrote:

> As promised, I am sending You a couple of extracts from the original documents that prove that Dr. Picker has made brazen changes in his book. These

are of course only a few examples for it is a huge amount of work to compare the documents with their counterparts in the book. Dr. Picker's book is not only missing all conversations after 1.8.42 but it is also missing a large part of the notes between 6.6.41 and 21.3.42. On the other hand, he has added various things in the time from 21.3.42 to 1.8.42 that are not to be found in the original documents.[35]

Genoud thought it interesting to have a look at the documents in Picker's possession. Had Bormann given him a copy of all of Heim's notes? Or had Bormann only let him see a part of Heim's work? Since he thought it would be unjust towards the public and the foreign publishers about to publish Picker's book not to tell them about the situation, he felt himself forced to go public with the matter. He then included a proposal for a press release for Mau to think about.[36] To the letter he had also attached five photocopies of the original document, as well as eight pages of typed copies (*Abschriften*) from various places in the original document.[37] Unfortunately, the photocopies are not present in the archival material at the IfZ.

Mau thanked Genoud for the photocopies and the other examples "from which the unreliability of Picker's published text can be clearly seen."[38] About a week later Mau wrote that he had showed Genoud's examples to the *Beirat* at the IfZ. While being careful enough to take the doubts concerning the reliability of Picker's text in the light of the material provided by Genoud into consideration, the *Kuratorium* and *Beirat* at the IfZ wished to hear from Professor Ritter and Picker before taking a firm stand on the matter. In the meantime, the IfZ had prepared a statement for the press that stated that it had come to the attention of the IfZ that a second text of this source had come to light and that it showed differences when compared to the text in *Tischgespräche*. The IfZ would do its best to get to the bottom of the problem of these differences. In this context, Mau thanked Genoud for the photocopies of note No. 64, which contained Picker's signature and his handwritten additions, thus giving it all the signs of an original document. However, Mau stated that it would be preferable to be able to compare *all* Genoud's original pages to Picker's copy. For example, for note No. 45 Genoud had only included two pages, which meant that at least one, probably containing his signature, was missing. If such a complete comparison showed that Picker had treated his text in a wrongful manner, Mau had no doubt that the IfZ would decide to take its hand away from *Tischgespräche*. The IfZ would then also not stand behind a second edition of the book.[39] Picker's notes in Genoud's possession thus had proofreading corrections and additions made to them.

However, there were no plans for a second edition of *Tischgespräche*. *Athenäum* did not expect the first edition to have sold out before the end of 1951 but confirmed that *if* a second edition would be printed then there would certainly be room for correcting obvious mistakes in the text. A re-arrangement of the text in its original chronological form, an idea that had apparently been suggested by the IfZ, was not possible though, according to Junker. The critique coming from government circles was certainly not pleasant, and some of it did concern, as Ritter has intimated, issues that both he and the publisher had tried to convince Picker of allowing. However, some of the critique also targeted Ritter's thematic arrangement of the text, and Junker made sure to point this out to him. Some within the Bavarian government had even questioned the authenticity of the document as a whole, but Junker hastened to re-assure Ritter that there could be no doubts of this.[40] It is worth asking the question why Genoud never ever agreed to such a complete comparison of the two manuscripts? He clearly did have in his possession a manuscript containing all the notes that were later published as *Libres propos*, *Table Talk*, and *Monologe*. I suspect that the reason Genoud refused was that he wanted to be able to keep bluffing if necessary and did not want to show the other players what cards he was holding.

Mau took the opportunity to meet Schmitz during a trip to Berlin and had a long conversation with him. After that, Mau wondered if Genoud could send him the six-pages-long comparison between the two texts as well as a complete list of the notes in his possession that he had given to a Mr Dohrn in Zürich, and which Dohrn had shown Mau. He also wondered if that was a complete comparison or if more had to be done.[41] The next day Genoud wrote Mau to tell him that his lawyer, Dr Runge, had filed a lawsuit with the court in Düsseldorf. He stated that he would quickly send Mau a comparison between the texts from July 1941 and March 1942 and that it would be interesting to hear Picker explain the differences. Genoud had also been in touch with the FRG/BRD Federal Criminal Police Office (*Bundeskriminalamt*), where it had been made clear to him that it was possible to determine when a document had been made. If Picker continued to adhere to the position that two versions of the documents had been made – one correct that he had published and one incorrect made for Bormann's personal use – then Genoud urged Mau to undertake a thorough scientific investigation of both Picker's and his own documents.[42]

What Genoud was talking about at the end here was the fact that Picker tried to explain the textual differences by stating that two variants of his notes had been made. Picker had stated in a newspaper interview that Bormann "liberally edited" (*freizügig bearbeitete*) the notes for use in the power struggle in the Nazi Party, thereby having "forged them in a sense" (*in gewissem Sinne verfälscht*).[43] Later on, as we have seen, Picker would show this to be untrue by actually correcting his own text for the second edition of *Tischgespräche* in 1963 so that it essentially agreed with Genoud's documents.

Genoud replied to Mau that he had not undertaken a complete comparison and that he also could not see the value in doing so, since it would be made by him and not by a neutral party. He had thought that the IfZ was such a neutral party but so far he had only lost valuable time, he said. Now he was waiting for an unequivocal decision from the IfZ; either the IfZ would back Picker's book or it would wash their hands of it. One could not be both judge and party to the case at once, he finally added in French.[44] Genoud certainly had somewhat of a point here, although it is unclear why he simply did not suggest another neutral party to do this comparison.

Mau replied that there seemed to be a misunderstanding behind it all. As far as he was concerned, he had stated that the IfZ could only take a stand if Genoud explicitly asked for it within the framework of his legal battle against Athenäum-Verlag. Since no such expressed demand had been forthcoming from Genoud, Mau had simply waited. Mau could not unilaterally decide on whether to take away the IfZ's backing from Picker's book. The IfZ's position was a difficult one, said Mau, and such a decision could not be made with ease. But if a choice had to be made, Mau would have to say that Genoud's claims to authenticity were better than Picker's "because they offer every guarantee that no subsequent intervention in the text had been made." Mau at the same time felt obligated also to try to get Genoud and Picker to come to an agreement and wondered if there was any way for Genoud to accept a compromise. He also sent Genoud a copy of a record of a discussion held at the IfZ on this issue for him to read and treat with discretion.[45]

Genoud replied:

> Interesting are the explanations of Dr. Picker, who would certainly have made a brilliant career as a magician. Despite all the bad experiences, I do not want to assume Dr. Picker to have bought the faithful Heinrich Heim – not for 30 pieces of silver but for 20 percent – to produce "original records" with his help. I'd rather think he found them in his hat, among the rabbits and pigeons. However, what is important is only the manuscript he presented to the publishing house and later, on 26 January, to Professor Ritter.[46]

This is the first evidence that Picker had offered Heim a share of the revenue for *Tischgespräche*. Apparently, Genoud had also at this point already met with Heim, since he could not otherwise have made statements regarding Heim's character.

The question is if Genoud ever actually had the original notes or only photocopies of them. There are a number of indications that the latter was the case. For instance, there is this exchange between Athenäum-Verlag and Dr Mau of the IfZ in November 1951 when Genoud had apparently made "his material" available to the IfZ in some form. Picker, wrote the publisher, "is himself in possession of a transcript of the version which Mr Genoud also has in his hands."[47] The German word *Durchschrift* means "copy." Note that it is not said that Picker had a copy while Genoud had the original. But then again *Athenäum* was a party in this case, so it may have had reason to downplay Genoud's manuscript. The way the letter is formulated it seems as if both Genoud and Picker had typed copies (or *Durchschriften*). Mau's reply to this letter actually strengthens this view. Mau wrote that the comparison between the Picker notes in Genoud's possession and the ones published in *Tischgespräche* differed and that Genoud had passages in it that were not in the Picker book, but Mau did not think – and this speculation on Mau's part is key – that it was likely that Picker had made more extensive notes for Bormann than he made for himself. If he really made two different versions of his notes, wrote Mau, then one had to assume that the ones he kept for himself would be more complete. "Until proven otherwise, we must assume that Mr. Picker and Mr. Genoud have the same documents." The IfZ would now look into the matter and make sure that if Ritter had made redactions that it really "concerns 'only very few places and completely inconsequential content.'"[48] We have to assume that Mau had not been confronted with an original manuscript consisting of pages signed by Heim, Bormann (or Picker), or anything like that at all at this point. If he had, he would never have been able to assume that Genoud's and Picker's notes were of equal nature.

In mid-December Athenäum-Verlag wrote to Mau and asked to be kept in the loop regarding the process of investigating Genoud's material that the IfZ was undertaking. Genoud had told the publisher that he would go to court to defend his rights, but it was thought that any such rights were rather weak.[49] The reply from Mau came just two days later. He stated that there was no doubt to the IfZ "that the texts in possession of Mr. Genoud are the notes by Mr. Heim and Mr. Picker kept by Bormann." This seems like an unequivocal thing to say. Surely Mau had by then seen the complete original that Genoud claimed to possess? In reality things were far less certain, and there is good cause for us to doubt whether the IfZ actually got to see Genoud's manuscript. The reason is that Mau wrote that according to "a list" (*Nach einem Verzeichnis*) that had been made available to the IfZ Genoud had 169 Heim notes, i.e. 123 more than Picker. Obviously, Mau would never have expressed himself this way if he had actually seen the original documents. He would then simply have referred to the fact that Genoud's manuscript contained that many notes by Heim. Nonetheless, Mau wrote that the IfZ recommended the publisher not to publish yet another edition of Picker's book without the inclusion of Genoud's material.[50] The conclusions of the IfZ were sent to Athenäum-Verlag where it caused some surprise as the IfZ, in the eyes of the publisher, in principle gave Picker right, but still stated that Genoud's material was somehow more precious (*Wertvollere*) than Picker's. According to Ahtenäum-Verlag, Genoud had no case and he could not publish his material either in Germany or elsewhere as long as he did not have the permission by Picker and Heim. Genoud's lawyer had not been able to make a convincing case for his claim to copyright to the publisher.[51]

This must indeed mean that the publisher, at this point, had not seen any original documents either, since it would have been impossible for them to consider Genoud's case as being without merit if they had been confronted with the original notes—then at least that fact would have been something worth considering. Not at any point in this whole affair was there any talk about Picker having only copies of the notes and Genoud having the original pages that Picker's manuscript was a copy of. Neither, and this is obvious from both the newspaper article reporting on it and from the court documents, did Genoud ever produce his originals in court in order to prove his case of authenticity and copyright. That is not the kind of behaviour one would expect from someone in possession of a sensational original document containing the words of Adolf Hitler. Genoud thought it very odd that

Ritter and the publisher had taken it upon themselves to cut portions of the text out.[52] He continued:

> Often these interventions change the meaning of Hitler's statements, which sometimes become quite pointless as a result. And on top of that, the incompleteness of the records and the confusion that Prof. Ritter calls "editing"! The overall result has very little in common with the Bormann notes as they are in my hands.[53]

It is surely interesting to see the fury with which Genoud opposed what he considered to be Picker's changes to the text and chastising him for having forged the notes and so on, even though he at that very moment was about to publish a text in French that he himself had taken the same liberties with. It is thus clear that Genoud was only playing a game here and that he was never genuinely upset about the changes made to the text.

Genoud nonetheless thanked Mau for trying to arrange a compromise but said that he was now past that stage and intended to stop Picker's book at any price.[54] He then suggested that the IfZ should demand that Picker hand over his manuscript to them. They could then ask Ritter if this was the same manuscript that he had had access to or if it differed from it. Genoud was of the opinion that Picker's manuscript was nothing more than a transcription of parts of Bormann's notes plus personal retrospective reflections made by Picker.[55] Genoud was of course correct in assuming that Picker had copied Heim's notes. Genoud also sent Mau new comparisons between the two texts; this time concerning the most obvious changes in notes 174, 175, 176, 177, 191, 193, 213, 214, 215, and 216. He included a list of notes dated after 1 August 1942 as well as two photocopies of pages 442 and 462 of his manuscript.[56] Genoud continued to send examples of the changes he claimed Picker had made. He sent photocopies of notes 88 and 156 in *Tischgespräche* (pages 799–802 in Genoud's manuscript) as examples of how Ritter's thematic arrangement sometimes changed the spirit and meaning of the text. In this case, the effect of Ritter having split a note dated 5 July 1942 (evening) in two was that a comparison between the political situations in England and Germany was turned into a comparison between Germany post-1933 and Germany pre-1933. Genoud also wanted a written statement from Mau regarding his current position towards the two texts.[57] Genoud did not say why he wanted such a statement from Mau, but this would become obvious during the lawsuit that Genoud was preparing at that time. None of the photocopies are still in the IfZ archive.

The case brought up by Genoud is interesting. In *Table Talk* the relevant part of the 5 July 1942 note reads:

> These very important facts have been largely overlooked in Britain because the country is ruled not by men of intelligence but by Jews, as one must realise when one sees how the intrigues of the Jews in Palestine are accepted

in Britain without comment or demur. One of our most important tasks will be to save future generations from a similar political fate and to maintain for ever watchful in them a knowledge of the menace of Jewry.[58]

In this version it is obvious that the second sentence refers back to the first one. However, when Ritter broke these two sentences apart – making the first sentence about Britain part of note 88 and the second sentence about Germany part of note 156 – this connection was lost, and Ritter must have thought that the mentioning of a "similar political fate" referred to the political situation in Germany *before* the Nazi takeover, and hence he inserted a parenthesis after "political fate" saying "(as the German from 1918 to 1933)."[59] The intention was of course to clarify to the reader what the text was referring to, but the result was the opposite and a change in meaning. Interestingly, this mistake is not corrected in the second edition of *Tischgespräche* from 1963. The reference to the German situation from 1918 to 1933 is still in the text although with the parentheses removed (thus the mistake is made even more a part of the text). Even though the sentence about Britain comes immediately before the sentence about Germany in the 1963 edition, the two sentences are still divided by being put in different paragraphs with some space between them, making it seem as if they are independent of each other when in fact they were originally not.[60]

Mau gave his view on the two texts in his reply:

> I would far prefer a new text edition, based on the notes in your possession, to a second edition based on Picker's documents. Your material has the advantage of purveying the table talk notes in the form in which Bormann preserved them, and that they also contain corrections from his hand, which at the same time shine a light on Bormann's personality, which is of interest to historical Research and is to be preferred. Your material also provides assurance that no subsequent corrections have been added to the notes. Dr. Picker has pointed out that he compiled his text version on the basis of three different set of records. The deviations shown by his text vis-à-vis your documents show that Dr. Picker has subsequently corrected by occasionally smoothing over, omitting, and supplementing from his memory, although there is no question that no intentions of forgery were at play.[61]

Unfortunately, we are not told what the three sources for Picker's text were. Furthermore, we cannot be sure it is true. Mau did apparently not appreciate the source-critical implications of the many changes to the text that Bormann had made. These were furthermore not the only changes that had been made to the text. As we shall see in Chapter 4, many changes and additions were made already at the proofreading stage. Mau then told Genoud that Picker had said that he was prepared to meet Genoud in Munich sometime between the 16th and 29th of February 1952 to discuss these matters.[62] Genoud, however, thought it best to wait until it was made clear if his suggestion for a settlement outside the court would be accepted or not.[63] Mau forwarded Genoud's standpoint to Picker's publisher, and did the same with the reply back to Genoud.[64]

In March 1952 the information about the existence of the correspondence between Martin Bormann and his wife had leaked to the German press, and Genoud was apparently not happy about it. He cited the article and said that Mau could surely understand that he now had the impression that the IfZ was not worthy of his confidence.[65] Mau was shocked to read about Genoud's reaction and promised that he or the IfZ had nothing to do with the rumour. The IfZ had been getting several questions about this article put to them from the government in Bonn as well. The article had mentioned that the letters were planned for publication, but the IfZ had no such information, stated Mau. The IfZ was not the source of either the information or the facsimile of one of the letters that had appeared with it, he assured Genoud. However, Mau called attention to the fact that an article in *Gazette de Lausanne* from 12 February 1952 contained a facsimile of half a letter. Genoud had jumped to conclusions that were not valid, Mau wrote, and he was waiting to hear Genoud's response.[66] Genoud later replied that he was glad to hear that the IfZ had nothing to do with the matter and added that with regard to the facsimile in the Lausanne newspaper *he* was the source of that.[67] Genoud himself was thus trying to rev up the expectations for his planned publication of the letters.

The first court case: who should own the copyright to the table talk notes?

Genoud did indeed file a lawsuit against Picker and Athenäum. The case was deliberated and decided upon during 1952 in Düsseldorf. This court case gives us some interesting information, at least regarding how the two parties chose to present their case to the court. It was, for example, stated by Genoud that Heim had been given the assignment by Bormann with Hitler's permission to make "stenographic records that Heim immediately dictated in the form of file notes to the secretary Miss Fugger, which were presented to Bormann to sign, who, if he considered it necessary, made small corrections." As proof of this Genoud put forth not only the note written by Bormann (see the facsimile in *Table Talk*, M.N.) to this effect but also testimony by Fugger and Heim.[68] It is unclear how Fugger and Heim actually testified – i.e. did they appear in person or was their testimony delivered in written form – and what they said exactly. I have also not been able to find out what Fugger's first name was.

It is noteworthy that Genoud apparently stated that he had no idea who had written down the notes after Heim left in 1942. The court documentation states that "These transcripts from the latter years 1942 to 1944 were made by a person who was not identified by name."[69] This is very odd considering that in *Monologe* both Müller's and Bormann's names are on several of the notes and that Genoud had informed Buchheim about Müller's contribution already in 1951. It is true, however, that quite a lot of the notes in *Monologe* do not have a name attached to them. Since we do not have access to the "originals", it is impossible to say for sure whether these notes were ever signed or not.

In court Genoud tried to argue that he was the sole holder of the publication rights because of the contract he had signed with Flammarion in 1951 (no date given) and through his agreement with the representative of Paula Hitler (she had changed her last name to Wolf in the 1930s; however I have decided to use her original last name throughout) on 20 November 1952.[70] The court, however, decided that Genoud did not have a case, i.e. that he held neither the copyright nor the publication rights to the notes in question. Contrary to what Genoud had tried to argue, the court confirmed Picker's conviction that Hitler's testament from 29 April 1945 was valid as a "Military Testament." This meant that all the rights to everything he left behind (including his words as recorded in these notes) now belonged to the Bavarian state. The court also concluded that Hitler's sister did not have any valid claim as Hitler's heir either. Genoud's agreement with her was therefore to be considered "an agreement with someone without rights" (*einen Vertrag mit einem Nichtberechtigten*), and he had not been able to prove that Hitler had bequeathed the table talk notes to his sister Paula. The law required Paula Hitler to have been expressly given the copyright by her brother in order for her to claim it; since such a document could not be produced by Genoud, the copyright was still technically Hitler's.[71]

There is something to be said about whether Paula Hitler had actually signed over the rights to Genoud, as well as the timing of it. The notarized paper from Paula Hitler's Nazi-sympathizing lawyer, Alfred Seidl, is in fact dated 17 July 1952.[72] I have tried to trace the negotiations between Genoud and Paula Hitler as far back as possible, and the earliest document I can find is a reference, in a letter from Paula Hitler to Genoud on 17 December 1951, to a letter from Genoud to her on 1 September 1951. Seidl was careful enough to point out in late November that the signing over of rights did not come with any sort of guarantee, whereby he meant that Paula Hitler could not be held responsible if the courts should happen to decide (which they did) that Hitler's testament was valid (which would make the Bavarian state the legal heir to his *Nachlass*).[73] Reasonably this is an indication of the fact that Genoud did not start to secure the publication rights until *after* Picker's book had been published.

Two days later Paula Hitler wrote a letter to Genoud in which she asked him and his friend Hans Rechenberg, politely but decidedly, to handle their business concerns with Seidl in Munich and not with her directly. The letter thus makes clear that Genoud and Rechenberg had been in contact with her (and perhaps they had even met in person). At this point it is clear that no agreement had been reached regarding the matter of the *Tischgespräche*, a matter that Paula Hitler said she did not want to ever speak about again – "At the same time, I refer once again to the original theme: *Tischgespräche* (of which no mention have been made since then) and that we should nevertheless try to agree on this basis for starters."[74] On the same day Rechenberg wrote to Paula Hitler and complained about her unwillingness to deal with Genoud in person. Apparently, she had cancelled a meeting with them the day before (set to take place just a few days later), a decision that had left them in an "embarrassing" situation with their lawyers. He and Genoud only wished to clear up the juridical situation regarding Hitler's table talks, Rechenberg stated. Genoud felt hurt, he continued, by Paula Hitler's action, having invested so much both emotionally and materially into this affair. As far as he could see, Genoud was the *only* person with any interest in safeguarding the interest of Hitler's heirs, and it went without saying that Genoud's efforts, which really came from the bottom of his heart, were made much more difficult due to the suspicion with which she had been treating him. This was especially sad, Rechenberg said, considering that Genoud had made considerable material sacrifices in order to get his hands on the original manuscript, and also considering that he did not wish to publish the original unless it was possible to do so "in a form true to the original text" – a weird formulation that only raises further questions. Also, in order to safeguard the translation rights Rechenberg urged her to talk to Seidl in order for the agreement to be completed.[75] It is reasonable to assume from this letter that Genoud and Rechenberg were getting desperate.

Genoud did thus obviously not appreciate Paula Hitler's attitude, and her wish not to talk about *Tischgespräche* again was not respected by him either. He brought the matter up again in correspondence with her at least as late as December 1953. In this letter it also becomes clear that Paula Hitler was unhappy with the way things had turned out. She complained that she could not imagine, when two years earlier she had suggested that all matters regarding *Tischgespräche* should be handled by the lawyer Seidl, that Seidl would come to guard Genoud's interests rather than hers. It was apparently Genoud who had paid Seidl for his work and not Paula Hitler, since she did not have any money to spend on lawyers, she said. Perhaps that was why this situation had occurred, she thought, although she had taken for granted that Seidl would even so be looking out for her interests. Hitler's sister was not pleased with Genoud at all at this point, and she wrote that even though Genoud had bothered to make sure he had the permission from Hitler's heirs he still treated them as if they were "receivers of alms." She also made abundantly clear to Genoud that he should think of a way to make all these issues disappear because she would not sign any agreement that was based on secrets or ambiguities of any kind.[76] The relationship between Paula Hitler and Seidl seems to have gone steeply downhill from there, and in the summer of 1954 Seidl had to inform Genoud that he was no longer representing her. The reason was that she clearly did not trust Seidl anymore and had either refused to answer his queries entirely or given only evasive answers.[77]

On 15 March 1953 Dr Helmut Krausnick of the IfZ wrote Genoud and stated that he and the IfZ were looking forward to the English edition with Trevor-Roper's preface. Krausnick asked if the time had not come for Genoud to provide the IfZ with the source material for his book. He assured Genoud that any publication of this text by the IfZ was not planned any time soon. The IfZ also wished to have a copy of *Table Talk* in order to evaluate its worth as a historical source. If

Genoud could send them Trevor-Roper's preface, perhaps in proof, the IfZ would be very grateful, Krausnick wrote.[78] Genoud stated that the legal battle continued since Picker had appealed the court's decision.[79] The IfZ eventually received a copy of *Table Talk* in July.[80] Krausnick repeated the request for Genoud to provide the IfZ with the original manuscript sometime later.[81] Once again it seems this request went unanswered.

The court decision must no doubt have been a huge disappointment for Genoud who had bet everything on a bluff and lost. Ironically, however, he lost even though, or rather because of the fact that, the court believed him. His strategy of portraying the notes as the result of the work by a team of stenographers had failed. It resulted in the court making the very reasonable decision that since the stenographers did not hold copyright, Genoud could not either. If this indeed was Hitler's words, then the copyright belonged with Hitler, or, as was now the case, with the Bavarian state. It is important to stress that the court did not forbid Genoud to publish in German.[82] Trevor-Roper's assessment of the outcome was that Picker had "captured the anyway insignificant market" in Germany, "while elsewhere M. Genoud's text (which is certainly more complete and less ill-arranged) has prevailed."[83] At this point, though, Trevor-Roper was of course already completely invested in Genoud's manuscript by having put his name on *Table Talk*. Heim, on the other hand, commented that it would be very dissatisfactory if Genoud was to publish his book "without having clarified the legal situation, without expert advice on translation and without comment by Heim as the main author, and finally without giving Heim the opportunity to convince himself of the authenticity and completeness of the manuscript."[84]

Picker also insisted that the notes – or at least Heim's notes – were a result of a stenographic recording process. Picker's incentive for doing this was of course that if Heim had been a stenographer then Heim, and per implication Genoud, could not claim a copyright of them. This also backfired on him, since the court decided he could not hold copyright either.[85] Picker actually realized what his argument meant for *his own* claim to copyright so he tried to argue that since Hitler was a "historical personality" the dictator could not claim copyright to these notes either. This argument, however, was not accepted by the court.[86] This false story would later not suit Picker so he then changed it to the true one. After all, how could it be stenographic notes if he himself did not know stenography?

Moreover, Picker had betrayed his own lie by having agreed to give Heim part of the revenue from *Tischgespräche* after Heim had appeared to claim his right after its publication. This was information given to Genoud by Heim.[87] This arrangement proved that neither Heim nor Picker had been stenographers and that both their contributions were to be considered creative literature to a similar degree. The deal, signed by Heim and Picker, had been struck on 27 February 1952, i.e. *before* the court case in Düsseldorf. It stated:

Agreement

The following fee agreement is signed between former State Councillor, Mr. Heinrich Heim, Munich, and former District Councillor, Mr. Dr. Henry Picker, Wilhelmshaven, for Dr. Picker's book: "Hitlers Tischgespräche im Führerhauptquartier 1941/2". Mr. Heim is entitled to 50% of the author's fee, which is accounted for by his table talk transcripts according to his share of the total number of pages in the book or the share of half of the total column number in the magazine prints. Mr. Heim is entitled to verify the accuracy of the settlement at any time by access to Dr. Picker's accounting.[88]

According to documentation in Werner Jochmann's private archive in Hamburg, Heim was paid DM 1,500 on 31 March 1952 for various re-prints of the notes in the magazines *Quick* and *News Chronicle*; readings of parts of the text on the radio station NWDR (*Nordwestdeutscher Rundfunk*); as well as for the sales of the book itself.[89] The same document seems to imply that there was also an earlier agreement made between the two, because it says that the payment was made according to "our agreement from 6.10.1951 and 27.11.1952."[90] The latter must reasonably be a mistake, since the agreement cited above is dated in February 1952. The real date should reasonably be 27 November 1951.

According to Heim, he had received this money, but by 1958 he and Picker had fallen out, partly because Picker had, in his eyes, "not exactly acted wisely." Heim did not specify it more than that. With Genoud, on the other hand, Heim had apparently had no problem at that point.[91] In 1980 Heim also acknowledged that Picker had given him a share of the income from the sales of the book in the early 1950s.[92] In 1972 he had complained bitterly to Werner Maser that Picker had not given him any part of the revenue for the second edition of *Tischgespräche* from 1963. He was upset with Percy Ernst Schramm too, whom he felt had not taken him seriously and who had not consulted him before publication. As a result, stated Heim, a number of mistakes regarding the history of the notes had been included in Schramm's edition, matters that Heim felt obligated to correct publicly at some point or another.[93]

Heim was at least offered some reimbursement. Nonetheless, he would later, when interviewed by John Toland in 1971, claim that he "was never consulted by any of the publishers" of his notes.[94] This was obviously untrue. Not only had the IfZ made several interviews with him, but also both Picker and Genoud were in contact with him at the time (indeed, as soon as they found out about his existence it seems). Toland taped his interview with Heim, and hence I was excited to find out that a copy of the interview was apparently located in the "John Toland Papers" at the Roosevelt Presidential Library. Unfortunately, however, it turned out that Toland used the same cassette for another interview and recorded over the Heim interview when talking to Egon Hanfstaengl – the son of Hitler's foreign press chief, Ernst "Putzi" Hanfstaengl. At least this is what archivist Virginia Lewick thought had happened after having double-checked with the LoC, which also has copies of Toland's papers and recordings.[95]

Heim claimed in an interview by the IfZ in 1952 that the reason for why he did not get involved in the legal battle between Genoud and Picker (in which he as the author of the notes actually considered himself entitled to take part) was that his trump card vis-à-vis Genoud was that he was the only one who could confirm the authenticity of the Genoud's manuscript, and he adds that it had indeed been questioned if *Libres propos* was not actually a forgery (just like Eva Braun's diaries). He thought that he would risk losing this position of strength if he got involved in the legal battle on either side.[96]

This interview with Heim is one of two made at about the same time (the second one was made only a couple of weeks later) by the same interviewer. In the first interview Heim stated that Genoud's manuscript was probably the most reliable because both the "author" (i.e. Heim) and Bormann had gone through them. However, it is hard to understand how he could make that statement with any certainty when he also said in the same interview that he had only been allowed to see a few of Genoud's manuscript pages. That Heim considered himself a co-author to the notes in Picker's book is obvious from the interview with him.[97] But in the second interview Heim contradicted himself and stated that when Genoud asked him to authenticate his manuscript before *Libres propos* was published, he had leaned towards Picker's German version "out of loyalty" (*aus Loyalität*). This supposedly led to a break between him and Genoud.[98] It is not entirely clear what "loyalty" Heim is referring to here, but it could be that he is talking about the agreement with Picker regarding royalties from *Tischgespräche*. It is perhaps possible to harmonize these statements if we assume that the reason for why Heim preferred *Tischgespräche* over *Libres propos* simply was that the former was published in German. In an interview from 1972 Heim explicitly denounced Genoud's versions completely by saying that it "is a material in which one encounters thousands of stupid mistakes." Heim also claimed he did not know how Genoud had acquired Bormann's manuscript, even though he had met Genoud and spoken to him.[99] All of this thoroughly contradicts what Heim apparently told John Toland in 1971.[100] We thus see that Heim's story changes somewhat over time and depending upon whom he was speaking to it seems.

Instead of claiming that Bormann was the author, Genoud stated in court that Hitler himself was the copyright holder.[101] This was in reality Genoud's way of claiming the copyright for himself, since he argued that he had bought the publication rights to Hitler's written estate from his sister Paula. Genoud had offered Mau's statement concerning the authenticity of the two texts, which he had requested as evidence in court.[102] This way he could now show that the head of IfZ considered his notes to be of better quality than Picker's. Mau of course had no idea that Genoud would use his statement in this way and must have been rather taken aback by it. Picker was certainly not happy about this and told Mau and Buchheim as much during a meeting in Munich on 2 July.[103]

During all this time Genoud had been working on a French translation of his notes to be published by Flammarion, the contract having been signed already in 1951. In June 1952 Genoud wrote to Mau and told him that *Libres propos* would be published in France on 3 July.[104] Mau then also received a copy of the book on 8 July.[105] It is not known why it was decided to split the book into two volumes or why the second volume was not published until 1954. His true motives for his actions unfortunately will probably never be known. Why did Genoud not publish his notes in German immediately? Trevor-Roper has stated that Genoud hurried to get a French edition out in order to claim copyright, something that could be done on a translation.[106] That would make sense if Picker had not been able to benefit from the profits of the sales of *Tischgespräche*; but since Picker could do so, then Genoud could reasonably do that too. Thus, that *cannot* be the true reason. Furthermore, Genoud eventually did decide to publish his text in German in the form of *Monologe* in 1980. Nothing new had happened by then that made the copyright situation any different than it was in the mid-1950s. The nail in the coffin for the copyright hypothesis, however, is the fact that the contract with Flammarion had been signed long before the copyright issue had been settled in court. Genoud had thus planned to publish an amended French version all along.

That the copyright issue was not the true reason is also shown by Genoud's answer to the question why he had not let the original German manuscript of the *Tischgespräche* be published, put to him at a seminar with the title "Freedom of information in contemporary historical research and its legal barriers" organized by the IfZ in 1977. There, Genoud did not mention anything about being afraid to lose control over this manuscript. Instead he said:

> If it has not yet come to the possibility of a German edition, as I planned with Professor [Eberhard] *Jäckel* years ago, perhaps more than ten years ago, it is quite simple, namely because no publisher has so far been found.[107] [Italics in original.]

Since it is absolutely impossible to trust what Genoud says without being able to confirm his statements with other independent sources, we cannot be sure that this was the real reason either. It most likely was not, because it does not really seem to agree with what we know about Genoud's handling of his manuscript. Moreover, there were many publishers that would have loved to be the one to publish this source in the original (in fact, it is hard to imagine any commercial publisher in Germany that would not have wanted to publish this text), so this statement is not very likely to be true.

How did Picker get hold of Heim's notes?

One of the most vexing questions in the history of the table talks is the issue of how Picker came to possess so many of Heim's notes. It is something that should not have been able to occur, at least not according to the official narratives concerning how the table talk notes were made. Since it is highly unlikely that Picker would have been able to gain access to those of Heim's notes that Heim had given to Bormann, it is obvious that Picker must have somehow been able to copy these notes somewhere else. The question is then: where, and under what circumstances, did this occur?

Genoud wondered about this too, and in a letter to Mau in July 1952 (on the back of which he asked Mau to forgive him for his terribly poor German).[108] Genoud was positive that the Heim notes in Picker's possession were nothing but copies, or carbon copies, of Heim's notes.[109] Then he quoted a statement made by Picker's lawyer in the Düsseldorf court, a statement which includes some new and interesting information regarding the provenance of the notes:

> Former State Councillor Heim and District Councillor Picker have, on the basis of Hitler's statements at the [dinner, M.N.] table and thereafter, made notes 'on the clock' – as the plaintiff correctly asserts – notes, or dictated transcripts no less. These notes, however, were not made for Martin Bormann privately, but for the Party Chancellery of the NSDAP. They were therefore not – as the plaintiff assumed – handed over to Bormann, as head of the Party Chancellery, in a single copy, but in two copies. After review by Bormann, both copies were sent to the Party Chancellery in Munich, into the hands of State Director Hanssen.[110]

Genoud wondered if that meant that Picker had had a third copy made.[111] Part of the answer to this riddle was provided by Heim in an interview made for John Toland's Hitler biography in the 1970s. Heim explained that he had been on a mission to Italy and when he came back to the office in Munich, he noticed some of his notes lying on Hanssen's desk, and next to these were a set of typed copies of them. When he asked Hanssen why these notes were lying on the desk, Hanssen replied that while Heim was gone he (Hanssen) had been replaced by a man (Heim could not remember if Picker's name had been mentioned or not) who had found the notes in the safe and had then copied some of them in the anteroom (*Vorzimmer*). Heim had then asked Hanssen to ask Bormann if such copies had been authorized and received a negative reply.[112] In October 1976 Heim actually wrote about this episode in a letter to the British newspaper *Daily Telegraph*, in which he stated that he had discovered this in August 1942, on his return from Rome.[113] Heim was obviously not remembering the timing of these events correctly, because by 1 August he was already back at the FHQ making his first note for Bormann since he had left for Italy in March.[114]

However, this story does not really make total sense, because why would the copies still be lying on Hanssen's desk if Picker had taken them with him? We have no indications that Picker had typed up more than one set of copies. But the information is interesting, since we know that at least some of the pages of the notes that Picker copied were also in Munich, perhaps even in the same safe (for more on this, see Chapter 4). John Toland summarized Heim's statements regarding how the notes were made like this in his book:

> Shortly after their arrival at Wolfschantze [sic], Bormann had suggested almost offhandedly to Heinrich Heim, his adjutant, that he surreptitiously note down what the Chief said. In order so that Hitler wouldn't know he was being put on record, Bormann instructed his adjutant to rely on his memory. But Heim wanted more accurate results and on his own initiative he began making copious notes on index cards which he hid on his lap. Bormann was taken aback but he gave Heim tacit approval to continue taking notes. "So the matter went on," Heim recalled, "without Bormann giving me any instructions, expressing any wishes or anything else except to silently show his happiness that in this way much would be preserved and not forgotten."[115]

The last part obviously cannot be true, since it contradicts Heim's position as stated unofficially to the IfZ in 1952, and in other sources cited so far in this book. Bormann was active in the process of finalizing the notes, so the idea that he only "silently showed his happiness" cannot be correct. However, the exact same phrasing was used by Heim in his recording for the BBC in 1953.[116] Moreover, Bormann's intention was to use the notes in his capacity as chief of the party chancellery, so he certainly did not only intend for Hitler's words to be "preserved" for posterity as memory. For him, these notes were a means to an end, and that end was to gain more power within the NSDAP and the Third Reich. Since this latter occasion is also closer to the events in time, we should reasonably assume that the unofficial information given in 1952 is more likely to be correct than what he said in more official interviews in 1953 and 1971. Heim certainly does not say that Bormann told him to rely on his memory in any of the interviews made with him for Toland's book.

There may actually have been yet another purpose for making these notes, namely to serve as a sort of official chronicle of the philosopher-king in his FHQ, in the vein of Hitler's idol Frederick the Great. At least Heim intimated as much in 1976 when he stated in the letter to the *Daily Telegraph* that he just could not understand how Picker had had the audacity to have some of his notes copied in Munich. "In our eyes", wrote Heim, "this was the property of the people, which should be preserved untouched for the future."[117] The notes were thus considered to be the common property of the German people; a future cultural heritage of sorts. This certainly gives the notes another character in a way that has important source-critical consequences. The "we" obviously did not include Picker, since he acted in a way that Heim did not approve of.

The second court case: Picker sues Genoud

By the summer of 1952 no one had yet seen any original notes from Genoud's manuscript. All he had ever shown to anybody were photocopies of documents. He had even refrained from showing the original notes during the first trial in Düsseldorf, and it had therefore also been questioned in court whether Genoud actually had the original documents. Genoud wrote to Mau in order to get him to assure the court that this was the case. According to Genoud, he had visited Buchheim and shown him the complete original document, 1,045 pages, to him. He also wrote that the first page consisted of a note with the word "Secret!" (*Geheim*) on it.[118] The second page was Bormann's note (the facsimile in *Table* Talk/*Monologe*, M.N.) that Mau had been given a photocopy of. About four-fifths of Heim's notes were not included in Picker's book, said Genoud, and a comparison between Picker's and his text between 21 March 1942 and 31 July 1942 (Picker's time at the FHQ) showed that Picker's text in *Tischgespräche* was about 20 percent larger. Genoud wanted to hear Mau's view on these matters.[119]

Mau replied that he and Buchheim were both convinced that Genoud's document, which they had both seen photocopies of, was authentic and original. It was documents containing the signature of all the scribes as well as handwritten additions and commentaries by Bormann. However, with regard to Picker's own notes Mau stated that Picker had convinced the IfZ that his own notes were indeed more detailed than the ones he gave to Bormann. Picker had only dictated a part of his notes.[120]

It seems as if Picker felt a bit strengthened by the ruling by the court in Düsseldorf, and, indeed, as if he became overconfident. Instead of being satisfied with a draw where neither he nor Genoud were granted copyright, he decided, after the publication of *Libres propos*, to sue Genoud for damages for copyright infringement. Apparently, Picker took the denial of Genoud's claim to copyright as an approval of his own claim. Picker thus filed a counter-lawsuit in the Regional Court (*Landesgericht*) in Oldenburg. This was a mistake, as it turned out, because the Oldenburg court ruled against Picker.

After this point there is a large gap in the material in IfZ with regard to this matter. The next document is dated in March 1953 and talks about the fact that after the result of the first court case, it seemed to Mau as if Genoud would have been prepared to make a deal, but that he now, after Picker had sued him for the publication of *Libres propos*, felt obligated to take matters into his own hands. By this time Mau knew about the upcoming publication of *Table Talk* and that this would be the basis for an American edition. He still hoped, however, that Picker and Genoud could come to terms so that a critical German edition could be published.[121]

On 18 March 1953 the municipal court in Oldenburg gave its verdict in the lawsuit that Picker had filed against Genoud. Picker had sued for damages due to loss of revenue caused by Genoud's statements in the press and in the preface to *Libres Propos* – where he claimed to be the sole holder of Bormann's copyright and the original documents – and his complaints to the IfZ, which had prolonged the selling of translation rights abroad as well as slowed sales in Germany. Picker also cited the postscript in *Tischgespräche* where it is stated that any changes to Hitler's utterances were indicated by italics.[122] Picker had, in other words, gone out of his way to make the case that the book represented Hitler's words as precisely as possible. This, naturally, did not strengthen Picker's case to be considered an independent author with a claim to copyright. Picker claimed that Genoud was responsible for the fact that the publisher had sold only 4,105 copies of the 13,000 printed by the end of September 1952.[123]

Genoud's *Libres Propos* had also claimed a part of the German market, stated Picker, and added that he had found copies of it in a bookstore even in his hometown of Wilhemshaven.[124] Picker now assumed that his copyright would be granted because he had not just taken part in Hitler's dinner monologues as an official scribe but also outside of work as a private guest. Since he had transformed Hitler's direct speech into indirect speech and partly shortened it, and through a productive process transformed it into something else than a mechanistic transcription, he thought he had a good case. Only in about 10 or so cases had he written Hitler's words down at the table on small cards that Bormann had given him for this explicit purpose, claimed Picker. Otherwise, he had not been obligated to make any notes whatsoever.[125] Picker was trapped in a Catch-22 situation here: he could not tell the truth and argue that he had in fact been quite liberal with the text because then he would have undermined the veracity of the text, and he could not argue that his notes very precisely portrayed Hitler's words because then he would undermine his own copyright claim. He thus tried to balance between these two positions and convince the court that the text was in a sense free enough to count as a literary product, and therefore should be granted copyright, but at the same time exact enough to be a true record of Hitler's words.

Genoud, on the other hand, did not have such a difficult time during this trial. He said that he had simply given his view on the copyright issue to interested members of the press and that he had not stated anything in his preface that Picker had not said in his own preface. In addition to this, Genoud had become convinced about his claim through conversations with Hitler's personal adjutant Julius Schaub and Hitler's personal photographer Heinrich Hoffman, among others. He furthermore insisted that Picker could not claim any copyright since he had simply purveyed Hitler's words, words that were the Führer's own. Since Picker had been in the HFQ on official business, he could not claim to have taken part in the dinners as a private individual. Genoud, too, took refuge in what Ritter and Picker had said about the nature of the text in *Tischgespräche* to support his case. Ritter had surely based his statements on what Picker had told him, said Genoud, and there was nothing in Picker's book that indicated that he had tried to mislead the public as to the nature of the text. He also referred to the verdict in the Düsseldorf trial as support for his claim.[126] The irony in this situation was of course that while Genoud had previously argued that his version of the text was the best one because Picker had made so many changes to his text, he now found himself arguing in the Oldenburg court that Picker's text was actually very accurate. The following was reported in the newspaper *Fränkische Nachrichten*:

> Picker argued that the table talks he, at the time, wrote down stenographically in his official capacity were his intellectual property. However, this view

was not recognised by the Oldenburg district court. On the contrary, Picker had only recorded and recreated someone else's intellectual property in protocol form without acquiring a copyright to it.[127]

Apparently, the journalist reporting the matter made a mistake when stating that Picker had claimed he had used stenography. There is actually nothing in the verdict from the court about Picker having made such a claim. It may be a misunderstanding based on what Genoud claimed during the proceedings. Genoud had claimed that "the plaintiff [Picker] was merely an official stenographer in Bormann's service." The verdict also states that Picker had gotten the author's copyright (*Autorenrechte*) to Heim's notes from Heim himself.[128] The court was of the same opinion as Genoud and stated that Picker was at the FHQ on official orders and that he thus could not separate his professional work from his private dealings. The court here used Picker's own description of his time at the FHQ as expressed in *Tischgespräche*, where he stated that he been stationed there, against him. Picker had thus not taken part as a guest of Hitler's, as he also had claimed, but as a professional. His notes were then not a private matter, and he could therefore not claim copyright to them either.[129] Picker seems to have tried to argue two contradictory things at once, namely that he was at the FHQ as both a guest and in his official capacity.

The court did indeed confirm the Düsseldorf verdict and gave Genoud right. Based on the case presented by Picker, the court ruled that he had not added anything of importance to the text, which was then simply a transcription of Hitler's table talks. No matter what you decided to call them when published, the copyright therefore belonged to the person who had initially uttered the statements in question, i.e. Hitler. Picker's statements in his preface now came back to stab him in the back. The court even stated that it was only the original copyright holder who had any right to make changes to the text. With direct reference to Picker's statements in his preface the court ruled that it could not be made any clearer that the text was *not* the personal work of Picker and that he, due to the statement that Hitler did not know that he made most of the notes, did not even have the permission to make the notes in the first place. The court said:

> It can hardly be stated more clearly that it is a non-authorized use of a work, and even according to the plaintiff's own presentation it is an illicit one.[130]

The argument that Hitler did not know about the notes being made was thus seen by the court as diminishing Picker's copyright claim even further. Note that the court's verdict had nothing to do with historical source criticism; it ruled on the question of legal copyright. In doing so they did not evaluate how the text had actually been changed or how exact it was from the beginning. The verdict was based on the evidence and arguments presented to the court.

Moreover, the court stated that neither could Picker claim to have gotten the permission by the rightful owner of Hitler's words by referring to the decision by the IfZ to publish the book, since the government owned the copyright to Hitler's works. The IfZ was not the government and could thus not give such permission. The Oldenburg court supported itself on the ruling by the court in Düsseldorf, which had concluded that Hitler's testament was valid and that it was thus the Dönitz government – and after it the Federal Republic – that became the heir to Hitler.[131] Picker had made a mistake when he thought that he, after having made a choice in his book between his official and private function at the FHQ in favour of the former, could then turn around and use his status as a private individual to claim copyright to his notes.[132] It is in a way rather strange that Picker expected it to be any different.

The court then cited the Düsseldorf ruling in order to make clear that it had already at that point been made abundantly clear that neither Picker nor Heim could claim to hold copyright over the notes:

> In the Düsseldorf judgment of 4.12.1952 it is also stated: "The authors of the transcripts, Heim and Picker, cannot be recognized as authors or editors. They only fulfilled the purely performing tasks of a secretary."[133]

This part of the Düsseldorf verdict was actually cited by Genoud in the Italian edition *Conversazioni segrete* in 1954 in order to illustrate both the illegitimacy of Picker's claims and the veracity of the recorded text.[134] It is thus hard to see the Oldenburg case as anything but a victory for Genoud and a hard loss for Picker even though Genoud was also not granted copyright; Picker brought the lawsuit and he lost.

The myth of the unsuspecting Hitler

In late 1954 Dr Helmut Krausnick at the IfZ asked Genoud to provide him with the original German wording of a passage in *Table Talk* dated 13/14 October 1941 where it said: "I write drafts of letters only concerning matters of vital importance. It's what I did, for example, for the Four Year Plan – and last year, when I was contemplating the action against Russia." This passage was important for the understanding of Hitler and his policies, said Krausnick.[135] It is not known if he received an answer to this request.

Apparently, in the mid-1950s Genoud, together with Heim, was contemplating making photocopies of his documents available to the public by letting libraries and archives in German-speaking countries subscribe to them.[136] This was of course just another effort for Genoud to make even more money off of his Nazi documents. Why nothing came of this idea is unclear, but perhaps there was simply no discernible interest from libraries and archives to pay for such access.

Picker writes in the second edition of *Tischgespräche* that the 10 or so notes that he got Bormann's explicit order to put down on paper acted as a sort of alibi for him when he made the rest of his about 190 notes. These orders also meant that he did not have to worry about embarrassing questions from the other guests, Picker writes. He also claims that Bormann on three occasions showed his notes to Hitler who corroborated that they represented his words in a manner that satisfied him.[137] The French journalist Pierre Péan also claims that Hitler gave Bormann the order to see to it that the notes were being made.[138] But Picker also writes that Hitler *ante facto* was made aware of *all* of his notes. When he left the headquarters late in the summer of 1942, he asked Bormann if he could take his private notes with him, notes that filled several notebooks. Bormann then, according to Picker, thought that the safest thing would be to ask for Hitler's permission before doing anything like that (a seemingly reasonable assessment). Hitler allegedly then gave a green light for Picker to take them with him, and a precondition for this was to have been exactly the fact that Picker had *not* used stenography and that it was not an exact representation of Hitler's every word. And if that was not enough, Hitler apparently also gave his permission for Picker to publish them after the war.[139] This is certainly a fanciful story. But how much of it is true?

The idea that Hitler, or Bormann, gave Picker permission to bring these notes with him is a figment of Picker's imagination. Bormann's former secretary, Ilse James, was adamant on this point when she described to Werner Jochmann her recollections about Picker and his activities in the FHQ:

> I have not yet sat down for a close study of Picker's book, but even at first glance I have noticed many false statements, distortions and inventions. [. . .] For example, the statement that Dr. Hanssen gave Dr. Picker the key to the armored safe in the Führerbau, extremely brazen – I think it is impossible! And the claim that he was given the notes for publication by Hitler or Bormann is naturally absolutely scandalous, as you rightly point out. Because Hitler of course did not know about the notes and even Bormann did not give Picker the transcripts to use for other purposes. I remember the first weeks of Picker's activity in the "Wolfsschanze", he was for us at that time – also probably for Bormann – we who were all used to Dr. Hanssen's and Heim's well thought-out and fine-tuned way of working, like an "Elephant in the Porcelain Shop"; that is how insensitive he appeared to me at the time. He had somehow become aware of the Heim notes; it is possible that Bormann had mentioned them and he [Picker] immediately began to assert himself in the same way. I still remember full well that at that time I refused to write these things for him, so coarse and simplified or even far from his own comprehension did what he want to write seem to me at the time. At the time, I carefully explained to him that I doubted that Bormann would approve of them. Moreover, it also appeared to me at the time that what he wanted to have produced was copies of his own transcripts rather than of those [notes] that had previously been produced by Bormann. I told him at that time that I had to ask Bormann, but, if I remember correctly, I limited myself to suggestions, because one did not want to "clash" [with Bormann].

In any case, he constantly wanted to make, or even have someone else write, his own notes after every meal and every tea hour, and these were by no means the same as Bormann's. Because *all* of Hitler's statements was not to be recorded, but only occasional and particularly interesting points were to be noted down.[140] [Emphasis in original.]

It is certainly very interesting that James claimed that Picker had approached her asking her to type up the copies of mostly his own notes. Note also that what she considered absurd was not that Picker had gotten access to Heim's notes in the *Führerbau* in Munich, but only that Hanssen would have given him the key to the safe in which the notes were kept. There may actually be something to James's description of Picker and his personality, however. Heim confirms this view, seemingly independently, as he stated to the American artist and science fiction writer Karen Kuykendall that he was recalled from Italy because Bormann had told the NSDAP HQ in Munich by the end of July that Picker had "proved himself unacceptable", and he thus wished Heim to return to the FHQ. Heim speculated that there must have been some sort of doubt about Picker's loyalty and that he was probably declared *persona non grata* due to his behaviour.[141]

I have already shown why the idea that no one knew about the notes being made is absurd, considering the fact that Bormann on many occasions used them in his daily struggles within the Nazi Party hierarchy. Here we see that James knew full well that these notes were being made and even what Bormann had ordered Heim (and Picker) to record. James does not touch upon how these notes were used by Bormann, however. In her statements it is as if they were simply collected for no other purpose than to be available for the future. As usual, we have to consider that these statements contain not only truths and conscious falsehoods but also unwitting mistakes due to flawed recollection.

Another person who could not understand how Bormann could allow Heim and Picker to make their notes without Hitler's approval was Kuykendall. Would not Bormann have taken a huge risk by doing this, if it were true that Hitler had strictly forbidden notes to be made, she asked Heim in her correspondence with him in the mid-1970s.[142] More importantly, Kuykendall had, when she interviewed Heim in 1973, gotten the distinct impression that Heim had said that Bormann in fact *did* get Hitler's approval. She even told John Toland this in a letter to him in 1976.[143] In fact, she was absolutely sure that this was what Heim had told her at that time, even though Heim later denied it. Kuykendall wrote:

You told me in a recent letter that Hitler did NOT know that he was being recorded, but in our interviews of 1973 you told me that Hitler DID know he was being recorded. My notes of that time read as follows:

"The idea to record was Bormann's; he felt that the Fuehrer's words should be preserved for posterity. He did not ask Hitler's permission at first, but he did inform him later and showed him Heim's notes (in German shorthand.) Hitler was surprised, but he did agree to let the recording continue, as long as it was done unobtrusively. Bormann would always show Hitler the transcripts from Heim's notes; only minor changes were made."

Therefore, if Hitler did NOT know he was being recorded, it seems to me that Bormann was taking a very risky chance of arousing the Fuehrer's wrath by doing something he was not authorized to do. . . . You didn't really clarify this point, in you last letter; Mr. Tiem felt that Hitler DID know he was being recorded, otherwise Bormann couldn't have gotten away with it. The sentence from your last letter, ". . . that what he (Hitler) said was strictly confidential, <u>even if notes were taken</u>," indicates that Hitler DID know he was being recorded, and that he had given his permission.[144] [Emphasis in original.]

As Kuykendall rightly pointed out to Heim, here he had provided not one, but two, clear statements that contradicted his official story and which actually indicated clearly that Hitler knew, or could reasonably suspect, that what he was talking about was being brought down on paper at some point (even if not exactly when he was speaking).

Heim never could give a good explanation for how both Kuykendall and her translator, Elefterios Tiem, could have gotten this matter so mixed up. There is indeed not only one misunderstanding in Kuykendall's notes, assuming that she made a mistake, but several points that she needed to have misheard for Heim to be correct, i.e. that she had made a mistake. Heim simply replied that:

> It is unclear to me how you could have come to this opinion in 1973, **[that I knew the Führer, through MB, became aware of my dictations and approved of them]**, apart from a few posts; Dora Kentmann spoke English, French and Russian and German and she also felt the beating; The error in understanding must therefore have been made by Elefterios, who interpreted before Mme Kentmann was there, his English had gaps [. . .]. I am sorry that because of this you find yourself on the wrong track and being forced to re-think. We – MB and HH – never imagined that our actions could violate AH's intentions; [. . .] What he said was sacred to us: A treasure that had to be protected [. . .]. [145] [Stricken through text has been stricken out in original; bold text in square brackets has been added by hand.]

Heim thus blamed the whole matter on Tiem's poor English. But this does not seem credible, but Kuykendall rather reluctantly admitted that: "O.K., there could have been a wrong translation or a misunderstanding on my part back in 1973" and agreed to change the wording.[146] But Heim also told Kuykendall another thing that in fact indicated knowledge on Hitler's part, namely that:

AH knew that we, as men of political leadership, unlike the generals, attentively listened to all of his words, but he rightly told himself that he – having spoken confidentially – was off the record, even when we put that which we heard down on paper.[147]

This certainly implies that Hitler knew that people were writing his words down afterwards. Interestingly, Heim also was of the opinion that Picker, in having withheld some of his notes from Bormann, had betrayed Bormann's trust.[148] But if that was the case, then why should we not also conclude that Bormann must have betrayed Hitler's trust by not telling *him* that notes were being made? This was a question that Kuykendall, too, continued to stress, even after she had agreed that there might have been a mistranslation or misunderstanding. It is obvious from her letter that she was not satisfied with Heim's tactic of dodging this important question. She also remarked that Heim had, as a reply to another of her many questions, stressed that Hitler was a person who really "took possession of his surroundings" and who was quick to notice things around him; Hitler, Heim had claimed, was "very observant."[149] Gerhard Engel also confirmed this characteristic of Hitler's to Kuykendall.[150]

Kuykendall, perceptively, could not avoid drawing the conclusion from this statement, which so clearly contradicted Heim's assertion that Hitler noticed absolutely nothing of what was going on around him as he spoke at dinner and fired another question at Heim:

> I wonder if Hitler didn't <u>suspect</u> that notes might be taken unobtrusively as he was speaking – with his acute powers of observation and his perception, he surely must have suspected that something was going on "under the table", so to say. COULD YOU COMMENT ON THIS, PLEASE?[151] [Emphasis in original.]

But she never received an answer that could explain the conundrum. In his reply, Heim instead claimed that Hitler, from his central place at the dinner table, could not see what anybody else in the room was doing and, moreover, when he spoke he did not keep eye contact with anyone, but rather stared into the air.[152] Instead of offering clarification, Heim continued to send rather mixed messages about this point:

> It means a lot to me to see You liberated from the idea that MB acted against the Führer's wishes when wanting to record his words without having secured AH's approval. You can be sure: AH, had he learned today what happened, would <u>thank</u> MB.[153]

On the one hand, Heim assured Kuykendall that Hitler knew nothing of what was going on; on the other hand, he assured her that Bormann absolutely did not go against Hitler's wishes when ordering notes to be made.

John Toland, too, had suspected that Hitler perhaps understood that notes were being made, and Heim was forced to issue the same assurance in that case, i.e. that: "if Mr. Toland believes that AH might have seen me write after all, he is mistaken."[154] Heim's version makes no sense at all. He states that Hitler, who sat in the middle of the long dinner table, could only see the persons sitting directly across from him; as if he could not see the people sitting along the table on both sides. Moreover, said Heim, and added a detail he had not included in his story before, he made his notes *under* the table, and in such a calm manner that nobody could have seen him.[155] One is astounded by this statement; no one could see it? Not even the persons sitting next to him? It simply does not hold up to scrutiny.

It is actually quite hard not to get the impression that Heim inadvertently supplied Kuykendall with ever more confirmations of the fact that Hitler must have understood that notes were being made. He also told her:

> Miss Karen, please believe me: There is <u>nothing</u> to suggest that the Führer wished for that which he had shown us, as it were, to be forgotten, because it seemed to us all – as I already said – to be perfect in content and form. [. . .] At the time, the inner circle was still made up of confidants relying upon one another, betrayal was yet unknown; and if the notes, as intended, rested in the hands of MB as the Head of the Party Chancellery – i.e. with the Führer's <u>deputy</u> – <u>there was</u> no danger of it being profaned: the recorded, we were allowed to tell ourselves, will later come to be of great importance for historical research.[156] [Emphasis in original.]

With the last words Heim almost quotes the Bormann facsimile which had appeared in *Table Talk* (and later would appear in *Monologe*). The language here is instructive; Heim used words usually reserved for religious texts when he said that there was no risk of Hitler's words being "profaned" in the hands of Bormann or the other faithful. Heim continued his statement of elation as if he was preaching the Gospel, stating that the conversations gave Hitler what he needed, namely relaxation; it gave the listeners a unique experience; and it gave the world a source that was an inexhaustible treasure trove.[157] None of this really strengthens Heim's claim that Hitler did not know about him making these notes. Rather, the opposite feeling is generated by these infatuated ruminations.

In fact, it seems more likely that Heim unintentionally had said a bit too much in Kuykendall's interviews (they had met three times in 1973)[158] with him, and he later had to retract what did not fit his official story. It is not at all unusual that people say too much in interviews; in fact, a lot of investigative journalism is based on this very tendency. It is first in hindsight that people realize that they have said something that they were not supposed to. This "risk" certainly increases if the interviewee likes the interviewer, which was very much the case here. Heim and Kuykendall found each other and became good friends. Their correspondence testifies to this; in 1974 Heim sent her a painting by Karl Leipold, one of Hitler's favorite artists, that she had framed, and on another occasion, in 1977, he sent her a recording of a Bach piece played by a friend of his. Kuykendall was obviously very pleased to receive these gifts from her friend.[159]

There is actually more evidence that supports this conclusion. First, Kuykendall had taped her interviews with Heim, so she should have been able to actually check what he had said, unless this particular statement had not been taped.[160] Second, it also turns out that Heim on other occasions in his interviews had said things that he, when he got to see his own words on paper, wanted to retract. Kuykendall had sent Heim a questionnaire based on matters that Heim had said in the interviews and that she wanted to follow up on. In several instances Heim had then stricken out phrases that Kuykendall claimed that he had himself used on the tape recording. Kuykendall told Heim that she would certainly not use these phrases if Heim did not want her to, but she felt it was very odd of Heim to now retract his earlier statements.[161] Heim did not resent Kuykendall for putting these questions to him. On the contrary, he thanked her for her "lovely letter" (he even wrote this letter in English) and stated that he could not remember what he had told her, but in response he stated: "I think, I would concede" to having said the things that Kuykendall claimed.[162]

The question that must be answered, however, is: why would Heim insist on this point if it were not true? The answer, I believe, can be found in the fact that Heim was a devout Hitler worshiper all his life. He had sworn loyalty to Hitler, and he would never "betray" his idol. Hitler could apparently, in Heim's eyes, do nothing wrong. He claimed that he had once heard Hitler curse his "fate" in a lapse of depression, complaining that he was loved by half the world and hated by the other half. Then he invents a new quote and puts the following words in Hitler's mouth: "why did not Heaven let me become an architect!" In another one of his many exaggerations, Heim at the same time claimed that no one had looked forward to peace as much as Hitler.[163] Heim's responses to one of Kuykendall's questionnaires are also extremely revealing and give us many clear clues as to how to understand his repetition of his mantra. To the question of whether there was anything in Hitler's character that he especially disliked, Heim said: "Nothing at all." He also insisted that Hitler "was a very brave man" and a "genius"; Heim considered Hitler to be outstanding in *all* intellectual fields. Hitler's staff all "revered him", according to Heim, who also confessed to having felt "inspired" by Hitler ever since he first heard him speak in 1920, and he "always had the feeling that he was a superhuman being above all others."[164] Once again we see this sacral language being used by Heim when speaking about his former boss.

But what possible motive could Ilse James have to further the myth that Hitler was unknowingly speaking freely in the table conversations? Well, her motivation could easily be the same as Heim's. The fact that Hitler in them does not really mention anything having to do with the persecution of the Jews and the Holocaust should provide us with a clue. James was, as were all the secretaries in the FHQ, basically an apologist who had no interest whatsoever in defaming Hitler. The reason for this was simple: anything bad that they divulged about Hitler would also make themselves look bad. If they knew what was going on, why on earth did they then stay true to Hitler to the very end? The safest strategy then became not to admit to any knowledge of the atrocities committed by their bosses Hitler and Bormann. Another fact in this particular case was that James had had her character deeply questioned by the American James P. O'Donnell in his book *The Bunker: The History of the Reich Chancellery Group* from 1978. O'Donnell claimed that James (then Krüger), among other things, had smuggled out a pouch of diamonds for the SS Chief Wilhelm Mohnke. She had since the end of the war consistently refused to speak about what happened during the last days in the Berlin bunker.[165] This was information that James, of course, characterized as a "completely made up and defaming characterization."[166] This seems to me to be ample reason for James to continue this fairy tale.

When did Genoud actually acquire the table talk manuscript?

This question might seem like it ought to have a very straightforward answer, but it turns out that it does not. Genoud's account of how and when he came to possess the table talk documents did not remain consistent over time and space. Several versions of events have been presented by Genoud and various researchers over the years. Willi Winkler states that Genoud paid 9,000 Swiss francs for the Bormann documents; lets on that the mysterious Italian government official may have been a man by the name of Rodolfo Siviero, but then again, maybe not; and refers to Theodor Schmitz. Schmitz could not remember if Genoud came to Italy in 1950 or in 1948, writes Winkler, but Genoud supposedly acquired the table talk manuscript through an Italian called Edilio Rusconi. Winkler presents no source for when Genoud got hold of the manuscript that is independent of the latter. Most of it is based on what Péan writes in his biography of Genoud and on an article in the *Kölner Stadt-Anzeiger* from 22 June 1961.[167] The latter article was also published in the *Süddeutsche Zeitung* the next day, i.e. 23 June, a piece that Schramm mentions in his preface to *Tischgespräche*. They must have the same source because the articles are basically identical.[168] The source is most likely Genoud who had prepared a statement in Italian on 23 March 1961 where he described how he got hold of the Bormann and Hitler documents.[169]

In an article in the *Wiener Library Bulletin* (sometime around 1954) Trevor-Roper wrote that "on acquiring physical possession of the papers . . . M. Genoud evidently made an agreement with Frau Bormann and with the trustee appointed by the Land Government of Bavaria to administer the affairs of the Bormann children." At the same time, he repeats the story about how Genoud had only just gotten his hand on the table talk manuscript when Picker published his book.[170] How he could have made a deal with Gerda Bormann, who died in 1946, is unclear. Trevor-Roper does not give us a source for his statement, nor does he seem to have reflected on this obvious mismatch in timelines.

According to the legend, which Winkler also propagates, the table talk documents came to Italy in one of the 27 wooden chests containing a lot of papers that Bormann wanted to save from the crumbling Third Reich. These supposedly travelled along with the families of the top Nazis, among them Gerda Bormann and eight of their nine children, into Italy during the spring of 1945. This route was called *Übersee Süd* (Oversea South) and referred to the plan of in the end shipping the fugitives out overseas to safety in South America. Winkler states that the documents were part of these documents, but he does not, in fact, present any evidence to back this statement up. The reference that he gives has to do with some of Hitler's aquarelle paintings. In addition, Winkler says that the chests were transported from Obersalzberg, where Bormann's family was living at the time.[171] There is one source that contains this information, however, and Winkler refers to it on another occasion but *not* to support this statement. In an article in *Der Spiegel* from early 1953 it is said that Wilma Schaub, the wife of one Hitler's personal adjutant Julius Schaub, remembered a call from von Hummel, Bormann's chief of staff, asking if she had something important in the house to bring for the evacuation over the Alps and into Italy. According to her, in one of the chests were also the table talk documents, which was brought to and stored in, a bunker outside the city of Bozen in northern Italy.[172] It is unclear, however, how Wilma Schaub knew what was in the chests. Heim was convinced that none of the copies in Munich had survived the war and ruled out the possibility that any of them had found their way into Italy via the "Übersee" route, but he did not say anything about Bormann's original.[173]

According to Péan, Genoud had just put the contract that gave him the rights to Bormann's papers in his pocket in the summer of 1951 when he stumbled across an article in the Italian newspaper *Corriere della Sera*, which stated that *Tischgespräche* was about to be published in Germany by the publisher Athenäum. In this version, Genoud thought that Rusconi had sold two versions of the manuscript. Blinded by rage, he supposedly wrote to a friend in Germany and asked him to send a copy of *Tischgespräche*. What happens next cannot be discerned from Péan's story, but after having read the book Genoud met with the CEO of Athenäum, Dr Junker, in order to come to an "agreement", but the publisher would have none of that and refused to make any kind of deal with the Swiss. Junker had, after all, IfZ in Munich behind him and was thus convinced that he was in the right.[174] This story has to be false, because when Genoud wrote to the IfZ on 29 July he asked them for two copies of Picker's book.

There are several things to notice here: 1) Genoud here says that Rusconi sold him the table talk manuscript, while he otherwise states that he only bought the Bormann letters from Rusconi; and 2) this story just seems a little bit too good to be true, a bit too much like a movie plot perhaps, especially with the part about having put the contract in his pocket when reading about Picker's book. Surely, such coincidences have happened, but is it really the case here? No, I am not convinced. It seems to be put together after the fact. Another reason to doubt the story is that the whole timeline seems to be built on Genoud's own information. Unfortunately, it is not clear on what kind of sources Péan bases his version of events on, since his book lacks proper references. But I received a statement written by Genoud on 7 May 1954 from his lawyer in which the whole thing is detailed.[175] It could be that Péan has based his version on something similar, if not in fact the same document, in which case we are back at square one, with no independent evidence to prove when Genoud bought the table talk manuscript.

As we have seen, the table talk documents were mentioned for the first time by Genoud himself in a letter to Buchheim of the IfZ on 29 July 1951 (see the beginning of this chapter). It is true that Genoud did not mention the table talk manuscript in his initial correspondence with the IfZ in late May that year, but are we really to believe that Genoud had acquired these documents between his first contact with the IfZ in May and 29 July? Could it be that Genoud knew about, and perhaps even had seen and bought the table talk documents already, by 1948? Genoud himself is clear on this point. He even states in writing that he did not hear about the existence of Hitler's table talk until 26 January 1950 (he admits to having heard about the existence of Bormann's letter exchange with his wife already in June 1948 though).[176] But do we have some solid evidence that can show that Genoud also knew about the existence of table talk documents in 1948?

Yes, in fact we do. The evidence is provided offhandedly by Genoud himself in an interview with him made by the British journalist Gitta Sereny and published in the British newspaper *The Observer* in 1996. Sereny quotes Genoud as stating the following: "I found out in 1948 that 'Table Talk' still existed . . . and that's what I wanted most of all."[177] Could Sereny have confused these documents with the Bormann letters? No, because the quote continues to say: "But I also heard of Bormann's letters to his wife."[178] This interview, at which time Genoud might have made a *faux pas*, proves that Genoud was lying about the time that he first heard about their existence. It is even worse since the wording, i.e. *still* existed, suggests that Genoud had heard that such notes had been produced even prior to that time and that he only discovered they *still* existed in 1948.[179] It could be mentioned here that Winkler refers to this article in his book, but without commenting on this piece of information.[180] *The Observer* had already in 1992 stated in an article, then in connection with the outrage concerning *The Daily Mail*'s publication of extracts from the recently recovered complete Goebbels diaries, that Genoud had "acquired control over the Nazi leaders' literary estates from their families in 1947."[181] If this is true, then Genoud acquired these rights much earlier than he later stated.

While Winkler states that Genoud came to Italy at some point in either 1948 or 1950, Péan states that he met Schmitz in 1950. Péan also claims that Genoud got wind of Bormann's correspondence with his wife in June 1948, just as Genoud told Sereny. From the text it is not completely evident what Péan based this on, i.e. whether it was either letters or perhaps an interview with Genoud.[182] It is, of course, very possible that Genoud did hear about the Bormann letters in 1948 and that he purchased them, but *only* the Bormann letters, in January 1950. That part of the story could thus be true. Genoud then put the lie about being offered the table talk documents at the same time into this real event. Indeed, it might be that what Genoud purchased in Italy in the summer of 1951 was, as an article in *Rheinischer Merkur* stated in July 1992, simply the right to Bormann's literary estate.[183] This, too, falls neatly into place with the information that Genoud got hold of the material earlier than 1951.

But there is even better confirmation that even 1948 may be too late a point for his acquiring of the table talk manuscript. The source in question is an article in

Der Spiegel from 1952, i.e. pretty close to the events described. It contains a story about Genoud and the recent publication of his *Libres propos* and it says, based on Genoud himself, that "in 1947 Genoud finally came into possession of the files." Since then they had been lying in a bank deposit box in a Swiss bank. The article proves that Genoud was lying when he stated that he bought the table talk manuscript in Italy in mid-1951, and the story about him just having put the contract in his pocket when he read about the publication of Picker's book is thus also a forgery. As it turns out, Genoud had already signed the contract with the French publisher Flammarion, in the summer of 1951, "a few weeks" before he found out about the publication of Picker's book.[184]

Why would Genoud lie about this? Well, one possible reason could be that he wanted to hide a criminal past. Interestingly, in the records of the German Federal Ministry of Justice (*Bundesministerium der Justiz*) there is an assertion that a U.S. military court in Frankfurt am Main (which apparently was Genoud's hometown for a while) convicted Genoud for the crime of "Aryanizing Jewish fortunes" in 1946.[185] This is a part of Genoud's life that has previously remained unknown despite the many biographies and articles written about him. Nobody places him in Germany so soon after the war, and certainly not Genoud himself. It is, however, easy to understand why Genoud would perhaps want to keep silent about it.

Genoud apparently stated the same time for his acquisition of the manuscript during the trial against Picker's publisher in 1952. According to *Der Spiegel*, Genoud told the court he got it "two years after the end of the war" (*zwei Jahre nach Kriegsende*), i.e. in 1947, and also disclosed that he had not bought it in Italy but had acquired it "in Bavaria in Martin Bormann's archive."[186] Note, however, that the same article also contains two obviously incorrect statements, namely that both Heim and Picker were stenographers and that Genoud had published *Libres propos* already in June 1951.[187] This means that the information about when and where he got the documents could be mistaken as well. Karl Laske, too, says that Genoud got his hands on a part of Bormann's archive at this point, although he is unclear as to what part it actually was.[188] I have found yet another article from 1952 that states that the original manuscript was "a thick stack of documents with a lot of marginal notes by Martin Bormann"[189] that had been lying:

> for several years in the vaults of various Swiss banks. That, at any rate, is what the director of the publishing house Flammarion claims. And so too claims the man who supplied him with the transcript of this alleged original manuscript: Monsieur François Genoud, a Swiss citizen.[190]

What is interesting is that the article says that what Genoud had was *not* the "supposed" original itself, but a transcript of it. Since the article was published in 1952 and speaks of the manuscript having laid in various bank deposit boxes for "a few years", it means that Genoud cannot have bought the manuscript only one year before this point. The CEO of Flammarion must obviously have been told this information by Genoud himself, so this proves that Genoud claimed to have gotten the table talk manuscript several years before 1951.

Yet another article from a French newspaper proves that Genoud's later dating of when he got his hands on the table monologues is false. The journalist George Maranz tells the story of the trial in Düsseldorf and writes about how he had met Genoud for the first time at the trial of the German General Hermann-Bernhard Ramcke in Paris in 1951. According to Maranz, Genoud had at that time offered to show him photocopies of Martin Bormann's correspondence with his wife. Genoud told the French journalist that he could not divulge exactly how he had gotten his hands on *the entire* Bormann archive ("la totalité des archives de Bormann"), but he ensured that he had secured the right to use this material as he saw fit. At the time, however, Maranz was unable to get the newspapers he was working for interested in this material and so the matter came to nothing. During their second meeting (which Maranz unfortunately does not date, but it could be during the Düsseldorf trial) Genoud told him that the documents had been brought to Italy by Mrs. Bormann at the end of the war and that "these papers came into my possession" shortly thereafter, a collection of documents that, according to Genoud himself, contained the complete table monologues from July 1941 to November 1944.[191] Ramcke's trial had ended already in March 1951, so if Genoud already had all the Bormann material by then, he must have purchased it earlier than in June that same year. That Genoud got his manuscript in 1947 must hence now be considered a proven fact.

It turns out that Genoud's lawyer, Cordula Schacht, thought that Genoud in fact got hold of the manuscript in Bavaria. In an email reply to Werner Jochmann's daughter, Renate Miron, in late September 2016 she stated the following:

> Genoud received the material of the Hitler talks from a certain Ministry official Heim in Munich. I think his name was Alfons Heim. He had in turn temporarily participated in Hitler's table rounds and subsequently recorded the speeches. I don't possess these documents. To my knowledge, the children of Genoud do not either.[192]

This is quite remarkable, and it goes completely against everything that Heim ever said about this matter (who consistently denied ever having kept any of his notes). This does not mean that we can immediately dismiss Schacht's information, however. While Schacht obviously remembers Heim's first name wrong, she does get the other details regarding the manuscript history right, especially the part about the notes having been written down after the conversations that they record. We must also assume that, since she knew Genoud well, Genoud would have told her about how he got hold of the table talk manuscript many times. Heim lived in Munich, and Péan tells us that Genoud spent a lot of time in Munich after the war and that he there became acquainted with (among many other old Nazis) none other than Heim.[193] What we don't know is when they first got to know each other. As always when it comes to second-hand witnesses and hearsay, it is impossible, absent corroborating independent evidence, to be sure that what is reported is true.

But why should we trust Genoud in this case, when he says he got the manuscript in 1947, but not when he says he got hold of them in 1951? I believe that the two really strong pieces of evidence that make us justifiable in choosing 1947 as the year for when Genoud laid his hands on the manuscript are:

1) The fact that this is what Genoud had told his publisher Flammarion (there was no reason for Genoud to tell the publisher that the manuscript had been lying for a few years if that was not the case).
2) The fact that this was the year apparently stated in court (it is hard to see what Genoud would gain by stating this year rather than a later one if 1947 was not true).

We can thus safely say, given the other evidence already cited, that Genoud laid his hands also on the manuscript, i.e. the text that was the basis for *Libres propos* and *Table Talk*, and later *Monologe*, in 1947.

However, there is yet other information that pertains to this question that we need to deal with. In an article in the German newspaper *Die Zeit* we find the astonishing statement that Genoud knew Bormann's secretary – in reality his chief of staff (*Stabsleiter*) – Helmut von Hummel, the man who Bormann had allegedly ordered to transport Heim's notes over the Alps at the end of the war. It says that von Hummel "relying on good long-distance connections with Genoud" managed the not-so-easy task of transporting all the chests with papers and whatnot. Furthermore, von Hummel supposedly "relieved" the entourage of one of the chests "on the way", and the article says that at that time "an old contact man of Hummel's appeared at the right moment: François Genoud." It was not known why Genoud was there or whom he was working for.[194]

Where this information comes from is not certain because the article does not refer to the source for this. The author does mention Karl Laske's and Péan's biographies, but this cannot be found in Péan's book. So, what about this information? Is it plausible? Let us first state for the record that Péan is not able to give a definite location for Genoud during the final months of the war. Genoud worked for the International Red Cross in Belgium, tending to families who had lost their homes in the bombing campaigns, and Péan says that Genoud was jumping across the borders repeatedly but does not specify what borders he is talking about.[195] Winkler also reports, based on a memorandum by the GDR secret police *Stasi* from an interview with Schmitz, that Schmitz recalled that when he met Genoud the first time the Swiss drove a car with French plates and introduced himself as a representative of the Red Cross.[196] Genoud began his service for the Red Cross on 13 March 1945, although it is unknown when he left.[197] The *Stasi* report in fact says nothing at all about the Red Cross; however, it is correct that Schmitz stated that Genoud both times he met him (not just the first, as Winkler claims) drove a car with French plates.[198]

Péan never mentions von Hummel in his book. Are we to believe that Péan missed this vital piece of information, i.e. that Genoud was in contact with Bormann's secretary during the war? There are some hints as to where this information could come from, though. The *Die Zeit* article also brings up the interviews that *Stasi* made with Schmitz. Could that be the source of this information? Winkler refers to this article, written by Hansjakob Stehle, but he does not comment upon this information. Winkler claims that Schmitz said that Siviero had stolen the chests containing the Bormann papers, but Stehle's article says nothing of the sort.[199] Stehle states that the Bormann papers were already gone when Schmitz came into the picture and that Genoud showed up in 1948 to negotiate for the right to publish them – according to Stehle, Schmitz said that Genoud by then already had *both* Bormann's correspondence and the table talk manuscript. Genoud is to have claimed that he had acquired the missing Bormann archive from an Italian source.[200] Jochmann later repeated this in *Monologe*, saying that after the German capitulation "an Italian Government official took possession of the whole content and sold it to François Genoud"[201] Even though Winkler sits on this source he still writes that Genoud got hold of the Bormann papers through Schmitz, and only in passing mentions the possibility, based on Stehle, that someone in Bormann's entourage may have been acquainted with Genoud.[202] The information in Stehle's article would make sense to a large degree considering that we now have established that Genoud got hold of the Bormann documents already in 1947.

Theodore Schmitz: Catholic priest and *Stasi* agent

Another very important fact that Winkler does not let the reader know is that Schmitz was working as an informant, or so-called *Inoffizielle Mitarbeiter* (IM), for *Stasi* in the GDR. More exactly, Schmitz was referred to as an IMF, which during the period 1968 to 1979 stood for Unofficial Employee of the Internal Defence with Enemy Connections in the Operational Area (*Inoffizielle Mitarbeiter der inneren Abwehr mit Feindverbindungen zum Operationsgebiet*). Schmitz, called "Theo" by his handlers, was recruited on 21 November 1968, declared that he was prepared to cooperate fully, and the operation was given the code name "Hase" by *Stasi*.[203] IMF was the highest level of informant according to the MfS regulations from January 1968. Dieter Grande and Bernd Schäfer have noted that one should be careful not to make too much out of the label "IM" because this could mean a lot of different things. The MfS was a pragmatic organization, they say, and did not really care whether those people that it considered to be IM were actually formally, and knowingly, working as informants for the MfS. Many of the IMs within the Church were unwittingly considered to be IM by the MfS.[204]

However, not everyone seems to share this view of the IMs. Jens Gieseke writes that the IM category included only people that had agreed, most often in writing, to work covertly and to conspire with the MfS. Moreover, the category of IM implied a rather close relationship between the IMs and the MfS agents that ran

them, writes Gieseke. In 1968 the MfS had about 100,000 IMs in active operation. Interestingly, when Gieseke lists the various types of IMs that the MfS had,
he does not mention the IMF category. He does mention a category called FIM,
i.e. *Führungs*-IM, which was a smaller group of IMs that ran their own IMs.[205] Perhaps, then, Schäfer and Grande are being a bit too generous to the IMs within the
Church that they write about in their book. No matter what category Schmitz was
actually in (IMF or FIM), however, he was clearly not an unwitting IM. From the
very first conversation between him and the MfS, he agreed to provide *Stasi* with
information about his and the Church's activities.[206]

From the very beginning Schmitz's role as guardian for the Bormann children
was a topic of the conversation, and Schmitz provided the *Stasi* with photographs
and letters exchanged with the children (as well as other related materials). Genoud
was mentioned by Schmitz as a person that the *Stasi* might be interested in already
during the second interview with him on 29 October 1968, although the table
talks themselves seem to have been of little interest to *Stasi*. Instead the focus was
on the Bormann letters.[207] Perhaps this was because at the time there were rumours
going around that Martin Bormann had managed to escape Berlin and lived in hiding somewhere. On 16 January 1969 Schmitz stated to his handlers that he had met
Genoud for the first time in 1952 when Genoud was preparing the publication of
what would become *The Bormann Letters*.[208] However, during the next interview
on 12 March 1969 Schmitz said that he had in fact met Genoud already in 1948,
and the meeting in 1952 was actually their second one. Moreover, the second
meeting supposedly took place in Rome, while Schmitz was there together with
the Berliner bishop (Wilhelm) Weskamm (1891–1956) (The *Stasi* records spell the
bishop's name "Weskamp", which is wrong.) At that time Genoud told Schmitz
that he had managed to get the famous British historian Trevor-Roper to write
a preface to the planned Bormann letter publication. According to the report,
Schmitz told his handlers that when they met in Rome Genoud had told him that
he had in fact met Trevor-Roper already in the spring of 1945 while the latter was
working as an officer for British Military Intelligence.[209] Genoud may very well
have said something along these lines to Schmitz back in 1952, but there is no
reason to think that it has anything to do with the truth. Certainly, Trevor-Roper
never mentioned anything about this meeting, and there is no reason for why he
should not have if it had been true.

Schmitz seems to simply have forgotten about the 1948 meeting the first time
around, because he could gain nothing by lying about this. Schmitz's story does
seem to hold up to scrutiny. It may be that Genoud secured the right to the
Bormann *Nachlaß* sometime after 1952, because in 1954 Schmitz sent a letter to
Genoud in which he attested to the fact that Genoud had the right to "safeguard" Bormann's archive on behalf of the heirs, and among this material, wrote
Schmitz, "are, in particular, documents and other items that were in the chests
that Mrs. Bormann sent to South Tirol for safekeeping in April 1945."[210] Schmitz's
statement that Genoud had managed to recruit Trevor-Roper to write the preface

to *The Bormann Letters* in 1952, even though they were not published until 1954, also checks out. In November 1952 Trevor-Roper sent a transcript of the Bormann letters, which had been provided to him by Genoud, to Weidenfeld. Included in the letter was an essay on the letters written by Genoud. Trevor-Roper had apparently met up with Genoud in Paris, at which point the latter had given him the documents in question.[211]

In fact, we have definitive proof that Schmitz had met Genoud before 1952 because on 1 November 1951 Mau wrote to Ritter about his recent meeting with Schmitz in Berlin. Schmitz then confirmed that Genoud had acquired the right to publish Bormann's papers.[212] If we assume that Schmitz agreed to sign over the publication rights to Genoud in 1948, then the meeting in Rome in 1952 may have been a very informal one where Genoud simply informed Schmitz about the progress of the publication of the letters. In fact, Schmitz told the *Stasi* that in 1952, during a stay in Rome, he had sent Genoud a telegram in which he provided his address and telephone number in Rome. Genoud had then called Schmitz and said that he looked forward to meeting Schmitz again. Genoud had told him that he was very busy at the moment and could not come to Rome to meet Schmitz this time around but said that he would come the next time Schmitz was in Rome. According to Schmitz, 1952 was also the year when he received a transcript of the German text in the Bormann letters from Genoud; these transcripts he had then given to his lawyer in West Berlin, and the *Stasi* received copies of these transcripts in early 1969.[213]

In the debriefings with his *Stasi* handlers Schmitz also tells a story about how the Bormann documents were transported southward that is slightly different from the version that has so far been spread in the literature. This fact may indeed be the best indication of it being closer to the truth of the matter. Schmitz claimed that Genoud had not been willing to answer his questions as to how he came to possess the documents, but stated that it was known to him, apparently through his interactions with Gerda Bormann, that at least the letters, as well as other valuable items between Martin and Gerda Bormann, had been in a chest that Gerda Bormann had left for safekeeping with the *Gauleiter* of Tirol, Hofer, in Innsbruck. Before Gerda Bormann passed away she had asked Schmitz to become the guardian of her children and had apparently told him about the valuable documents in the chests left with Hofer so that Schmitz could, if necessary, use these in order to make sure that the children were taken care of financially. Schmitz had, he stated, asked Genoud about the whereabouts of this chest, but the Swiss had claimed that he did not know.[214]

Schmitz had met several times a week with Gerda Bormann between 20 January and 22 March 1946. By March 1969 Schmitz also stated that the originals of the Bormann letters and the rest of Bormann's personal archive lay in a safe deposit box in a bank in Switzerland; or at least Genoud had said as much to him. Schmitz also said that Gerda Bormann had told him that she had left five chests with Hofer in Innsbruck. The letters, as well as the other documents, were transported from

Martin Bormann at the FHQ to his wife in the Obersalzberg by a special courier, the *SS-Obersturmsbannführer* Franz Spögler. According to the *Stasi* files, Spögler had been a part of the group led by famous *Waffen-SS Obersturmbannführer* Otto Skorzeny (famous for having freed Mussolini from his captors in 1943) and had been serving as a bodyguard for Mussolini's girlfriend, Clara Petacci. After the war Spögler became the manager of a hotel (*Gasthof Spögler*) in the town of Longomoso (Klobenstein-Ritten) in Bozen, Italy.[215]

Spögler's name has never before come up in this context, but the matter is somewhat complicated by the fact that, according to Italian, there were apparently two Franz Spöglers who were both natives of Longomoso. The Franz Spögler who served in Skorzeny's unit and was a bodyguard for Petacci (1915–1989), and one (b. 1927) who was drafted in October 1944 and served in the 31st *SS-Freiwilligen-Grenadier-Division* and who is a local politician in Longomoso. The former was, again according to the Italian wiki page, an owner of a hotel when he joined the SS as a volunteer in September 1939.[216] A thread on a German *Wehrmacht* online forum started by what appears to be a grandchild of the politician Franz Spögler also makes it evident that the two Spöglers were not related.[217] We thus have ample reason to assume that the Spögler referred to by Schmitz and the one who owned the *Gasthof Spögler* in Longomoso are the same person.

Winkler says that he believes that Stehle's statement about Genoud's contacts with von Hummel is nothing but a rumour.[218] However, Stehle also says that a spy that we know was close to Genoud, by the name of Paul Dickopf, had as one of his main tasks was forwarding information to Bormann's party headquarters in Munich.[219] Since we know that Genoud knew Dickopf, it is not unreasonable to assume that Dickopf put Genoud into contact with someone in Bormann's entourage, perhaps von Hummel. It is also worth noting that Stehle was a trained historian and not a journalist. Moreover, a document from the Swiss Secret Police in 1955 states that Genoud was suspected of having been spying for Nazi Germany during the war, from around April 1940 onwards. The Swiss Secret Police had wiretapped his phone and surveyed his mail, but this had not yielded any confirmation of these suspicions.[220] Martin Bormann, the son of Martin and Gerda Bormann, commented on Stehle's article in several letters to the publisher in the summer of 1997. It does not seem as if he had much criticism regarding the details, and there is perhaps no reason to assume that he knew anything about it. He had told Stehle over the phone that he had no information about Genoud because he had never met him.[221] He criticized Stehle for not giving Schmitz the benefit of the doubt and for not assuming that he had helped the children out of good intentions only.[222] Stehle also got the year for when Bormann's siblings returned to Germany wrong. But Stehle also got things right. Bormann says that it was correct that Genoud had appeared at a baptizing that Schmitz performed in Lübeck and presented him with two photos of the Bormann children taken from his trove of documents.[223] Schmitz stated that he would gladly pass these comments on to Stehle.[224] Bormann later told him that Stehle never replied.[225]

Bormann also commented upon another of Stehle's articles called "Martin Bormann: Stalin's Mann in Berlin?" published in *Die Zeit*. The article suggested that Martin Bormann was still alive and living in the Soviet Union. This was not a new idea, said Bormann. The first time it had appeared was in 1949–1950 when he was at a boarding school in Ingolstadt in Canisius-Konvikt, and it had given him great angst. He knew his father's attitude towards Christianity and was now afraid that he, as a Christian and thus a "traitor of National Socialism", must now be on his father's "killing list." The possibility that his father was now living in the Soviet Union, and therefore had a real chance of reaching him, made him afraid. At the time, he took his bike and went to see his uncle, Albert Bormann, who was then living in a work camp by the Rebdorft monastery in Eichstätt. According to his recollection, Albert Bormann calmed him by saying: "Don't let yourself go crazy. That has a totally different context. I can guarantee you that your father never thought like that."[226] Note that Martin Bormann Jr. was wrong about his father having considered Christians to be traitors of National Socialism. There were many Nazis who considered themselves Christian, and Bormann does not appear to have considered them traitors.[227]

The *Der Spiegel* articles show that Genoud constantly changes the story about how the notes came about. Any questions about where the table talk documents come from are carefully avoided by Genoud, who at this early stage does not seem to be willing to share any details regarding this part of its history. There is no mentioning of Gerda Bormann bringing the manuscript to Italy, nothing about buying the manuscript from an Italian government employee, nothing like that at all. Instead Genoud shares with the journalist that Hitler had given Bormann permission to capture his words for posterity. The story is full of wonderful details that Genoud reasonably cannot have had any clue about. For example, Bormann installed a man at the end of the dinner table each day who sat ready, with sharpened pencil, to jot down the Führer's every word. Picker and Heim are mentioned by name – strangely enough Picker is said to have been the first to take notes only to be replaced by Heim – and Genoud apparently also stated that from September 1942 on an unknown employee of Bormann continued to take notes. Then we are told that Bormann, all through this time, worked with the notes on a daily basis; according to Genoud, Bormann made a great number of footnotes to the text and clearly noted when Hitler was being earnest or when he was ironic. Genoud, continuing to spin his web of deceit, decorates his story with yet more details. In November 1944, he says, the manuscript and some other papers from the party headquarters started to wander off. At first, Gerda Bormann had got them and kept them "in a safe place." While on a temporary visit in Milan, Italy, a few weeks after he had signed the contract with Flammarion in Paris, he allegedly read some very disturbing news in *Corriere della Sera*, namely that the *Tischgespräche* had been published in Germany.[228]

Note that this is the third story regarding when he found out about Picker's book that Genoud gives. It is now clear that what Genoud writes in the document entitled "Note sur l'affaire des aquarelle" regarding the manuscript is a clever lie (perhaps some of it is true, but it is almost impossible to entangle eventual truths from within all the lies). Genoud could, however, be telling us the truth when he says he got the Bormann letters from Rusconi and the table talk manuscript from Siviero. The information about these persons is a little bit too detailed for it to be totally made up, it seems, and this separation is supported by independent sources. However, *the timing* of the acquisition is a whole different matter. Siviero and Rusconi are the likely sources of these documents. One must then assume that it is these two Italians that Genoud is referring to in his introduction to *The Bormann Letters* when he says he "received" the documents "directly from the people who saved them."[229] As it turns out, Rusconi and Siviero knew each other and may even have worked together.

Rudolfo Siviero (the "007 of art") and Edilio Rusconi: the sources of Genoud's documents?

The Italian stated to have sold the table talk documents to Genoud, Rudolfo Siviero, was a dubious character. He was a failed poet and aspiring autodidactic art historian who had been a committed fascist during Mussolini's time in power, but he had joined the resistance when Germany occupied Italy in 1943 (while this may sound like an odd turn, it really was not – it was perfectly natural for an ultra-nationalist to oppose foreign occupation). According to the curator of Museo Casa Rodolfo Siviero in Florence, Attilio Tori, Siviero sympathized strongly with Mussolini's nationalist Fascist movement but was not an anti-Semite. Having been recruited by the Italian Secret Service in the mid-1930s, Siviero was sent to Ehrfurt in Germany in September 1937 to report on the anti-Semitic Congress arranged there by the Hitler regime. Siviero acted under the cover of being a representative of an Italian university student organization, even though he had never in fact attended university. He apparently came to spend a lot of time in Erfurt and Berlin, until he for some unknown reason had to leave Germany in 1938. Tori speculates that it may have been because the Germans had found out that he was working for the Italian Secret Service. Mussolini's decision to erect racial laws similar to those in Germany was a big disappointment to Siviero, states Tori, but he continued to be loyal to the regime until the Allied invasion of Italy in 1943. Siviero remained with the Fascist Secret Service but came to play a double game and established contacts with both the resistance and the British forces in Italy. Eventually, however, his scheme was discovered, and he was arrested and imprisoned. He was saved by a high-ranking officer in the Secret Service, who was also acting as a double agent, and could flee to the southern Allied-occupied part of the country towards the end of the war, after having been set free. During this time, he established a lot of contacts that allowed him to make the transition to peacetime smoothly.[230]

Siviero was made minister plenipotentiary in the Italian government in 1946, an honorary position that he received for his work in the Italian resistance. As such he worked for a long time with recovering stolen artwork to Italy, an activity that gave him the nickname "the 007 of art." In 1984 there was an art show in Palazzo Vecchio in Florence and on display were a number of water colour paintings by Hitler that Siviero allegedly had received from Bormann's wife in 1946. Siviero had then taken the paintings to Florence with the idea of putting them on display there, although it apparently took until the 1980s for that to actually happen.[231] Rusconi, who later became a famous publisher and movie director in Italy, apparently worked under Siviero, so there is a solid connection between these two characters.[232] This is also the one fact that makes it almost certain that Genoud was telling the truth on this issue. However, the fact that Siviero was a famous person in the early 1950s, precisely for having recovered stolen art works to Italy, may have made him the perfect patsy for Genoud.[233] But there is independent evidence that Siviero used his position in order to get his hands on paintings, which he then sold illegally, for considerable amounts of money.[234]

Dr August Priesack, an old Nazi and expert on Hitler paintings, has even accused Siviero of stealing the 20 paintings in his possession. Siviero apparently never spoke about the Hitler paintings, or how he got hold of them, during his lifetime. His last will and testament did not mention them, even though the assistant director of Casa Museo Rudolfo Siviero in the 1980s, Emma Micheletti, claimed that the paintings had in fact been a "gift" donated to the museum by Siviero. The only person he confided in seems to have been his sister, Imelda Siviero, who took the details regarding this affair to her grave.[235] The fact that Priesack claims this is certainly interesting, considering that Winkler has Schmitz saying the same. It is not at all improbable that this might actually be true. If we assume that Schmitz got this information from Gerda Bormann, then it is even more reasonable to assume it is correct. It certainly sounds more plausible than the idea that Bormann's wife would simply give the paintings, as well as the table talk documents one would have to assume, to a man who has no known connection to her whatsoever. According to Tori, there is no reason to think that Siviero would *not* have stolen this material if he had had the opportunity to do so. From his days in the Secret Service, Siviero was used to doing things in a morally questionable manner. He was a man of action and was good at getting things done, according to Tori.[236]

By the time Siviero formally began his work for the Italian Ministry of Foreign Affairs in April 1946 Gerda Bormann was already dead, and while it is possible that Siviero might have met her in Merano before this point, it seems less likely than the hypothesis that Sivero got his hands on the material in some other, perhaps illegal, way. Furthermore, the correspondence from this time that has been preserved in Siviero's archive at Museo Casa Rodolfo Siviero in Florence shows officials in Bolzano writing to Siviero in Rome at the *Ufficio per il Recupero delle Opere d'Arte e del Materiale Bibliografico of the Ministero della Pubblica Istruzione*, and the other way around. This seems to indicate that Siviero did not have Bolzano as his regular workplace.[237] However, he *did* indeed work in Palazzo Ducale in Bolzano some-times.[238] He also did travel to Germany a lot on missions to recover stolen artwork. For example he spent approximately two weeks in Munich, probably at the CCP, in March 1948.[239] This means that Siviero was in Munich at the same time as Heim's proof pages were discovered at the CCP (see Chapter 4), and perhaps at the same time as Genoud as well. Another fact that seems to implicate Siviero in something shady is the fact that his diaries for the crucial years 1946–1948, which are otherwise preserved chronologically intact between 1921 and 1983, are missing at the *Accademia delle Arti del Disegno* (the Academy of Art and Design) in Flor-ence, which he became president of in the 1970s. Tori suspects that the friend of Siviero who made them available after Siviero's death probably saw to it that they disappeared, most likely because they contained matters that were not flattering to Siviero's memory.[240]

So, it seems that Siviero was the right kind of character, in the right kind of position, for both acquiring and selling the table talk documents. In fact, there is credible evidence to doubt whether Siviero was the amazing saviour of stolen art that he made himself out to be. On 5 December 1954, the Italian magazine *L'Europeo* published an article in which Siviero claimed that he had persuaded the Americans not to take a large number of stolen Italian artwork removed from Flor-ence in 1944 as war booty from the Germans. Siviero also stated that he had per-suaded the Allies to instead transport the artwork back to Florence. These claims came to the attention of Frederick Hartt, an art historian and former lieutenant in charge of the Tuscany branch of the Monuments, Fine Arts and Archives (MFAA) Section of the American Military Government (AMG) in Italy 1944–1945, who wrote to the editor-in-chief of *L'Europeo*, Michele Serra, to inform her that Siviero was actually lying about this whole matter. Not only had Siviero not been involved in this operation and was trying to take credit for work performed by the U.S. 5th Army, but he had been explicitly excluded from it by the Hartt and his superiors because they did not trust him.[241]

Siviero had also greatly exaggerated the number of artworks involved, claim-ing it to have been over 3,000 when in fact there had been about 800. Siviero had also claimed in the article that he had managed to convince the Americans that the Germans had not actually stolen the artwork at all, but that they had simply removed them in order to protect them from the bombardment of Italian cities. This, and the charge that the Allies had planned on taking these pieces of art as war booty, was especially serious, Hartt thought, because it was nothing but a rehashing of old Nazi/Fascist propaganda.[242] Hartt wrote a reply to the article to which Sivi-ero then replied, attacking Hartt's motives and denied ever having been prohibited from taking part in the operation in question.[243]

In a letter to Serra, Deane Keller, a professor of drawing and painting at Yale University (and former captain of the AMG 5th Army MFAA), told her that he had met Siviero the first time in Siena 4–5 July 1944. They had talked a bit about art stolen by the Germans, and Keller had made a mental note that he was not sure where Siviero belonged ideologically, i.e. if he was still a Fascist sympathizer or not.

In the winter of 1944–1945 Keller then met Siviero again as the latter approached him at the HQ of the AMG in Florence wanting to be let in on the operations to recover stolen art. Keller had not promised Siviero anything at that time, he later stated, and after consulting with his superiors, he was told not to use Siviero in any capacity whatsoever. In the letter to Serra, Keller stressed that he had the documentation to prove all of this was true.[244] Now, the statement that Siviero had talked about the stolen artwork with Keller at their first meeting in Siena is a bit odd, because according to Hartt most of the artworks had not yet been stolen, and no one actually knew about the first German theft on 3 July until 25 July when it was discovered by the British novelist Eric Linklater, then a major.[245] So how did Siviero know about this before anyone else did?

Keller's letter to Serra also includes a small piece of the puzzle regarding Rusconi, because Rusconi is actually mentioned here. Keller wrote that a few civilians were involved in the operation and among those was "a professional packer from Trento sent by Sig. Rusconi of the Superintendency there." The artwork was packed and then shipped by train from Bolzano.[246] Rusconi thus worked as a senior official at the local Italian government in Trento in 1945. Trento is located about 50 km south of Bolzano, which in turn is about 30 km southeast of Merano (where Gerda Bormann lived during the last months of her life).

Siviero did not take kindly to Hartt's attempts to rectify the lies that he had peddled to *L'Europeo*. Once Hartt's article had appeared in the magazine Siviero had apparently complained loudly to the Fulbright Commission, which was funding Hartt's stay in Florence at the time. When this did not work as he had planned, Hartt stated in a letter to Francis T. Williamson at the U.S. Embassy in Rome, Siviero pulled some strings with the Italian police and Hartt received a phone call from the Carabinieri who wanted to question him regarding some activities that he had been involved with during his time with the MFAA. Hartt was indeed questioned by the police, and from the persistence with which one question in particular was asked (Hartt refused to answer most questions related to his official duties with the MFAA and simply referred the Carabinieri officer to the U.S. Embassy), Hartt thought that Siviero was trying to tie him to illegal exports of stolen artwork that had allegedly taken place while Hartt was with the MFAA.[247]

Hartt looked deeper into this matter and could report back to Williamson a while later that Siviero was indeed weaving an intricate web of lies around his personality. He concluded that Siviero based his claims of having been involved in the operation on lists that had been published after the AMG 5th Army had returned the artwork to Florence. Siviero had provided very precise and correct information regarding the dates of the German thefts (3 and 19 July and 22–26 August) and also claimed to have been concerned with these works of art long before Hartt arrived in Florence. However, Hartt pointed out that he arrived in Florence on 14 August 1944, so if Siviero was telling the truth, then he had been working for the Germans. Several names of American officials that Siviero referred to in order to validate his story had in fact not taken up their positions until after the artworks had been returned, and Siviero could thus not have interacted with them. Moreover,

Hartt had discovered that Siviero kept a card file on indiscretions made by Italian officials who could be of use to him or who might get in his way. Siviero had also received a suspended sentence for impersonating a policeman. According to Hartt, Siviero was universally feared and hated by the people working for the Italian Fine Arts Administration.[248] If Siviero was indeed working for the Germans, it would explain how he knew about the theft of 3 July 1944 when talking to Keller only a day or two later.

Now we get back to Genoud's claim that he suspected the Italian seller had "duped" him. For a long time, I did not see what was odd about this claim, other than that it was part of a story that seemed too fanciful to be true. But then I realized that the lie is actually hiding a truth inside it. It is a matter that may prove to be the key to the whereabouts of the original table talk documents. The question that suddenly struck me was this: why would anyone who had just bought an original Bormann manuscript think that the seller had sold a copy of the same text to someone else? The answer is: there would be no reason. However, *if* Genoud never had the original manuscript, but *only a photocopy* of it, which a number of independent sources indicate, then it becomes perfectly understandable why such a statement would make sense in Genoud's world. Hence, what Genoud is saying here may well be true, although he placed it inside a lie. This would explain not only why he waited until 1951 to go "public" with his manuscript even though he had acquired it already in 1947/48, but also the odd statement that he thought he had been double-crossed by Siviero.

A note from an interview that David Irving made with Genoud (attended also by historian Elke Frölich) in Lausanne in 1971 may in fact provide the final proof. In the notes that Irving has published on his website he states that "the originals of the Tischgespräche documents are in his hands at this moment – ribbon copies, cream tinted paper, Din A4."[249] There is no reason that Irving would call the pages in Genoud's possession "copies" if they were not photocopies. In fact, Heim, too, divulges this information in an interview in 1975 where he told the interviewer: "Mr. Genoud has copies of Martin Bormann's transcripts, which he then sent to his wife for safe-keeping."[250] Thus, it has been established: Genoud never had the original documents. The originals are perhaps still out there somewhere, waiting to be discovered.

So, what does this all mean? Well, it means that even though Genoud's photocopy of the table talk documents is also lost, and may be in the possession of his living heirs or his secretive lawyer Cordula Schacht, the original documents may still be in Italy, perhaps in Siviero's personal papers somewhere in Florence. While this may seem unlikely, we should remember that the original of Alfred Rosenberg's diary, which had disappeared mysteriously after having been used by the U.S. chief counsel, Robert Kempner, in the trial against Rosenberg at the International Military Tribunal (IMT) at Nuremberg in 1946, was recovered in 2013 after having been lost for over 60 years. It turned out that Kempner had kept the diary, alongside an incredible amount of other original Nuremberg documents, among his personal possessions until his death in 1993, whereupon the diary had passed to Jane Lester, his aide and translator at Nuremberg (and lifelong mistress) who, in turn, had then handed it to Herbert Richardson, an ordained minister and former theology professor who ran a small academic publishing house in Lewiston, New York, for safekeeping. The whole story is told by one of the former FBI agents who tracked down the diary and brought it into the possession of the United States Holocaust Memorial Museum (USHMM).[251] This is just to show that the idea of a government employee keeping a major historical document of vital importance for the understanding of the Third Reich is not only a conceivable or plausible idea – it has been done before and by much more prominent people than Siviero.

Conclusion

This chapter has dealt with the history of Genoud's manuscript, and I have tried to clear up the many uncertainties relating to its provenance. One important issue has been the question of when, where, and from whom Genoud actually acquired the manuscript. Unfortunately, it has not been possible to give certain answers to all of these problems. However, by the use of a lot of new archival material from several European countries, I have been able to shed new light on at least parts of this history.

The comparison between Genoud's and Picker's texts has been continued in this chapter. Genoud chose to go directly to the IfZ and its director, Dr Mau, and to lobby his case with them instead of doing so in the media. Genoud certainly did manage to convince Mau and the IfZ that Picker had manipulated the text published as *Tischgespräche*. However, the result of this campaign was not what Genoud had hoped. The IfZ did not recall Picker's book; nor did they publish Genoud's manuscript. Mau instead simply let Genoud know that the IfZ did not plan to publish a second edition of *Tischgespräche*. Indeed, this seems to have been the main result of the discovery that Picker's text was not unedited; the IfZ decided to disconnect itself from the table talks and to concentrate on other matters. The second edition of *Tischgespräche* was instead published by a commercial publisher, and Picker would correct his text and pretend as if nothing had happened.

The chapter has also covered the trials in both Germany and France where Genoud and Picker sued each other, respectively. The court cases dealt with the claims to copyright to the table talk texts, which both Genoud and Picker argued they held. Genoud basically argued on behalf of Hitler's heir, his sister Paula, from whom he had acquired the publication rights. This case had its strength in that Genoud in a way represented a direct relative to Hitler, the purported source of the words in the table talks. The weakness of his case was obviously that Genoud could not claim any legal rights for himself. Also, Genoud was trying to get the copyright not only to Heim's (and Bormann's and Müller's notes) but also to Picker's notes in his possession. Picker, on the other hand, argued that he held the copyright to the text that he had authored. That was obviously his strongest argument to copyright; the weakness was that Picker lied and claimed that he had made stenographic notes. This was to be his downfall. Genoud argued that a stenographer could not claim copyright to the words they record, since that was the intellectual property of, in this case, Hitler. The court in Düsseldorf agreed with this judgement and decided the case against Picker. On the other hand, the court did not think that Genoud had any copyright either. Thus, Genoud both won and lost this case. In one way he did achieve his goal though: Picker had painted himself into a legal corner by falsely claiming that he had used stenography. This was also a claim that he would later drop. In the future he would instead reverse strategy and argue that Heim was the one who had used stenography, while he himself (Picker) had not, and therefore Genoud could not claim any copyright over either Heim's or Picker's notes in his manuscript.

It has been established that Genoud lied about when he laid his hands on the table talk manuscript. Instead of having happened in mid-1951, as he would later claim, we have seen that the evidence points to him having acquired it already in 1947. The evidence also indicates that Genoud had kept the manuscript in a Swiss bank vault for several years. We have seen that Theodore Schmitz, the Catholic priest who became the legal guardian of the Bormann children after the death of Gerda Bormann in 1946, was an informant for the East German secret police *Stasi*. I had hoped that the records from the *Stasi* interrogations with Schmitz would give an insight into how Genoud got hold of his manuscript, but it turned out that Schmitz did not know. It appears likely that Genoud purchased the manuscript, along with the Bormann letters, from the two Italians Rudolfo Siviero and Edilio Rusconi. Exactly how Siviero and Rusconi came to possess these documents is unknown, but I have been able to establish a connection between the two Italians, which means that this story seems more likely to be true.

Notes

1 Letter from Buchheim to Genoud, 29 May 1951; IfZ; ID 103/19; Korrespondenz G.
2 Letter from Genoud to Buchheim, 25 June 1951; IfZ; ID 103/19; Korrespondenz G.
3 Letter from Buchheim to Genoud, 10 July 1951; IfZ; ID 103/19; Korrespondenz G.
4 Letter from Genoud to Buchheim, 25 July 1951; IfZ; ID 103/19; Korrespondenz G.
5 Letter from Genoud to Buchheim, 29 July 1951; IfZ; ID 103/19; Korrespondenz G.
6 Letter from Erna Waltz to Genoud, 1 August 1951; IfZ; ID 103/19; Korrespondenz G.
7 Letter from Erna Waltz to Buchheim, 2 August 1951; IfZ; ID 103/19; Korrespondenz G.
8 Aktennotiz by Buchheim from his conversation with Genoud, 11 August 1951, p. 1; IfZ; ID 103/19; Korrespondenz G.
9 Der Bundesbeauftragte für die Unterlagen des Staatssicherheitsdienstes der ehemaligen Deutschen Demokratischen Republik (henceforth: BStU); Ministerium für Staatssicherheit (henceforth: MfS); AIM 2717/75, Band II; "Treffbericht", Berlin 13 February 1969 (interview took place on 16 January 1969), pp. 2–3.
10 See Trevor-Roper's introduction in: *The Bormann Letters: The Private Correspondence between Martin Bormann and his Wife from January 1943 to April 1945. Edited with an introduction and notes by H. R. Trevor-Roper* (London: Weidenfeld and Nicholson, 1954), p. xxii. Trevor-Roper seems to have misinterpreted Schmitz when he stated what kind of cancer Gerda Bormann suffered from, however, because in the typed copy of Schmitz's letter it says "Unterliebskrebs", which must mean that she must have had uterus cancer; see: typed copy of Schmitz' letter, 20 November 1953; CCLO; HTRP; Vol. Sac. Dacre 3/8/1.

Trevor-Roper and Weidenfeld had met with Genoud already in September 1953 to discuss the publication of Bormann's letters (Sisman, Adam, *Hugh Trevor-Roper: The Biography* (London: Weidenfeld & Nicolson), p. 214). Apparently, this title was not a big success because Weidenfeld never printed a second edition. It does not even seem to have gone through a second printing. In fact, the letters are since long out of print, in contrast to *Table Talk* that is still readily available, and the edition from 1954 is today somewhat of a rarity. According to Sisman (ibid.) the publication rights for the American market were sold by Weidenfeld. However, it was not published there until 1981 when a re-print appeared from AMS Press, New York.

11 Letter from Genoud to Trevor-Roper, 24 November 1953; Letter from Nicolas Thompson to Trevor-Roper (with transcript of Schmitz's letter attached, dated 20 November 1953), 25 November 1953; CCLO; HTRP; Vol. Soc. Dacre 3/8/1.

12 The 22nd is probably the correct date since this is the one stated by Schmitz (see: ibid.).

13 Printed card thanking for congratulations, dated October 1941; Diözesanarchiv Berlin (henceforth: DAB); V/75–1–3; Nachlaß Theodor Schmitz (NTS).

14 Repositur 75: "Schmitz. Theodor", p. 1; DAB; Archive directory DAB Abteilung V.

15 Letter from Bormann to Schmitz, 28 June 1997 (with copy of letter from Bormann to *Frankfurter Allgemeine Zeitung*), p. 2; DAB; V/75–1–2; NTS. This is all that remains of Schmitz's involvement in this matter in his personal papers.

16 Ibid., pp. 4–5. Bormann states that the children hardly knew their father.

17 *The Bormann Letters . . .*, pp. xxii–xxiii. It is perhaps interesting to note that Karl Wolff is mentioned as a source for a Hitler aquarelle painting listed on an auction site for Nazi memorabilia. It says there that Wolff presented the painting as a gift to the caretaker of Palazzo Ducale in Bolzano, Italy, a man by the name of Gino Marri. Wolff's Waffen-SS troops used the palace as HQ at the end of the war. No source is stated, however, so it is hard to corroborate this information (for this, see: www.hermann-historica.de/auktion/hhm72.pl?f=NR_LOT&c=7142&t=temartic_R_D&db=kat72_R.txt, accessed: 2016–07–13.

18 See Genoud's introduction in: *The Bormann Letters . . .*, p. viii.

19 Letter from Trevor-Roper to Thompson (with attached galley insertion), 4 December 1953; CCLO; HTRP; Vol. Soc. Dacre 3/8/1.

20 "NOTE á l'intention de Monsieur le Dr Balsinger" signed by Police Inspector Pache in Berne 18 February 1952, pp 1–3; Box 128; from the private archives of Pierre Péan, Paris, France.

21 von Lang, J., *Der Adjutant . . .*, p. 324.

22 Ibid., pp. 331–337. Wolff managed to reduce his sentence and save his life only because he had negotiated the capitulation of the German forces in Italy with the Western Allies before the end of the war (ibid., pp. 255–273).

23 Laske, K., *Ein Leben . . .*, pp. 83–84.

24 Letter from Bormann to Schmitz, 28 June 1997 (with copy of letter from Bormann to *Frankfurter Allgemeine Zeitung*), pp. 1–5, quotes on p. 4; DAB; V/75–1–2; NTS.

25 Höhne, Heinz, *Der Orden unter dem Totenkopf. Die Geschichte der SS* (Augsburg: Weltbild Verlag, 1992), pp. 528–531.

26 "Note confidentielle" signed by Police Inspector Pache, p. 2; Box 128; from the private archives of Pierre Péan, Paris, France.

27 Letter from Weber to Lüthi, 22 January 1952, pp. 1–2; Box 128; from the private archives of Pierre Péan, Paris, France.

28 Letter from Schmitz to Genoud, 7 April 1954; Box 130; from the private archives of Pierre Péan, Paris, France. There is no trace of any correspondence with Genoud, or even any documents pertaining to Schmitz's guardianship of the Bormann children, in his papers at *Diözesanarchiv* in Berlin.

29 Aktennotiz by Buchheim from his conversation with Genoud, 11 August 1951, p. 1; IfZ; ID 103/19; Korrespondenz G.

30 Ibid., pp. 2–3.

31 Ibid., p. 3.
32 Letter from Paschoud to Athenäum-Verlag, 13 August 1951, pp. 1–2; IfZ; ID 103/19; Korrespondenz G.
33 Letter from Buchheim to Genoud, 19 September 1951; IfZ; ID 103/19; Korrespondenz G.
34 Letter from Genoud to Athenäum-Verlag, 29 October 1951, pp. 1–2; IfZ; ID 103/19; Korrespondenz G.
35 Letter from Genoud to Mau, 29 October 1951, p. 1; IfZ; ID 103/19; Korrespondenz G.
36 Ibid., pp. 1–2.
37 Ibid., p. 2.
38 Letter from Mau to Genoud, 2 November 1951; IfZ; ID 103/19; Korrespondenz G.
39 Letter from Mau to Genoud (see also the text for the press release attached to the letter), 8 November 1951, pp. 1–2; IfZ; ID 103/19; Korrespondenz G.
40 Letter from Junker to Ritter, 14 September 1951; BAK; N 1166; Vol. 364.
41 Letter from Mau to Genoud, 10 December 1951; IfZ; ID 103/19; Korrespondenz G.
42 Letter from Genoud to Mau, 11 December 1951; IfZ; ID 103/19; Korrespondenz G.
43 "Bormanns Geist geht um" in *Der Fortschritt*, 26 October 1951.
44 Letter from Genoud to Mau, 13 December 1951; IfZ; ID 103/19; Korrespondenz G.
45 Letter from Mau to Genoud, 18 December 1951, pp. 1–2; IfZ; ID 103/19; Korrespondenz G.
46 Letter from Genoud to Mau, 2 January 1952, p. 1; IfZ; ID 103/19; Korrespondenz G.
47 Letter from Athenäum-Verlag to Mau, 12 November 1951, p. 1; IfZ; ID 101/2.
48 Letter from Mau to Athenäum-Verlag, 15 November 1951, pp. 1–2; IfZ; ID 101/2.
49 Letter from Athenäum-Verlag to Mau, 11 December 1951; IfZ; ID 101/2.
50 Letter from Mau to Athenäum-Verlag, 13 December 1951; IfZ; ID 101/2.
51 Letter from Athenäum-Verlag to Mau, 4 January 1952; IfZ; ID 101/2.
52 Ibid., p. 1.
53 Ibid., pp. 1–2.
54 Ibid., p. 2.
55 Ibid.
56 Ibid.
57 Letter from Genoud to Mau, 1 February 1952; IfZ; ID 103/19; Korrespondenz G.
58 *Hitler's Table Talk. . .* (1953), p. 563.
59 *Hitlers Tischgespräche. . .* (1951), p. 314.
60 *Hitlers Tischgespräche. . .* (1963), p. 442.
61 Letter from Mau to Genoud, 7 February 1952, p. 1; IfZ; ID 103/19; Korrespondenz G.
62 Ibid., pp. 1–2.
63 Letter from Genoud to Mau, 11 February 1952; IfZ; ID 103/19; Korrespondenz G.
64 Letters from Mau to Genoud, 15 and 21 February 1952; IfZ; ID 103/19; Korrespondenz G.
65 Letter from Genoud to Mau, 20 March 1952; IfZ; ID 103/19; Korrespondenz G.
66 Letter from Mau to Genoud, 24 March 1952, pp. 1–2; IfZ; ID 103/19; Korrespondenz G.
67 Letter from Genoud to Mau, 3 April 1952; IfZ; ID 103/19; Korrespondenz G.
68 Copy of Genoud's complaint before the court, 18 March 1952, pp. 2–3; IfZ; ID 103/19; Korrespondenz G.
69 "Urteil" from the court in Düsseldorf, 4 December 1952, p. 2; BAK; Bundeministerium der Justiz; B 141/422750; "Verlagsrecht. Urheberrechte und Verlagsrechte an dem Nachlaß Adolf Hitler; Nachdruck und Neuauflage von Hitlers 'Mein Kampf'"; Vol. 1.
70 Ibid.
71 Ibid., pp. 4–6, 8–23, quote of p. 23.
72 Copy of the notarized deed in: CCLO; HTRP; Vol. Soc. Dacre 6/6/1. The document from the notary public, however, did not state that Genoud owned the rights, but that Paula Hitler did – and that this right included any translations of the texts.
73 Letter from Paula Hitler to Genoud, 17 December 1951, p. 1; Letter from Seidl to Genoud, 20 November 1951; from the private archive of Pierre Péan, Paris, France.

74 Letter from Paula Hitler to Genoud, 22 November 1951; from the private archive of Pierre Péan, Paris, France.
75 Letter from Rechenberg to Paula Hitler, 20 November 1951, pp. 1–2; from the private archive of Pierre Péan, Paris, France.
76 Letter from Paula Hitler to Genoud, 7 December 1953, pp. 1–2; from the private archive of Pierre Péan, Paris, France.
77 Letter from Seidl to Genoud (including a carbon copy of a letter Seidl had written to a lawyer by the name of Voegeli telling him of his decision to stop representing Wolf), 1 June 1954; from the private archive of Pierre Péan, Paris, France.
78 Letter from Krausnick to Genoud, 5 March 1953; IfZ; ID 103/19; Korrespondenz G.
79 Letter from Genoud to Krausnick, 21 May 1953; IfZ; ID 103/19; Korrespondenz G.
80 Letter from Krausnick to Genoud, 24 July 1953; IfZ; ID 103/19; Korrespondenz G.
81 Letter from Krausnick to Genoud, 21 August 1953: IfZ; ID 103/19; Korrespondenz G.
82 There is nothing in the many newspaper articles that were published regarding the trial that said that Genoud could not publish his manuscript in German. See the many clippings in: IfZ; ID 34; Band 86.
83 Draft article by Trevor-Roper (itself undated), p. 3; CCLO; HTRP; Vol. Soc. Dacre 3/8/1. This was a draft for a short article about the Bormann *Nachlaß* that Trevor-Roper wrote for Dr Alfred Wiener, head of the Wiener Library in London, and the "Wiener Library Bulletin"; see: Letter from Trevor-Roper to Alfred Wiener, 17 November 1953; CCLO; HTRP; Vol. Soc. Dacre 3/8/1.
84 Typed transcript of an interview with Heim by Dr. Freiherr von Siegler in Munich on 1 July 1952 on the behalf of the IfZ (dated 2 July 1952), pp. 1–2; www.ifz-muenchen. de/archiv/zs/zs-0243_1.pdf, accessed: 2012–11–16.
85 Ibid., p. 7.
86 Ibid.
87 Copy of Genoud's complaint before the court, 18 March 1952, p. 3; IfZ; ID 103/19; Korrespondenz G.
88 "Vereinbarung", 27 February 1952 signed by Heim and Picker; WJN; Binder: Schriftwechsel: A – K 1977.
89 "Honorarberechnung für Herrn Ministerialrat Heinrich Heim", undated 1952, signed by Picker; WJN; Binder: Schriftwechsel: A – K 1977. This note also stated that: "Settlement and payment are subject to the proviso that Mr. Heim can prove his copyright if it is contested."
90 Ibid. "unserer Vereinbarungen vom 6.10.1951 und 27.11.1952"
91 Letter from Heim to Hans Grimm, 9 November 1958, p. 2; WJN; Binder: Schriftwechsel: A – K 1977.
92 "Eidstattliche Erklärung", 13 February 1980, p. 2; WJN; Binder: Schriftwechsel: A – K 1977. "Dr. Henry Picker hat hat mir als prozentualen Anteil am Ertrag der ersten Verlagseinkünfte Anfang der fünfziger Jahre einige Beiträge zukommen lassen."
93 Letter from Picker to Maser, 11 October 1972, p. 2; WJN; Binder: Schriftwechsel: A – K 1977.
94 Toland, J., *Adolf Hitler* (Vol. II), p. 782. Note that the two-volume edition of Toland's book has Heim's comments on a different page than in the shortened one-volume edition (there the page number is 682). Toland's book, by the way, is a testimony to the fact that oral history does not necessarily make a work better or more reliable. Toland made more than 100 interviews with witnesses during the early 1970s, and while the interviews themselves (kept at the Roosevelt Presidential Library) are an interesting source material for historians today, they did little to guarantee the book's trustworthiness. Toland's book should generally not be cited without independent corroboration.
95 Email from Lewick to me, 6 October 2016.
96 Letter from Dr. Freiherr von Siegler to Dr. Carl Dietrich Erdmann 15 November 1952, p. 1; Notes made by Dr. Freiherr von Siegler of a conversation with Heim, 5 November and 14 November 1952, pp. 1, 3, 5; www.ifz-muenchen.de/archiv/zs/zs-0243_1.pdf, accessed: 2012–11–16.

97   Ibid., p. 4.
98   Typed notes from a conversation between von Siegler and Heim 19 November 1952, p. 2; www.ifz-muenchen.de/archiv/zs/zs-0243_1.pdf, accessed: 2012–11–16.
99   Notes from an interview with Heim by Falk Wiesemann 23 January 1972, p. 10; www.ifz-muenchen.de/archiv/zs/zs-0243_2.pdf, accessed: 2012–11–16.
100 Toland, J., *Adolf Hitler* (Vol. II), p. 782 (p. 682 in the one-volume edition).
101 Copy of Genoud's complaint before the court, 18 March 1952, p. 5; IfZ; ID 103/19; Korrespondenz G.
102 Copy of Genoud's complaint before the court, 18 March 1952, pp. 7–8; IfZ; ID 103/19; Korrespondenz G.
103 Aktennotiz by Picker, 2 July 1952; IfZ; ID 103/19; Korrespondenz G.
104 Letter from Genoud to Mau, 20 June 1952; IfZ; ID 103/19; Korrespondenz G.
105 Letter from Mau to Genoud, 8 July 1952; IfZ; ID 103/19; Korrespondenz G.
106 Rosenbaum, R., *Explaining Hitler . . .*, p. 74. Rosenbaum does not take this seriously either.
107 *Wissenschaftsfreiheit ind ihre rechtlichen Schranken. Ein Colloquium. Herausgegeben vom Institut für Zeitgeschichte* (München: R. Oldenbourg Verlag, 1978), p. 46.
108 Letter from Genoud to Mau, 30 July 1952, pp. 1–2; IfZ; ID 103/19; Korrespondenz G.
109 Ibid., p. 1.
110 Ibid.
111 Ibid.
112 German transcription of interview with Heinrich Heim 13 May 1975, p. 2; FDR PL; JTP, 1962–1983; Series II "Adolf Hitler"; Box 46. The first interview with Heim was made on 17 March 1971; this transcript is from one of three follow up interviews made in 1975.
113 Heim's letter is quoted by Anton Joachimsthaler in: Schroeder, C., *Er war mein Chef . . .*, p. 355 (footnote 226).
114 *Monologe . . .*, p. 320.
115 Toland, J., *Adolf Hitler* (Vol. II), pp. 788–782 (p. 682 in the one-volume edition).
116 Manuscript for Heim's recorded statement to the BBC, 14 September 1953, p. 9–10; WJN; Binder: Schriftwechsel: A – K 1977. These paragraphs are so similar, that unless Heim had memorized exactly this phrase, one would be tempted to think that Toland had translated it from this manuscript.
117 Heim's letter is quoted by Anton Joachimsthaler in: Schroeder, C., *Er war mein Chef . . .*, p. 355 (footnote 226).
118 This page appears as a facsimile in the Italian edition of Genoud's book: *Conversazioni segreti . . .*, see page before title page.
119 Letter from Genoud to Mau, 30 July 1952, p. 1; IfZ; ID 103/19; Korrespondenz G.
120 Letter from Mau to Genoud, 9 August 1952, pp. 1–2; IfZ; ID 103/19; Korrespondenz G.
121 Letter from Mau to Gerhard von Reutern, 12 March 1953; IfZ; ID 101/2.
122 Rechtsstreit Dr. Henry Picker gegen François Genoud. Urteil vom 18.3.1953; pp. 1–2; IfZ; ID Go 02.10.
123 Ibid., p. 2.
124 Ibid., p. 3.
125 Ibid.
126 Ibid., pp. 3–4.
127 "Streit um Hitlers Tischgespräche" in *Fränkische Nachrichten*, 10 April 1953.
128 "Rechtstreit Dr. Henry Picker gegen François Genoud. Urteil vom 18.3.1953", p. 2; IfZ; ID Go 02.10.
129 Ibid., p. 6.
130 Ibid., p. 5.
131 Ibid.
132 Ibid., p. 6.

133 Ibid.
134 *Conversazioni segreti . . .*, p. VI.
135 Letter from Krausnick to Genoud, 14 December 1954; IfZ; ID 103/19; Korrespondenz G. See also: *Hitler's Table Talk. . .* (1953), p. 57.
136 Letter from Heim to Grimm, 7 October 1956, p. 2; WJN; Binder: Schriftwechsel: A – K 1977.
137 *Hitlers Tischgespräche. . .* (1963), pp. 509–510.
138 Péan, P., *L'extrémiste . . .*, p. 165.
139 *Hitlers Tischgespräche. . .* (1963), pp. 513, 515–517.
140 Letter from Else James to Jochmann, 21 November 1979, p. 1; WJN; Binder: Schriftwechsel: A – K 1977.
141 Letter from Heim to Kuykendall (typed version), 3 April 1978, p. 3; UALSC; PKK MS 243; Series II; Box 2, Folder 5.
142 Letter from Kuykendall to Heim, 25 July 1977, p. 1; Letter from Kuykendall to Heim, 20 September 1977, p. 2; UALSC; PKK MS 243; Series II; Box 2, Folder 5.
143 Letter from Kuykendall to Toland, 5 December 1976, p. 2; UALSC; PKK MS 243; Series II; Box 2, Folder 9. Kuykendall told Toland this as part of a series of comments on specific information stated in his book, pointing to how Toland said (on p. 682) that Hitler did not know notes were being made. Interestingly, Toland provided detailed replies to *all* other questions and comments posed to him except this one (see earlier: Letter from Toland to Kuykendall, 7 January 1977, p. 1). Toland was the one who suggested Heim to Kuykendall and provided his address to her. Toland was in fact quite enamoured by many of the old Nazis that he had interviewed for his book. He said that Heim was "like a bird on a bush" that had to be approached "quietly and cautiously." He deplored the treatment of Leni Riefenstahl who was now "in a sad state." Toland thought Riefenstahl was "a remarkable person" and said he had "grown fond of her." He complained that she had "gotten an awful deal since the war", and celebrated her photographs of African "Blacks", which showed "an understanding . . . that her 100 % anti-Fascist critics don't have." About Richard "Rix" Schultze-Kossens (who was an SS officer who became a long-time Adjutant to Hitler) Toland said that "I regard him as a dear friend." According to Toland, this SS man, who was an unrepentant Nazi and had been a part of the innermost Nazi circle, "was an idealist and he had absolutely no knowledge of the ghastly plans of Hitler to eliminate the Jews." Schultze-Kossens and his wife were "pure people", and perfectly "decent", although it was certainly hard for Americans to understand this fact, Toland said. Toland then compared the Nazi atrocities against the Jews with what the Americans, who were also "good people", were doing in Vietnam (see: letter from Toland to Kuykendall, 15 October 1972, p; letter from Toland to Kuykendall, 23 January 1973). After her visit to Germany in 1973, Toland wrote to Kuykendall to tell her that she was fortunate to have met so many important people. But, he said, her "attitude didn't hurt." Most researchers behaved "like district attorneys", complained Toland, and said that "After Vietnam and Watergate [I] can't see how any American can afford to be self-righteous." (See: postcard from Toland to Kuykendall, 26 August 1973). Clearly, Kuykendall, too, was taken in by these die-hard Nazis, because she also became friends with the Schultze-Kossens and kept exchanging letters with them for many years (See: letter from Kuykendall to Toland, 5 December 1976, p. 1). To Speer she wrote, the day she (probably) received the postcard from Toland: "I enjoyed so very much meeting with you and talking with you this summer; I feel that I've learned a lot about Hitler that I didn't know before." (Letter from Kuykendall to Speer, 27 August 1973; BAK; N 1340; Vol. 33.)
144 Letter from Kuykendall to Heim, 20 September 1977, p. 2; UALSC; PKK MS 243; Series II; Box 2, Folder 5.
145 Letter from Kuykendall to Heim, 28 February 1978, p. 1; UALSC; PKK MS 243; Series II; Box 2, Folder 5.
146 Letter from Heim to Kuykendall, 3 April 1978, p. 2; UALSC; PKK MS 243; Series II; Box 2, Folder 5.

147 Letter from Heim to Kuykendall, 26 August 1977, p. 3; UALSC; PKK MS 243; Series II; Box 2, Folder 5.
148 Ibid.
149 Letter from Kuykendall to Heim, 28 February 1978, p. 1; UALSC; PKK MS 243; Series II; Box 2, Folder 5.
150 Letter from Engel to Kuykendall, 29 January 1974, p. 3; UALSC; PKK MS 243; Series II; Box 2, Folder 3.
151 Letter from Kuykendall to Heim, 28 February 1978, p. 2; UALSC; PKK MS 243; Series II; Box 2, Folder 5.
152 Letter from Heim to Kuykendall, 3 April 1978, p. 2; UALSC; PKK MS 243; Series II; Box 2, Folder 5.
153 Ibid., p. 1.
154 German transcription of interview with Heinrich Heim 25 February 1975, p. 5; FDRPL; JTP; Series II "Adolf Hitler"; Box 46. The first interview with Heim was made on 17 March 1971; this transcript is from one of three follow-up interviews made in 1975.
155 Ibid. For the table placements, see also: FDRPL; JTP; Series II "Adolf Hitler"; Box 46; German transcription of interview with Heinrich Heim 13 May 1975, p. 1.
156 Letter from Heim to Kuykendall, 3 April 1978, p. 2; UALSC; PKK MS 243; Series II; Box 2, Folder 5.
157 Ibid.
158 Letter from Kuykendall to Heim, 6 August 1974, p. 1; UALSC; PKK MS 243; Series II; Box 2, Folder 5.
159 Ibid.; Letter from Kuykendall to Heim, 23 January 1977, p. 1; UALSC; PKK MS 243; Series II; Box 2, Folder 5.
160 Letter from Kuykendall to Heim, 19 March 1974, p. 1; UALSC; PKK MS 243; Series II; Box 2, Folder 5.
161 Ibid., pp. 1–2. See also: Heim's answers to Kuykendall's questionnaire, 13 September 1973 (in same vol. and folder), pp. 1–13.
162 Letter from Heim to Kuykendall, 8 April 1974, p. 1; UALSC; PKK MS 243; Series II; Box 2, Folder 5.
163 Letter from Heim to Kuykendall (typed version), 3 April 1978, p. 6; UALSC; PKK MS 243; Series II; Box 2, Folder 5.
164 Heim's (translated) answers to a questionnaire from Kuykendall, undated 1974, pp. 2–8; UALSC; PKK MS 243; Series II; Box 2, Folder 5.
165 "The Woman from Hitler' Bunker" in *Evening News*, 30 March 1979; WJN; Binder: Schriftwechsel: A – K 1977. After the war she had married British Army Captain Leslie James, believed to have been one of her interrogators after she was caught fleeing from Berlin, who by 1979 was a tutor at Cambridge University, but both of them had refused to speak about how they met.
166 Letter from Else James to Jochmann, 9 June 1980, p. 2; WJN; Binder: Schriftwechsel: A – K 1977.
167 Winkler, W., *Der Schattenmann . . .*, pp. 53–55, 318.
168 *Hitlers Tischgespräche. . .* (1963), p. 22. "Italiener in größte Kunstschieberei des Jahrhunderts verwickelt. Hitlers 'Geheimmagazin in die Schweiz verkauft. Erste Spuren der aus Italien Verschwundenen 600 Kostbarkeiten" in *Kölner Stadt-Anzeiger*, 22 June 1961, p. 2; "Sitzen die Bilderdiebe im eigenen Land? Italiener soll Gemälde aus Hitlers Bozener Geheimmagazin verschachert haben" in *Süddeutsche Zeitung*, No. 149 (23 June 1961), p. 5. The *Süddeutsche Zeitung* says that the article is "their own report" from Rome, and the *Kölner Stadt-Anzeiger* says, likewise, that their article is "from our correspondent" in Rome. However, that is obviously at best a half-truth, since the content of the articles is identical. The only interesting difference is that the latter newspaper spells Genoud's name (which is mentioned twice) wrong: "Genout."

169 Genoud, François, "Dichiarazione", 23 March 1961. A copy of this document was given to me by Frau Cordula Schacht.

170 Undated article by Trevor-Roper: "Table Talk Aftermath" in *Wiener Library Bulletin*, p. 2; Christ Church Library, Oxford; Hugh Trevor-Roper Papers; Vol. Soc. Dacre 6/6/1.

171 Winkler, W., *Der Schattenmann . . .*, pp. 40–41, 313.

172 "Hitler-Film: Wie ihn keiner sah" in *Der Spiegel*, 1/1953, p. 25.

173 Notes from interview with Heim by Falk Wiesemann on 23 January 1972, p. 11; www.ifz-muenchen.de/archiv/zs/zs-0243_2.pdf, accessed: 2013–08–07.

174 Péan, P., *L'extrémiste . . .*, pp. 165–168, 183–184.

175 Genoud, François, "Note sur l'affaire des aquarelles", 7 May 1954. Thanks to Frau Cordula Schacht for sharing this document with me.

176 Ibid., p. 1. I received a copy of this document from Frau Cordula Schacht. Exactly why Genoud wrote it Frau Schacht does not know (email to the author, 2013–08–21).

177 Sereny, Gitta, "The Truth Is, I Loved Hitler" in *The Observer*, April 28, 1996, p. 7.

178 Ibid.

179 Interestingly enough, the document Genoud wrote contains a reference to the contract that he supposedly signed with Rusconi's lawyer, a man by the name of Urbani, on 27 July 1951, and it says that a copy of this contract was attached to the document (Genoud, François, "Note sur l'affaire des aquarelles", 7 May 1954, p. 1). However, this contract also now seems to be lost. His lawyer Cordula Schacht at least claims not to know of its whereabouts (email to the author, 2013–08–21).

180 Winkler, W., *Der Schattenmann . . .*, pp. 14, 19.

181 Harrison, David and Merritt, John, "Agent of Hitler Cashes in on Press War" in *The Observer*, 12 July 1992. I thank Jil Sörensen of *Der Spiegel* for making this article available to me.

182 Péan, P., *L'extrémiste . . .*, pp. 164–165, 167.

183 von Barmettler, Stefan, "Kniefall vor dem obersten Lügner" in *Rheinischer Merkur*, 24 July, 1992. I thank Jil Sörensen of *Der Spiegel* for having made this article available to me.

184 "Hitler-Erbe: Zwanzig Millionen" in *Der Spiegel* 28/1952, p. 21. "1947 endlich will Genoud in den Besitz der Akten gelangt sein."
   Winkler has actually used precisely this article, but he mentions none of this in his book. He says, based on the article, that Genoud was offering Bormann's correspondence like it was candy, or pornography (not clear to whom though), in the courtroom during the trial against General Major Hermann-Bernhard Ramcke in France in 1951 (Winkler, W., *Der Schattenmann . . .*, pp. 69). But this is not what the article actually says. *Der Spiegel* states that it was German journalists that were being offered a peek at photocopies of the letters, not in the courtroom but at a café called "Flore" on Boulevard St Germain ("Hitler-Erbe: Zwanzig Millionen" in *Der Spiegel* 28/1952, p. 21). Pierre Péan, too, obviously quotes this article but does not comment upon this either (Péan, P., *L'extrémiste . . .*, p. 190). Trevor-Roper also knew about this article: See clipping; CCLO; HTRP; Vol. Soc. Dacre 6/6/1. Ramcke had been promoted to general of the paratroopers by Hitler in the fall of 1944 for his fanatical defence of the city of Brest in France (which was the reason he was being tried for war crimes in 1951). See: Pyta, W., *Hitler . . .*, p. 522.

185 Letter from Erwin Fischer to Dr. Diedrich Hinrichs, 28 May 1982, p. 3; BAK; Bundesministerium der Justiz; "Arbeitsgruppe: Veröffentlichungen aus den schriftlichen Hinterlassenschaften ehemaliger NS-Größen"; B 141/422755; Vol. 7.

186 "Verlagsrechte: Hitlers Erben" in *Der Spiegel* 49/1952, 3 December, p. 32.

187 Ibid. *Der Spiegel* ought to have known that this was incorrect because it had reported in July that same year that the book had just come out (2 July) ("Hitler-Erbe: Zwanzig Millionen" in *Der Spiegel* 28/1952 (9 July), p. 21.)

188 Laske, K., *Ein Leben . . .*, p. 93.

189 "Wem gehören Hitlers Tischgespräche?" in *Neustädter Tageblatt*, 3 August 1952.

190 Ibid.

191 Maranz, George, "L'heritage' litteraire' d'Hitler se disputera devant les tribunaux"; Box 130; clipping from the private archives of Pierre Péan, Paris, France.
192 Email from Renate Miron to me, with copy of Schacht's reply to Miron's inquiry as to the whereabouts of the manuscript used for *Monologe*, 27 September 2016. At the same time Schacht made clear that she was not actually holding Genoud's papers, but had stepped in for Genoud in the arrangement that he had had with the heirs of Goebbels's papers.
193 Péan, P., *L'extrémiste . . .*, p. 208.
194 Stehle, Hans Jakob, "Martin Bormann in west-östlichen Zweilicht" in *Die Zeit*, 24/1997, 6 June, 1997.
195 Péan, P., *L'extrémiste . . .*, pp. 141–142, 151.
196 Winkler, W., *Der Schattenmann . . .*, pp. 53, 316.
197 Péan, P., *L'extrémiste . . .*, p. 142.
198 "Treffbericht", Berlin 13 February 1969 (interview took place 16 January 1969), p. 3; BStU; MfS; AIM 2717/75, Band II.
199 Winkler, W., *Der Schattenmann . . .*, p. 316, *n*33.
200 Stehle, H., "Martin Bormann . . ." in *Die Zeit*, 24/1997, 6 June, 1997.
201 *Monologe . . .*, p. 10. Apparently, the text initially said "an Italian Fascist leader" (*ein italienischer Faschistenführer*), but Jochmann changed this to "Regierungsbeamter" after having discussed the formulation with Genoud; for this, see: Werner Jochmann Nachlaß (in the hands of Professor Ursula Büttner, Hamburg); Binder: Schriftwechsel: A – L 1980; Letter from Jochmann to Genoud, 22 January 1980, p. 2.
202 Winkler, W., *Der Schattenmann . . .*, pp. 45, 53–54.
203 In April 1993 the Catholic Church in the former GDR created a working group to go through the documentation of the MfS in order to establish the extent and quality of the Church's contacts and collaboration with the MfS. The MfS conducted this operation, called *katolischen Linie*, between 1950 and 1989. The result was presented in 1998 in a book by Dieter Grande and Bernd Schäfer, and it revealed 252 known IMs among the Catholic clergy, laymen, and the political party Christian Democratic Union (CDU). Schmitz is actually mentioned on one occasion in Grande and Schäfer's book. Apparently, the *Stasi* was also bugging Schmitz's apartment between 22 September 1964 and 23 October 1972. According to Grande and Schäfer, this bugging operation was code-named "Hase" However, they do not seem to have been aware that Schmitz was an IMF because they do not connect his codename "Theo" to Schmitz. For this, see: Grande, Dieter and Schäfer, Bernd, *Kirche im Visier. SED Staatssicherheit und katolische Kirche in der DDR* (Leipzig: Benno Verlag, 1998), pp. 11, 14–15, 47, 59. This means that the MfS had been listening to the meetings and conversations held in Schmitz's apartment for over four years before they actually approached him and recruited him to act as IMF. It is reasonable to assume that the MfS during the bugging had collected information that they then used to pressure Schmitz and convince him to accept the role of an IMF. The MfS memorandum from the recruitment meeting with Schmitz on 21 October 1968 makes clear that Schmitz was asked how he intended to compensate for having broken the norms and laws of the GDR, and it continues by saying that the "candidate" understood his situation very well and had no interest in that the information about him collected by the MfS should be made public ("Bericht", Berlin 4 November 1968 (interview took place 21 October 1968), pp. 4–5; BStU; MfS; AIM 2717/75, Band I).
204 Grande, D. and Schäfer, B., *Kirche im Visier . . .*, pp. 37–40.
205 Gieseke, Jens, *Die Stasi 1945–1990* (München: Pantheon, 2011), pp. 112–115.
206 "Bericht", Berlin 4 November 1968 (interview took place 21 October 1968), pp. 1–6; BStU; MfS; AIM 2717/75, Band I.
207 Ibid.
208 "Treffbericht", Berlin 13 February 1969 (interview took place 16 January 1969), p. 1; BStU; MfS; AIM 2717/75, Band II.

209 "Treffbericht", Berlin 15 March 1969 (interview took place 12 March 1969), pp. 5–6; BStU; MfS; AIM 2717/75, Band II.
210 Letter from Schmitz to Genoud, 7 April 1954; Box 130; from the private archives of Pierre Péan, Paris, France.
211 Letter from Trevor-Roper to Weidenfeld, 13 November 1952; CCLO; HTRP; Vol. Soc. Dacre 6/6/1.
212 Letter from Mau to Ritter, 7 November 1951, p. 4; IfZ; ID 101/1; Korrespondenz Hermann Mau 1950–1952 A – Z.
213 "Treffbericht", Berlin 13 February 1969 (interview took place 16 January 1969), pp. 3–4; BStU; MfS; AIM 2717/75, Band II.
214 Ibid., pp. 1–2.
215 "Treffbericht", Berlin 15 March 1969 (interview took place 12 March 1969), pp. 2a, 5, 10; BStU; MfS; AIM 2717/75, Band II. This hotel actually still exists, but now under the name "Sporthotel Spoegler."
216 https://de.wikipedia.org/wiki/Franz_Spögler; https://it.wikipedia.org/wiki/Franz_Spögler, accessed: 2017–06–28.
217 www.forum-der-wehrmacht.de/index.php/Thread/27966-Franz-Spögler/, accessed: 2017–06–28.
218 E-mail from Winkler to the author 2013.09.09.
219 Stehle, H., "Martin Bormann. . " in *Die Zeit*, 24/1997, 6 June, 1997.
220 "Note confidentielle" signed by Police Inspector Pache, p. 1; Box 128; from the private archives of Pierre Péan, Paris, France.
221 Letter from Bormann to Schmitz, 28 June 1997 (with copy of letter from Bormann to FAZ), pp. 1–5; DAB; V/75–1–2; NTS.
222 Ibid., p. 4. Bormann adds that the children were not 11, as Stehle stated in the article, but 10 (from 9 births, because there were twins).
223 Ibid., p. 5.
224 Letter from Schmitz to Bormann, 11 July 1997; DAB; V/75–1–2; NTS.
225 Letter from Bormann to Schmitz, 28 June 1997 (with copy of letter from Bormann to FAZ), p. 1; DAB; V/75–1–2; NTS.
226 Ibid., p. 2.
227 For more on this, see for example: Steigmann-Gall, R., *The Holy Reich . . .*, passim.
228 "Hitler-Erbe: Zwanzig Millionen" in *Der Spiegel* 28/1952 (9 July), pp. 21–22.
229 *The Bormann Letters . . .*, p. viii.
230 Conversation with Attilio Tori on 1 August 2016, Florence, Italy.
231 See the introductory note by the Alderman for Cultural Activities in the Florence Municipality, Giorgio Morales, in: Colletti, Enzo and Mariani Riccardo, *The Water Colours of Hitler: Recovered Art Works. Homage to Rudolfo Siviero* (Alinari: Florence, 1984), p. See also: www.museocasasiviero.it/ww4_siviero/rodolfosiviero.page, accessed: 2016–06–25; as well as: www.monumentsmenfoundation.org/the-heroes/first-hand-participants/siviero-rodolfo, accessed: 2016–07–08. Much information is also contained in: Lambert, Marc, *Un peintre nommé Hitler* (Paris: Éditions France-Empire – ECS, 1986), pp. 120–157. According to an article in *The New York Times*, Siviero's sister, Imelde Siviero, put 20 of these paintings (19 of which were said to be genuine) up for auction in Trieste, Italy, in November 1992. No one was willing to pay the asked $400,000 for the paintings, due perhaps to an injunction by the Italian Culture Ministry a few days earlier that forbid the paintings leaving the country. The paintings were returned, and the auctioneer did not think they would be offered for sale again; see: www.nytimes.com/1992/11/21/world/hitler-works-shunned.html, accessed: 2016–07–13.
   Nonetheless, a few of the paintings were indeed offered for sale again.
232 Stehle, H., "Martin Bormann . . ." in *Die Zeit*, 24/1997, 6 June 1997. Stehle's article was referenced in: "Edilio Rusconi vendette lettere di Bormann" in *Le Idee*, 6 June 1997.
233 Siviero had published a book on this subject in 1948: Siviero, Rudolfo, *Sulle opere d'arte italiane recuperate in Germania* (Rome: Accademia nazionale dei Lincei, 1948).

In 1950 and 1952 he published other texts detailing the recovering operations, see: Rovati, Frederica, "Italia 1945: il recupero delle opere d'arte trafugate dai tedeschi" in *ACME – Annali della Facoltà di Lettere e Filosofia dell'Università degli Studi di Milano*, Vol. LVII; Fascicolo III; Settembre – dicembre 2005, p. 265; www.ledonline.it/acme/allegati/Acme-05-III-08-Rovati.pdf, accessed: 2016–06–24.

234 Rovati, F., "Italia 1945 . . ." in *ACME* . . ., p. 282; www.ledonline.it/acme/allegati/Acme-05-III-08-Rovati.pdf, accessed: 2016–06–24.

235 Lambert, M., *Un peintre . . .,* pp. 145, 152–153, 157. Lambert presents a series of hypotheses regarding how the paintings could have ended up in Siviero's hands, including the suggestion that he may have been a part of the network that arranged the flight of Gerda Bormann and the rest of the Nazi entourage in April 1945, but he presents no evidence in support of any of this (ibid., pp. 155–156).

236 Conversation with Attilio Tori on 1 August 2016, Florence, Italy.

237 Letter from Giulio Motter to Siviero, 13 August 1946; Letter from Rupnik to Siviero, 31 March 1947; Letter from Siviero to the office in Bolzano, 3 October 1951 Museo Casa Rodolfo Siviero (henceforth: MCRS), Florence, Italy; Personal Papers of Rodolfo Siviero (henceforth: PPRS).

238 Letter from Siviero to Superintendent Mannoni, 8 June 1948; MCRS; PPRS.

239 Permit for Siviero (and five other Italians) to visit Munich, 10 March 1948; MCRS; PPRS.

240 Conversation with Attilio Tori on 1 August 2016, Florence, Italy.

241 Letter from Frederick Hartt to Michele Serra, 3 January 1955, pp. 1–4; National Gallery of Arts; Gallery Archives; RG 28 (henceforth: NGA); MFAA-D Frederick Hartt Papers, 28MFAA-D1 "Siviero Controversy, 1955–1956" [NGA; 28MFAA-D1].

242 Letter from Frederick Hartt to Ardelia Hall, 6 January 1955, pp. 1–3; NGA; 28MFAA-D1.

243 Letter from Frederick Hartt to Frank Snowden, 9 February 1955, pp. 1–2; NGA; 28MFAA-D1.

244 Letter from Deane Keller to Michele Serra, 14 February 1955, pp. 1–2; NGA; 28MFAA-D1.

245 Letter from Frederick Hartt to Francis T. Williamson, 21 March 1955, p. 2; NGA; 28MFAA-D1. Linklater is actually mentioned in the table talks because Goebbels gave one of his books to Hitler for him to read.

246 Letter from Deane Keller to Michele Serra, 14 February 1955, p. 2; NGA; 28MFAA-D1.

247 Letter from Frederick Hartt to Francis T. Williamson, 20 February 1955, pp. 1–2; NGA; 28MFAA-D1.

248 Letter from Frederick Hartt to Francis T. Williamson, 21 March 1955, pp. 1–3; NGA; 28MFAA-D1. Siviero would tell basically the same lies in a publication from the Accademia delle Arti di Disegno in Florence to celebrate the thirtieth anniversary of the liberation in 1975; see: Siviero, Rudolfo, *La difesa delle opere d'arte. Testimonianza su Bruno Becchi* (Florence: Accademia delle Arti di Deisegno, 1976). This booklet was bilingual featuring the same text in both Italian and English.

249 "Note on an interview of M. François Genoud at his home, Fontanettaz 25, Lausanne, Geneva, from 5 to 11 p.m., 21 June 1971"; www.fpp.co.uk/Hitler/Genoud/Interview_210671.html, accessed: 2016–07–08.

250 FDRPL; JTP; Series II "Adolf Hitler"; Box 46; German transcription of interview with Heinrich Heim 1 October 1975, p. 2.
   The first interview with Heim was made on 17 March 1971; this transcript is from one of three follow-up interviews made in 1975. This statement was made "off the record" as Heim had asked the interviewer to turn off the tape recorder.

251 Wittman, Robert K. and Kinney, David, *The Devil's Diary: Alfred Rosenberg and the Stolen Secrets of the Third Reich* (New York: HarperCollins, 2016), pp. 1–61. The diaries themselves were finally published in full in the original language in 2015: Jürgen Matthäus und Frank Bajohr (Hg.), *Alfred Rosenberg. Die Tagebücher von 1934 bis 1944* (Munich: S. Fischer Verlag, 2015).

4

THE HEIM PROOF PAGES

How a revolutionary discovery and its
implications went unnoticed

How Heim's proof pages were found: the CCP gallery
assistant Joseph Ehrnsberger

Heim's proof pages tell us that they were not found by the Americans at the
CCP, but by a German national called Joseph Ehrnsberger who lived on *Herzog
Wilhelm Straße* 4 in Munich.[1] A look at a map reveals that this address is located
perhaps not even a kilometre away from the former NSDAP headquarters. Joseph
Ehrnsberger was employed at the CCP in Munich from August 1945 as a gallery
assistant. Unfortunately, we do not know when he left the CCP. This was not a
terribly important position, since the gallery assistants were almost as low as you
could go in the organizational hierarchy at the CCP.[2] The question still remains
how Mr. Ehrnsberger came into possession of the pages and where the rest of
the manuscript had gone. We also do not know exactly when Ehrnsberger found
the pages.

As we saw in Chapter 3, the Italian who most probably sold Genoud the table
talk documents, Rudolfo Siviero, was at the CCP in March 1948. But since we do
not know when Ehrnsberger left the CCP, it is impossible to know if Ehrnsberger
and Siviero were there at the same time. If they were, there is a possibility that
Siviero was there at the time when Ehrnsberger found Heim's proof pages. Something that makes this scenario at least a little bit plausible is the timing of when the
proof pages arrived in Washington, D.C., i.e. September 1948. If Ehrnsberger had
found these documents long before 1948, they would likely have been shipped to
the United States much earlier. But if they were found in or around March 1948,
it would make sense why they did not arrive in the United States before that point
in time.

An amusing detail in connection with this is that David Irving has stated
that in 1971 he showed these proof pages to Genoud but he does not say

what Genoud had to say about them.[3] Irving, writing to Trevor-Roper in December 1972, also claimed to have tracked down Ehrnsberger's widow, who was allegedly:

> astounded by this fact [i.e. by the information that her husband supposedly found these notes], said her husband had had no other similar papers – but that during the war he had been a Munich city official responsible for looking after the property of bombed-out families.[4]

As with so much of the information coming from David Irving, it is indeed hard to know whether to trust this account or not. Although it is quite difficult to see any immediate reason for why Irving would lie about this fact, it is an established fact that Irving very frequently lies and distorts the facts in his books, as well as when he appears in court (this was shown to be true in the libel case of *David Irving v. Deborah Lipstadt/Penguin Books* in 2000).[5] Thus there is little reason for us to assume that he is more likely to tell the truth in private correspondence with bona fide academics (a category loathed by Irving). In any case, we are certainly justified in doubting Irving unless we have independent corroborating evidence that what he says is accurate.

It thus seems as if Ehrnsberger may have been working for the NSDAP *Parteikanzlei*, i.e. for Bormann's organization, because the *Parteikanzlei* was charged with providing help for victims of the Allied bombings.[6] It is perhaps only a strange coincidence that Ehrnsberger thus had the same duties in Munich at about the same time as Genoud assisted bombing victims for the Red Cross. It could be that Ehrnsberger was a party member, and in that case, there may be files on him in the NSDAP archive or in the local archive in Munich. This could shed more light on this man and how it came to be that he was working for the Americans directly after the war.

Mau goes to the United States

While Ritter was working on the *Tischgespräche* manuscript, Mau at the IfZ was working to get access to the German documents captured by the Allies. Fortunately for Mau and the IfZ, these ambitions had the backing of the US High Commissioner, i.e. the Chief of the Office of HICOG, John J. McCloy, who ordered that the IfZ should get all the support it needed in its endeavour to gain access to Nazi documents. Through HICOG the IfZ got access to transcripts from the Nuremberg trials, as well as a collection of Nazi pamphlets. However, the IfZ still lacked access to central collections, documents that very soon became available to historians outside Germany. Ritter was a vocal advocate of the idea that German historians needed to be the ones writing the history of the NS era, because, as he argued, the German people might not want to accept history written by foreigners, and those who had not lived through the NS era could never understand this matter as well as German historians could.[7] The latter argument was, of course, a rather dubious and unscientific one.

Nevertheless, Ritter was not the only German historian to feel this way. Mau, too, was suspicious of the possibility to write good history based on e.g. the Nuremberg transcripts until such time that German historians had a chance to inspect the original documentation in order to avoid the suspicion that the victors had been selective in what they shared with the Germans. Astrid M. Eckert writes that Mau seized the opportunity when Bernard Noble, the head of the Historical Office of the US State Department, visited Germany in March 1951 and managed to get the backing of both him and Director Shepard Stone at HICOG for an invitation to go to the United States.[8]

Mau had in fact been lobbying the Americans before Noble's arrival. In February 1951 he had spoken to representatives of HICOG regarding the need for the IfZ to find out as soon as possible what German archival material the Americans had in their possession – especially in the LoC, the State Department, and the Hoover Library. The Americans said that this would be done as soon as possible and stated that Mau should be given the opportunity to visit the United States to do the necessary research. Dr James Reed, the director of the Education and Cultural Relations Division, and Dr Edgar Breitenbach, the former director of the CCP in Munich, were then appointed as contacts for Mau and the IfZ.[9] All of this was thus already in place when Noble arrived in March.

But Noble had invited Mau without consulting all the other branches of the US government that had been involved in capturing German documents, and if it had not been for McCloy's backing, it is likely that Mau's visit in the summer of 1951 would have been cancelled. As it turned out, neither the LoC nor the DRB were at all interested in greeting Mau before a policy paper on the captured documents had been finished. After some internal wrangling Noble and McCloy managed to arrange for Mau to be able to see most of the documents in American hands that were of interest to the IfZ (which basically excluded foreign policy, the *Wehrmacht*, and the war in general), and Mau was diplomatic enough not to bring up the issue of the return of the documents to Germany during his visit. Despite their initial uneasiness, however, Mau did gain access to all the material at the LoC. He also visited the National Archives and the Hoover Institution, but could not visit the Departmental Records Branch (DRB) because the British had not yet given their consent to this.[10]

It was when he was going through the captured documents kept at the LoC that Mau discovered the extant proof pages of Heim's notes. On 19 June 1951 Mau wrote the following about the documents he found at the LoC in a report back to the IfZ:

> Some part is still disordered and unvetted and not yet in the catalogue. [. . .] I have taken notes of a few more, especially of an interesting portfolio with

a few architectonic sketches and keyword notes from Hitler for speeches (apparently early), as well as handwritten corrected records of the State Official Heim of table talks from the spring of 1942, partly printed in the Picker book, partly not printed. Valuable clue to checking the trustworthiness of the Picker's edition.[11]

Tischgespräche was published that summer, while Mau was in the United States, after Ritter had been able to convince the IfZ that such a publication was the right thing to do. It would reveal "the 'grotesqueness of this leadership'", Ritter insisted.[12] The Americans in HICOG, however, among them Dr Reed, stated to Mau that a publication of the *Tischgespräche* at that point, and under that title, might have unwanted consequences. Mau, on the other hand, underlined that it must be considered good that the IfZ published this important source in such a serious form.[13] According to Mau, Picker was very interested in cooperating with the IfZ, and he thought that Picker only had a wish to preserve Hitler's word for history in mind when making his notes. He had turned down an offer of $20,000 from an American publisher because he wanted to be sure that the text would be treated in a credible manner. However, Picker had stated that he was not really happy about his relationship with Ritter, and he was particularly unsatisfied with Ritter's initiative to sort the notes into themes. But he also realized that by letting Ritter publish them, the notes gained in credibility compared to if he was to have published them on his own.[14] As we have seen, these feelings were more than returned by Ritter.

Mau had thus made perhaps the most important discoveries with regard to the history of the table talks. However, the true importance of these documents was not fully realized at the time. In a letter to Ritter from the summer of 1951 Mau wrote, almost offhandedly:

> By the way, I discovered some notes by Heim from January/February 1942 in the Library of Congress. Some of them are not handed down by Picker. A comparison of the transcripts printed in your edition with the Library of Congress manuscripts revealed – except for very few [dis] agreements – agreement.[15]

Ritter brought this find up in his correspondence with *Athenäum* in September, where he reported that Mau "in the USA, parts of the Heim manuscript that have remained unknown to Dr. Picker has been found." Considering this development Ritter wished to know if a second edition of *Tischgespräche* was being planned and if it would be possible to correct the many printing errors and mistakes he had discovered – mistakes that he claimed had nothing to do with him.[16] From this it is obvious that Ritter, and perhaps also Mau, at this stage considered the documents found in the United States to be the "original" version of Heim's notes, i.e. the document that Picker had copied his Heim notes from. Indeed, the idea that these were anything else than that does not seem to have been entertained by anyone at this stage.

In the eyes of the Athenäum Verlag, even though none of their representatives had actually seen the newly discovered documents, Mau's find showed that Picker's manuscript was genuine. The same was true for the documents that had been forthcoming from Switzerland, which obviously was a reference to Genoud.[17] Now, the only way in which Genoud's manuscript and the LoC pages confirmed that Picker's text was "genuine" was that in the cases where they overlapped, which *Athenäum* at this point knew nothing about; thus, it corroborated that such notes had been made. However, this did not show that the statements they record were accurate representations of Hitler's words, and at the end of the day, that was what was of real importance after all.

Editorial changes in Picker's text

Junker's colleague Gerhard Reutern at *Athenäum* wrote to Ritter in early October. In principle, Reutern said, the material discovered in the United States by Mau was of great interest; however, according to Mau, only a small part of it was of real interest to an eventual second edition of *Tischgespräche*. It was not necessary to enlarge the book greatly, he thought, and the new text could be considerably reduced through editorial "eliminations."[18]

Ritter was critical towards Reutern's unwillingness to really contemplate the changes that should be made in a second edition of *Tischgespräche*, foremost because he expected it to be extremely difficult to argue his case before the IfZ *Beirat* unless he could present in detail how the book should be changed. He also thought it was a huge mistake that he had advised the IfZ to support the publication of *Tischgespräche* without signing a contract that stipulated that the commentary that he had wanted to include also should be included, or the IfZ would refuse to partake in the publication. Ritter stressed, however, that the issue of whether Mau considered the documents he had discovered in the United States to be of small or great significance was completely beside the point. Now that they had been discovered, Ritter said, they simply had to be included in a second edition, either in their chronological context or in an appendix.[19]

Athenäum was not convinced, however. According to Junker and Reutern, any changes would have to be made with Picker's permission. The publisher then claimed that according to the information available to it, the Heim material was extremely important and should be published in a special volume by the IfZ, something that apparently came as a complete surprise to Ritter – and it is indeed not clear how *Athenäum* had gotten this impression. Perhaps this was the result of confusion between the proof pages and Genoud's manuscript. Genoud had meanwhile appeared and he was apparently in possession of material from Bormann's archive. The copyright to this material was highly questionable, *Athenäum* stated, considering the fact that it concerned a text "that has undoubtedly been independently written down, edited, and selected by Picker and Heim. Moreover, these transcripts are not likely to correspond with Hitler's original copies."[20] *Athenäum*'s argument here is thus that the text did not really correspond to what Hitler had said; it is rather doubtful that the full implications of this assumption were drawn.

In early October, Picker met with Heim at his home in Wilhelmshaven and Picker wrote a so-called memorandum (*Vermerk*) regarding their conversation, a copy of which he sent to *Athenäum* who then, in turn, shared it with Ritter.[21] This memorandum seems to have been a sort of alibi to confirm Picker's previous narrative concerning the history of his manuscript and to explain the differences between his own and Genoud's manuscript. Indeed, he likely shared it with Ritter for exactly this reason. As Picker put it, Heim "asked [me], and authorized himself, to guard his interests . . . connected to my book." Heim was at this time still suffering from health issues due to his years as a captive in the American internment camp, so that he had to lead a withdrawn existence.[22] Unfortunately, we do not have access to Heim's version of this meeting. The only source we have is Picker's memorandum. Since Picker is writing for his own cause here, and since we know that he tended to invent stories to support his claims and "rights", we simply cannot simply take him at his word.

The problem with Picker's memorandum is that he provides many details regarding how Heim said he made his notes that Heim never mentions elsewhere. For example, Picker states that Bormann on several occasions after Hitler had spoken in the Officers' Mess (*Casino*) asked Heim to make notes of what had been said on a particular subject. Bormann is also said to have made his own notes for those occasions when Heim's recollections differed from his own.[23]

Picker claimed to have Bormann's permission to record Hitler's utterances "that were important for either politics or state bureaucracy", although it was not known to him whether Bormann had, in turn, gotten Hitler's permission to do so. Picker points out that both Engel and Heim had been adamant about the point that Hitler would never have given his permission to such a thing. But he still claimed that Hitler had confirmed the correctness of the content of his notes on no fewer than three occasions "which were also marked in the margin by Bormann with a blue pen – F (seen and approved by the Führer)." Picker argued that Bormann had probably done so in these specific cases because he wished to protect himself when using these notes as "Führer orders." Then he claims that Heim nonetheless had stressed to him that he, after Picker had left the FHQ in August 1942, had had to make his notes in secret so that Hitler did not notice him.[24] Once again, without corroborating independent evidence, we cannot trust Picker's story. The only thing that is indeed likely to be true is the motive for Bormann wanting to have records of Hitler's statements, i.e. because these were important to him for political and administrative reasons. Picker never produced any original notes containing Bormann's handwriting proving that Hitler had "authenticated" anything.

Ritter felt that this information changed everything. It gave a wholly different story regarding central points of the history of how his manuscript came about. It was certainly very unfortunate that Picker had not presented this information before the publication of *Tischgespräche*, because Ritter's introduction now appeared to be based on a mistaken understanding of its history. This certainly made his discussions with the critics of the book even more difficult, he said. The idea to publish Heim's newly discovered notes in an IfZ volume appeared to Ritter to be a "grotesque" idea, and he concluded, dismissively, that the only thing that mattered to *Athenäum* was apparently if they could make a profit. Neither could he understand why *Athenäum* was wasting valuable time regarding a second edition. What were they waiting for, he asked?[25] It is significant and indicative of Ritter's lack of critical thinking that he apparently bought Picker's new story wholesale and never questioned it.

Meanwhile, Genoud and Picker had met in order to try and arrive at a common understanding. This was not possible, however. Genoud intended to publish his manuscript abroad, and it was not possible to get Genoud to agree to let *Athenäum* see the material in his possession. With Heim, on the other hand, things had gone very smoothly, *Athenäum* reported, and he and Picker had come to an agreement. Now *Athenäum* was waiting for a decision concerning what would happen regarding the right to use the material.[26] Ritter complained to *Athenäum* that the critique against the book had been so hard that even his reputation as a scholar had been questioned, and because of this he could not, again, put his name to a book that did not exactly correspond with his demands.[27]

Mau's discovery of the notes at the LoC made it apparent that Picker's and Heim's texts were not exactly similar. In early November Mau wrote to Ritter to tell him about the latest developments. By that time Genoud had sent photocopies to Mau that, to him, proved that Picker had made many changes also to his own notes. The copies that Genoud had provided to Mau contained Picker's signature, which were indisputable proof of their authenticity, even though the signature for note No. 45 was missing. His conclusion was "that the Picker text contains omissions, insertions, and cosmetic changes." This included some omissions of Hitler's statements about the Pope, which Picker claimed had been done out of respect for Catholics.[28] It would now be important to determine whether Picker had actually not produced a text for print that differed from the original material. The rest of the IfZ board members now assumed that Ritter had only seen the manuscript Picker intended to publish.[29]

By 9 November Ritter had been made privy to Genoud's photocopies of notes No. 45 and 64 in *Tischgespräche* that he had provided to the IfZ, i.e. notes made by Picker dated 24 June and 22 April 1942, respectively. One had to conclude from these photocopies, said Ritter, that the documents had to be genuine since "it contains clearly recognizable corrections in Dr. Picker's handwriting."[30] Furthermore, Ritter could conclude that this text:

is only partially in agreement with our text. Apart from some stylistic changes that Mr. Picker appears to have made, it is a matter of deletions and additions.[31]

From Genoud's documents could thus be concluded that the text published as *Tischgespräche* was quite different from the one in Genoud's manuscript. Since Genoud's copies included Picker's proof changes, this also tells us that the process of creating the notes was similar to the Heim case. In this case, however, these are changes made *after* the dictation to Bormann's secretary, and unfortunately Ritter does not give us any details regarding what these redactional changes were.

Ritter was now becoming increasingly convinced that he had been duped by Picker, and perhaps also by *Athenäum*. He detailed some of the differences between the text printed in *Tischgespräche* and Picker's notes in Genoud's manuscript, and among these were several examples of Picker having made omissions (parts included in *Libres propos* and *Table Talk*). In one case Picker had also added a smaller part in place of one of these omissions. Ritter also concluded that *Tischgespräche* had differences also when compared with the proof pages. He was thinking specifically of a difference in wording in the note dated 18 January 1942. He remarked that this was not a difference shown by Genoud, but by Mau, which must reasonably mean that Genoud did not provide a copy of this document to the IfZ. If the IfZ would not agree to publishing a scholarly edition containing the "true" text, Genoud was threatening to make even more enlightening disclosures.[32] He also questioned *Athenäum*'s idea that the discovered proof pages were so many that it was impossible to print them all in an affordable volume.[33] It turned out that it was indeed a matter of the publisher having confused these documents with Genoud's much bigger manuscript.[34]

Ritter's comments to the photocopies of Genoud's documents that Mau had sent to him are also interesting. Ritter had the following to say about these:

> Very strange are the considerable discrepancies between the Heim text in the form published by Picker and the form that Mr. Genoud holds in his hands. Some of these are purely stylistic changes, due to the rather imperfect form of Heim's records, which, like the records of Picker, are not quite literal, even if they move into direct speech and based on stenographic notes. These may only have been stenographic keywords: Sometimes the records were downright incomprehensible in their brevity, so that at my suggestion individual explanatory words – but then put in brackets – were inserted, as is now also obvious from the comparison. Sometimes Picker's text also seems to offer something like a different reading of the original stenographic notes, e.g. in point 175, 3 paragraph: (300 years instead of 30 years).[35]

Ritter also remarked that Picker had material that Genoud did not have, such as No. 213 "Visit to Italy" (*Besuch in Italien*) and No 215 (last passage), which Picker simply "could not have made up."[36] Ritter drew the following conclusions:

> It is noteworthy that most of the places missing in Picker contain hateful tirades against priests and Jews. Mr. Picker once assured us that Bormann always exaggerated Hitler's statements of this type. Whether the deviation is due to this is difficult to assess. All in all, I cannot imagine that Mr. Picker has caused all these deviations on his own. His attitude was always very cautious, especially towards the Heim manuscript. He once stressed, among other things, that Mr. Heim was probably still live and could still assert his own author rights. One should therefore not change his texts where they, in this form, are not really understandable. Hence, only the following explanation is possible: that there must actually be two different versions of the Heim notes, one of which was handed over to Picker. The best way forward would be to clarify this through a discussion with Mr Heim, who is supposed to live in Munich.[37]

Ritter stated further that without more information he would not consider Genoud's text as the one to measure against, "least of all against Picker's texts, who still owns his own documents (which I would like to see for myself in Oldenburg)."[38] Ritter was thus, it seems, somewhat biased in favour of *Tischgespräche*, which is not strange considering that he had invested so much of his own credibility in this volume.

By January Picker had sent his complete manuscript to Athenäum-Verlag. Interestingly, it is said that Heim was ready to buy his notes from Genoud: "It is true that he is in possession of some of the texts written by Mr. Heim that are missing from our book and which Mr. Heim is willing to buy from Mr Genoud. . . . It would be in the interests of all concerned if Mr. Genoud were to decide to now give them up and to be content with compensation for them." The publisher wanted this matter cleared up as soon as possible because the German edition had already been sold out, and it was important for the negotiations with foreign publishers to once and for all be clear on the final version of the text.[39] Ritter thought that he had, through discussions with Picker, been able to gain some insights into how the text had been produced.[40] He could not, however, remember having seen the passages present in Genoud's manuscript in Picker's notes, and he had to assume that these deletions had been made before the manuscript he got to see was made. Certain names had been deleted by either Ritter or Junker (such as Crown Prince Rupprecht, in note No. 124; Prince Lippe-Biesterfeld, in note No. 45; Ambassador Luther, in note No. 64, etc.).[41] Luther was still alive, and Ritter thought it best to protect the old man from critique in the press. The former chief of the *Reichsbank*, Hjalmar

Schacht, was said to be a "swindler" (*Beschwindler*), so this word was taken out, too. The part about the Dutch Prince Rupprecht had to be taken out, according to Ritter, since the critique against the Dutch royal family would otherwise have been too damaging. Some critique of Churchill was taken out on the initiative of the publisher. Martin Niemöller's name was not in the version that he had access to.[42]

In late March or early April 1952, the IfZ received the complete manuscript for *Tischgespräche* from Picker. The manuscript had 542 pages, and the first 200 pages of *Tischgespräche* were compared to this manuscript and many differences were found. The manuscript contained handwritten changes, which apparently (most often) were not part of Ritter's text. In some cases, *Tischgespräche* contained things that were not present in the manuscript.[43]

Some examples of the differences

Let us have a closer look at the latter difference and see what it might tell us about the process of creating these notes. In his proof pages Heim had typed the following:

> The old gentleman [Hindenburg, M.N.] thought of him [Papen, M.N.] as a kind of greyhound, but **[,]** I think **[,]** liked him very much. Papen treated him very cleverly. Papen made himself deserving, too. The first impetus came from him: He completed the intrusion into the Holy Constitution **[!]** That he could not do more was obvious.[44] [Bold text in square brackets are handwritten additions.]

Picker's version in *Tischgespräche* from 1951 instead reads:

> The old gentleman liked him very much. Papen has treated him very cleverly.[45]

Obviously, the version found in the first edition of *Tischgespräche* is a much shorter version of what can be found in Heim's proofs. It is worth noting that the longer version had not been added by hand by Heim but was already present at this stage of typing up this proof text. The really interesting thing is that when we go to the second edition of *Tischgespräche* from 1963 we find this:

> The Old Gentleman thought of him as a kind of greyhound, but I think, liked him very much. Papen treated him very cleverly. He made himself deserving, too. The first impetus came from him: He completed the intrusion into the Holy Constitution. That he could not do more.[46]

While this version is longer and more similar to the one in Heim's proof pages, it is not identical. The fact that Schramm does not comment upon most of this paragraph not being present in the first edition of *Tischgespräche* shows that he did not take his job as editor and commentator seriously enough. Instead he only notes that the last sentence ended like that in the manuscript.[47] This was indeed the case; the *Ms. 63* used by Schramm reads exactly like this. It is certainly ironic that Picker claims that he had corrected Heim's note ("*Für die Richtigkeit: Picker*").[48] We are offered no explanation as to why the text is changed compared to the first edition.

Schramm's lack of critical thinking has been noted before, of course. In fact, in 1964 the German political scientist Eric Voegelin dedicated several lectures in his series on Hitler and the Germans at Munich University to Schramm and *Tischgespräche*. The lecture in question was called "Descent into the Academic Abyss" and addressed Schramm's introduction to the 1963 edition of *Tischgespräche* and his, in Voegelin's view, inability to understand Hitler analytically, as well as making many remarks on the poor prose. Voegelin did not view the content of *Tischgespräche* itself in a critical light, however. At the same time, he also defended Schramm against those critics who had implied that he had made excuses for Hitler and National Socialism.[49] This only further illustrates that even those who have been critical of the table talks have not been critical enough and in the correct sense.

Ritter noted that in *Tischgespräche* the following phrase in the note dated 27 March 1942 in Picker's manuscript was quite different from the published version:

> dann sei ihm ein charakterloses Schwein wie Churchill, das 30% der Tageszeit besoffen sei, doch noch hundertmal lieber als Cripps.[50]
>
> [Translation:] *then a characterless swine like Churchill, who is drunk 30% of the day, is a hundred times more preferable to him than Cripps.*

In *Tischgespräche* it simply said:

> Wenn er zu wählen habe zwischen Cripps und Churchill, dann sei ihm Churchill doch hundertmal lieber als Cripps.[51]
>
> [Translation:] *If he had to choose between Cripps and Churchill, then Churchill is a hundred times more preferable to him than Cripps.*

This note is not included in *Monologe*, since Picker's notes were excluded from that edition, so we do not know how it read in German there, but it still offers an enlightening example of how Picker treated his notes and of the reliability of his statements and explanations. In 1951 Picker explained the difference by claiming that the phrase "characterless swine" was Bormann's addition – a product of his "redneck-drastic language regulation" (*landwirtschaftlich-drastische Sprachregelung*).[52] If that was true, then it is certainly highly surprising to find it *ad verbatim* included in the 1963 edition of *Tischgespräche*.[53] Picker also did not explain how Bormann's additions had been included in his own manuscript.

Now, it is interesting to note that the version of Picker's note in *Libres propos* and *Table Talk* is a bit different still. It reads:

> Between Churchill and Cripps I have no hesitation in choosing. I prefer a hundred times the undisciplined swine who is drunk eight hours of every twenty-four, to the Puritan.[54]

This is, as usual, based on Genoud's version in *Libres Propos* which reads:

> Entre Churchill et Cripps, mon choix est fait. Je préfère cent fois le cochon sans caractère, ivre huit heures sur vingt-quatre, au puritain.[55]
>
> [Translation:] *Between Churchill and Cripps my choice is made. I prefer a hundred times the swine without character, drunk eight hours out of twenty-four, to the puritan.*

We see that the translation in *Table Talk* is a bit liberal at some places compared to the French original wording. Note also that while *Libres propos* and *Table Talk* has "eight hours out of twenty-four", Picker instead has "30 percent" which is essentially the same amount. Picker probably sanitized the part calling the British prime minister a drunkard because this was an obvious insult to Churchill.

This note is interesting also for another reason, namely that the order of the various parts in this long note is different in *Table Talk* and in *Tischgespräche*. The part cited earlier is stated as having taken place during an evening session in *Tischgespräche*, while it is included during the midday session in *Table Talk*. In *Table Talk* there is no entry during the evening at all. Large sections found in the second edition of *Tischgespräche* cannot be found in *Table Talk*.[56] There are also parts in the second edition of *Tischgespräche* that are not present in the first edition.[57] As usual, Schramm does not comment upon this fact, nor does he say anything about the fact that in the manuscript used for the 1963 edition there are handwritten changes made by Picker in these paragraphs.[58]

As already mentioned, the parts of the 27 March note that are not in the first edition of Picker's book contain redactional changes, which show that they were most likely literary constructions inserted much later by Picker. For example, we find:

> Lorenz **[spricht]** mit Hochachtung von Keitel, der um 8 Uhr morgens aufsteht und um 9 Uhr mit der Arbeit beginnt, obwohl er als 60jähriger nachts oft nicht vor 12 Uhr zu Bett kommt und nach **[der]** Übernahme des Oberbefehls über das Heer durch den Führer auch noch die Heeres-Verwaltung zu besorgen hat.[59] [Bold text in square brackets are handwritten insertions.]
>
> [Translation:] *Lorenz **[speaks]** with respect of Keitel, who gets up at 8 am and starts work at 9 am, although as a 60-year-old he often doesn't get to bed before 12 pm at night and after **[the]** takeover of the command over the army by the Führer also has to handle the Army's administration.*

It seems as if Picker at first mistook the word "spricht" for the word "erzählt" and only later discovered his mistake. But if Picker was really copying an original with the word "spricht" in it, that option seems less likely to be true. Instead, this is likely an example of when Picker's change was one motivated by aesthetic reasons and that he was rewriting this paragraph from scratch.

There is also a case where a large part of a sentence that was included in the first edition was apparently forgotten by Picker as he typed up the *Ms. 63*, which made him add the missing passage by hand:

> Möglich auch, daß das, was der Mond als Atmosphäre um sich hatte, unsere Erde an sich gerissen hat, womit **[sich die Lebensbedingungen der Menschheit auf der Erde]** von Grund auf verändert hat.[60] [Bold text in square brackets is handwritten insertion.]
>
> [Translation:] *It is also possible that what the Moon had around it as an atmosphere usurped our earth, changing **[the living conditions of humanity on Earth]** from the ground up.*

In *Monologe* the end of this passage is a bit different as it reads: "may have changed from the ground up." (*von Grund auf mögen geändert haben.*)[61]

The *Beirat* at the IfZ had a meeting on 5 November after which a statement was released to the press to the effect that the IfZ distanced itself from *Tischgespräche*. This upset Picker quite a lot, and he consequently sent Mau a long letter in which he did his best to offer a refutation of Genoud's highly successful effort of questioning the veracity of his manuscript. Picker's defensive tract offers a number of interesting pieces of information and clues to the nature of Picker's manuscript. Picker starts off his defence by attacking Genoud's character by stating that in his conversation with Genoud, the latter had stated that *Tischgespräche* had been introduced by a man, i.e. Ritter, "who was compromised by 20 July" – a reference to the assassination attempt on Hitler and Ritter's opposition to Hitler during the war – and that the book therefore from the outset was "suspect" from the point of view of the three-fourths of the potential buyers that had been going through the denazification process. According to Picker, *Athenäum* could confirm this statement by Genoud.[62]

He also stressed that Genoud almost only had material produced by Heim and Picker himself, and he and Heim were the only witnesses to the conversations. He also stressed that in the negotiations that he and *Athenäum* had had with Genoud, the latter had on at least three occasions made claims that did not correspond to the facts, as identified by Picker. Apparently, Genoud's lawyer, who had initially bombarded the publisher and Picker with demands, had not been heard from since Picker had pointed out that Genoud was simply a fencer of stolen property even despite the fact that he had tried to gain legal rights to Bormann's estate after the fact. He also said that Genoud's claim that the District Court (*Amtsgericht*) in Berchtesgaden had verified the legality of his claims had turned out to be fraudulent.[63]

Picker also brought forth the reasonable objection that he could not understand why the IfZ had not demanded that Genoud should present the original documents before engaging in negotiations with him. The IfZ could not make an informed judgement regarding Genoud's claims "from a foreign agent on the basis of some photocopies or uncertified transcripts." This was also a reasonable point to make. Picker also criticized Mau for having refused to visit him in Wilhelmshaven and "to study my original recording of the transcripts of Mr. Heim and myself and the Bormann notes also in my hand, dictated on the basis of our original recording." Picker had not sent these to Mau in Munich because he was concerned that they might be lost, but he stressed that a scientific evaluation was absolutely impossible to conduct without the documents in his possession.[64] What Picker says here is certainly significant. The claim here is that he possessed not one original manuscript, but two. One of them apparently contained the text (handwritten or typed) as it was *before* it was dictated to Bormann's secretaries, and the other was a copy (handwritten or typed) of the dictated version of the text, which he called "Bormann notes." The irony of his critique against Genoud is, of course, that Picker would then himself launch into an effort to rebut Genoud's points regarding differences in the texts, which Picker had critiqued because they were based on original documents Genoud had not presented, without providing the originals, on which his rebuttal was based, to the IfZ.

Picker then again came back to a description of how he and Heim had made their notes in the context of addressing the differences between the various texts. He wrote:

> In addition, I would like to stress that the original recordings of Mr. Heim and myself already represent a selection of Hitler's several hours long table talks. A complete recording would have yielded a multi-volume work and would also have been technically unworkable, because we were lawyers and not stenographers and with an attempt – not to be concealed at all – at such a comprehensive recording of Hitler's "Round Table" would have forfeited Hitler's trust and even subjected us to the harshest punishment. With the recorded texts, however, we, especially as lawyers, have allowed ourselves to be most precise. What we dictated from our original records as a "note" for Bormann represented a second selection that took into account Bormann's party-political historical points. Therefore, taking into account everything that seemed historically important, my book publication made it necessary to go back to the original recording, since I own a copy of the manuscript submitted to you by Mr. Genoud that I always consulted for comparison.[65]

Picker made the startling claim that *Tischgespräche* had never been said to be the version of Heim's and Picker's notes that were dictated to Bormann's secretary and subsequently included in the Bormann manuscript. His published notes were, he said, quite a lot more detailed and longer than the ones he dictated to Bormann's secretary. Thus, he could not be responsible for the different wording in Genoud's manuscript – a difference that he claimed he knew about even before Genoud came along and presented his text "which was determined, e.g. the sharper formulation, by Bormann's purposes." He said that a look at even one of the pages from Genoud's manuscript would show "that Bormann corrected them without regard to the signing of a note by Mr. Heim or me, rewrote pages or even demanded 'a more precise elaboration', even though . . . even a reproduction of Hitler's statements in indirect speech had to come at the expense of historical fidelity."[66] Picker thus admitted that *Tischgespräche* did not contain the original text.

No matter how frustrating the fact that we cannot draw any trustworthy information from Picker's statements may be for us as historians, we cannot relax the source-critical standards just because we are tempted by having a testimony from a primary eyewitness in front of us. Picker clearly has an agenda and an indisputable motive for presenting matters in a way that strengthens his claim to authenticity; he is trying to fend off potentially disastrous consequences for his manuscript, and by implication for *Tischgespräche*, in this declaration.

Now, however, we get to the *really* interesting part, namely where Picker makes a detailed comparison between Genoud's and his own "original" text(s). Picker here uses two phrases to separate the two texts that he apparently was in possession of, i.e. 1) "original" and 2) "Bormann notes" (*Bormann-Vermerke*). For example, he says regarding one difference, that the version in *Tischgespräche* is correct because it was what Hitler had said "according to the original" and that it was "also explicitly corrected with ink in my copy of the Bormann notes."[67] Apparently, then, someone had made proof corrections by hand with a pen to the version of the text that Picker had dictated to Bormann's secretary. It seems as if the handwritten corrections had been made by Picker himself, because in another similar case he states that a certain phrase had been used by Hitler according to his "original" notes, "but it did not fit the purpose of the Bormann note and was therefore supplemented with ink only in my copy."[68]

Picker implies that the dictation followed *after* a sort of editorial meeting with Bormann where the latter expressed his opinions as to what should be part of the text – a note dated 7 April 1942 – and what should not. Picker writes that:

> "They are not even honest" and "with hypocritical words and" are present in both my original and my Bormann-Vermerke copy, i.e. Bormann, in whose underlying confrontation with the churches it fit excellently into, wanted to have heard it while I hadn't heard it.[69]

What Picker is saying here is that Bormann wanted to have a passage that Picker had not heard inserted into the text and that he had then added this sentence within parentheses to both his original notes and to the copy of the dictated text. In fact, there is good reason to assume that Picker may be divulging a bit of truth here regarding what the proofreading process looked like. There is evidence also from Heim's testimony, as well as from an analysis of his proof pages, which certainly seems to imply a similar creation process. Nonetheless, in the *Ms. 63*, as well as in the book itself, we find these phrases included in Picker's text.[70] Apparently, by then Picker considered it fitting to include Bormann's remarks. What Picker said about Genoud's, and his own texts, could of course still be true, although it looks increasingly less likely to be the case.

Another such case we find in a note dated 9 April 1942 in which Hitler also rants about religion. The *Ms. 63*, as well as the second edition itself, contains a longer paragraph, squeezed in between two other paragraphs, that is not in the edition from 1951. However, we do find a corresponding passage in *Table Talk*.[71] The *Ms. 63* also contains a handwritten sentence that is actually in the 1951 edition, and thus appears to be a case of where Picker, again, forgot to include this part of his text when he typed up the *Ms. 63*. At the same time the manuscript entails other minor handwritten changes and additions that are *not* in the first edition but that subsequently appear in the 1963 edition of *Tischgespräche*. A phrase in the 1951 edition, which has been typed into the manuscript, has also been stricken out and does not appear in the 1963 edition.[72] It seems very unlikely that Picker forgot this long paragraph when preparing the 1951 edition; the missing text is instead a result of a wilful omission on his part. The fact that it appears in the 1963 edition also shows that it was written after 1951.

The phrases quoted earlier, which are not to be found in *Tischgespräche*, refers to one of Picker's own notes, so we cannot find Genoud's German version of it in *Monologe*. However, in *Table Talk* it says: "these people aren't even honest" and "in the most unctuous style", which in *Libres propos* reads: "*ces gens-là ne sont même pas honnêtes*" and "*dans le style le plus onctueux*."[73] It is obvious that *Table Talk* has translated its phrases from the French text; it is, indeed, a direct translation word for word. This cannot, of course, be taken as proof that Picker is telling the truth here; we would at least need to have a look at either of his copies of the text to see if these phrases have indeed been added in the way he says they have, and this still would not constitute proof of these phrases being due to Bormann intervening in the creation process. It would make Picker's claim a bit more plausible, however, and it certainly sounds like something that Bormann could have added. That, in and by itself, does not count as evidence though, because, as we know, arguments from so-called "internal evidence" to the effect that some utterance suits "the character" of a certain individual, or "sounds like" a certain person, are too unreliable, and hence invalid as evidence.

What is suspect about Picker's argument here is the fact that he claims that these phrases were added by hand by him in *both* his "original" notes and in the version that he dictated to Bormann's secretary. But, reasonably, any addition made as a result of Bormann having intervened, which ought to have taken place prior to the dictation, should have resulted in these phrases already being in the dictated version. They certainly were present in the manuscript that Genoud had in his possession. Unless we are meant to assume that both Bormann and Picker added these phrases by hand after the dictation had been made, this makes little sense. But why would Bormann bother to try and convince Picker that some phrases should be added to Picker's own copies when he could simply add them to his own? There was really no need to tell Picker unless he wanted the phrases to be part of the final dictated version of the text. But then, again, they ought to have been included in Picker's copy of the dictated text too. What is also unfortunate is that Picker does not include any of Heim's notes in this declaration. If we had access to Genoud's manuscript, this puzzle could be easily solved, but at present that is impossible. Note that it can still be the case, and very likely is the case, based on the other evidence that we have, that such interventions in the proofing process were actually made by Bormann in cooperation with Heim, Picker, and Müller.

Ritter apparently did not see any problems with this at all. According to him, it was entirely up to the person witnessing the conversations to decide what to include and exclude from the text, and even redactional changes of words and phrases in the original notes, such as "stylistic improvements" or the like, did not constitute a problem for him "unless they change the meaning of the word spoken by Hitler."[74] How quotes from such a source should be handled is not addressed by Ritter, and neither is the question of how the reader could ever hope to know whether the changes made had altered the content or intent of Hitler's statements. First, that is a context-dependent issue, and, second, it is a matter that can only be determined on a case-by-case basis with full knowledge of the changes that have been made. In either case, the resulting text cannot be said to be of the same character as the version of the text that has not gone through a similar editing process. This should be obvious to a very historian.

The only thing that Ritter deplored was that he had not been privy to the actual amount of things that had been removed from the text, he told Picker. If he had been, he would have changed the last point in his endnote and stated clearly that certain names and phrases had been removed in order to protect still-living persons and their reputation. Ritter, however, wished to know, since he was trying to defend the book against attacks, if the manuscript that Junker had shown him when they met in Freiburg in early 1951 was "a new copy made for the purpose of publication, or if it was a manuscript created at the headquarters itself, which you made ready for publication through handwritten additions?" Furthermore, he noted that this was the first time that he had heard anything about a difference between the original notes and those intended for Bormann's personal use.[75] Then he added:

> It is clear from the photocopies that Mr. Genoud sent to Munich, which I have had presented to me, that Mr Genoud did not have a text with hand-written modifications, but a clean copy without any substantial insertions

or corrections, but which were corrected by you by hand in some places, and signed at the end. Are these facts to be understood as to mean that you have dictated the texts at the Headquarters twice? Once for your own use and once in modified form for Bormann's use? Furthermore, that you each have a copy of both versions? [. . .] Do you also have a copy of the previously unprinted records of Mr. Heim discovered by Dr. Mau in Washington? Only if I am aware of the amount of manuscripts at hand can I participate with any use in the further debate.[76]

From this letter we can draw some interesting information: 1) Genoud's manuscript did entail some minor handwritten additions at some places, but not of the kind described by Picker (then again we do not know exactly which notes Ritter had seen) and not of the kind present in Heim's proof pages; 2) Picker's manuscript that he had given to *Athenäum* did contain handwritten additions, and this is of importance when we look at the manuscript used for the second edition of *Tischgespräche* in 1963; and 3) that the copies of Picker's notes in the Genoud's manuscript in some places contained corrections made by hand by Picker, as well as at the end of one note, his signature. The latter point thus seems to confirm a part of Picker's story, i.e. that he in some instances actually *did* make changes to the version intended for Bormann *after* it had been dictated.

On 25 November Picker replied to Ritter and explained that the manuscript given to Athenäum was a newly prepared version aimed specifically for the publication of *Tischgespräche*, since Picker did not want to risk losing any of his two original manuscripts by putting them in the mail.[77] According to Picker, Bormann did not handle the signed notes with the respect of a "civil servant" but instead shamelessly changed and shortened the text "with the generosity of a former estate inspector [. . .] and sharpened the formulations with a kind of redneck language." Picker argued that this was a violation on his text, which was reporting Hitler's utterances in an way that was "historically impeccable."[78] Picker then, interestingly, also commented upon Heim's notes, and what he had not let *Athenäum* publish from them, as well as the pages found by Mau in Washington:

Of the Heim records, as far as they are in my hand, I have only not released a brief passage about Hitler's post-war reckoning with the clergy, as it represents a repetition of things said elsewhere. The three unprinted Heim notes that Dr. Mau found in Washington are unknown to me. However, Mr Heim is prepared to check their accuracy.[79]

From this then we should be able to conclude that Picker and Heim, at this point in time, stood in contact and that they had perhaps discussed Mau's discovery. Picker was of the opinion that is was historically more valuable to publish a few "correct" notes than to publish 20 notes "additionally trimmed by Bormann's shortenings and changes due to Bormann's crude language." Genoud was well aware of this fact, Picker claimed, and this was the reason that he had provided examples to IfZ that had not been as tampered with by Bormann, as some of the other notes that Picker had in his possession. Picker thought that the IfZ should publish yet another statement saying that *Tischgespräche* contained the text without Bormann's changes, as well as pointing out that Genoud's manuscript had been stolen from Bormann's private archive. He added that the reason for why he and Heim had not already chosen to do away with Genoud through legal action was that it had come to his attention that Genoud had no money with which to pay for the legal fees. No matter who won the lawsuit, Picker and Heim would end up footing the bill, Picker claimed.[80]

A few days later Mau wrote to State Secretary (*Staatssekretär*) Dr Strauss at the *Bundesjustizministerium* stating that he had the impression that Genoud wanted to keep his manuscript secret, since he himself had suggested that any comparison between his manuscript and Picker's book should be made by a representative of the IfZ in Genoud's hometown of Lausanne.[81] Picker did reply to Ritter's questions a few days later, and although we do not have the actual letter, we do have Ritter's summary of its content. According to this summary, Ritter concluded that Picker had in his possession:

> 1) handwritten transcripts, each of which You each time produced after the table session before the dictation, 2) a copy (partly a carbon copy, partly a main copy) of the typed transcripts made for Bormann.[82]

From this we can then conclude that Picker did not still have his "original" supporting notes, i.e. the ones that he claimed to have made while Hitler was speaking. What he claimed to have were the handwritten recollections, made *after* the event, which were used as a basis for his dictations to Bormann's secretary. He also claimed to have not only carbon copies of his dictated notes but also, which is certainly surprising, that some of these that were "original" copies. How he came to possess these is not explained in Ritter's letter.

One fact that is enormously hard to understand is how Ritter, after all of this had been divulged and the details regarding Picker's manuscript still had not been settled, could tell Picker: "I share your view that Bormann's texts are worthless for publication, compared with your transcripts."[83] This simply was not a reasonable statement to make, and it is evidence of a high level of credulity and an equally large lack of critical thinking on Ritter's part.

How many copies of the table talks were originally made?

The preceding section naturally brings us to the issue of how many copies of the table talk notes were actually produced by Picker and Heim. This question might not seem to be a difficult one, or perhaps even an important one, but it is in fact not easy to answer at all, and, as it turns out, it is really a central issue to try and sort out if we wish to understand what kind of sources we are dealing with here. For the historian, thus, this task should be an urgent one. This will become even more obvious once we start to discuss the proof pages of Heim's notes in more detail.

The notes that Picker produced were, according to Heim, the fourth set ever produced. Heim was initially convinced that the two copies that had been sent to Munich had been destroyed during the war and that Genoud had a photocopy of Bormann's copy.[84] However, in an interview from 1972 Heim phrased himself a little differently. He then said that Bormann had produced one proofed copy first, but that he had not felt that this sufficed, so he had two more copies made. Heim uses the word *Durchschlag*, which basically means carbon copy.[85] According to Jochmann, what happened was that a first draft was produced based on Heim's notes, which was then proofread and corrected by Heim himself. From this proof a final version with two copies were produced.[86]

According to Heim, the notes were produced as follows: first he typed up a version based on his stenographic supporting words (from the dinner conversations where such could be made, M.N.), and then he made necessary changes to it (this is most likely the proof pages found at the LoC). After that, one "original" and two copies were typed up (the time in between is uncertain). The "original" Bormann kept for himself, and the two copies were allegedly sent to two different departments at the party headquarters in Munich.[87] Note that the concept of "original" is not really a meaningful one to use in this context, because it is purely a matter of definition which version is to be considered the "original." The only sense in which this term has any meaning at all is if it is used only to refer to the copy of the typed notes that was not a carbon copy. Still, the word is confusing, since it leads the reader to believe that the text contained in it was somehow "original", and thus more reliable than any other version.

Here it is necessary to observe that Heim's proof pages do not seem to be the result of a dictation process. The key to understanding this is provided by Gerhard L. Weinberg in the introduction to *Hitlers zweites Buch* (Hitler's Second Book) where he remarks, as proof for this book having been the result of Hitler's dictation, that there are spaces before commas and periods in the text. This, writes Weinberg, happened because the person taking the dictation had prepared for the next word and was not prepared for the sentence to end.[88] We do not see this in Heim's proof pages.

As Heim in 1958 was discussing the possibility of publishing his so-called original notes, which were in Genoud's possession with the *völkisch*-nationalist publisher Hans Grimm, he wrote that the idea that he and Picker had been stenographers was an invention made by Genoud. The reason was, according to Heim, that Genoud thought that the publication of the notes would be questioned unless the reader found himself face to face with Hitler in the text. Genoud's lie was thus crafted specifically in order to trick the reader into thinking that they were reading Hitler's exact words. Heim included a copy of a note, which he had received from

Genoud, in the letter to Grimm (unfortunately this is not present in Jochmann's archive where I found a copy of this letter), which showed only the spirit and theme of Hitler's thoughts. Heim had made Genoud aware of this fact already in 1952, he wrote, but Genoud did not seem to care. Heim wrote:

> One day there will have to be the publication of these sources. My transcripts look like the page that Genoud presented to the Institute of Contemporary History [IfZ]: 24.II.42. But Genoud does not feel compelled to do so because, apparently, neither side has questioned the authenticity of his documents; and he had no interest in it to begin with, because my first page states that the following could be heard <u>in this vein among other things</u>. Genoud presumably said to himself, and perhaps not without reason, that the publication will be in question if the readers did not have Adolf Hitler directly in front of them. So, Picker and I became stenographers and stenographers <u>could</u> only be acting on instructions. When I first saw G., in the summer 1952, he was already fixed on this reading, and it was thus, although G. in the meantime had learned from me what had actually happened, transferred into the English and certainly also the U.S. edition. This also had the benefit for G., who had battled Picker in court in 1952/53, by not having to ask us for our consent: Stenographers are not copyright holders. (Picker told me he couldn't stenograph at all.)[89] [Striking out and underlining in original.]

Heim simply came to accept Genoud's fancy invention that he and Picker had been stenographers and the readers, including historians to this day, took the bait and went with it. Although this document comes from Jochmann's archive, he strangely never mentions this at all when critiquing Picker's claim (in the 1963 edition) that his 36 Heim notes were based on the stenographic originals. Instead, Jochmann makes it sound as if Picker is the one who made this idea up – noting that a stenographer could not claim copyright.[90] Perhaps this was in order not to further undermine the value of Heim's notes.

Picker tells a somewhat different story than Heim. According to him, Bormann had two collections of notes, one in a safe in the so-called *Führerbau* in Munich and one in *Berghof*, Obersalzberg, in the Bavarian Alps. Picker states that Bormann had collected them to act as a sort of encyclopaedia (Picker uses the word *Nachschlagematerial*) for himself and for the head of Rudolf Heß's department. Hence, Picker does not seem to have had the impression that two copies were sent to Munich and the two departments at the headquarters there. Instead, he places *one* manuscript there, which he assumes was lost in a fire by the end of the war and one at Hitler's alpine retreat, the *Berghof* at Berchtesgaden. Picker furthermore writes, as we have seen, that Bormann received two copies of his notes, some of which were complete and some of which were not.[91] The story of a copy at the *Berghof* also appears in Gitta Sereny's biography of Albert Speer, but it is not stated from where, or whom, she got this information.[92] The table talks should thus be used in basically the same way as the material recorded and collected by the OKW historians Scherff and Scheidt, according to Picker. This particular parallel has not been acknowledged by any historian prior to this study.

Here Picker's version gets some surprising support from Bormann's former secretary Ilse James (born: Krüger), who is otherwise scathing in her condemnation of Picker as a liar and a fraud, when she states the following:

> Martin Bormann did not leave these notes in his office – neither in Wolfschanze, Berlin, Munich, nor Obersalzberg. He sent these – I believe first at irregular intervals – to his wife on the Obersalzberg for safekeeping. I have seen for myself that from time to time how he put notes of this kind in a brown envelope (of which he held a stock), sealed it and addressed it to "Mrs. Gerda Bormann, personally," probably sometimes along with a personal letter. If he temporarily kept copies of the notes, he placed them in his desk drawer (which is probably how Dr. Picker acquired the Heim notes) and then later sent them to his wife. In the Wolfsschanze he did not have an armoured safe, nor in the office. Nothing essential was ever kept in the armoured safe in Berlin. His wife must have had the notes with her for a long time before she took them to South Tirol.[93]

James does not say anything about a copy being sent to Munich, but we know that at least one copy must have been kept there (Heim's proof pages is evidence of that, and we have independent testimony that attest to this as well). However, the fact is that she here seemingly confirms Picker's statement that a copy was sent to Obersalzberg. The idea that Bormann did not keep a copy of the notes for himself, but instead sent these to his wife, of course makes no sense considering the purpose for which they were produced, which was, after all, to be used by Bormann in his machinations for more influence and power in the Third Reich – and we know that he used them in this way. Independent and reliable evidence shows James's assertion to be incorrect.

The *Führerbau* was the house in which the Munich Agreement of 1938 was signed, and it was physically attached to the NSDAP headquarters, the "Brown House" (*braunes Haus*). This would mean that Picker and Heim both point to almost the same location for at least one of the copies. This is therefore almost certainly correct. The really interesting part of it, however, is that the *Führerbau* became the CCP for the US Army after the end of the war used in their effort to collect and re-distribute the enormous amount of art that the Nazis had stolen. The CCP, which would bring the pages to the LoC in 1948, was thus based in the building directly next to where at least one of the manuscript copies was stored. The *Führerbau* was virtually untouched by the bombings, while the "Brown House" was completely destroyed. If there were a manuscript in that building, it is likely to have burned up. Heim is most trustworthy in this case because he was actually stationed in the "Brown House" from the autumn of 1942 until the end of the war.[94] Nonetheless, some of his proof pages survived, perhaps because they were locked in a safe.

Other important records also found by the Americans in the *Führerbau* were the archives of *Atelier Troost*, the architecture and interior design firm of Paul Ludwig Troost and his wife Gerdy Troost. Paul Troost had been Hitler's favourite architect before his death in 1934, designing many official Nazi buildings in Munich and Berlin, including the *Führerbau* itself, and his legacy was carried on by the fanatical Hitler devotee Gerdy Troost, who did a lot of interior design work for Hitler after the death of her husband.[95] This building thus housed a lot of important files produced by the Hitler regime.

According to the manuscript reference librarian at the Manuscript Division at the LoC, Patrick Kerwin, Heim's proof pages arrived there "from the Department of the Army via Craig H. Smyth" who was in charge of the CCP in Munich.[96] However, Smyth's organization was abolished in June 1946.[97] Does this mean that Smyth held on to these documents until September 1948? No, not necessarily, because the Americans kept their CCP in Munich until August 1951.[98] The documents are listed in historian Gerhard Weinberg's *Guide to Captured German Documents* from 1952. This was the first guide of its kind and the first to ever mention these documents.[99] Weinberg, as it happens, had one recommendation for the author of this book, namely: "never believe Genoud."[100] According to Kerwin, the existence of them at the LoC was virtually unknown before this point.[101] However, as we have seen, they were known to Mau, Ritter, and the IfZ from the summer of 1951. In the May issue of the LoC *Quarterly Journal of Current Acquisitions* from 1948 we are told that "transfers from the Department of the Army have brought in the Hitler Library and other collections that belonged to Nazi leaders, but these are not yet sufficiently catalogued to permit a final report at this time."[102]

In November 1948 yet another small article on the Nazi material was published in the journal, and although the notes with Hitler's utterances are not mentioned it is reasonable to assume that they were part of the collection described.[103] The next article on this material was published in May 1952 and detailed some of the material acquired by the LoC from various government branches after 1946. The Hitler Papers are mentioned here but the utterances are not.[104] The IfZ tracked these publications carefully, and a report about this issue of *Quarterly Journal of Current Acquisitions* can be found in its archive.[105] By 25 September 1952 copies of the pages were made from microfilm at the LoC and sent to Mau in Munich.[106] The copies seem to have been ordered in July.[107] From October 1952, then, Heim's proof pages had then found their way back to Munich, where they could then be seen by anyone who bothered to look.

Evaluating Heim's proof pages

The evidence suggests, beyond any reasonable doubt, that Heim's proof pages are genuine. For example, they start with the phrase: "Among other things, the boss expressed himself along the following lines of thought:", which Heim in an interview with the BBC in 1953 had remarked were missing from *all* printed editions of the notes he had seen.[108] This was also Weinberg's personal view in 1951, and it remains so still today. The main reason for this is, according to him, that some of the notes are typed on the backside of Bormann's personal stationary (see image 1 below).[109]

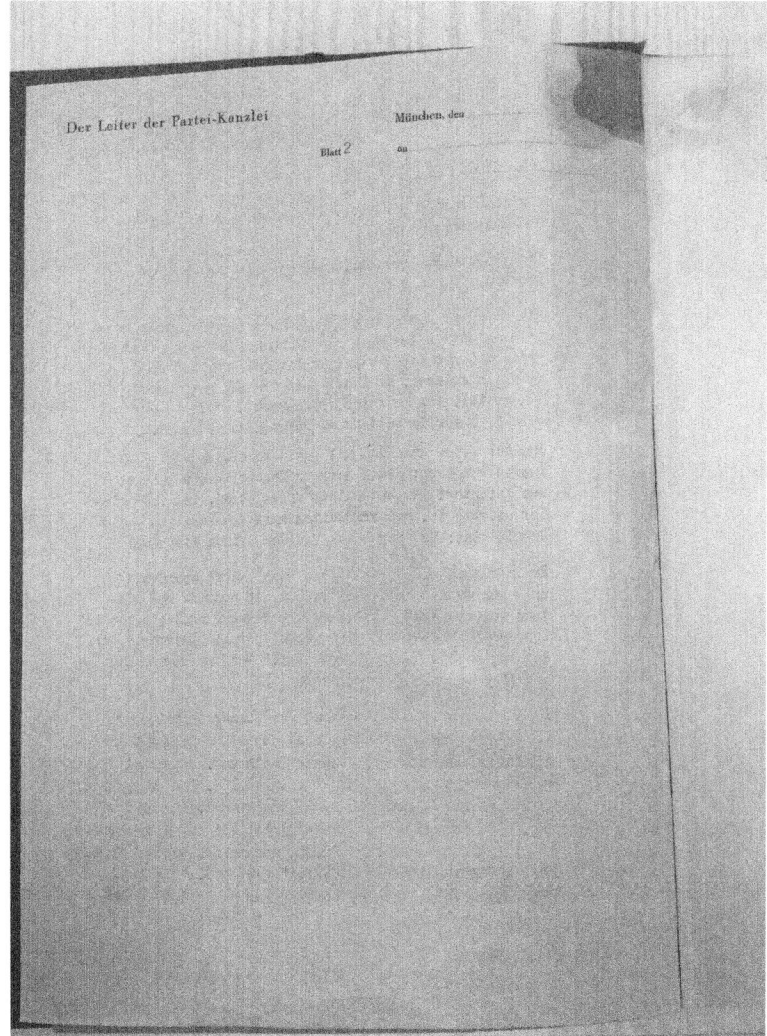

Der Leiter der Partei-Kanzlei   München, den

Blatt 2   an

IMAGE 1   Bormann's stationary from the NSDAP HQ in Munich; printing on the backside the first page of Heim's preserved proof notes. Courtesy of Bundesarchiv, Berlin-Lichterfelde.

Photo by the author.

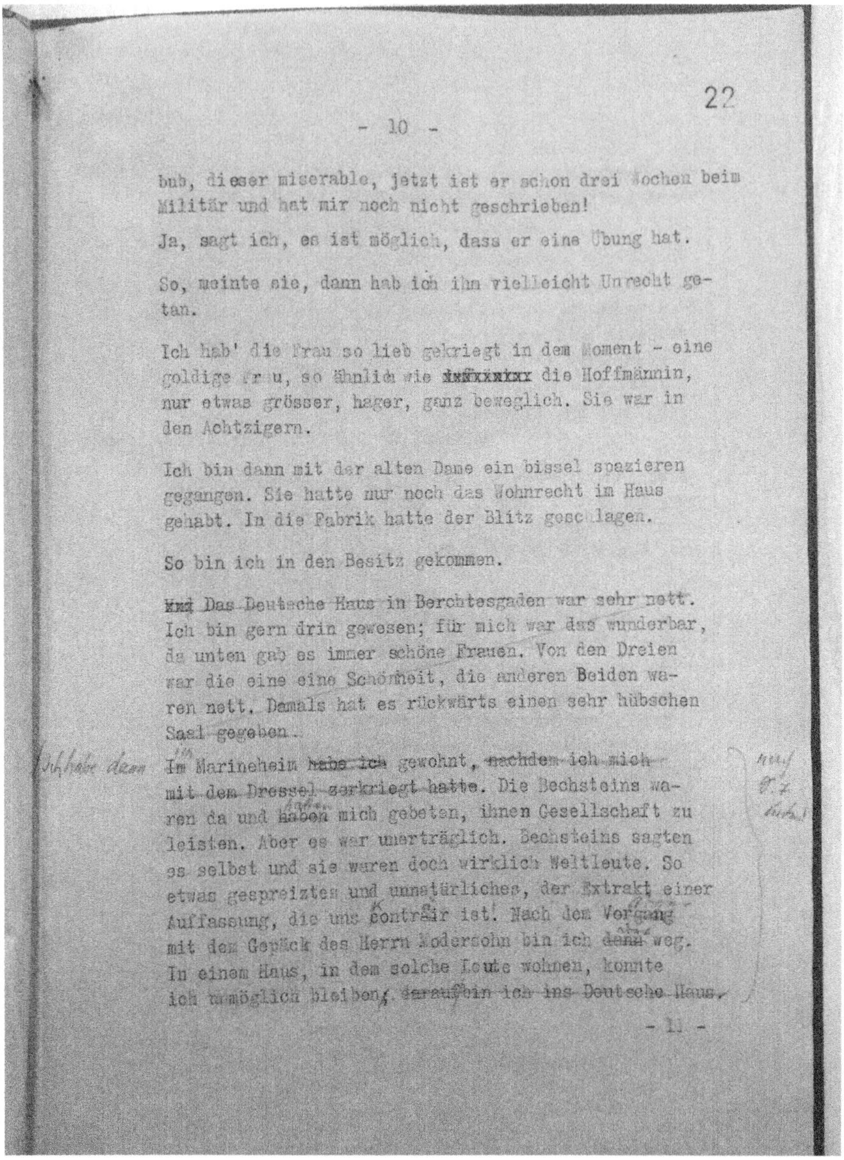
22

\- 10 -

bub, dieser miserable, jetzt ist er schon drei Wochen beim Militär und hat mir noch nicht geschrieben!

Ja, sagt ich, es ist möglich, dass er eine Übung hat.

So, meinte sie, dann hab ich ihm vielleicht Unrecht getan.

Ich hab' die Frau so lieb gekriegt in dem Moment - eine goldige Frau, so ähnlich wie [illegible] die Hoffmännin, nur etwas grösser, hager, ganz beweglich. Sie war in den Achtzigern.

Ich bin dann mit der alten Dame ein bissel spazieren gegangen. Sie hatte nur noch das Wohnrecht im Haus gehabt. In die Fabrik hatte der Blitz geschlagen.

So bin ich in den Besitz gekommen.

~~Und~~ ~~Das Deutsche Haus~~ in Berchtesgaden war sehr nett. Ich bin gern drin gewesen; für mich war das wunderbar, da unten gab es immer schöne Frauen. Von den Dreien war die eine eine Schönheit, die anderen Beiden waren nett. Damals hat es rückwärts einen sehr hübschen ~~Saal gegeben~~.

Ich habe dann Im Marineheim ~~habe ich~~ gewohnt, ~~nachdem ich mich mit dem Dressel verkriegt hatte~~. Die Bechsteins waren da und haben mich gebeten, ihnen Gesellschaft zu leisten. Aber es war unerträglich. Bechsteins sagten es selbst und sie waren doch wirklich Weltleute. So etwas Gespreiztes und Unnatürliches, der Extrakt einer Auffassung, die uns konträr ist. Nach dem Vorgang mit dem Gepäck des Herrn Rodersohn bin ich ~~dann~~ weg. In einem Haus, in dem solche Leute wohnen, konnte ich unmöglich bleiben; ~~daraufhin ich ins Deutsche Haus~~.

\- 11 -

IMAGE 2 One of Heim's proof pages. Courtesy of Bundesarchiv, Berlin-Lichterfelde.

Photo by the author.

Moreover, the notes are not carbon copies (*Durschlag*) but original typed pages. There are, however, several places where blue ink that obviously comes from blue carbon paper (*Blaupapier*) has "bled" through the paper. However, these marks are redactional changes, made with a pen through a piece of carbon paper, that were made *after* the text was typed up. What also speaks for these being "original" pages is the fact that there are no unintended blue smudges from the carbon paper elsewhere on the pages, which would be normal when carbon copies are concerned. The notes could well have been typed up using a so-called *Reiseschreibmaschine*, i.e. a smaller kind of traveller's typewriter, that was fitted into a custom-made suitcase.[110]

The pages contain a large amount of handwritten additions and changes to the text, some of which are quite massive, i.e. sometimes several new paragraphs have been added to the text. As we shall see later on, all these changes match perfectly the text published in *Monologe*. What we have here is thus typed proof pages that preceded the final version of the manuscript that Genoud later got his hands on. Even more importantly, the changes also appear in Picker's version of Heim's notes, which proves that Picker copied a version of Heim's text that came *after* these proof pages. All in all, then, the brunt of the evidence suggests that these pages were typed up at the party chancellery in the "Brown House" in Munich and that they are proof pages that have gone through some kind of editorial process.

There are several other features to these pages that are of interest to us here as well. First, while pages 3–18[111] all have tears in the upper left corner indicating that they were once stapled together and subsequently ripped loose, pages 19–22 (which have page numbers 7–10 in the proof pages) do not. Instead, these bear the marks of the staple that has been carefully removed in their upper left corner. The missing corners then re-appear on pages 23–41. The odd part is that pages 13–26 are part of the same note (dated 16–17 January 1942). Pages 43–47 (notes dated 20, 22, and 24 January) have their corners intact (they bear rust marks made by a paper clip instead). These latter pages are also the only ones that have text on *both* sides of the page. Moreover, instead of handwritten changes and additions being made by pencil, these have theirs made by a pen.[112] It almost looks as if another person made these because the handwriting looks rather different from the ones made with a pencil; whereas the latter are smooth and elegant, the changes made by a pen look sloppy and unsophisticated.[113]

The part about "German House" (*Deutsche Haus*) at the bottom of page 10 (see image 2 above) referred back to a paragraph immediately preceding the paragraph about the Bechsteins, where it was also mentioned. This preceding paragraph has also been stricken out, and it contains a statement about how wonderful it was for Hitler to stay there because there were always beautiful women there. Without any context it is said that "one of the three was a real beauty, the other two were pretty."[114] These parts, partially re-formulated, we then find re-inserted in the text by hand (pencil) on page 7 where the "German House", or "*Dreimäderlhaus*" (i.e. the "Three girls house"), in Berchtesgaden is mentioned.[115] Here we also find a handwritten proof editing in the margin referring back to page 10.[116] Now the part about the three women is easier to understand. The question is why these parts of the text were not typed in the

23

- 11 -

Im Deutschen Haus habe ich - immer mit Unterbrechungen -
eineinhalb bis zwei Jahre gewohnt. Erst vorn und dann
immer im gleichen Zimmer hinten heraus.

Ja, mit diesem Berg bin ich eng verbunden. Vieles hat
sich dort getan, ist entstanden und vergangen, es sind
mit die schönsten Zeiten meines Lebens. Ich hänge auch
an dem ersten Haus. Meine grossen Pläne sind alle dort
entstanden. Immer habe ich nette Freunde dort gehabt.
Wieviel Zeit konnte ich mir noch frei machen! Jetzt
ist man wie ein Viech dauernd angehängt. Es sind jetzt
nur die paar Stunden, die ich hier sitze.

Für die Baronin bin ich ein interessanter Mensch gewesen. Eckart hatte ihr gesagt, ich habe hier einen jun-
gen Freund, der wird einmal ein ganz bedeutender Mann
werden. Sie wollte wissen, was ich tue. Ich sagte, ich
sei Schriftsteller.

Wie war es bei Dietrich Eckart so nett, wenn ich in
der Franz-Joseph-Strasse zu ihm gekommen bin! Wie hat
er für das Annerl gesorgt! Wie er gestorben war, hat
sie mir bitterlich weinend gesagt, für ihr Leben werde sie einen so uneigennützigen Menschen nicht mehr
finden. Er hatte immer, wenn er umzog, sein Bett dabei
und die Kaffeemühle. Wir sind heute alle einen Schritt
weiter gekommen, darum merken wir nicht, was er damals
war: ein Polarstern. Alles, was die anderen geschrieben haben, war so platt. Wenn er einen abgekanzelt hat,
das war so geistreich! Ich war damals stilistisch noch
ein Säugling. Ich habe nur etwas Beruhigendes: dass es
ihm auch nicht herausgequollen ist, sondern dass Er-
gebnis eines gewissenhaftesten Bemühens war. Ich kann
Sachen, die ich vor zehn Jahren geschrieben habe, gar-

- 12 -

IMAGE 3   Page from Heim's proof notes. Courtesy of Bundesarchiv, Berlin-Lichterfelde.
Photo by the author.

right place from the beginning? Perhaps the reason for the surrounding pages
missing the top corners is that pages 7–10 were taken out in order to be edited.

Let us consider the fact that page 10 ends with a full sentence, i.e. the sentence
mentioning "German House", and does not continue on page 11. It seems to start
anew on the following page, as if it had not been mentioned already immediately
before on the previous page. This is most likely because pages 7–10 looked different

originally; then they were taken out, were re-written, and were then put back into the manuscript. But in doing so new mistakes were obviously made. The reason for the handwritten redactions and the moving of large chunks of text seems to have been to create some chronological order in the statements about where and when Hitler lived while in Berchtesgaden during the latter half of the 1920s, because on page 7 "German House" and *Haus Wachenfeld* are mentioned before the Naval Officers' hotel *Marineheim* – the full name of this hotel was *Prinzessin Adalbert Marine-Offizersheim Hotel Antenberg* – is mentioned on page 10. But Hitler's short stay at *Marineheim* came before he established himself in *Haus Wachenfeld*.[117] The exact timing of these events is uncertain because there is a lack of documentation.

These proofs give witness to what the process of creation of the *Monologe* notes looked like. In this sense they are unique, because no other evidence provides us with such an unbiased and independent testimony to this creation process. I chose to use the word "creation" consciously, because this is indeed what the process that Heim went through; i.e. a wilful act of constructing Hitler's words. The pages were most likely typed by Heim himself, and as such they would represent his attempt at rec-reating Hitler's words *before* dictating to Bormann's secretary. The manuscript simply contains too many typing errors and manual changes for them to have been made by a professional typist. The many typing mistakes and additions also prove that the notes were indeed not made from stenographic notes to any significant extent.[118] The pages contain not only changes that are not in the *Tischgespräche* version, as compared to in *Monologe*, but also, and this is absolutely crucial, text that did not make it into the manuscript that later became *Monologe*. One such example will suffice to illustrate this point. It is the note dated to the night between 8 and 9 January 1942:

Comparison between *Monologe* and Heim's Proof Pages[119]

Monologe	*Heim's Proof Pages*
Der Religionsunterricht wurde bei uns nur von Priestern gegeben. Ich war der ewige Frager. Den reinen Prüfungsgegenstand habe ich beherrscht wie kein anderer. Mann konnte mir deshalb nichts machen. In der Religion habe ich lobenswert und vorzüglich gehabt, dafür im sittlichen Betragen ungenügend.	Der Chef sprach sich u.a. dem Sinne nach **[wiefolgt]** aus:
Aus der Bibel habe ich mit Vorliebe die bedenklichen Themen genommen. Bitte, Herr Professor, was versteht man darunter? Eine ausweichende Antwort. Ich frug wieder und wieder, bis dem Professor Schwarz schließlich die Geduld riß: "So, und jetzt endlich setzen Sie sich!"	Der Religionsunterricht wurde bei uns [nur] von Priestern gegeben. Ich war der ewige Frager. Den reinen Prüfungsgegenstand habe ich beherrscht wie kein anderer. **[Man]** konnte mir deshalb nichts machen. In der Religion habe ich lobenswert und vorzüglich gehabt, dafür im sittlichen Betragen ungenügend.
	Aus der Bibel habe ich mit Vorliebe die bedenklichen Themen genommen: Bitte Herr Professor, was versteht man darunter? **[Eine ausweichende Antwort]**. Ich frug wieder und wieder, bis **[dem Prof. Schwarz]** schliesslich die Geduld riss: So und jetzt endlich setzen Sie sich!

(Continued)

Monologe	*Heim's Proof Pages*
[Translation:] *Religious instruction was only given to us by priests. I was the eternal questioner. I mastered the exam subject matter like no other. One could therefore not do anything to me. In religion I have had commendable and excellent, but insufficient in conduct. From the Bible I loved to address the questionable topics. Please, Professor, what does this mean? An evasive answer. I asked again and again, until the professor Black finally lost patience: "So, and now finally sit down!"*	[Translation:] *Among other things, the boss expressed himself along the following lines of thought [as follows]: Religious instruction was given to us [only] by priests. I was the eternal questioner. I mastered the exam subject matter like no other. [One] couldn't do anything to me because of that. In religion I have had commendable and excellent, but insufficient in conduct. From the Bible I loved to address the questionable topics: Please Professor, what does this mean? [An evasive response]. I asked again and again until [Prof. Schwarz] finally lost patience: So, and now finally sit down!*

Source: Text in bold and within square brackets in the LoC pages are handwritten changes; stricken-over text is typed text that has been stricken out. The ° denotes a word that has been typed in between the lines and then stricken out.

From this example only, all illusions of the *Monologe* text faithfully reproducing Hitler's statements are obsolete and to no avail. The notes are in fact just as much a literary product as Picker's. They are both based on real utterances by Hitler, but since we are in no position to be able to sort out the "original" and *ad verbatim* from the literary creations, the whole text is, and must indeed be treated as, problematic and as, at best, a summarizing memorandum of what was said.

What is more, what is here ascribed to Hitler regarding his grades is false. As far as we know Hitler's conduct was never deemed "insufficient" during his school years in Linz and Steyr 1900–1905. During all those years he received the grade "appropriate" (*entsprechend*), or as it was also called some years "satisfactory" (*befriedigend*), or a 3 on the 5-point grade scale. His grades in religion were, as far as we know, never "commendable" (*lobenswert*), a 2, or "excellent" (*vorzüglich*), a 1. In his last school year, the only year for which we know his grade in religion, he received a 4 (*genügend*) in the first semester and a 3 (*befriedigend*) in the second semester.[120] Most likely, therefore, what Heim's notes tell us is fiction. It could be fiction created by Hitler himself, of course, but nothing indicates that Hitler aced his exams in religion. This seems to be a lie that was intended to explain how someone who kept sabotaging religion class and hounding the teacher could still manage to get such good grades in the subject. Reality is put on its head in these notes, and this has nothing to do with the truth. Thus, the lies about his school grades in *Mein Kampf* are continued and expanded in *Monologe*.

There are actually more inaccuracies in this note. It is said that Hitler came to live in *Haus Wachenfeld* in 1928[121]; however, the bulk of the available evidence, according to Christoph Püschner and Ulrich Chaussy, points to the spring of 1927 being the correct time.[122] Chaussy and Püschner point out that Jochmann – in a footnote in the very beginning of the note dated 16–17 January 1942 – writes that Hitler rented *Haus Wachenfeld* already in 1925 and that he then purchased it in 1929. For some inexplicable reason Jochmann does not explain why he contradicts the year given in the text that he annotates. Moreover, Jochmann's statements are both wrong. Chaussy and Püschner also show that Martin Bormann, in a letter dated 27 December 1941, wrote that: "By chance, the Führer learned in 1927 that the small house Wachenfeld was for rent; the Führer immediately sprang into action."[123] Perhaps Jochmann simply did not notice that Hitler gave a different year. Apparently, and a bit stranger, Bormann made no effort to correct the incorrect dating in his own manuscript.

These proof pages clearly show signs of having been created in a process of writing. The numerous changes in the text can hardly be the result of Heim suddenly remembering that Hitler in fact said it in another way than originally written in the proof text. Rather, we see a process whereby the text is worked over; phrases are changed and re-written in order to find a formulation that suited the author. Did Hitler even say these things on this particular occasion? There is no way to be certain about this. However, the fact that the parts have been moved around in this manner at least suggests that it is not at all impossible that they were entirely invented and inserted into the text at an even earlier stage. Since the process by which the notes were created is largely opaque, we have no way of being sure how many versions the text went through before reaching its final form. All we can know for sure is that the preserved proof pages pre-date the manuscript version that was later published as *Monologe*. It is likely that these changes were the result of some kind of editorial conference between Heim and Bormann, although it is not Bormann's handwriting. The handwriting is most certainly Heim's, as can be determined by a comparison to other examples of Heim's handwriting.

But how do we know that these notes were written in Munich? Could not the pages have been written at the FHQ and taken to the party chancellery afterwards? I argue that there is one fact that speaks conclusively against that possibility, namely that the notes are part of a series and not at all randomly preserved. The proof pages contain notes No. 100, 110–116, and 120 in *Table Talk* (or No. 89, 97–103, and 106 in *Monologe*) and they are all from January 1942. This means that they were part of a larger manuscript containing at least notes 100–120. Now, it would surely be an amazing coincidence if both the first and last note in this proof manuscript happened to be preserved. Statistically it is more likely that there originally were many more notes on both sides of these numbers. In *Tischgespräche* we find some of Heim's notes dated between 1 January and 11–12 March 1942, i.e. notes No. 75–158 in *Monologe*. This means that it is likely that notes No. 75–158 were also part of the same pile of proof pages as the surviving documents.

Moreover, why would such a large number of proof pages be transferred to Munich? The simple answer seems to be that there is absolutely no reason to do this if the final version of the table talks had been produced already at the FHQ. Thus, it appears that the only reason for these proof pages to end up in Munich at all is that they, and the final version of the notes, were actually finished there. Heim probably took some sort of draft notes with him when he left the FHQ in mid-March 1942. While in Munich he must have typed up the proofs for these and a number of other notes, which he then subsequently edited, perhaps after an editorial conference between Bormann and Heim prior to finally producing the final version of the table talk notes.

The strongest argument for the proposition that such a conference took place is that the additions are of such character that Heim cannot have dared to make them without Bormann's knowledge; indeed, it seems extremely unlikely that he did not confer with Bormann before making them. Heim was after all Bormann's assistant and subservient to him. The same one of Bormann's secretaries, i.e. a woman with the last name Fugger[124] (as noted at the top of each note in *Monologe*), typed up all of these January notes, and it could very well have been made in one sitting at the "Brown House." Note that neither Fugger's nor Heim's name appears on the proof pages.

So, when were these notes produced, i.e. at what point did Heim come to Munich? Well, as it turns out, when Heim left the FHQ in March 1942 his first mission was to help his close friend, the painter Karl Leipold, prepare an art exhibit in *Haus der Deutschen Kunst* in Munich. It is not completely clear how long Heim stayed in Munich, but after finishing the work with Leipold, Heim went to Rome, Italy, on business (talking to the widow of the painter Friedrich Stahl about his estate, as well as some matters having to do with architecture), after which he returned to Munich in late July. In August he was back at the FHQ for a while, after which he returned to Munich and the party HQ – located right next to the *Führerbau* – in the fall of 1942 after leaving the FHQ for good. He remained in Munich until the end of the war, working on the planned reorganization of Europe after a Nazi war victory.[125] Leipold had contacted Heim before the art exhibit and said that he, being 79 years old, could not manage this huge project on his own. Bormann had therefore, according to Heim, instructed him to assist Leipold.[126] Hitler, apparently, was so impressed by Leipold's work that he bought the artist's entire collection in 1942.[127]

Interestingly, Heim told Karen Kuykendall (who was working on a book about Hitler's attitude to the arts), first in 1973 and then again in 1978, that Picker had copied his notes, not in the FHQ, but in Munich. Heim also lambasted Picker for not having shown his own notes to Bormann, like he himself had. He wrote:

> At the same time, Picker had his notes, published in Munich and Stuttgart, and, in addition, a part of mine – without informing me – copied in the anteroom of Bormann's office in the *Führerbau* in Munich; the publication was also made without me being told about it or having asked for my agreement.[128]

Heim told the same story to the British newspaper *Daily Telegraph* three years later, thereby confirming Picker's claim that he had a secretary type up the copies.[129]

> What I do not understand when I look at the behaviour of my replacement [i.e. Picker] during the period from mid-March to the end of July 1942 is that he – instead of putting it on his (Martin Bormann's) table (having had the honour of being his adjutant) – deprived the *Reichsleiter* of a whole lot of notes. It would have reflected positively <u>on</u> him if he had shied away from keeping a copy to himself, but no: He also had to make a part of my notes into his own by having copies of them produced, in an unexplained way, in the *Führerbau* in Munich.[130]

According to Heim, who claimed to have checked Bormann's schedule between 8 and 22 June 1942, a period from which there are no monologues recorded, Bormann and Hitler were actually in the *Führerbau* in Munich on 10 June.[131] Heim's point was that this also places Picker there at that time. Note that Heim is most likely mistaking the "Brown House", in which the NSDAP party HQ was located, with the *Führerbau*, which was an official representational building only, in the passages earlier. It is unlikely that the proof pages were found in the *Führerbau* because of the widely different uses of these buildings; more likely is that they were found in the ruins of the "Brown House" and were then taken to the Americans in the CCP/*Führerbau* by the CCP gallery assistant Joseph Ehrnsberger. This places Picker in Munich during the time that Heim was in Italy, which supports Heim's claim that Picker copied his notes there.

This is an important piece of information for us when trying to reconstruct what actually happened during the summer of 1942. Due to Heim's statements to Kuykendall, we know for sure that Heim must have produced the proof pages found after the war, as well as the final version of these notes, sometime between mid-March and 10 June that year. We know this because the notes had to be in Munich when Picker copied them – both the proofs and the originals, since it makes no sense for the proofs to have arrived in Munich once the final notes had been typed up – and Heim must have arrived in Italy before 10 June, since he was not in Munich when Picker arrived there together with Hitler and Bormann.

There is thus a window from mid-March until early June where Heim could have typed up the notes. Even if he left Munich before the beginning of June, he still had one and a half month, which is more than enough to type up the proofs and amend them. What is the most pertinent matter to stress here, again, is that *this means that at least the notes dated January 1942 were finalized some three and a half to four and a half months after the statements that they record were made.* From a source-critical point of view that is a lot of time that certainly adversely affects the reliability of the text.

The reason for Heim leaving the FHQ is a bit interesting. In the statement to the court in Munich in late 1948 Heim had said that he had been told by Bormann by the end of 1942 that he wished to replace him. Heim claimed that he had asked Bormann to be sent to the front, but the latter had instead decided to send him to Munich. Heim remained in Munich until 30 April 1945 when the Americans occupied the city. Interestingly, after the war he did not mention anything about the notes he had made for Bormann. Instead, he told the court a number of other duties he had performed for the *Reichsleiter*.[132] The fact that Heim left the FHQ at that time is probably not a coincidence.

Ilona Arnold, a stenographer at the party chancellery in Munich, said in a statement to a court after the war that up until sometime in 1942 Bormann had a personal assistant in the party HQ called K. W. Hanssen (for whom Arnold had been taking dictations). However, at some point that year "there was . . . a big conflict" between Bormann and Hanssen. Arnold claimed not to know what had caused this break between the two, but after that point Bormann did not want any more personal assistants, she said. The reason was ostensibly that Bormann did not wish to risk a repetition of this experience.[133] The break between Bormann and Hanssen, which led to the latter being fired, is confirmed also by another witness.[134] It is likely that the conflict between Bormann and Hanssen has to do with the fact that the latter allowed Picker to copy Heim's notes, which were lying on a desk in Hanssen's office (see later).

According to Arnold, Hans Müller was one of several people that Bromann, after the break with Hanssen, delegated Hanssen's former tasks to.[135] Interestingly, Arnold does not mention Müller having been sent to the FHQ, however, and this may be an important point. Perhaps this is an indication that the notes in Genoud's table talk manuscript that has Müller as a note-taker was actually recorded in Munich at the *Parteikanzlei* based entirely on Bormann's recollections, or in Berlin, where Müller also worked. Perhaps Müller wrote down what Bormann told him and then dictated to one of the secretaries. Ironically, one witness claimed after the war that Müller was a deeply believing Christian who condemned the methods that the party used in its fight against the churches.[136]

Bormann spent almost all of his time at Hitler's side. Picker places Hitler, and thus also Bormann, in Munich on 27 April and 10 June 1942, at which time Bormann could very well have had time to meet with Heim to perhaps edit some notes. Heim was based at the "Brown House" also while working on the art exhibit. It is then also likely that the additions to the proof pages were made by Heim while in Munich between March and July – exactly the period in which Picker replaced him at the FHQ.

Significant changes made in the proof pages

Many changes are of such a nature and detail that they cannot possibly be an *ad verbatim* account of what Hitler said at the time, but rather must be additions made up at a much later stage. There are several examples one could give of this, but a few will have to suffice here. For instance, there is a small addition, again, in the note dated 8/9 January 1942, where Hitler is apparently talking about dictating a theatre play to his sister when he was 15 years old.

Comparison between notes dated 8/9 January 1942 in *Monologe* and in Heim's proof pages[137]

Monologe	*Heim's proof pages*
So bin ich auf und ab gesaust und habe meiner Schwester diktiert; ich habe das in zahllosen Auftritten mit einer glühenden Phantasie ausgemalt.	So bin ich auf und ab gesaust und habe meiner Schwester diktiert. **[Ich habe [das] in zahllosen Auftritten mit einer glühenden Phantasie ausgemalt.]**
[Translation:] *So I scoured up and down and dictated to my sister; I have pointed that out in countless appearances with a glowing imagination.*	[Translation:] *So I scoured up and down and dictated to my sister. **[I have pointed [that] out in countless appearances with a glowing imagination.]***

Source: Text in bold and within square brackets in the proof pages are handwritten changes; stricken through text is typed text that has been stricken out manually.

The explanatory and contrived character of the added sentence becomes glaringly apparent when one reads the proof page and when one sees that it was added by hand in a later proofreading process.

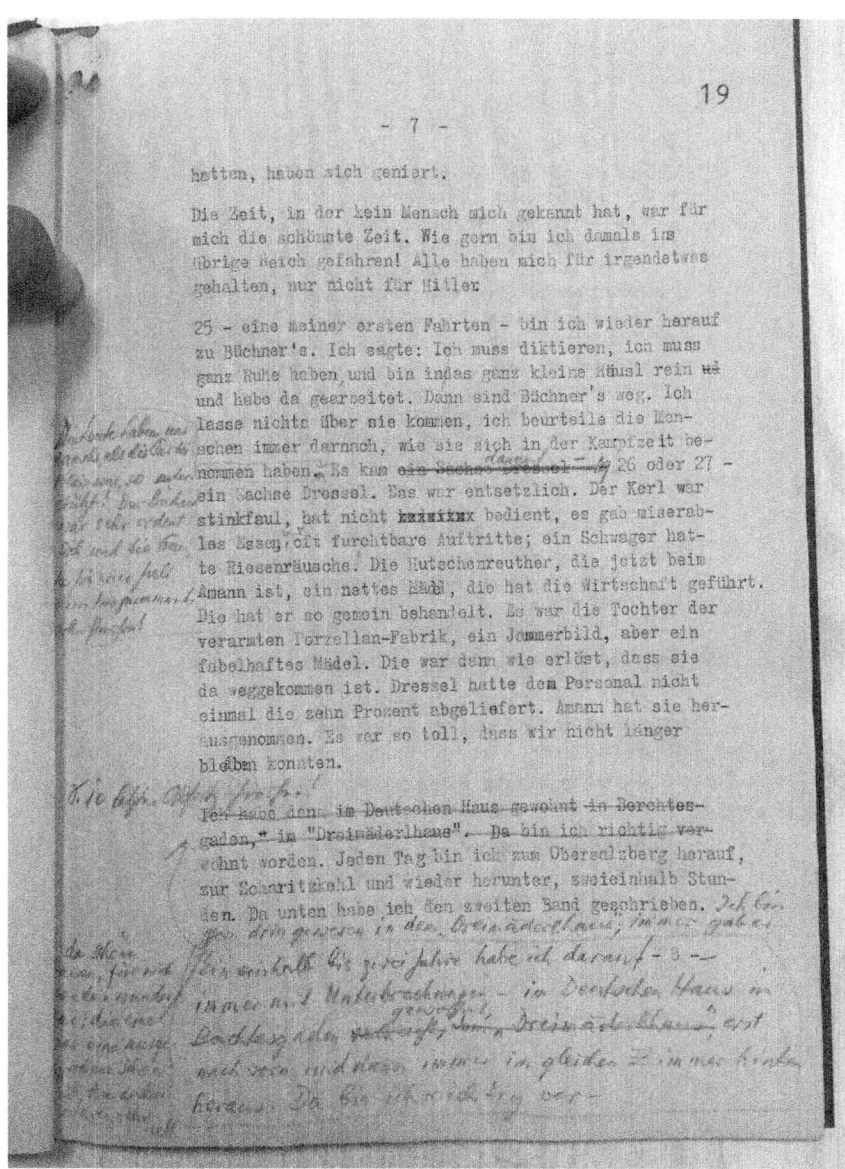

IMAGE 4   One page from Heim's proof notes. Courtesy of Bundesarchiv, Berlin-Lichterfelde.

Photo by the author.

Comparison between notes dated 16/17 January 1942 in Heim's proof pages and *Monologe*[138]

Heim's proof pages	*Monologe*
25 – eine meiner ersten Fahrten – bin ich wieder herauf zu Büchners. Ich sagte: Ich muß diktieren, ich muß ganz Ruhe haben, und bin in das ganz kleine Häusl rein und habe da bearbeitet. Dann sind Büchners weg. Ich lasse nichts auf sie kommen, ich beurteile die Menschen immer danach, wie sie sich in der Kampfzeit benommen haben. **[Die Leute haben uns damals, als die Partei klein war, so unterstützt! Der Büchner war sehr ordentlich, und die Frau, ja sie war halt eine temperamentvolle Person!]** Es kam [darauf] – 1926 oder 1927 – ein Sachse Dressel.	1925 – ein meiner ersten Fahrten – bin ich wieder herauf zu Büchners. Ich sagte: Ich muß diktieren, ich muß ganz Ruhe haben, und bin in das ganz kleine Häusl rein und habe da bearbeitet. Dann sind Büchners weg. Ich lasse nichts auf sie kommen, ich beurteile die Menschen immer danach, wie sie sich in der Kampfzeit benommen haben. Die Leute haben uns damals, als die Partei klein war, so unterstützt! Der Büchner war sehr ordentlich, und die Frau, ja sie war halt eine temperamentvolle Person! Es kam *darauf* – 1926 oder 1927 – ein Sachse Dressel.
. . .	. . .
wöhnt worden. **[Eineinhalb bis zwei Jahre habe ich darauf – immer mit Unterbrechungen – im Deutschen Haus in Berchtesgaden gewohnt, erst nach vorn und dann immer im gleichen Zimmer hinten heraus. Da bin ich richtig ver-].** Jeden Tag bin ich zum Obersalzberg herauf, zur Scharitzkehl und wieder herunter, zweieinhalb Stunden. Da unten habe ich den zweiten Band geschrieben. **[Ich bin gern drin gewesen, in dem "Dreimäderlhaus", immer gab es da schöne Frauen, für mich war das wunderbar; die eine war eine ausgesprochene Schönheit, die anderen waren sehr nett.]**	Eineinhalb bis zwei Jahre habe ich darauf – immer mit Unterbrechungen – im Deutschen Haus in Berchtesgaden gewohnt, erst nach vorn und dann immer im gleichen Zimmer hinten heraus. Da bin ich richtig verwöhnt worden. Jeden Tag bin ich zum Obersalzberg hinauf, zur Scharitzkehl und wieder herunter, zweieinhalb Stunden. Da unten habe ich den zweiten Band [von "Mein Kampf"] geschrieben. Ich bin gern drin gewesen, in dem "Dreimäderlhaus", immer gab es da schöne Frauen, für mich war das wunderbar; die eine war eine ausgesprochene Schönheit, die anderen waren sehr nett.
[Translation:] *25 – one of my first rides – I'm back up to Büchner's. I said: I have to dictate, I have to have complete peace, and I am in the very small house and have worked there. Then Büchner's are gone. I don't let anything come at them, I always judge people by how they behaved in fight time. **[People so supported us back when the party was small! Büchner was very tidy, and the woman, yes she was simply a spirited person!]** There was a Sachse Dressel [in addition] – in 1926 or 1927 – a Sachsonian Dressel.*	[Translation:] *In 1925 – one of my first rides – I was back up to Büchner's. I said: I have to dictate, I have to have complete peace, and I am in the very small house and have worked there. Then Büchner's are gone. I don't let anything come at them, I always judge people by how they behaved in fight time. People were so supportive of us back when the party was little! Büchner was very tidy, and the woman, yes she was simply a spirited person! In addition there was – in 1926 or 1927 – a Sachsonian Dressel.*
[. . .]	*[. . .]*

Heim's proof pages	Monologe
iled. **[One and a half to two years I lived – with constant interruptions – in the German House in Berchtesgaden, first in the front and then always in the same room at the back. That's when I was really spoiled.]** *Every day I went up to Obersalzberg, to the Scharitzkehl and down again, two and a half hours. Down there I wrote the second volume.* **[I liked to be in it, in the "three girls house," there were always beautiful women there, for me that was wonderful; one was a true beauty, the others were very pretty.]**	*One and a half to two years I lived – with constant interruptions – in the German House in Berchtesgaden, first in the front and then always in the same room at the back. That's when I was really spoiled. Every day I went up to Obersalzberg, to the Scharitzkehl and down again, two and a half hours. Down there I wrote the second volume [of "Mein Kampf"]. I liked to be there, in the "Three Girls House," there were always beautiful women there, for me that was wonderful; one was a true beauty, the others were very pretty.*

Source: Text in bold and within square brackets in the proof pages are handwritten changes; stricken through text is typed text that has been stricken out manually.

The additions here are so many and of such magnitude and character that they cannot reasonably be explained by arguing that Heim had forgot to include them there when he first typed up the text. Moreover, these notes from 8/9 and 16/17 January are from the nightly tea conversations, which means that they were re-created completely from memory without any supporting notes. They are too detailed to be things that Heim remembered correctly after even more time had elapsed between him hearing Hitler speak and typing up the first draft. Clearly these are redactional additions made in order to "improve" on the text. Indeed, it is doubtful if these additions stem from Heim originally; rather they probably stem from Bormann.

Yet Thomas Weber cites this very note frequently in his book *Wie Adolf Hitler zum Nazi wurde*, unaware of all the editing that lay behind the final product in *Monologe*. Weber even quotes the parts where Hitler supposedly cites conversations taking place in 1923 as if they accurately reflects what was being said.[139] Weber uses these quotes (where Dietrich Eckart reportedly called Hitler "Wolf") to support his conclusion that Hitler, in 1923, saw himself as a "wolf" and leader of a "pack."[140] However, this note from mid-January 1942 cannot be used to verify what Hitler thought of himself almost 20 years earlier. This is not to say that what Weber argues is not true; only that the table talks cannot be used to corroborate it.

The proof pages are the key to figuring out the source-critical value of Heim's notes, and therefore of *Monologe*. Jochmann knew about these pages, as we shall see later on in this book, but clearly did not understand how they affected the value of the manuscript as a representation of Hitler's words. What the proof pages show beyond any reasonable doubt is that the notes were a literary product to a much larger extent than what has so far been acknowledged by historians. These pages testify to the process whereby Heim (and probably Bormann) both recreated and created

Hitler's utterances, and they also imply that the process was much more drawn out than previously known. Instead of being made in immediate connection to the conversations, as claimed by Heim, the proof pages show that text was rearranged and added over a longer period of time. How much time that elapsed between the when Heim typed up the first draft text, and when the handwritten additions were added, is unclear. However, I have argued that there is good evidence for assuming that several months may have passed between the production of the first draft text and the additions being added, and finally before the final version of the notes was produced. The final version of the text seems to have been typed up in Munich, *not* in the FHQ as historians have previously assumed (based on Heim's testimony).

It just so happens that Weinberg has made some further contributions to the study of the table monologues. By chance I stumbled upon such an occasion in his preface to *Hitlers zweites Buch* from 1961.[141] Weinberg discusses a remark in a note dated 17 February 1942 about Hitler's second unpublished book that appears in *Table Talk* and in *Libres propos*, but that is missing in *Tischgespräche*. The phrase, in *Table Talk*, reads:

> In 1925 I wrote in *Mein Kampf* (and also in an unpublished work) that world Jewry saw in Japan an opponent beyond its reach.[142]

In *Libres propos* we find the following phrasing:

> En 1925, j'ai écrit dans *Mein Kampf* (et également dans un texte non publié) que la juiverie mondiale voyait dans le Japon un adversaire hors de sa portée.[143]
>
> [Translation:] *In 1925 I wrote in* Mein Kampf *(and also in an unpublished text) that World Jewry saw in Japan an opponent beyond its reach.*

The phrasings are extremely similar and show that *Table Talk* was translated from the French also in this case. This is evident from how the passage reads in *Monologe* where it says:

> 1925 habe ich in "Mein Kampf" und einer anderen, nicht veröffentlichten Schrift, geschrieben, daß das Weltjudentum in Japan den letzten nicht anfreßbaren Gegner sieht.[144]
>
> [Translation:] *In 1925 I wrote in "Mein Kampf" and another, not published text, that World Jewry saw in Japan the last unreachable opponent.*

There can be no doubt as to what source *Table Talk* was translated from. The English and French texts do not contain a phrase corresponding either to "the last" opponent or to "its" ("*sa*" in French). We can also notice that the parenthesis is not present in *Monologe* and that it is also somewhat differently phrased. However, I seriously doubt that this passage purveys what Hitler actually said. The whole sentence seems contrived; i.e. what possible reason would Hitler have to include the cumbersome and awkward phrase "and another, not published text"? It seems rather obvious that this phrase has been put in there by someone else (by either Heim or Bormann) just to make a point.

We can compare also with how Weinberg chose to re-translate this passage from English into German in 1961:

> Im Jahre 1925 habe ich in *Mein Kampf* (und auch in einem unveröffentlichten Werk) geschrieben, daß das Weltjudentum in Japan einen Gegner sehe, an den es nicht herankönne.[145]
>
> [Translation:] *In the year 1925 I wrote in* Mein Kampf *(and also in an unpublished work) that World Jewry sees, in Japan, an opponent that it could not approach.*

Now it becomes really interesting, because it turns out that not only is the text in *Tischgespräche* (1951) different, but it also differs compared to the text in the manuscript for the 1963 edition. In *Tischgespräche* (1951) neither *Mein Kampf* nor any other book is mentioned in this context. It simply states:

> Ich habe 1925 geschrieben, daß das Judentum in Japan den letzten nicht anfreßbaren Gegner sieht.[146]
>
> [Translation:] *I wrote in 1925 that World Jewry saw, in Japan, the last unreachable opponent.*

However, in the manuscript to the 1963 edition of *Tischgespräche* we find the following text:

> Ich habe 1925 **[in "Mein Kamp" und einer anderen nicht veröffentlichten Schrift]** geschrieben, daß das Welt-Judentum in Japan den letzten, nicht anfreßbaren Gegner sieht.[147]
>
> [Translation:] *I wrote in 1925 **[in "Mein Kampf" and another unpublished text]** that World-Jewry saw, in Japan, the last unreachable opponent.*

The bold text indicates that the passage, which is identical to *Monologe*, has been added by hand to the carbon copy manuscript. It is likely that it is Picker himself who has made this change because it differs markedly from the handwritten comments to the text inserted by Schramm. The latter uses a pencil and his handwriting is difficult to read, whereas the former uses a pen and writes rather clearly. There is no other plausible candidate for these editorial changes. However, this proves that Picker had simply left this part out in the 1951 edition, since the German text later published in *Monologe* was not available at the time.

What is also significant here is that the passage is actually incorrect. The part about Japan does not appear in the first volume of *Mein Kampf*, which is what the year 1925 implies, but in the second volume published in December 1926. It is true, however, that the chapter in question, chapter 13, was a mixture of texts that went back as far as April 1924, but these parts had been lifted out of the first volume in 1925 and instead reappeared, re-worked and interlaced with text based on the pamphlet *Die Südtiroler Frage und das Deutsche Bündnisproblem* (The South

Tirol Issue and the German Alliance Problem) published in the spring of 1926, in the second volume. The part about Japan and the Jews appears at the very end of the chapter.[148] Gerhard Weinberg shows that this passage had been part of the pamphlet published that spring, however he mistakenly claims that Hitler had dictated this section to the CEO of Franz Eher Verlag, Max Amann, in 1925.[149] There is no credible evidence of Hitler having dictated any part of *Mein Kampf* to Amann.[150] In fact, this section (as is the rest of the text) of *Die Sütiroler Frage...* was identical to the passage ending up in *Mein Kampf*.[151] But considering that *Die Südtiroler Frage ...*, whose foreword is dated 12 February 1926, as Othmar Plöckinger has shown, was based om material that Hitler had already begun working on while in the Landsberg prison, and the fact that it forms a coherent whole,[152] it could be that the part about Japan and the Jews was actually written in Landsberg in 1924. However, there is no way to know exactly when this passage was written.

Likewise, this passage clearly implies that the remark about the unpublished work dates also *that* book to 1925. This is especially clear in *Monologe*'s version of the text. This is, however, entirely incorrect since Hitler's second book was not written until 1928, as Weinberg conclusively proves. But there is an independent source that corroborates the mistaken date as apparently having been talked about in Hitler's entourage. Weinberg quotes Hitler's secretary Christa Schroeder (who had apparently also seen this book manuscript) in Albert Zoller's book *Hitler privat* from 1949 as saying: "Already in 1925 Hitler had, in complete secrecy, begun to write a book on foreign policy."[153] Weinberg reasons that Schroeder can only have gotten this date from Hitler himself, since she did not start to work for him until 1933, and thus it must be due to a flaw in Hitler's memory, he writes.[154]

Weinberg reasons that either this unpublished work was mentioned by Hitler and later excluded by Picker, or either Heim or Bormann inserted it at a later stage. For obvious reasons he could never imagine that Genoud had tampered with the text in *Table Talk* and *Libres propos*. He goes on to say that Heim is unlikely to have dared to add something like this if Hitler had not said it and would anyway most likely not have known about this book in any case. There is perhaps some merit to that, although Heim had known Hitler since the early 1920s. Bormann, on the other hand, could easily have had the audacity to add this phrase, Weinberg writes, but he cannot see any reason for him to do so. His conclusion, therefore, based also upon the many other missing phrases and passages in Picker's book, is that Bormann excluded the remark from the version of the manuscript shown to Picker. Weinberg also concludes from this that Picker's version is a later, and therefore more edited, variant of the text.[155] We now know for a fact that Weinberg was wrong regarding his reasoning about Picker and *Tischgespräche*. We know this since the phrase is inserted by hand in Picker's manuscript for the second edition.[156] The omission must have been Picker's, and the other omissions from the first edition that then appear in the second edition, many of which have already been detailed in this book, prove this.

Moreover, Weinberg argues that it is all the more likely that the utterance is authentic, since it is incorrect, and thus a product of Hitler not remembering correctly. He adds in support of this conclusion that Hitler had trouble getting things right when referring to his own personal last will and testament, too, which he had dictated less than four years earlier.[157] It is doubtful if this was due to an inability to remember the correct facts, however. Hitler lied and obfuscated purposefully when it came to his own biographical history. The fact of the matter is also, as Weinberg points out, that Hitler makes no reference to Japan in *Hitlers zweites Buch* that is in any way similar to the one cited earlier.[158] Jochmann, as usual, does not tell us at all what he makes of this. He simply refers to page 723 in the second volume of *Mein Kampf* and to page 171 in *Hitlers zweites Buch* where Japan is mentioned, but not at all in the same context (there is absolutely no talk about Jews and their attitude to Japan here).[159] Jochmann is thus giving a reference to a passage that is obviously *not* what Hitler is talking about according to *Monologe*, even though Weinberg had shown this to be incorrect in the very book that Jochmann is referring to.

Odd similarities between Genoud and Picker

While there is no doubt that Genoud had an authentic manuscript, there are some very interesting similarities between *Libres propos* and *Tischgespräche* on the one hand, and Heim's proof pages and *Monologe* on the other hand, that need to be addressed when we try to evaluate the genealogy of these manuscripts.

The first example comes from a note dated 18 January 1942, i.e. it is one of the notes included in Heim's proof pages. Hitler is here recorded as speaking about when the party programme and the party itself were founded and why he does not want to change the party programme. In *Tischgespräche* Hitler says:

> Mit diesem Programm wurde die Bewegung am 24. Februar 1919 gegründet.[160]
>
> [Translation:] *With this programme, the movement was founded on 24 February 1919.*

Interestingly, Genoud has the same in his edition, namely:

> C'etait déjà le nôtre le jour de la foundation du Parti, le 24 février 1919.[161]
>
> [Translation:] *It was already ours on the day of the foundation of the party, on 24 February 1919.*

Genoud's version, in which the phrase "this programme" is not mentioned (because it is referring back to the previous sentence where the programme *is* mentioned), is of course repeated in *Table Talk*.[162] The intriguing thing is that the given year is incorrect. This fact was pointed out by Schramm in the second edition of *Tischgespräche* – Ritter had not corrected it in the first edition – since the mistake was repeated in the *Ms. 63*.[163] The party programme was announced that day in 1920, one year later than both sources say. This seems like an excusable mistake for one writer to make, but when two make it, especially under the circumstances discussed here, then the historian might get to thinking that Genoud based his date on Picker. Jochmann has put the correct date in himself but says nothing, as usual, about Genoud. Jochmann writes the year like this: "[1920]."[164] He did this because in his manuscript the year was missing, just as in Heim's proof page where it simply says:

> wurde die Bewegung am 24. Februar gegründet.[165]
> [Translation:] *the movement was founded on 24 February.*

This is how we know that Picker and Genoud (and Trevor-Roper based on the latter) added the year on their own. This proves beyond reasonable doubt that Genoud was looking at Picker when he wanted to find out what year the party was founded as he was preparing his French translation.

Here we must digress a bit in order to understand what this statement really means. The NSDAP was not really founded on 24 February 1920. In fact, there is still considerable confusion in the literature regarding when the party actually changed its name and became generally known as the NSDAP. Anton Joachim-sthaler states that the name change from DAP to NSDAP had been formally decided on 1 February 1920, but he actually gives no source for this claim. Sven Felix Kellerhoff notes that a formal name change did not even take place on 24 February. The 25 points of the party programme was dictated to the party secretary, Ferdinand Wiegand, on 22 February 1920. The date 24 February 1920 was when the 25 points were read aloud publicly for the first time, namely in the *Hofbräuhaus* in Munich. This date was then used in Nazi propaganda to mark the constituting meeting of the NSDAP, even though it was nothing of the sort. The meeting was never announced as a foundational meeting at the time, and it was not thought of as such. The announcements for the meeting only spoke about the DAP and Hitler was not even mentioned as speaker.[166]

In fact, the police report from the meeting states that Hitler had read the "Program of the German Workers' Party" (*Program der deutschen Arbeiterpartei*), and a report in the *Völkischer Beobachter* from 28 February stated that the programme points "come close to the principles of the programme of the German Socialist Party."[167] Moreover, the party actually officially changed its name to NSDAP a few days *after* the meeting on 24 February 1920 (although the name change had been decided upon already on 1 February), and the term "National Socialist" was nowhere to be found in the party programme. Legally, moreover, the NSDAP did not exist until 30 September that year, when it was registered as *Nationalsozialistische Deutsche Arbeitsvereins Deutschland* (NSDAVD). The protocol from the founding meeting of the NSDAVD gave 5 January 1919 as the foundational date for the NSDAP.[168] The latter date was, of course, when the DAP, and *not* the NSDAP, had originally been founded. The police report from the meeting on 24 February 1920 still only mentioned the DAP.[169]

Kellerhoff points out that a police report mentioned the name "NSDAP" on 6 April, and that Hitler first used it in a speech in Rosenheim on 2 May 1920.[170] However, Kellerhoff's conclusion is a bit imprecise because another police reports still has Hitler talking about "das Programm der DAP" as late as 11 May 1920.[171] Apparently, Hitler was himself not using the new party name regularly by early May; in fact, whenever he proclaimed the 25 points of the party programme he did so by referring to the party as DAP. The first time that a report mentions

Hitler using the name NSDAP is on 12 May 1920.[172] But this did not mean that Hitler made a clear break, since on 19 May Hitler again talked about the party as the DAP.[173] The *Völkischer Beobachter* still referred to the party as the DAP as late as 19 June 1920.[174] *Rosenheim Tageblatt* referred to Hitler still calling the party the DAP on 21 June 1920, and the name NSDAP is talked about for the first time in a newspaper report in the *Münchener Neueste Nachrichten* on 30 June 1920 as they reported on a speech held on 24 June.[175] Still, Hitler's notes for a speech in Munich in July uses the name DAP.[176] The police report from Hitler's speech in Munich on 6 July also mentions the DAP party programme.[177] The first time a report mentions Hitler ending a meeting with a salute to the NSDAP is on 15 July 1920. The police report actually uses both names.[178] Karl Riedl, the first treasurer of the NSDAP, recorded in his diary that one point of a meeting of the party board (*Ausschuß*) on 8 July 1920 had been the name DAP, and Eberhard Jäckel notes in an editorial comment in *Sämtliche Aufzeichnungen* that at the time the name DAP "was a nuisance to many" and that Hitler was adamantly arguing against "a dilution of the name."[179] In August 1920 Rudolf Heß (who had been a member since 1 July) called the party both "National Socialist Workers' Party" (*nationalsozialistische Arbeiter – Partei*) and "German Workers' Party" (*Deutschen Arbeiterpartei*) in a typed statement.[180] The fact is that Hitler used DAP in his notes for a speech even as late as mid-1922.[181] It thus seems as if the old name lived on for quite some time before it was replaced by NSDAP, and it was only from July 1920 onwards that the latter name became more generally used. Even so, we know from correspondence that Heß used the names NSDAP and DAP interchangeably still in July 1925 as, for example, in a reply to a party supporter dated 29 July.[182]

But there is yet another reason to mistrust Hitler's statement as recorded by Heim in this case, and that is *the reason given for why Hitler did not want to change the party programme*. On 13 November 1922 Hitler held a long speech at an NSDAP meeting in Munich in which, according to the police report, he said:

> The programme of the movement is a temporary programme. The leaders refuse to set up new ones after achieving the goals set out in the program in order to enable the continued existence of the party.[183]

Hitler even specified that the main point of the programme was contained in the idea that no Jew could ever be a German citizen (*Staatsbürger*), since a Jew could not be *Volksgenosse*.[184] This was actually a point that Hitler made forcefully on many occasions. The *Völkischer Beobachter* reported on 25 November 1922 (from an NSDAP meeting held on 22 November) that Hitler underlined:

> That a party must never be an end in itself; but must only form a means to a higher end. If a party is only given to the organization, it is absolutely harmful, because its principle is: First the party, then the fatherland. On the other hand, it must be noted that parties also survive themselves. [. . .] Therefore, the parties forge their temporary programmes as being valid for eternity, in order to bait their constituents and maintain the party organization. Another

hoax is also popular here: One must not fully fulfill the small material things of the programme, because then no one else would vote [for the party]. In these cases, the party has become an end in itself, and the party big wigs care little if the motherland perishes over it.[185]

On 17 August 1923 the *Frankfurter Zeitung* reported the following from a speech that Hitler had held three days earlier:

The National Socialists have no program for a hundred years, they are only a movement for the liberation of the people. Their task is to forge the people together in holy hatred against their oppressors.[186]

These statements are clear in their implications, namely that once the goals of the NSDAP party programme had been fulfilled there would be no real reason for the party to continue to exist, and no new aims should be created in order to justify the prolonging of the life of the party. Indeed, Hitler's view seems to be that he expected the party to wither away after this point. This likely had to do with Hitler's insistence on the point that the party should be a non-parliamentary and revolutionary party. This was the vision up until the putsch in November 1923, and it was only after the reformation of the NSDAP in 1925 that the parliamentary way became the strategy for the party. The involvement in the parliamentary democratic system required a totally different kind of party structure and organization, a bureaucratic and modern party structure – one that resembled that of the established Weimar Republic parties.[187]

The parliamentary strategy was initiated by Hitler's co-conspirator in the failed 1923 coup, Erich Ludendorff, during Hitler's time in prison. Rudolf Heß wrote on 21 October 1924, after the *Reichstag* had been dissolved, that Hitler was of the opinion that the *völkisch* bloc should not get involved in the parliament again. Heß thought that it must have annoyed Hitler that he had retreated from all business concerning the party, and that he could not meddle in this matter. Hitler's total resistance to a parliamentary strategy was repeated by Heß in a letter on 27 November that year.[188] Hitler nevertheless reluctantly had to accept the *fait accompli* that he was presented with, but parliamentarism should be used in order to combat democracy by obstructing the democratic process.[189] Later, however, he would claim that he was the originator of this idea. He had chosen the legal path, he told the audience at *Bürgerbräukeller* in Munich on 8 November 1935, because of the many dead that the bloody coup attempt had resulted in back in 1923. Many people had questioned his choice, Hitler proclaimed, and asked how the party could ever work legally. Then he cited a fictional conversation in which he replied to these people: "What do you want? Should you teach me how to fight? Where were they when we hit off? I do not need any instruction from you about revolution or legality."[190] Many years later Hitler would brag about how "the so-called National Socialist Revolution has defeated democracy inside democracy with democracy!"[191]

It may even be that before 1924 Hitler did not expect the NSDAP to actually ever come to power in Germany, at least not in his lifetime. The fact that Hitler talked about himself as only being "the drummer" (*der Trommler*), and expressing doubt as to whether or not there would actually be a man ready to shoulder the responsibility of leading Germany to victory, during this same period may indicate as much.[192] In a letter on 27 November 1924 Heß stated that Hitler had told him that it would take several generations before reality had adjusted to the ideology and vice versa. His aim was set in the very distant future, Hitler said, and perhaps he would only have the honour to "soften the earth" (*den Boden zu lockern*), i.e. to prepare the ground, and to place a pole in it; a pole that would point to an earlier great era in human history. It would be up to another coming great personality to continue his work in the future, Hitler stated to Heß.[193] Still by New Year's 1932 Hitler reminded the members that the party was only a means to an end, not an end in itself, and that it only had a right to exist as long as it was dedicated to the struggle for the National Socialist idea of a future *Volksgemeinschaft*.[194]

But after 30 January 1933 matters changed a great deal for Hitler. In his New Year's proclamation on 1 January 1936 Hitler stated that the party was "the firm and indestructible bearer of the German will to live."[195] Two years later he would state that the NSDAP would lead the nation in the coming centuries as the guarantor of the future of the German people.[196] The party was now called "the eternal, politically sustaining National Socialist Party."[197]

This also relates to the issue of whether Hitler thought of the regime as a revolutionary one or not. The case for this view was made forcefully by Rainer Zitelmann in 1987, while Peter Longerich in his Hitler biography from 2015 states that the revolution was transformed into evolution after Hitler on 6 July 1933 proclaimed that "the revolution is not a permanent state" (*Die Revolution ist kein permanenter Zustand*). In the same speech he announced the revolution was now to become evolution. Zitelmann does not deny this but points out that this statement was contradicted by many others that Hitler made after that point. For example, Hitler said on 30 January 1934 that the revolution should continue during the coming year.[198] Moreover, Hitler made his 6 July statement one day after the Catholic *Zentrum* party had been dissolved and two days before the concordat (*Reichskonkordat*) between Nazi Germany and the Vatican was signed. Clearly this was propaganda intended to put fears about the party's radical agenda both domestically and in the Vatican to rest, and the fact that Longerich takes it seriously is a bit odd.

Only a few weeks before, on 16 June 1933, Goebbels spoke in Hamburg about the National Socialist revolution at which time he made perfectly clear that the revolution was only now beginning.[199] Hitler clearly was of the view that the revolution would go on. On 19 March 1934 he said in a "revolutionary appeal to the old fighters" (*Revolutionsappell der alten Kämpfer*) in Munich that the National Socialist revolution had to go on. A worldview needed a lot of time to revolutionize the minds of the people, Hitler said. One could not become a National Socialist in a year, and several generations would pass before everyone had buried the sign of victory in their hearts. Only at that point could the revolution be considered finished and the German people saved, he said.[200] Yet on 13 July that year, almost exactly one year after the first time, he said, using very similar words, that "the revolution is not a permanent state for us."[201] This, however, came right on top of the mass murder of his opponents in SA (as well as a number of conservative politicians), whom Hitler had accused of trying to bring about a second revolution. Hitler was trying to fight a struggle on two fronts here; on the one hand *against* the revolutionary SA, and on the other *for* the continued spreading of National Socialist ideology throughout German society. Thus, we cannot take this instance too seriously either. Some months later, on 9 November 1934, he pointed out that the party was not at the end of its mission, but only at the beginning.[202] But one of the most telling passages come from a speech made in January 1940 in which he stated that Germany was now at the beginning of "the eighth year of the National Socialist revolution."[203] Goebbels, too, made it abundantly clear in a speech on 30 January 1942, marking the ninth anniversary of Hitler coming to power, that National Socialism was an ongoing revolution.[204] The same point was forcefully made when he spoke in Heidelberg to members of the National Student Leadership (*Reichsstudentführung*).[205] Then, in January 1944 Hitler noted "the twelfth year of the re-organization of our people" and about how the revolution had to be carried on further.[206] It is indeed hard not to give Zitelmann credit here, i.e. Hitler clearly thought of his years in power as a continuing revolution.

What Hitler said here shows that what Heim records is a later development and not the original reason for why the programme should not be altered. Obviously, after the Nuremberg Laws of 1935 the goals of the party programme had already been fulfilled. The NSDAP had by then become exactly what Hitler criticized in 1922, i.e. an organization filled with "party big wigs" (*Parteibonzen*) that had outlived its purpose and was only hurting the nation. According to the logic of what Hitler stated in 1922, the party should then cease to exist. But the party *did* still exist and was more prevalent than ever before. Hitler even said on 6 July 1933 that the "party has now become the state."[207] This was a point that Hitler would make on increasingly more occasions during the 1930s. On 13 September 1935, i.e. two days before the Nuremberg Laws were established as the law of the land, he underlined that there could be no separation between the *Führer* and his followers, and therefore no separation between the *Führer* and the party.[208] The *Führer* was the party, and the party is the *Führer*, he declared on 18 September.[209] In a speech on 7 September 1937 he also underlined that the movement, the NSDAP, and the state were now one and the same and the only true authority in the nation.[210] Also, on 24 February 1941 he pointed out that "the people and the Wehrmacht, the party and the state – they are now an insoluble entity."[211] To put forward the earlier view in this later situation would be to acknowledge that he had changed his views. Thus, Hitler may well have said what Heim records, but it is not the truth.

This may also be the reason for why Hitler started to claim that it was his political opponents that had called him "the drummer" (*Trommler*). In several speeches in the 1930s he brings up this point. The first time was in a speech to the Industrial Club in Düsseldorf in 1932, where he rhetorically questioned why it would be a bad thing to whip up national sentiment in the German people.[212] Hitler brought this point up again in February 1936 when he stated that his opponents had for several years called him *Trommler*.[213] Now, the fact that Hitler saw himself only as Trommler before 1924 was shown by Albrecht Tyrell in his book *Vom "Trommler" zum "Führer"* in 1975.[214] But clearly this was a matter that Hitler thought necessary to adjust to make it fit his later view of himself better.

Thus, *Monologe* follows the false story told in *Mein Kampf* in this case as well. It was only later that this date came to denote the beginning of the so-called new party, the NSDAP. Once again, then, we see how the table talks spread Nazi myths and propaganda. The mistake regarding the year seems excusable for one writer to make, but when two make it, especially under the circumstances discussed here, then the historian has to draw the conclusion that Genoud based his dating of this event on Picker's *Tischgespräche*. This is how we know that Picker, Genoud (and Trevor-Roper, based on the latter) added the year *ante facto*.

More importantly, the statement regarding the party programme having remained unchanged is not true. In fact, in the letter from 14 July 1921 in which Hitler announced his decision to leave the party, he stipulated as one of the conditions for re-entering that "every further change of the name or of the program should once and for all not be undertaken for a period of six years."[215] This obviously suggests that the party programme had been changed on more than one occasion since 24 February 1920. In reality the programme was amended five times between 1920 and the party meeting in Bamberg 14 February 1926. The need for the Bamberg meeting was also brought on because of the demands for a re-writing of the party programme from many within the NSDAP, and a working group had been formed, led by Gregor Straßer, which met for that purpose in Hannover on 22 November 1925. This group convened even though Hitler had repeated the claim that the programme was immutable in August that year. Historians have claimed that it was only after the Bamberg meeting, from which Hitler emerged as the undisputed victor, that the party programme was finally secured.[216]

However, this seems to be not entirely correct. Obviously, the demands for changes continued also after the Bamberg meeting, since Hitler had to address this issue yet again at the NSDAP "Leader Day" (*Führertagung*) in Passau on 12 August 1926. Hitler stated that it was of utmost importance that the party programme should not be changed, because people would not be willing to lay down their life for an ever-changing programme. This decision, he once again stressed, was immutable.[217] Yet, Gottfried Feder stated in a publication of the programme in 1927 that this did not mean that the programme could not be elaborated upon. Only *the spirit and basis* for it were immutable.[218] The version in *Monologe* does agree with how Hitler depicts this matter in *Mein Kampf*, however, where he also defended the idea that the programme should be unchangeable.[219]

There are other falsehoods in Heim's notes to point to as well. For instance, in the note dated during the night between 27 and 28 September 1941 Heim states that Hitler said:

> Who knows, if my parents had been wealthy enough to let me attend the academy, I don't think I would have been able to get to know social hardship from the ground up.[220]

This refers to Hitler's years in Vienna and him not having attended the art school of his dreams. However, the idea that Hitler did not attend college because his parents were not rich enough is not true. In reality, Hitler tried to get in (twice, even) but failed because he was simply not talented enough. Joachimsthaler remarks that many other youngsters from modest backgrounds were able – through thrift, dedication, and hard work – to advance in life. Hitler simply lacked the necessary qualities at that time.[221] Once again, then, we find that *Monologe* is propagating lies about Hitler at a time when, according to Heim, Hitler was supposedly most open and sincere. Did Hitler actually say this, and in that case why did he lie to his entourage (or at least convince himself that this was true)?

Another example of such odd similarities between Genoud and Picker can be found in the note dated the next day on 19 January 1942. In both *Monologe* and Heim's proof page we find:

> Ich hatte fortgesetzt Schwierigkeiten, meine Männer vor Duellen zu bewahren. Ich habe das dann einfach verboten. *Ein paar meiner* besten Leute sind *mir* durch solche Dummheiten zusammengeschossen worden.[222] [Italics added.]
>
> [Translation:] *I continued to struggle to save my men from duels. I just banned that then. A couple of my best people have been shot up [and lost] to me by such stupidities.*

The German first-person dative form "*mir*" is awkward in English, but it is important to include it for comparative purposes. As it happens, Picker has a different wording here instead of "*meiner*"; he has also used the plural instead of the singular form; the first-person dative form "*mir*" is not included. It reads:

> *Einige unserer* besten Leute sind durch solche Dummheiten zusammengeschossen worden.[223] [Italics added.]
>
> [Translation:] Some of our *best people have been shot up by such stupidities.*

When we then turn to *Libres propos* what do we find? Indeed, we find that Genoud follows Picker in this case as well. Writes Genoud:

> *Nous avons* perdu de cette façon stupide quelques-uns parmi les meilleurs *des nôtres.*[224] [Italics added.]
>
> [Translation:] *In this way* we have *lost some of the best* of ours.

The French *quelque-uns* (some) corresponds to the German *einige* in and the last phrase in the French edition, *des nôtres* (of ours), corresponds to the second word in the German version, *unserer*. This is clearly a phrasing that Genoud could not have made by mistake and just happened to get the plural form instead of the singular in exactly the same manner as Picker. *Monologe*'s wording better corresponds to the rest of the paragraph, where first-person singular is used. In Picker's and Genoud's editions Hitler suddenly switches to first-person *plural* in the last sentence. Even with only these two examples it must be considered proven that Genoud, at least in these cases, modelled his text on *Tischgespräche*. And while we could perhaps explain the first example by Genoud taking a quick look at Picker, because he perhaps could not remember what year the NSDAP was founded, the second example is harder to explain that way. The question becomes why he would do such a thing? Genoud's French version of this, and thus also *Table Talk*, is quite different from that of *Monologe*.

But there are more examples. Yet another interesting similarity we find in an entry dated 2 August 1941, where Picker has Hitler saying:

> Deshalb konnte ich Torgler laufen lassen, während ich *Thälmann* zurück-halten *mußte*.[225] [Italics added.]
>
> [Translation:] *That is why I could let Torgler go while I had to restrain Thälmann.*

Then, when we go to Genoud we find the following:

> Aussi j'ai pu laisser courir Torgler, tandis que j'ai *dû* garder *Thaelmann*.[226] [Italics added.]
>
> [Translation:] *Also, I could let Torgler go while I had to hold [on to] Thälmann.*

As we see Genoud, too, has the name "Thälmann" as well as the past tense of the irregular verb *devoir* (have), i.e. *dû* that means "had to." Why is this important? It is important because *Monologe* includes neither of these. In *Monologe* we instead find:

> deshalb konnte ich Torgler laufen lassen, während ich ihn zurückhalte.[227]
>
> [Translation:] *therefore I could let Torgler go, while I had to restrain him [referring back to the name of Thälmann mentioned at two sentences earlier, M.N.].*

The fact that *Monologe* does not have either "Thälmann" or an equivalent to Picker's "mußte" here is significant. If only one of them appeared in Genoud's edition, we could perhaps argue that it was a coincidence, but that becomes hard to do when we take both into consideration. It is obvious that Genoud must have made his translation from Picker in this case as well. This does not mean that Genoud's manuscript is forged obviously, only that he in some cases based *Libres propos* upon *Tischgespräche*. Why on earth he would do this is, of course, a question we will probably never get a conclusive answer to. While these examples may seem like small drops amidst a large ocean, they are, in fact, enough to affect the character of all the water around them – what used to be sweet water has turned salty, or at least brackish, from the exposure.

In August 1979, not long before the publication of Jochmann's edition, the historical specialist at the Manuscript Division at the LoC, Eugene R. Sheridan, wrote to Trevor-Roper and informed him that the papers in the LoC that Trevor-Roper, in his preface to his second edition of the *Table Talk*, had stated that Irving had made him aware of were in fact the same as those that appeared in *Table Talk*.

Apparently, Trevor-Roper had not investigated this matter. He also included a copy of the entry from 19 January 1942, in which Hitler speaks about duels. Sheridan stated that

> The numerous pencilled corrections they contain indicate they may well be the first typed drafts of Heinrich Heim's notes . . . and the fact that they were discovered in Munich in 1945 suggests that they might be the last surviving remnants of the set of <u>Bormann-Vermerke</u> that was, as you write, 'kept in the Führerbrau [sic] in Munich and . . . Burnt at the end of the war.'[228]

Note that Sheridan made a mistake regarding the year when the notes were found. If this was correct, Sheridan wrote, then a comparison between these notes and those in Genoud's possession might reveal "some interesting insights about the principles of selection Bormann followed in compiling this valuable historical source."[229] Sheridan's assessment of Heim's proof pages concurs with the one presented here, which indeed seems to be the only reasonable explanation. Sheridan was also right in assuming that a comparison between them would yield interesting results.

It is most likely Sheridan's handwritten references to *Table Talk* that appear on the cover pages to Heim's proof pages.

Conclusion

The discovery of Heim's proof pages at the LoC in the early 1950s by the director of the IfZ, Dr Mau, is perhaps the single most important discovery ever made with regard to the history of the table talks. However, despite this fact, no historian actually understood the real significance of these documents for the question of how reliably Heim's notes convey Hitler's words. The proof pages for a long time were simply seen as a confirmation that Genoud's manuscript was genuine. Astonishingly, no one ever seems to have bothered to ask what the many changes to the draft text meant from a source-critical perspective. It was as if changes to the memorandum did not imply that the fidelity was negatively affected by this practice. In reality, however, these handwritten changes testify to the fact that the notes are a carefully crafted literary product where Heim (assisted by Bormann) made an effort to formulate the statements ascribed to Hitler in, according to their view, the best possible manner.

Much of the most surprising facts about Heim's notes have been uncovered only by studying the original documents now kept in the *Bundesarchiv* in Berlin. These documents revealed many important facts that could not be gained from either paper or digital copies – because they were not visible – and among them were the discovery that these notes had been written at the NSDAP party HQ in Munich and *not* at the FHQ, as had always been claimed. The notes, dated in January 1942, were not written down and proofread until sometime after mid-March 1942 after Heim had been replaced by Picker at the FHQ. This is the only plausible explanation for the totality of the evidence, including the fact that the proof pages were brought to

Munich in the first place, where they were discovered by a gallery assistant, German national Joseph Ehrnsberger, working at the American CCP, i.e. in the former *Führerbau*. My investigation of the documents in the archive also revealed the fact that these notes were only a small part of a larger series of notes that had once been held together by staples – notes covering at least the period January to March 1942. Unfortunately, the rest of these proof pages have been lost. This all means that Heim finished his notes several months after the conversations that are recorded in them, which is yet an even greater problem from a source-critical perspective.

It was also at the NSDAP HQ in Munich that Picker copied his share of Heim's notes during the summer of 1942. There are several witness statements that testify to this, and we can therefore rather accurately reconstruct how Picker went about acquiring these notes. Picker had replaced Bormann's assistant K. W. Hanssen there for a short while and during this time he had gained access to Heim's notes. As a consequence of this, Bormann seems to have become quite angry with not only Picker, but with both Hanssen and Heim too. Bormann had Hanssen replaced by Hans Müller (who would later make some table talk notes for Bormann during 1943), and Heim was sent back to Munich. It is perhaps also not at all insignificant that Müller was stationed in Munich. Whether he made his notes in Munich or on location at the FHQ is unknown. I have not been able to confirm that Müller was actually stationed at the FHQ, but that does not mean that he was not. Perhaps the most likely scenario is that Müller made his notes in the same way as Heim, i.e. a draft version of the text was drawn up at the FHQ and the final version was then finished at the Party HQ in Munich sometime later.

We have also seen that the notes contain many statements that either are untrue, for example, repeating known lies originally published in *Mein Kampf* or that cannot have been uttered by Hitler. It seems obvious that the table talks were not at all a record of Hitler's most inner thoughts and unguarded statements, as they have been claimed to be by so many people, experts and lay people alike, over the years. We find in them the same kind of Nazi propaganda and myths that we find elsewhere in Hitler's official statements and publications. Some instances of when Genoud edited his text based on Picker's book have been discovered due to the reading of Heim's proof pages, as when Hitler is said to have claimed that the NSDAP was founded on 24 February 1919. In Heim's proof pages (as well as in *Monologe*) there is no year given, yet in *Libres propos* and *Table Talk* we find the year 1919. This is a mistake; the real year should be 1920. This has to be because Genoud copied Picker's mistake in *Tischgespräche* in 1951.

Notes

1 See handwritten message on the top of note "Führerhautquartier, 18.1.1942, abends." In fact Carrier in his article assumed that the name in question was "Schrasberger", but that was due to a mistranslation. We can be sure that the address given was Ehrnsberger's home address because the *Münchener Stadadressbuch* in 1950 lists an Ursula Ehrnsberger at this address (e-mail correspondence from Matthias Röth, Archivoberinspektor in Munich, to the author 2013–10–10).
2 Smyth, Craig Hugh, *Repatriations of Art from the Collecting Point in Munich After World War II* (The Hague: Maarssen, 1988), pp. 55, 105. The story of how I found this out is quite

amazing. I had corresponded with Dr Stephan Klingen, who is the head of the Photography Department at the Zentralinstitut für Kunstgeschichte in Munich, which is housed in what used to be the *Führerbau*, on another matter. Just by chance I asked him if the name Joseph Ehrnsberger meant anything to him, and he replied that he thought he remembered that Ehrnsberger had worked at the CCP. Then I found his name in Smyth's book on a list of newly hired German civilians. I had not seen it prior to this, because it simply had not occured to me that Ehrnsberger could have worked for the Americans.

3   See David Irving's interview notes, 21 June 1971; www.ifz-muenchen.de/archiv/zs/zs-0243_2.pdf, accessed: 2012–11–16.
4   Irving to Trevor-Roper, 24 December 1972; CCLO; HTRP; Vol. Soc. Dacre 6/21, p. 2.
5   For this, and more on the trial, see: Guttenplan, D. D., *The Holocaust on Trial: History, Justice, and the David Irving Libel Case* (London: Granta Books, 2001); Evans, R. J., *Lying About Hitler. . .*; for the complete trial transcript, see: www.hdot.org/trial-materials/trial-transcripts/#, accessed: 2016–10–26. I want thank Don Guttenplan for drawing my attention to these online transcripts.
6   Longerich, P., *Hitlers . . .*, p. 184.
7   Eckert, A. M., *The Struggle for the Files . . .*, pp. 336–337.
8   Ibid., pp. 337–338.
9   "Aktennotiz" by Mau, 16 February 1951; IfZ; ID 103/202.
10 Eckert, A. M., *The Struggle for the Files . . .*, pp. 338–339.
11 Report from Mau to IfZ regarding his visit to the United States, 19 June 1951, pp. 1–2; IfZ; ID 101/1; Korrespondenz Hermann Mau 1950–1952 A – Z.
12 Eckert, A. M., *The Struggle for the Files . . .*, pp. 339–340.
13 "Aktennotiz" by Mau, 24 April 1951; IfZ; ID 103/202.
14 Ibid.
15 Letter from Mau to Ritter, 22 July 1951, p. 2; IfZ; ID 101/1; Korrespondenz Hermann Mau 1950–1952 A – Z. The letters at the end of some of the words in the transcript have disappeared.
16 Letter from Ritter to Junker, 8 September 1951; Bundesarchiv, Koblenz (henceforth: BAK); N 1166; Vol. 364.
17 Letter from Junker to Professor Dr. Erich Kaufmann, 26 September 1951, p. 2; BAK; N 1166; Vol. 364.
18 Letter from Reutern to Ritter, 2 October 1951; BAK; N 1166; Vol. 365.
19 Letter from Ritter to Reutern, 5 October 1951; BAK; N 1166; Vol. 365.
20 Letter from Athenäum Verlag to Ritter, 10 October 1951, p. 1; BAK; N 1166; Vol. 365.
21 Ibid., p. 1.
22 "Vermerk" by Picker, 8 October 1951; BAK; N 1166; Vol. 365.
23 Ibid.
24 Ibid.
25 Letter from Ritter to Athenäum Verlag, 16 October 1951; BAK; N 1166; Vol. 365.
26 Letter from Athenäum Verlag to Ritter, 19 October 1951, pp. 1–2; BAK; N 1166; Vol. 365.
27 Letter from Ritter to Athenäum Verlag, 31 October 1951, p. 1; BAK; N 1166; Vol. 365.
28 Letter from Mau to Ritter, 7 November 1951, pp. 1–2; IfZ; ID 101/1; Korrespondenz Hermann Mau 1950–1952 A – Z.
29 Ibid.
30 Letter from Ritter to Athenäum Verlag, 9 November 1951, p. 1; BAK; N 1166; Vol. 365; *Hitlers Tischgespräche. . .* (1951), pp. 118–122, 143–145.
31 Letter from Ritter to Athenäum Verlag, 9 November 1951, p. 1; BAK; N 1166; Vol. 365.
32 Ibid., pp. 1–2.
33 Ibid., p. 4.
34 Letter from Junker to Ritter, 19 November 1951; BAK; N 1166; Vol. 365.
35 Letter from Ritter to Mau, 18 January 1952, p. 1; IfZ; ID 101/1; Korrespondenz Hermann Mau 1950–1952 A – Z.
36 Letter from Ritter to Mau, 18 January 1952, p. 1; IfZ; ID 101/1; Korrespondenz Hermann Mau 1950–1952 A – Z.

37 Ibid., p. 2.
38 Ibid.
39 Letter from Athenäum-Verlag to Mau, 28 January 1952; IfZ; ID 101/2.
40 Report by Ritter "Mein Anteil an der Publikation von 'Hitlers Tischgesprächen'," 18 November 1951, p. 3; IfZ; ID 101/1; Korrespondenz Hermann Mau 1950–1952 A – Z.
41 Ibid., p. 4.
42 Ibid., p. 5.
43 "Aktenvermerk" undated (late March or early April) 1952, pp. 1–3; IfZ; ID 103/202.
44 Bundesarchiv, Berlin-Lichterfelde (henceforth: BABL); NS 6; Vol. 819; "18.1.1942, abends", p. 2 [Document 33]. "Der alte Herr hat ihn für eine Art Windhund gehalten, aber[,] ich glaube[,] doch ganz gern gehabt. Papen hat ihn sehr geschickt behandelt. Papen hat sich auch verdient gemacht. Der erste Anstoss kam von ihm: Er hat den Einbruch in die heilige Verfassung vollzogen[!] Dass er nicht weiter konnte, war klar." See also: *Monologe . . .*, p. 212.
45 *Hitlers Tischgespräche. . .* (1951), p. 410. "Der alte Herr hat ihn ganz gern gehabt. Papen hat ihn sehr geschickt behandelt."
46 *Hitlers Tischgespräche. . .* (1963), p. 157. "Der Alte Herr hat ihn für eine Art Windhund gehalten, aber ich glaube, doch ganz gern gehabt. Papen hat ihn sehr geschickt behandelt. Er hat sich auch verdient gemacht. Der erste Anstoß kam von ihm: Er hat den Einbruch in die heilige Verfassung vollzogen. Daß er nicht weiterkonnte"
47 Ibid.
48 Document 36; BAK; N 1128; Vol. 31.
49 Voegelin, Eric, "Descent into the Ecclesiastical Abyss: The Catholic Church" in *The Collected Works of Eric Voegelin, Vol. 31, Hitler and the Germans*. Translated, Edited, and with an Introduction by Detlev Clemens and Brendan Purcell (Columbia: University of Missouri Press, 1999), pp. 110–154.
50 Letter from Ritter to Athenäum Verlag, 9 November 1951, p. 1; BAK; N 1166; Vol. 365.
51 *Hitlers Tischgespräche. . .* (1951), p. 56.
52 Letter from Picker to Mau, 12 November 1951, p. 5; BAK; N 1166; Vol. 365.
53 *Hitlers Tischgespräche. . .* (1963), p. 218. Schramm notes regarding a sentence containing the phrase "like the men of the leading French social class (1789)." that this is an "addition of the Bormann version (B.-V. from 27.3.1942 evening)." However, it is unknown where he has gotten this information because there is no such comment in *Ms. 63*; see: Document 121 (27 March 1942); BAK; N 1128; Vol. 31.
54 *Hitler's Table Talk. . .* (1953), p. 369.
55 *Libres Propos. . .* (Vol. II, 1954), p. 13.
56 *Hitlers Tischgespräche. . .* (1951), pp. 55–57; *Hitlers Tischgespräche. . .* (1963), pp. 216–219; *Hitler's Table Talk. . .* (1953), pp. 367–373. Schramm notes this in a footnote, although, as always, referring to the American paperback edition from 1961, making the page references different as compared to the English and American editions of 1953 (see: *Hitlers Tischgespräche. . .* (1963), p. 212).
57 *Hitlers Tischgespräche. . .* (1963), pp. 215–216.
58 Document 118–119 (27 March 1942); BAK; N 1128; Vol. 31.
59 Document 118 (27 March 1942); BAK; N 1128; Vol. 31.
60 Document 49 (25 January 1942); BAK; N 1128; Vol. 31. See also: *Hitlers Tischgespräche. . .* (1951), p. 299; *Hitlers Tischgespräche. . .* (1963), p. 167.
61 *Monologe . . .*, p. 233. There are other slight differences between the texts in *Monologe* and *Tischgespräche*, too.
62 Letter from Picker to Mau, 12 November 1951, p. 1; BAK; N 1166; Vol. 365. The "Vermerk" is dated 8 October 1951.
63 Ibid.
64 Ibid., p. 2.
65 Ibid.
66 Ibid., p. 3.
67 Ibid.
68 Ibid., p. 4.

69 Ibid., p. 5.
70 Document 180 (7 April 1942); BAK; N 1128; Vol. 31; *Hitlers Tischgespräche. . .* (1963), pp. 260–261.
71 Document 189 (9 April 1942); BAK; N 1128; Vol. 31; *Hitlers Tischgespräche. . .* (1951), p. 359; *Hitlers Tischgespräche. . .* (1963), p. 267; *Hitler's Table Talk. . .* (1953), pp. 419–420.
72 Document 188 (9 April 1942); BAK; N 1128; Vol. 31; *Hitlers Tischgespräche. . .* (1951), p. 359; *Hitlers Tischgespräche. . .* (1963), p. 266.
73 *Hitler's Table Talk. . .* (1953), p. 412; *Libres Propos. . .* (Vol. II, 1954), p. 53; *Hitlers Tischgespräche. . .* (1951), p. 357. In *Tischgespräche* Niemöller's name has been removed from this context, and instead the text says simply "dieser Pfarrer"; in both *Table Talk* and *Libres propos*, however, Niemöller's name is present. This proves that Genoud had a text in which his name appeared.
74 Letter from Ritter to Picker, 21 November 1951, p. 1; BAK; N 1166; Vol. 365.
75 Ibid.
76 Ibid., pp. 1–2.
77 Letter from Picker to Ritter, 25 November 1951, p. 1; BAK; N 1166; Vol. 364.
78 Ibid.
79 Ibid.
80 Ibid., pp. 1–2.
81 Letter from Mau to Strauss, 27 November 1951; IfZ; ID 101/7; Korrespondenz Hermann Mau: Bundesministerium 1951–1952. Mau was writing to Strauss regarding a telephone conversation that had had the day before concerning Genoud, and the letter he had sent to the IfZ.
82 Letter from Ritter to Picker, 3 December 1951; BAK; N 1166; Vol. 365.
83 Ibid.
84 Typed transcription of conversation between Heim and Dr. Freiherr von Siegler, 5 November 1952, p. 2; www.ifz-muenchen.de/archiv/zs/zs-0243_1.pdf, accessed: 2013–08–10.
85 Anteckningar från intervju med Heim av Falk Wiesemann, 23 januari 1972, p. 11; www.ifz-muenchen.de/archiv/zs/zs-0243_2.pdf, accessed: 2013–08–17.
86 *Monologe . . .,* p. 8.
87 Typed record of an interview of Heim by Dr. Freiherr von Siegler, 5 November 1952, p. 2; www.ifz-muenchen.de/archiv/zs/zs-0243_1.pdf, accessed: 2013–08–10.
88 Hitler, A., *Hitlers zweites Buch . . .,* p. 15.
89 Letter from Heim to Grimm, 9 February 1958, pp. 1–2; Werner Jochmann Nachlaß (in the hands of Professor Ursula Büttner, Hamburg) (henceforth: WJN); Binder: Schriftwechsel: A – K 1977.
90 *Monologe . . .,* p. 16.
91 *Hitlers Tischgespräche. . .* (1963), pp. 506–507, 513.
92 Sereny, Gitta, *Albert Speer: His Battle with the Truth* (New York: Alfred A. Knopf, 1995), pp. 728–729.
93 "Anmerkungen zur 'Einfeuhrung'." attached to letter from Ilse James to Jochmann, 30 December 1979, p. 1; WJN; Binder: Schriftwechsel: A – K 1977.
    The letter also brings forth much critique of Picker's statements. Jochmann had sent his introduction to *Monologe* to James for her to read through and correct; see: Letter from Jochmann to Else James, 18 December 1979; WJN; Binder: Schriftwechsel: A – K 1977.
94 *Monologe . . .,* p. 11.
95 Stratigakos, Despina, *Hitler at Home* (New Haven: Yale University Press, 2015), p. 137. Stratigakos states incorrectly that the CCP was housed in the "Brown House."
96 Email from Kerwin to the author, 2012–12–06. Smyth has described his experiences in Munich in: Smyth, Craig Hugh, *Repatriations of Art from the Collecting. . ..* This book does not mention these documents.
97 www.archives.gov/research/foreign-policy/related-records/rg-239.html, accessed: 2013–08–28.
98 Whitney, M'Lisa, *M 1946. Records Concerning the Central Collection Points ("Ardelia Hall Collection"): Munich Central Collecting Point, 1945–1951* (Washington, DC: National

Archives and Records Administration, 2009), p. 2; www.archives.gov/research/micro-film/m1946.pdf, accessed: 2013–09–04.

99 Weinberg, Gerhard, *Guide to Captured German Documents*, Research Memorandum No. 2, Vol. 1 (Alabama: Human Resources Research Institute, Maxwell Air Force Base, December 1952), p. 55.

100 E-mail from Weinberg to the author, 15 September 2013.

101 E-mail from Kerwin to the author, 6 December 2012.

102 Eaton, Vincent, L. and Goff, Frederick R., "Other Rare Acquisitions" in *Library of Congress Quarterly Journal of Current Acquisitions*, Vol. 5, No. 3 (May 1948), p. 53.

103 Stuurman, Douwe, "The Nazi Collection: A Preliminary Note" in *Library of Congress Quarterly Journal of Current Acquisitions*, Vol. 6, No. 1 (November 1948), pp. 21–22.

104 "Manuscripts" in *Library of Congress Quarterly Journal of Current Acquisitions*, Vol. 9, No. 3 (May 1952), pp. 145–146.

105 "Deutsches Archivmaterial in der Library of Congress" by Fritz T. Epstein, pp. 1–3; IfZ; ID 200/2.

106 Copy of "The Library of Congress Order for Photoduplication", 25 September 1952; WJN; Binder: "Schriftwechsel".

107 Letter from Mau to Library of Congress, 28 July 1952, pp. 1–2; IfZ; ID 200/2.

108 Franz-Willing, Georg, "Hitlers Tischgespräche" in *Klüter Blätter. Monatshefte für Kultur und Zeitgeschichte*, Jahrgang 32 (Dezember 1981), Heft 12, p. 26.

109 Email from Weinberg to me, 18 September 2013.

110 See: ibid., pp. 3–47. These facts are *only* obvious from a close inspection of the original documents in the *Bundesarchiv*. It is not apparent even in digital, and certainly not on xeroxed, copies. I want to thank archivist Sven Schneidereit at the *Bundesarchiv* Berlin-Lichterfelde for all the kind assistance.

111 These page numbers refer to the pagination made by the *Bundesarchiv*. It is a bit mis-leading since the archive also paginated the small notes taped to the first page of each note, which list the corresponding note number in *Table Talk*. This means that for each of the nine notes there are nine "redundant" paginations in the document collection. Since the title page has been given the number "1" the actual note starts at page number "3" (and the preceding *Table Talk* reference is on page number "2").

112 "Hitler Privat-Gespräche", See backside of the first note "8./9.1.1942", pp. 3–47; BABL; NS 6; Vol. 819.

113 Ibid., p. 11.

114 Ibid., p. 10.

115 The "Three women house" is a phrase with an interesting history. It was the name of a house on *Schreyvogelgasse* 10 in Vienna built sometime either in 1700s or the 1800s. There is a legend tied to this building, namely that the composer Franz Schubert had romantic relationships with the three daughters – Hannerl, Hederl, and Heiderl – of a glass master by the name of Franz Schöll. In reality, the building likely had nothing to do with Schubert because the legend was based on the novel *Schwammel – Ein Schubertroman* by Rudolf Hans Bartsch published in 1912. This book was then turned into a musical called *Das Dreimäderlhaus*, performed for the first time in 1916, and for two movies with the same name in 1918 and 1958, respectively. There are now several hotels called "Dreimäderlhaus" and apparently one was located in Berchtesgaden. The odd thing is that the text seems to imply that there were actually three girls living there, one of whom was beautiful and the other two who were pretty.

116 Ibid., p. 7. As far as I can tell the notation says: "*S. 10 lezter Absatz* [unreadable]!".

117 Chaussy, Ulrich and Püschner, Christoph, *Nachbar Hitler. Führerkult und Heimatzerstörung am Obersalzberg* (8, aktualisierte Auflage) (Berlin: Ch. Links Verlag, 2017), pp. 39–46.

118 The same points have very convincingly been made with regard to how Hitler created the first volume of *Mein Kampf*; see: Kellerhof, S. F., *"Mein Kampf"* . . ., pp. 56–57.

119 *Monologe* . . ., p. 185; "Hitler Privat-Gespräche"; "8/9.1.1942", p. 1; BABL; NS 6; Vol. 819.

120 Heiden, Konrad, *Adolf Hitler. Eine Biographie. Ein Mann gegen Europa. Zweiter Band* (Vol. II) (Zürich: Europa-Verlag, 1937), see facsimile of grades (Document 2) at the

end of the book; Bavendamm, Dirk, *Der junge Hitler. Korrekturen einer Biographie 1889–1914* (Graz: Ares Verlag, 2009), p. 144. Franz Jetzinger only mentions Hitler's "4"; see: Jetzinger, Franz, *Hitlers Jugend. Phantasie, Lügen und die Wahrheit* (Wein: Europa-Verlag, 1956), pp. 98–103.

121 *Monologe . . .*, p. 206.

122 Chaussy, U. and Püschner, C., *Nachbar Hitler . . .*, pp. 46, 232 *n*3.

123 Ibid., p. 232 *n*3; *Monologe . . .*, pp. 202, 439 *n*60.

124 I have not been able to find out what Fugger's first name was nor where she was located at the time that these notes were written.

125 *Monologe . . .*, p. 12; Longerich, P., *Hitlers . . .*, p. 129; University of Arizona Library, Special Collections (UALSC); Papers of Karen Kuykendall, MS 243 (PKK MS 243); Series II: Interviews and Correspondence, 1971–1978 (Series II); Box 2, Folder 5; Letter from Heim to Kuykendall, undated March 1973, p. 2. It is evident from Kuykendall's reply that this letter was sent sometime in March. The art show, which was part of the exhibition called *Große Deutsche Kunstausstellung*, which took place eight times between 1937 and 1944, was opened on 4 July 1942 by Goebbels, and contained a total of 1213 paintings by 680 artists. The special exhibit featuring Leipold contained 22 of his works. For more on the role, and importance, of art for Hitler, his understanding of himself, and the construction of the Third Reich, see: Schwarz, Birgit, *Geniewahn: Hitler und die Kunst* (Vienna: Böhlau Verlag, 2009).

126 Letter from Heim to Kuykendall, 7 October 1977, p. 6; UALSC; PKK MS 243; Series II; Box 2, Folder 5.

127 Handwritten answer to a questionnaire sent to him by Kuykendall, 13 September 1973, p. 12; UALSC; PKK MS 243; Series II; Box 2, Folder 5.

128 Letter from Heim to Kuykendall, undated March 1973, p. 3; UALSC; PKK MS 243; Series II; Box 2, Folder 5. It is evident from Kuykendall's reply that Heim wrote this in March.

129 Heim's letter is quoted by Anton Joachimsthaler in: Schroeder, C., *Er war mein Chef . . .*, p. 355 (footnote 226).

130 Letter from Heim to Kuykendall, 3 April 1978, p. 2; UALSC; PKK MS 243; Series II; Box 2, Folder 5.

131 Letter from Heim to Kuykendall, 15 October 1974, p. 2; UALSC; PKK MS 243; Series II; Box 2, Folder 5.

132 Staatsarchiv München; SpkA K 659: Heim, Heinrich; "Erklärung in eigener Sache für die Spruchkammer X in München" signed by Heim, 19 November 1948, p. 3. Copies of the StAM documents have been provided to me by Professor Wolfram Pyta in Stuttgart, and I extend my deep gratitude to him for having shared his personal archival material with me.

133 Testimony by Ilona Arnold, 28 February 1949, pp. 1–2; Staatsarchiv München (StAM); SpkA K 1207: Müller, Hans.

134 Testimony by Alexander Klein, 28 October 1948, pp. 2–3; StAM; SpkA K 1207: Müller, Hans.

135 Testimony by Ilona Arnold, 28 February 1949, pp. 3–4; StAM; SpkA K 1207: Müller, Hans.

136 Testimony by Lina Ullman, 23 March 1948, pp. 1–2; StAM; SpkA K 1207: Müller, Hans.

137 *Monologe . . .*, p. 187; "Hitler Privat-Gespräche"; "8/9.1.1942", p. 5; BABL; NS 6; Vol. 819.

138 *Monologe . . .*, pp. 205–206; "Hitler Privat-Gespräche"; "16./17.1.1942, nachts", p. 7; BABL; NS 6; Vol. 819.

139 Weber, T., *Wie Adolf Hitler zum Nazi wurde . . .*, pp. 374, 387–389. These parts do not appear in *Becoming Hitler*.

140 Ibid., p. 387.

141 Hitler, A., *Hitlers zweites Buch . . .*, pp. 16–19.

142 *Hitler's Table Talk . . .* (1953), p. 314.

143 *Libres propos* . . . (Vol. I, 1952), p. 304.
144 *Monologe* . . ., p. 280.
145 Hitler, A., *Hitlers zweites Buch* . . ., p. 18.
146 *Tischgespräche.* . . (1951), p. 205.
147 Document 67 (17 February 1942); BAK; N 1128; Vol. 31.
148 *Hitler, Mein Kampf* . . . (Band II), pp. 1541, 1621 **[299]**.
149 Hitler, A., *Hitlers zweites Buch* . . ., p. 18.
150 Plöckinger, O., *Geschichte eines Buches* . . ., pp. 126–129.
151 Hitler, Adolf, *Die Südtiroler Frage und das Deutsche Bündnisproblem* (München: Franz Eher Verlag, 1926), p. 46.
152 Plöckinger, O., *Geschichte eines Buches* . . ., pp. 95–96, 102.
153 Hitler, A., *Hitlers zweites Buch* . . ., p. 18. "Schon 1925 hatte Hitler ganz heimlich ein Buch über Außenpolitik zuschrieben begonnen." See also: Zoller, A., *Hitler Privat* . . ., p. 155.
154 Hitler, A., *Hitlers zweites Buch* . . ., p. 19.
155 Ibid., pp. 17–18.
156 Document 63 (8 February 1942); BAK; N 1128; Vol. 31.
157 Note that all of this goes against the well-attested incredible memory that Hitler is supposed to have possessed. He could supposedly easily remember details that he had read a long time ago and is reported to have impressed his generals with his precise memory of military matters, history, etc. (Christa Schroeder talks about this in detail in: Zoller, A., *Hitler Privat* . . ., pp. 36–43. According to Schroeder, Hitler's memory was complete, and he could without problem remember names, books, numbers, details from when and where he had met a person the first time, details in movies and plays, and so on.) Hitler's bodyguard Rochus Misch has described Hitler's memory as photographic, something that he says Hitler proved over and over (Misch, R., *Der Letzte Zeuge* . . ., p. 143). Misch also states that it was strictly forbidden to mention politics or military matters during the evening conversations (*Feierabend*) that took place after dinner and tea (ibid., p. 132). But when it came to his own life, Hitler seems to have had an extremely poor memory. There is certainly a pattern here. The question is what it means. There are plenty of other reasons to question this idea too. Not least the fact that Hitler insisted upon having his military conferences recorded by stenographers due to his increasing conflicts with the military brass speaks heavily against the idea that Hitler having photographic memory was a widespread and accepted idea (ibid., p. 143). Why would there ever be a need for stenographers if everyone knew Hitler had a flawless memory and never questioned that fact?
158 Hitler, A., *Hitlers zweites Buch* . . ., p. 18.
159 *Monologe* . . ., p. 456 (endnote 196).
160 *Hitlers Tischgespräche.* . . (1951), p. 198. Schramm notes in the second edition that this is wrong but does not comment upon the fact that Genoud makes the very same mistake.
161 *Libres propos.* . . (Vol. I, 1952), p. 218.
162 *Hitler's Table Talk.* . . (1953), p. 224.
163 *Hitlers Tischgespräche.* . . (1963), p. 159; *Hitlers Tischgespräche.* . . (1951), p. 198; BAK; N 1128; Vol. 31; Document 38 (18 January 1942).
164 *Monologe* . . ., p. 213.
165 "Hitler Privat-Gespräche"; 18./19.1.41 nachts, p. 1; BABL; NS 6; Vol. 819.
166 Joachimsthaler, A., *Hitlers Weg begann* . . ., pp. 265–270; Kellerhoff, Sven Felix, *Die NSDAP. Eine Partei und ihre Mitglieder* (Stuttgart: Klett-Cotta, 2017), p. 48. Nonetheless, the idea that the party changed its name to NSDAP on 24 February 1920 is still being put forth in new literature on the subject, see for example: Taylor, Cory, *How Hitler Was Made: Germany and the Rise of the Perfect Nazi* (Amherst: Prometheus Books, 2018), pp. 131, 136.
167 *SA*, pp. 110–111 (Document 83). The DSP was another *völkisch* party active in Germany during the same period. From August 1920 to the summer of 1921 there were discussions about merging the NSDAP and DSP into a new party called *Deutsche*

Nationalsozialistische Arbeiterpartei (DNSAP). Drexler argued for this option while Hitler argued against it. Hitler eventually won the debate and got his way after having dramatically left the party on 14 July 1921, at the same time as he put forth clear demands for accepting to rejoin the party. Drexler, as well as the *Parteiausschuß*, who understood Hitler's importance for the NSDAP and who did not want to risk a breakup of the party, decided to consent to Hitler's demands and to grant him dictatorial powers within the NSDAP by electing him chairman at a meeting on 29 July 1921. Once the NSDAP had grown big enough not to risk being swallowed up by the other rightwing organizations Hitler actually changed his mind, and on 20 October 1922 the DSP, under Julius Streicher, merged with, and became part of, the NSDAP (ibid., pp. 284–292, 305).

168 Weber, T., *Wie Adolf Hitler zum Nazi wurde . . .*, p. 250; Joachimsthaler, A., *Hitlers Weg begann . . .*, pp. 274–276.
169 *SA*, pp. 109–110 (Document 83).
170 Kellerhoff, S. F., *Die NSDAP . . .*, pp. 48–49; *SA*, pp. 129–130 (Document 97).
171 *SA*, pp. 132–133 (Document 100). At this time Hitler even made the crowd repeat: "Long live the German Workers' Party!" Interestingly, the editors of the volume nonetheless use the name NSDAP in the headlines for these documents.
172 Ibid., p. 133 (Document 100).
173 Ibid., p. 134 (Document 101).
174 Ibid., p. 149 (Document 110).
175 Ibid., pp. 150, 152 (Document 111 & 112).
176 Ibid., p. 154 (Document 115).
177 Ibid., p. 159 (Document 118).
178 Ibid., p. 162 (Document 120).
179 Ibid., p. 161 (Document 119).
180 *Rudolf Heß. Briefe 1908–1933. Herausgegeben von Wolf Rüdiger Heß. Mit einer Einführung und Kommentaren von Dirk Bavendamm* (München: Georg Müller Verlag, 1987), p. 263 (No. 280).
181 *SA*, p. 648 (mid-1922).
182 Eberle, Henrik (ed.), *Briefe an Hitler. Ein Volk schreibt seinem Führer. Unbekannte Dokumente aus Moskauer Archiven – zum ersten Mal veröffentlicht* (Bergisch Gladbach: Gustav Lübbe Verlag, 2007), p. 60.
183 *SA*, p. 727 (Document 421).
184 Ibid.
185 Ibid., p. 735 (Document 428).
186 Ibid., p. 974 (Document 557).
187 For the point about party restructuring, see: Herbst, Ludolf, *Hitlers Charisma. Die Erfindung eines deutschen Messias* (Frankfurt am Main: S. Fischer Verlag, 2010), pp. 197, 218–258.
188 *Rudolf Heß. Briefe . . .*, pp. 354–355 (No. 357 & 358).
189 Kershaw, I., *Hitler 1889–1936. . .* (Vol. I), p. 228; Ullrich, V., *Adolf Hitler. . .* (Vol. I), p. 195.
190 *HRP* I/2, p. 553 (8 November 1935).
191 *HRP* II/4, p. 1658 (30 January 1941).
192 *SA*, p. 966 (Document 554).
193 *Rudolf Heß. Briefe . . .*, p. 356 (No. 358).
194 *HRP* I/1, p. 172 (31 December 1932). Published in *Völkischer Beobachter* on 1 Januari 1933.
195 *HRP* I/2, p. 562 (1 January 1936). This was actually read by Goebbels on national radio.
196 *HRP* I/2, p. 774 (1 January 1938).
197 *HRP* I/2, p. 872 (12 June 1938). ". . . die ewige, politisch tragende nationalsocialistische Partei. . . . "

198 Zitelmann, R., *Hitler: Selbstverständnis . . .*, especially pp. 39–86; Longerich, P., *Hitler . . .*, pp. 343–346. He does not mention Zitelmann at all in this context. See also: Ullrich, V., *Adolf Hitler. . .* (Vol. I), p. 502; *HRP* I/1, p. 286 (6 July 1933).

199 *GR* I, pp. 113–123 (16 June 1933).

200 *HRP* I/1, p. 371 (19 March 1934).

201 *HRP* I/1, p. 412 (13 July 1934).

202 *HRP* I/1, p. 459 (9 November 1934).

203 *HRP* II/3, p. 1461 (30 January 1940).

204 Heiber, Helmut (ed.), *Goebbels Reden 1939–1945*, Band II (München: Wilhelm Heyne Verlag, 1972), pp. 83–84 (30 January 1942).

205 Ibid., pp. 240–257 (9 July 1943).

206 *HRP* II/4, pp. 2085–2086 (30 January 1944).

207 *HRP* I/1, pp. 286–287 (6 July 1933). See also: Longerich, P., *Hitler . . .*, p. 344.

216 *HRP* I/2, p. 529 (13 September 1935).

209 Longerich, P., *Hitler . . .*, p. 456.

210 *HRP* I/2, p. 719 (7 September 1937).

211 *HRP* II/4, p. 1669 (24 February 1941).

212 *HRP* I/1, pp. 89–90 (27 January 1932).

213 *HRP* I/2, p. 581 (24 February 1936).

214 Tyrell, Albrecht, *Vom "Trommler" zum "Führer". Der Wandel von Hitlers Selbstverständnis zwischen 1919 und 1924 und die Entwicklung der NSDAP* (München: Wilhelm Fink Verlag, 1975).

215 *SA*, p. 438 (Document 262).

216 Kershaw, I., *Hitler 1889–1936. . .* (Vol. I), p. 278; Longerich, P., *Hitler . . .*, pp. 164–165; Plöckinger, O., *Geschichte eines Buches . . .*, pp. 105–107.

217 *HRS* II/1, p. 44 (Document 21).

218 See Werner Jochmann's comment in an endnote in: *Monologe . . .*, p. 441.

219 *Hitler, Mein Kampf. . .* (Band II), pp. 959–965, 1159–1163 **[1–4, 97–99]**.

220 *Monologe . . .*, p. 72.

221 Joachimsthaler, A., *Hitlers Weg begann . . .*, p. 37.

222 *Monologe . . .*, p. 214; "Hitler Privat-Gespräche"; 19.1.42, abends, p. 1; BABL; NS 6; Vol. 819.

223 *Hitlers Tischgespräche. . .* (1951), p. 321.

224 *Libres propos. . .* (Vol. I, 1952), p. 219.

225 *Hitlers Tischgespräche. . .* (1951), p. 197.

226 *Libres propos. . .* (Vol. I, 1952), p. 21.

227 *Monologe . . .*, p. 52.

228 Sheridan to Trevor-Roper, 19 August 1979, p. 1; CCLO; HTRP; Vol. Soc. Dacre 6/6/2.

229 Ibid., p. 2.

5

THE PUBLICATION OF *HITLER'S TABLE TALK* AND THE ROLE OF HUGH TREVOR-ROPER

Introduction

Trevor-Roper first learned about the *Tischgespräche* in 1951 shortly after the publication of the book. In a letter to his good friend Bernard Berenson in September 1951 he wrote that he had read Picker's book while he travelled through Spain. After reading the book he said that he was thinking of writing something on the mind of Adolf Hitler so as to set the record straight regarding Hitler's character – he was not a charlatan that just happened to come to power by accident (as claimed by Alan Bullock, M.N.), wrote Trevor-Roper, but a man with a conviction and a plan. He felt that *Tischgespräche* confirmed this view.[1]

This must have been a new idea, perhaps one that had occurred to Trevor-Roper only after reading *Tischgespräche*, because in *The Last Days of Hitler* he had himself painted Hitler as an unrepentant nihilist. He had then frequently referred to Hermann Rauschning's books, including *Die Revolution des Nihilismus* from 1938, which he considered to be totally genuine and he made "no apology for recommending it" even though its authenticity had already been doubted. Rauschning was, Trevor-Roper stated defiantly, "completely reliable."[2] At that time it had been completely and totally obvious to him that Rauschning had laid bare "the essential nihilism of the Nazi philosophy"; Hitler's actions were all "in conformity with this nihilistic ideal this absolute love of destruction"; he went on to tell his readers that "nihilism was always implicit, and often explicit" in Hitler's ideology, again referring to Rauschning; during early 1945 "despair only intensified the nihilism", he wrote, and he claimed that Goebbels, too, at war's end, had preached "an ideological nihilism."[3]

All references to *Die Revolution des Nihilismus* are glaringly absent from the essay "The Mind of Adolf Hitler" that was eventually published in *Table Talk*. The word "nihilism" is only mentioned once, and then only when he repeats Hitler's own claim to have read Schopenhauer, "the philosopher of nihilism", during the First World War (he actually says that Hitler carried Schopenhauer's works around "in his pocket", which is incompatible with the claim in the text where Hitler is said to have carried a five-volume edition with him, which in itself is not very credible, since it could not fit into his pocket). He does, however, still refer to Rauschning's book from 1933 *Hitler Speaks* (*Gespräche mit Hitler*) on several occasions.[4] The claim about having carried five volumes of Schopenhauer (a note dated 19 May 1944 and made by Hans Müller)[5] in the field is interesting in its own right because Hitler told other versions of this story on other occasions to other people. Hans Frank writes in his memoirs that Hitler told him (not clear when) that during the later war years he carried a frayed paperback (*Reclam-bändchen*) copy of Schopenhauer's *Welt als Wille und Vorstellung* (*The World as Will and Representation*).[6] Otto Dietrich gives yet a slightly different version: he states that Hitler had talked about having carried "a small edition of Schopenhauer's collected works" in the field.[7] Interestingly, Hitler said much the same to the group of generals and officers gathered at the Platterhof in Berchtesgaden on 26 May 1944, i.e. just a few days after Müller's note was made.[8] Julius Schaub also confirms that Hitler told his closest associates a story like this. According to him, Hitler had claimed that he "as a constant companion [had] carried a small volume of Schopenhauer during the war."[9] Frank's, Dietrich's, and Schaub's versions sound more credible, since they do not require Hitler to have carried around five whole volumes. It is worth noting though that Schaub does not state explicitly *which* war he is referring to; what makes the whole matter a bit uncertain is the fact that he includes this story between stories about the war in Poland in September 1939 and the attack on France in May 1940. It could thus be that Schaub is in fact talking about the Second World War here and that this therefore is not the same as the story told in *Monologe*.

This means one of two things, namely that either Müller misheard or misremembered what Hitler said or Hitler actually told him a different story. What we do know is – via a letter from the state prosecutor in Bavaria, Martin Dresse, to the prison in Landsberg on 4 December 1923 – that Hitler received the five volumes of Schopenhauer's collected works, as well as writing utensils, delivered to his cell in the end of 1923. This edition of Schopenhauer's works had been published in 1920.[10] Therefore it cannot have been these volumes that Hitler carried with him in Flanders. Hitler does not seem to have owned these volumes before; instead, they were sent to him by a supporter on the outside. Hitler thus did own Schopenhauer's collected works at one point in his life, but we cannot know if he actually read them. Let us now return to Trevor-Roper's introductory essay in *Hitler's Table Talk*.

Trevor-Roper started his essay by criticizing other historians, including Bullock, for having regarded Hitler as a mere "charlatan", "a consummate actor and hypocrite", "a mere illiterate, illogical, unsystematic bluffer and smatterer", and "a diabolical adventurer animated solely by an unlimited lust for personal power";[11] all these were of course things that Trevor-Roper himself had subscribed to in *The Last Days of Hitler*. Now, after having read *Tischgespräche* and the texts contained in the *Table Talk*, Trevor-Roper had, very conveniently, seemingly forgotten about all of this. Now, instead, historians should contemplate the undeniable "genius" of the "demobilised corporal" who managed to build an empire across the European continent. Indeed, Trevor-Roper concluded triumphantly, "I have laboured this point because I wish to maintain – contrary, as it happens, to all received opinion – that Hitler had a mind." Hitler was, he now stated while seemingly marvelling at the fact that no one had ever understood this before him, "a systematic thinker and his mind [was], to the historian, as important a problem as the mind of Bismarck or Lenin."[12]

He much later told Eberhard Jäckel, when commenting on the latter's book *Hitlers Weltanschauung* (*Hitler's Worldview*, which was the book that really cemented the view of Hitler as an ideologically convinced actor), that it "has always seemed to me extraordinary that commentators have refused to recognize what is so obvious when one examines the evidence."[13] That he himself had been equally unable to recognize this seemed to be a point lost on him. Trevor-Roper in fact still claimed in his introduction to *The Testament of Adolf Hitler* in 1961, as well as in the German edition of this text *Hitlers politisches Testament* in 1981, that Rauschning's *Gespräche mit Hitler* was an authentic and reliable source to Hitler's thoughts.[14] He did this even though the inauthenticity and unreliability of this book had been pointed out to him already in 1960. Gerhard Meinck, author of *Hitler und die deutsche Aufrüstung 1933–1937* (1959), told Trevor-Roper that he had not used Rauschning in his book because "the conversations had not taken place in the form" that Rauschning claimed. Instead, it was likely that Rauschning had produced his book by mixing statements that he had indeed heard Hitler utter, with Rauschning's own ideas, and, perhaps, also with matter taken from *Mein Kampf*.[15] Trevor-Roper replied in a for him, it seems, very typical way. He stated that he had always suspected that Rauschning's book was not *ad verbatim*, but as remembered by him, and that "therefore there may be some room for error." However, he still thought that "the content, in general, justifies itself on internal evidence."[16] Once again, the method of verifying a source based on internal evidence proved to be a treacherously inaccurate way of going about establishing authenticity.

Meeting Genoud

Pierre Péan has shown that Genoud and Trevor-Roper started a cordial correspondence during the winter of 1951–1952.[17] According to Adam Sisman, this occurred shortly after Trevor-Roper found out "that what appeared to be a more authoritative text of Hitler's *Table-Talk* was to be published in France" by a certain François Genoud. Sisman writes that it was Trevor-Roper that then contacted Genoud regarding the possibility of publishing an English edition, and this may very well be true, even though we know that Genoud had already decided to publish in English by that point.[18]

In August 1952 Trevor-Roper met with François Genoud in Lausanne and the Swiss told him all of his views about Hitler and National Socialism and laid bare his anti-Semitism.[19] Genoud was a very shady character to say the least. Besides being a lifelong Nazi ever since meeting Hitler in person at the age of 17 in 1932 up until his suicide in 1996, he also financed the Venezuelan terrorist Carlos "The Jackal" and his activities and was involved with not only the Palestinian terror leader Wadi Haddad but also the West German terror group RAF. All of this and more can be found in the several biographies of Genoud that has already been written.[20] More pertinent for us in this case is, however, is the fact that just as dedicated as Genoud was to National Socialism and Hitler, just as unscrupulous was he when it came to selling old documents that the major Nazi criminals had had in their possession. Genoud was used to moving in dubious circles and to making up stories about his intelligence activities during the war. He was in the business of making money off of his documents and to rectify what he thought to be misinterpretations regarding his Nazi heroes. Genoud was convinced that Hitler had found a way beyond capitalism and communism and, to him (as to Bormann), the much-hated Christian culture (the famous so-called third way of Fascism).[21]

Trevor-Roper too had the wish to make money on these types of documents, and therefore his and Genoud's desires proved to be a poor mixture, at least from the perspective of the historian interested in source-critical issues pertaining to these documents. Trevor-Roper's letters to his literary agent show just how acutely aware he was of his own value as an expert to newspapers, magazines, and book publishers who turned to him in order to get a seal of approval and editorial comment; in short: to authenticate them. In fact, it had been that way ever since Trevor-Roper had published his famous book *The Last Days of Hitler* in 1947, a book that had propelled him to fame all over the world.[22] Genoud's documents also really did increase in value after Trevor-Roper had gone on the record attesting to their authenticity. As we shall see, the unfortunate mix of pecuniary and reputational interests also meant that Trevor-Roper, on occasion, consciously or unconsciously, became a bit lazy when looking at the documents that were laid before him – forgeries did not pay as well as authentic documents that could be published, after all.

Genoud told Trevor-Roper that the manuscript had been in Gerda Bormann's hands by the end of the war, and although he could not be specific about how he had gotten the manuscript he promised it was fairly purchased (together with the other Bormann material – a fact which contradicted his earlier untrue statement that he had purchased the table talk manuscript last). They came, Genoud said, "from Frau Bormann's hands, directly or indirectly, into those of 'a certain Italian', and had afterwards, directly or indirectly, been acquired by him." Genoud did not say that he had purchased anything from Frau Bormann directly, but that he had purchased the rights to Bormann's written estate from the trustee appointed by the Bavarian state to manage the family's affairs and who was the guardian of the Bormann children (Theodore Schmitz, M.N.). He also said he had purchased the publication rights from Hitler's sister, Paula Hitler, and gave Trevor-Roper a copy of "a notarial deed confirming his legal acquisition of Paula Hitler's rights." By this point the lawsuits had been filed, and Genoud was certain to win the copyright case. Picker had no right whatsoever, according to Genoud. He was planning on publishing the table talk in due course, but not the Bormanns' private letters due to their intimacy, at least not until the Bormann children were of age and could express their views (as we have seen, this was originally Schmitz's condition for letting Genoud publish the letters at all). He then claimed that his publication in French had been precipitated by Picker's publication, which had violated Genoud's copyright. Bormann had made only two copies, and Genoud had one of them he claimed, and any other copy was therefore invalid and unauthorized. Trevor-Roper wrote that Genoud also claimed that Picker had falsified the notes and "showed me numerous incidents in which Picker had altered the sense of the documents compiled by Heim." Genoud nevertheless recognized that he might well lose the lawsuit in Düsseldorf, where he as plaintiff would have to prove his right rather than merely disprove Picker's, but he was convinced that Picker could not show that he had any rights at all, and because of this Genoud proceeded to manoeuvre Picker into filing a lawsuit against him, so that Picker would then have the burden of proof. He did this by publishing in French, which infringed on Picker's planned French edition (this contradicted the reason for publishing in French he had just given). Picker filed a lawsuit in a French court claiming 30 million francs. Genoud was confident that Picker could not win this case. His hope was that a previous defeat in France could affect the outcome in Germany.[23] As we will see, this account conflict somewhat with what Trevor-Roper wrote regarding Genoud's intentions to Eduard Baumgarten about a year later. It is also not at all clear why Genoud simply could not have challenged Picker's copyright, one that he said he was sure that Picker did not have, by publishing his own German text.

Still, even though he had now access to this new source material and time to study it well, Trevor-Roper managed to make glaringly inconsistent judgements of Hitler's character in his introductory essay. For example, he states that Hitler "was a complete and rigid materialist."[24] He made this statement even though the *Table Talk* itself points to the exact opposite conclusion; it has Hitler raging against materialism, which he considered to be a hallmark of the Jews. For example, the last note in *Table Talk* has Bormann restating Hitler's opinion on Jesus saying that according to Hitler Jesus was an Aryan who "fought against the materialism of His age, and, therefore, against the Jews."[25] If there is one thing that we can say about Hitler it is that he was decidedly *not* a materialist, but an idealist. This is a well-known basis of Hitler's worldview – National Socialism – and it ought to have been apparent to Trevor-Roper that this judgement was wrong.[26]

Immediately after Genoud had published the first volume of *Libres propos* he had also serialized parts of it in *France Soir*. This exactly mirrored the publication of parts of *Tischgespräche* in the German magazine *Quick*. In the summer of 1952 Trevor-Roper wrote a letter to his friend Berenson and asked if he had now had time to read *Tischgespräche*, which he thought was "of great historical importance." By then Trevor-Roper knew that Genoud (whom Trevor-Roper called an ex-Nazi) claimed to have "the entire original text" of the table talks. He also told Berenson that he looked forward to the pending court case. He said that he had been contacted by the British Foreign Office because a former SS officer by the name of Eugene Dollmann had offered to obtain some valuable original Hitler manuscripts for them. Trevor-Roper commented on this in the following way: "I suspect – though it is mere surmise – that Genoud's title is really bad & that he is trying to off-load the documents before the trial exposes him!"[27] Thus, it seems as if Trevor-Roper initially doubted Genoud's reliability, but that he quickly dropped these suspicions.

In connection to this, it is worth mentioning that Heim had also raised a claim against *France Soir*, and he had authorized Picker to defend his rights by signing them over to him. Heim wrote in a letter, apparently requested by Picker:

> I object to the publication of my transcripts of Hitler's table talks in *France Soir* and in the publishing house Flammarion. I authorize Dr. H. Picker [. . .] to exercise my rights on his behalf, which I am ceding to him.
> Munich, 1 July 1952.[28]

This was certainly a rather surprising act of hostility against Genoud, whom Heim had otherwise not deemed to be an enemy of any kind. But then again Heim flip-flopped between sometimes supporting Genoud, supporting Picker, and trying to stay neutral between the two. But this shows that Heim was not entirely honest when he claimed that he had not taken sides in the lawsuits Genoud and Picker exchanged with each other. Picker seems to have assumed that Heim, through this authorization, had signed over the copyright for Heim's notes to him. Heim, on the other hand, later made clear to Picker that the copyright could not be signed over to another author, and he had not intended this with the earlier arrangement.[29] This seems to imply that Heim thought that *he* had the copyright.

Picker's falsifications that Genoud talked about – which Trevor-Roper says that Genoud had shown him examples of – i.e. the differences between Picker's and Genoud's notes, are to be found in Trevor-Roper's papers as typed comparisons between entries in German (written by Genoud).[30] The text from Genoud's manuscript as shown there agree with the text as published in *Monologe*.

Genoud did not seem stressed at all in August 1952 when he wrote to Trevor-Roper to tell him that he was negotiating with several publishers for the English edition but had made no commitment to any of them. Weidenfeld was not one of them at that point apparently.[31]

In September, i.e. after their first meeting in August, Genoud wrote to Trevor-Roper saying that he would consider Trevor-Roper's validation of his documents as a tremendous help in the French court case:

> In my opinion, only the historical value of the documents in question should be taken into account. In this respect, it would be very important to me that your testimony could be produced. You are indeed the expert unanimously recognized as the most qualified in this matter, and I am sure that an objective opinion on your part would have immense weight.[32]

Genoud wished to know if he could refer to Trevor-Roper, if necessary, both in the French and German lawsuits. By this time Trevor-Roper had decided to help Genoud find a publisher in Britain, and Genoud thanked Trevor-Roper heartily for this effort.[33] Trevor-Roper apparently even agreed to testify on behalf of Genoud if needed.[34] He was indeed also successful in finding a publisher for Genoud's text.

On 17 October 1952 the CEO of the publishing house Weidenfeld & Nicholson, George Weidenfeld, wrote to Genoud and offered him a deal for an English translation. He did so definitely without having seen the product he was buying, and he appears to have acted only on Trevor-Roper's assurance that Genoud and his manuscript could be trusted. This was also before the outcome of the lawsuit, but Weidenfeld trusted Trevor-Roper's assessment – "his authority, which I respect very much", he said – that Genoud's case was a strong one. This was indeed quite a gamble, but one that would turn out to pay off handsomely for everyone involved, even though Genoud did not gain copyright from the courts. Weidenfeld also wrote that he would very much like to conclude the contract as soon as possible before he went on a planned trip to the United States. Perhaps he and Trevor-Roper could meet Genoud in either Paris or Lausanne to finish the matter, he suggested.[35] Genoud quickly accepted Weidenfeld's offer and agreed to meet him and Trevor-Roper in Paris at Hotel Kléber at their convenience. He only stipulated some changes to the terms – to his advantage, of course – and delivered some criticism against Weidenfeld for the poor terms offered.[36] George Weidenfeld writes about this encounter in his autobiography and adds regarding the manuscript's journey from Bormann's hands to Genoud's that some of Gerda Bormann's papers "found their way to Lausanne."[37] Genoud then wrote Trevor-Roper to thank him for having arranged the deal with Weidenfeld and also praised him for having published an article in *The Sunday Express* – entitled "Hitler's Sister: A Lawsuit" – about Genoud's documents. Genoud wrote: "Thanks to you, these documents are highlighted in front of the English public."[38] Genoud apparently considered that by doing this Trevor-Roper had also validated his documents for an English audience.

It is thus obvious for any observer that Trevor-Roper had already strayed far outside the proper boundaries with regard to his role as a historian and academic. Instead of critically assessing the document in question, he had proceeded to ensure that it was instead published as quickly as possible. Trevor-Roper validated this document, which he was benefiting from financially, to several generations of historians and laymen alike. The publication of *Table Talk* and his introductory essay made it virtually impossible for Trevor-Roper to later publicly question the content of the text without risking to totally embarrass himself in front of his academic colleagues and the world at large.

Lost, and added, in translation

The translation of the table talks turned out to be not as straightforward as might initially have been expected. It seems as if the publisher was not happy with the work done by the original translator Norman Cameron. Weidenfeld wrote to Trevor-Roper on 8 January 1953 and told him that the translation would be completed only by 15 January because he had "had to use a second translator, Colonel Stevens (do you remember Stevens and Best?), whom I sent to Montreux, where he has been translating from the German direct under Genoud's supervision. The whole of next week will be used to iron out stylistic differences between the two translations, so that by the end of that week you would have the complete raw material."[39] However, Stevens had in fact *not* been translating from a German text. In paragraph III of the contract it was stated:

> III. The translation into English will be made on the basis of the French version by François Genoud and it is agreed that the licensor will permit the translator appointed by the licensee to examine at any time in Switzerland the original German version insofar as this is required by the work of translation.

We know that he really received these contracts because Trevor-Roper acknowledged this in a letter in October 1952 where he also stated that he would get back to Weidenfeld regarding his views on the contract text.[40] Unfortunately, these comments are nowhere to be found in Trevor-Roper's papers. In Trevor-Roper's papers there is a transcript of the contract in French, most likely from Genoud himself, where the fifth paragraph stipulated that:

> The assignee undertakes to proceed immediately with the English translation and to have this translation carried out in record time, based on the French text of the Flammarion edition.[41]

This French version, which apparently is an early draft of the contract, thus states that it was due to a wish to gain time that the translation should be done from the French edition, but this cannot be anything but a red herring. It does not take less time to translate from French than from German, especially not when the translator sometimes will have to double-check his translation by comparing it to a German text. It was just that Genoud was unwilling to let the translator see the complete German text (the true reason for which still remains obscure).

Thus, this simply cannot have been unknown to Trevor-Roper as he wrote the last words in his introduction to the *Table Talk* on 16 March 1953. He had had access to at least three copies of this paragraph before that time. It is not known how Trevor-Roper responded to this paragraph, or if he ever questioned what the motive for this stipulation was. But we do know that he did not mention any of this to his readers. Instead he stated that: "The text used for this edition of Hitler's Table-Talk is the text of the original *Bormann-Vermerke*."[42] He did this, just as he would do 20 years later in the second edition in 1973, knowing that what he was saying was not true. This is a cardinal sin by any historian, since it seriously puts the authenticity and fidelity of the text in doubt. The public and all historians that were bound to use this source in their writings had a certified right to be informed about this odd translation process and utterly irregular handling of the manuscript.

Even more odd is Trevor-Roper's reaction when we consider the fact that Weidenfeld wrote to Trevor-Roper in February 1953 saying:

> We are now engaged in re-checking the first half of the translation, which as you know *had to be made from the French*, but was subsequently revised by the second translator, who worked from the original German.[43] [Italics added.]

Perhaps he unconsciously pushed this knowledge out of his memory because it was so devastating. Granted, it may also be explicable if one considers that Hitler and National Socialism was not Trevor-Roper's main occupation at any time in his career.[44]

But how do we make sense of Weidenfeld's statements when we know for a fact that the English text corresponds in almost every instance with *Libres propos* and not with *Monologe*? The reference to a first half seems to correspond perfectly to the part of the text covered by the first volume of *Libres propos* (probably translated by Norman Cameron), and the second translator who had worked from the German was thus in that case Stevens. This would agree with Stevens's statement that he translated his part of the text from a German text; albeit it would leave the issue of why he did not say that he had also re-checked the other part unanswered (although that is admittedly a minor problem). Because of all of this Weidenfeld's letter indeed demands a satisfactory explanation – one that ties up all these loose ends – since it is completely inconceivable that Weidenfeld would say that the text had been re-checked against a German text if that was not the case. It was apparently a process that took a longer period of time.

Once again, we find that all of these perplexing facts are easily explained under the proposed γ-hypothesis, i.e. that Genoud supplied Stevens with a manuscript that was a re-translation of the French text into German. That would explain how the English text, in large parts, could still *look* like it had been translated from the French – even though Stevens, Weidenfeld, and Trevor-Roper may have thought that it was not. It could thus also be that the reason for why Trevor-Roper did not mention this fact in 1953 was because he thought that the text had been re-checked against the German original. But even so, Trevor-Roper should have mentioned these facts when talking about the text and what it was based on because it certainly had bearing on the text's claim to be completely reliable. Since this strange way of going about the translation would have put the text's authenticity, or at least reliability, in serious doubt, Trevor-Roper did not bother to do so.

But who was this Colonel Stevens that Weidenfeld had sent to Switzerland, and who was this Best that he also mentioned? Well, the two had been involved in a dramatic set of events during the war very directly related to Hitler himself. Lt. Col. Richard Henry Stevens had been the head of the Passport Control Office in The Hague for the British Secret Intelligence Service in The Netherlands from 1939. On 9 November that year Stevens and Captain Sigismund Payne Best were abducted by either the German *Abwehr* or *SD-Ausland* outside the small town of Venlo in The Netherlands (creating the famous so-called "Venlo Incident") and taken to Germany. They were accused of having aided in the failed assassination attempt on Hitler in Munich, in reality orchestrated solely by Georg Elser, that had taken place the day before. They spent the rest of the war in the Sachsenhausen and Dachau concentration camps (KZ) before being released in April 1945. Ironically, Elser was also imprisoned in Sachsenhausen before he, too, was transferred to Dachau in early February 1945. But while Stevens and Best were released in April, Elser was instead murdered. Stevens, who prior to his mission in Europe had served in the Rajput Regiment in the Indian army was, according to *The Times*, also a "distinguished linguist." After the war he worked as a translator in Paris and London, e.g. for North Atlantic Treaty Organization (NATO) between 1951 and 1952.[45] There is some contradictory information about Stevens in the various sources. It has also been said that Stevens was in fact freed by Allied forces in South Tirol in 1945 and that he was by then no longer part of MI6 since he had named names of British agents while in the KZs.[46] Stevens was in fact something of a linguistic *savant* it seems, apparently being fluent not only in Greek (his mother was Greek) but also in Arabic, Hindustani, Malay, German, French, and Russian. His German was apparently so good that he was able to adopt the alias Richard Fuchs and pose as a German national in Dachau.[47]

The historical coincidences are piled on even more by the fact that Stevens then in 1953 found himself translating Picker's note dated 3 May 1942 in which Hitler is talking about the assassination attempt in Munich.[48] Neither Stevens, Best, nor Elser is mentioned here, however, which is odd considering Stevens's background. It could at least have deserved a footnote. But there are other interesting things contained in this note, namely the inaccuracies in Hitler's alleged statements. The note says that Hitler left the *Bürgerbräukeller* ten minutes early on 9 November 1939 because of an urgent conference in Berlin that he had to attend.[49] There are several mistakes and inaccuracies here. First, the assassination attempt occurred on 8 November. This was the traditional day of celebration of the failed coup in 1923 and of the so-called martyrs who had died during this uprising. Had Hitler really forgotten what date that took place and on what date he held his Memorial Speech (*Gedenkrede*) even though he had held this speech on the same location and date ever since 1925? Second, the statement that he had left ten minutes early and therefore escaped unscathed is also not true. The celebration was planned to take place between 8:30 p.m. and 10 p.m., but Hitler had been forced to change his normal plan because of the bad autumn weather that prevented him from flying to Berlin the next day as planned. Instead, he had to take the train the same evening at 9:31 p.m. and he thus had to leave early. The bomb was set to go off at 9:20 p.m., which under normal circumstances would have been halfway into Hitler's speech. But Hitler began speaking earlier than planned and then cut his speech short, leaving at 9:07 p.m.[50] It was thus not because of an urgent conference that he had to leave; that is incorrect. Had Hitler forgotten about the true reasons or did he consciously make up this inaccurate story? Certainly, some of the people listening, such as

Bormann, must have known this was incorrect. There is a curious connection to Gerhard Ritter here as well. It turns out that Ritter, just like the Nazis, seems to not have accepted the truth regarding Elser, i.e. that he alone was responsible for the assassination attempt. Instead Ritter still as late as 1955 referred to Elser as a "communist foreign spy" (*Auslandsspitzel*) and even suggested that he was probably a Gestapo agent or perhaps even a tool of Himmler himself.[51]

Trevor-Roper later wrote to Weidenfeld and complained that he was referred to as an editor of *Table Talk* in advertisement for the book. He thought that criticism against the editing, which he himself would also make, reflected unfairly upon him. He asked if this error could be corrected.[52] *Table Talk* was also serialized, this time in the *Sunday Express* starting in early March 1953 and in the advertisement it said that Hitler's words had been "revealed through a team of shorthand writers."[53] The serialization began almost two months before the book was released on April 24.[54]

There are many differences between the English and German texts as they appear in *Table Talk* and *Monologe*. These differences are very often due to variations in the text introduced either by Genoud in the French edition or, seemingly, by Stevens as he translated the text. The examples are simply too many to be shown here, but some of the most glaring examples will serve to illustrate this important point. It is not known why Stevens chose to introduce phrases that are to be found neither in the German nor the French texts, and they cannot always be explained by introducing English idioms instead of German idioms. There are also other odd differences between the two versions, such as the fact that even though they contain the same notes (apart from the part of Picker's notes that do not appear in *Monologe*) they have been divided differently so that some notes that are one single note in *Monologe* are two notes in *Table Talk*.

In *Table Talk* we find that the entry dated 11–12 March, the last entry before Picker's notes begin, has the number 173 and the entry dated 1 August has number 274.[55] *Libres propos* and *Table Talk* do indeed have 173 entries for this period, while *Monologe* has only 158.[56] There is thus a strange variation in how Jochmann on the one hand and Trevor-Roper and Genoud on the other numbered the notes. Even more odd is the fact that this difference in numbering seems to only affect the notes contained in volume I of *Libres propos*, because from 1 August and onwards the number of notes in *Monologe* and the volume II of *Libres propos* correspond exactly. Since *Table Talk* was translated from the French it has the same division as *Libres propos*. Furthermore, we know that the translators used *Libres propos* also for those notes that are not in Picker's book because the short descriptions of the content that appear at the head of each entry are present in both books. They do *not* appear in *Monologe*. We have no particular reason to expect that Trevor-Roper could remember how many of Picker's entries that appeared in Genoud's manuscript, since he at most saw them in passing before the publication of the first edition in 1953.

The reason behind the numerical deviation is that a number of entries that are included in the same note in *Monologe* has been divided into two or more notes in *Table Talk*/*Libres propos* (Vol. I). It starts already in the beginning when note 3, dated 11/12 July 1941, in *Monologe* has been turned into notes 3 and 4, both dated "Night of 11th and 12th July 1941", in *Table Talk*.[57] Then comes a series of notes whose internal order is different.

Order of notes in *Monologe* and *Table Talk*[58]

Monologe	*Table Talk*
1.10.41	1.10.41
27/28.9.41 and 9.10.41	27/28.9.41 and 9.10.41
9/10.10.41	9/10.10.41
10.10.41	25/26.9.41 and 9/10.10.41
25/26.9.41 and 9/10.10.41	10.10.41
10/11.10.41	10/11.10.41

The three individually numbered notes from 19 October 1941 in *Table Talk* have been collected under the same heading in *Monologe*.[59] Oddly, *Monologe* places a note dated midday 30 October 1941 before the note dated 29 October. *Table Talk* has the more logical order in this instance.[60] This reversal is even stranger, considering that in *Monologe* this note is followed by one dated to the evening 30 October. *Table Talk* separates between the notes dated evening 1 November and night 1–2 November 1941, while *Monologe* includes the latter in the former.[61] This has not been a consistent choice on Jochmann's part, because the notes from midday and evening on 1 January 1942, for example, are given separate headings in both versions.[62] Then *Table Talk* puts the conversation from 2 November at midnight, while *Monologe* puts it at midday.[63] In *Monologe* the note dated 10 January 1942 comes before the one dated the day before. In *Table Talk* that is not so, and then *Monologe* dates one short note 12 January, while *Table Talk* dates it 13 January, which in turn come before the one for the night of 12–13 January.[64] This is probably a mistake on the part of Genoud in *Libres Propos* that has been transmitted to *Table Talk* in the translation process. *Table Talk* has a long note that is dated midday 23 January that is instead dated 25 January in *Monologe*.[65] While *Table Talk* has three separate notes for the evening of 18, evening of 19, and night of 19–20 February 1942, *Monologe* has them all under one and the same number.[66] These examples are what lie behind the difference with regard to numbering of the notes in *Table Talk/Libres propos* and *Monologe*.

There is also one entry that appears in *Table Talk* that does not appear in Jochmann's *Monologe*. It is a note dated 15 June 1943 and that, among other things, deals with intellectual and artistic property in industrial society.[67] It is unknown why this is missing in *Monologe*. At least Jochmann does not say anything about having left any notes out. We know, however, that he *did* leave certain notes in Genoud's manuscript out of *Monologe*, most likely as a result of Genoud having put in his veto against them being included. This conclusion is made even more probable by the fact that these notes are not included in either *Libres propos* or *Table Talk*. Copies of them are still in Jochmann's archival material; ironically the only copies that are still in there. The rest of the manuscript is nowhere to be found. It is one note made by Bormann entitled "Goethe on smoking" (*Goethe über das Rauchen*), with manuscript page numbers 1016–1017, and one called "Excerpts from the Führer speech on 27.1.1944" (*Auszüge aus der Führerrede vom 27.1.1944*), with page numbers 1022–1034.[68] The page numbers show that they were in fact part of Genoud's manuscript, and this makes Jochmann's statement in *Monologe* that the notes in the original manuscript were "re-printed unedited [and] preserving the chronological order" false.[69] He had left out at least three notes from the volume.

In fact, one of the very few indications that Stevens ever saw an original manuscript page are two footnotes attached to one of Picker's notes, more precisely one dated 5 April 1942 (this one is therefore not present in *Monologe*). These footnotes indicate that Bormann had commented by hand on the note itself. The first one, attached to an entry where Himmler suggested that all French children deemed to have "Germanic blood" should be taken from their parents and put in German boarding schools, states: " 'Sinister theory!' (MS. note by Bormann.)", and the other: " 'In Himmler's entourage, Rost Van Tonningen always worked against Mussert.' (MS. note by Bormann.)"[70] However, this is an illusion. In reality these notations were translated from *Libres propos*, but since it is to be found in the illusive second volume, the chances that anyone would ever notice this fact was rather minimal.[71] This is also why it has remained unknown until now. But here it once again gets interesting to compare the two versions. In Genoud's French version the first footnote says: " 'Théorie nébuleuse!' (Note manuscrite de Bormann.)"[72] But the French *nébuleuse* means "unclear", "vague", or "imprecise." The word "sinister", chosen by the translator of *Table Talk*, does not relate a correct view of what the French text says here (and looks odd in context). Since the original German manuscript is not available anymore, we have no way of knowing what the handwriting really says, if there were any at all.[73]

A comparison between the two notes in *Table Talk* and *Libres propos* shows that the former has been translated completely based upon the latter. There are also paragraphs in *Table Talk* that are italicized and these are italicized in *Libres propos* as well, while they are not italicized in *Tischgespräche*. The summary of the content in the beginning of the note is also exactly the same in *Table Talk*.[74] This is of course true for *all* the notes between 24 March 1942 and 30 November 1944. But the second volume of *Libres propos* was not published until one year after *Table Talk*, so this fact must mean that Stevens had access to a version of *Libres propos vol. II* already in 1952/53. Moreover, the text in the first edition of *Tischgespräche* is divided in two parts (let us call them A and B), since Ritter chose a thematic disposition for this book.[75] But since the chronologically ordered second edition of *Tischgespräche* published the text as it was, we can compare the two, and what we find then is that A ended up after B in the 1951 edition (on pages 420–421 and 66–69, respectively).[76] In *Libres propos* and *Table Talk*, however, the order is B and A, i.e. it follows how the two parts appear in *Tischgespräche* of 1951.

This presents us with a dilemma. If Genoud really had Picker's original notes and published them as they were, then we must assume that Picker for some reason decided to reverse the order in the second edition of his book (we do not know in what order the two parts occurred in the manuscript that Ritter based his edition on). The other possibility is that Picker placed the A and B in a different order in his two manuscripts, i.e. the one that he gave to Bormann and the one he kept for himself. In that case it is simply a coincidence that Ritter happened to place them in the right order in the first edition of *Tischgespräche*. A third possibility, then, is that Genoud did not actually have this note but based it upon Ritter's edition of *Tischgespräche* in which the first part of the text came second.

A comparison between the last Heim entry before he was replaced by Picker, dated 11/12 March 1942 – i.e. the last entry in the first volume of *Libres propos* – and the first Heim entry after his return to the headquarters, dated 1 August 1942, in *Table Talk*, *Monologe*, and the second volume of *Libres propos* is also extremely interesting. At first, it appears that the 1 August entry proves that it was translated from Genoud's photocopied German manuscript.[77] The reason for why we can be pretty sure that a German text was used when translating this note is that in *Table Talk* there is a comment added to the entry saying:

> *Note by translator.* The text for this day is very disjointed and confusedly written (with even grammatical mistakes in the German).[78] [Italics in original.]

However, the text in *Table Talk* clearly follows the French in *Libres propos*, which does not contain such a comment; for example, there are three italicized parts in *Libres propos*, one at the very beginning of the note describing the topic of discussion and two further down where injections by Keitel (see later) and Bormann are described. This is copied in *Table Talk* but it does not appear in *Monologe*, and these parts are also differently worded in the latter version.[79] Furthermore, Jochmann says nothing about any grammatical mistakes in *Monologe*.[80] This is indeed very strange because if the German was so bad it ought to have created a problem for Jochmann as well, i.e. should he publish the note as it was or should he correct the grammatical mistakes? The note by the translator also implies that he had done his best to produce a text that was comprehensible and less confused. What would indicate that this happened is the fact that the English text is perfectly intelligible. An even more peculiar fact, however, is that there does not seem to be any grammatical errors in Jochmann's version – nor does it look "disjointed and confusedly written." This is even more strange considering that the English translation follows the German rather well (even though it was clearly translated from the French version of the text) – for it is unreasonable to assume that it is a coincidence that the translation into English and the correction of the text in German produced a basically identical result, not least because of the great liberties taken by the translator on most other occasions.

It is as if Stevens was working from *another* German text than that which later appeared in *Monologe*; indeed, he *must* have been. The reason for why the text contained grammatical errors and was "disjointed and confusedly written" is unknown, but since the text in *Monologe* does not suffer from these problems, Stevens cannot have had access to the same text. Did someone with poor command of the German language write it? Genoud's first language was French, and he is certainly the most obvious candidate for the authorship of the note that Stevens had. Genoud cannot reasonably have had Heim's original note in front of him when he typed the version that Steven's had access to because why would the German then be confused and the note disjointed? It is more likely that Genoud had re-translated the French text from *Libres propos* into German – we know he later did this in the case of *Hitlers politisches Testament* (see Chapter 6).

The evidence that a German text was used is clear. The note contains a section where Hitler on Bormann's initiation criticizes the Catholic Church and (briefly) Jehovah's Witnesses.[81] We know that the translator must have had access to some kind of German text in this case, because in *Table Talk* it says: "Bible Students (*Bibelforscher*)." The German term does not appear in *Libres propos*, which instead has "Témoins de Jéhovah." However, in *Monologe* it says "Bibelforschern."[82] Note that *Table Talk* has "*Bibelforscher*", while *Monologe* has "*Bibelforschern.*" In context, the latter dative form is the correct one. This could perhaps be an example of the grammatical errors in the German text that Stevens was using. On the other hand, the difference could also be due to Stevens having chosen to state the nominative form of the word. Moreover, the wording is much more similar to the German text in *Monologe*, yet the text is at the same time clearly influenced by *Libres propos* as far as the layout is concerned. This becomes evident from a side-by-side comparison.

Comparison between *Table Talk*, *Libre propos*, and *Monologe*[83]

Table Talk	Libres propos	Monologe
Field Marshal Keitel expressed the opinion that we had much the same situation now with the Bibel Students (*Bibelforscher*). *Hitler replied:* [Italics in original.]	*Keitel fait cette réflexion: "Dans ce domaine, il me semble que nous n'avons pas grand' chose à envier aux Américains. Je pense à notre secte des Témoins de Jéhovah."* *Hitler répond:* [Italics in original.] [Translation:] *Keitel made this reflection: "In this area, it seems to me that we do not have much to envy the Americans. I'm thinking of our cult of Jehovah's witnesses."* *Hitler responds:*	Der Generalfeldmarshall wirft ein, ähnlich sei es bei uns auch mit den Bibelforschern gewe-sen. Der Chef: [Translation:] The General Field Marshall interjects, it is comparable here with the Bible Researchers. The boss:

While *Table Talk* clearly resembles *Monologe* more, there are details that agree completely with *Libres propos*. The italicized phrase "Hitler replied" directly corresponds to "Hitler répond" in *Libres propos*, for example. The paragraph even has a line space before and after it in both *Table Talk* and *Libres propos*, which does not appear in *Monologe*. That cannot be an accident either. The extra information about America in *Libres propos* is likely to be Genoud's creation. Moreover, the fact that the text in *Table Talk* and *Libres propos* is italicized proves that the translator must have had a copy of *Libres propos* vol. II in front of him.

A close reading reveals some other additions to the text that appear in *Table Talk* that cannot be found in *Monologe*. For example, in *Table Talk* Hitler says:

> It is perfectly true that the British swallow everything they are told. At the moment, nevertheless, there is a certain amount of murmuring over faked reports. To justify the bluff, those at the head of affairs are reduced to telling the discontented that these false reports are being spread in order to deceive the enemy. A large portion of intelligent Britons say: "We are waging war by bluff, *and it's the only way we can wage it!*" **Whether they believe that they are really bluffing us, is a very different matter.** In the autumn of 1939 they declared that there were already a million Britons in France! Even I estimated their strength at between thirty-five and forty divisions, whereas in reality they had twelve or fifteen – a mere 350,000 men! I cannot imagine the publication of a deliberate lie in the German official communiqué; *but they don't mind how many they publish in their reports*, and one realises now the extent to which they are hoodwinking their own people.[84] [Italics and emphasis added.]

In *Libres propos* we find the following:

> Il est vrai que le public anglais avale toutes les bourdes. En ce moment pourtant, il est visible que l'opinion britannique commence à se montrer réticente. Pour justifier leur bluff, les dirigeants en sont réduits à expliquer à ceux qui protestent qu'ils font cela pour tromper l'adversaire. *Il n'y a pas d'autre façon, disent-ils, de conduire la guerre.* Eh bien, nous pouvons les assurer qu'ils font erreur s'ils pensent nous intimider en agissant de la sorte! Rappelons-nous qu'en automne 1939 ils prétendaient avoir débarqué en France plus d'un million de leurs soldats. Pour ma part, j'avais calculé qu'ils avaient débarqué de trente-cinq à quarante divisions. En réalité, c'était de douze à quinze, soit environ trois cent cinquante mille hommes![85] [Italics added.]
>
> [Translation:] *It is true that the English public swallows everything. At the moment, however, it is evident that British opinion is beginning to be reluctant. To justify their bluff, the leaders are reduced to explaining to those who protest that they are doing this to deceive the opponent. There is no other way, they say, to conduct the war. Well, we can assure them that they are mistaken if they think they can intimidate us by doing so! Let us remember that in autumn 1939 they claimed to have landed in France more than one million of their soldiers. For my part, I had calculated that they*

had landed between thirty-five and forty divisions. In reality, it was twelve to fifteen, or about three hundred and fifty thousand men!

The version that Jochmann published has a somewhat different wording still, and is shorter:

> Gewiß, die Masse nimmt dort gläubig hin, was ihr gesagt wird; aber man hört jetzt doch auch viele Stimmen des Unmuts über Falschberichtung. Die Führung entschuldigt sich damit, in Rücksicht auf uns müsse man so schreiben. **Ein großer Teil der intellektuellen Engländer sagt: Wir führen Krieg mit Bluff!** Sie bilden sich ein, daß sie uns damit einschüchtern können. 1939, in Herbst, haben sie klärt, sie hätten jetzt bereits über eine Million Engländer in Frankreich! Ich hatte mit 35 bis 49 Divisionen gerechnet. Dabei hatten sie dort 12 bis 15 Divisionen, etwa 350 000 Mann! *Dieses Lügen, das können wir nicht. Ich könnte mir nicht denken, daß in den deutschen Heeresbericht bewußt eine Lüge hereinkommt. Das machen die eiskalt! Nun sieht man ja auch, wie sehr sie ihr eigenes Volk beschwindeln!*[86] [Italics and emphasis added.]
>
> [Translation:] *Of course, the masses accept in faith what they are told; But you can now hear a lot of voices of displeasure with false reporting. The leadership apologizes by saying that with consideration to us one has to write like this. A large part of the intellectual English says: We are waging war with bluff! They are imagining that they can intimidate us with it. In 1939, in autumn, they clarified that they already had over a million Englishmen in France! I had expected 35 to 49 divisions. They had 12 to 15 divisions there, about 350,000 men!* Lie like this, we can't. I could not envision that a lie would deliberately come into the German Army report. They do it without a care! Now you can also see how much they swindle their own people!

The version in *Monologe* thus contains many things (the italicized part) not present in either *Table Talk* or *Libres propos*. The bold sentence in *Monologe* – "a large part of the intellectual English" – has a very similar counterpart in *Table Talk* – "A large portion of intelligent Britons say" – but *not* in *Libres propos* where neither intellectual English nor intelligent Britons can be found. We now can also see that the bold sentence in *Table Talk* does not appear in either *Libres propos* or *Monologe*. Obviously, it cannot be a misinterpretation of: "They are imagining that they can intimidate us with it." *Table Talk* appears to be a mixture of the French and the German texts, with some added on peculiarities.

We are thus faced with two options here: either Stevens made the emphasized sentence in *Table Talk* up or there was really a sentence like this in the German text that he was translating from. I argue that for several reasons the former option seems highly unlikely; first, it is very hard to see what the motivation would be for Stevens to do such a thing and, second, it is hard to understand how he could make such a bold move and risk getting caught. Rather, then, the latter option is likely to have been the case, i.e. Stevens translated a German text that actually had such a sentence in it. Genoud likely went overboard with his own interpretation of what Hitler was thinking and let his imagination run amok.

That Hitler really thought that the British were conducting a bluff war can be ascertained from other independent evidence. According to Goebbels's diary, Hitler had stated something similar on 20 June 1939 at the Berghof regarding the British security guarantee to Poland. Hitler had said that he did not believe that the British would come to Poland's rescue. "Es blufft nur", or "they are just bluffing." Volker Ullrich has noted that it is hard to know if Hitler actually meant what he said or not.[87] It was not a very strange opinion at all; it was, after all, simply a recognition of the fact that the war was also a propaganda war and one where both sides were trying to obfuscate their actions as much as possible in order to hide their true goals and actions from their opponents. The Allies, and especially the British, made frequent and often successful use of deception and decoy operations during the war, not only during the preparations for the D-day landings in June 1944. It was a tradition that went back to the First World War.[88]

It also mirrors something that Hitler said in a speech on 4 September 1940. He was making a series of ironic remarks where he claimed that the British had put their hopes on a number of symbolic so-called generals in their fight against Germany. First, there had been "General *Revolution*" (i.e. the hope that a revolution in Germany would oust the Nazis from power), then "General *Hunger*", and finally "General *Winter*." Then he stated:

> Die Engländer sollten . . . ihren bedeutendsten eigenen General vielleicht zum britischen Reichsgeneralfeldmarschall zu erheben: nämlich den General *Bluff*. Das ist ihr einziger Verbündeter. . . . Uns allerdings schlägt man mit diesem General nicht mehr. Mit ihm kann man das britische Volk vielleicht dumm machen, aber das deutsche Volk hat England genügend kennengelernt.[89] [Italics in original.]
>
> [Translation:] *The English should [. . .] perhaps elevate their most important general of their own to the British General Field Marshall: namely General* Bluff. *This is their only ally. [. . .] But we are no longer defeated by this general. With him you may be able to make the British people stupid, but the German people have gotten to know England well enough.*

It is obvious that this utterance is related to that recorded by Heim in *Monologe*. However, it is also equally obvious that there are important differences between the versions. Perhaps most importantly, the idea of a British "bluff" has now been transformed from a sarcastic remark on Hitler's part into an honest phrase used by British intellectuals. Already on the face of it this statement is ludicrous; Hitler did not know what Britain's intellectuals thought on this matter. But the fact that Hitler used this metaphor in this way in a public speech tells us one important thing about the Hitler that Heim recorded on 1 August 1942: it does not represent Hitler's innermost thoughts on this matter. Instead it transmits a clear propaganda phrase, and it once again shows that the table talks do not present us with the private and unguarded Hitler. Neither can this be a reference to the so-called Phony War, since the first usage comes *after* the Phony War is over. Here we encounter the same problem as with Hitler's lies about his own personal history, which he seems to have convinced himself of. But without access to Hitler's mind we simply cannot be certain what he really believed or not. All we can be certain of is that it was not true.

There are more examples of the same kind of variations between the text in this particular note. A while later *Table Talk* has Hitler saying the following:

> The Church has succeeded in striking a very pretty balance between the life on earth and in the Hereafter. *On earth, they say, the poor must remain poor and blessed*, for in Heaven the earthly rich will get nothing; *and the unfortunate poor on earth believe them!*[190] [Italics added.]

The French text reads as follows:

> L'Eglise a fait un savant mélange des choses de ce monde et des choses de l'autre monde. Les pauvres croient qu'ils sont destinés de tout éternité à la pauvreté et que les enfants de leurs enfants doivent demeurer dans cet état jusqu'à la consommation des siècles – les riches, eux, n'ayant pas accès au paradis![191]
>
> [Translation:] *The Church has made a clever mix of things of this world and things of the other world. The poor believe that they are destined for all eternity to poverty and that the children of their children must remain in this state until the end of the centuries – the rich, they, have no access to Paradise!*

However, in the German we find:

> Die Kirche hat es verstanden, das Diesseitige mit dem Jenseitigen auszugleichen. Die Armen haben geglaubt, sie müßten arm sein *und mit Kind und Kindeskind arm bleiben*, denn die anderen, die hier reich sind, ins Himmelreich gehen sie nicht ein![192] [Italics added.]
>
> [Translation:] *The Church has been able to balance this life with the afterlife. The poor have believed that they must be poor* and to remain poor with child and grandchild*, because the others who are rich here [on earth] cannot enter the Kingdom of Heaven!*

Once again, the italics in the English paragraph shows additions to the text not present in the German, and conversely the italicized parts in *Monologe* show phrases that do not appear in *Table Talk*. The first sentence in all versions is essentially the same. It is the second sentence that differs between them. While *Libres propos* and *Monologe* are basically the same, *Table Talk* is the odd one out again. The italicized part in *Monologe* has clearly been left out in *Table Talk*. Likewise, there is nothing either in *Monologe* or *Libres propos* that could justify a translator to add "they say" and the word "blessed." In fact, the English text makes Hitler sound more critical of the Church than he does in the German and French versions. We have no way to know for certain why these differences are there. It could of course be that the German text that Stevens had access to contained statements that correspond to what we find in *Table Talk*, but it could also be that this is an expression of Stevens's creative mind. We see another example of this just a little bit further down in *Table Talk* where Hitler states:

> No science remains stationary. In my eyes the ability of mankind to reject a proven untruth is one of its virtues.[93]

In *Libres propos* we find:

> Il n'existe aucune discipline de la connaissance qui ne soit en état de constante évolution. A mes yeux, la bonne foi humaine consiste à repousser le mensonge avéré.[84]
>
> [Translation:] *There is no discipline of knowledge that is not in a state of constant evolution. In my eyes, the good faith of mankind is to repel the proven lie.*

But the German has a slightly different wording:

> Es gibt kein Wissen, das sich nicht ständig ändert. In meinem Augen gehört es zur Aufrichtigkeit des Menschen, daß er an Unwahrheiten nicht festhält.[95]
>
> [Translation:] *There is no knowledge that does not change all the time. In my eyes, it is part of man's sincerity that he does not hold on to falsehoods.*

First, "Wissen" does not mean "science" but rather "knowledge" in general, and second the word "Aufrichtigkeit" means "honesty" rather than "virtue." But more importantly, this passage contradicts other views on science and the scientific method that Hitler expressed over the years. What we find in the table talks cannot be understood as Hitler's "real" view on this topic. In reality, Hitler expressed conflicting opinions on the subject throughout his life. For example, when Hitler made Rosenberg the head of ideological schooling in the party on 21 January 1940 he announced that Rosenberg was to start building a library for the so-called college (*Hohe Schule*) that after the war was supposed to become "the central site for National Socialist research."[96] That implies ideology production, not an interest in objective scientific research. At the same time, he told Rosenberg that the proposal for the school's organization risked being criticized for politically directing the science, something that the Church had tried to do for so long. This was not good, he told Rosenberg. The interesting thing here is that Rosenberg expressed surprise at what he called "the Führer's positivistic remark" which was something new for him. But he noted that due to Hitler's strong belief in Providence (*Vorsehung*) both worlds existed within him.[97] This shows that Hitler here expressed a view that Rosenberg did not recognize.

On the other hand, Hitler was of the opinion that it was precisely the fact that the Church did *not* let its central ideological tenets be changed by scientific results that gave it its strength and durability, and he held this up as a role model for the NSDAP. That was why the 25 points of the party programme should never be changed, he said. People could not be convinced of the necessity of blind faith in ideological dogmatic statements if these tenets of belief were allowed to change. This would only create doubt among the adherents to the ideology. Just as the Church had refused to change its dogmas when they contradicted science, the NSDAP had to adopt the same stance, he argued.[98] The problem with science was precisely its fundamental tendency to change its position on the nature of the world as new evidence and results became available. In a speech in Plauen on 12 June 1925 he stated that a political movement's strength lay in its ideological unity, and the belief in the correctness of the ideological tenets had to remain even if science was to point in another direction. Science and research kept changing through the ages, but ideology could not be allowed to do that.[99]

Thus, the statement recorded in the table talk text to the effect that Hitler thought that it was a strength of humanity to revise false doctrines was obviously not true in a general sense. It held true for when he criticized the Church's outdated dogmas or another opponent's political views, but not when it came to National Socialist teachings. As a general rule, then, it is obvious from the historical record that Hitler was never interested in science unless its results could be applied in the service of National Socialism. Ideology always came first for him and would remain dominant whatever the sciences concluded. He was, as always, only in favour of "objectivity" when it served his purposes, i.e. it was as crude a subjectivism as could be imagined. This was not due to a calculated strategy or of cynicism on Hitler's part; he was simply blind to the contradiction entailed in the ideological views that he held. Logical thinking was never Hitler's forte – a fact that only goes to show just how little he had actually studied philosophy – and he probably did not realize that he was holding and espousing ideas that conflicted with one another.

Let us now get back to the table talk texts again. On another occasion Hitler comments upon his fear that the fact that Christianity's ever-changing perception of the afterlife was tied up to so many small earthly things that when these minor matters started to fall apart, people would turn to the materialism of Bolshevism, with the following sentence: "That is deeply worrying" (*Das ist das Tieftraurige*). In Trevor-Roper's edition, however, this has been translated as: "And that is a terrible tragedy."[100] *Tieftraurig* does not mean "tragedy", but rather "deeply sad" or "deeply worrying." The change in meaning is clear. And even if the difference in meaning is not always that great, even though it is certainly a fact, it does point to a liberty taken in the translation process that is both unnecessary and potentially deceiving to the reader. For a historian, or anyone who wants to quote Hitler as to his views in a matter, however, it becomes crucial that the translation can be trusted down to the minutest details. To make an idiomatic translation is not good enough; it has to stay as true as possible to the original text.

There is also a minor mistake in the part about the Church, where in the English version Bormann brought up the subject of *"the gifts which France made almost every day to the Church, and on which the power of the Church was thriving mightily."*[101] [Italics in original.] This makes little sense. What would it mean for France to give the Church "gifts"? It turns out that this is a translation error. In *Monologe* (as in the French and Italian editions) it is the Spanish dictator Franco, not "France", who is mentioned by Bormann. However, in the French and Italian text it is explicitly said that Franco did the Church in Spain favours. In *Monologe* only Franco is mentioned.[102] This makes much more sense also because Hitler had been talking about a book about Spain that he had read, and both versions later have Hitler mentioning Franco. Stevens must have misread "France" as "Franco", which makes one wonder if he in fact had a hand-written text in front of him, and no one ever caught the mistake when proofreading the text. In fact, the mistake remains in the second edition of *Table Talk* published in 1973.[103] The word "gifts" in *Table Talk* appears odd in this context, and the word "favours" would seem to have been a much better fit. But the word used in *Monologe* is "Schenkungen", which means "gifts" or "donations." The latter might have been a better choice in this context. This again indicates that Stevens in this case seems to have worked from a German text that did not include the part explicitly referring to Spain.

The highly corrupted translation in *Table Talk* has nonetheless acquired a kind of official status, as if a translation could somehow be the final and only possible way to translate a text into another language. This argument was used by David Irving in the libel trial against Professor Deborah Lipstadt as a proof that his rendering of Hitler's utterances was correct, in fact better than e.g. Richard J. Evans's own translation of the same passages. Irving stated that "Weidenfeld & Nicholson published the edition of Hitler's table talk back in about 1949, with an introduction by Hugh Trevor-Roper, a very good volume . . . and that is the translation I have used. . . . The official translation. I have not changed one dot or comma of the official translation as published by Hugh Trevor-Roper."[104] Here Irving obviously gets the year of publication wrong, placing it four years prior to 1953, but he also uses an argument from authority in order to claim that *Table Talk* is an excellent source. There is no such thing as an "official" translation of Hitler's table talks. This is just yet another example of how dishonest, although clever, Irving is, since he on other occasions would make the exact opposite argument, i.e. that one would have to consult the original German text to get a reliable version of what was said at a certain instance. Irving is simply making the argument that suits his *ad hoc* purpose.

But it turns out that Irving was in fact lying when he claimed he had gone back to the original German documents in this case. The reason is that Irving claimed that he received copies of Genoud's manuscript pages and that he used them for his book *Hitler und seine Feldherren* (*Hitler and His Generals*).[105] If Irving used copies of Genoud's original, we would, of course, expect the quotes in this book to be identical with those in Jochmann's *Monologe*. However, they are not, and they seem to indicate that he in fact used Trevor-Roper's *Table Talk* and Picker's *Tischgespräche* instead. Now, most of the references in the book pertain to Heim's notes (which Irving simply quotes as "Tischgespräch") and are not *ad verbatim* quotes, so it is impossible to check what the source actually is. The few quotes that he actually includes show, however, when compared with *Monologe* on the one hand and *Table Talk* and *Tischgespräche* on the other, that the manuscript used for *Monologe* cannot be the source. The only quote that appears in Monologe will serve well to illustrate this point. In *Hitler und seine Feldherren* it says:

> Die einzige Kolonie, die er gern wieder hätte, wäre unser Kamerun – sonst nichts. (Heim)[106]

But according to *Monologe* Heim's note from 18 October 1941 actually says:

> Nur unser Kamerun möchte ich wiederhaben, sonst nichts.[107]

This is clearly not the same wording. But if we take a look at the same sentence in Trevor-Roper's *Table Talk* we find the following:

> In any case, the only colony I'd like to have back would be our Cameroons – nothing else.[108]

We can clearly see that Irving's phrase "die enzige Kolonie", which does not appear in Jochmann, must have come from Trevor-Roper's "the only colony"; even the idiosyncratic " – " sign is repeated by Irving. Then Irving's phrase also contains the strange change into third-person singular, but this is something that appears in every quote in his book – Irving has changed words here and there (nothing major, but still very unnecessary and points to carelessness). Thus, we can conclude that Irving has simply changed the wording of the English edition. One could of course question if the similarity is due to Irving re-translating the English into German or if he got some type of document from Genoud that was worded this way in German (perhaps the same document that *Table Talk* was then translated from).

Moreover, what Hitler is saying in *Monologe* regarding colonial possessions is not true, and it once again points to the importance for scholars to be critical of the content in the table talks. In early March Hitler had told the British ambassador, who had offered to give Germany back some of her colonies, that the colonial question was not yet ripe for settling. He instead wanted to wait maybe as long as ten years to solve this issue. The point though was that Hitler indeed *did* want Germany's former colonies returned, only he wished to negotiate from a position of strength and dictate to Britain what they should give him.[109] Interestingly, the British journalist Ward Price includes a statement in his book *I Know These Dictators* from 1937 that agrees with what Hitler is saying in the table talks. Ward writes that:

> Officially, the aim of Germany is stated to be the recovery of all her former colonies. But there is reason to suppose that German statesmen might be satisfied with 'a rounded-out Cameroons.' By this is meant a West African colony based upon the original German territory there, which is now divided between the adjoining British Nigeria and French Equatorial Africa.[110]

While this agrees with the table talks, it is the complete opposite of Hitler's real intentions. With this context we must ask: is it only a coincidence that the table talk Hitler is saying the same things as Nazi propaganda was saying before the war? No, this is rather a result of the fact that the table talks may have been intended for publication at some point after the war. Those present must have known that this was not Hitler's true position on this matter.

After all, detailed discussions were had on this issue during the war, and plans made, for how the colonies in Africa would be divided as spoils among the victorious Axis Powers. Germany was planning on grabbing considerable holdings in Central Africa. This is apparent from many documents from the German Foreign Ministry during the war, for example, the notes by Under State Secretary (*Unterstaatssekretär*) and *SS Oberführer* Ernst Woermann from a discussion within the Foreign Ministry from 21 January 1942, i.e. the day after the Wannsee Conference. From this document it is also clear that Hitler took active part in such colonial discussions. The expectation was that England would lose all its colonies in Africa. The French possessions in equatorial Africa would be the centre of the new German colonial empire, which would include eastern Nigeria, Cameroon, Uganda and Kenya, German East Africa, and perhaps also northern Rhodesia. Belgian Congo would also be added to this empire in some way or another. Discussions between Hitler/Ribbentrop and Franco/Suñer had been held on this topic in Hendaye already on 23 October 1940, so it was not the case that Hitler had changed his mind a year later when Heim made his note.[111] Colonial possessions after the war were always the aim.

It also fits nicely with Hitler's demands that Germany should be compensated for its loss of colonies after 1918 that he started to bring forth every now and then from 1937. Max Domarus thought that this was not really an honest expression of his true opinions as Hitler had proclaimed in *Mein Kampf* that the former colonial policy of the *Kaiserreich* was outdated, and that the expansion should occur in the East instead.[112] But Hitler had noted in a letter to the *Gauleiter* of Baden-Elsaß, Robert Wagner, already on 22 November 1929 that the aim was to get the German colonies back. The third point in the party programme concerned mainly land and colonies in Europe, but the NSDAP would not say no to colonies overseas either, he said.[113] Even the so-called "Hossbach proto-col" (*Hoßbach-Niederschrift*), which was never intended for public consumption or propaganda purposes, contains a clear case for when the former German colonies could be given back; i.e. in a situation where Britain found itself in an emergency while Germany was very strong. Germany could not expect to get a share of Britain's colonies otherwise.[114]

Publicly in his propaganda, however, Hitler was not as forthcoming. In his infamous speech to the *Reichstag* on 30 January 1939 Hitler brought this up again and stated that Germany had no territorial demands towards Britain or France other than the "Wiedergabe unserer Kolonien."[115] He once again repeated this claim in his speech to the *Reichstag* on 28 April 1939.[116] Moreover, it was also part of Hitler's demands in the negotiations with Britain shortly before the invasion of Poland. Germany wished to either have its colonies back or get some of Britain's colonies as compensation.[117] He mentioned the issue in a speech on 6 October, as well in his annual 8 November speech.[118] Furthermore, Jodl states in his diary that Hitler, after German tanks had reached the French coast at Abbéville, had said that: "The British can at any time have a separate peace after giving back our colonies."[119] The issue about the British having stolen the German colonies in 1918 and 1919 came up again in January 1941, and Hitler stated that he had never asked for anything that actually belonged to Britain.[120] This indicates that Hitler was not letting the *Wehrmacht*, which he did not really trust anyway, in on his real plans either.

It is important, however, not to confuse Hitler's demand for the former German colonies with his plans to conquer *Lebensraum* in Eastern Europe. The colonies could not solve the problem of ensuring a secure food supply for Germany, he declared to the military leadership gathered at the *Reichskanzlei* on 23 May 1939, because deliveries from those colonies could easily be stopped by a naval blockade (as during the First World War). The "problem of sustenance" (*Ernährungsproblem*) would be solved by the colonizing of Eastern Europe. Only there would Germany have total control of production and delivery routes.[121] The African colonies were instead a matter of prestige to Hitler – having colonies was part and parcel of what it meant to be a great power. Hitler seems to have taken the loss of its colonies as an insult to Germany's honour, and he spoke of "the theft of the German colonies" by the Versailles powers.[122]

In several other cases, however, Irving quotes passages that are not in either *Mono-loge* or *Table Talk*, but that appear only in Picker, and thus *must* be quoted from there. Once again though Irving does not refer to Picker, but simply to "Tischgespräch" followed by a date.[123] Another example is when Irving cites Hitler as saying:

> Bei diesem Kampf würden wir uns sogar mit dem Teufel verbünden, um zu siegen.[124]
>
> [Translation:] *In this struggle we will even ally ourselves with the Devil in order to win.*

This entry, dated to 17 May 1942, is missing in Jochmann because it is one of Picker's notes. But the wording in *Tischgespräche* is quite different:

> daß wir bei diesem Kampf um Sein oder Nichtsein uns sogar mit dem Teufel verbünden würden, um zu siegen.[125]
>
> [Translation:] *that we will even be allied with the Devil in this struggle for existence or non-existence in order to win.*

This particular one, however, also appears in *Table Talk*. Here we can see that Irving's quote leaves out a part of the sentence and moves some words around. Once again, if we look at *Table Talk* we find:

> that the present conflict is one of life or death, and that the essential is to win – and to that end we are quite ready to make an alliance with the Devil himself.[126]

Granted, this version differs from both of the sentences earlier, but the fact that the part about a fight to the death appears earlier in *Table Talk* could explain why Irving leaves that particular part out. But *Table Talk* simply follows *Libres propos* here in which we see the following phrasing of this passage:

> que dans ce conflit où il s'agit de notre vie ou de notre mort, l'essentiel est de vaincre – et qu'en vue de cette fin nous contracterions alliance avec le diable en personne.[127]

We clearly see that *Table Talk* is based entirely upon *Libres propos* here. The theme of making a pact with the Devil was an old one for Hitler. He had, for example, used it in a speech on 23 May 1928, but then in the context of the fight against Hitler's archenemy France.[128] The phrases "life or death" and "the essential is to win" both attest to this, since they are too similar to be a coincidence. There are two possibilities to explain the difference between Genoud's and Picker's versions of this note by Picker. Either Picker changed his own note before the publication of *Tischgespräche* so that it mentions none of these phrases or Genoud's handiwork is again at play here.

Hitler also made a similar statement in a speech on 23 May 1928, in the *Bürgerbräukeller* in Munich. Speaking about the fact that France was the sworn enemy of Germany and that all efforts must be directed towards preparing the nation for a new war against this foe, Hitler said the following:

> Wenn heute der Satan käme und sich mir als Verbündeter antragen würde, gegen Frankreich würde ich ihm die Hand geben (stürmischer Beifall).[129]
>
> [Translation:] *If Satan came and was to join me as an ally against France then I would give him the hand (thunderous applause).*

This seems to show a remarkable persistency in terms of metaphorical language on the part of Hitler considering that there were 14 years in between these occasions. Exactly the same religious imagery and very similarly formulated too.

That Irving and Picker end in the same way could be due to a grammatical peculiarity in the German language, which places infinitive phrases at the end of sentences, or it could be because Irving looked at Picker when translating the phrase. Then again, the *Table Talk* version is different in implication, something that might suggest that Irving did not use *Table Talk* in this case. Perhaps he simply misquoted Picker – although there is of course a possibility that Genoud's version of Picker's note had a different wording. All in all, there is only one quote in Irving's book that appears in *Monologe* and this does not concur with the German text as published in *Monologe*. Irving's book thus provides no evidence of him having used any part of the manuscript that later was published by Jochmann in 1980.[130]

Irving, in fact, admitted to this fact during the libel trial against Deborah Lipstadt in 2000. There, when pressed on the issue by Lipstadt's attorney, he stated that:

> When I wrote the *Hitler's War* in the 1970s, I had the English text in front of me, when I reissued it in Germany I contacted the Swiss owner of the original Martin Bormann files, who had the original German texts and I obtained from him on that occasion German texts of these passages. But I did not translate it, Mr. Rampton. The translation was done by either Trevor-Roper or by Weidenfeld and I have used the exact words.[131]

Let us start by making perfectly clear that this makes no sense whatsoever. First, *Hitler und seine Feldherren*, upon which *Hitler's War* is based, was published in 1975, but already in the first edition of *Hitler's War*, which was published in 1977, Irving thanked Genoud in his "Acknowledgements" for having "supplied key extracts from Bormann's personal files."[132] Second, it makes absolutely no sense to gain access to the German original text and still use a highly flawed translation. Third, Irving did not use the exact words from *Table Talk*. It is as if Irving just cannot manage to tell the truth at any time, no matter how small the detail.

When Lipstadt's attorney, Richard Rampton, questioned why Irving had chosen to use "a terrible translation" when the original text was available to him, Irving had great difficulty explaining his choices, but continued to claim that, in his view, *Table Talk* offers "an adequate translation."[133] For Irving, of course, the quality of the translation was of secondary importance at best, since for him his quote-mining exercises were only a means to an end, namely to exonerate Hitler from all responsibility for the Holocaust. "No documentary evidence exists that Hitler was aware that the Jews were being massacred", Irving wrote triumphantly in his book.[134]

But, as we have seen, Irving is actually lying about using *Table Talk* as his source in these instances, and we know this because many of the passages that he quotes are not in *Table Talk* but only in *Tischgespräche*, which he indeed *did* translate himself in *Hitler's War*. This is even more ironic considering that during the trial Irving explained his decision to use the *Table Talk* translation (which he in fact did not) by referring to criticism of his book by other historians who did not recognize his quotes precisely because they were *not* as in *Table Talk*. Thus, Irving claimed to have decided to use *Table Talk*; yet he still claimed to have used the original German text in the German edition of the book.[135] The contradiction is total.

Another such example from the trial was the phrase taken from a note dated 25 October 1941 in *Table Talk* that says:

> Let nobody tell me that all the same we can't park them in the marshy parts of Russia! Who's worrying about our troops? It's not a bad idea, by the way, that public rumour attributes to us a plan to exterminate the Jews. Terror is a salutary thing.[136]

According to Irving, this was "an accurate transcript of the original official, shall we say, translation of the Hitler table talk." Irving used this passage because it apparently stated, if taken at face value without any source-critical evaluation, that Hitler did not know about the fact that the Germans were indeed exterminating the Jews. Rampton pointed out that the phrase "Terror is a salutary thing" was in fact not in the German text (as published in *Monologe*), which Irving acknowledged to be true and said that when he discovered this he had changed his quote, although he kept the rest of the *Table Talk* translation (even though he also said that if he had had the German text available at the time *Hitler's War* was published he would have translated it differently altogether).[137] This contradicted his statement to have had access to the German original text via Genoud. The text in *Monologe* looks like this:

> Sage mir keiner: Wir können sie doch nicht in den Morast schicken! Wer kümmert sich denn um unsere Menschen? Es ist gut, wenn uns der Schrecken vorangeht, daß wir das Judentum ausrotten.[138]
>
> [Translation:] *Nobody should tell me: We cannot send them into the marshes! Who is then concerned about our people? It is good if the fear that we exterminate the Jews precedes us.*

The English translation in *Table Talk* stems entirely from *Libres propos*, and it was Genoud who had made the changes to the text. This fact does not seem to have been known by any of the witnesses at the trial, since if it had been there would not have been so much speculation about how this mistranslation could have occurred.[139] The last part about the fear of extermination of the Jews has some resemblance to something that Hitler wrote in *Weisung Nr. 33* dated 23 July 1941 where he said that acts of resistance against the German forces could not best be stopped simply by punishing those guilty of active resistance before a court, but "especially if the occupying power spreads such a fear" that it alone would quell any effort to resist among the people.[140]

Irving's book is a mess in many ways, but particularly from a source-critical point of view. He often uses very unconventional reference systems, his endnotes in *Hitler's War* are often filled with long comments and quotes without any references to sources, and for many quotes in the book there are no sources at all. For example, pages 351–354 contain a lot of information and direct quotes, yet there are no endnotes at all for these pages.[141] When Irving incorrectly cites *Table Talk* he provides no reference for that entire page in the endnotes either.[142] To add to the confusion, although he lists both *Tischgespräche* and *Table Talk* in his bibliography, Irving never refer to these titles in his endnotes. Instead he uses the generic "Hitler's Table Talks" and includes Werner Koeppen's notes there as well. This odd practice makes it hard to know what he is quoting from, which was no doubt Irving's intention all along.[143]

According to Genoud, as reported by Péan, Stevens is supposed to have asked to translate the German original instead of the French translation because he wanted to speed the translation process up, something that Genoud states he agreed to on the even stranger condition that Stevens was to pretend, officially, that he had translated the French version.[144] That makes absolutely no sense at all. More importantly, it does not match what actually happened. First, we know from the comparisons made by both Richard Carrier and myself of the various editions that *Table Talk* was translated almost entirely from the French text. Second, it was never announced publicly that Stevens had translated from a French copy. It is extremely difficult to understand why anyone would ever agree to such a thing. All that would do would be to sow seeds of doubts about the reliability of the translation in the reader's mind. Any translation not made from the German original would have absolutely no weight in the scholarly community and that would in turn be completely self-defeating for Genoud. That is also why Trevor-Roper consistently claimed that *Table Talk* had been translated from the German original. No, the whole story feels like a very poor construction to explain away the fact that Genoud could not let the translator and Trevor-Roper have access to that part of his manuscript, which would show the deviations not only between the manuscript and Picker's German but also those between former and his own French edition

Trevor-Roper's questionable handling of Genoud and his documents

Already it has become obvious that Trevor-Roper had great trouble separating his academic self, and the responsibilities that this entailed, from his personal desire and ambition to be involved in the publication of Genoud's various documents. In many ways the 1950s and 1960s was a golden age for anyone interested in Hitler and Nazi Germany. Streams of memoirs and source volumes were being published by former Nazis and historians alike, and new Nazi documents were being discovered all over the place. The historical actors themselves were often still alive and more than eager to try and align the historical record with a narrative that best suited their own personal interests. Trevor-Roper was at times surprisingly open about the fact that he used Genoud as a way to further his reputation and that he did not bother to be especially critical towards the texts that Genoud brought to him. But this was of course long before the days of social media.

Following an article about Genoud in *The Sunday Times* in July 1967 entitled "Swiss Banks told: reveal the Khider 'millions'" Trevor-Roper wrote to the foreign editor at the newspaper, Frank Giles, asking if he could get some more information on Genoud from him or from the journalist who had written the article, Ingrid Etter. Trevor-Roper stated, privately and confidentially, that he knew Genoud "personally quite well, and have always had good relations with him." He stated that he knew that some of his activities were "pretty shady" but that he never pressed Genoud about them. The reason was that Genoud, according to Trevor-Roper, could be "very useful as a source, if carefully handled." Trevor-Roper continued: "I hope, one day, to make some further discoveries through him, provided my good relations with him remain undamaged: we operate on the basis that each knows the other and play fair."[145] Giles replied to Trevor-Roper and said that he would pass on Trevor-Roper's request to Etter.[146] These lines provide the explanation for why Trevor-Roper was never more critical of Genoud's person and his alleged originals and why he did not reveal any of his suspicions to the wider public. He saw in Genoud a source of income and, unquestionably, of fame – the fame that came from being the first scholar to present a coveted Nazi document in print for the first time. "Playing fair" in this context apparently meant: "Don't ask uncomfortable questions."

In his biography of Genoud, Winkler cites a letter from Trevor-Roper written in 1964 to an American college student to basically the same effect, i.e. that Trevor-Roper had some doubts regarding Genoud's sources but he refrained from saying anything about this because he did not want to lose any privileges with Genoud.[147] In fact, the student, Louis Schmier, was a doctoral student at the University of North Carolina, Chapel Hill, and Schmier had written to Trevor-Roper in January 1964 to ask him for assistance in his planned dissertation work on Martin Bormann. Trevor-Roper did reply, and in his second letter Schmier asked if Trevor-Roper could tell him about the extent of Genoud's material and if Trevor-Roper could help Schmier to get in contact with him "for further exploration of these files", if Genoud was still alive. This, however, seems to have been a bit threatening to Trevor-Roper's position as Genoud's primary output source and he replied:

> it would be quite useless for me to put you in touch with him. As far as I know he is still alive, although he did not answer my last letter when I proposed a meeting in Switzerland: but he may have been travelling then. He is a business man, and I do not know what his business is: probably something rather shady. I never ask him any questions, and on that basis we get on very well together. He declines to see anyone on these matters, and my relations

with him are on a strictly business footing. When he has a document which he wants to publish, he relies on me to vouch for its genuineness, if I think it's genuine: that is all. Of course I have my suspicions about his sources, but I keep the bargain too and do not express them![148]

Trevor-Roper was clearly protecting his own interests here. He even suggested that Genoud may very well have died, although he could not be sure, as if Genoud was an old man on the brink of death. It is indeed hard to imagine a more discouraging letter than this from a famous Oxford professor to an aspiring doctoral student. Whatever Schmier decided to do is unknown, but the correspondence with Trevor-Roper ended there. It would probably have taken a lot for him to continue his effort to get in contact with Genoud after that treatment. As we have seen, it could hardly be considered truthful to say that Genoud refused to see anyone in these matters. And he definitely did not react badly in general to questions about his sources; Trevor-Roper had others put them to him in private on many an occasion. Trevor-Roper could certainly have volunteered Genoud's address if he had really wanted to help Schmier, but he chose not to do this, no doubt because he did not want any competition with regard to Genoud.

About the same time as Trevor-Roper wrote to Giles he received a letter from an anonymous person. The letter was simply signed "Dick" and the address was 21 Queen Anne's Gate in London – a very fancy address in the very centre of London, opposite St James's Park just a few hundred meters from the Parliament, Buckingham Palace, and the Home Office and not very far from MI6 HQ. It was probably from someone inside British intelligence and it stated that Genoud had been a German Intelligence Service agent run by the Nazi *SD*-officer Paul Dickopf during the war (Dickopf was an NSDAP member and an agent for the *SD* in Switzerland, M.N.) and that "We [i.e. British intelligence, M.N.] learned as early as 1952 that Genoud was claiming to possess many Nazi documents and to be the literary executor of Hitler and Bormann." Furthermore, he writes that "Genoud is not currently of interest to us and you probably know far more about him than we do."[149] This makes it seem as if Trevor-Roper had sent a letter to some old colleague inside MI6 requesting information about Genoud after reading the *Sunday Times* article. In early August Trevor-Roper received the information he had requested from Etter-Vellino (based in Geneva).[150] Paul Dickopf was not just anybody. He was one of many former Nazis employed by the Allies in the FRG after the war. By January 1947 he was working as an intelligence agent for the American occupation authorities in Germany.[151] He later became the fourth president of the German Federal Criminal Police Office (BKA) 1965–1971 as well as president of Interpol 1968–1972, whose HQ, ironically, was housed in the same building as the former Gestapo, at which time he was a paid agent working for the Central Intelligence Agency (CIA). In this position Dickopf recruited many former Nazis into Interpol.[152] The fact that Genoud had worked for Dickopf may not be of little importance to the story of how he got his hands on the table talk manuscript, but I have unfortunately been unable to find more information about this

Yet another example of the similarities is note No. 257 in *Table Talk* (No. 102 in *Libres propos* Vol. II and No. 159 in *Monologe*)[153] which begins:

> *Conversation turned to a book entitled "Juan in America" which Bormann had recently lent to the Fuehrer. In it the author paints a picture of the unbelievable conditions which reigned in the intellectual and political circles of the United States, and of the astonishing credulity of the American citizen. Hewel stated that this credulity was not an exclusively American characteristic, and that in Britain, too, the people swallowed everything they were told. Hitler said:* This reminds me of the Häusser reunion which I attended in Stuttgart, where exactly the same sort of thing occurred.[154] [Italics in original.]

In the French it reads:

> *Conversation general sur un livre, intitulé* Juan in Amerika, *que Bormann, quelques jours aupavarant, avait donné à lire au Führer. L'auteur y brosse un tableau des conditions incroyables dans lesquelles s'exerce l'activité intellectuelle et politique aux Etas-Unis et de la crédulité du citoyen américain. Hewel souligne que cette crédulité n'est pas propre aux Américains et qu'en Angleterre également le public gobe tout ce qu'on lui raconte. Hitler intervient:* Cela me fait penser à la reunion de Häusser à laquelle j'ai assisté à Stuttgart.[155] [Italics in original.]
>
> [Translation:] General conversation about a book, entitled Juan in Amerika, which Bormann, a few days earlier, had given to the Führer to read. The author paints a picture of the incredible conditions under which intellectual and political activity takes place in the United States and the credulity of the American citizen. Hewel points out that this credulity is not unique to the Americans and that in England also the public gobble up everything that is told to him. Hitler intervened: *It reminds me of the Häusser reunion, which I attended in Stuttgart.*

But in Jochmann's *Monologe* we instead find the following:

> Das Tischgespräch geht um das Unglaubliche der kulturellen und politischen Zustände in Amerika, wie es ein Buch schildert, das R[eichsleiter] B[ormann] dem Chef vor einigen Tagen gegeben hat. Der Gesandte H[ewel] unterstreicht, daß nicht nur in Amerika, sondern auch in England alles gläubig hingenommen wird, was man dem Volk vorsagt, und sei es noch so blöde. Der Chef erinnert sich der Haeuser-Versammlung, die er in Stuttgart erlebt hat. Genauso sei das da gewesen![156]
>
> [Translation:] *The table discussion is about the unbelievable state of the cultural and political conditions in America, as described in a book that R[eichsleiter] B[ormann] gave to the boss a few days ago. The envoy H[ewel] emphasizes that not only in America, but also in England, all that is said to the people is accepted on faith,*

> *no matter how stupid. The boss remembers the Haeuser Meeting he experienced in Stuttgart. That same was the case there!*

It is obvious that the English translation concurs with the French rather than with the German. The choices of words, formulations, and syntax of the sentences are conclusive proof of this. The formulation of the first sentence shows immediately that *Table Talk* follows the French; e.g. both include the title of the book in question, while *Monologe* does not. Both the French and English editions use the word reunion, but the German uses *Versammlung* instead, which is not the same word and would not render "reunion" if translated into English. While the French phrase *assister à* translates as "to attend" or "to be present at", the German verb *erleben* is akin to "to experience", "to undergo" or "to witness." Furthermore, the word *Häusser* in both the English and the French shows that Stevens cannot have had a document that said *Haeuser*, in which case he would never have chosen the spelling in the French edition. Yet another difference is the absence of the word *Reichsleiter* (or an equivalent of that term) in both the French and the English and the fact that this apparently was abbreviated to "R. B." in Jochmann's manuscript.

Let us now turn to the fact that both *Table Talk* and *Libres propos* includes the book title *Juan in America* (written by Scottish writer Eric Linklater and published in 1931)[157] while *Monologe* does not. Jochmann instead includes this title (together with a short biography of the author) in one of the endnotes.[158] This difference is actually much more interesting than it seems at first. In *Monologe*, Jochmann does not tell us how he knew the title of the book, so we might assume that he consulted the English or French version, since there is absolutely no reason for him not to include it in the note itself if it had been in his manuscript (not even if it was only as a handwritten addition by Bormann). However, this seems to be exactly what happened. According to a notation in Jochmann's archive, the title of the book was mentioned in handwriting in the margin, i.e. it was added afterwards and was not in the typed text itself.[159] Jochmann says nothing about this in *Monologe*. It therefore seems unlikely that this is the same text that Stevens had access to. Moreover, the subject of the book (set as it is in the year before the Wall Street crash focusing on the American Prohibition era and the resulting gangster rule) does not seem to fit well with the topic of the note. Jochmann apparently made no comparison to the other editions, so there is no way for us to know what he made of the differences between them and his text.

But even the few things that *Libres propos* and *Monologe* have in common are extremely intriguing to look at. I am here thinking about the fact that where the French uses the verb *souligner* ("to underline" in English) the German has the directly corresponding verb *unterstreichen*, while the English has the verb "to state." It is an interesting and odd choice of word because it really does not correspond to either the French or German word. It also proves that the second volume of *Libres propos* is not simply straight a re-translation of the English into French. On the other hand, *Table Talk* agrees with *Monologe* when it says "where exactly the same sort of thing occurred" and the German has *Genauso sei das da gewesen*. *Libres propos* has no such sentence at all. The rest of the text for this date follows *Monologe* at times and *Libres propos* at other times. It is as if the note is a mixture of the two texts. An example is the following sentence, which appears inside a long paragraph that otherwise follows *Monologe*:

> If I had not decided in 1936 to send him the first of our Junker aircraft, Franco would never have survived.[160]

Here the French has the following:

> Si je ne m'etais pas décidé, en 1936, à lui envoyer nos premiers Junkers, Franco n'aurait pas réussi.[161]
>
> [Translation:] *If I had not decided, in 1936, to send him our first Junkers, Franco would not have succeeded.*

But in *Monologe* we instead find:

> Wenn 1936 ich mich nicht entschlossen hätte, die ersten Ju's zu schicken, wäre Franco nicht durchgekommen.[162]
>
> [Translation:] *If I hadn't decided to send the first Ju's in 1936, Franco wouldn't have made it through.*

While the difference is certainly not huge, the English sentence follows the French perfectly, including the use of the pronouns "him" and "our", which are totally absent from the German text. Sometimes the text is a direct mixture of the two versions (Note: *italics* – from the French; **bold** – from the German):

> *During the first World War* major operations generally came to an end about the end of November or the beginning of December, and the front became comparatively quiet. I remember well *that we had some very hard fighting at the end of October 1918*, and then on the 27th down came the rain, and everything **was washed out**.[163]

In *Libres propos* we find the following sentences:

> Pendant la guerre mondiale, les operations cessaient généralement vers la fin de novembre ou le début de décembre, et le front s'immobilisait. Je me rappelle qu'en 1918 nous avons encore livre de durs combats fin octobre, le 27. Alors la pluie se mit à tomber, puis la neige, et bientôt ce fut la fin.[164]
>
> [Translation:] *During the world war, operations generally ceased in late November or early December, and the front came to a standstill. I remember that in 1918 we still fought hard at the end of October, the 27th. Then the rain began to fall, then the snow, and soon it was the end.*

But in *Monologe* we instead see:

> Im allgemeinen sind Ende November, Anfang Dezember im Westen die Kriegshandlungen zu Ende gewesen, sie klangen dann immer aus. Wir haben noch Kämpfe gehabt Ende Oktober, am 27. Oktober; dann begann es plötzlich, zu regnen und zu schneien, und dann ist die Geschichte ersoffen.[165]
>
> [Translation:] *In general, at the end of November, at the beginning of December, the war in the West came to an end, it increasingly rang out. We still had battles at the end of October, on October 27th; then it suddenly started to rain and snow, and then the history is filled with water.*

As we can see, the first part of the paragraph follows the French translation almost perfectly. It is towards the end that the English agrees with the German instead, although there are parts that do not correspond well to either of those. The phrase "was washed out" corresponds reasonably well to the word *ersoffen* (from the verb *ersaufen*, which means "to drown" or "to fill with water"), and here the French ending is completely different. In *Table Talk* Stevens states that it started to rain on the 27th but the date in German text could just as well be interpreted as referring to the battle, meaning that the rain and snow started *after* this point. Interestingly, *Table Talk* does not mention it snowing, which is odd if Stevens text contained this information. Or did he simply forget it?

A fascinating example of the differences is also a note dated 4 January 1942 where Hitler is said to have stated that the tank as a weapon would not survive the war. This is referred to by Wolfram Pyta in his Hitler biography.[166] The reason for Hitler's view was the development of a new anti-tank grenade, the so-called "hollow charge." In *Table Talk* we find the following:

> The Hollow charge means the death of the tank. Tanks will have finished their career before the end of the war. We haven't used the hollow charge so far, but there's no more reason to wait, since Italy has suggested to us a similar weapon. Secrets are badly kept amongst the Italians, and what Italy has to-day, the rest of the world will have soon! If the others have it, there'll be nothing left for us to do, either, but to pack up our tanks. With the help of this weapon, anyone at all can blow up a tank.[167]

However, the odd thing is that the part about the hollow charge is missing in *Monologe*:

> Die . . . ist das Ende der ganzen Panzerwaffe. Der Panzer wird das Ende dieses Krieges nicht mehr erleben. Wir haben die . . . bis jetzt nicht verwendet, aber Italien hat sie uns angeboten, und was Italien hat, hat die übrige Welt. Geheim bleibt das nicht. Haben es die anderen auch, dann können wir

wie sie einpacken. In der Zukunft ist jedermann in der Lage, einen Panzer mit einer . . . total zu zertrümmern.[168]

Naturally, we would expect Jochmann to have included the name of this weapon if it had been in the manuscript page he had access to. The inescapable conclusion from its absence appears to be that this word (or words) was not present in Jochmann's photocopy. In the case of *Juan in America* where the title of the book had been added by hand Jochmann included it in an endnote. But in this case there is not such endnote and this, too, seems to lead to the conclusion that there was nothing added here. Unless Jochmann chose not to include it, of course, or simply forgot about it. This makes one wonder where the term "hollow charge" comes from in *Table Talk*. As in the other instances, this is taken from *Libres propos*:

> La charge creuse signifie la mort des blindés. Les blindés auront terminé leur carrière avant la fin de cette guerre. Nous n'avons pas utilisé la charge creuse jusqu'à maintenant, mais il n'y a plus de raison d'attendre puisque l'Italie nous a proposé une arme analogue. Or chez les Italiens les secrets sont mal gardés, et ce que l'Italie a, le reste du monde ne tarde pas à l'avoir aussi! Si les autres l'ont, il ne nous restera plus, à nous aussi, qu'à remiser nos panzers. N'importe qui, à l'aide de cette arme, pourra faire sauter un blindé.[169]

As usual, we can see that the *Table Talk* passage in its entirety has been translated based on the French edition. Pyta, in fact, uses other sources for concluding that Hitler was talking about "Hohlgranate", but he does not mention the fact that this information is not in *Monologe*.[170] The most interesting question is certainly *why* Heim's note did not contain the term. One can speculate that it was due to 1) secrecy or 2) that Heim did not remember the term as he was writing his text. However, I believe that the name of the weapon was probably added by hand in the margin and the reason for it being absent in *Monologe* is simply that Jochmann forgot to include it. That is the only reasonable explanation for how Genoud could include it in the French edition. Of course, there is perhaps no need to point out that Hitler was utterly mistaken in assuming that the tank had played out its role.

I will now present an explanatory hypothesis that I believe can account for all of the problems presented here – let's call it the y-hypothesis. According to y: Stevens translated a German text that was different from the one later published in *Monologe*, perhaps a text that was a re-translation into German from Genoud's French text. The hypothesis also assumes that Genoud in the process made some further changes to the text, such as adding phrases that were missing in the French.[171] This would explain that certain phrases are only to be found in *Monologe* and *Table Talk*. The validity of a scientific hypothesis is determined by its explanatory power, which is in turn determined by how well it fits the available evidence. We must thus test it, and, preferably, compare it to other hypotheses in an effort to falsify it.

Let us then try to falsify the γ-hypothesis by formulating a number of competing hypotheses: *1)* Stevens used *both Libres propos* and the manuscript that was later published as *Monologe* but followed the French almost entirely, only using the German text for minor details here and there that were missing in the French text, but not correcting all the other inconsistencies in the French text. This would also require that Genoud forgot these phrases when typing up the manuscript for *Libres propos*. While the latter is quite possible, the former requirements for *1)* to be true is so improbable that we can write it off. It would require Stevens to have added a few minor details in order to "correct" the translation but at the same time ignore a mass of glaring inconsistencies and faulty translations that remained in the text. Moreover, Stevens's letter has also stated things (se later in the beginning of chapter 6) that directly contradict *1)*, and for this hypothesis to be true we would have to make even one more *ad hoc* assumption, namely that Stevens lied to Trevor-Roper (or that he had forgotten about it). Once again this is so unlikely that we can disregard it. To assume: *2)* that the similarities are just coincidental is not credible either – in fact it is so improbable that we can confidently say that hypothesis *2)* is false. Equally improbable is: *3)* that Genoud only had one German manuscript and the reason we see differences between *Table Talk* and *Libres propos*, on the one hand, and *Monologe*, on the other, is that Jochmann changed it. Any other hypothetical explanations are hard to imagine.

Having discarded hypotheses *1)*, *2)*, and *3)* we are left with the γ-hypothesis. As it turns out, under the explanation provided by γ all pieces of the puzzle fall neatly into place. Genoud translated the French text for *Libres propos* back into German, which he then supplied to Stevens. The γ-hypothesis thus proves that Stevens had a German text at his disposal *that was different from the one that Jochmann had access to* almost 30 years later. The question now becomes: *Why* did Genoud produce such a text? While we may not be able to get at Genoud's motivation in this particular case, it actually appears to fall into a pattern regarding his *modus operandi*. The history of *Hitlers politisches Testament* in fact is an example of exactly the same procedure whereby Genoud first translates a German text into French and publishes it, then translates the French into English and publishes that, it, and then re-translates it into German only to finally publish a German version that is slightly different from the French and English versions (see Chapter 6).

Moreover, a further similarity between the notes in *Libres propos* (both volumes) and *Table Talk* is that none contain information as to in which headquarters they were uttered. Only the date and time of day are given. In *Monologe*, as in *Tischgespräche* and in Heim's proof pages, however, the place is also included. It is quite unlikely that the English would be identical to the French in this sense if it had not been translated from a text that did not include the location where the conversations took place. Why, for example, Genoud or Weidenfeld would insist on these particular matters being the same in *Table Talk* is hard to understand.

This discussion has presented convincing evidence confirming the γ-hypothesis as an explanation for the similarities between *Table Talk* and *Libres propos*. No other explanation can satisfactorily explain *all* the similarities and discrepancies in one single blow without resorting to absurdities or extreme improbabilities.

Trevor-Roper and the second edition of *Table Talk* from 1973

Trevor-Roper dealt with the discrepancies between Genoud's English text and Picker's second edition from 1963 in his preface to the second edition of *Table Talk* from 1973. He wrote that Picker quite naturally regarded his own version as the best one and even mentions the alterations that Pickers claimed Bormann was to have made. Trevor-Roper does not comment upon this more than to say that Bormann would no doubt have answered Picker that he, too, was present at the conversation and that his recollection was as good as anyone else's. This was thus in effect an acceptance of the fact that Bormann had perhaps edited the text published in *Table Talk*. Trevor-Roper then wrote:

> However, I do not think that the occasional textual discrepancies between the two versions are of great importance. As Dr. [Andreas] Hillgruber [Schramm's co-editor of *Tischgespräche*] notes, although the order of the subjects discussed is somewhat differently given, the substance of the two versions, where they coincide, is in all material respects the same.[172]

It is somewhat alarming and saddening to see that Trevor-Roper apparently did not understand, or care, about the significance of textual discrepancies in a record that he claimed to be Hitler's own words. Variations in the text meant that one could not be certain about what Hitler had actually said, and it certainly proved beyond a doubt that what was published in *Table Talk* was not a stenographic record. This is to leave aside all the other source-critical problems with these texts that have already been discussed at length in this book.

In preparing to write the second preface Trevor-Roper asked David Irving for help. Trevor-Roper stated that he had persuaded Weidenfeld to re-issue *Table Talk* and in the new preface he would deal with the textual question. He had a vague memory, he wrote, that Irving had once told him that he had found yet other notes of Hitler's table talk, and Trevor-Roper now wondered if Irving would let him note this in the text. Trevor-Roper also asked if Irving had ever met Picker, and if so, if he regarded him as "reliable and objective." He wanted to be fair towards Picker, Trevor-Roper wrote, but added that the former clearly had an interest in portraying himself as being "much more than a mere note-taker." Picker wanted the world to believe that only he had a truthful recollection of what the Führer had said and that "any correction of it by Bormann must be falsification."[173] Irving replied some days later and stated that the table talk notes that Trevor-Roper referred to must be Werner Koeppen's notes that Irving had sent Trevor-Roper "some time ago to look at." In this letter he also told Trevor-Roper about Heim's proof pages located at the LoC. It is equally obvious from Irving's letter that he sent Trevor-Roper copies of these pages. Irving wrote that he had compared these to Genoud's manuscript and found that "the Heim version" was, in his words, "a fair copy of these enclosed January 1942 pages, incorporating in the typescript the handwritten amendments." He also said that he would have his assistant look into the Picker issue a bit, since she was more knowledgeable in this area than he was, but his general opinion was that Heim was more trustworthy than Picker.[174] At this point then, Trevor-Roper knew about basically all the facts presented in Chapter 4 in this book. However, he either did not realize what the proof pages meant or he decided not to address the source-critical problems that their existence created. It is also quite astonishing that Trevor-Roper, a famous Hitler scholar, had apparently lost or misplaced the copies of both Heim's proof pages and Koeppen's notes that Irving had sent him. Was he just sloppy or did he simply not care enough about the issue to actually keep track of the existing sources?

In early January 1973 Trevor-Roper thanked Irving for having sent him the documents for him to take a look at, and he was returning them to Irving, who surely was waiting for them, and he added that the preface for the second edition had already been sent to the publisher but he had sent a new paragraph containing information about Irving's documents that he hoped would be included.[175] Of course, Trevor-Roper did not say anything about having actually seen Heim's proof pages in his 1973 preface. To finish it off Trevor-Roper wrote that:

> One day – when the original German text of the <u>Bormann Vermerke</u> [Genoud's manuscript, M.N.] is available and other obstacles have been removed – it will be possible to present a complete record of Hitler's surviving Table-Talk. Meanwhile, M. Genoud's text remains by far the fullest continuous record, and the only record in English, of an important historical document.[176]

What Trevor-Roper means when he says that the German text is not available is unclear. Perhaps he simply meant a published version. And what did he mean by "a complete record"? Did not *Table Talk* contain all the notes in Genoud's possession (except for the three entries which we know where left out)? Trevor-Roper does provide some new additional information regarding Genoud's manuscript in this preface. In making a comparison between how many of Picker's and Heim's notes that appear in *Table Talk*/Genoud's manuscript and *Tischgespräche* he states that 138 entries are common to both versions, that Picker prints only 36 Heim notes supposedly taken down between 5 July 1941 and 11 March 1942, and that Genoud's manuscript had 173 entries in that same period. Trevor-Roper also states that 101 of Picker's notes survived in the manuscript. Trevor-Roper specifically makes sure to say "*Bormann-Vermerke*" and does not hint at the fact that *Libres propos* had been used when translating the text.

More astonishing things were about to happen, however. The very same day as his letter to Baumgarten on 18 March 1973, Trevor-Roper wrote a letter to

Mrs. Hilary Walford, editor at Weidenfeld & Nicolson, asking her to undertake some research in the company's archive to find out if Stevens had in fact translated from the German original or, as he now suspected, from the French. He stated at the same time that this issue "may be of greater interest than it seems." This was of course an understatement if there ever was one, but the remarkable fact is that Trevor-Roper, despite this, perhaps in order not to create a panic at the publisher, wrote:

> The answer to this question does not affect the authenticity of the <u>Table Talk</u>, or the reliability of Stevens' version, which is beyond question; but it might prove the key to a larger problem in which I am interested.[177]

Whatever the larger problem that he referred to was remains unknown. It is certainly quite alarming if Trevor-Roper really thought that this did not affect the reliability of Stevens's version – we now know that it definitely *did* distort the text. This is not just an anachronistic judgement of Trevor-Roper because every historian should in this situation be able to understand that the translation cannot be trusted. Mrs. Walford replied to Trevor-Roper some days later stating that all the documentation regarding the original publication had been lost, including the original contract, but the company had received a copy of this contract from Genoud when they had negotiated the terms for the new edition of *Table Talk* and she included a xeroxed copy of the original contract, in French (as well as an English translation).[178]

Trevor-Roper thanked for the copy of the contract, which "answers my question" regarding the translation process.[179] Nonetheless, we find Trevor-Roper claiming that the 1973 edition contained the translation of the *Bormann-Vermerke*.[180]

This whole affair is indeed very odd considering that Weidenfeld had sent Trevor-Roper two copies of this same contract, which included everything they had agreed upon, already in October 1952.[181] Trevor-Roper had thus misplaced the contract too.

And no matter what the situation was in 1953 this does not in any way excuse Trevor-Roper leaving the information out in 1973 as well. For it is highly telling that Trevor-Roper did not mention, or even hint at, *any* of this in his 1973 preface.[182] One could argue that, judging from Trevor-Roper's correspondence with Irving, he barely had time to include a new paragraph on the documents that Irving had found. This was either in early January 1973 or between Christmas and New Year's 1972. Thus, he perhaps did not have the possibility to incorporate this knowledge or these suspicions in the preface. The critique delivered here would then have no ground because one cannot criticize someone for including something that one is not aware of. However, this pleading on Trevor-Roper's behalf does not seem to be entirely justified, because there was a possibility to include a separate note with this vital information even after the book had been printed (this is a common practice). Since it is not known exactly when the book was printed, it is not possible to say whether Trevor-Roper could have added this information to his preface or not. But despite all these indications that something was not right with the *Table Talk* text, he did not mention anything about it; no doubt because of the great damage he thought that this would mean to the English edition that he edited, and to his reputation as a historian.

Conclusion

This chapter has revealed many astonishing facts regarding how *Table Talk* was translated and published and about famous British historian Hugh Trevor-Roper's role in this, as well as about his relationship with Genoud. We have seen that Trevor-Roper certainly was more than willing to cut corners when it came to matters having to do with source criticism as long as it benefited him financially and his reputation as a scholar and expert historian of Nazi Germany and Hitler.

Rather amazingly, it has been shown that *Table Talk* was not translated from the original German, as Trevor-Roper claimed in his introduction to the book. Instead, it was translated almost entirely from the French based upon Genoud's two volumes of *Libres propos* published in 1952 and 1954. Trevor-Roper knew this full well because he had been informed of it at the time and he had also seen the contract between Genoud and Weidenfeld & Nicolson, which stipulated that the translation had to be done this way. It is not clear *why* Genoud insisted on this. Nonetheless, we have also seen that there is, on occasion, evidence in the text that clearly points to a German text having been used in a few instances, although it is not at all clear which German text this was. Trevor-Roper never told his readers about these facts, not even after having re-discovered that the text had been translated from the French (a matter he had apparently forgotten) as he was working on the new introduction for the second edition of *Table Talk* published in 1973. I have also provided cogent reasons, and evidence, for the hypothesis that Stevens on occasion likely translated a typed German text, provided to him by Genoud, which purportedly was identical to the original text but that in reality differed from latter. It was, apparently, a combination of Genoud's French translation and the German text published in 1980.

Trevor-Roper volunteered his reasons for not being more critical in public about Genoud's documents several times in his private correspondence over the years. There, Trevor-Roper stated that he was not questioning Genoud as hard as he could have been because he wished to remain on friendly terms with him in order to be able to benefit from further documents that Genoud might want to publish in the future. This became a very lucrative and beneficial arrangement for Trevor-Roper indeed; he came to publish a number of Genoud's documents. Besides *Table Talk* Trevor-Roper wrote the introduction to, and assisted in the publication of, *The Bormann Letters* in 1954 and *Le testament politique d'Hitler* in 1959, the latter also published in English as *The Testament of Adolf Hitler* in 1961 and in German as *Hitlers politisches Testament* in 1981.

All of this has shown that *Table Talk* should never ever be used by historians when citing anything from the table talk notes. The translation was not only made from the French, but it also contains formulations added by the translator, Colonel Stevens, and excludes certain parts later included in *Monologe*. There is nothing holy or official about a translation and translations should, if citations are indeed necessary, therefore be made by each scholar based upon the German versions of the text. However, when citing or referencing *Monologe* (or *Tischgespräche*) scholars must consider the many source-critical problems that have been revealed in this book.

Notes

1 Davenport-Hines, Richard (ed.), *Letters from Oxford: Hugh Trevor-Roper to Bernard Berenson* (London: Weidenfeld & Nicolson, 2006), p. 74.
2 Trevor-Roper, Hugh, *The Last Days of Hitler* (London: Macmillan & Co., 1947), p. 4.
3 Ibid., pp. 4, 51–52, 85–86.
4 See: Trevor-Roper's essay "The Mind of Adolf Hitler" in *Hitler's Table Talk. . .* (1953), p. xxix, for the references to Rauschning, see: pp. x, xvii, xxvii, xxix–xxxi.
5 *Monologe . . .*, p. 411. Note that the dating is uncertain. This entry has no fewer than three different dates in three various editions of the table talks. It has the dates 18 May in *Libres propos* and 16 May in *Hitler's Table Talk*. See: *Libres propos. . .* (Vol. II, 1954), p. 343; *Hitler's Table Talk. . .* (1953), p. 718. These differences cannot be explained, and it is not the only example of such differences.
6 Frank, H., *Im Angesicht des Galgens . . .*, p. 40. See also: Weikart, R., *Hitler's Religion . . .*, pp. 18, 298 *n*7 who refers to the wrong page in Frank's book (p. 46).
7 Dietrich, O., *12 Jahre mit Hitler . . .*, p. 92.
8 For this see: Weikart, R., *Hitler's Religion . . .*, pp. 18, 298 n7.
9 Rose, O. (ed.), *Julius Schaub . . .*, p. 228. "als ständigen Begleiter im Kriege ein Bändchen Schopenhauer bei sich getragen."
10 Fleischmann, P., *Hitler als Häftling . . .*, p. 89.
11 Trevor-Roper's essay "The Mind of Adolf Hitler" in *Hitler's Table Talk. . .* (1953), p. vii.
12 Ibid., pp. viii–ix.
13 Letter from Trevor-Roper to Jäckel, 26 May 1969, p. 1; CCLO; HTRP; Vol. Soc. Dacre 6/6/1.
14 Trevor-Roper, H. R., "Einleitung" in *Hitlers politisches Testament . . .*, pp. 18–19.
15 Letter from Meinck to Trevor-Roper, 24 June 1960, pp. 1–3; CCLO; HTRP; Vol. Soc. Dacre 1/1/M.
16 Letter from Trevor-Roper to Meinck, 5 July 1960; CCLO; HTRP; Vol. Soc. Dacre 1/1/M.
17 Péan, P., *L'extrémiste . . .*, p. 188.
18 Sisman, A., *Hugh Trevor-Roper . . .*, pp. 213–214. Sisman writes: "the issue of who owned Hitler's copyrights was untested in the courts, and the position was further complicated by the claim of the stenographer who had taken down the table-talk and who had licensed the German edition" (ibid., p. 214). Sisman thus includes the incorrect statement that Picker used stenography.
19 Undated handwritten memorandum by Trevor-Roper, pp. 1–5; CCLO; HTRP; Vol. Soc. Dacre 6/6/1.
20 See: Winkler, W., *Der Schattenmann. . .* ; Péan, P., *L'extrémiste. . .* ; Laske, K., *Ein Leben. . .*.
21 Winkler, W., *Der Schattenmann . . .*, pp. 18–19, 33, 72–73, 108–116.

22 Sisman, A., *Hugh Trevor-Roper . . .*, pp. 302, 476.
23 Undated handwritten memorandum by Trevor-Roper, pp. 1–5; CCLO; HTRP; Vol. Soc. Dacre 6/6/1. The document from the notary public, however, did not state that Genoud owned the rights but (incorrectly) that Paula Hitler did – and that this right included any translations of the texts (see copy of the notarized deed in: CCLO; HTRP; Vol. Soc. Dacre 6/6/1).
24 Trevor-Roper's essay "The Mind of Adolf Hitler" in *Hitler's Table Talk. . .* (1953), p. xxxiii.
25 *Hitler's Table Talk. . .* (1953), p. 721.
26 See for example: Kellerhoff, S. F., *Die NSDAP . . .*, pp. 25–27.
27 Davenport-Hines, R. (ed.), *Letters from Oxford . . .*, pp. 93–94.
28 Note written and signed by Heim, 1 Juli 1952; WJN; Binder: Schriftwechsel: A – K 1977.
29 Letter from Heim to Werner Maser, 1 November 1972, p. 1; WJN; Binder: Schrift-wechsel: A – K 1977. See also: Letter from Picker to Maser, 11 October 1972; WJN; Binder: Schriftwechsel: A – K 1977.
30 See typed pages by Genoud, p. 6; CCLO; HTRP; Vol. Soc. Dacre 6/6/1. A comparison is necessary to see if there are any differences between this German version of Genoud's text and Jochmann's volume.
31 Genoud to Trevor-Roper, 29 August 1952; CCLO; HTRP; Vol. Soc. Dacre 6/6/1.
32 Genoud to Trevor-Roper, 19 September 1952; CCLO; HTRP; Vol. Soc. Dacre 6/6/1.
33 Ibid.
34 Genoud to Trevor-Roper, 3 October 1952; CCLO; HTRP; Vol. Soc. Dacre 6/6/1.
35 Weidenfeld to Genoud, 17 October 1952; CCLO; HTRP; Vol. Soc. Dacre 6/6/1.
36 Genoud to Weidenfeld, 21 October 1952; CCLO; HTRP; Vol. Soc. Dacre 6/6/1.
37 Weidenfeld, George, *Remembering Good Friends: An Autobiography* (London: HarperCollins, 1995), p. 290. Unfortunately, Weidenfeld writes very little about the publication of *Table Talk*.
38 Genoud to Trevor-Roper, 21 October 1952; CCLO; HTRP; Vol. Soc. Dacre 6/6/1.
39 Weidenfeld to Trevor-Roper, 8 January 1953; CCLO; HTRP; Vol. Soc. Dacre 6/6/1.
40 Trevor-Roper to Weidenfeld, 23 October 1952, p. 2; CCLO; HTRP; Vol. Soc. Dacre 6/6/1.
41 "Entre les soussignes" undated 1952; CCLO; HTRP; Vol. Soc. Dacre 6/6/1.
42 See "A Note on the Text" in: *Hitler's Table Talk. . .* (1953).
43 Weidenfeld to Trevort-Roper, 25 March 1953; CCLO; HTRP; Vol. Soc. Dacre 6/6/1.
44 Gina Thomson pointed this last point out to me during a conversation in her home in London on 2013–09–23.
45 Longerich, P., *Hitler . . .*, p. 711; Kershaw, I., *Hitler 1936–1945. . .* (Vol. II), p. 274; Ullrich, V., *Adolf Hitler. . .* (Vol. II), pp. 96–100; Eberle, Henrik and Uhl, Matthias (eds.), *Das Buch Hitler. Geheimdossier des NKWD für Josef W. Stalin, zusammengestellt aufgrund der Verhörprotokolle des Persönlichen Adjutanten Hitlers, Otto Günsche, und des Kammerdieners Heinz Linge, Moskau 1948/49* (Bergisch Gladbach: Gustav Lübbe Verlag, 2005), pp. 108–111, 625. See also obituary over Stevens in: "Lt.-Col. R. H. Stevens" in *The Times* [London, England], 14 February 1967, p. 12. *The Times Digital Archive*. Web. 29 April 2015. See also: Ullrich, V., *Adolf Hitler. . .* (Vol. II), pp. 93–101.
46 Eberle, H. and Uhl, M. (eds.), *Das Buch Hitler . . .*, p. 625. Eberle and Uhl does not say what their source is for this information, however.
47 www.venlo-zwischenfall.de and www.mythoselser.de/texts/stevens.htm, accessed: 2019–06–13.
48 *Hitler's Table Talk. . .* (1953), p. 451.
49 *Hitlers Tischgespräche. . .* (1951), p. 230; *Hitler's Table Talk. . .* (1953), p. 451.
50 Ullrich, V., *Adolf Hitler. . .* (Vol. II), pp. 93, 97.
51 Ibid., pp. 99–100.
52 See manuscript for letter later phoned in, 5 March 1953; CCLO; HTRP; Vol. Soc. Dacre 6/6/1.

53 "Sunday Express" in *The Times* [London, England], 27 February 1953, p. 6. *The Times Digital Archive*. Web. 29 April 2015.

54 For the release date, see: "Multiple Display Advertisements" in *The Times* [London, England], 15 April 1953, p. 8. *The Times Digital Archive*. Web. 29 April 2015.

55 *Hitler's Table Talk*. . . (1953), pp. 360, 602.

56 The reason is that *Monologe* keeps entries made during the day, evening, and night in one and the same entry, while *Table Talk* and *Libres propos* sometimes make different entries of these even though they have the same date.

57 *Monologe* . . ., p. 40; *Hitler's Table Talk*. . . (1953), pp. 5–6.

58 *Monologe* . . ., pp. 74–77; *Hitler's Table Talk*. . . (1953), pp. 47–51.

59 *Monologe* . . ., pp. 95–96; *Hitler's Table Talk*. . . (1953), pp. 74–76.

60 *Monologe* . . ., pp. 111–116; *Hitler's Table Talk*. . . (1953), pp. 94–100.

61 *Monologe* . . ., pp. 118–119; *Hitler's Table Talk*. . . (1953), pp. 102–103.

62 *Monologe* . . ., p. 166; *Hitler's Table Talk*. . . (1953), p. 163. See also the notes from midday and night of 3 and 4 January 1942. There are several other examples as well.

63 *Monologe* . . ., p. 121; *Hitler's Table Talk*. . . (1953), p. 106.

64 *Monologe* . . ., pp. 193–194; *Hitler's Table Talk*. . . (1953), pp. 199–200.

65 *Monologe* . . ., pp. 227–229; *Hitler's Table Talk*. . . (1953), pp. 233–236.

66 *Monologe* . . ., p. 283; *Hitler's Table Talk*. . . (1953), pp. 318–319.

67 *Hitler's Table Talk*. . . (1953), pp. 706–707.

68 Photocopies of "Goethe über das Rauchen" and "Auszüge aus der Führerrede vom 27.1.1944"; WJN; Binder: Schriftwechsel: A – K 1977.

69 *Monologe* . . ., p. 34.

70 *Hitler's Table Talk*. . . (1953), pp. 401–402. Meinoud Rost van Tonningen was a Dutch Nazi leader and one of the most prominent collaborators with the Nazi occupation forces in The Netherlands during the war. Anton Mussert was the leader of the National Socialist Movement in The Netherlands (*Nationalsozialistische Bewegung in Nederland*). Bormann's note is interesting because it was not only Himmler who supported van Tonningen against Mussert; Hitler did so too.

71 *Libres propos*. . . (Vol. II, 1954), pp. 43–44.

72 Ibid., p. 43.

73 In the second edition of *Tischgespräche* from 1963 Percy Ernst Schramm includes Bormann's handwritten notations in the footnotes, choosing to translate (obviously based on *Table Talk*) the first phrase into "Finstere Theorie" (*Hitlers Tischgespräche*. . . (1963), p. 253). *Finster* could be translated in a number of ways, for example "dark", "gloomy", "horrible", or "awful." The fact that Schramm states that this comment occurs in the *Bormann-Vermerke* shows that he was not aware of the fact that the text had been translated from Genoud's second volume of *Libres propos* (which he, as we have seen, did not think had ever been published). The supposed handwriting by Bormann does not appear on the *Ms. 63* (BAK; N 1128; Vol. 31; Document 170 (5 April 1942)).

74 *Hitler's Table Talk*. . . (1953), pp. 401–407; *Libres propos*. . . (Vol. II, 1954), pp. 43–49; *Hitlers Tischgespräche*. . . (1951), pp. 66–69, 420–421.

75 See: *Hitlers Tischgespräche*. . . (1951), pp. 66–69, 420–421.

76 *Hitlers Tischgespräche*. . . (1963), pp. 252–256.

77 *Libres propos*. . . (Vol. I, 1952), pp. 349–350; *Hitler's Table Talk*. . . (1953), pp. 360–361, 603–608; *Monologe* . . ., pp. 317–323.

78 *Hitler's Table Talk*. . . (1953), p. 603.

79 Ibid., pp. 603–608; *Libres propos*. . . (Vol. II, 1954), pp. 235–239; *Monologe* . . ., pp. 320–323.

80 *Monologe* . . ., p. 320.

81 *Hitler's Table Talk*. . . (1953), pp. 604, 606–607; *Monologe* . . ., pp. 320–322.

82 *Hitler's Table Talk* . . . (1953), p. 604; *Libres propos*. . . (Vol. II, 1954), 235; *Monologe* . . ., p. 159. In the American edition of *Table Talk* a mistake has been made, and the text says "Bibel Students (*Babelforscher*)" instead; see: *Hitler's Sercret Conversations* . . ., p. 490.

83 *Hitler's Table Talk* . . . (1953), p. 604; *Libres propos.* . . (Vol. II, 1954), p. 235; *Monologe* . . ., p. 159.

84 *Hitler's Table Talk.* . . (1953), p. 604.

85 *Libres propos* . . . (Vol. II, 1954), p. 236.

86 *Monologe* . . ., pp. 320–321. It really says "das machen *die* eiskalt!" here. The word *die* (here: the) doesn't really make sense in this context, since would literally translate to "That will make them ice cold." It would make more sense if it had said: "das machen *sie* eiskalt!" because then *sie* (they) would refer to the British and them stone cold lying to their own people, literally "They make it ice cold." It is not known if this is because Heim's note actually said *die* or if it is a spelling error that happened as the text was set for printing. It just so happens that "eiskalt" is given by Christa Schroeder as an example of a word that Hitler often used. Her example, however, is that Hitler used to say this about his own action, i.e. "'da bin ich eiskalt'", or "then I am ice cold." (Schroeder, C., Er war mein Chef . . ., p. 71). This could be an indication that Heim remembered this word correctly. On the other hand it could also just be a case where Heim used a word that he knew was part of Hitler's specific vocabulary.

87 Ullrich, V., *Adolf Hitler.* . . (Vol. II), p. 32.

88 See for example: Rankin, Nicholas, *Churchill's Wizards: The British Genius for Deception, 1919–1945* (London: Faber & Faber, 2005).

89 *HRP* II/3, pp. 1578–1579 (4 September 1940). Hitler made similar statements, mentioning General Winter again, half a year later as well. This time the bluffing is not referred to, however; see: *HRP* II/4, p. 1669 (24 February 1941). He brought up the idea of the British using bluff tactics as one of their weapons in the war again in a speech at the end of 1943. For this, see: ibid., pp. 2053–2054 (8 November 1943).

90 *Hitler's Table Talk.* . . (1953), p. 606.

91 *Libres propos* . . ., (1954), pp. 237–238.

92 *Monologe* . . ., pp. 321–322.

93 *Libres propos* . . ., (1954), p. 238.

94 *Hitler's Table Talk.* . . (1953), p. 606.

95 *Monologe* . . ., p. 322.

96 *HRP* II/3, pp. 1446–1447 (21 January 1940).

97 Matthäus, J.& Bajohr, F. (Hg.), *Alfred Rosenberg* . . ., p. 315 (7 February 1940).

98 *Hitler, Mein Kampf.* . . (Band II), pp. 1161–1165 **[98–100]**. See also: Herbst, L., *Hitlers Charisma* . . ., pp. 188–189.

99 *RSA* I, p. 93, Document 50 (12 June 1925).

100 *Hitler's Table Talk.* . . (1953), p. 607; *Monologe* . . ., p. 322.

101 *Hitler's Table Talk.* . . (1953), p. 606.

102 *Monologe* . . ., p. 321; *Libres propos.* . . (Vol. II, 1954), p. 237; *Conversazioni segrete* . . ., p. 644. Ironically, the Italian historian Augusto Donaudy states in the preface to this book that *Libres propos* was a "l'egregia e fedelissima traduzione in lingua francese dei *Borman-Vermerke* [sic]", i.e. an excellent and faithful translation in French of the original *Bormann-Vermerke* (ibid., p. VI).

103 *Hitler's Table Talk.* . . (1973), p. 606.

104 "Trial Transcript", day 4, p. 170; www.hdot.org/day04/#, accessed: 2016–11–28.

105 In email correspondence with the author 2013–08–07 Irving stated: "He gave me Xerox copies. Perhaps half a dozen all told. He also showed me the Leitz Ordner of the whole set of them." And on Irving's website he states: "Genoud allowed me privileged access to the original German documents for *Hitler's War*." (www.fpp.co.uk/Hitler/Table_Talk/Picker.html, accessed: 2013–09–30). Note that Irving gives the English title (published in 1977), although the German edition was published first. Irving is overall rather careless regarding details on his website. For example, he writes that Weidenfeld's edition of *Table Talk* "was published in about 1949" (www.fpp.co.uk/Letters/Hitler/Law200603.html, accessed: 2013–09–30). The correct year is of course 1953. This faulty date is the same as that which he stated in the trial, as seen earlier.

106 Irving, David, *Hitler und seine Feldherren* (Frankfurt am Main: Verlag Ullstein, 1975), p. 791. Interestingly, Hitler mentions Cameroon also in *Mein Kampf*, but there he writes it off completely as being unviable as part of Germany colonial policy, which was to be directed only towards Eastern Europe; see: Kellerhof, S. F., *"Mein Kampf"* . . ., pp. 27–28. Apparently, he had changed his mind later on.

107 *Monologe* . . ., p. 94.

108 *Hitler's Table Talk.* . . (1953), p. 74.

109 Linne, Karsten, *Deutschland jenseits des Äquators. Die NS-Kolonialplanungen für Afrika* (Berlin: Ch. Links Verlag, 2008), p. 48; Dülffer, Jost, "Kolonialismus ohne Kolonien. Deutsche Kolonialplaene 1938", in Franz Knipping and Klaus-Jürgen Müller (eds.), *Machtbewußtsein in Deutschland am Vorabend des Zweiten Weltkrieges* (Paderborn: Ferdinand Schöningh, 1984), pp. 247–270 (quotation, p. 250); Simms, Brian, *Hitler: Only the World Was Enough* (London: Allen Lane, 2019), pp. 203–204.

110 Price, W., *I Know These* . . ., p. 146.

111 *Akten zur Deutschen Auswärtigen Politik 1918–1945. Aus dem Archiv des Auswärtigen Amts* (henceforth: ADAP), *Serie E 1941–1945. Band I. 12. Dezember 1941 bis 28. Februar 1942* (Göttingen: Vandenhoeck & Ruprecht, 1969), pp. 277–278 (Document 157).

112 *HRP* I/2, pp. 672–673, 716, 740 (30 January, 7 September & 3 October 1937).

113 *RSA* III/2, p. 475 (Document 103).

114 *HRP* I/2, p. 751 (5 November 1937). See also: *HRP* I/2, p. 967 (8 November 1938).

115 *HRP* II/3, p. 1064 (30 January 1939).

116 *HRP* II/3, p. 1159 (28 April 1939).

117 *HRP* II/3, p. 1272 (27 August 1939). Britain did not accept either of these options; see: ibid., p. 1279.

118 *HRP* II/3, pp. 1384, 1408, 1410 (6 October & 8 November 1939). See also: Longerich, P., *Hitler* . . ., p. 695.

119 *HRP* II/3, p. 1514 (20 May 1940). According to testimony after the war, Hitler stated at the HQ of Army Group A on 24 May that getting the colonies from Britain was "desirable, but not crucial"; see: ibid., p. 1515. Naturally, this must be considered less trustworthy considering when it was stated and the long time that had passed since the words reported were uttered.

120 *HRP* II/4, p. 1659 (30 January 1941).

121 *HRP* II/3, p. 1197 (23 May 1939).

122 *HRP* II/3, p. 1206 (4 June 1939). See also: *HRP* II/3, p. 1455 (30 January 1940).

123 Irving, D., *Hitler und* . . ., pp. 355, 376, 387, 402–403. In one instance Irving even dates a *Tischgespräch* to 23 March 1942 (ibid., p. 796). The problem is that this date is not in Jochmann, who has a large gap between 11/12 March and 1 August, and it is not included in Trevor-Roper's edition either. The only edition that has this particular entry is Picker (*Hitlers Tischgespräche.* . . (1951), p. 134). The fact that Irving mixes quotes like this without giving proper references is of course not good.

124 Irving, D., *Hitler und* . . ., p. 376.

125 *Hitlers Tischgespräche.* . . (1951), p. 88.

126 *Hitler's Table Talk.* . . (1953), p. 489.

127 *Libres propos.* . . (Vol. II, 1954), p. 126.

128 Cited by Gerhard Weinberg in the foreword in: Hitler, A., *Hitlers zweites Buch* . . ., p. 25.

129 Hitler, A., *Hitlers zweites Buch* . . ., p. 25.

130 Irving does, however, reproduce a facsimile of one entry that appear in Jochmann on his website, and this particular one concurs *ad verbatim* to Jochmann's text (see: *Monologe* . . ., p. 106; www.fpp.co.uk/Hitler/Table_Talk/Picker.html, accessed: 2013–09–30).

131 "Trial Transcript", day 4, p. 172; www.hdot.org/day04/#, accessed: 2016–11–28.

132 Irving, David, *Hitler's War* (London: Hodder and Stoughton, 1977), p. vii.

133 "Trial Transcript", day 4, p. 172; www.hdot.org/day04/#, accessed: 2016–11–28.

134 Irving, D., *Hitler's War*, p. 331.

135 "Trial Transcript", day 4, pp. 175–175; www.hdot.org/day04/#, accessed: 2016–11–28.

136 *Hitler's Table Talk. . .* (1953), p. 87.

137 "Trial Transcript", day 5, pp. 18–19; www.hdot.org/day05/, accessed: 2016–11–28.

138 *Monologe . . .*, p. 106.

139 Almost the entire day 17, and the questioning of defence witness Christopher Browning, is devoted to this issue, see: "Trial Transcript", day 17, passim; www.hdot.org/day17/, accessed: 2016–11–28.

140 Hubatsch, W. (ed.), *Hitlers Weisungen . . .*, p. 167. See also: Ullrich, V., *Adolf Hitler. . .* (Vol. II), p. 232.

141 Irving, D., *Hitler's War*, pp. 351–354, 854.

142 Ibid., pp. 331, 851.

143 Ibid., pp. 827, 832, 847.

144 Ibid., pp. 188–189. Péan does not question Genoud and seems to be unaware of Carrier's findings.

145 Trevor-Roper to Giles, 11 July 1967; CCLO; HTRP; Vol. Soc. Dacre 6/6/1.

146 Giles to Trevor-Roper, 13 July 1967; CCLO; HTRP; Vol. Soc. Dacre 6/6/1.

147 Winkler, W., *Der Schattenmann . . .*, p. 82. It is perhaps surprising that Trevor-Roper was so open about his uncritical attitude to his sources, but this must mean that he genuinely could not see what the problem was. It is not entirely clear to what document this letter refers because Winkler does not specify it.

148 Schmier to Trevor-Roper, 18 January 1964; Trevor-Roper to Schmier, 22 January 1964; Schmier to Trevor-Roper, 14 February 1964; Trevor-Roper to Schmier, 18 February 1964; CCLO; HTRP; Vol. Soc. Dacre 1/1/S (File: Schmier).

149 "Dick" to Trevor-Roper, 20 July 1967; CCLO; HTRP; Vol. Soc. Dacre 6/6/1.

150 Giles to Trevor-Roper, 2 August 1967, and attached confidential report on Genoud from Ingrid Etter-Vellino; CCLO; HTRP; Vol. Soc. Dacre 6/6/1.

151 Letter from the Chief of the Swiss state police to the police in the canton of Berne, 15 January 1947; Box 127; from the private archives of Pierre Péan, Paris, France.

152 "Deutsche Interna für die USA. BKA-Chef war CIA-Agent" in NTV, 19 June 2011; www.n-tv.de/politik/BKA-Chef-war-CIA-Agent-article3613461.html, accessed: 2019–10–01; Posner, Gerald, "Interpol's Nazi Affiliations Continued After War" in *The New York Times*, 6 March 1990, Section A, p. 22.

153 The difference is due, not only, to the fact that *Monologe* does not contain Picker's notes (in which case it ought to be No. 174 in *Libres propos* (if Picker's notes are removed). The last Heim note in *Monologe* (11/12 March 1942) is No. 158 while the same in *Libres propos* is No. 173. Thus, the division is inexplicably different. Jochmann says nothing about this.

154 *Hitler's Table Talk. . .* (1953), p. 603.

155 *Libres propos. . .* (Vol. II, 1954), p. 235.

156 *Monologe . . .*, p. 320.

157 In the essay "Aus Gottes egienem Land" in *Das eherne Hertz*, pp. 421–427, Joseph Goebbels mentions this book and derides the Americans for having no culture. The essay is dated 9 August 1942 and states that Linklater's book "Gerade in diesen Tage kommt das Buch. . . 'Juan in Amerika' in deutscher Übersetzung heraus", and that one "muß dieses Buch . . . gelesen haben, um die Amerikaner von heute richtig zu verstehen." (Goebbels, J., *Das eherne Hertz* (Munich: Zentralverlag der NSDAP, 1943), p. 422). What Goebbels is saying is that the book had not yet been published but was about to be so in a few days. Since the note states that Bormann had given the book to Hitler a few days earlier than August 1 it would mean that he got it before it was published. It is also an interesting coincidence that Hitler should speak about Stuttgart since the book was published by a company based in Stuttgart (or was that the reason why he mentioned it?). This means

that Genoud *could* have gotten the title of this particular book from reading Goebbels's essay in this NSDAP book. This would explain why Genoud gave the German title instead of, say, the French (*Juan en Amérique* was published in France in 1944). The book was used as a major propaganda tool by Goebbels's *Reichspropaganda-ministerium* and was spread in large numbers both in Germany and at the front. The official reason was that this book was deemed to serve as a better proof of the bankrupt American culture than any material produced by the state (see endnote by Werner Jochmann in: *Monologe . . .* (for the official function of this book, see: p. 462)). This was thus not just any kind of obscure book, but one that was very well known at the time; and, hence, most likely by Genoud too. Goebbels wrote in his diary on 26 July 1942: "I read the book of the Scotsman Linklater 'Juan in America'. It's the most spirited, witty ridicule of culture and public life in the US I've ever seen. I will arrange for this book to be distributed to a greater extent to German intellectuals. This book works against America more than a hundred pamphlets and memoirs, mainly because it is so amusingly written and can be read out in a river. I would like to compare it in its effect with regard to the United States with the book 'Self-Portrait of a Gentleman' on England at the time." See: *TBJG* II/5, p. 189 (26 July 1942). Interestingly, Goebbels claims that it was *he* who had sent the book to Hitler, and he reports from his visit to the *Werwolf* FHQ by Winniza, the Ukraine, on 19 August 1942: "The Führer has read the book of Linklater 'Juan in America', which I had sent him, with the greatest interest and pleasure. He gives it to all acquaintances and strongly advises them to read it. He very much agrees that I should send several thousand copies of this excellent book to people of the party, officers of the Wehrmacht, and to intellectuals. It is more effective than any propaganda brochure." See: *TBJG* II/5, p. 356 (20 August 1942).

158 *Monologe . . .*, p. 462.
159 See a list of questions regarding certain notes in Genoud's manuscript, p 1; WJN; Binder: "Schriftwechsel A – K 1977".
160 *Hitler's Table Talk. . .* (1953), p. 607.
161 *Libres propos. . .* (Vol. II, 1954), p. 239.
162 *Monologe . . .*, p. 323.
163 *Hitler's Table Talk. . .* (1953), p. 604.
164 *Libres propos. . .* (Vol. II, 1954), p. 236.
165 *Monologe . . .*, p. 320.
166 Pyta, W., *Hitler . . .*, p. 406.
167 *Hitler's Table Talk. . .* (1953), pp. 177–178.
168 *Monologe . . .*, p. 177.
169 *Libres propos. . .* (Vol. I, 1952), pp. 173–174.
170 Pyta, W., *Hitler . . .*, pp. 407, 752. The technical issue of the thickness of the steel on the tanks, and the inability of the enemy to penetrate it (as well as the inability of British and French tanks to withstand German anti-tank weapons) had been the theme of Hitler's ruminations just before the invasion of Poland in 1939; see: *HRP* II/3, p. 1270 (27 August 1939).
171 Generally speaking, it is preferable not to have to add *ad hoc* assumptions to a hypothetical explanation. However, this principle is not universal, and it will become obvious why this is not a problem in this case during this course of our investigation.
172 *Hitler's Table Talk. . .* (1973), p. viii. The manuscript for the new preface is located in: Christ Church Library, Oxford; Hugh Trevor-Roper Papers, p. 2; Vol. Soc. Dacre 6/6/1. Winkler states in the end of his book that Trevor-Roper's papers are located at Cambridge, even though he twice refers to letters in this archive giving the correct location (Winkler, W., *Der Schattenmann . . .*, pp. 311, 322, 351).
173 Trevor-Roper to Irving, 15 December 1972; CCLO; HTRP; Vol. Soc. Dacre 6/21.
174 Irving to Trevor-Roper, 24 December 1972; CCLO; HTRP; Vol. Soc. Dacre 6/21, pp. 1–2.

175 Trevor-Roper to Irving, 7 January 1973; CCLO; HTRP; Vol. Soc. Dacre 6/21. The manuscript copy of the preface for the second edition in Trevor-Roper's archive referred to earlier does not contain the additional information about Irving's documents and must thus have been written before this was added.

176 *Hitler's Table Talk. . .* (1973), p. x. When Oxford University Press re-published the *Table Talk* in 1988 the preface to the second edition was not included. Instead it was identical to the original edition from 1953 (see: *Hitler's Table-Talk. . .* (1988). This was probably to mark the 35-year anniversary of the first edition.

177 Trevor-Roper to Hilary Walford, 18 March 1973; CCLO; HTRP Vol. Soc. Dacre 6/6/1.

178 Copy of contract attached to letter from Wiedenfeld and Nicolson to Trevor-Roper, 23 March 1973, p. 1; CCLO; HTRP; Vol. Soc. Dacre 6/6/1.

179 Trevor-Roper to Hilary Walford, 30 March 1973; CCLO; HTRP; Vol. Soc. Dacre 6/6/1.

180 *Hitler's Table Talk. . .* (1973), p. viii.

181 Weidenfeld to Trevor-Roper, 22 October 1952; CCLO; HTRP; Vol. Soc. Dacre 6/6/1. These two copies are not present in this volume.

182 *Hitler's Table Talk. . .* (1973), pp. vii–x.

6

THE TESTAMENT OF ADOLF HITLER

The last table talk or a clever forgery?[1]

Introduction

As was already mentioned, Genoud was sitting on a number of manuscripts, one with a more spurious provenance than the other, which he turned into publications during the 1950s and 1960s. Besides Genoud, Trevor-Roper was the one consistent factor in all of these publications. In 1954 they had published parts of the correspondence between Martin and Gerda Bormann under the title *The Bormann Letters*.[2] Then, in 1959, Genoud published *Le testament politique*.[3] The alleged original document purportedly consisted of notes made by Martin Bormann himself dictated to him by Hitler mostly in February 1945 (one entry dated in April was also included). It was thus a sort of "table talk II" and was portrayed as a continuation of the table talk notes that had previously been published in *Table Talk*. This text was then translated and published in English in 1961 and given the identical title *The Testament of Adolf Hitler* (henceforth: *The Testament*) with an introduction by Trevor-Roper.[4] Finally, in 1981 a German edition with the equally similar *Hitlers politisches Testament* was also published.[5] These were rather confusing titles considering that Hitler's actual private and political testaments were two completely different documents dictated by Hitler to his secretary Traudl Junge in the bunker under Berlin on the night of 29–30 April 1945.

This chapter delineates the history of *The Testament* and argues that these texts very likely are forgeries; in any case their provenance is so dubious that no serious historian should ever use them unless new sources come to light that can prove their authenticity. Note that I am talking about texts in plural; this is motivated because, as we shall see, the various published editions are similar in style and content but not identical in their wording.

But isn't it difficult to forge such a large amount of text in a way that still makes it look authentic to experts? The answer has to be no, and there are many examples one could provide of when historians have been fooled by something that they really wanted to be authentic. For example, there was East German (and later Minister of Justice in the GDR) Max Fechners's forgery of Goebbels's diaries. Winkler writes that Fechner related Goebbels's pathos without it even once sounding fake.[6] Another example are the so-called Hitler diaries forged by Konrad Kujau in the 1980s. It is true that Speer already in Spandau felt as if *Table Talk* contained traces of Goebbels's hand, and Fest as well states (no doubt based on Speer) that he thinks that Goebbels created certain passages. Fest used the French edition and remarks that it had no doubt been re-worked a bit (obviously oblivious to the fact that Genoud had reworked it) and even acknowledges that the original has been lost.[7] The entertaining thing is that Speer nonetheless seems more convinced by this redacted document than he did by Picker's *Tschgespräche*. If one were to paraphrase Speer, one could say that an incorrect text could purvey a correct image.[8]

Even though several historians have used the various editions of these texts in their works,[9] there are also those who have refused to do so. Ian Kershaw's judgement about this text was unambiguously sceptical, as it should have been, and he wrote in his mammoth Hitler biography:

> The main problem with the authenticity of the text is that no reliable and certifiable German version exists. It is impossible, therefore, to be certain. A great deal has to be taken on trust; and even then, no safe mechanism for checking is available. . . . [The] English version contains a very loose and untrustworthy translation of the German text – itself not guaranteed to be identical with any long-lost original or the lost copy of that original – which was eventually published only in 1981. . . . Further examination of the text in the meantime – though this was not mentioned by the German publishers – by Professor Eduard Baumgarten had established that the translation back into German from the French (carried out by a Dutchman) contained between the lines a second German text, written in the hand of François Genoud. The available German text is, therefore, at best a construct; neither the original nor the copy of that original exists. Baumgarten tended, since the content was consonant with Hitler's thinking and expression, to accept the authenticity of the text. There is, however, no proof and, therefore, no reliable German text whose authenticity can be placed beyond question.[10]

He also – mistakenly, I should add – states that these notes "came to light" in 1951 (Kershaw may here be confusing the alleged original document with the original document of the table talks, the *Bormann-Vermerke*) and volunteers the admission that the "tone of the monologues is unmistakingly Hitler." But at the same time, he also states that Hitler's many secretaries seem to have been unaware of these being taken down by anyone (see also later in this chapter). At least one of them questioned their authenticity, although she thought it might be a compilation of Hitler's thoughts. She even ruled out the possibility of Bormann having recorded Hitler's words precisely because of the fact that Hitler forbade *ad verbatim* records of his off-the-cuff statements.[11]

Sometimes this document has been used, perhaps inadvertently, by reference to a work that has made use of it. Such is the case in the first volume of Frank McDonough's new history of Nazi Germany. On one occasion McDonough cites something that Hitler allegedly said in February 1945 about the Munich Agreement in 1938. McDonough refers to Fest's Hitler biography. Fest, on his part, cites *Le testament politque*.[12] Recently, Brendan Simms has also "with considerable reluctance" refrained from using these texts due to my previously published peer-reviewed article on this topic, which Simms calls a "forensic examination."[13] Kershaw and Simms have thus had the integrity and the necessary source-critical acumen not to use sources with such dubious provenance such as these.

The beginnings: a new text of questionable provenance

The long and rather strange history of these texts began, as far as Trevor-Roper was concerned, in 1958. On 26 April that year Genoud wrote to him to inform him about these notes and wondered if he would like to read them. Trevor-Roper was intrigued and replied that he would very much like to do that. He consequently asked if Genoud could send him a copy of the text. Genoud was of course delighted to hear this, but told Trevor-Roper that he had already parted with his only *French* text. This text he had sent to Stevens for translation into English, but he would ask Stevens to send this copy to Trevor-Roper when he was done with it, or even better, the English translation made from it. The so-called "original" in German Genoud did not want to part with, he said, because the rights of Hitler's heirs were not protected. He could, however, show Trevor-Roper the German text on location in Switzerland. He never specified what kind of an "original" this actually was. "We are in the same situation as with the Table Talk six years ago", wrote Genoud, once again reminding Trevor-Roper of the fact that *Table Talk* had been translated from the French too.[14] This affair had thus already become rather strange. There were at this point already apparently two versions of this text: one French text and alleged German one.

In early June Stevens wrote to Trevor-Roper and said that he had received Genoud's French documents containing the text and that he would "translate them and get in touch" with Trevor-Roper. He also wrote that he would "have preferred to translate direct from the original German (as I did in my share of Hitler's Table Talks)." He would send Trevor-Roper the translated text as soon as it was completed. Trevor-Roper thanked Stevens heartily and suggested that they would meet in London after he had read it. Stevens sent Trevor-Roper the translated text on 24 June 1958 for him to read.[15] *Nota bene*: Stevens does not write that he translated from the German original manuscript, but "the original German". It is of course easy to make too much of this, but considering all the other information regarding the translation process that has come to light, this also indicates that Stevens did not have the original manuscript at his disposal, but another German text that Genoud had likely told him was an exact transcript of the original text. Trevor-Roper then wrote to Genoud in early October saying that he had received Stevens's translation and that he had found it "very interesting."[16]

In his introduction to *The Testament* Trevor-Roper claims that by the end of February "Hitler had completed his work: Only once thereafter – on April 2 – did he add a last postscript." He also includes a made-up story of how Hitler himself told "a Nazi official" who he had ordered to leave Berlin for Bad Gastein to remove the gold reserves from the Thuringian salt mines and that Bormann would entrust him with a document that he was to bring to safety. Bormann then supposedly gave this man a sealed package containing the notes which were to be preserved "in the Party Archives."[17] Trevor-Roper had been told this story by Genoud and Rechenberg when he met them in Paris in November 1958.[18] According to this story, the documents were then preserved in a bank vault in Bad Gastein. Without mentioning Rechenberg by name Trevor-Roper clearly presents him as the man who was entrusted by the former Reich Minister for Economic Affairs (1938–1945), Walter Funk, then imprisoned in Spandau in Berlin, to destroy the documents that Funk had smuggled out of Berlin at the end of the war. Funk supposedly was afraid that the documents in Bad Gastein would incriminate him even further in the eyes of the Allies. Rechenberg did as he was ordered, we are told; "after extracting some personal papers, he was to burn the rest 'The rest' was Hitler's last *Table Talk*." This of course made no sense at all. Funk thus did *not* destroy the personal papers, but only *The Testament* as if *that* document was what would incriminate him further. But before burning the original Rechenberg had them photocopied, Trevor-Roper says, which he then secretly kept for himself. The absurdities continue when he claims that Funk, upon his release from prison in May 1957, agreed to the "*fait accompli*", even though he was not at all pleased with Rechenberg for having preserved the document, as long as his own role was not divulged.[19] It is interesting to note that when *The Times* published a short review on *The Testament* in 1961 it repeated the claim that "they were taken for safe keeping to a bank in Bad Gastein, and eventually rescued for publication."[20]

Trevor-Roper thus met with Genoud and his companion Hans Rechenberg in Paris in November 1958. At that time, he was allegedly shown the illusive photocopy of the original document. This information was given to German sociologist Eduard Baumgarten in the early 1970s, and Baumgarten included it in a footnote in his manuscript for a book about the history of *The Testament* text that he was working on in 1973.[21] Trevor-Roper had been told by Genoud and Rechenberg that Funk wanted to meet him and that he had agreed to publication of the document as long as it was done by Genoud and Trevor-Roper together. Funk's name was to be kept out, though. However, even though Trevor-Roper's memorandum of the conversation from this meeting in 1958 says that Rechenberg had made a photocopy of Funk's document, *it never says that Trevor-Roper had been shown the photocopy at the meeting.*[22] This is very odd. How could he not have found this to be an important fact to write down? There is nothing in his notes about either having seen the photocopies and nothing about Bormann's signature on each page. This is probably the best evidence we have that there is something off with Trevor-Roper's later claim about having seen the photocopy in Paris in 1958. It is simply unthinkable that he would not have included this information in his memorandum if he had actually seen it with his own eyes. From a source-critical perspective, it is extremely problematic that the only primary source written directly after the meeting does not contain any information about this.

It is not until a year later, in November 1959, that we have evidence of Trevor-Roper first mentioning that he had actually seen photocopies of some document. He did this in a letter to Brian Melland (who had been the chief of the British Army Historical Section's Enemy Document Section [EDS] from 1948, M.N.). Melland had written to him after having read an article in the *Sunday Express* in April and May 1959 which talked about *Le testament politique*. The article had stated that the authenticity of the photostatic copies of the notes had been validated by Trevor-Roper. He wished to know if these notes would appear in print any time soon.[23] In his reply Trevor-Roper told Melland: "I have seen the originals, or rather (since the originals were burnt) the photostatic copies of them, and I know the whole history of them." Apparently, then, Trevor-Roper had some trouble distinguishing between an original and a photocopy of that said original. But, he said, he could name no names until death had intervened. He went on to say that these notes had just been published in French and he did not know when, or even if, they would ever be published in another language.[24]

In this letter, however, Trevor-Roper never mentions anything about personally having seen Bormann's signatures on these photocopies. Moreover, can we really trust Trevor-Roper to be telling the truth here, or did he claim that he had seen the photocopies in order to allay any suspicion on Melland's part that they forgeries?

In fact, Trevor-Roper actually never says that he had personally seen Bormann's signature in the introduction to *Le testament politique/ The Testament* either. There he only says that Bormann's "large, loose, formless signature is there" and that this attested to the documents' authenticity of "the typewritten pages." The same is true for the version of the introduction included in the German edition. In the French version it even says that the signature appeared "*at the bottom* of the typed pages" [italics added].[25] It is unknown why the English and German text do not mention this latter detail. But this could mean that he had simply been told by Genoud that the documents contained Bormann's signature. Trevor-Roper even said in 1961, while reiterating the claim that he had seen "the German documents", that it was impossible to prove the authenticity of the Testament but that he nonetheless was "satisfied from both internal and circumstantial evidence that it is genuine."[26] Once again he did not mention personally seeing the many signatures on these documents.

That piece of information only appears in the historical record about 12 years later. In March 1973 Trevor-Roper wrote to Baumgarten telling him about the meeting in Paris in 1958 that he had seen the photocopy "only in the Hotel Belfast" (a very fancy hotel in the middle of Paris, M.N.) where he had met Genoud and Rechenberg. He thus had no opportunity to really validate the document. At the same time Trevor-Roper also said that although Genoud had offered a meeting with Funk, Trevor-Roper had not taken him up on his offer. This was a decision that he now regretted and thought that he perhaps should have "in the interest of historical accuracy."[27] It was in the same letter that he told Baumgarten that he remembered clearly that every page of the document had Bormann's unmistakable signature on it.[28] Here he went back to the version included in the French introduction, which had later been removed from the English version of the same text. But can we trust Trevor-Roper on this point? It turns out that Trevor-Roper at the same time stated that he had never ever seen any handwriting by Bormann except his signature and that he had been told that Bormann had lost one or more fingers on his right hand and that this was the reason for his "loose and ungainly" signature.[29] This is absurd. Trevor-Roper had seen plenty of documents written by Bormann by hand in connection with the publication of both *Table Talk* and, not least, *The Bormann Letters*. It is even more absurd considering that Trevor-Roper mentions Bormann's letters in his letter to Baumgarten.[30] His personal archive also contains some copies of these letters. Incredibly, Trevor-Roper had completely forgotten about seeing both them and Bormann's notes by 1973. He later changed his statement in another letter after this lapse of memory had been pointed out to him by Baumgarten. He said: "When I wrote to you on 18th March 1973 I had evidently forgotten that note by Bormann which I had seen and myself published in 1953!"[31] Evidently, he still did not remember having seen Bormann's letters.

Moreover, Trevor-Roper's claim that he had seen Bormann's signature was actually a *confirmation* to a question posed by Baumgarten who wished to know: "Do you remember having seen Bormann's <u>signature</u> at the end of each chapter, or even at the bottom of every page?"[32] The question is a bit odd; why were alternatives given here when Trevor-Roper had already mentioned this in his French introduction in 1959? Was the signature at the end of each note or on every page? This was not something that Trevor-Roper had mentioned to Baumgarten before, which is really strange if he indeed had seen the signatures. This was instead information that Genoud and Rechenberg had given Baumgarten in 1973. Thus, everything that Trevor-Roper stated in his reply was simply a reiteration of a statement that Genoud and Rechenberg had made in conversations with Baumgarten. There is thus a good chance that Trevor-Roper may indeed simply have imagined that he had actually seen these signatures, the existence of which he might well only have been told about, just as he imagined never ever having seen Bormann's handwriting before.

In 1962 the German journal *Der Spiegel* ran an article on this document and referred to Genoud's French edition but said that the many quotes were "based on Genoud's German document." At the same time, it was noted that Genoud refused to give up the German text. The quotes included in the *Der Spiegel* article do agree with the text in *Hitlers politisches Testament*, but this says nothing about the authenticity of the text. One quote was mistakenly said to be from 2 February (a date not included in *Hitlers politisches Testament*) when in reality it is dated 2 April.[33] Winkler notes that Genoud skilfully directed this publication too by not letting the journalists check the provided German text against an original.[34]

Trevor-Roper had, however, apparently been quite convinced of the document's authenticity because to a question regarding this point coming from David Irving (who thought it was a forgery) in late 1967 he repeated that the style and context, Bormann's signature, and Genoud's story about how the document came to him and the fact that Trevor-Roper could not see the motives for Genoud to produce a forgery all pointed towards authenticity. Trevor-Roper did admit, though, that it was difficult to penetrate the mind of the perfect forger and that highly qualified scholars had devoted enormous amounts of time to producing forgeries for nothing more than the private satisfaction of having fooled the experts. Because of this, Trevor-Roper wrote, one could not "reason confidently in such a matter." But as the evidence stood, he was inclined to believe it was genuine.[35] Nevertheless, in public Trevor-Roper "reason confidently" with regard to Genoud's Hitleralia. It is also hard to believe that Trevor-Roper could really not imagine why a Nazi sycophant would want to forge a document that both glorified Hitler and was sure to make him money.

Irving had pointed out to Trevor-Roper that according to Heinz Linge's calendar, Bormann was with Hitler "on only seven of the 18 days in February 1945 listed as the dates on the Genoud notes." He also provided a transcript of these dates. Irving felt that this indicated that the notes were forgeries and added that none of the people he had interviewed had seen Bormann make these notes and that in the case of *Table Talk* the dates were all from the right days.[36] Trevor-Roper, however, was not convinced by this argument and replied that since Heinz Linge's diary was not available for the earlier period, such a comparison could not be made. One exception was the last note in *Table Talk*, which not only was made by Bormann himself but that also has him intervening in the conversation, and for this day Linge's diary has no meeting with Bormann either. This seemed to be solid proof against Irving's hypothesis and method of evidence, since the table talk notes were genuine. Also, he said that no one had ever suggested that the notes had to have been made under interview-like circumstances on the days that they were dated.[37] This latter point was certainly contradicted by the full title of *Hitlers politisches Testament*, which claimed that the notes were "dictations" (*Diktate*).

On 26 May 1969, Trevor-Roper wrote to German professor of history at Stuttgart University, Eberhard Jäckel, and congratulated him on having been able to "obtain" the German text of *The Testament*. Trevor-Roper had recently read Jäckel's book *Hitlers Weltanschauung*, which Jäckel had sent to him, and in it Jäckel had quoted a sentence from a note dated 4 February in his book and stated in a footnote that Genoud had been kind enough to allow him to cite "the unpublished German original wording."[38] The quote in Jäckel's book is indeed identical to the text in *Hitlers politisches Testament*.[39] Apparently, Jäckel had initially written to Trevor-Roper asking him if *he* supply the original German wording of certain passages in the belief that he had the original text in his possession. At that time Trevor-Roper had given Jäckel Genoud's address and told him to contact the Swiss for this information. Jäckel did so and Genoud had told him that he could not show him the whole text, but he could supply the individual German phrases that Jäckel needed. Genoud said he needed three weeks to do this because he had to contact Rechenberg who allegedly had the German transcript. After three weeks, a timeliness that is indeed a reason to get suspicious, Jäckel reportedly got a letter with the phrases from Genoud. Trevor-Roper for some reason considered this to be confirmation that Rechenberg had the text in question.[40]

But this could not be considered to be a confirmation of anything, and it just shows just how uncritical Trevor-Roper was. All of this depended on a story that Genoud had told Jäckel, who had no idea if what Genoud had said was actually true. From this Trevor-Roper equally erroneously concluded that Jäckel had "obtained" the original German text. Trevor-Roper wrote:

> P.S. May I congratulate you on your diplomatic skill in obtaining the German text of the 1945 table-talk from François Genoud? I wish we could persuade Genoud to allow the publication of that text in the original language – and indeed to allow scholars to compare his text of the earlier table-talk with that of Picker, as now published by Percy Ernst Schramm.[41]

This seems to have made Trevor-Roper even more certain about the authenticity *The Testament* text. After thinking about Irving's objections a lot, he said in a letter to Irving on the very same day, he noted that Jäckel was now also convinced of the text's authenticity.[42] At first, we might be tempted to interpret the fact that the quotes in *Der Spiegel* and *Hitlers Weltanschauung* agree with the German text that was later published as a confirmation of authenticity. This would be a huge mistake, however. It tells us nothing about its authenticity.

We have, it turns out, good reason to doubt that the claim that Rechenberg had the German transcript is true. In March 1971 Genoud wrote to a lawyer by the name of Udo von Busekist in Düsseldorf whom he assumed was the executor of Luise Funk's, Walter Funk's widow, last will and testament (she had died in October 1963). Genoud was mistaken, however, because von Busekist told him that he had indeed not been the executor of the estate, but he told him that Frau Funk's sole heir was a Horst Walter, now the head of the Daimler-Benz Niederlassung auto store in Wuppertal, whom he thought that Genoud was surely familiar with. However, the literary papers (*literarischen Nachlasses*) had *not* been part of what Frau Funk had given to Walter, von Busekist said. Instead, this material had been given to Mr. Rechenberg.[43]

Baumgarten's own involvement in this affair lasted several years (and never resulted in any published findings in the end). Baumgarten was in May 1972 under the impression that Genoud had "good reasons for fearing" that Walter had destroyed the photocopy of this valuable document, although he could not offer an explanation as to why anyone would want to do this.[44] Interestingly, Albert Speer had mentioned Horst Walter in passing in his memoirs *Erinnerungen* published in 1969. Speer wrote that Funk had told him in Spandau prison about a drinking party at the *Waffen*-SS staff HQ in the fall of 1943 where "Funk's adjutant and friend for many years, Horst Walter, now [Sepp] Dietrich's adjutant, took part."[45] Now it becomes clear why Walter became involved in this case. The question is of course if Horst Walter's appearance in Genoud's and Rechenberg's story related to *The Testament* in 1971, reasonably soon after the publication of Speer's memoirs where Walter is mentioned, is accidental.

But this too turned out to be a misunderstanding. In a handwritten notation in the margin on this letter Baumgarten wrote that Rechenberg had in fact only been given the publication rights to Funk's private papers, but he had *not* been given the papers themselves. This had been made clear to Baumgarten through conversations with Rechenberg, whom he had met in München on 5 February 1973, as well as with Walter.[46]

I have not been able to find Genoud's initial letter to Rechenberg, but in Rechenberg's response it is evident that it was he who had told Genoud that von Busekist was the executor of Frau Funk's estate; he had been told that this was the case by (former *SS-Oberführer* and *Ministerialdirektor* in the *Reichswirtschaftministerium*, M.N.) Dr. (Gustav) Schlotterer. The documents in question had, as far as Rechenberg could remember, been returned to Funk by Genoud in connection with them having been shown to Trevor-Roper and in preparation for a conversation between Trevor-Roper and Funk. Rechenberg then stated that he no longer had any knowledge about these matters and that he had not found any time to order and arrange Funk's private papers since 1963, thus contradicting his statement to Baumgarten that he had not been given any papers. "In any case, the documents that You mention are *not* among the notes that remained from Funk's lifetime that were handed over to me." As a postscript he added that the documents could perhaps be in Walter's possession.[47] Genoud thus had to be reminded of what he himself had done with the document. His next move in his effort to try and locate it was thus to contact Horst Walter.

This did not happen until most a year later, in early 1972, when, despite von Busekist having told him that Walter did not have the documents he sought, Genoud wrote a letter to him, since he was the lone heir of Luise Funk, he said. Genoud told him that among the documents in Funk's personal papers were among other documents "notes from Riechsleiter Martin Bormann from the year 1945." Photocopies of these notes had been given to him in 1959 for his use by Funk himself, Genoud wrote, and "I personally handed them back to him in early 1960 for a planned meeting with the historian Professor Trevor-Roper [obviously, this was not the correct year – either Genoud was mistaken or he lied]. Now, I need these documents really urgently." He also referred Walter to an agreement he had made with Funk on 24 October 1957 and included a copy of this agreement in the letter.[48] However, this agreement had nothing to do with the alleged Bormann notes from 1945, but instead with Funk giving Genoud the publication rights to his memoirs *Wer Regiert das Geld? Erfarungen eines Notenbankpräsidenten (Who Controls the Money? Experiences of a Central Bank President)* It is unclear why this would be relevant in this context.[49]

This certainly makes it seem as if there indeed were photocopies of this document at one point. Why else would Genoud write to Walter in order to try and retrieve them?[50] Genoud asked Walter to tell him about the extent of written papers that Funk's widow had had in her possession at her death.[51] But Genoud claimed that Funk had given *him* the photocopies in 1959. This contradicts what he had said to Baumgarten and Trevor-Roper where it always was Rechenberg who had been in possession of the photocopies. Was Genoud simply trying to make his claim to the documents seem more legitimate? Or had he and Rechenberg been lying to Baumgarten and Trevor-Roper? The latter scenario is unlikely to be true simply because it would serve no function. It was as if Genoud was fishing for anything that he could get from Walter, and he was trying to validate his claim to any documents by referring to his rather irrelevant agreement with Funk from 1957. Unfortunately, we do not have access to Walter's response to this request from Genoud. One also starts to wonder if Rechenberg was in fact playing Genoud as well. Perhaps Genoud really thought there were photocopies of the typed notes that he may have been given by Rechenberg. Perhaps he paid a handsome sum of money for this text.

But what kind of documents were these notes that he tried to retrieve from Walter really? In fact, this is not at all clear. Genoud never mentioned Hitler in his letter to Walter. Why did he not include this central piece of information? How could Walter know what notes Genoud was looking for without a more precise description than that? Was he actually looking for the photocopies of the text that was later published as *Hitlers politisches Testament* or some other notes that Bormann had made? In fact, the precise nature of these notes was never mentioned in any of the letters. As we have seen, Trevor-Roper never met with Funk, apparently due to a lack of interest on Trevor-Roper's part. It should, however, be noted here that we do not know if Funk had actually agreed to a meeting – the only source for this information is Genoud and Rechenberg who constantly lied about matters related to this topic. The interesting thing is that while Trevor-Roper thought that the fact that Genoud wished for him to meet Funk was "evidence" that Funk would have confirmed Genoud's story of the document's origin, he apparently was by that point not convinced about its authenticity.[52] Obviously, since they never met, Trevor-Roper never got such a confirmation, although he still acted as if he had.

In this context, a letter from the former Chief of the Reich Chancellery (1933–1945), Hans Heinrich Lammers, to Genoud from 31 March 1959 is interesting to dissect. If the letter is authentic, it is evidence that Genoud had given Lammers access to a text said to be Hitler's statements to Bormann in February and April 1945. Lammers stated that he could for the most part well remember Hitler having made utterances such as those entailed in Bormann's notes. He added that he was not surprised that Bormann could remember Hitler's statements almost *ad*

The Testament of Adolf Hitler **289**

verbatim because he was after all just an interpreter (*Dolmetscher*) of Hitler's words and not someone who made politics based on his own thoughts.[53]

However, we do not know if Lammers saw the photocopies, which is highly doubtful, or more likely a typed text sent to him. If Genoud had sent Lammers a typed text that he *said* was a transcript of notes originally made by Bormann, then Lammers may well have simply believed him. Lammers never mentions anything about Bormann's signature being on the documents that he had read and validated. Moreover, it is not really evident why Genoud felt that he needed this testimony from Lammers in the first place if he had photocopies of the original notes with Bormann's signature all over them. It is obvious that the letter from Lammers was not intended for Genoud's own consumption, but to be used as a proof of authenticity for others, as a substitute for an original that they were never allowed to see. We have already seen that Genoud did *not* let Trevor-Roper or Stevens read the photocopies in 1959 since he specifically stated to Trevor-Roper that he did not want to part with this document. Why would Genoud lie about this if the photocopies indeed existed and were kept by Funk? We can therefore exclude the possibility that he sent a copy of the photocopies to Lammers. Rather, he had sent Lammers the same German typed text that he had in his possession all along.

Trevor-Roper seems to have borrowed Lammer's last statement for his introduction to *The Testament* where he says that Bormann was a better "interpreter" of Hitler's words than Goebbels because "he had no ideas of his own to distort."[54] The similarity to what Lammers wrote in his letter to Genoud is striking. It is likely that Genoud used the letter from Lammers in the process of convincing Trevor-Roper that the document that he was putting his name on was in fact genuine. This again should make us question whether Trevor-Roper had actually ever seen the photocopies of this document. Genoud's refusal to show Trevor-Roper the photocopies in 1959 as he was working on the introduction to *Le testament politique* and *The Testament* also makes no sense if Trevor-Roper had already seen them in Paris in November 1958. Genoud had then nothing to lose by showing them again.

Nonetheless, Trevor-Roper stated with impressive firmness in the preface to *Hitler's Politisches Testament*, and in words that are similar to his discussion with Baumgarten, that:

> They are doubtlessly authentic: their history, their content, and Bormann's well-known signature proves this.[55]

Thus, Bormann's signature and the history of the manuscript had now all of a sudden become definite proof of its authenticity. This must be considered rather dishonest by Trevor-Roper, since his true thoughts on this matter were far more ambiguous than that. The preface to this book is also strange for another reason. At the end Trevor-Roper added the following phrase to it: "(unchanged wording of the text from 1961)."[56] Not only is that a weird thing to say no matter what the circumstances are, but it is even more weird considering that it cannot possibly be true. The text namely contains proof that material was added after that point and even after 1980, because Trevor-Roper writes the following regarding the history of the *Bormann-Vermerke*:

> It was not until 1980 that they were published in Germany by Werner Joch-mann under the title "Monologe im Führerhauptquartier 1941/42", based on Heinrich Heim's notes.[57]

There is of course no way that Trevor-Roper could have written this in 1961 since *Monologe* was published in 1980. The introduction had thus in fact been changed. The question is then why on earth Trevor-Roper would pretend that it was the same? Most likely answer: Trevor-Roper forgot that he had added this bit and intended only to assure the reader that the text was the same. The effect, however, became quite the opposite. Moreover, this statement also hid the fact that this introduction did not contain the detail about Bormann's signature at the bottom of the pages that appeared in the original French edition.

In May 1972, however, Baumgarten would tell Trevor-Roper, based on infor-mation given to him by Genoud, that it was *Rechenberg* who had sent the photo-copy to Funk and that the document after the death of Funk's wife was in the hands of an unnamed man in the Ruhr area (i.e. Horst Walter). This was a lie of course. At the same time Genoud told Baumgarten that he could no longer access the German transcript and that he therefore recommended re-translation into German from the English text.[58] Thus, what Genoud told Baumgarten was bogus.

The text that Jäckel had been given access to was, of course, not the original, but part of a typed text which Genoud claimed to be a transcript of the lost pho-tocopy of the original. Genoud likely had this in his possession all along, since he could give Jäckel access to quotes from this text in 1968/69. The "three weeks" were probably intended to lend credence to this ruse and to convince Jäckel of the reality of it all. However, by mid-1972 this typed transcript had also been lost, Baumgarten said. Genoud claimed it had been returned to Funk shortly before his death.[59] This was the third version of events that Genoud would tell and this, too, was an obvious lie. Funk had died on 31 May 1960. Thus, Genoud could not have given the typed text back to Funk because he evidently still had it when he let *Der Spiegel* see parts of it in 1962 and when Jäckel got to see parts of it in 1968–1969. Moreover, in the previous versions of the events it had always been the *photocopy* that had been returned to Funk (regardless of who had actually given it to him), and this was said to have happened already in 1959. Genoud would continue to toy with various scholars, who would engage in the futile effort of wrestling the so-called 'original' text of these notes from Genoud over the coming years.

Trevor-Roper and Genoud reconnected at some point after Trevor-Roper had written to Jäckel in 1969, and on 25 October 1971 they dined together in Laus-anne, Switzerland. At that time Genoud asked Trevor-Roper if he would be will-ing to take part in a publication of the German text of *The Testament*. This must reasonably also mean that Genoud had ready access to the text. Trevor-Roper apparently answered in a general manner, knowing, he said, that Genoud's words were one thing and his actions another.[60] What is interesting is that this is *after* Genoud had written to Rechenberg in April and asked him where the document was, but *before* he wrote to Luise Funk's heir Horst Walter in January 1972 to ask him where Bormann's notes were.[61] Genoud thus offered Trevor-Roper to publish the German text before he had it. Are we supposed to believe this version of events simply because documents seem to corroborate it? Are not these letters definite proof that there actually was an authentic text behind *The Testament* text? Well, it might seem that way, but let us remember that Genoud shared his correspondence with Baumgarten and Trevor-Roper. Thus, it could well be that he shared letters intended to strengthen his and Rechenberg's scam. Rechenberg was, after all, in on the lies and would no doubt have played along. Something that points to this interpretation being true is the fact that Horst Walter's reply to Genoud's letter was apparently *not* shared with them.

Astonishingly, Baumgarten was at this stage apparently not the least suspicious of Genoud, it seems, because he told Trevor-Roper that he was pretty angry at the IfZ that kept distrusting Genoud. It seemed to Baumgarten as if the IfZ could have published this document in German years ago "had they only been . . . a little less impatience with certain puzzling idiosyncrasies and mystifications" on the part of Genoud. By this point, too, Baumgarten had actually re-translated the English text into German and Genoud had even suggested to him that they should have this version published. Baumgarten did not think this was a good idea, however. It would be "a thankless task", as he put it, firstly because Genoud himself did not think that this translation reminded him of Hitler's way of talking, and secondly because Albert Speer, who had apparently been offered the chance to read this re-translation, had said that it was "far beyond" Hitler's way of thinking. This suggested to Baumgarten that he would need to work together with "a fullfledged philologist" if his "private working-paper retranslation should ever be transformed into a public edition." Baumgarten did not feel competent to do this.[62]

Here, then, Baumgarten was admitting to having forged a German version of an English translation of a text that no one had seen and to try and pass it off as authentic in a publication. Unfortunately, we do not have access to Baumgarten's re-translation so we cannot evaluate in what way, or if at all, it differed from the version eventually published. But one can also wonder why Genoud let Baumgarten go through the trouble of doing this when Genoud evidently had the text that later became *Hitlers politisches Testament* all along; the fact that Jäckel's quote from it agrees with this published text proves this. Why Genoud would want to publish a re-translation when he evidently had a text already, as proven by the citations in *Der Spiegel* and *Hitlers Weltanschauung*, is unclear.

Naturally it turned out that Genoud was lying about this part of the story as well. Baumgarten later (unclear exactly when) visited Horst Walter and talked to him about this matter. However, instead of confirming Genoud's and Rechenberg's version of events, the man instead said that he had never seen the text in question and Funk had never spoken to him about any such document.[63] This is yet another strong indication that there never was any photocopy of such a text. Now Genoud and Rechenberg changed their story. According to Baumgarten, they now claimed that the authenticity of the photocopy had been validated by a colleague of Trevor-Roper's from Oxford who had accompanied him to Paris in November 1958. The photocopy had allegedly been returned to Genoud and Rechenberg on the day of the meeting. This was, however, also brazen lies and Trevor-Roper denied all of this.[64] Clearly, Genoud and Rechenberg appear to have been compulsive liars.

Amazingly, Genoud and Rechenberg now told Baumgarten that Funk himself had said that he had never seen the content of the "package" Hitler gave him for safekeeping and which he had allegedly ordered Rechenberg to burn without opening it in 1946 and that Funk by 1958 was of the opinion that "it could very well have been a non-authentic transcript or some sort of summary." Yet they claimed to have returned the photocopy to Funk after the meeting in Paris in 1958 and they also said that Funk had then had Lammers and Arthur Axmann (the leader of *Hitler-Jugend* 1940–1945) assure that they recognized their master's voice in the document.[65] Why would Genoud and Rechenberg make such a startling admission to Baumgarten? Well, the most likely reason seems to be that they were creating a story that made it possible for them to insist that the document was genuine no matter what anyone said. After all, if Funk did not see the content of the package, he could not have told Walter about it. Many questions remain though. They had previously said that Funk had been displeased when he found out that Rechenberg had made a copy of the document, which implies that Funk *did* know what was in the package. How could Funk say that it was probably a non-authentic transcript if he had never seen the content of the package? Had Genoud and Rechenberg shown Funk a transcript of a text that they claimed were Bormann's notes of Hitler's words and gotten the response that it could be a forgery? Also, Funk cannot have shown the document to Lammers and Axmann since 1) it contradicts the claim that Funk never saw the text and 2) it is obvious from Lammers's letter to Genoud from March 1959 that he had not seen this text before. Furthermore, Funk would not authenticate a text he never saw and could not have been planning to publish it.

Jäckel wrote to Trevor-Roper in August 1972 that his "efforts to obtain the original text of the Bormann notes from Mr. Genoud are still disheartening and have so far led to nothing but enormous confusion."[66] Baumgarten's rather odd attitude towards source criticism is apparent in a letter to Trevor-Roper from June the same year where he writes that a publication in German based on the original text would not really add anything to the content of the French and English editions, since what Hitler thought on these subjects "is sufficiently clear and authentic in these two translations." Nonetheless, the lack of such a German version was "annoying" (*ärgerlich*). He then went on to complain that some of the English formulations did not sound like Hitler at all.[67]

Baumgarten's statement is also a bit odd considering that the English (and French) text appears to be a very direct translation of the German in *Hitlers politisches Testament*, or the other way around, so if the formulations did not at all sound like Hitler in English, how come it sounded exactly like Hitler in German? It makes no sense at all. Moreover, how can these versions agree so well unless they were based on the same text? It seems impossible. It seems as if only one of two explanations is plausible: 1) either the German text had been translated from the French (from which the English also had been translated, as we shall see) or 2) the French and English editions had been translated from a German text that Genoud had produced before 1959 (and kept in his possession although lying about this fact).

A few months later, Genoud told Baumgarten that Trevor-Roper had agreed, no less, to publish the German text together with Genoud and Baumgarten, and the latter even visited Trevor-Roper regarding this matter in Oxford on 15 May 1972. Baumgarten said he had his doubts about how correct Genoud's claim was because he had talked to Jäckel who had also agreed with Genoud to publish the German text. It looked to Trevor-Roper as if Genoud "chose to forget this agreement with Jäckel" when courting Trevor-Roper and Baumgarten on the same matter.[68] Even if Baumgarten had his doubts initially, Genoud seems to have charmed him into trusting him more or less completely during 1973. In late July that year Baumgarten met with Genoud in Freiburg, incidentally the same city where Genoud as a teenager had met Hitler in 1932 and become a loyal "convert." After this meeting Baumgarten wrote that his impression was: "This man is fundamentally <u>honest</u> – and he is a very <u>friendly</u> person, besides." Genoud had told him that although his doubts about the authenticity of *The Testament* text "objectively" were very precise and exact, Baumgarten would be much better off, subjectively speaking, to simply grant Genoud his complete trust. Since they last met, said Genoud, he had examined his conscience and reached the conclusion that his translation in *Le testament politique* "was only in 'good French'" but in all other aspects "strictly true to the text though." No changes to content or structure had been made, Genoud promised. Therefore, there could be no talk about a "Genoud version" added to the Bormann version. Genoud now seemed to be ready to retract his veto "against a complete German re-translation."[69] Here Baumgarten was openly telling Trevor-Roper that the German edition would be a re-translation into German from the French translation of a purportedly authentic original text that no longer existed. However, due to the fact that the German quotes in *Der Spiegel* agree *ad verbatim* with the text as published as *Hitlers politisches Testament* we know that Genoud had already retranslated the French text a year after the publication of *The Testament* at the latest.

Trevor-Roper re-discovers that *The Testament* was translated from the French

On 13 March 1973 Baumgarten wrote a long letter to Trevor-Roper and told him that Rechenberg had said that the manuscript was full of spelling errors, and that "Heim concludes that Bormann wrote each chapter <u>himself</u> in [sic] the machine – probably the same night, since Hitler often began the next chapter the following day."[70] Note that there is no evidence that Bormann's other notes were full of spelling errors. Moreover, Heim had never seen the original text, so he was in no

position to make statements about this matter. Baumgarten also wrote that Rechenberg had told him that:

> the photocopies were <u>technically very bad:</u> [with] black spots. Did Genoud
> tell you that he had made meaningful additions in his translation? He assured
> me that the list of content at the head of each chapter were written by him
> (Genoud).[71]

This shows that Genoud had admitted that he had manipulated his manuscript.
Trevor-Roper of course never mentioned any of this to his readers. Baumgarten
also stated, among else, that it seemed to him as if the English translation at times
diverged from the French edition. Stevens appeared to have "translated mostly from
the French", he wrote, because it is extremely similar" (*weil ungemein ähnlich*) but
that he had used the German original text where Genoud's translation had been
too free. "That is how it looks at least."[72] Trevor-Roper replied that he could not
remember Genoud having said anything about adding matters to the text and that
the photocopies he had been shown "were perfectly readable."[73] This is conclusive
proof of the fact that Genoud had tampered with the texts and that if Trevor-Roper
actually saw a photocopy at all, it was not the same text that was later published.

The "list of content" mentioned here referred to the short introductions that
summarize the content in every note. These introductions, however, are not identical between all three versions. The English is entirely based on the French edition,
and we know this because these summaries are often different in *Hitlers politisches
Testament*. A great example of this difference is the introduction to note No. 5
dated 13 February 1945 where almost nothing is the same in the German version.
Genoud obviously decided to sit down and write new introductions to his text. For
example, one sentence in the English edition says: "The futility of racial hatred"
which corresponds well to the French "Against the hatred of races."[74] In the German version, however, we find: "Race pride as precondition for agreement with
other great races."[75] It is not that any of these describe the content in a bad manner;
it is just that they describe different aspects of what is being said in the text.

All of this awoke Trevor-Roper's dormant critical thinking. Five days later
he wrote back telling Baumgarten about his realization that *The Testament* was
not based on the German original but on the French translation, thus presenting
Baumgarten's conclusion as his own. Not only had they kept the German text from
Baumgarten, Trevor-Roper said:

> I now suspect that they concealed it even from Colonel Stevens. You write
> that you have the impression ('dass Herr Stevens meist aus dem Franzosis-
> chen übersetzt hat (weil ungemein ähnlich)' and that he has only resorted to
> the German text where Genoud's French version was too free. This implies
> that Stevens had at his disposal <u>both</u> a French <u>and</u> a German text.[76]

Trevor-Roper then, rhetorically it seems, states that he could not see why Stevens would use the French version since he knew German perfectly. He then

mentioned an occasion when he, while working on the new edition of *Table Talk* in 1973 discovered a mistake that proved to him that Stevens had indeed used Genoud's French edition for his translation. Stevens's mistake only made sense if he had used Genoud.

> In other words, I now think that Genoud supplied to Stevens <u>not</u> the German original but his own French version of 'T.T.1' [Table Talk I, M.N.]; and he may easily have done the same with 'T.T.2' [*The testament*, M.N.].[77]

It was unfortunate that Stevens had since died, wrote Trevor-Roper, so that one could not ask him about it.[78] But Trevor-Roper did not need to consult Stevens in order to find this out. He would only have had to consult his own correspondence with Stevens and Genoud from that period because there it was always made perfectly clear that Stevens translated the text from the French.

Trevor-Roper then listed three things that seemed to prove authenticity, namely: 1) Bormann's signature on each page, 2) Genoud's and Rechenberg's accounts of its origin, and 3) its own internal evidence. However, Trevor-Roper said:

> On these bases, I do not regard (1) and (2) as strong. Bormann's signature could easily be forged, and Genoud and Rechenberg are not trustworthy witnesses.[79]

Thus, in private Trevor-Roper himself considered the signature on the documents, the existence of which are dubious, not to be a good proof of authenticity. He also considered Genoud and Rechenberg to be unreliable. Instead it was the internal evidence, and the fact that Trevor-Roper could not see why Genoud would have an interest in forging a Hitler document, that spoke mostly for authenticity.[80] That is indeed not a very strong, or even decent, case for authenticity.

Baumgarten planned on censoring Trevor-Roper's judgement in the introduction to his planned book. He asked Trevor-Roper if he could replace his rather damaging words with something different, such as with the phrase: "I do not regard (1) and (2) as unassailable by distrustful critics." Baumgarten wrote by hand in the margin of the proof sent to Trevor-Roper:

> may I change your wording in this manner – instead of saying: "Bormann's signature could easily be forged, and Genoud and Rechenberg <u>are not trustworthy</u> witnesses" [You wrote this in <u>private</u> and would perhaps not like to see it "put in print" – (see your letter of 18. March!)[81] [Underlined in original.]

By this addendum Baumgarten showed that he understood exactly what harm these words could do to Trevor-Roper and *Table Talk* and he, one must say, decided to conspire together with Trevor-Roper against their readers in order to hide this information from the public.

So, what did Trevor-Roper say about Baumgarten's suggestion? Did he take the bait and agree to falsifying his own *true* judgement regarding the text and its authenticity? Yes, indeed he did. Trevor-Roper replied, referring explicitly to the passage quoted earlier, that he would "prefer the prudently amended passage" of his letter to read: "'On these bases, (1) and (2) are clearly not unassailable', and stop there."[82] But the essence of this change was the same – it concealed Trevor-Roper's doubts about the texts authenticity from the readers. When Baumgarten some years later quoted this letter to the participants of an IfZ seminar, he in fact included Trevor-Roper's true judgement, but this was of course to a much smaller and specialized audience than the planned book was meant for.[83]

Trevor-Roper, however, vacillated with regard to his source-critical conclusions about the text. He clearly wanted the text to be authentic and so he decided to turn a blind eye to the many and clear indications of fraud. He told Baumgarten that he might be the only person except Genoud and Rechenberg who could confirm that a German text actually had existed at one point because he had seen:

> a photocopy of it. It had to be shown to me, for I would not have accepted its authenticity otherwise. It may, of course, even so, be a forgery; and it could be that Genoud's reluctance to reveal it spring from a fear of exposure. On the other hand, he has been equally reluctant to reveal his German text of 'T.T.1' and we know that T.T.1 is perfectly genuine; and he has refused to publish the German text of the Bormann letters, whose authenticity, is unquestioned. Therefore it seems that we must look elsewhere for the cause of his sensitivity.[84]

Trevor-Roper chose to accept the claim of authenticity based on very flimsy evidence. Trevor-Roper thought that Genoud was afraid to lose control over the material and its publication rights and the economic profits that sprang from it. According to Trevor-Roper, the court proceedings had shown that anyone was allowed to publish Hitler's writings if they were in possession of them, "without troubling about legal copyright. On the other hand, translations into other languages were protected by copyright." That was why Genoud only allowed publication of translations, he said. That was the only way he could retain control over his material. Trevor-Roper was confident that this was the reason from his many conversations with Genoud who was "terrified of allowing his German texts to be seen." He had thus far not allowed anyone to see the texts of either the table talks, the testament, or the Bormann letters unless there was an absolute need. Genoud's fear had nothing to do with the authenticity of his material, concluded Trevor-Roper in his letter.[85]

But this made no sense either. The copyright question had no bearing on the issue of why Genoud and Rechenberg had never shown the German text to anyone. Showing it to the translator could not be considered a security risk. The argument that anyone in possession of a Hitler document could publish it without bothering about copyright also contradicted what Genoud had said on so many other occasions, namely that he could not publish the text until the copyright holders' claims had been secured. Moreover, the final publication of *Hitlers politisches Testament* in

1981 demonstrates that this argument was untrue since the risk of losing control of the text was not smaller then than it had been before.

Continuing doubts and the exposure of more lies

In an undated note recording a telephone conversation between Trevor-Roper and Baumgarten on 7 July 1974 Trevor-Roper states that Baumgarten now doubted Genoud's story of how he had obtained the testament text and that he thought that the story told by Genoud and Rechenberg was "a falsification designed (presumably) to enable them to publish the document without producing the original." Nonetheless, Baumgarten still thought that the text was genuine and that Genoud in fact had the original and that he had obtained it at the same time as the table talk manuscript, i.e. "from Frau Bormann in Merano, by purchase, and that he cannot publish the original, lest he be sued by Bormann's heirs from infraction of their copyright." To his credit, Trevor-Roper was not entirely convinced by this argument.[86] All of this was Baumgarten's own fantasy. How Baumgarten could consider the text as authentic even though he thought Genoud and Rechneberg had lied about how they got it is a conundrum, and why they would not want to produce the original if they had one is also unclear.

Baumgarten's research into the story told by Funk/Rechenberg/Genoud had resulted in important findings. He told Trevor-Roper in October 1974 that a new book about Rudolf Heß, written by an American Spandau prison guard, spoke about Funk having been given the assignment to transport the gold to the southern borders of Germany and that he had had the gold buried there in April 1945.[87] Baumgarten did not mention the title of the book, but it must be the book *Heß* written by the Eugene K. Bird (the first American guard in Spandau and later director of the prison). It had been published in German in 1974, and in one paragraph it stated that Funk had been given the mission in early 1945 to transport more than 100 tonnes of gold to Thuringia, a part of which was captured by American troops on 8 April (in reality it was found already the day before, M.N.). It then says that the rest of the gold reserve (consisting of 728 gold bars weighing 25 kilograms each, and over a billion *Reichsmark* worth of bank notes as well as other valuables and jewels) was shipped to Bavaria in "Mitte April" where it was buried near Walchensee as part of an agreement between Funk and Colonel (*Oberst*) Franz Wilhelm Pfeiffer, who was the head of the Mountain Ranger School (*Gebirgsjäger-schule*) in Mittelwald.[88]

But was this really true? Let us try and sort out what actually happened. Funk had visited Goebbels on 27 January asking if he, considering the military situation, "at least should evacuate the most important parts of the Reichsbank of Berlin." To Goebbels this was a very bad idea that could only start a series of nefarious rumours, and the military situation was not as bad as to justify such an evacuation. "I categorically rejected this", he wrote. Just over a week later, however, Goebbels mentions in his diary on 7 February 1945 that discussions were held between himself, Bormann, and Lammers regarding the evacuation of "the most important executives and management materials from Berlin . . ., to Thuringia." According to Goebbels only the 120 or so "forces" (*Kräfte*) and "the most necessary management documents" should be evacuated. Funk was mentioned in connection with this, the implication being that while the *Reichsminister* (Funk was not mentioned by name, only by title) should oversee this evacuation, he should of course remain in Berlin personally. Every evacuation of persons and material had to be cleared by the chief of the Reich Chancellery, Lammers, and every evacuation that had not received such prior authorization was to be regarded as desertion and punished by death.[89]

Exactly at what point Funk had gone against Goebbels's expressed orders and transported the gold reserve from Berlin is not known; the time window from 27 January to 7 April is quite large. Now, what about the information in Bird's book to the effect that a part of the gold reserve had been evacuated out of Thuringia in mid-April. Even on the face of it, this seem absurd. The Americans had occupied the area by then, so how could the Nazis transport anything out of there? On 9 April 1945, Goebbels stated something in his diary (this is in fact the last entry ever dictated by Goebbels) that proved that it could not be true that Funk had been assigned a mission by Hitler to transport the Nazi gold reserve from Bad Gastein to Thuringia on 17 April 1945. Goebbels's diary showed that the gold reserve, which had already been hidden in Thuringia for some time by then, had fallen into American hands, and Goebbels blamed Funk for having transported the gold (and art treasures) against Goebbels's express protests to Thuringia from Berlin in the first place.[90] Goebbels berated Funk for having let himself been convinced by his advisors to ship the gold reserve and art treasures to Thuringia from Berlin, and adds that if he had been the Führer, then he "would have known what to do next", obviously referring to having Funk executed, but added that he assumed "that those responsible are not held accountable in any way." In Germany it was now possible to do whatever one wanted, because there was no one who had the strength to punish such "crimes" anymore, he complained.[91] Yet even though this story had been proven false by 1974 at the latest, this fiction was still included as fact in Trevor-Roper's introduction in *Hitlers politisches Testament*.[92] In Goebbels's diary it says:

> Now, with a reprehensible disregard of duty, they have let the most valuable possessions of the German people fall into the hands of the enemy. I learn from enquiries with the national railways that some lax measures have been taken to transport the gold and art treasures from Thuringia to Berlin, but this has been prevented by the Easter days. One could rip all one's hair out if one imagines that the national railways celebrate Easter while *all our gold stock is seized by the enemy*.[93] [Italics added.]

This entry proves that the entire gold reserve had been captured. Which means that there was nothing left for Funk or anyone else to transport to, and bury in, Bavaria.

The gold reserves were thus found in a salt mine in Merkers on 7 April by the 90th Infantry Division of the US 3rd Army, and the Paris edition of the newspaper *The Stars & Stripes* wrote about the find on April 9, the same day that Goebbels made his diary entry (which means he heard about it on 8 April).[94] The timeline thus does not fit the Funk story either. Neither Genoud nor Baumgarten, nor Trevor-Roper, seem to have been aware of these facts at that point, however. Perhaps Funk made this assertion up unbeknownst to Rechenberg and Genoud. But then again, perhaps Funk never made such an assertion at all; perhaps Genoud and Rechenberg simply made the whole thing up. This, in and by itself, is enough to prove that Genoud was lying again.

But the most convincing evidence against the Funk story comes from the witnesses that Baumgarten interviewed. No fewer than four people – Christa Schroeder, Admiral von Puttkamer, Otto Günsche, and Colonel von Below – all confirmed that Funk had been nowhere near the bunker in Berlin either in March or April 1945. According to Schroeder and Günsche, Hitler furthermore did not trust Funk enough to endow him with such an important document, if it had in fact existed.[95] The question for Baumgarten was then: *how* did Funk come to possess the sealed package with the 18 notes ostensibly taken down in the bunker in Berlin? Could he have gotten it from Bormann directly, he asked? Was Hitler oblivious to Funk laying his hands on it? Or could it be that Funk received the manuscript from Hitler somewhere outside the bunker on April 17, for instance, in Hitler's private apartment? Baumgarten noted in connection with the last question that the notes dated in February 1945 – if in fact they did take place at all, he added – had to have been recordings of utterances that were made outside the bunker in any case. There were, in his view, three possible such locations.[96] Baumgarten was clearly desperate to find a way to confirm his belief that the notes were authentic.

The answers to these questions were not at all unimportant, said Baumgarten, but were of central importance for the evaluation of the trustworthiness of these 18 notes. Baumgarten wrote:

> The answers [. . .] are of weight f i r s t and f o r e m o s t for a correct assessment of the nature and extent of Hitler's authorship of the 18 "Hitler-Bormann notes". Did Hitler himself compose them in their logical style? Or did Bormann pull them together retrospectively from back and forth wandering, only casual ruminations of Hitler during situation meetings and other occasions, thematically arranged and in addition to "speeches" composed in dictation form? Much depends on this either/or for the assessment of the "spiritual power" of the defeated Hitler in February and April 2, 1945. If Hitler <u>personally</u> gave the order to Funk, it is probable that he was also personally involved in the composition of the notes in a directed and progressive manner from point to point as the author and ultimate arbiter of his affairs.[97] [Emphasis in original.]

Schroeder thought that the notes might have been a summary of statements written down by Bormann at some point and that Bormann absolutely was in a position "to reproduce entire passages of Hitler literally." But, she added, "the statements may also have been made by other knowledgeable people."[98] Another of Hitler's secretaries, Gerda Christian, had been presented with a photocopy of one of the pages by Genoud (it is unclear if she meant a photocopy of the original or of Genoud's transcript), and she considered it "not . . . authentic." It could perhaps be a summary of utterances, she stated in a letter to Schroeder in 1975, but she was totally convinced that Hitler would never have dictated anything like this to Bormann. Hitler was totally against putting any of his way of thinking on paper, according to Christian, who claimed that Hitler once, as a response to a suggestion that she should write his words down using stenography, stated " 'no, then I would no longer speak so freely.'"[99] We should, when pondering these issues, be aware of the fact there is indeed no solid evidence that Funk ever possessed the photocopies in question.

Let us remember that Hitler ordered all his personal papers both in Berlin and in Berchtesgaden destroyed so that nothing would remain. This task was given to his personal adjutant Julius Schaub who saw to it that all of the records in Hitler's safes were burnt.[100] Everything that Genoud and Rechenberg had said about Funk being given documents to preserve would go directly against Hitler's later order to destroy all his personal papers. It is thus not likely to be true. But was not Hitler's last will and testament from 29 April 1945 taken out of Berlin in the final days of the war? Yes, that is true. However, that document was of a completely different kind than the notes discussed in this chapter. The reason for why Hitler's real political testament was smuggled out of Berlin was a simple and instrumental one: it contained Hitler's orders regarding who was to assume power after his suicide.

Despite all of this, in January 1975 Baumgarten again wrote Trevor-Roper to tell him the great news that he had managed to get his hands on "the original text" (*den Urtext*) of Hitler's *Bunkergespräche*. He included it in his letter, but it is unfortunately not present in Trevor-Roper's archive. However, it was of course not really the original text, but a typed copy of a typed copy of a supposed photocopy, as Baumgarten put it. Nonetheless, Baumgarten was still certain that the text was genuine. He also asked Trevor-Roper if he remembered seeing the words "utterances by the Führer" on the top of every page.[101] Once again, Baumgarten, based on Genoud and Rechenberg, presented a different version of how the text had been produced. The text had been produced for Baumgarten by Genoud shortly before this point in time, i.e. in 1974/75, based on a transcript made by Funk himself (!) of the photocopy of poor quality made by Rechenberg in 1946. Funk had in fact made no fewer than *two* transcripts of the document, Baumgarten said and both Lammers and Axmann had validated the content. He noted that he had not been able to compare this text to Funk's transcript of the photocopy.[102]

Trevor-Roper asked no critical questions. Instead, he simply congratulated Baumgarten on his "diplomacy and perseverance" and said that he never really believed that Baumgarten would succeed in "extracting from Genoud the original German text of that document." It was "a miracle", according to Trevor-Roper, "and a very useful miracle too, enabling you to settle the vexed problem of authenticity." Exactly how this issue could be settled by this transcript of a transcript of an alleged photocopy Trevor-Roper did not say. As a reply to Baumgarten's question Trevor-Roper stated that he could not recall seeing these words on top of every page. He added that his natural reaction "is to feel that, if I had seen it, I would have positively remembered it." He did remember seeing Bormann's signature on each page, but he could not say that the words listed by Baumgarten were there. On the other hand, he could say that they were not there either.[103] Trevor-Roper clearly did not remember the content of what he had allegedly seen.

More indications of fraud: analysis from the internal evidence

I have spent a lot of time criticizing Trevor-Roper and Baumgarten for having relied on so-called internal evidence when evaluating their source, and I could therefore perhaps justifiably be criticized for doing the same in an effort to show why *The Testament* is very likely a forgery. However, what I am doing in this part is actually not a source-critical fallacy, and I will explain why. While it must be concluded that an analysis of the internal evidence of a text alone is not a reliable method to establish whether a text really is what it claims to be, we can use independent sources to evaluate whether the statements in the text that we are analysing are likely to be authentic or not, and therefore if the document itself is likely to be genuine. The point is that we can never determine if a text is genuine by simply looking at content because a good forgery is by definition good enough to fool even the best-trained experts by imitating the style of the original. Historians must be able to corroborate authenticity by other means, i.e. by 1) investigating the original text (this includes forensic analyses of the paper, ink, and so on), 2) analysing the context (including the purported history of the document and all that we already know about the author from other sources), and 3) using independent evidence that supports authenticity. In this case we do not have access to any originals and are then unfortunately wholly dependent upon the independent evidence. The independent evidence must then be compared to the text we want to authenticate, and *only* then can reference to the internal evidence be valid methodologically. While content that contradicts everything we know about an author's views *can* be used (under the right circumstances – there are possible exceptions obviously) to invalidate a text, we *cannot* use content that *corresponds* to an author's known views to validate it.[104] Once again, this is because that is exactly what we should expect also of even a half-decent forgery.

There are actually many more things that indicate that *The Testament* was in some way or another forged. Baumgarten noted in October 1974 that the dates on the last two entries (actually it was the three last entries because there are two notes dated 26 February, M.N.), 26 February and 2 April 1945 (with no entries at all in March), corresponded exactly with the dating of Bormann's letters to his wife as published in *The Bormann Letters*. Those, too, were dated 26 February, then nothing in March, and finally one dated 2 April. This could of course be a coincidence, said Baumgarten, but it seemed unlikely. He wrote:

> For example, it now appears that Genoud, in his French translation, has not only added the preceding summary of the contents to the chapters, but also the dating could have been invented, at least in part, by him.[105]

But that is not all. It turns out that of the 18 notes in *Hitlers politisches Testament* 13 of them have corresponding dates in *The Bormann Letters*, and 3 of these 13 are dated on the same day (note that there are only 14 dates in total, since several of the 18 notes have the same date).[106] Baumgarten does not mention this fact at all. It may be of considerable importance that Genoud in fact addresses the dating and the fact that there are no notes dated in March (which is also the case in *The Bormann Letters*), in his preface in *Le testament politique*. He writes:

> Why do these stop on February 26? Why this thirty-five-day interruption between the seventeenth and eighteenth? Why, after this long silence, this one and only note dated April 2 – and then nothing?[107]

It is obvious that the publisher's introduction to *Hitler politisches Testament* for a large part is based upon this introduction by Genoud. Several points included in Genoud's French introduction, including the part about the dating, appears, translated word for word into German, in the German edition.[108]

To me, however, this seems like questions that are completely unnecessary to ask with regard to the notes themselves. Genoud is for some reason drawing attention to something that really needs no explaining. So, what if there are long breaks? There are even longer ones in *Bormann-Vermerke*, but Genoud never bothered to ask these types of questions about them. An erratic record is actually to be expected, considering not least that the documents had survived through the fog of war. Asking why something starts and ends on a certain date is totally meaningless unless one is referring to another case with the same interruptions. Only *then* do they become noteworthy and demand an explanation. It seems as if Genoud is, perhaps inadvertently, referring to *The Bormann Letters* and drawing attention to his bluff – as if he was aware that this coincidence called for an explanation – and wished to forestall critical questions.

Trevor-Roper's official evaluation of this absurd story was that there could be no doubt about the documents' authenticity and even claimed to have seen Bormann's signature at the bottom of each page (as we shall see, there are good reasons to doubt that claim): "their history, their content and Bormann's own familiar signature attest it at every point."[109] The same evaluation was included in the introduction to the German edition in 1981.[110] Trevor-Roper never mentions the many doubts about the authenticity that he had nevertheless had over the years, or many of the other problems with the text. From the looks of it, then, Genoud (or perhaps Rechenberg) may have used the dates of the Bormann letters as a model when ascribing dates to at least the last two entries in *The Testament* text, and possibly all of the notes.[111]

There are indeed certain things in the notes themselves that indicate forgery. In note No. 16, dated 26 February, Hitler is supposed to have said:

> Churchill did not appreciate the generosity and chivalry that I have proved to England a hundred times by avoiding the extreme. I deliberately spared the fleeing Britons at Dunkirk.[112]

This seems to be confirmed by Christa Schroeder who also claims that Hitler spared the British on purpose and that he once said to her that the reason he let the British get away was: "Because I wanted to save human lives."[113] This seems to corroborate authenticity. However, it cannot be ruled out that Schroeder did not get her idea from reading the text later published as *Hitlers poilitisches Testament*. We know for a fact that Baumgarten gave this text to her in 1975. Therefore, we cannot trust her as a source regarding Hitler's intentions at Dunkirk. This rather seems to be part and parcel of Schroeder's effort to defend, and in a sense rehabilitate, Hitler, and she also claims that she was sure that he had suffered in his soul from the bombing of Britain. Moreover, the claim itself is absolute nonsense.[114]

Karl-Heinz Frieser brings this hypothesis up in his *Blixtkrieg-Legende*, and even quotes *Hitlers politisches Testament* as being Hitler's words taken down in a protocol, although he states that out of all of the suggested explanations none has caused so much irritation as this one.[115] According to Volker Ullrich, who cites Schroeder's version, there was no truth in this statement whatsoever.[116] Hitler referred to Dunkirk as a major victory, and as the annihilation of the British Expeditionary Forces (BEF) on 5 June.[117] Longerich also shows that Hitler's so-called "peace offer" towards Britain in his speech to the *Reichstag* on 19 July 1940 was intended to give the British one last chance at accepting peace, and thereby also to spare the empire. Preparations for an invasion of the British Isles, although only as a last resort, had already been under way for some time.[118] However, the fact that Hitler did not, although he was trying to come off as peaceable towards the British, bring up Dunkirk as an example of when he showed leniency against British forces in his 19 July speech (nor did he do so in his 4 September speech) makes it very unlikely that what *Hitlers politisches Testament* relates is true.[119] Rather, it reflects a much later reinterpretation of the events. This is not conclusive proof that the entry is a forgery of course; it could simply be that Bormann is giving the propaganda version of events.

It is easy to see how, in hindsight, people could believe that the famous "halt order" of 24 May 1940 was issued with this in mind. But this is a myth, probably originating with the Chief of Army Group A Gerd von Rundstedt, ex-chief-of-staff when the latter was being interrogated by Lidell Hart after the war.[120] Indeed, Rundstedt himself offered this explanation too shortly after the war.[121] Firstly, the halt order only applied to the tank divisions. This is absolutely crucial for the evaluation of this statement. Instead, it was the *Luftwaffe* that was supposed to finish off the encircled British forces.[122] Göring telephoned Hitler on the 23rd arguing that it should be the ideologically convinced *Luftwaffe*, and not the conservative *Wehrmacht*, that dealt the final blow to the British. Secondly, this had coincided with a decision by Rundstedt to issue a preliminary halt order to Kleist's and Hoth's Panzers the night of the 23rd in order to keep the German forces concentrated. Thus, it was ultimately Rundstedt, and not Hitler, who had made this decision. When Hitler then visited Rundstedt's HQ on the morning of the 24th he simply found himself agreeing to *fait accompli*. Only thereafter was Hitler's halt order sent, which made Rundstedt's preliminary order permanent. If anyone deserves to be blamed for the halt order and the escape of the BEF at Dunkirk, it is Rundstedt. But in reality, it was not a question of simply letting the British off the hook. The *Luftwaffe* did its best to kill as many British soldiers, and sink as many ships, as they could, and the German infantry, too, made sure that the British had their hands full inside the encirclement.[123] It has been noted that while the *Luftwaffe* had had colossal successes in the early stages of the campaign, it had also suffered enormous losses. In reality, the *Luftwaffe* was in great need of a pause itself in order to regain strength. No fewer than 1005 aircraft had been lost, and Karl-Heinz Frieser argues that even though Göring may have influenced Hitler's decision to agree to halt the tanks, it is likely that this only played a minor role.[124]

Thirdly, the idea that Hitler wanted to save the BEF is also amply contradicted by the order issued by Hitler on 24 May, which said that the next goal was to destroy the encircled British and French forces and that it was the task of the *Luftwaffe* to do this. The *Luftwaffe* was to make sure that they did not escape to England. The term "annihilation" (*Vernichtung*) of the enemy forces is all over the *Weisung* No. 13.[125] It is true that most of the generals in the *Oberkommando des Heeres* (OKH) did not understand the reason behind the halting of the attack. They wanted to press on to the coast and finish off the Allied forces. But Hitler, who supported Rundstedt (to whom he had left the final decision regarding the halt) and Göring, disagreed. The decision perhaps suited Hitler also for another reason, namely that it proved a point to the OKH, not least to the critical Halder and Brauchitsch, that *he*, and nobody else, was the ultimate authority also on military matters.[126]

The *Wehrmacht* liaison officer at FHQ, General Gerhard Engel, noted on the 23rd that Göring had suggested the "annihilation of the British in Northern France", and while the army people in the FHQ were extremely upset by this, Engel reports Hitler as "enthusiastic" (*begeistert*). Hitler was stressing the ideological dependability of the *Luftwaffe* as opposed to that of the army. By the 27th Göring was claiming great success for the *Luftwaffe*'s endeavour.[127] In reality, the *Luftwaffe*'s effort was rendered rather inefficient. This was, in part, due to bad weather, partly by the Stukas bombs burying themselves too deep in the sand before exploding (thus causing much less damage), and partly because of the new British fighter plane Spitfire that plucked German fighters and bombers out of the sky with a high degree of efficiency.[128]

Hitler had actually intervened and ordered a halt on 17 May, too. At that point Hitler had been nervous about the security of the German southern flank, ranting to his generals that they were jeopardizing the whole operation. Peter Longerich ascribes both these halt orders to Hitler's wish to make a "power demonstration towards the Army leadership."[129] Warlimont explained Hitler's angst about the tank divisions had to do with his experiences during the First World War from which he had taken the idea that tanks could not be safely operated in marshy terrain in Flanders.[130] This is considered Hitler's "true" motive for supporting Rundstedt's halt order in *Blitzkrieg-Legende*. The OKH had in fact transferred Rundstedt to another part of the front but had done so without Hitler's knowledge. When Hitler discovered this when he arrived at the front on 24 May, he immediately declared the OKH decision null and void. Hitler thus supported Rundstedt mainly because he could not stand that the OKH had tried to circumvent him. An example had to be made, and Hitler made sure to put the OKH in its place.[131] After two days, once it had become obvious that the evacuation was actually very successful, Hitler realized that he had made a mistake and ordered a full onslaught on Dunkirk.[132] The same point is made by Warlimont.[133]

Furthermore, the *Haltbefehl* saved not only a considerable number of British troops but also many French (and other) troops. Under constant bombardment from the *Luftwaffe* the evacuation managed to extract no fewer than 198,315 British and 139,911 Allied (of which most were French) soldiers from Dunkirk. Julian Jackson, in his *The Fall of France*, actually refers to the note in *The Testament*, although he rejects the notion of it being seriously meant by Hitler. However, of course, he does not question the authenticity of the note itself.[134] So did Hitler wish to do the French a favour, too, by letting nearly 140,000 French troops cross the English Channel? That is indeed very doubtful. For this utterance to be authentic to Hitler, it must either be a glaring example of self-deception or a deliberate lie designed to fool the world. Even though Hitler was not a stranger to self-deception, in this case it seems very unlikely to be the explanation for the counterfactual statement in this source.

One of the few Hitler historians who seems to have lent this idea some credence is John Toland. He not only treats *The Testament* as authentic (which most other historians have also done), writing that Hitler "told Bormann that he had purposefully spared the English", but he also refers to two other instances when Hitler supposedly said things to the same effect, namely to his "naval adjutant", i.e. Karl-Jesko von Puttkamer, and to Hans Linge. However, Toland gives us no good references for these statements so we cannot be expected to take them seriously; in the case of Puttkamer, there is no source at all, and in the case of Linge the reference is to secondary literature. Toland did interview Puttkamer, who he contradictingly says unequivocally stated that any such idea belonged "to the realm of fables." But he then refers to two other persons who gave statements, while in no way corroborating the particular statement under discussion here, to the effect that Hitler liked the English and really did not want to go to war against them. One of these persons is the former French ambassador to Berlin, André François-Poncet (interviewed by Toland in 1971), who, as we should recall, wrote the afterword to *Le testament politique de Hitler*. François-Poncet had thus read this statement and was well familiar with it, and so we could assume that his judgement and memory must have become tainted by this over the years.[135]

The most likely explanation for the entry in *Hitlers politisches Testament* is that someone, Genoud being a likely candidate, who did not know about Rundstedt's role in this matter forged the note in question with the intention of trying to exculpate Hitler *ante facto* and explain away what in fact had been a huge blunder on his part.

Yet another reason for not trusting the version presented in *Hitlers politisches Testament* is that Hitler himself at the time clearly did not see the evacuation at Dunkirk as a benevolent gesture or a victory for Britain. On 6 April 1941, in preparation for the attack on Yugoslavia and Greece, he told his soldiers on the southeastern front to fight the enemy "until the last Englishman has found his 'Dunkirk' in Greece!"[136] This would be an odd way to express a wish to annihilate the enemy if he had deliberately spared the British at Dunkirk. Then, on 4 May, Ribbentrop had a conversation in Berlin with the former U.S. ambassador to Belgium, John Cudahys. According to the minutes from the meeting made by Hitler's personal interpreter Paul Schmidt, Ribbentrop was clearly trying to impress Cudahys by projecting strength and telling the Americans that Germany had won the land war in Europe and Africa and there was nothing that anyone, not even the United States, could do about this fact. It would not serve American interests to intervene in the war, Ribbentrop stated. A landing of American troops in Europe would never succeed; the result was bound to "develop into an American Dunkirk."[137] Not only does this show that Ribbentrop did not consider Dunkirk to be a blessing for the British, but it shows that the whole evacuation was generally interpreted as being a complete disaster at the time.

Ribbentrop's rant did not project strength or confidence at all. This impression is only strengthened by Hitler's statements about the United States made to Japanese Ambassador Hiroshi Oshima just over a month later, on 14 July. Hitler went on and on about how the armaments manufacturing in Europe was much better than that in the United States, and he scorned the American soldiers. As so often Hitler fell back on his experiences during the First World War when interpreting things during this war. He had seen the American soldiers, he said, when they met tired German troops on the Western Front, and the Germans had still incurred huge losses on the Americans. He would let them land on the continent only to destroy them. To make good soldiers it took more than dollars, Hitler assured Oshima. Hitler told him that one could not build a giant effective army in only a few years. An effective war machine took hundreds of years of tradition to build; it took idealism and self-sacrifice on the part of the soldiers. The Americans had none of that, he concluded, and he did not fear the United States either materially or militarily. But even despite all these assurances of the US military's incompetence, he would prefer it if the Americans stayed out of the war in Europe, and he still considered the United States a threat to Germany in Europe and to Japan in East Asia; a threat they had to combine their strengths to destroy.[138]

This view of Americans soldiers was diametrically opposed to the one he had expressed on 14 October 1928 when he stated in a speech that the United States had gathered the best of the European race, which had been emigrating to the new continent for hundreds of years, and he talked about: "The shiny human material that America had sent against us in world war was largely sprouted from German peasant blood." The United States was growing into a racial danger for Europe, Hitler had then stated.[139] Brendan Simms has interpreted Hitler's statements to Oshima in 1941 as him "protesting too much" and, referring to Hitler's statements in 1928, that "his bluster revealed the extent of his anxiety about the looming struggle with the overwhelming might of the United States."[140] It is not clear whether Hitler's views had in fact changed or if he was simply being insincere in either 1928 or 1941. It is likely that Hitler's statements to Oshima contained both truths and falsehoods and exaggerations. While it is likely true that he did not value American armaments and military tradition very highly, he probably did respect the size of the American economy and its armed forces. He clearly would rather not fight the Americans if he could avoid it. Yet he never hesitated to declare war on the United States when Japan had attacked Pearl Harbor only a few months later. Thus, Hitler's attitude towards the United States was ambiguous, but it fit perfectly with the Nazi view of its enemies in general: even though the enemy (such as the Jews) were inferior they could still posed an enormous threat to Germany, such a threat that they had to be physically annihilated. It did not make sense, but then not much in National Socialism ever did.

One more example that gives us yet another reason to be very suspicious about this text is related to something that Hitler is claimed to have said on 13 February 1945: "I have fought the Jews with an open visor" (*Ich habe die Juden mit offenem Visier gekämpft*), conjuring up the image of a knight that fights his enemy (perhaps a mighty dragon) without putting down his visor.[141] This metaphor *mit offenem Visier* does exist in both French and English, but the English and French editions do not use this metaphor at all. The English translation, which was based on the French, stated: "I have always been absolutely fair in my dealings with the Jews." The latter seemed to Baumgarten as too refined a statement for Hitler to make, while he considered the German version coarser and therefore completely authentic.[142] It just so happens that Heim referred to this exact passage in a letter to Werner Jochmann in 1980. In connection with a discussion about the Nazi treatment of the Jews, Heim wrote: "Have you seen Martin Bormann's transcript about A. H.'s utterance on this subject from 13.II.1945?"[143] This should not be interpreted as a confirmation of the authenticity of *Hitlers politisches Testament*, however, because Heim had no knowledge about the history of this text.

Coincidentally, or perhaps not, Hitler used the exact same phrase in *Mein Kampf* although in another context, namely when he wrote about how religious and political matters should not be mixed. Hitler stated that one should not do via a political party what one did not have the courage to do "with an open visor" (*mit offenem Visier*), or out in the open.[144] He also at one point says that the NS ideology should openly confess its intentions to the world: "already on the visor shall we be known."[145] This fact can, of course, not be taken as proof that *Hitlers politisches*

Testament is genuine either, since any forger worth his or her salt would certainly have taken recourse to *Mein Kampf* to find inspiration. The *offenem Visier* metaphor specifically was obviously not used very often by Hitler, and we know this because 1) it occurs only once in *Mein Kampf* and 2) it does not appear anywhere in either *Monologe* or *Tischgespräche* (which it reasonably should do if Hitler had a habit of using it). Nor is it used in Hitler's unpublished second book. How convenient, then, that it should appear again in Hitler's purported last statement to the world. This phrase is like a knot that neatly ties *Mein Kampf* and *Hitlers politisches Testament* together, closing the loop. It is almost as if somebody is trying to convince the reader that it really is Hitler speaking in the text. Yet another reason for us not to trust the note from 13 February 1945 is that Hitler is there portrayed as having stated that the Jews were in fact not a race at all, but only a "spiritual community" (*Gemeinschaft des Geistes*), and that from a genetic point of view there was no such thing as a Jewish race.[146] But this goes against everything we know about Hitler's views on this topic from all other sources. In *Mein Kampf*, for example, Hitler wrote the exact opposite of this, namely that the Jews were only a race and absolutely not a religious or spiritual community. The Jews lacked the necessary idealistic character to form such a spiritual community.[147] Hitler repeated this position in the manuscript to his second book, and in notes dated 5 November 1941 and 27 February 1942 Heim records utterances to this effect too.[148] In short, this statement cannot have been made by Hitler.

There are more factors that point to *Hitlers politisches Testament* being at least partly a forgery. Notes No. XII and XIII are dated 20 and 21 February 1945, respectively, and this coincides with dates on Bormann's letter to his wife.[149] The problem for the proposition that Bormann made these notes in the bunker in Berlin (let us remember that according to the German edition Hitler dictated to Bormann) is that Bormann was not with Hitler during these days. In fact, he was not even in Berlin. We know this because Bormann's diary, which was found by Soviet troops during the last days of the war, places him *en route* to the Party HQ in Munich on the morning of the 20th, and he remained in Munich for the rest of the day. In Munich he met with Helmuth Friedrichs and Gerhard Klopfer – i.e. the two highest-ranking Nazi officials after Bormann in the *Parteikanzlei*; Friedrichs's deputy, Heinrich Walkenhorst; Bormann's adjutant, Wilhelm Zander (incidentally one of the three people who would later smuggle Hitler's real testament out of Berlin); and another official of the party HQ, Dr. Schmidt-Römer.[150]

He was apparently back in the north on the 21st because the diary has him meeting with his personal assistant (*persönliche Referent*) Hans Müller (the same Müller who noted down some of Hitler's utterances in 1943 included in *Monologe*) in *Lager Zossen* (Zossen is a city just south of Berlin and *Lager Zossen* was the HQ of the German General Staff). He was back at Berlin HQ (*Hauptquartier Berlin*) on the 22nd.[151]

This conclusively shows that the dating of the notes in *Hitlers politisches Testament* simply cannot be authentic but *must* be fictional. This, of course, does not prove that the notes themselves are forgeries, but it makes it even more likely considering all the other evidence that points to this conclusion.

Heim thought that the notes from 1945 were authentic, but he did not believe that Hitler had dictated them to Bormann. "In my opinion, these are not dicta-tions by the Führer", he wrote to Karen Kuykendall in October 1975. Instead, he thought that Bormann had done just like he, Heim, had done in 1941–1942, i.e. with the use of supporting words "written down from memory" what he had heard Hitler say.[152] However, he thought, typically considering his Hitler worship, that the utterances were characterized by "astonishing clarity and ravishing vibrancy."[153] Then, he stated the following:

> but he probably read his notes to the Führer, at which time edits could have been made if something was unclear or had to be supplemented. Your guar-antor's [Heim] opinion on M[artin] B[ormann] culminates in the assertion that: *he had no imagination, he never created anything.* . . . To get AH to speak this way in 1945, he [Hitler] needed as a catalyst the knowledge-seeking attentiveness of a counterpart who took the word from his lips, a man who would be able to capture what had been experienced. And that at this deci-sive moment, in AH's eyes, MB was the man of the people to whom he could safely entrust his hitherto unspoken knowledge, is not to be attributed to a coincidence, but had a long history.[154] [Italic phrase in English in original.]

Now, this is certainly interesting. But first note that Heim's judgement about Bor-mann not being able to create anything himself (in italics) is exactly what Lammers had written to Genoud, who in turn had fed this statement to Trevor-Roper for him to include in his introduction to *The Testament*. This makes one wonder if Heim had read this and now repeated it to Kuykendall or if this is just an amaz-ing coincidence. Heim was not present in Berlin in 1945 so he had no idea about whether the notes were authentic or not or how they, in that case, were made. But considering that Heim always stressed that Hitler never knew that notes were being made when *he* had written down what he remembered of Hitler's statements, it is quite extraordinary that he was so adamant that Hitler knew about these notes and even suggested that Bormann likely had read the notes to Hitler. There is no way that he could have known this, and there is no reason for him to assume it, unless Bormann had done so in the past.

But we actually have an example of someone from the Nazi old guard that doubted the authenticity of at least parts of this source. Willi Krämer, a Nazi who had worked under Goebbels, wrote to Heim in February 1986 asking him some questions about Hanna Reitsch's book *Höhen und Tiefen*[155] (*Highs and Lows*):

> This astonishes me: That our ideological opponents have not yet used the ominous passages in the "Knaus Book" [a reference to *Hitlers politisches Testa-ment*, M.N.] for their propaganda, or is this "best-seller" saved for a special

situation? Having read Hanna Reitch's fourth chapter particularly thought-fully, I am firmly convinced that the two passages in the "Bormann-papers", published in the "Knaus-Buch", pages 122 and 125, are forged! Will you help me find the truth?[156]

There is no trace of Heim's reply to Krämer's letter at the IfZ, but since Heim had recommended the book to Jochmann, one has to conclude that he thought it did record Hitler's words. What two passages was Krämer referring to in his letter to Heim? Initially, I had expected to find specific references to *The Testament of Adolf Hitler* (remember that when *Höhen und Tiefen* came out in 1978 the German edition *Hitlers politisches Testament* had not yet been published) in Reitsch's book saying that these were untrue,[157] but it turns out that she does not mention this document at all. However, in *Hitlers politisches Testament* there are on pages 122 and 125 two explicit references to Hitler having exterminated (*ausgerottet*) the Jews.

These must have been the passages that Krämer suspected, and wished, were forged. Krämer was no doubt just like Heim insisting that Hitler could not have known anything about the extermination of the Jews and therefore he could not have been talking about it in this open fashion. But what is the connection to Reitsch's book in this context then? Well, in chapter 4 in her book Reitsch defends Hitler against charges of war crimes, in effect a form of Holocaust denial on her part, and actually talks about how magazines had published what she claimed to be a forged interview with her where she made statements that she had never made. She specifically mentions an article that first appeared in *Stars and Stripes* under the title (in German) "Eyewitness Account of Hitler's Last Days by Hanna Reitsch" written in first person. Not only that, Trevor-Roper is mentioned explicitly as having used this forgery in his best-seller *The Last Days of Hitler* in 1947. She claims that she naively wrote to Trevor-Roper telling him that he was the victim of a scam – she had not written this eyewitness testimony.[158] In his book, Trevor-Roper refers not to *Stars and Stripes* but to a series of articles in *News Chronicle* on 28, 29, and 31 December 1945. It could be that the same article had been re-printed. He does, however, at the same time state that "Reitsch's narrative has been checked carefully against other sources, and no material statements is based on her account alone without explicit indication." Granted, Trevor-Roper's portrait of Reitsch in his book is not a flattering one. He describes Reitsch as "vain", "egotistical", "insufferable", "an ardent Nazi", a "tiresome" and "some-what incomplete type of woman" who "had long worshipped at the shrine of Adolf Hitler."[159] Naturally, Reitsch could not have been happy with Trevor-Roper's characterization of her, even though it was the truth, and it is understandable if she felt the sting and wished to hit back by claiming it was a false source. There-fore, one cannot take the fact that Reitsch claimed that what he wrote was untrue as evidence that it actually was.

But could not the fact that Krämer thought that these blatant admissions of hav-ing exterminated the Jews be interpreted as evidence *for* authenticity? It is an argu-ment from a so-called "criterion of embarrassment", a common source-critical method of analysis used to tease out authentic statements from false ones.[160] At first this line of argumentation might seem very convincing. After all, what kind of Nazi would forge a document admitting to this crime? It must then be genuine. But let us remember that Heim had also read these passages and he still thought that the text was genuine. It could be that whoever forged the document at least privately thought of the Holocaust as Hitler's greatest achievement and did not consider it to be an embarrassment at all. Moreover, these passages are not really any more of an admission of genocide than some of the statements recorded in the table talks. After all, Hitler is not speaking about gassing millions of Jews to death in Auschwitz, Treblinka, and other camps or shooting thousands of Jews to death; these passages could just as well be interpreted as metaphoric, cultural, political, or spiritual extermination.

The central point here though is, that even though the phrase *mit offenem Visier gekämpft* is a German idiom used to describe a situation when one has not been shunning a conflict situation, it is not very commonly used. Nowhere else is Hitler ever (or Goebbels, or anyone else of the top Nazis, for that matter) recorded as having used this phrase. However, there is an occasion on which it was used, and it may or may not be a coincidence. In 1940 Otto Straßer, Hitler's old rival in the NSDAP, published his book *Hitler et moi* (*Hitler and I*; or *Hitler und Ich* in German), which was allegedly based on notes made by Straßer immediately after the conversations in question; at one point he even writes that his text is based on "stenographic notes" (des notes sténographiées).[161] By now, we all know how much credence we should give any claims of stenographic notes: i.e. not much. Straßer did not base his book on stenographic notes.

Nonetheless, *Hitler et moi* is highly relevant for the discussion here. It turns out that Straßer has a whole chapter in the book with the familiar title: "Battle with an open visor" (Combat à visière ouverte). He also writes that after one of their many arguments and conflicts, and after Hitler purportedly spoke to him in threatening language about sending the SA thugs after him: "I decided to battle his hypocrisy with an open visor."[162] Considering that the phrase is used also in French one has to wonder why Genoud chose not to use it if it was in a genuine German text? Adding to this and strengthening the argument that this text was forged, we have the fact that Rechenberg was actually a friend of Otto Straßer's brother Gregor, and thus he reasonably knew Otto as well.[163] Now, is this simply a matter of coincidence? To be sure, it is certainly not impossible. But, again, how probable is it? Rechenberg had certainly read *Hitler et moi* and perhaps Genoud had as well. While it is not possible to determine this probability with any degree of certainty, it should, at the very least, make us even more suspicious of Rechenberg's claims that this text is genuine.

The best textual evidence of forgery

However, the best textual evidence that *The Testament* is a forgery is to be found towards the end of the second entry, dated 6 February 1945, in the typed manuscript containing the English text for *The Testament*, i.e. the translation made by Stevens. A minor handwritten correction in this text tells a lot about how it was translated. The text is speaking about how Frederick the Great was in such a grave military situation during the Seven Years War that he contemplated suicide, but that the death of the Tsarina Elisabeth of Russia in January 1762 saved him and led to the breakup of the coalition against Prussia. The fourth sentence in the second paragraph starts: "Then, *a few* days before the date he had chosen [for his suicide, M.N.]."[164] [Italics added.] This agrees with the text in the French edition where it says: "Or *quelques* jour savant ce terme."[165] [Italics added.]

However, in the typed manuscript "a few" has been added by hand by someone. Originally, the typed text said "three" instead of "a few", as in "three days later."[166] It is not evident who added these words, but it could be Trevor-Roper's handwriting. Why is this significant? It is significant because in *Hitlers politisches Testament* the same sentence starts: "And *three* days before the gallows deadline" (*Und drei Tage vor der Galgenfrist*) [Italics added].[167] Since the "three" in the typescript cannot be a mistaken translation from the French, this word *must* come from a text that said something different than the published French text. It must have come from a typescript that (at least in this instance) was identical to the text later published in 1981. It could have been a German text. Yet, everything else shows that the English text was translated from the French and not from the German – and other evidence proves this as well, as we have seen. In the entry dated 14 February 1945, for example, the typescript has stricken out the word "divorce", which was a direct translation of the French *divorce*, and typed in the more correct English word "discrepancy."[168] This was a mistake that was very easy for an English speaker to make, since the words are homonyms in English and French, but it could not have been made if the German text had been the basis for the translation. The formulation in *Hitlers politisches Testament* is entirely different, so the correction of this error was not made based on a German text.[169]

So, what does this mean exactly? Well, there are several possibilities. But one thing is for certain: even if Stevens got the word "three" from a German text handed to him by Genoud, which may or may not have been the same German text that was eventually published as *Hitlers politisches Testament*, this is in no way evidence that this German text is genuine. We still have no idea where this text came from or what it looked like. What this *does* mean, however, is that Genoud had in his possession a text that said "three" instead of "a few" in 1961 at the latest, although it is unknown if it was in German or in French. As we shall see, the word "three" is also extremely significant for the question of the text's authenticity. The pertinent question in this context is: Where does the concept of "three days" come from? What is the source for this idea?

After the unexpected death of Elisabeth of Russia everything changed in Prussia's favour; Russia then sued for peace and exited the grand coalition against Frederick II. This was an obvious comparison to Hitler's situation in February 1945. In *The Testament* Hitler also says "behold, the Tsarina died" and states that if something now were to happen to Churchill "everything would change in a flash!"[170]

The similarities to Frederick II's situation during the Seven Years War was a common theme also in Goebbels's diaries during this period. On both 24 January and 12 February 1945 Goebbels compared Hitler to Frederick the Great.[171] The role of Frederick the Great as an inspiration for Hitler has been dealt with in great detail by Wolfram Pyta.[172]

Of the 14 dates in *The Testament* 5 appear also in Goebbels's diary, namely 6, 7, 10, 13 February, and 2 April.[173] However, only on the first of these, i.e. the one with the same date as the note in *The Testament* under discussion here, do we find a small overlap of subjects. In *The Testament* we find Hitler insisting that the situation is not without hope, and that the war was not yet lost. This is a subject that comes up also in Goebbels's diary that day (but Frederick II is *not* here).[174] No other overlap of conversation subjects occurs, however. One could perhaps be tempted to see the coincidence of one theme on 6 February as proof of authenticity for *that* entry at least. But that would be a mistake. Hitler repeated this mantra over and over during the last months of the war both in his speeches and in his private conversations.[175]

Frederick II is mentioned in Goebbels's diary on 27 February 1945, the first date included in the then newly discovered diary entries from 1945 published in English in 1978 (based on an original in German published in 1977) with an introduction by none other than Trevor-Roper. There Goebbels states that "we must be as Frederick the Great was and act as he did." Hitler agree with him, Goebbels says, and he goes on to state how much Hitler reminded him of the former Prussian king. Goebbels says he had told Hitler that he had recently read a book on Frederick II by Thomas Carlyle and that Hitler knew this book very well (a facsimile of one of these diary pages is even included in the book). He also says he recited parts of the book to Hitler. Frederick II is mentioned many more times by Goebbels during the last months in his diary.[176] Now, these diary entries did not become public until a microfilm copy of them appeared in East Germany and were offered to the publisher Hoffman & Campe in October 1972.[177] Thus, they were not available to Genoud or Rechenberg in 1959. These facts might also make us think that *The Testament* is authentic. However, that is a *non sequitur*.

First, as already shown, it is important to note that references to Frederick II from both Goebbels and Hitler were very common, both in private and in public, during the war.[178] For example, on 28 February 1945, the day after his diary entry, he brought this up in a speech on the radio. These "striking" parallels between Hitler and Frederick II had even been the topic of the movie *Der große König* (*The Great King*) that had been produced in time for the celebration of Hitler's fifty-third birthday on 20 April 1942.[179] The Prussian king had, of course, also been a frequent theme in Hitler's table talks.[180] Hitler mentioned him on several occasions in *Mein Kampf*, in his unpublished second book, and many times in many of his speeches over the years.[181] The traces even go much further back than that. Hitler brought up Carlyle and Frederick the Great during the trial against him in 1924, and then mentioned Carlyle and his book again in a speech in Munich on 30 July 1927.[182] We thus have two recorded occasions when

Hitler mentioned Carlyle's book in his speeches. Interestingly, on 2 May 1928 Hitler, as a reply to two NSDAP party members at a meeting, who had stated that Frederick the Great allegedly carried a vial of poison (*Phiole mit Gift*) with him during the Seven Years War and that this was a sign that he was prepared to die rather than give up his honour, taunted the German foreign minister (and former chancellor) and liberal *Deutsche Volkspartei* politician Gustav Stresemann for not being prepared to do the same. Contrasting Stresemann to the towering figure of Frederick the Great, Hitler asked if anyone really believed that Stresemann carried a vial with poison with him in Geneva (at the League of Nations, M.N.).[183] This very long speech was published as a special issue of *Völkischer Beobachter* on 5 May 1928.[184] Note that it was not Hitler who claimed that Frederick had carried a vial of poison with him – he repeated what others had said: an important detail to remember. It appears to have been a rather common story about Frederick II floating around at the time.

All of this means that any reference to Frederick II in *The Testament* cannot be interpreted as a sign of authenticity. Instead, it must be considered one of the most obvious references for any reasonably skilled forger to make. This is not just hypothetical speculation. We actually have evidence that this is *exactly* what a forger of Hitler documents would do, and in fact did do. The first time that Frederick II appears in a supposedly official Hitler document is in Eberhard Jäckel's source volume *Sämtliche Aufzeichnungen* in a note dated 5 October 1916 where Frederick II is pictured in a drawing. Why do I bring this up here? Well, because this document is a forgery made by the forger Konrad Kujau.[185] This proves that a forger wishing to pass off a document as genuine indeed would choose to include a reference to Hitler's favourite monarch.

It turns out that the forger Kujau was not far off the mark on this one. In fact, the first evidence we have of Hitler studying the history of Frederick II is an architectural guide to Berlin written by Max Osborn in 1909 which Hitler purchased in a small bookstore in Fournes in northern France in late November 1915. We know this because Hitler signed it stating the place, month, and year of purchase. The book survived not only the First World War but also the Second World War, and it was a part of the remaining books of Hitler's private library that eventually found their way to the United States and the LoC. Timothy Ryback has shown that especially the chapter about Frederick the Great shows many signs of having been well-read. Eventually, Hitler came to possess a large number of biographies of the king. Hitler did not read them all apparently, since, for example, the four surviving copies of a large collective edition have been preserved still in the wrapping from the publisher.[186] Kujau of course did not know about Hitler's book purchase in November 1915, so the close proximity in time between this event and the forged document is entirely coincidental. This is important to remember when we evaluate the likelihood of the note dated 6 February mentioning Frederick II in close proximity to authentic documents mentioning him, being forged.

Hitler also used Frederick the Great as a comparison in a conversation with the Chief of the General Inspection for the Tank Troops (*Chef der Generalinspektion der Panzertruppe*) on 29–30 December 1944. Here the change of regent in Russia is mentioned, but the context is entirely different than in *The Testament* because here Hitler says that it was not the miracle itself that was of greatest importance, but rather Frederick II's will to never give up *before* this miracle happened. This appears to have inspired Hitler's hope that the grand coalition against him would crumble due to ideological differences between the Allies.[187] He had done the same in a conversation with an Italian delegation in April 1944.[188] Note, again, that the issue here is not whether Hitler ever talked about Frederick the Great or whether he ever compared the difficult situation in Second World War to that of the Prussian king during the Seven Years War. We know he did. The issue is whether he actually said what, and when, *The Testament* claims he did. There are, after all, a number of details regarding this story that we see for the first time in *The Testament* and in no other source.

On 12 April 1945 President Roosevelt died unexpectedly, and this was apparently interpreted by both Hitler and Goebbels as a sign from God that matters were about to turn in Germany's favour. Albert Speer, for instance, tells us that this was explicitly compared to the death of Elisabeth of Russia. It is only *after* 12 April that we have evidence of Hitler uttering his belief that this was as significant as it had been for Frederick II back in 1762. Speer claims that Hitler was extremely excited by these news, although he at the same time makes clear that it was Goebbels who talked about it the most.[189] Nicolaus von Below, on the other hand, clearly ascribes this enthusiasm only to Goebbels and states that Hitler viewed Roosevelt's death "more soberly, without great optimism."[190] According to Toland, who supports himself on Fritz Hesse's book *Hitler and the English* from 1954 (a translation of *Das Spiel um Deutschland* from 1953), Ribbentrop noticed Hitler's elation on the morning of 13 April and stated in anger that "the scoundrel" Goebbels had managed to convince Hitler that this was a turning point in the war.[191] As we see, the various versions of the events do not entirely match each, but this is only to be expected. Did Hitler view the death of Roosevelt as a sign from God? Yes, he most likely did, and von Below's statements, which are the ones that differ the most from the other accounts, are probably downplaying Hitler's reaction a bit. Speer, on the other hand, is likely boosting Hitler's excitement to an equal degree. Speer's book was not published until long after *Le testament politique* and can thus not be the source for these statements.

The question then becomes if we can find the information in *The Testament* in a source that was available by the late 1950s. It turns out that there indeed were such sources. For instance, in 1955 Hans Frank mentions in his memoirs that Hitler had at some point (Frank does not say when this happened) talked about how Frederick the Great had been on the verge of losing the Seven Years War if the Russian empress had not died "at the very last moment".[192] He does not mention anything about suicide, though. Frank's memoirs were published in good time for anyone who would seek to use its content for a publication in 1959. But there is yet another, and much better, candidate.

It turns out that all of the information included in *The Testament* is to be found already in Trevor-Roper's *The Last Days of Hitler* from 1947. Based on an entry in Count Schwerin von Krosigk's diary dated 15 April 1945 Trevor-Roper recounts how Goebbels some days earlier had told von Krosigk that he "had recently been reading aloud to the Fuehrer, to solace him in his universal discomfort. He was reading from his favourite book, Carlyle's *History of Frederick the Great.*" In Carlyle's book, says von Krosigk, it was described how the king stated to his minister Count Finckenstein that if there was no change in his desperate situation by 15 February 1762, he would take poison. Finckenstein then, according to Carlyle (Trevor-Roper points out that von Krosigk misquotes Carlyle and the facts; actually, Frederick II had written to Marquis d'Argenson), told the king to be brave and that his sufferings would soon be over; a change in fortune was about to occur. On 12 February the Czarina died, von Krosigk states. This was "the Miracle of the House of Brandenburg."

Here we thus have a source that establishes *three days* between the deadline for the alleged suicide and the death of Elisabeth of Russia. According to von Krosigk's diary, who reported Goebbels's words, this had caused Hitler's eyes to tear up from emotion. It was von Krosigk who called Goebbels on the morning after Roosevelt's death to give him the news. Then Goebbels told him how he the day before had talked to some officers at General Theodor Busse's HQ in Küstrin and laid out his expectation for a change in fortune just as in the case of the Miracle of the House of Brandenburg during the Seven Years War. The officers then allegedly asked him "What Czarina will die this time?" As he was driving home on 12 April Goebbels had heard the news of Roosevelt's death and he had then immediately called General Busse and triumphantly announced to him that "the Czarina is dead." Goebbels next rang Hitler on the phone and told him about the good news too: "My Fuehrer, I congratulate you! Roosevelt is dead!"[193] All of this is uncritically repeated by e.g. Alan Bullock, Joachim Fest and Ian Kershaw.[194]

But there are differing accounts of these events. According to an interview that John Toland did with Busse in 1963, Busse had called Goebbels on 13 April asking him if Roosevelt's death was what he had been referring to the day before whereupon Goebbels allegedly said "Oh, we don't know. We'll have to see."[195] Interestingly, Frederick II himself used the phrase "the miracle of the House of Brandenburg" after the battle of Kunersdorf in August 1759, when his armies had been almost completely annihilated and had only been saved by his enemies inability to agree amongst themselves.[196] Trevor-Roper mentions, and cites, the part about Frederick the Great in his introduction to *The Testament*, but he does not bring up the fact that he had himself written about this based on von Krosigk's diary in *The Last Days of Hitler*.[197] It is likely that he had forgotten about this.

The important fact here is that what Trevor-Roper says about von Krosigk citing Carlyle inaccurately is correct. A most important detail is that Carlyle does *not* talk about Elisabeth of Russia having died on 12 February 1762; instead, he gives the correct date 5 January.[198] Carlyle does cite a letter from Frederick II to his lover Marquis d'Argens dated 18 January 1762 where it says:

> "you judge correctly of the whole situation I am in, of the abysses which surrounds me; and, as I see by what you say, of the kind of hope that still remains to me. It will probably not be till the month of February [Turks, probably, and Tartar Khan; great things coming then!] that we can speak of that; and that is the term I contemplate for deciding whether I shall hold to CATO [Cato, – and the little Glass tube I have!] or to CAESAR'S COMMENTARIES," and the best fight one can make.[199]

Here, Carlyle has Frederick II mentioning a "glass tube", perhaps containing poison although this is never stated explicitly, which he would use should he decide to do as Cato,[200] and perhaps commit suicide, or to fight on like Caesar. However, the glass tube is not mentioned in the actual letter. There we instead find simply (Frederick II, the great German nationalist hero, ironically wrote in French):

> You judge very well the current situation I am in, the abyss that surrounds me; and I see, from what you tell me, that you are guessing that there remains hope for us. It will not be until February that we will be able to talk about it with certainty, and that is the timeframe I have suggested for myself to decide if I will stick to Cato's opinion, or if I will follow *Caesar's Commentaries* [*on the Gallic Wars*, M.N.].[204]

The part about a "glass tube" is an interpolation made by Carlyle who was quite fond of adding bits like this to his quotes.[202] Reasonably, Carlyle *must* thus also be the original source of the idea that Frederick II carried a poison capsule with him.

The entry in *The Testament* thus seems to be constructed on what we find in von Krosigk's diary as presented in Trevor-Roper's *The Last Days of Hitler*. It is also interesting that we find no prediction of the death of any of the Allied leaders in connection with the discussion of Carlyle's book in Goebbels's diaries. The closest he comes is on 23 March when he again says that he had "recently been reading Thomas Carlyle's book on Frederick the Great." Here he basically cites a part of the book, writing "at the darkest hour a bright star arose and Prussia was saved when he had almost given up all hope. Why should not we also hope for a similar wonderful turn of fortune!"[203] Interestingly, Christian Goeschel includes a reference to this episode in an article in *Journal of Contemporary History* from 2006. His version is a little bit different, however. He writes:

> Goebbels is said to have read out passages from Carlyle's history of Frederick the Great to Hitler in the bunker. In these passages, Frederick the Great contemplated suicide by poisoning himself when the military situation seemed hopeless to the Prussians in 1757 during the Seven Years War.[204]

The idea that this did not actually happen right before the death of Elisabeth of Russia in 1762 but instead in 1757 is a new piece of information. The source that Goeschel builds upon for this is Kershaw's Hitler biography.[205] The problem is that Kershaw never says that this took place in 1757. He tells the story as it appears in Trevor-Roper's *The Last Days of Hitler*.[206] Goeschel seems to have added the year 1757 by inferring it from Goebbels's radio speech on 28 February 1945 (published in *Völkischer Beobachter* on 1 March), which he also references, in which the propaganda minister cited a letter that Frederick II had written to his sister in March 1757 where he stated that the only options for people like them, in the difficult situation he and his troops found themselves, were victory or death.[207]

Goebbels's diary often seems to actually contradict what von Krosigk says Goebbels told him about Hitler's reaction to comparisons with Frederick II. Goebbels was in fact frustrated that Hitler would not act as Frederick II had towards untrustworthy underlings, and Goebbels was here talking specifically about Göring whom he wished Hitler should remove. But Hitler refused to do so even though Goebbels used Carlyle's book on several occasions to try to sway him, and Goebbels complained about this and said it was the greatest difference between Hitler and the king.[208] However, in mid-March Hitler actually had used Frederick II as an example when he was furious at Sepp Dietrich's *SS Leibstandarte* for not having done what he ordered. According to Otto Günsche, Hitler screamed that Frederick II had indeed not shied away from punishing several regiments for cowardice.[209]

According to his diary from 4 March 1945 Goebbels was "now immersed in Carlyle's book" and he found it a great source of inspiration and consolation in those dark days.[210] In fact, Goebbels writes that he gave Hitler a copy of Carlyle's book on 11 March 1945.[211] The book that Goebbels handed Hitler was allegedly an abridged version (which still totalled more than 2,100 pages) of Carlyle's many-volume work and it was of course in German and not in the original English.[212] Ryback does not know what edition Goebbels gave Hitler (and it is not clear where the number of pages comes from). There were a number of abridged editions published in German over the years. Ryback agrees that it is not at all likely that Hitler ever read the multi-volume editions.[213] This would mean that Hitler did not already possess a copy of this book that he allegedly knew so well before that point.

Did Hitler ever read Carlyle's book? The short answer is we do not know, although we can be absolutely certain that he never read all 21 volumes of Carlyle's work. In fact, Ryback says that: "I truly doubt that he ever owned a copy."[214] At the very least, it means that Hitler did not yet possess a copy on 6 February when *The Testament* has him referencing the miraculous death of Elisabeth in 1762. As we have seen, however, we do have two examples of Hitler mentioning Carlyle's book; during his trial in 1924 and in a speech in 1927. Thus, we know he knew *of* it (and perhaps also read, or even owned, a version of Carlyle's text at one point). After that we find no reference to Carlyle in any source, primary or otherwise, where Hitler talks about Frederick the Great. It was clearly Goebbels and not Hitler who was obsessed with Carlyle's book and with Frederick the Great as an example during this period.

According to Ernst Hanfstaengl's memoirs, Hitler had a copy of Franz Kugler's biography of Frederick II originally published in 1840 in his bookshelf in his apartment in Munich in the early 1920s.[215] It may not be entirely without importance that Carlyle's book (or books) is not to be found among the many volumes that survived the war and that are now held at Brown University and LoC. Considering that so many of Hitler's books disappeared from the bunker in Berlin, and from Hitler's house in Berchtesgaden, at the end of the war this does not at all mean that Goebbels was lying or that he never owned the book. It could be in an archive in Moscow or in private hands somewhere. The chance that such a book was taken by a GI is even greater if Goebbels had signed it and written a dedication to Hitler in it. Sometimes these books appear in the most mundane places such as yard sales, used bookstores, among books discarded for free by public libraries, and in boxes in attics. Sometimes they are sold for large sums of money at fancy auction houses in London or New York. Most often, however, they are probably never discovered or made available to the public. Many such books have surely been thrown away by people who did not realize what they had in their possession or have burned up in fires in houses, garages, or storage facilities.

In Trevor-Roper's book, then, was all the information that anyone about to forge a Hitler document from this period needed. The only way that this would not be a forgery based on *The Last Days of Hitler* is if von Krosigk related exactly what Goebbels actually told him, if the mistakes are thus Goebbels's and not von Krosigk's, and if Goebbels then told Hitler the exact same story. What speaks against this hypothesis is that this explanation depends upon on von Krosigk having been able to perfectly remember what Goebbels had told him; von Krosigk's diary entry is dated 15 April 1945 and describes matters that Goebbels had told him several days before.[216] Trevor-Roper never says exactly how long before though. But von Krosigk says in his diary that his conversation with Goebbels took place "on Monday" (*am Montag*).[217] Since 15 April 1945 was a Sunday this means that the conversation took place on 9 April, a whole week earlier.[218] He thus did not have all these statements fresh in his memory, and we therefore have to assume that he could not remember exactly what Goebbels had said. This is especially true since the conversation was quite long; it is summed up on no fewer than six whole pages in the diary. This further increases the likelihood that the mistaken dating is von Krosigk's doing; in fact, it makes it almost certain. Anyone who argues that von Krosigk could keep Goebbels's words *ad verbatim* in his head for a whole week has all the facts about how the human brain and memory works against them, and need to provide a convincing argument for that assumption.

There is no primary source *except* von Krosigk's diary where Goebbels ever put the dates 12 and 15 February 1762 in this story nor where he ever talked about Elisabeth having died "three days" before Frederick II's alleged deadline to commit suicide. Goebbels in fact never mentions this suicide either. As far as we know, the only person ever stating the same details that we find in *The Testament* is von

Krosigk in his diary as cited by Trevor-Roper in *The Last Days of Hitler* in 1947. This means that we are forced to treat the pertinent details in von Krosigk's diary as if Goebbels never actually said them. This is a strong nail in the coffin for the claim to authenticity of *The Testament*.

Another early published source may even have provided Genoud and Rechenberg with the impetus to invent a political testament document in the first place. In Albert Zoller's interview book with Hitler's former secretary Christa Schroeder, a book that was published in 1949, Schroeder tells Zoller about something that supposedly happened "at the end of 1944":

> At the end of 1944 Hitler indicated to me the intention to dictate a very long treatise. I was to be prepared during the following days. But he never followed through on his intention. I am convinced that it concerned his political testament.[219]

This is thus said to have happened only a few months before the notes contained in *The Testament* are dated. This could of course also be interpreted as evidence *for* authenticity. Perhaps Hitler simply chose to dictate it to Bormann instead? But let us remind ourselves that Schroeder herself did not think that *The Testament* was authentic and that Hitler would not have dictated such a thing to Bormann. She never saw or heard of Hitler having dictated anything to Bormann during those last months. Are we really to believe that Hitler changed his mind and decided to dictate his political testament in secret even though he had announced his intention to do so more or less openly to Schroeder not long before, and that he then dictated a political testament, albeit a short one, *again* to Traudl Junge on 29 April 1945? No, that is not at all probable. It is also clear that Goebbels did not know of *The Testament*, because when he in the early morning of 29 April 1945 wrote his appendix to Hitler's political testament, he did not feel he had to distinguish between this "political testament" and another existing document that was also a political testament.[220] Neither did Bormann on the note attached to the political testament from 29 April addressed to *Großadmiral* Dönitz.[221] If Hitler had already dictated a political testament to Bormann, there would be no need for a second one. But to a forger, the statement by Schroeder quoted earlier provides the perfect alibi for a document said to have been Hitler's political testament; it even contained the title of the document published by Genoud in 1959 (albeit this is informed speculation).

The fact that that von Krosigk's diary entry is dated 15 April, which is *three days* after Roosevelt's death on 12 April, may not be a coincidence. In von Krosigk's version, Elisabeth of Russia is then said to have died on 12 February 1762, *three days* before 15 February that was Frederick II's purported suicide deadline. It could thus be that von Krosigk mixed up Roosevelt's death date with Elisabeth's when retelling this story in his diary and made the three days that had elapsed since Roosevelt's death into the period between Elisabeth's death and the alleged deadline for Frederick II's suicide.

Let us now have a look at the known chronology. We have Goebbels writing in his diary on 27 February 1945 that he had "recently" been reading Carlyle's book and that he on 27 February had repeated passages from it to Hitler. This means that 27 February is the earliest point in time that Hitler could have been given the mistaken information related in von Krosigk's diary by Goebbels (this assumes that von Krosigk correctly remembered what Goebbels told him). If Hitler had been told this earlier, then it would make no sense for Goebbels to write as if he had not done so. In that case he would surely have written that he "again" told Hitler about this. The note in *The Testament*, which is the only source to contain all the information found in von Krosigk's diary, is dated 6 February. We now have a chronological problem on our hands: how could Hitler talk about something on 6 February when he did not hear about it until 11 days later on 27 February? The answer is, of course, he could not. The note dated 6 February in *The Testament* simply *has* to be a forgery.

A German text is finally published

In 1977 the IfZ arranged a seminar that focused on the legally problematic issues for the historical sciences connected to the fact that important historical source material was held in private hands. At this seminar Genoud repeated his assertion that the uncertainties regarding the copyright were the reason why he did not publish *Hitlers politisches Testament* in 1959.[222] During the preparation for the colloquium, Baumgarten stated in a letter to the director of the IfZ, Martin Broszat, that:

> No matter whether Mr. Genoud can be present on [both] Friday and Saturday (which he hopes), I would ask you to see him [either] together, or alone, on Saturday, in order to present the "situation" on the subject of the Hitler-Bormann document (II.1945;2.IV.45), as I see you now, and ask for your opinion and advice.[223]

Genoud was, however, very happy to accept the invitation to the colloquium from Broszat, and he wrote that he would like to bring his daughter and his wife with him to Munich.[224] Broszat briefed Genoud about what points might be brought up during the discussion, and among these was "the problem of Hitler's table discussions and the bunker talks of 1945, the tradition of which is only available in English or French [. . .]." Broszat stated that Genoud, if the IfZ had understood matters correctly, in the 1950s had said that "on the other hand, the original German text of the Bormann notes on which these publications were based should be published by a German publisher." It was a tremendous handicap for historians that these important sources were not available in their original language, wrote Broszat. The IfZ had heard that Genoud had indicated to a Dr Hoch in October 1973 that he was talking to German publishers about these sources, but on the other hand "we hear that the original German-language documents no longer exist or are no longer accessible." Brozsat therefore wished to know if 1) the German manuscript wording (*Manuskriptfassung*) for *Table Talk* of 1953 and *Le testament politique* were available (either in Genoud's or someone else's hands) and 2) whether he was still opposed to a publication of these texts in German. If the IfZ did not get a satisfactory answer to these questions, it had to be assumed, based on the other information that the IfZ had access to, that the German texts, either completely or partly, were no longer accessible. Such a statement by the colloquium would cause quite a stir in the historical community, Broszat wrote.[225]

Perhaps this message got Genoud a bit shaken because he seems to have produced a typescript of the German text rather quickly which he apparently showed to Baumgarten. This is of course a bit odd considering that Baumgarten had had a version of this text in his possession since 1975. But this document actually contained no fewer than two *different* German versions of the text. During the IfZ seminar Baumgarten made the astonishing announcement that Genoud's typed manuscript contained a second text that was handwritten between the lines of the other text. That text between the lines was the version later published, and an analysis had concluded that it was written in Genoud's handwriting as it looked in 1958. Genoud had assured him that this handwritten text corresponded *ad verbatim* with the original German text.[226] This aligns very well with the conclusion presented earlier, namely, that the text that Genoud showed *Der Spiegel* and Jäckel in 1962 and 1969, respectively, had been produced already before 1959 and that Genoud lied when he told Baumgarten in 1973 that he no longer had access to it.

David Irving claims that Genoud gave him "a copy of the complete typescript of the Testament" in 1979. The exchange supposedly took place in a hotel in Paris. Irving in fact has a facsimile of one of these pages on his website, a page he claims to have gotten a copy of from Genoud himself. The facsimile shows a page of typed text that has been partly stricken out and supplemented with new text between the lines, which corresponds to the text in *Hitlers politisches Testament*. Allegedly, Genoud later told him that he made the whole thing up stating: "'But it is just what Hitler would have said, isn't it?'" He claims on his website that the whole typescript is now to be found at the IfZ in Irving's deposited material there called *Sammlung Irving*.[227] The IfZ archivists have not been able to locate such a document, however. What *is* in the collection is an undated note written by Irving describing how he received the fake testament from Genoud and what it looked like.[228]

Even though Irving is a known falsifier of history (which has been proven in a British court) and a Holocaust denier, he nonetheless seems to be on the right side of history with regard to *The Testament*. His *reason* for considering it to be a fake, however, is less pleasant and it is only begrudgingly that I find myself sharing his basic evaluation of this particular document. Irving bases his conclusion on basically the same reason that the Heim's Nazi friend Krämer (see earlier in this chapter) dismissed it as a forgery too, namely because it contains parts where Hitler brags about having exterminated the Jews. Since Irving claims that Hitler never knew anything about the mass murder of Jews during the war, he simply has to claim this document is a fake by default. His decision is thus not based on rational analysis of the evidence, but on an *a priori* held ideological assumption that he cannot depart from lest his whole worldview and identity crumble. This should make us suspect that this facsimile (and the alleged document it is a part of) may in fact be a forgery made by Irving in order to prove all the other historians wrong. However, the fact that Baumgarten divulged this information – based on it having been shown to him by Genoud – already in 1977 disproves this assumption.

Amazingly enough, for Baumgarten, this very fact still became a proof for the authenticity of the text. Indeed, it seems as if Baumgarten could never be convinced that the document was not genuine. At the same time, however, he concluded that the only real "proof" of authenticity that was actually available (considering that the original was lost and that even the authenticity of *that* text could be doubted) was the internal evidence of the text itself – i.e. it sounded so much like Hitler that it *had* to be Hitler. Baumgarten got this line of reasoning directly from Trevor-Roper.[229] This was horribly bad source-critical reasoning. Why Genoud had chosen to write down that authentic text between the lines of another (then) by necessity forged text we are not told, because the question never seems to have been asked by anyone.

Naturally, none of this was later mentioned in *Hitlers politisches Testament* published by Albrecht Knaus Verlag in 1981. In the foreword, which may have been written by Werner Jochmann, the manuscript's dubious history was kept from the readers who were simply told that Genoud had been given a photocopy of the original by his friend Rechenberg (who in his turn was said to have gotten it from Funk), thus establishing a purportedly authentic provenance of the document. Since nothing was said about the subsequent loss of the photocopies, or of the retranslation into German from the French, the readers were thus led to believe that Genoud still possessed the photocopy and that the book in front of them was in turn based upon that original text.[230]

Privately, Trevor-Roper was apparently thrown between hope and despair regarding Genoud's texts. In 1978 he even wrote to Genoud asking him to once and for all tell the truth about the authenticity of the *Hitlers politisches Testament* because both Irving and Baumgarten, surprisingly, believed it was a forgery. Genoud then sent Trevor-Roper a copy of the letter from Lammers from 1959.[231] We must here remind ourselves about Rheindorf's conclusions regarding Engel's, and others', so-called "authentication" of Picker's and Heim's notes, namely that we cannot reasonably expect anyone to be able to remember specific formulations that Hitler may or may not have used decades later. Lammers, by the way, never had a representative at the FHQ, although he had visited from time to time.[232] We have already seen that Trevor-Roper must have borrowed from Lammers' letter when writing his introduction in 1959 so it seems a bit odd that Genoud would then send this very document to Trevor-Roper again when he asked about its authenticity. Had Trevor-Roper never seen Lammers's letter before after all? In that case, should we assume that the part in the introduction about Bormann not having a mind of his own was perhaps incidental or maybe suggested to him by Genoud?

After so many years of fruitless hopes and efforts on the part of several historians *Hitlers politisches Testament* was eventually published by Albrecht Knaus Verlag in 1981, the same publisher that Werner Jochmann had worked with on *Monologe*. Genoud seems to have agreed to publish *Hitlers politisches Testament* because the cooperation with Knaus had previously gone so smoothly. Presumably, that meant that the publisher had not asked too many bothersome questions about the text's authenticity. In an interesting overlap, Knaus asked Jochmann in the summer of 1980 if he was interested in assisting with the publication of *Hitlers politisches Testament* just as he had done with *Monologe*. It is not known what Jochmann's reply was.[233] In the end, however, it does not seem as if Jochmann was involved in this work. It turns out that it was Baumgarten who was the scholar tasked with working on the manuscript, although it is not known what he actually did. We know that Baumgarten was involved because Knaus wrote to Heim (of all people) in January 1981 and told him that he had had a meeting in Frankfurt with Genoud and Baumgarten, "who is now preparing the 'Bormann-Dictations', i.e. *Hitler's political will* for publication in my publishing house." [Italics in original.][234]

Knaus had met Genoud in Heim's hometown of Munich the first time (it seems) during the summer of 1980, and they had spoken about the possibility of publishing the German text. In a letter to Jochmann he said that even though the authenticity of this text had been questioned, and even though its history was murky, it would be a mistake to withhold Hitler's last wishes from the German people. Knaus wondered if Jochmann did not agree. He stated that Genoud had given him the German text when they met in Munich, as well as both the French and English versions. [Of course, this was not the original – indeed it could not have been, since that was not in Genoud's possession any longer, according to him – so it is not clear why Knaus would put any trust in it at all]. At the same time Knaus asked Jochmann if he thought that they should include Trevor-Roper's introduction as well. Trevor-Roper had since become Lord Dacre, Knaus remarked, and his stature had certainly not decreased. In connection with this Knaus mentioned that he had also spoken to Eberhard Jäckel about this text, who was an authority on the subject to Knaus because he had recently (that same year in fact) published a book containing Hitler's earliest writings and speeches up until 1924 (the book was *Hitler. Sämtliche Aufzeichnungen 1905–1924*, M.N.). Jäckel considered the evidence for authenticity convincing enough, Knaus said. Everyone knew that Hitler had a remarkable memory, and there were recollections in this text that only Hitler could be the source of, Jäckel had apparently said to Knaus.[235] Jäckel, as we need to remember, had also been quite deeply involved in the effort to entice the German text from Genoud about a decade earlier. Knaus never went into any detail regarding what in the text that could only have come from Hitler's supreme memory.

Now, it is important to know when we evaluate Jäckel's statements regarding this text's authenticity that he had very recently been completely duped by the forger of Hitler documents Konrad Kujau, who would become known as the man behind the Hitler diaries scam a few years later. Jäckel was in the summer of 1980 convinced that the Hitler diaries were authentic after having seen one of the 'originals' (i.e. Kujau's forged handwritten documents, M.N.) in September 1979 (Jäckel had even offered to edit them), and Trevor-Roper would also make the tragic mistake of going on the record authenticating them. In Jäckel's case it was even worse than that because he had, in his search of material to include in his book about Hitler's early writings and speeches, been shown several forged Hitler poems on that same day in September, which he subsequently, convinced they were real, had included (no fewer than 75 of them) in his book.[236] Jäckel was thus no better than any other Hitler expert at determining authenticity by analysing content and style. Moreover, confirmation bias was no doubt at work here, in the sense that these historians *wanted* very much for these documents to be real.

As already stated, it is not known what exactly Jochmann replied, but it seems that he did not write the opportunity off completely because he apparently called Knaus five days later, and in the letter that Knaus wrote to him the day after this conversation it does seem as if Jochmann was interested in the matter because Knaus sent him the German text (and the French and English versions as well). Knaus now asked if he did not think that it would be very "pompous" to publish it with both the English introduction by Trevor-Roper and the French introduction by André François-Poncet and added with a blue pen: "If you can agree." Knaus would be excited to hear what Jochmann thought about this and told him that he foresaw a quick publication planned for the spring of 1981. Then they could put Hitler's last utterances behind them once and for all.[237] As far as we know, things went along as planned, both introductions were included. Perhaps Jochmann is even the author of the publisher's own "preface" (*Vorbemerkung*) to the book.

It may not be entirely coincidental that the publication of *Hitlers politisches Testament* happened at a time when there was a resurgence of interest in Prussia and Frederick the Great in Germany, even in East Germany, in the 1980s – a Prussian Wave (*Pruessenwelle*). In West Berlin there an exhibit on the Prussian historical legacy opened in 1981 and this was accompanied by a number of popular books on Prussia. In East Germany Erich Honecker ordered that the statue of Frederick II that had previously been standing on the parade street *Unter den Linden* in central Berlin, and which had been removed in the early 1960s, should be placed there again and he ordered the nation's historians to celebrate the Prussian heritage as being progressive and an early example of socialism.[238] Genoud may well have decided to try and profit from this renewed interest by finally publishing the German text in which Hitler was speaking about the Prussian hero King during the final days of the Third Reich.

Ironically, too, Trevor-Roper himself dismissed David Irving's book *Hitler's War* in 1977 with the following clear-sighted methodological point:

> When a historian relies mainly on primary sources, which we cannot easily check, he challenges our confidence and forces us to ask critical questions. How reliable is his historical method? How sound is his judgment?[239]

The same question could be directed at both *Table Talk* and *Monologe*, since both books are based on a primary source that is not only difficult, but even impossible, to check. It was near impossible while Genoud was still alive, since he refused to let anyone see the original German manuscript, and it certainly is impossible now, since no one knows where it is.

An odd postscript

In the early 2000s Trevor-Roper would make a series of rather weird statements with regard to this text. Historians kept digging into the history of *The Testament* and in effect produced new challenges to the established truth on the subject. With all the credibility that Trevor-Roper had invested in *The Testament* and considering all the statements that unequivocally insisted on the document's authenticity that he had made in public, one would think that he would have had a high degree of certainty in his own judgement. That does not seem to have been the case, however. In fact, he appears to have never actually trusted Genoud.

In correspondence with historian Richard Carrier in 2002 Trevor-Roper stated that although he considered on balance that most of the evidence "supports the claim of authenticity", he at the very same time told Carrier "but because of lingering doubts I have never cited the work as evidence." This is quite astonishing. Let us remember that this is the same document that Trevor-Roper himself, in his preface to *Hitlers politisches Testament*, judged to be "undoubtedly authentic" (*zweivellos echt*). So, on the one hand, he attests to its authenticity to the whole world, but on the other, he does not cite it because of lingering doubts. Reasonably, he can never have been that convinced of it being genuine. Trevor-Roper continued to make amazing admissions. He told Carrier that even if it was to be shown to be a forgery, he did not think that Genoud was behind it. That would be contrary to his interests, according to Trevor-Roper, because if he was exposed, he would damage the claim of the other genuine documents that he had collected. Instead, Trevor-Roper's suspicions would fall on Rechenberg.[240] Trevor-Roper may, as we have seen, actually not be wrong in suspecting Rechenberg, but his inability to see that Genoud could have had an interest in peddling a fake Hitler document is hard to understand or believe. Moreover, how could Genoud have been exposed when there was no original? This was, in that case, the whole point of the elaborate cover story regarding its provenance that he and Rechenberg had attached to the document.

In addition, Trevor-Roper wrote that he had always found Genoud to be straightforward, although somewhat difficult to deal with because of his unwillingness to show his original documents (which Trevor-Roper still ascribed to nervousness about copyright). He did not believe that Genoud deliberately distorted the texts, but added that, "I have not made a close textual study." Thus, Trevor-Roper thought Genoud to be in general trustworthy.[241] Neither could Trevor-Roper comment on Carrier's findings that Genoud's French translation could not be trusted.[242] This, too, was a stunning statement coming from a former Regius Professor of History at Oxford University. Trevor-Roper knew that the text had been translated from the French *and* that Genoud had added material to it. But considering his history of forgetting even the most important and obvious details and facts related to the documents that he endorsed and validated, we should perhaps not be all that surprised if Trevor-Roper had forgotten this fact again.

Conclusions

This chapter has investigated the authenticity of the texts published first in 1959 as *Le testament politique*, then in 1961 as *The Testament*, and lastly in 1981 under the title *Hitlers politisches Testament*. It is important to underline that we are talking about three separate texts, because even though they are similar, they are *not* identical. Many historians have cited these documents largely uncritically since they were published, despite the fact that no original document is available. The many uncertainties connected to this source ought of course to have been pointed out by first Hugh Trevor-Roper in 1959 and 1961 and then by the German publisher Knaus in 1981. That neither of them did so was certainly to shy away from their responsibilities towards their readers. If they had done so, there might have been no need to write this chapter.

We have seen that the story of how Genoud got this text from the former director of the Nazi German *Reichsbank*, Walter Funk, is untrue. Several witnesses have independently stated that Funk was never in a position to be given these documents – he was not present in the bunker in Berlin and was not trusted enough to have been given such a document. Furthermore, Hitler's secretaries Christa Schroeder and Gerda Christian did not think that Hitler had dictated anything to Bormann, even though they thought that it could perhaps be a summary of things that Hitler had said at some point or another. However, the author of this text is completely unknown. Trevor-Roper claimed to have seen photocopies of documents at a meeting in Paris in November 1958. But there are a number of problems with this claim. First, this information is not in his notes made immediately after the meeting. It appears first in the form of an offhand remark in his introduction to *Le testament politique* in 1959, and then in later statements to various people. Surely, he would have mentioned such an important fact in his notes if it had happened. Second, even if he did get to see some photocopies of some document, he never had the opportunity to actually compare the content of these photocopies with the text that Genoud published in French in 1959. Third, Trevor-Roper later on expressed serious doubts about the veracity of these documents in his private correspondence.

According to the evidence, the French text was at least once re-translated into German by Baumgarten and efforts were made to pass it off as the real thing. Eventually, a document containing the German text was presented by Genoud but then in the form of a transcript in Genoud's handwriting from about 1958. This text appears between the lines of a typed document containing a completely different, and entirely unknown, text, which by necessity has to be a forgery too. Where the text eventually published as *Hitlers politisches Testament* actually came from is still not known, and it will likely never be known, but we do know for sure that the stories told of its history by Genoud and Rechenberg are not true.

Moreover, I have shown that the text contains statements that cannot reasonably have been uttered by Hitler and that cannot be the result of misunderstandings on Bormann's part either. Such examples are the ideas expressed in the note No. 16 dated 26 February that Hitler willingly let the British at Dunkirk get away, and the statement in the note No. 5 dated 13 February saying that the Jews were not a race but only a religious community. All the independent evidence both before and after this date completely contradicts these statements. In these sources Hitler expressly says that the Jews were *nothing but* race, and in fact incapable of forming a religious or spiritual community. This also strongly suggests that these statements are not genuine. The particular distortion of Hitler's view of the Jews actually fit perfectly into Genoud's political agenda to further Arabic nationalism, which has been well described in the biographies about him, since it could serve as a cogent argument against a Jewish nation-state: Israel. After all, race was the core of a nation and a people (*Volk*) according to the National Socialist worldview, which was an ideology that Genoud subscribed to.

The dating of several of the notes also shows that this text cannot be trusted. Two of them, notes No. 12 and 13 dated 20 and 21 February 1945, record statements made on days when Bormann was not in Berlin and thus could not have listened to Hitler speak. One of the most suspicious features of *Hitlers politisches Testament* is also that the dates on the three last entries – notes No. 16 and 17 dated 26 February and note No. 18 dated 2 April – correspond exactly to the dating of the letters published in *The Bormann Letters* in 1954. Five notes out of 18 are therefore suspect of having been tampered with. Add to this is the fact that Genoud addressed this lacuna in his preface to *Le testament politique* in 1959. The fact that Genoud never mentions *The Bormann Letters* in this context is like an inadvertent admission of guilt on his part – he seems to know that this demands an explanation but cannot explicitly explain why without betraying his own deceit.

But the best piece of textual evidence that *The Testament* is a forgery comes from the note dated 6 February 1945 where Hitler is made to speak about Frederick II and the death of Elisabeth of Russia in 1762. I have shown that the "three days" mentioned in *Hitlers politisches Testament* has to be based on von Krosigk's diary cited by Trevor-Roper in his *The Last Days of Hitler* from 1947. It contains information that von Krosigk appears to be the source of when summarizing, on 15 April 1945, his conversation with Goebbels on 9 April. But there is no independent evidence that can corroborate that Goebbels ever stated the precise information that we find in von Krosigk's diary and in *The Testament*. Goebbels's diary also shows that Hitler did not possess Carlyle's book until Goebbels gave it to him on 11 March, i.e. over a month later than the note in *The Testament*. Since the details in von Krosigk's diary and *The Testament* are the same, they must, if the text is genuine, ultimately stem from Goebbels. Then, again, if the text is authentic, then Hitler repeated things that Goebbels had told him about Carlyle's history of Frederick II. But we know from Goebbels diary that the first time he spoke to Hitler about this book was on 27 February. Therefore, Hitler could not have given Bormann this information already on 6 February. And all of this is on the assumption that von Krosigk remembered exactly what Goebbels had told him a week earlier; this is in itself too unlikely to have happened. The note has to be a forgery.

Considering all that has been shown in this chapter, the burden of proof should reasonably be on the person arguing *for* authenticity. Reference to the "internal evidence" is simply not a reliable or valid method for historians to use when trying to establish this text's authenticity. This method is also generally unreliable and has failed spectacularly in many other cases in the past. A prime example of this is the forged Hitler diaries in the early 1980s that fooled all the experts who analysed them, including the handwriting analysts, as well as the 75 forgeries included by Eberhard Jäckel in his source volume *Sämtliche Aufzeichnungen*. In the case of *Hitlers politisches Testament* we simply have too many indicators that should cause any careful and critical historian to doubt its veracity. Historians should therefore refrain from using this source and ought to consider it a forgery until reliable and incontrovertible evidence that it is genuine is presented.

Notes

1 I have previously dealt with the English and German editions of these texts in: Nilsson, M., "Hugh Trevor-Roper and the English Editions . . ."; Nilsson, M., "Constructing a Pseudo-Hitler? . . .".
2 *The Bormann Letters. . ..*
3 *Le testament politique. . ..*
4 *The Testament of Adolf Hitler. . .* (1961). There was also an unauthorized English edition published in 1978 in the United States. by the American neo-Nazi L. Craig Fraser (then in his twenties). See: *The Testament of Adolf Hitler: The Hitler-Bormann Document, February–April 1945. With an Introduction by L. Craig Fraser* (Noontide Press, 1978). L. Craig Fraser now appears to be the district attorney for the Dublin Juridical circuit serving Laurens, Treutlen, Twiggs, and Johnson counties in Georgia. His introduction is an explicit celebration of Adolf Hitler as the supreme and awesome leader of the white race. I have not been able to confirm this, but a blog from 2015 suggests as much. See: Wood, Alan (blog post), "A District Attorney in Georgia Wrote an Introduction in a Book Praising Hitler", 10 April 2015; http://gwmac.com/a-district-attorney-in-georgia-wrote-an-introduction-in-a-book-praising-hitler/, accessed: 2019–10–29.
5 *Hitlers politisches Testament. . ..*
6 Winkler, W., *Der Schattenmann . . .*, p.93. However, Fechner did not pretend that his forgery was true. On the contrary, he had a political and pedagogical point with his forgery, which he even admitted to in the afterword to the book! Fechner's message was: this is how Goebbels would have written if he had been honest about his views.
7 Speer, A., *Spandauer Tagebücher*, p.633; Fest, J., *Hitler. . .*, p.1150, note 109.
8 Another example of a forgery that fooled basically everyone involved is the famous (or perhaps infamous) forged biography of the eccentric billionaire Howard Hughes that the writer Clifford Irving produced in the 1970s. Irving forged not only Hughes's spoken expressions but also his handwriting in several long letters that managed to fool all the experts that scrutinized them. Thanks to his thorough research Irving was able to convince even the most critical publishing lawyers that he had become a good friend of Hughes, whom no one had seen in over ten years. Even persons that had met Hughes and were considered experts on him were fooled by both the letters and the finished "biography". The publishing house McGraw-Hill paid around one million dollars to Hughes, with a check put out to H. R. Hughes, which Irving's wife managed to cash

via a Swiss bank account under the fake name Helga R. Hughes. The book had already been printed before Hughes himself vehemently denied that Irving had been commissioned by him to write his biography. The real Hughes (who had a very distinct way of speaking) had already, prior to this, denied this in a phone conversation with the Time-Life journalist Frank MacCulloch, who had been the last person to interview Hughes 14 years earlier. But after having read Irving's material, and cross examined him about his alleged meetings with Hughes, MacCulloch still became convinced that Irving was telling the truth and that the phone call came from an impostor! (See: Brown, Mick, "You Couldn't Make It Up" in *The Telegraph*, 28 July 2007; www.telegraph.co.uk/culture/3666824/You-couldnt-make-it-up.html#, accessed: 2012–10–28.) Irving's bluff goes to show that you can fool almost anybody, especially when the people you are trying to fool really want the lie to be the truth.

9 See for example: Bullock, A., *Hitler. . .* (1962), pp. 769–772; Fest, J., *Hitler . . .*, pp. 735, 776–777, 842, 876–877, 989, 1011–1014; Haffner, Sebastian, *Anmerkungen zu Hitler* (Munich: Kindler Verlag, 1978), p. 29; Pyta, W., *Hitler . . .*, pp. 636, 643; Goeschel, Christian, *Mussolini and Hitler: The Forging of the Fascist Alliance* (New Haven: Yale University Press, 2018), pp. 292–293.

10 Kershaw, I., *Hitler 1936–45 . . .*, pp. 1024–1025. For a discussion about this text, see also: *Wissenschaftsfreiheit ind ihre rechtlichen Schranken . . .*, pp. 43–52.

11 Kershaw, I., *Hitler 1936–45 . . .*, p. 1024.

12 McDonough, Frank, *The Hitler Years: Triumph 1933–1039* (London: Head of Zeus, 2019), pp. 348, 467 *n*175; Fest, J., *Hitler . . .*, pp. 776–777, 1122 *n*213.

13 Simms, B., *Hitler . . .*, p. xxiii.

14 Letter from Genoud to Trevor-Roper, 26 April 1958; letter from Trevor-Roper to Genoud, 6 May 1958; letter from Genoud to Trevor-Roper, 16 May 1958; CCLO; HTRP; Vol. Soc. Dacre 6/6/2.

15 Letter from Stevens to Trevor-Roper, 2 June 1958; letter from Trevor-Roper to Stevens, 13 June 1958; letter from Stevens to Trevor-Roper, 24 June 1958; CCLO; HTRP; Vol. Soc. Dacre 6/6/2.

16 Letter from Trevor-Roper to Genoud, 1 October 1958; CCLO; HTRP; Vol. Soc. Dacre 6/6/2.

17 Trevor-Roper, H. R., "Introduction" in *The Testament of Adolf Hitler. . .* (1961), pp. 7–11.

18 Facsimile of a memorandum of conversation entitled "History of TT2" by Trevor-Roper from the meeting in Paris in November 1958 in the proof manuscript for Baumgarten's planned book "Das Hitler – Bormann Dokument"; CCLO; HTRP; Vol. Soc. Dacre 6/6/1.

19 Trevor-Roper, H. R., "Introduction" in *The Testament of Adolf Hitler. . .* (1961), pp. 9–11. For the same story see: "Mitteilungen zur Geschichte des Manuskripts der Hitler-Diktate" in the proof manuscript for Baumgarten's planned book "Das Hitler – Bormann Dokument", pp. 19–22; CCLO; HTRP; Vol. Soc. Dacre 6/6/1.

20 "Hitler's Table-Talk" in *The Times* [London, England], 23 March 1961, p. 17. *The Times Digital Archive*. Web. 29 April 2015.

21 "Mitteilungen zur Geschichte des Manuskripts der Hitler-Diktate" in the proof manuscript for Baumgarten's planned book "Das Hitler – Bormann Dokument", pp. 17, 19–20; CCLO; HTRP; Vol. Soc. Dacre 6/6/1. Baumgarten was nephew of Max Weber. He had joined the SA in 1933 and the NSDAP from 1937. Martin Heidegger, who was his dissertation advisor, eventually denounced Baumgarten, who he thought was not really a dedicated Nazi. Baumgarten could nonetheless continue his academic career thanks to his contacts in the party. After the war he was defended by several academic colleagues and could then also use the letter from Heidegger denouncing him as "proof" that he was never a convinced Nazi.

22 Facsimile (dated November 1958) and original (undated) of a memorandum of conversation entitled "History of TT2" by Trevor-Roper from the meeting in Paris in November 1958 in the proof manuscript for Baumgarten's planned book "Das Hitler – Bormann Dokument"; CCLO; HTRP; Vol. Soc. Dacre 6/6/1. Trevor-Roper only

writes that he had been asked by Rechenberg and Genoud not to tell Funk that they had a photocopy of the document.

23 Letter from Brian Melland to Trevor-Roper, 13 November 1959, pp. 1–2; CCLO; HTRP; Vol. Soc. Dacre 3/8/1.

24 Trevor-Roper to Melland, 16 November 1959; CCLO; HTRP; Vol. Soc. Dacre 3/8/1.

25 *The Testament of Adolf Hitler. . .* (1961), pp. 7, 11; *Hitlers politisches Testament . . .*, p. 23; *Le testament politique . . .*, pp. 22, 25.

26 Trevor-Roper to John Biggs-Davison, 24 November 1961, p. 7; CCLO; HTRP; Vol. Soc. Dacre 1/1/D.

27 Letter from Trevor-Roper to Baumgarten, 18 March 1973, p. 1; CCLO; HTRP; Vol. Soc. Dacre 6/6/1.

28 Ibid.

29 Ibid.

30 Ibid., p. 3.

31 Trevor-Roper to Baumgarten, 26 May 1973, p. 1; CCLO; HTRP; Vol. Soc. Dacre 6/6/1.

32 Letter from Baumgarten to Trevor-Roper, 13 March 1973, p. 4; CCLO; HTRP; Vol. Soc. Dacre 6/6/1.

33 "Hitler-Testament: Lateinisches Gift" in *Der Spiegel* 3/1962, pp. 28, 30.

34 Winkler, W., *Der Schattenmann . . .*, p. 114.

35 Letter from Irving to Trevor-Roper, 24 November 1967; HTR to Irving, 20 December 1967, p. 2; CCLO; HTRP; Vol. Soc. Dacre 6/21.

36 Ibid. In reality there were only 14 days because some of the notes have the same date on them.

37 Letter from Trevor-Roper to Irving, 20 December 1967, pp. 2–3; CCLO; HTRP; Vol. Soc. Dacre 6/6/1.

38 Jäckel, Eberhard, *Hitlers Weltanschuung. Entwurf einer Herrschaft* (Tübingen: Rainer Wunderlich Verlag Hermann Leins, 1969), pp. 72–73.

39 *Hitlers politisches Testament . . .*, p. 43.

40 Memorandum by Trevor-Roper from a meeting with Baumgarten on 15 May 1972, p. 1; CCLO; HTRP; Vol. Soc. Dacre 6/6/1.

41 Letter from Trevor-Roper to Jäckel, 26 May 1969, pp. 1–2; CCLO; HTRP; Vol. Soc. Dacre 6/6/1.

42 Trevor-Roper to Irving, 26 May 1969; HTR to Irving, 20 December 1967, p. 2; CCLO; HTRP; Vol. Soc. Dacre 6/21.

43 Letter from von Busekist to Genoud, 10 March 1971; CCLO; HTRP; Vol. Soc. Dacre 6/6/1.

44 Letter from Baumgarten to Trevor-Roper, 8 May 1972, pp. 1–2; CCLO; HTRP; Vol. Soc. Dacre 6/6/2.

45 Speer, Albert, *Erinnerungen* (Berlin: Propyläen Verlag, 1969), p. 343.

46 Letter from von Busekist to Genoud, 10 March1971; CCLO; HTRP; Vol. Soc. Dacre 6/6/1.

47 Letter from Rechenberg to Genoud, 24 April1971; CCLO; HTRP; Vol. Soc. Dacre 6/6/1.

48 Letter from Genoud to Walter, 4 January 1972; CCLO; HTRP; Vol. Soc. Dacre 6/6/1.

49 See agreement between (and signed by) Genoud and Funk, 24 October 1957; CCLO; HTRP; Vol. Soc. Dacre 6/6/1.

50 Letter from Genoud to Walter, 4 January 1972; CCLO; HTRP; Vol. Soc. Dacre 6/6/1.

51 Ibid.

52 "Anhang I" of the proof manuscript for Baumgarten's planned book "Das Hitler – Bormann Dokument", p. 3; Christ CCLO; HTRP; Vol. Soc. Dacre 6/6/1. This was the working title of the book that was prepared R. Piper & Co Verlag. It is unknown why the book was never published, but most likely because Genoud did not release the German text.

53 Letter from Lammers to Genoud, 31 March 1959; private archive of Pierre Péan, Paris. Photo of the original document in the author's possession.

54 *The Testament Adolf Hitler. . .* (1961), p. 7.

55 *Hitlers politisches Testament . . .*, p. 26. This was also stated in the English edition, something that was quoted by e.g. *The Times* in its review of the book ("Hitler's Table-Talk" in *The Times* [London, England], 23 March 1961, p. 17. *The Times Digital Archive*. Web. 29 April 2015).

56 *Hitlers politisches Testament . . .*, p. 40. We have no reason to believe that it was not Trevor-Roper who wrote this. Whenever the publisher added something to the text, it seems to have been clearly indicated (ibid., pp. 20–21).

57 *Hitlers politisches Testament . . .*, p. 20. Note that Trevor-Roper gives the wrong time span for the documents in Jochmann's book, which includes the same period as his own English edition.

58 Memorandum of conversation between Trevor-Roper Baumgarten, 15 May 1972, p. 1; CCLO; HTRP; Vol. Soc. Dacre 6/6/1.

59 Letter from Baumgarten to Trevor-Roper, 8 May 1972, p. 2; CCLO; HTRP; Vol. Soc. Dacre 6/6/2.

60 Undated typed memorandum from the meeting by Trevor-Roper; CCLO; HTRP; Vol. Soc. Dacre 6/6/1.

61 Letter from Rechenberg to Genoud, 24 April 1971; letter from Genoud to Walter, 4 January 1972; CCLO; HTRP; Vol. Soc. Dacre 6/6/1.

62 Letter from Baumgarten to Trevor-Roper, 8 May 1972, p. 2; CCLO; HTRP; Vol. Soc. Dacre 6/6/2.

63 Letter from Baumgarten to Trevor-Roper, 13 March 1973, p. 3; CCLO; HTRP; Vol. Soc. Dacre 6/6/1.

64 Ibid., p. 2; Letter from Trevor-Roper to Baumgarten, 18 March 1973, p. 1; CCLO; HTRP; Vol. Soc. Dacre 6/6/1.

65 Letter from Baumgarten to Trevor-Roper, 13 March 1973, pp. 2–5; CCLO; HTRP; Vol. Soc. Dacre 6/6/1.

66 Letter from Trevor-Roper to Baumgarten, 26 August 1972 (this carbon copy is actually undated, but the date is apparent from Baumgarten's reply on 26 September); CCLO; HTRP; Vol. Soc. Dacre 6/6/2.

67 Letter from Baumgarten to Trevor-Roper, 15 June 1972, p. 1; CCLO; HTRP; Vol. Soc. Dacre 6/6/2.

68 Undated typed memorandum by Trevor-Roper; CCLO; HTRP; Vol. Soc. Dacre 6/6/1.

69 Letter from Baumgarten to Trevor-Roper, 23 July 1973, pp. 1–2; CCLO; HTRP; Vol. Soc. Dacre 6/6/2.

70 Baumgarten to Trevor-Roper, 13 March 1973, p. 6; CCLO; HTRP; Vol. Soc. Dacre 6/6/1. Heim assumed that the spelling errors were due to Bormann not being used to handling a typewriter. Bormann did not trust his secretaries to do the typing for him, afraid that they would spread the knowledge to a third party, he claimed ("2. Mitteilungen zur Geschichte des Manuskripts der Hitler-Diktate", p. 32; CCLO; HTRP; Vol. Soc. Dacre 6/6/1).

71 Baumgarten to Trevor-Roper, 13 March 1973, pp. 6–7; CCLO; HTRP; Vol. Soc. Dacre 6/6/1.

72 Ibid., p. 4.

73 Letter from Trevor-Roper to Baumgarten, 18 March 1973, p. 2; CCLO; HTRP; Vol. Soc. Dacre 6/6/1.

74 *The Testament of Adolf Hitler. . .* (1961), p. 50; *Le testament politique . . .*, p. 78.

75 *Hitlers politisches Testament . . .*, p. 64.

76 Trevor-Roper to Baumgarten, 18 March 1973, p. 2; CCLO; HTRP; Vol. Soc. Dacre 6/6/1.

77 Ibid.

78 Ibid.

79 Ibid.

80 Ibid.

81 "Anhang I", p. 3; CCLO; HTRP; Vol. Soc. Dacre 6/6/1. Baumgarten also included Trevor-Roper's statement that he had seen Bormann's "unmistabeable [sic] monogram"

on each page and that this was "perfectly known" to him (ibid., p. 10). This manuscript, apparently under the working title "Das Hitler – Bormann Dokument" was prepared not for Knaus, which later published the text, but R. Piper & Co Verlag. It is unknown why the book was not published by Piper.

82 Trevor-Roper to Baumgarten, 26 May 1973, p. 1; CCLO; HTRP; Vol. Soc. Dacre 6/6/1.

83 *Wissenschaftsfreiheit und ihre rechtlichen Schranken . . .*, p. 49. Here however, Baumgarten dates Trevor-Roper's letter to 1971, which thus is an error.

84 Letter from Trevor-Roper to Baumgarten, 18 March 1973, p. 3; CCLO; HTRP; Vol. Soc. Dacre 6/6/1.

85 Ibid. For the part about Stevens, see also: Letter from Baumgarten to Trevor-Roper, 13 March 1973, p. 7; CCLO; HTRP; Vol. Soc. Dacre 6/6/1.

86 Undated typed memorandum entitled "François Genoud" by Trevor-Roper, p. 1; CCLO; HTRP; Vol. Soc. Dacre 6/6/2.

87 Letter from Baumgarten to Trevor-Roper, 19 October 1974, p. 2; CCLO; HTRP; Vol. Soc. Dacre 6/6/2.

88 Bird, K. Eugene, *Heß. Der "Stellvertreter des Führers" Englandflug und britische Gefangen-schaft Nürnberg und Spandau* (Herrsching: Manfred Pawlak Verlagsgesellschaft, 1974), pp. 97–98.

89 *TBJG* II/15, p. 241 (27 January 1945); p. 328 (7 February 1945).

90 Notes by Baumgarten after his meeting with Rechenberg and Genoud, 15 July 1974, p. 1; CCLO; HTRP; Vol. Soc. Dacre 6/6/2. See also page from Goebbel's diary 9 April 1945 attached to this document.

    Trevor-Roper, when writing his memorandum, stated that Goebbels's diary entry was from 19 April. This mistake made the timeline work for Trevor-Roper, since Funk then claimed to have transported the gold two days earlier (Undated typed memorandum entitled "François Genoud" by Trevor-Roper, p. 1; CCLO; HTRP; Vol. Soc. Dacre 6/6/2). I believe that the mistake is explained by the fact that Trevor-Roper misheard Baumgarten (the conversation was in German and over the phone), because the ninth, *neunte* in German, sounds similar to *neunzehnte* (nineteenth in German).

91 *TBJG* II/15, p. 690 (9 April 1945). It is interesting to note that this particular part of the diary entry is missing in the edited version of the diaries that was published by Hoff-man & Campe in 1977 under the title Goebbels, Joseph, *Tagebücher 1945: Die Letzten Aufzeichnungen* (Hamburg: Hoffman & Campe Verlag, 1977). This book was translated into English, edited and introduced by Hugh Trevor-Roper, and published in 1978 (*The Goebbels Diaries*. Edited and Introduced by Hugh Trevor-Roper (London: Book Club Associates, 1978), pp. 297–300).

92 *Hitlers politisches Testament . . .*, pp. 24–25.

93 Ibid., p. 690 (9 April 1945).

94 "Reich's Hoard of Gold, Cash Is 'Legitimate Prize of War'" in *The Stars and Stripes* [Paris Edition], 9 April 1945. This newspaper was produced for the US Armed Forces by the Information and Education Division; www.wartimepress. com/archives.asp?TID=Paris&MID=Stars%20and%20Stripes%20-%20All%20 Editions&q=168&FID=10, accessed: 2016–05–30.

95 Notes by Baumgarten after his meeting with Rechenberg and Genoud, 15 July 1974, p. 1; CCLO; HTRP; Vol. Soc. Dacre 6/6/2.

96 Ibid., p. 2.

97 Ibid.

98 Schroeder, C., *Er war mein Chef . . .*, p. 275.

99 Ibid., p. 257. "'nein, dann spreche ich nicht mehr so frei.'" Wolfram Pyta accepts this statement, although he cites the phrase as: "Dann hätte ich nicht so sprechen können!", and refers mistakenly to "p. 355, footnote 229", which does not contain this informa-tion (for this, see: Pyta, W., *Hitler . . .*, p. 666). The idea that Hitler stated that he would not have spoken "so freely" is hard to take seriously, however. For example, Hitler had told Goebbels in late January 1940 that he was planning on writing down everything that occupied him at the moment as a form of testament, or as Goebbels put it: "the Gospel of National Socialism." For this, see: Ullrich, V., *Adolf Hitler. . .* (Vol. II), p. 106.

100 Rose, O. (ed.), *Julius Schaub . . .*, pp. 347–359.

101 Baumgarten to Trevor-Roper, 17 January 1975, pp. 1–2; CCLO; HTRP; Vol. Soc. Dacre 6/6/1.

102 Ibid., p. 2.

103 Trevor-Roper to Baumgarten, 24 January 1975; CCLO; HTRP; Vol. Soc. Dacre 6/6/1.

104 It might be interjected that an exception to this rule would be if the text contains matter that only the purported author could possibly know. But in order to establish if that is in fact the case, we would have to consult independent evidence, and thus the validation is not made using only internal evidence. Certainly, we cannot conclude with absolute certainty that a text is a forgery (or contains forged passaged) even if it contains matter that completely contradicts everything we know about the author, but we would still be justified in rejecting it until such time that we find independent evidence that can corroborate it. Absolute certainty is not possible to attain (except in deductive logic). Historians, just as all empirical scientists, operate with probabilities, and the probability for a hypothesis being either true or false is always higher than 0 and lower than 1. An hypothesis is increasingly more likely to be true the closer the probability of it gets to 1 (a 0.5 probability means that the hypothesis is just as likely to be false as it is to be true), and it is increasingly *less* likely to be true the closer the probability of it being true gets to 0.

105 Letter from Baumgarten to Trevor-Roper, 19 October 1974, p. 2; CCLO; HTRP; Vol. Soc. Dacre 6/6/2.

106 *Hitlers politisches Testament . . .*, pp. 42–127; *The Bormann Letters . . .*, pp. 167–198.

107 *Le testament politique . . .*, p. 8.

108 *Hitlers politisches Testament . . .*, pp. 7–9.

109 Ibid., p. 11.

110 *Hitlers politisches Testament . . .*, pp. 24–26.

111 *The Bormann Letters . . .*, pp. 194–198. There are, in fact three short letters from Bormann to his wife dated 2 April.

112 *Hitlers politisches Testament . . .*, p. 113.

113 Schroeder, C., *Er war mein Chef . . .*, p. 272. See also p. 105. Indeed, the plan called *Seelöwe* was developed for precisely this reason.

114 Ibid., p. 105. At the same time, one must acknowledge that Schroeder includes other things in her recollections that find support in independent sources. For instance, she states that Hitler did not want to destroy the British army completely, since this was the guarantor of the British Empire. If the army was destroyed, so would be the empire, and that was not in the interest of Germany.

115 Frieser, Karl-Heinz, *Bliztkrieg-Legende. Der Westfeldzug 1940* (Munich: R. Oldenburg Verlag, 1995), pp. 388–391.

116 Ullrich, V., *Adolf Hitler. . .* (Vol. II), pp. 121–122, 134–135. See also: Nilsson, M., "Constructing a Pseudo-Hitler? . . .".

117 *HRP* II/3, pp. 1520–1521 (5 June 1940).

118 Longerich, P., *Hitler . . .*, pp. 729–732.

119 *HRP* II/3, pp. 1540–1559, 1573–1583 (19 July & 4 September 1940).

120 Horne, Alistair, *To Lose a Battle: France 1940* (Basingstoke: Papermac, (1969) 1990), p. 615.

121 Frieser, K.-H., *Bliztkrieg-Legende . . .*, p. 369; Kershaw, I., *Hitler 1936–1945 . . .*, p. 295.

122 *Generaloberst Halder. Kriegstagebuch. Band I. Vom Polenfeldzug bis zum Ende der Westoffensive (14. 8. 1939–30. 6. 1940). Bearbeitet von Hans-Adolf Jacobsen in Verbindung mit Alfred Philippi* (Stuttgart: W. Kohlhammer Verlag, 1962), p. 318.

123 Horne, A., *To Lose a Battle . . .*, pp. 610–616. See also: Evans, R. J., *The Third Reich at War . . .*, 2008), p. 129.

124 Frieser, K.-H., *Bliztkrieg-Legende . . .*, pp. 386–388.

125 Fest, J., *Hitler . . .*, p. 859; Hubatsch, W. (ed.), *Hitlers Weisungen . . .*, pp. 62–64.

126 Horne, A., *To Lose a Battle . . .*, pp. 611–613; Fest, J., *Hitler . . .*, p. 859.

127 *Heeresadjutant bei Hitler 1938–1943. Aufzeichnungen des Major Engels. Herausgegeben und kommentiert von Hildegard von Kontze* (Stuttgart: Deutsche Verlags-Anstalt, 1974), pp. 80–81.

128 Toland, J., *Adolf Hitler* (Vol. II), p. 705 (p. 610 in the one-volume edition).

129 Longerich, P., *Hitler . . .*, pp. 724–725.

130 Warlimont, Walter, *Im Führerhauptquartier der deutschen Wehrmacht 1939–1945. Grundlagen, Formen, Gestalten* (Frankfurt am Main: Bernard & Graefe für Wehrwesen, 1962), pp. 112–114.

131 Frieser, K.-H., *Bliztkrieg-Legende . . .*, pp. 368, 391–393.

132 Kershaw, I., *Hitler 1936–45 . . .*, p. 296.

133 Warlimont, W., *Im Führerhauptquartier der deutschen Wehrmacht . . .*, p. 114.

134 Jackson, Julian, *The Fall of France: The Nazi Invasion of 1940* (Oxford: Oxford University Press, 2003), pp. 95–97. The number of troops vary greatly in the literature; Frieser states 247,000 British and 123,000 French: Frieser, K.-H., *Bliztkrieg-Legende . . .*, p. 377.

135 Toland, J., *Adolf Hitler* (Vol. II), p. 706, (p. 611 in the one-volume edition).

136 *HRP* II/4, p. 1691 (6 April 1941).

137 *ADAP, Serie D: 1937–1941. Band XII. 2. Die Kriegsjahre. Fünfter Band. Zweiter Halbband. 6. April bis 22. Juni 1941* (Göttingen: Vandenhoeck & Ruprecht, 1969), pp. 586–588 (Document 451).

138 "Aufzeichnung des Gesandten Hewel" in *ADAP, Serie D: 1937–1941. Band XIII. 2. Die Kriegsjahre. Sechster Band. Zweiter Halbband. 15. September bis 11. Dezember 1941* (Göttingen: Vandenhoeck & Ruprecht, 1970), pp. 831–833 (Anhang II).

139 *RSA* III/1, p. 151 (Document 36). See also: ibid., pp. 162–163 (Document 37).

140 Simms, B., *Hitler . . .*, p. 425.

141 *Hitlers politisches Testament . . .*, p. 69.

142 Baumgarten to Trevor-Roper, 16 July 1973, p. 5; CCLO; HTRP; Vol. Soc. Dacre 6/6/2.

143 Letter from Heim to Werner Jochmann, 3 January 1980, p. 2; WJN; Binder: Schriftwechsel: A – K 1977.

144 *Hitler, Mein Kampf . . .* (Band I), p. 349 **[121]**.

145 *Hitler, Mein Kampf . . .* (Band II), p. 1689 **[331]**. ". . . schon am Visier soll man uns erkennen."

146 *Hitlers politisches Testament . . .*, p. 68. The use of the phrase "vom genetischen Standpunkt" is also a bit suspect, since genetics was not a subject that in any way was a theme common to Hitler.

147 *Hitler, Mein Kampf . . .* (Band I), pp. 777–779, 781–799, [317–325].

148 Hitler, A., *Hitlers zweites Buch . . ., s. 220; Monologe . . .*, pp. 130–131, 279.

149 *Hitlers politisches Testament . . .*, pp. 95–102; *The Bormann Letters . . .*, pp. 189–191.

150 Besymenski, L., *Die letzten Notizen . . .*, p. 144. In fact, none of the entries in Bormann's diary mentions anything related to the notes published in *Hitlers politisches Testament*. Note that Besymenski's book was first published in Russian and that the German edition was translated from Russian to German. It also suffers from the Marxist orthodoxy expressed in its analysis of Bormann and National Socialism. For instance, Besymenski states that Gerhard Roßbach's *Freikorps* had battled the "the proletarian revolution in Latvia" in the 1920s (ibid., p. 24).

151 Ibid., p. 145.

152 Letter from Heim to Kuykendall, 25 October 1975, p. 1; UALSC; PKK MS 243; Series II; Box 2, Folder 5.

153 Ibid.

154 Ibid., pp. 1–2.

155 Reitsch, Hanna, *Höhen und Tiefen 1945 bis zur Gegenwart* (München: Herbig Verlag, 1978), pp. 56–65. Hanna Reitsch was one of the best women test pilots in the Third Reich, working for the *Luftwaffe* between 1937 and 1945. She was a fanatical Nazi and trained around 70 so-called "SO" (Selbstopfer) pilots for a "kamikaze" mission towards the end of the war. Her idea was to make manned V1 rockets that would be

piloted straight into its targets. Hitler never authorized the missions, however, so none were really performed. But she apparently received permission to initiate test flights. She stayed in Berlin and in Hitler's bunker until the very end and flew the last aircraft out of Berlin; see: Iken, Katja, "Nazi-Starpilotin Hanna Reitsch: Für Hitler flog sie durch die Hölle" in *Die Zeit*-Online, 29 March 2012; www.spiegel.de/einestages/nazi-starpilotin-hanna-reitsch-a-947526.html, accessed: 2016–08–03.

156 Letter from Krämer to Heim, 22 February 1986; IfZ; ED 416; Vol. 2.

157 Unfortunately, I have previously mistakenly stated in an article that Reitsch cited this text: Nilsson, M., "Constructing a Pseudo-Hitler? . . .", p. 14.

158 Reitsch, H., *Höhen und Tiefen . . .*, pp. 63–64.

159 Trevor-Roper, H. R., The Last Days of Hitler (London: Macmillan & Co., 1947), pp. 161–162, 188.

160 This criterion is common in New Testament studies, especially by the scholars in the so-called Jesus Seminar, when theologians are trying to establish which statements ascribed to Jesus were actually said by him.

161 Straßer, Otto, *Hitler et moi* (Paris: Éditions Bernard Grasset, 1940), p. 118. The book was later re-published in German in 1948.

162 Ibid., pp. 114–115. "j'étais décidé à combattre son hypocrisie à visière ouverte. . . . "

163 Letter from Baumgarten to Trevor-Roper, 13 March 1973, p. 5; CCLO; HTRP; Vol. Soc. Dacre 6/6/1.

164 *The Testament of Adolf Hitler. . .* (1961), p. 40.

165 *Le testament politique . . .*, pp. 67–68.

166 Typed manuscript for *The Testament of Adolf Hitler*, p. 7; CCLO; HTRP; Vol. Soc. Dacre 6/6/1.

167 *Hitlers politisches Testament . . .*, p. 52.

168 Typed manuscript for *The Testament of Adolf Hitler*, p. 18; CCLO; HTRP; Vol. Soc. Dacre 6/6/1. See also: *Le testament politique de Hilter . . .*, p. 88; *The Testament of Adolf Hitler. . .* (1961), p. 59.

169 For this, see: *Hitlers politisches Testament . . .*, p. 73.

170 *The Testament of Adolf Hitler. . .* (1961), p. 40. Peter Longerich cites this passage in his Hitler biography, see: Longerich, P., *Hitler . . .*, p. 636.

171 Cited in: Ullrich, V., *Adolf Hitler. . .* (Vol. II), pp. 608–609.

172 Pyta, W., *Hitler . . .*, pp. 623–653. In this chapter Pyta also cites *Hitlers politisches Testament . . .*, p. 636.

173 *TBJG* II/15, pp. 313–330, 346–353, 371–382, 662–666.

174 Ibid., pp. 320–321.

175 Ibid., p. 253 (28 January 1945); p. 273 (30 January 1945); p. 378 (13 February 1945); pp. 485–486 (12 March 1945); *HRP* II/4, pp. 2179–2188, 2195–2198, 2203–2206, 2211–2212 (1 & 30 January, 24 February, 11 March 1945). However, there are 25 pages missing from the 2 April entry in Goebbels's diary (*TBJG* II/15, p. 666) so we do not know whether there would be overlapping themes there.

176 *The Goebbels Diaries*, pp. xxxix, 1–2. See also: Longerich, P., *Goebbels . . .*, pp. 659–660.

177 *The Goebbels Diaries*, p. xxxvii; Winkler, W., *Der Schattenmann . . .*, pp. 269–279.

178 Heiber, H. (ed.), *Goebbels Reden 1939–1945* (Band II), pp. 111–115, 200–201, 238, 244, 265, 274–275, 409, 413–414, 436, 443–446.

179 Longerich, P., *Goebbels . . .*, pp. 511–512.

180 *Hitler's Table Talk. . .* (1953), pp. 14, 31, 66, 80–82, 84, 109, 124, 126, 130, 260, 336, 360, 384, 402, 408, 476, 540, 646, 660.

181 *Hitler, Mein Kampf. . .* (Band I), pp. 303, 573, 633, 685, 813 **[98, 244, 251, 276, 330]**; (Band II), pp. 1555, 1641–1642 **[267, 308–309]**; Hitler, A., *Hitlers zweites Buch . . .*, pp. 76, 109, 139, 141–142, 168–169, 171; *SA*, pp. 143, 175, 187, 367, 377, 583, 608, 619–620, 717, 743, 775, 923, 955, 957, 982, 986, 1013, 1021, 1032, 1034; *RSA* I, pp. 88, 111, 252, 275; *RSA* II/1, pp. 400–401, 408, 431; *RSA* II/2, pp. 552, 585, 630, 664, 682, 715, 723, 770, 776–777, 796, 812, 827–828, 830, 835; *RSA* III/1, pp. 52, 93, 172, 271, 283, 300; *RSA* III/2, pp. 42, 117, 146, 187, 212, 267, 276, 399; *RSA* III/3, pp. 174, 254, 321, 448; *RSA* IV/1, pp. 172, 287; *RSA* IV/2, pp. 93, 149;

RSA IV/3, pp. 66, 76, 242–243; *RSA* V/1, pp. 71, 75; *RSA* V/2, pp. 44, 107, 254, 310, 368, 384–385; Gerhard L. Weinberg actually comments that Hitler, when talking about the great bravery of Frederick II in putting it all on the line, forgot about the importance of historical chance events such as the death of Elisabeth of Russia in 1762 (ibid., p. 142 *n*1). For the references to Wagner, Luther, and Frederick II, see also: Longerich, P., *Hitler . . .*, pp. 127, 140.

182 *SA*, p. 1198, 1202–1203 (Document 625); *Der Hitler-Prozess 1924. Wortlaut der Haupt-verhandlung vor dem Volksgericht München I. Teil 4: 19. – 25. Verhandlungstag. Herausgege-ben und kommentiert von Lother Gruchmann und Reinhard Weber unter Mitarbeit von Otto Gritschneder* (München: K. G. Saur, 1999), pp. 1573, 1578; *RSA* II/1, p. 425 (Document 159).

183 *RSA* II/2, pp. 827–828 (Document 268).

184 Ibid., p. 80.

185 *SA*, p. 77 (Document 41). Kujau also forged the Hitler diaries.

186 Ryback, T. W., *Hitler's Private Library . . .*, pp. 8–9, 20–21, 25, 50–51, 194, 223–225, 228, 264, 247.

187 Warlimont, W., *Im Hauptquartier . . .*, pp. 519, 525; Heiber, Helmut (ed.), *Lagebe-sprechungen im Führerhauptquartier. Protokollfragmente aus Hitlers militärischen Konferenzen 1942–1945* (Stuttgart: Deutsche Verlags-Anstalt, 1962), pp. 280, 291–292 (this speech is also cited by Warlimont).

188 Ullrich, V., *Adolf Hitler. . .* (Vol. II), pp. 464–465.

189 Speer, A., *Erinnerungen*, p. 467. Magnus Brechtken has pointed out that Trevor-Roper's *The Last Days of Hitler* also depended on Speer for much of the information; Speer thus from very early on was able to affect history by acting as a witness for historians; see: Brechtken, M., *Albert Speer . . .*, p. 282. Speer also claims that Hitler came to him holding a newspaper article in his hand shouting and asking if Speer had seen the news. This sounds less likely to be true. Yet this story has been repeated uncritically in the literature; see e.g. Longerich, P., *Hitler . . .*, p. 991; Evans, R. J., *The Third Reich at War . . .*, pp. 721–722. Evans accepts every bit of this narrative. Volker Ullrich also cites Speer and says that Hitler's general reaction as portrayed by Speer was confirmed by the testimony of stenographer Gerhard Hergesell in April 1948 (Ullrich here cites Anton Joachimsthaler's *Hitlers Ende* from 1995). He also brings up the fact that Nicolaus von Below has another opinion but does not go into the possible reasons for this difference: Ullrich, V., *Adolf Hitler. . .* (Vol. II), pp. 625, 832 *n*157.

190 von Below, Nicolaus, *Als Hitlers Adjutant . . .*, p. 408.

191 Toland, J., *Adolf Hitler*, p. 861. For a devastating critique of Hesse's book, see: Kraus-nick, Hemlut, "Legenden um Hitlers Aussenpolitik" in *Vierteljahrshefte für Zeitgeschichte*, 2. Jahrgang 1954, 3. Heft/Juli, pp. 217–239.

192 Frank, H., *Im Angesicht des Galgens . . .*, pp. 358–359.

193 Trevor-Roper, H. R., *The Last Days . . .*, pp. 106–110. Trevor-Roper actually con-tinues to talk about Carlyle and the ideological affinities between him, Hitler and the Germans who believed in an authoritarian "great man" (ibid., pp. 252–254). A typed transcript of the original document (supplied by Trevor-Roper) is located at the IfZ in Munich and can be accessed online, see: Schwerin von Krosigk's diary "The Begin-ning and the End", 15 April 1945, pp. 18, 20; www.ifz-muenchen.de/archiv/zsa/ZS_A_0020_04a.pdf, accessed: 2019–10–17.

194 Bullock, A., *Hitler. . .* (1952), pp. 712–713; Fest, J., *Hitler . . .*, p. 1000; Kershaw, I., *Hitler 1936–1945 . . .*, pp. 791–792. Kershaw bases his version on Trevor-Roper and Speer.

195 Toland, J., *Adolf Hitler*, p. 861.

196 See comment in footnote in: *RSA* V/2, p. 254 *n*4.

197 Trevor-Roper, H. R., "Introduction" in *The Testament of Adolf Hitler. . .* (1961), pp. 6–7.

198 Carlyle, Thomas, *History of Frederick II of Prussia, Vol. XX. Frederick the Great – Friedrich Is Not to Be Overwhelmed: The Seven-Years War Gradually Ends – 25 April 1760–15 Feb-ruary 1763*, p. 491.

199 Ibid., pp. 476–477.
200 An apparent reference to Cato the Younger who was one of the leaders in the rebellion against Caesar in the Roman Civil War and who committed suicide in 46 BCE rather than to face the humiliation of being captured and pardoned and thereafter be in Caesar's debt. Cato and his suicide became a role model for the Stoic philosophers. Cato, however, did not kill himself by drinking poison, but by cutting his own stomach open. For more on Cato and suicide in the Roman times, see: Griffin, Miriam, "Philosophy, Cato, and Roman Suicide: II" in *Greece & Rome*, Vol. 33, No. 2 (October 1986), pp. 192–202.
201 Letter from Frederick II to Marquis d'Argens, 18 January 1762, in: *Œuvres de Frédéric le Grand*, Vol. 19, pp. 318–317; http://friedrich.uni-trier.de/fr/oeuvres/19/317/text/, accessed: 2019–10–24.
202 This was confirmed by Professor Tim Blanning, an expert on Frederick the Great (and the author of a recent biography on him), in an email to me on 25 October 2019. On a direct question from me, Blanning replied: "The interpolation in square brackets are from Carlyle himself. He was fond of doing this."
203 *The Goebbels Diaries*, p. 215. See also: Ullrich, V., *Adolf Hitler. . .* (Vol. II), p. 609.
204 Goeschel, Christian, "Suicide at the End of the Third Reich" in *Journal of Contemporary History*, Vol. 41, No. 1 (January 2006), p. 157 [pp. 153–173].
205 Ibid.
206 Kershaw, I., *Hitler 1936–1945 . . .*, p. 783.
207 Heiber, H. (ed.), *Goebbels Reden 1939–1945* (Band II), p. 446; see also mentioning of Frederick II on p. 436. This letter is also cited by Carlyle but there is nothing about suicide here; see: Carlyle, T., *History of Frederick II of Prussia . . .*, pp. 106–107. For the original in French, see: Letter from Frederick to his sister Amelie, 25 March 1757 (Document 8772), in: *Politisches Korrespondenz Friedrichs des Großen*, Vol. 14, p. 412; http://friedrich.uni-trier.de/de/politKorr/14/412/, accessed: 2019–10–23.
208 *The Goebbels Diaries . . .*, pp. 183, 197, 251 (20, 21 & 27 March 1945).
209 Eberle, H. & Uhl, M. (eds.), *Das Buch Hitler . . .*, p. 334. Hitler's anger with Dietrich is corroborated by Christa Schroeder. See Zoller, A., *Hitler privat . . .*, pp. 219–220. She never mentions Frederick II in this context however.
210 *The Goebbels Diaries . . .*, p. 39 (4 March 1945).
211 Ibid., p. 102 (11 March 1945). See also: Ullrich, V., *Adolf Hitler. . .* (Vol. II), p. 609.
212 Ryback, T. W., *Hitler's Private Library . . .*, pp. 223, 225, 228.
213 Email from Timothy Ryback to me on 27 October 2019.
214 Ibid.
215 Ullrich, V., *Adolf Hitler. . .* (Vol. I), p. 138.
216 Trevor-Roper, H. R., *The Last Days . . .*, p. 106.
217 Schwerin von Krosigk's diary "The Beginning and the End", 15 April 1945, p. 16; www.ifz-muenchen.de/archiv/zsa/ZS_A_0020_04a.pdf, accessed: 2019–10–27.
218 This date, 9 April, also just happens to be the date on Goebbels's last diary entry. This entry contains no corroboration of the information in von Krosigk's diary. Goebbels mentions neither von Krosigk nor Frederick II.
219 Zoller, A., *Hitler privat . . .*, p. 156. On the other hand, *The Testament* has Hitler saying things that directly contradict things that Schroeder says in Zoller's book. On such example is his views on Japan and the Japanese. In Zoller's book Schroeder says that Hitler was always aware that his alliance with Japan stood in sharp contrast to his racial ideology and that the Japanese were inferior. In *The Testament*, however, Hitler is very positive towards the Japanese and he even explicitly says that he has "never regarded the Chinese or the Japanese as being inferior to ourselves" (ibid., p. 157; *The Testament of Adolf Hitler. . .* (1961), pp. 53, 76–78). It is almost as if it is a retort to what we find in Zoller's book. Schroeder says things that are contradicted by the table talks as well; the Japanese issue is only one of those.
220 *The Goebbels Diaries . . .*, pp. 331–332 ("Appendix by Dr. Joseph Goebbels to Adolf Hitler's Will and Testament, 29 April 1945", 29 April 1945).

221 See image of the handwritten note by Bormann attached to the political testament given to Dönitz, 29 April 1945, on a blog post by Dr. Greg Bradsher on the National Archive website; https://text-message.blogs.archives.gov/2016/01/19/the-search-for-hitlers-political-testament-personal-will-and-marriage-certificate-part-iii/, accessed: 2019–10–29.

222 *Wissenschaftsfreiheit und ihre rechtlichen Schranken . . .*, pp. 47–48.

223 Letter from Baumgarten to Broszat, 14 September 1977; IfZ; ID 507/1; Öffentliches Kolloqium zum Thema: "Die Informationsfreiheit der zeitgeschichtlichen Forschung und ihre rechtlichen Schranken".

224 Letter from Genoud to Broszat, 31 August 1977; IfZ; ID 507/1; Öffentliches Kolloqium zum Thema: "Die Informationsfreiheit der zeitgeschichtlichen Forschung und ihre rechtlichen Schranken".

225 Letter from Broszat to Genoud, 1 September 1977, pp. 2–3; IfZ; ID 507/1; Öffentliches Kolloqium zum Thema: "Die Informationsfreiheit der zeitgeschichtlichen Forschung und ihre rechtlichen Schranken". This letter must have been sent before Genoud's letter of 31 August had arrived in Munich. Genoud stated in his letter that he had just come back from a longer journey and had thus just read Broszat's letter from 28 July.

226 For this, see: Laske, K., *Ein Leben . . .*, pp. 155–157, 159.

227 www.fpp.co.uk/Hitler/docs/Testament/GenoudMS.html, accessed: 2019–10–15. Irving has the weird habit of writing about himself in the third person, making it appear as if someone else has written what is to be found on his website.

228 Email from acting archive chief Thomas Schütte at the IfZ to me on 5 November 2019.

229 *Wissenschaftsfreiheit und ihre rechtlichen Schranken . . .*, p. 49.

230 *Hitlers politisches Testament . . .*, p. 12.

231 Trevor-Roper to Genoud, undated but around New Year's 1977; Genoud to Trevor-Roper, 6 January 1978 and Lammers to Genoud, 31 March 1959; CCLO; HTRP; Vol. Soc. Dacre 6/6/2. For the original, see: Letter from Lammers to Genoud, 31 March 1959; Box 130; from the private archives of Pierre Péan, Paris, France.

232 Notes from interview with von Below 16 October 1951; BAK; N 263 (Nachlaß Rheindorf); Vol. 192; Document 10. I want to thank Professor Wolfram Pyta for sharing his copies of Rheindorf's papers with me.

233 Letter from Knaus to Jochmann, 17 July 1980, p. 1; WJN; Binder: "Schriftwechsel A – K 1977".

234 Letter from Knaus to Heim, 19 January 1981; IfZ; ED 416; Vol. 2.

235 Letter from Knaus to Jochmann, 17 July 1980, pp. 1–2; WJN; Binder: "Schriftwechsel A – K 1977".

236 For this, see: Harris, Robert, *Selling Hitler* (London: Arrow Books 2009 (1st edition by Faber & Faber Ltd, 1986)), pp. 118–121. There is much more on both Trevor-Roper's and Jäckel's roles in this affair in this brilliant book. Jäckel would discover his mistake only half a year later, in February 1981 and had to make an announcement in an academic journal that he had been fooled. To his credit, Jäckel became a bit more critical of the Hitler diaries after this experience, an attitude he kept even as he was asked to assess their authenticity in April 1983 (ibid., pp. 135–136, 334–335). By then the diaries had already been dismissed as forgeries by most historians who had looked at them.

237 Letter from Knaus to Jochmann, 25 July 1980; WJN; Binder: "Schriftwechsel A – K 1977".

238 Liulevicius, Vejas Gabriel, *The German Myth of the East: 1800 to the Present* (Oxford: Oxford University Press, 2009), p. 226.

239 Quoted in: Evans, R. J., *Lying About Hitler . . .*, p. 10.

240 Letter from Trevor-Roper to Carrier, 17 October 2002, pp. 3–4 (a copy of the letter was sent to me by Carrier).

241 Ibid., p. 2.

242 Ibid.

7

WERNER JOCHMANN AND THE *MONOLOGE IM FÜHRERHAUPTQUARTIER* EDITION

The publication of Genoud's "original" manuscript

Introduction

In this final chapter I will address the events concerning the publication of *Monologe*, i.e. the German edition of the text previously published in French and English as *Libres propos* and *Table Talk*. Much of this chapter depends upon documents from the historian, and editor of the volume, Werner Jochmann's private archive; a source material never before used by any historian who has paid attention to the history of the table talks. This material, which is in private hands, sheds a new and interesting light on the process that led to the publication of this manuscript. Initially, I had hoped to find a copy of Genoud's manuscript in this archival material, but unfortunately it turned out that no such document was to be found. The only manuscript I found was the typed proofs for the book. The archive contained many other interesting documents, however, as will become evident in the chapter.

In the beginning was the word

Unfortunately, there are still a lot of things that we do not know regarding the first, and only, edition of Genoud's manuscript in German and how it came to be published. The personal papers of Werner Jochmann is far from complete. Many documents that we would want, and even expect, to be there are simply not present, and the same is true for the French journalist, and Genoud's biographer, Pierre Péan's Genoud material that does not contain anything on the Jochmann edition. Research at the IfZ also turned up nothing at all relating to this affair. Perhaps the most disappointing of all is the fact that there is no documentation on the initial stages of the process, and thus we have no idea how or why Jochmann was selected to do the work, when and why Genoud decided to publish the manuscript, and so on. Even so, the following will shed much needed light on

Monologe and will contribute significantly to our understanding of this important historical source.

Because of what has been said earlier, it is unknown when Jochmann and Genoud made contact the first time, but there is a good chance that it may have been 1977 when the German academic publisher Hoffmann & Campe approached Jochmann to inquire if he would be interested in taking part in the publication of Goebbels's diaries.[1] Considering that Genoud controlled the publication rights to Goebbels's private papers, it is not unreasonable to assume that Jochmann at least must have heard of him in connection with this offer being made. Jochmann was still working on this in the summer of 1978, while also working on *Monologe*, and by then he was certainly aware of Genoud's role because he told the latter about his work on the Goebbels material in a letter.[2]

This is all the more likely since by January 1978 – thus very soon after the colloquium at the IfZ; perhaps Genoud got an offer from Knaus at the event – Genoud had given Jochmann "part I" (as well as part IV, M. N.) of the text for what would be *Monologe* and was about to send him "part II" and part "III" as well. These were most likely the same four parts in which both *Table Talk* and *Monologe* are divided. In a letter to Jochmann, Knaus stated that seeing the result of the research that Jochmann had made, it was obvious to him that the introduction to the book would have to address the differences compared to Picker's book, although Picker should absolutely not be made the main subject of discussion.[3] Perhaps it was felt that this would give Picker and *Tischgespräche* too much attention.

Apparently, though, Jochmann had not been completely satisfied with the division of the manuscript into four parts. He must have said something about this to Knaus, who then repeated it in a letter to Genoud. The letter from Knaus to Genoud, which Genoud now responded to, is not present in Jochmann's archive, so it is not possible to know exactly what Jochmann had objected to or expressed. Genoud, however, stated that he was "surprised" (*erstaunt*) that Jochmann could not "decide" what to do based upon the two parts of the manuscript and the English and French editions, which he was sure Jochmann had access to.[4] It could perhaps be that Jochmann was still not completely committed to the project and that he wanted to see the whole manuscript before deciding to accept the task assigned to him.

Genoud then told Knaus, in order to avoid any misunderstandings, that it was the first time in 27 years that he had parted with this text and that he had only done so because he had full confidence in Knaus and that he and no one else would keep it (except obviously Jochmann) and not make any copies of it. These conditions were to be upheld until the book had been published. Until the last two parts of the manuscript had been turned over to Knaus and Jochmann, Genoud thought it would be a good idea to deliberate some more on the conditions for their cooperation. For example, Genoud thought that a publication in the spring of 1980 was too late because of Heim's advanced age; Genoud apparently wished that Heim should be alive and able to read the book. The autumn of 1979 seemed more reasonable to Genoud, not least considering that the manuscript, according to him, was ready to print as it was and was already well known.[5] Knaus asked Jochmann not to take Genoud's expression of surprise too seriously. Genoud explained to him over the phone that he simply assumed that Jochmann had access to the English and French editions and that he could make a decision based on that. In early March Knaus wrote Jochmann again and wondered if the latter could perhaps agree that these editions and the two parts of the manuscript that he had so far received could be enough to give an answer whether he would take on the assignment. Knaus had set a meeting with Genoud to take place in Munich in March at which time Genoud would hand him the last two parts of the manuscript. He was of the opinion that the Swiss would most likely try to get him to give an offer for the whole deal at that meeting, but Knaus had no intention of making any such offers at the moment.[6]

Genoud did not send Jochmann the two parts in the mail because he was afraid that the text would get lost (he had already had that experience with a Goebbels letter, he said). Instead, he would hand them over personally to either Jochmann or Knaus, just as he had done with parts I and IV. Genoud remarked that until such time as these parts could be delivered, Jochmann could still get a perfectly good idea of the content by looking at the two parts he had already gotten, as well as *Table Talk* and *Libres propos*. The only thing that would have to be changed was that Picker's notes would be taken out. He did not specify why Picker's notes would have to be excluded, but it stands to reason that Picker and Genoud must already have had some sort of discussion on the topic. At this point Genoud and Jochmann had met at least once in Hamburg.[7] Jochmann, Knaus, and Genoud then met again in Munich later the same month.[8]

By June 1978 a contract for the book between Albrecht Knaus Verlag and Jochmann had been drawn up. The book had been given the working title *Hitlers Tischmonologe*.[9] The contract included translation rights for the whole world, but this particular part had to be taken out just a little while later because Genoud had changed his mind and did not want to give the publisher this right.[10] This is why there is no direct English translation of *Monologe* to this day. It is not clear why Genoud acted this way. What is clear from the correspondence in Jochmann's archive is that Jochmann did *not* have access to the original *Bormann-Vermerke*, but only to a copy of it. This is obvious from a letter Jochmann sent to Genoud in July 1978:

> In Portfolio II I am missing pages 190–193, namely the talks of 19 and 20 November 1941, which, according to your page count, must be available and have also been included in the English edition. *I suspect that, by mistake, these 4 pages were not copied.* May I ask you to look at your copy and when you have time make a copy of the missing sheets and send them to me? It is not extremely urgent, but I wanted to tell you straight away.[11] [Italics added.]

This proves, conclusively and beyond all reasonable doubt, that Jochmann did not have access to the original manuscript, but only (at best) a photocopy of it, and that thus *Monologe* too was based on rather shaky foundations from a source-critical perspective. Several other documents corroborate this conclusion.[12]

Genoud sent Jochmann the missing pages two weeks later, and at the same time he said that Jochmann probably did not have pages 1016–1017 (where Hitler spoke about smoking) and 1022–1034 (part of a speech Hitler had held in January 1944) either. Genoud sent Jochmann these pages a few days later.[13] Interestingly, these are the only pages that are still in Jochmann's archive. As already mentioned, these pages were never a part of either *Table Talk* or *Libres propos* and was consequently not included in *Monologe*; neither are the pages signed by whoever wrote them down. Note that there was never any talk about missing pages or something akin to that in all the correspondence surrounding the publication of *Table Talk*, even though the latter two notes are not included there and Trevor-Roper's archive is much larger and more detailed than Jochmann's. The translator of *Table Talk*, Stevens, certainly never mentioned anything like this either, which he reasonably would have if the situation was similar in that case. This is yet another indication that Stevens never saw even a photocopy of the original. Indeed, since Genoud did not have the original but only a photocopy of it, Jochmann thus got copies of a photocopy. A large part of the *Bormann-Vermerke* was still missing however, namely, Picker's notes in Genoud's possession. In late December 1978 Genoud finally promised he would send Jochmann the Picker documents. These, too, were not made available as originals, but only as photocopies. This was not because Genoud wished to have them included in the book, but because Genoud wanted Jochmann to compare them to Picker's *Tischgespräche* so that he could see the differences for himself.[14]

Jochmann readily understood the fact that the notes did not represent Hitler's words in any direct sense after he had corresponded with Heim on how the notes were made. Often two or three hours' worth of ramblings had been summarized into just a few pages, he noted. Jochmann even suggested to Genoud that this fact should be reflected in the title of the book (something that was later forgotten it seems). Jochmann wished to get away from the word *Tischgespräche*, considering that Picker had used that too, and after consulting with Heim he also had come to realize that it was not so much conversations (*Gespräche*) as it was monologues (*Monologe*). Also, since Bormann himself had written a handful of notes (and signed them), he thought that Bormann's name should be mentioned in the title as well (Jochmann does not mention that fact that the last entry had not been signed by Bormann). Furthermore, they were not protocol-like recordings, wrote Jochmann, but rather summary notes intended for internal use in the NSDAP. All of this meant that the source as such had to be viewed in an entirely different way than how Picker had tried to make the world believe. But, stated Jochmann, these were simply suggestions and he himself had several objections to his own proposals.[15]

Apparently, these unmentioned objections won out because it is certainly safe to say that Jochmann did not make these source-critical points clear to his readers in *Monologe*; neither was Bormann's name mentioned in the title of the book. Had

Jochmann taken care to point out that the notes presented in *Monologe* were not to be cited as Hitler's words, but rather as a summary of some of the themes on which Hitler spoke, historians would most likely have used them quite differently compared to how they now are used.

In May 1979 Knaus had to intervene on Jochmann's behalf and explain to Genoud that the copies of Picker's notes were essential to Jochmann being able to do finish the book.[16] Genoud explained the delay in delivering the Picker copies by saying that he had been travelling a lot lately, and while he had had the intention to bring the copies to Hamburg himself, this had not been possible. He also stated that it had been hard to make readable copies of the old "war paper" (*Kriegspapier*). He wrote that "the paper has become very dark and the text very light." But with the Xerox machine the copies turned out fine in the end, he said.[17] Note the eerie similarity between this description and the one given by Rechenberg about the purported original for the political testament text (see Chapter 6). It would take until the summer of 1979 for Jochmann to actually get copies of Picker's notes. Unfortunately, these are also nowhere to be found in his archive.

The historian Werner Maser, too, had received a few pages, apparently from Heim, which he used when writing his Hitler biography *Adolf Hitler: Legende, Mythos, Wirklichkeit* that was first published in 1971. Maser writes on two occasions that he quoted from a reproduction of the original manuscript containing Heim's notes from 8–9 January 1942:

> Cited from the reproduction of the original manuscript of Heim's notes from 8–9 January 1942, authenticated by Heinrich Heim (Reproduction in the author's possession).[18]

The quote makes clear that Heim had authenticated this note as being his. Strangely enough, Maser later states that this reproduction was in Heim's possession and not his own. This makes one wonder if what Maser writes in the quote cited earlier was a mistake or if he also kept a copy of this note.[19] Maser also cites a Heim note from 16–17 January 1942, which he states Heim authenticated in July 1968. Apparently, this reproduction was in Heim's private possession too.[20] These are the only two "original" notes that Maser, via Heim, had access to; all other quotes and references to Heim's notes are to those in Picker's *Tischgespräche*. These were, however, copies of Heim's proof pages, and one must then assume that Heim had received copies of these from somewhere.

An incomplete source-critical evaluation

One of the most obvious issues that Jochmann had to address in his introduction to *Monologe* was of course that of the text's reliability. To his credit, Jochmann did include more on this matter than Trevor-Roper had, but he still left glaring holes in his analysis. This review is interesting because it shows how source-critical acumen can very easily be negatively affected by dependencies of various kinds. One of the first issues where Jochmann got lost was in whether Hitler knew that his musings were being recorded in some way.

As we have already seen, Heim repeatedly and consistently claimed that Hitler had no idea that he was taking notes.[21] He would state the same in an interview with John Toland in 1971. Toland later wrote that:

> Heim was constantly faced with two problems: to select the most meaningful reflections (sometimes what he was writing down was superseded in importance by Hitler's next words) and to keep the Führer from seeing what he was doing.[22]

This of course lessened the degree of certitude with which Heim could hope to capture Hitler's statements, and this should have been a main point of discussion in Jochmann's introduction. This was not the case, however.

Moreover, Jochmann, just like Toland, relied completely on Heim's version (which is interesting, since Heim is alone in insisting that Hitler knew nothing about the notes) and used this to question Picker's reliability.[23] Picker, for sure, did lie about many things, but that does not mean that he lied about everything; e.g. it does not mean that he lied about Hitler knowing about Bormann's underlings making some sort of memoranda based on his statements. I believe that Heim gives a skewed picture of what actually happened in this case, it is utterly improbable that both Heim and Picker could make notes for two whole years without Hitler even once noticing or hearing what was going on.[24] Furthermore, Heim actually had a very good motive for insisting on this point, something which cannot be said about Picker, namely his attitude towards Hitler and *Tischgespräche*'s character overall. Heim, as it turns out, was a hardcore Nazi and a member of the so-called "old guard", i.e. those who had lived through the *Kampfzeit* and the failed revolution in November 1923. Heim had joined the NSDAP in July 1920, and was still a believing Nazi after the war. Heim was of the opinion that the table talks cleared Hitler, who he thought had been portrayed negatively ever since the war ended (the parallels to Genoud are striking here). The notes contained nothing about the Holocaust, or the mass murder of, or Eastern Europeans, for example. Instead, Hitler comes across as something of a philosopher-king, a thinker and a visionary, and even, in some cases, as a rather jovial character. Heim even says in an interview that Hitler's greatest skill was his ability to think wide – that Hitler possessed a humanistic width that everyone else was lacking, according to him.[25]

Heim can here only be referring to Hitler's widely witnessed dilettantism, which for Heim thus was Hitler's greatest strength. Heim had completely embraced Hitler's ideal when it came to knowledge and education. Even more enlightening is the fact that Heim at the same time tried to convince the world that the infamous November Pogrom of 1938 was a spontaneous uprising of ordinary Germans and that both Hitler and Goebbels were highly upset by the whole thing. He also claimed to be convinced that Hitler knew nothing whatsoever about the Holocaust.[26] The latter claim was also used by David Irving as evidence that Hitler did not know about the Holocaust in the libel case against Lipstadt. Irving stated that he had questioned Heim in great detail as to whether the Holocaust was ever discussed and had gotten the reply that this had never been talked about. From this Irving drew the inept conclusion that this must then imply that Hitler knew nothing about it because, as he said, he was convinced that he had gained Heim's trust (and that of the other adjutants' whom he had interviewed), the implication being that Heim would have told Irving about such discussions had they taken place.[27] Why Hitler would ever discuss the mass murder of Jews with Heim present is a question that Irving does not seem to have even considered asking.

Heim was such an old school Nazi that he had corresponded with Heß while the latter was in prison in Landsberg after the failed coup attempt.[28] Heim was also one of the over 100 Nazi dignitaries to be invited to the inspection of the KZ Dachau that was arranged by Himmler on 3 May 1936.[29] This is thus the only source for Jochmann's assumption that Picker is a liar in this instance. Picker was an apologist too, but he was not as fervent in his pro-Nazi apologia as Heim was. Considering that there was so much bad blood between Picker on the one hand and Heim and Genoud on the other hand – a conflict that apparently even resulted in Knaus being unable to use Picker's notes in Genoud's possession in *Monologe* – it is not at all unreasonable to assume that this affected Jochmann's judgement.

Jochmann writes, and here it at first seems as if he makes a good point, that it would have made little sense for Bormann to treat the notes as a secret intended for the inner NSDAP circles, only and to keep them safe, while at the same time agree to let Picker keep the notes for private use.[30] This line of reasoning seems reasonable until one thinks about the fact that 1) we know for sure that Picker did take a large amount of notes with him when he left the FHQ, and 2) we also know for a fact that Bormann received some of Picker's notes. Now, Jochmann does not try to explain how point 1) was possible. Did Picker smuggle out his notes from under Bormann's nose? That seems like a considerable risk to take for some pieces of paper even if they were memoranda of the Führer's words. Would Picker not have risked serious repercussions had he been caught smuggling his notes out? When Picker left, the war was still going well for the Germans, and there was no way that Picker could know that Hitler would not win the war and become the undisputed master of the European continent. If that had come to pass, it would be even more risky to steal the notes without clearance from a higher authority. Picker could certainly not publish his notes under such circumstances, and then the whole reason for taking them vanishes into thin air.

Jochmann even accepted the statement that Hitler was uttering his words unhindered by outside forces because he felt safe in this small relaxed atmosphere of confidants. "All the information points in this direction", he states confidently. Yet "all the information" in this case is only one source, and that is Heim. This was especially true for the exclusive nightly gatherings around the tea table, according to Jochmann, when Hitler absolutely did not count on his utterances being written down. Then Jochmann does something quite strange. He claims that Picker himself acknowledges this fact and states that Picker most likely saw to it to copy, especially the nightly monologues. This is an odd statement considering the fact that out of the 36 Heim notes in *Tischgespräche* only 13 were made at night.[31] This makes no sense. If Jochmann's logic was sound, we should expect the nightly notes to have made up a much larger part of the Heim notes in Picker's possession. Certainly, we should then expect them to have made up at least half of them.

One could also comment that the nightly entries were, after all, based on no notes at all. Jochmann does not mention this. This ought to make the nightly notes the *worst* source we have if we were interested in Hitler's true thoughts on a matter. Of course, Jochmann might argue, Picker did not know that at the time and therefore may have reached for the bigger apples further up the tree. But perhaps more importantly, these entries are not special in any way, content wise, which really takes the edge off of Jochmann's argument because *this* even Picker must have realized. Add to this the fact that out of the 158 Heim notes that appear in Jochmann, no fewer than 63, or about 40 percent, were such nightly monologues. Picker's 13 nightly entries do not seem like much (they make up 36 percent of the total) in this context, since he could easily have chosen 36 such notes if he really prioritized them.

Jochmann then gives some examples of when, according to him, Picker had made mistakes in the reproduction of Hiem's notes, but all along he simply assumes that Genoud's manuscript is the one to be trusted. In this case Jochmann was right, however, because as we have seen previously in this book Picker did make small changes to the text in both his own and in Heim's notes. Jochmann points out that in the end of one note in Picker's book, Picker had added a phrase that is missing from Genoud's version of the same text, which had been signed by Picker himself. On another occasion Bormann apparently wrote in the margin of one note that it was incorrect because Picker had, during the long conversation, lost track of who had said what and had not represented the Führer's words correctly.[32] This is of course very interesting, and for the historian it would have been very valuable to have more precise information about this mistake. Here Jochmann also takes a surprisingly uncritical position to Bormann's own ability to remember what Hitler and someone else had said. Bormann may well have been correct, but we cannot be certain. And since Genoud's original is missing, it is impossible to know what the notation in the margin said exactly.

When Jochmann then criticizes Picker for considering the notes in his possession his private property, and thus putting a scientific-critical edition of all the table talk notes on hold for an unforeseeable future, one can only marvel at the lack of critical review on his part towards François Genoud who until 1978 had guarded his manuscript with such care and jealousy – not letting anyone even see his manuscript in its entirety (not even Heim). Genoud considered his manuscript at least as much as his private property as Picker did his text, yet Jochmann has nothing negative to say about Genoud. How could he have become so selective in his scrutiny? We get another example of this selectivity when he goes on to describe Bormann's motivation for having Hitler's words written down in the first place. According to Jochmann, Bormann hoped to be able to control the intellectual-political development of the NSDAP by creating a compendium of Hitler's views on matters of importance for this purpose. He also gives examples of occasions when Bormann used Heim's notes for direct political purposes, in one instance even giving a copy of one of them to Minister of Justice Thierack so that he could conduct his work according to the Führer's wishes, something that Thierack apparently also did.[33] This is undoubtedly true, but it creates some problems for Jochmann's other claims and for the handling of his sources.

Firstly, and this has already been pointed out, this type of action contradicts Heim's statement that Hitler did not know about the notes. How could Bormann keep distributing such documents without this ever getting back to Hitler? Secondly, Jochmann here blatantly contradicts Heim, whom he trusts so deeply in other instances, because Heim insisted that Hitler's words were absolutely *not* meant to be taken at face value as if they were the final product of a lot of pondering and formulation. Heim was adamant that Hitler's utterances were only thoughts uttered in the spur of the moment – in fact, that was precisely why Hitler did not want his words to be written down verbatim, according to Genoud, i.e. as unfinished ideas. Heim even says that whoever did not understand this did not understand Hitler. According to Heim, then, the Bormann that Jochmann presents did not understand Hitler, and of course Jochmann cannot argue that. Hence, he conveniently forgets about Heim's testimony in this case without letting the reader know why he trusts Heim in one case but not in another.

Hitler's former secretary Christa Schroeder inadvertently confirms that the notes cannot have been made by the use of stenography. Her description of the *Teestunden* seems to preclude any such notes from being made, especially if they were supposedly "secret." She states that around the small round table were gathered Hitler, a doctor, one military as well as one personal adjutant, Bormann, two secretaries (Schroeder was one of them), and Heim. By the way she tells the story, however, i.e. by noting that Heim was acting on Bormann's secret orders when he made the notes that had since been published by Jochmann, it makes one wonder if Schroeder is simply re-telling Heim's version as given in *Monologe*.[34] This cannot be ruled out, and it seems that this is indeed very plausible.

Genoud for his own reasons did not follow Heim's version either, although he also portrays the table talk notes to be Hitler speaking freely and thus honestly. In fact, the title of his French edition speaks for itself: *Libres propos sur la Guerre et la Paix* – free utterances on war and peace. Genoud, however, claims that Hitler *did* know that his words were being recorded for history, although he says that Hitler did oppose that the notes should be made "mechanically", since he wanted to be able to "forget" that his utterances had been collected; otherwise, he would feel paralyzed, Genoud said. Despite these admissions Genoud apparently did not feel that this would make Hitler less candid or lessen the value of the notes as an historical source to Hitler's true thoughts and ideas.[35] Where Genoud got this information from is a mystery. It is worth noting that Heim would stress the same point to Karen Kuykendall in the 1970s. Hitler's statements were made "off the cuff" and should never be interpreted as the final word on any topic. According to Heim, Hitler tested the waters by floating ideas among this group of listeners in order to see what their reactions would be.[36]

Ironically, however, it seems that this version is thus the one that is closest to the truth, so perhaps Genoud was basing himself on Heim here. Jochmann ignored Genoud's statements completely in his introduction and did not address why his version of events differed from Genoud's. In fact, Jochmann keeps quiet about the source of the manuscript he uses and about the French version that Genoud published. Perhaps that was wise because Genoud conveys a lot of information about how the notes came into being that he could not possibly have known, and much of it seems to be simply the products of Genoud's own mind combined with information that was already known. For example, in his preface to *Libres propos* Genoud recounts which persons were habitually present during the monologues, listing Keitel, Jodl, Bormann (of course), Dietrich, the doctors Morell and Brandt, and the photographer Heinrich Hoffman. Genoud takes pains to make it clear to the reader that Hitler had no reason whatsoever to hide his true thoughts from these men: "He has no reason to hide his thought or distort it when addressing them."[37] All these men were of course well-known associates and confidantes of Hitler and all of them are mentioned by Picker in his foreword.[38] But even if what Genoud says was absolutely correct, that still does not mean that Hitler could be expected to speak freely on every subject. To assume that would be a fallacy. Furthermore, Genoud seems to assume that Hitler's version, or mental projection, of reality agreed with actual reality – a notion that seems unlikely considering the many instances and subjects when historians have shown Hitler's view of the world to be less than consistent with the facts.

Genoud certainly, just like Heim, also had a strong motive for wanting to portray the notes as a faithful (although perhaps not *ad verbatim*) representation of the private and unguarded Hitler. The Führer says exactly what Genoud wants him to say, as if it was Genoud himself speaking through Hitler. If no skeletons could be found in this closet, then they could not possibly come tumbling out from behind another door closet either. In reality, of course, the notes, as we have seen in the previous chapters, are of a totally different character. As Martin Vogt has noted, nowhere does Hitler in these conversations or monologues even touch upon subjects related to political or military secrets (things that one of course would expect to find in a collection of notes that discloses the unguarded Führer). Instead, what characterizes Hitler's utterances is often their banality and mundaneness.[39] What is clear is that if this source lets us pick the Führer's brain, one better not expect too much. If anything, the notes seem to show a Hitler that is constantly aware of what he is saying.

Jochmann did not really where to stand regarding these matters. He holds on to the view that the table talks recorded candid remarks that Hitler did not know were written down, but does away with the idea that it is a faithful *ad verbatim* representation of the Führer. At least that is the impression that one gets when

Jochmann writes that even though Heim tried his best to recollect Hitler's words the way they were uttered:

> they remain subjectively filtered. [. . .] This makes it clear that this is merely a meaningful representation, [that they] sum up long discussions, and less important or very specific presentations were occasionally left out.[40]

Even though this was in a sense a disqualification of Heim's notes, which should really have led to the conclusion that what we are citing when we quote *Monologe* is not Hitler but Heim's recollection of the former (sometimes also edited by Bormann – although we do not know to what degree), a real discussion of what this means for historians is never presented. Instead, Jochmann has a hard time making up his mind about which Hitler it actually is that is present in *Monologe*. On the one hand, he states, in contradiction to most research on Hitler, that Hitler possessed an impressive width of knowledge in most areas (except in the humanities), and he often struck his conversational partners with his ability to easily define the common denominator between various problems and come up with a solution to them (Jochmann comes dangerously close to sharing Heim's romantic view of Hitler's intellectual abilities here). But at the same time, he was of course forced to conclude that *that* Hitler is absent in Heim's notes and that the monologues captured by Heim presents a babbling Hitler who simply cannot be considered to have carefully considered every word before uttering them. It seems, just like Heim said, although Jochmann did not say this, to be rash remarks made off the cuff. Jochmann is also forced to state as a fact that Hitler did not reveal his motives for his actions or go into detail concerning political or military issues – not even in this closest of circles and among friends. The Heim notes thus testify to Hitler's great self-control, and even "Hitler's distrustful retention", Jochmann says. Nonetheless, he managed to combine this realization with his contradicting statement that Heim's notes show the candid Hitler that expressed himself freely – after all that's what makes his source so unique.[41] It simply does not add up.

  Jochmann did do some things right, however. For instance, he correctly dismissed Picker's claim to have gone back to Heim's original stenographic notes, although not for the right reason. Jochmann says, amazingly, that this might be of personal interest to Picker but not at all to the public interested in science and politics. He also comments on Picker's statement that Bormann edited the notes according to his liking by saying that this cannot be corroborated by Jochmann's source – i.e. Genoud's manuscript – and that it sounds crude and inconsequential.[42] Jochmann thus thought that it was of no consequence if Picker had actually gone back to Heim's stenographic originals. That is an astonishingly inaccurate and clueless statement coming from a historian. On the contrary, *if* that were true then it would have huge implications for which notes were more reliable. Jochmann says that all notes were signed either by Heim, Picker, or Bormann, But we actually know this cannot be completely true, since at least the very last note, which was written by Bormann, did not have Bormann's signature on it.

Hitler certainly knew that at least Bormann was recording things that he said. Jochen von Lang writes that Bormann made his own notes by way of short supporting words, which he then used to support his own politics (Albert Speer also mentions this when he says that Bormann was always quick to pull out a small piece of paper from his pocket and take quick notes whenever Hitler would speak about religion). If necessary, Bormann could even convince Hitler himself with the help of these notes, writes von Lang. In case he got caught doing something he should not and was reprimanded by Hitler, he could always claim only to have had the Führer's best interests in mind.[43]

None of what has been said here means that Ron Rosenbaum's conclusions about the table talks have any support in the evidence. He writes in his book *Explaining Hitler* that, at best, the *Table Talk* (he uses the English translation) shows a forged Hitler that "even though the words are (for the most part) Hitler's, nonetheless it's almost as false a creation as the 'Hitler Diaries.'" This did not mean that Rosenbaum thought someone else had forged the notes, even though that is indeed what the comparison implies. The difference would be that here it was Hitler himself who stood for the forging, according to Rosenbaum, who also was of the opinion that Hitler had given a green light to these notes and that "Hitler relished the idea that he was speaking for history." What he bases this on is not clear, however. On occasion he comes much closer to Picker's own view, which is true, namely that the text is an editorial re-construction of Hitler's words. Even so, he is convinced that we can somehow find the "true" Hitler in there somewhere (although he does not give us a hint as to how that would be possible if it was so fake).[44] Rosenbaum committed two simultaneous mistakes here: 1) he overestimated the extent to which the table talks contain Hitler's own words and 2) he underestimated how much they differ from the completely bogus Hitler diaries.

Jochmann does mention some details on how the notes were created in his introduction to *Monologe*. He writes, for example, about Heim:

> to the extent possible he discretely wrote down occasional supporting words, and sometimes even one or two noteworthy phrases. . . . During the nightly *Teestunden* . . ., however, there were no opportunity to even writes down a single word. Since this intimate circle remained gathered around Hitler until the first hours early the next day, the notes from the conversations could not be dictated until the next morning.[45]

Obviously, Jochmann's use of the word "notes" (*Aufzeichnungen*) in the last sentence must be a mistake, since he has just claimed that there were no such notes on the basis of which a dictation could be made. It is also symptomatic that Jochmann only mentions Heim, although *Monologe* also contained notes made by Müller and Bormann. He says nothing about how they created their notes, nor does he discuss the potential problems with not having any information about this process. Neither does he really go into detail regarding the source-critical issues raised by the recording process that he describes here.

This version of events has been repeated in many history books, even as late as 2018 in the second volume of Volker Ullrich's Hitler biography.[46] Heim assured Jochmann under oath that he had made "occasional notes of supporting words" (*zeitweise stichwortartige Notizen*) and that he on the basis of these had dictated the entire text to Bormann's secretary the next day. He also says that Picker had falsely claimed that his notes were "stenography."[47] We can here see how flawed information gets recycled by historians in ways that appear to give independent evidence for the myth, but that in reality are only re-writings of the same source (which is, in this case, Heim himself).

As already mentioned, the absolute majority of the notes were dictated to, and thus typed up by, one of Bormann's secretaries by the name of Fugger. The secretary taking the dictation put her "mark" on the transcript and is stated as "Fu" in *Monologe* together with the author of the note in question. In Heim's case the notation "H/Fu." can be seen under the date of the respective notes in the book.[48] Jochmann, again, does not discuss what these facts regarding how the text he introduces meant for *Monologe* as a historical source. All he says is that:

> Now, however, the records give only an insufficient picture of Hitler's remarks. Heim took notes at noon and evening during the larger circle of talks "to have a support for the most important details." But even then, he was only able to summarize, on a few pages when the meal was over, that which had been discussed in great detail in some cases. For the long monologues during the nightly tea hours, he was completely dependent on his memory.[49]

Jochmann also adds that Heim did not write anything down concerning military subjects or matters having to do with technology, since he was not well acquainted with these topics.[50] Note what this implicitly means, but what Jochmann does not realize or say, namely, that Heim could not remember matters that he did not already know rather well. In other words, what we find in *Monologe* may to a considerable extent be Heim's own words written down in his best effort to impersonate Hitler's way of speaking. In correspondence with Jochmann, Heim wrote that:

> It is, as You say: the line of thought and the essentials, which we wished to record in order to preserve what we heard from being forgotten. . . . [That] means: what A. H. occupied himself with goes way beyond that which can now be read.[51]

An odd find in Jochmann's archive

As already mentioned, Genoud's original manuscript is still missing and nobody alive today seems to know where it is. Genoud's lawyer, Cordula Schacht, who was the one that Genoud left most of his papers to before his suicide in 1996, has stated to me that the manuscript was not part of his estate when it was turned over to her. It thus seems to have vanished sometime between 1980, when Joch-mann had access to it, and 1996.[52] Jochmann, furthermore, says very little about the original in his preface. He does not say what kind of manuscript it was, nor about how he came to gain access to it or where it went afterwards. Sir Ian Ker-shaw stressed the same point in an email to me in which he simultaneously said that he had actually been acquainted with Jochmann for a while in the 1980s and that he always saw him as a very "careful and conscientious [sic] historian." For precisely that reason Kershaw always trusted *Monologe*. However, after taking my initial findings under consideration, he was struck by the fact that Jochmann says almost "nothing at all about the text on which his edition is based." Kerhsaw's conclusion was that I had "provided some cogent reasons for some scepticism with regard to the textual authenticity on the Jochmann edition of the Heim Aufzeichnungen."[53]

Jochmann also includes facsimiles of two handwritten pages signed by Heim where the latter talks in more or less general terms about the notes he made. It is not clear why Jochmann included these pages. One could get the impression that they are intended to somehow strengthen the claim to authenticity, however, that is not the case. Firstly, the text is not part of a correspondence between Jochmann and Heim because the notes are taken from Heim's interview with the BBC on 14 September 1953. Jochmann thus knew about the BBC interview but remained silent about the fact that Heim in that same interview stated that he had not himself been allowed to see Genoud's manuscript. In a review of *Monologe* Georg Franz-Willing noted this too, saying that is was odd of Jochmann to use the interview in this limited way.[54] All of this is strange, to put it mildly. One has to also, I believe, put into the equation the fact that Jochmann must reasonably have been consider-ing himself extremely fortunate to have been selected by Genoud for publishing the long sought-after German "original". This might in and of itself have dimin-ished his critical faculties somewhat.

Winkler stresses precisely the fact that Genoud, who was a sophisticated man, was a master at manipulating historians interested in the Third Reich (which made Genoud's market pretty wide, to say the least). He always saw to it that he gave the scholars just enough (or little) to keep them interested and to make them bid over one another. The originals, however, he kept to himself as long as possible if it concerned authentic documents, and perhaps indefinitely if they were forgeries. The thrill for Genoud lay in the secrecy, says Winkler.[55]

Jochmann also includes a few facsimiles of pages from Genoud's manuscript at the end of *Monologe*. But there is an astonishing fact that needs to be mentioned in this context. Among only three facsimiles that Jochmann includes in his book, one of them appears also among Heim's proof pages. These pages look almost com-pletely identical; they include the same hand-ritten corrections in the exact same place, the same mistyping by the typewriter, and even the same smudges on the paper. Yet the corrections are not completely identical, so it does not appear to be the same page. Now, how is this possible? Were the same corrections and changes done three times, i.e. once on each copy of the manuscript? That certainly seems like a tedious way to go about proofreading.

Jochmann's comments about the proofreading process are rather short and at times even a bit contradictory. On the one hand he states in his preface that as far as it was possible to know, there was little reason for proofreading. Furthermore, he states that in the manuscript that he used Bormann had only made a few additions to the text, which Jochmann notes as they appear in the book. This conflated Heim's proof pages with the final version of the notes. He continues by saying that whether or not some additions were made during the process of producing the final original could not be said with any degree of certainty, even though he had copies of Heim's proofs in his possession, and he seems to conclude that this was not the case based on the fact that Heim had denied it and that the documentation (unclear what he refers to) spoke against it. But then he goes on to repeat Heim's version of things, namely that Heim had worked the first version over and corrected it, after which an original and two copies had been produced. So eventually he ends up confirming that there was a proofreading after all.

The problem of the corrections on the facsimile page in *Monologe* was long a mystery to me until I had the opportunity to research Jochmann's papers pertaining to the publication of *Monologe*. Because it turns out that this page actually *is* the same page as the one in Heim's proof pages, although it is not a facsimile of the original page but of a copy of it. I found a series of copies of Heim's proof pages in Jochmann's archive, and on one of them Jochmann himself (probably) had filled in the faded handwriting on the page with a pencil. *That* is why there are minute differences to the handwritten changes on the original proof page. The pages *appear* to be different, but they are actually the same. It was not Jochmann who had made the copies, however. Instead, these are the copies ordered from the LoC by Dr Hermann Mau of the IfZ in the early 1950s, and Jochmann had then later received copies of these copies (although it is unknown from whom, or exactly when, he received them).[56]

Unfortunately, there is no clue as to why Jochmann chose to include a facsimile of a copy of a microfilmed document from the LoC when he reasonably had access to the original final version of that same page via Genoud. The only reasonable answer to this conundrum is that this page was not present (as an original) in the manuscript Jochmann got from Genoud. If you have access to both an original page, part of the manuscript you have been given exclusive access to for the first time, and a copy of a proof page of that note, which is of such bad quality that you need to fill in the handwriting yourself in order for it to be legible – and, on top of that, it comes from a completely different source – you simply do not choose to publish the latter copy.[57]

Now a whole set of interesting questions are begging to be answered. If this page was not in Genoud's manuscript, why did Jochmann choose to publish this particular page at all? He ought to have had plenty of pages to choose from when selecting a third facsimile page, so why did he not choose a page that *was* present in original in the manuscript, and why would he not tell his readers about this? There is certainly nothing special about the content of this page that makes the choice understandable. Jochmann's choice is perplexing to say the least.

The very last facsimile is a note dated during the night between 27 and 28 July 1941. This is note 11 in *Monologe*. What is interesting about this note is that Bormann's signature appears on the left together with the handwritten date "30.7", i.e. 30 July. This must reasonably mean that Bormann signed the note on that date.[58] This is two days after the statements were allegedly made by Hitler, indicating that it took a few days for it to be finished before the latter signed off on it. This note is part of a group of notes made around the same time that have no author name attached to them. We thus do not know who made them. Bormann's signature on this particular facsimile page could mean that Bormann wrote, or dictated, them all. But we cannot be sure that this conclusion is correct, and Jochmann of course never addresses this issue.

The table talks on trial again

Picker tried to stop Knaus from publishing not only his own notes but also the 36 Heim notes that he had published in *Tischgespräche* in 1951. This meant that the table talks once again appeared in a German courtroom. Picker's argument was an interesting and potentially successful one. He argued that the version of Heim's notes that he had published were truer to the original because he had gone back to Heim's stenographic originals and had had them transcribed. According to Schramm's preface to *Tischgespräche*'s second edition in 1963, and Schramm bases this on Picker's own account, Bormann let Picker see just a small part of Heim's notes, perhaps as part of a deal where Bormann got access to some of Picker's private notes. The ones he got, however, had been edited by Bormann already and so did not correspond to Heim's original notes, Schramm wrote. But because the stenographic originals were still lying in a desk drawer in *Wolfsschanze* Picker was able to, with the help of a secretary who could read stenography, re-create the text in its original wording. Therefore, one could in *Tischgespräche* see the words "corrected for the record: Picker" on every note made by Heim.[59] This appears also in the typed copy of Picker's manuscript that Schramm and Hillgruber used for the second edition of *Tischgespräche* in 1963, but then as "F. d. R.: Picker". Schramm added the full version (as in the printed edition) by hand on the first page of the manuscript copy.[60]

Picker actually hinted at as much already in the first edition of his book.[61] In his own introduction he wrote:

> This book is a historical document of a unique nature. Because I was also able to save Hitler's statements (which were in direct speech) co-stenographed by Mr. Heim from 21 July 1941 to 11 March 1942, insofar as Hitler's secretary [Bormann, M.N.] gave me [access] to round off my observations, from extermination, the reader can live side by side with the deliberations of the dictator for a whole year – often day by day.[62]

Now why would Picker lie about Heim having used stenography in a book that he could at least suspect that Heim would read? Yet, Picker still lied about this. In fact, Picker did not think that Heim was still alive at the time he wrote his first introduction. But as we have seen, there was a much more mundane reason for Picker to insist that Heim had used stenography. Picker no doubt had the German copyright law in mind here, according to which a stenographer had no copyright (*Urheberrecht*) to his own notes, since he has only written down someone else's words.

But this was at the same time a risky strategy because this would not obviously place the copyright to these notes in Picker's hands, but with the German federal government. Picker's way of going about things was also less than optimal from a source-critical perspective. Heim's notes would obviously purvey Hitler's words better than Picker's own notes if Heim had actually used stenography. Thus, Picker would actually make his case weaker (both regarding copyright and exactness of representation), not stronger, by this act. By 1963 Picker's false claim had become even riskier, since by then he knew full well that Genoud had a manuscript containing both his own and Heim's notes. As historians we are presented with an interesting problem here. Because if what Picker says is correct, then we should expect that those of Heim's notes that Jochmann and Picker have in common ought to differ from each other, and this difference ought to reflect Bormann's changes to Heim's text. I, of course, realized that Picker's statements should thus be able to be either corroborated or disproven by Jochmann's book. This exact way of going about things was actually suggested by Schramm in 1963, long before Genoud's manuscript became available in German.[63]

But then in the 1976 edition of *Tischgespräche* Picker goes even further and states that Hitler himself promised to let Picker publish his notes, with the precondition that any publication of them would have to be coordinated with the publication of Hitler's memoirs and that this promise had been forwarded by Bormann to Walkenhorst at the NSDAP HQ in Munich. Walkenhorst had even testified to this fact in court in May 1958, according to Picker himself.[64] This seems very unlikely to be true, not least considering the fact that Hitler himself demoted Picker from his position as *Reichsamtsleiter* on 1 November 1944.[65] In a newspaper article from September 1961 we are told that the court in 1958 had believed Walkenhorst's testimony and that Picker had prevailed in his battle for copyright of the notes over Hitler's sister Paula.

Various witnesses had made it clear that the records of Picker were not stenographic notes created in an official capacity but as private works by Picker, who, upon his departure from the headquarters was given permission to take his scripts with him and publish them after the war. This permission had only been conditional on Picker coordinating his publication if Hitler himself were to write his memoirs after the war.[66] This decision overturned the decision by the Municipal Court (*Landesgericht*) in Oldenburg from 1953.

Up until 1980 the Heim notes that *Tischgespräche* and *Table Talk* had in common had only been published in German by Picker so there was not really any other German text to compare *Tischgespräche* to. The publication of *Monologe* changed this situation entirely. The problem for Picker was that such a comparison shows that the Heim notes in *Tischgespräche* and in *Monologe* agree *ad verbatim*, with only minute variations (such as the positioning of some words or a missing or different word) on very few occasions. Picker's claim to have gone back to an unedited version of Heim's notes could therefore not be true. Picker was caught red-handed in a gigantic lie. This was no doubt one of the reasons for why he now tried to stop Knaus from publishing the 36 Heim notes included in *Tischgespräche*: Picker knew that he would be shown to be a brazen liar. Hints to the fact that Picker was lying were of course already there for those who wanted to see them. The introduction in 1951 had not mentioned anything about Picker having gone back to an original stenographic record that differed from the version later edited by Bormann. The information that Bormann changed both Heim's and Picker's texts appeared first in the second edition of Picker's book in 1963.

Picker used the same argument in the Municipal Court in Munich in 1980, i.e. that Hitler himself had given him the sole copyright of his notes, but now placed this event in April 1943, thus cleverly placing this promise *before* Hitler's demotion of him in 1944. But a decision that has been overturned once can be overturned again. The court in Munich did not find Picker's claim credible and thus dismissed the lawsuit against Knaus. Picker now backtracked a bit and admitted had he not received this promise from Hitler himself, but from Bormann (a claim that was equally dubious). The court also stated that due to the fact that Heim had not kept a stenographic record of everything Hitler said, this meant that Heim had *post facto* added the rest and this made him at least partly the author of the notes:

> that the formulations in their concrete form largely come from the witness Heim. Therefore at least a co-copyright of the witness Heim cannot be excluded.[67]

This reasonably undermined the fidelity of Heim's notes even further, but no one seems to have noticed that, or at least no one paid any attention to it. There was also enough bad blood between Picker and Genoud to explain why Picker would not want Genoud to profit from the publication of these entries. Picker perhaps tried to get even with Genoud. In a letter to Trevor-Roper in 1981, Genoud commented on what he had written in his preface to *Libres propos* regarding the idea that Bormann had gotten Hitler's permission to make the notes. He did this after the verdict in the case between Picker and Knaus had been announced. Apparently, he felt some pressure to try and explain away a glaring contradiction, namely, why it was that *he* (and Picker, M.N.) claimed that Hitler knew that notes were made while Heim insisted that Hitler did not? Genoud wrote (in French) to Trevor-Roper:

> If I were to write today, I would insist that Hitler reluctantly allowed Bormann to have notes taken, that Bormann feared that Hitler would change his mind if he was annoyed. This explains why Bormann told Heim and Picker, the secretaries, that the Führer did not know.[68]

This was an odd claim because Picker had never argued that Hitler was unknowing. Genoud added that Heim and Picker had no doubt always known about Hitler's attitude to this matter and if Picker now had changed his mind that was simply because he wanted to claim copyright over the notes. Then he stated:

> In summary, it is obvious that Bormann would not have systematically noted Hitler's words – and this for more than a year – without having been authorized to do so. As Bormann feared that the Führer would change his mind, it was essential for him to convince all those concerned that he did not know.[69]

Once again, thus, Genoud argues in contrast to Heim, and comes close to my argument, namely that it was unreasonable to assume that Hitler did not know about this frequent and prolonged activity. Of course, Genoud made all of this up; he had no idea what Bormann was thinking or his reasons for doing what he did. He also inadvertently rebutted the idea that it was a faithful record of Hitler's words – perhaps without realizing it himself. However, Genoud's story once again seems to make no sense. Are we really supposed to believe that Bormann told Heim and Picker that Hitler did not know that they were making notes although that was not so? How could Picker and Heim not discover that this was a lie? One also has to ask if Heim and Picker were not afraid to make notes without the Führer's explicit permission. What would happen to them if they were exposed? Perhaps more importantly, we know for a fact that Picker did *not* buy this argument (if it was indeed ever made), since he argues that Hitler knew.

Picker detailed during the trail that Heim had made stenographic notes on small cards, the size of postcards, which he had then stuck up the sleeve of his uniform. Heim actually confirmed these details, although he insisted that there were no such cards from the 13 notes (out of the 36) from the statements uttered at night.[70] Picker claimed that he had found cards containing stenographic notes for 35 of Heim's 172 notes (this number is interesting because it agrees with the number of Heim notes in *Libres propos* and *Table Talk* but differs from the number in *Monologe*) and that he gave them to a secretary who then transcribed them. Picker apparently showed a similar card (somewhat smaller than a normal postcard) in the court. He had not used the typed notes, which had passed by Bormann's desk, he insisted, but the original stenographic records. Heim, on the other hand, stood by his statement that he only made some occasional supporting words on one or two small cards during the conversations in question. It was absolutely impossible to fill 10 or 15 such cards, he stated.[71] However, he admitted that sometimes "I have noted down keywords that could also be made up of a half, or a whole, sentence." He also added that "My notes were stenographically made." Since he had to hide the card under his plate, he often could not even look at the card as he was making a notation. He only made such notes when he was unsure about something and wanted to be certain that he understood it correctly.[72]

In an interview with a German-speaking assistant to John Toland in 1975, Heim then said:

> these my stenographic notes, or those written by hand without shorthand, were only a basis for the record.[73]

This "basis" (*Unterlage*) was something more extensive than a few supporting words; it was a longer handwritten text draft that acted as a first draft for the typed proof copy of the text. What Heim appears to be saying here is that he produced a set of stenographic notes *after* the conversations that they summarize, which functioned as a first draft. This is not just wild speculation on my part. There is in fact solid evidence that Heim had a habit of working like this; I have found several drafts of letters that Heim wrote using stenographic shorthand, which he then re-wrote in normal handwriting and sent off.[74] Does this mean that Picker was actually telling the truth about having consulted Heim's "original" stenographic notes? No, it does not, since Picker's version of Heim's notes include the changes made during the later proofreading process.

It is doubtful that the term "original" is a meaningful word in the context of the table talks. There is no escape from the problem of subjectivity; the notes remain subjective recollections coloured by whatever agenda that may have motivated Heim and the other authors to make them in the first place. The process by which Bormann's and Müller's notes were made will remain clouded in uncertainty until some new source material becomes available that can shed light on it. The same is true for Picker's notes. We are often not in any position to say with certainty how reliable they are or to evaluate how they came about because the "originals" are lost and are thus inaccessible to historians. All we have to go on is Picker's and Heim's own statements, and these cannot be trusted unless we can verify them with independent sources.

The situation is not helped by the fact that there are so many contradictory, false, and unsupported claims spread about the table talks in the literature. For example, John Toland states in his Hitler biography from 1976 that Heim had made "copious notes on index cards which he hid on his lap."[75] This surely does imply that much of the content in the notes was written down as Hitler spoke. However, in the transcribed version of Toland's interviews with Heim, the latter says nothing of the sort. Toland thus seems to have interpreted Heim a bit freely. Initially, I was hoping to be able to confirm or disconfirm the accuracy of this claim by consulting the taped interview in the "John Toland Papers" at Franklin D. Roosevelt Library (FDRL) in Hyde Park, New York, to see if Heim gives any additional information there that was not included in the transcribed text. Unfortunately, it turns out that these recordings are lost, if they were ever there in the first place. The LoC does not have a copy of the tapes either. What seems to have happened is that Toland later recorded another interview on the same tape and then accidentally recorded over the Heim interview. In the finding aids it says that the interview should be on the tape, but neither the FDR Library nor the LoC actually listened to the tapes when they got them; they simply assumed that the information given to them by Toland was correct.[76]

Heim was not in the possession of his cards with the stenographic supporting notes on them anymore because he had burnt them together with his entire archive, he told the court in Munich.[77] This all indicates, or rather proves, that the absolute majority of the content of the notes that appear in Genoud's, Trevor-Roper's, and Jochmann's volumes was more or less made up, from memory to be sure but still, by Heim (and Bormann). In a letter to German historian Werner Maser in November 1972 Heim gave yet another similar, but still somewhat different, account of how he made his notes:

> "Heim protocols" or "Heim stenogram": the word protocol doesn't seem to me to be a good choice – it belongs to the field of official language, but regarding [the term] "Heim stenogram" the following point should be made: my stenography skills are very limited and I was happy if I from time to time could write down a keyword without anyone noticing it; during nightly tea it was impossible to record even one word.[78]

Werner Jochmann did not mention this in such detail in his introduction to *Monologe*, even though he had access to this information and thus knew very well that Heim's notes were nowhere near as exact as they have been made out to be. Jochmann had access to a wealth of information regarding this source-critical problem, but he chose not to tell his readers about most of them.

Picker's wife then gave her testimony and claimed that she clearly remembered having spoken to Heim (together with her husband) on 6 October 1951 in their home in Wilhelmshaven. Heim had allegedly said that he "had made stenographic notes of what Hitler said, as exact as possible, and then from that dictated the Bormann reports." He had done this in order to minimize potential conflict with Bormann regarding the content of Hitler's monologues. The reason for why she could still remember all of this so clearly, she said, was that she had often discussed this matter with her husband, as well as with Gerhard Engel, Julius Schaub, and Heinrich Walkenhorst, who was chief of the NSDAP Personnel Department in München.[79] These representatives of the party apparently stood by this story with signed affidavits.[80] Schramm states that a photocopy of Engel's affidavit from 1953 is present in Bundesarchiv.[81] Picker also included another such testimony from Engel dated in May 1964 in the third edition of his book.[82] Heim, on the other hand, denied that Engel could have any knowledge about how exact these notes were because he had not seen either Picker or himself make them.[83]

In Hans Frank's memoirs *Im Angesicht des Galgens* the editor of the book states in the endnotes that, according to Julius Schaub, Frank had been inspired to get a team of stenographers to write down all his statements and speeches and so on, when he heard:

> that the Führer's conversations during his frequent nightly round table were taken down stenographically on Bormann's orders, Frank felt the urge the

ambition to do the same. He also set up his circle just as in the Führer Head-quarters – the tables were put together in horseshoe form, over which Frank presided.[84]

This is presented by the editor as the *Entstehungsgeschichte*, or creation history, of Frank's diaries, and there is no critical discussion of this story. No source is referred to other than the fact that Schaub had said it. We are not told to whom Schaub told this story, when he did so, or how Schaub knew any of the things he claimed to know. Observe that if this is true, then it seems to con-tradict Heim's statement about Schaub, because how could Frank have heard about how Hitler arranged the stenographic recording of his table talks if Hitler were not aware of them being recorded? Thus, either Schaub never told Heim that Hitler did not know or the editor of Frank's book is not telling the truth. Or perhaps Schaub told whatever lie he thought that the person in question wanted to hear.

In either case, since we know that Hitler did not arrange for a team of stenog-raphers to record his table talks, Frank cannot have been inspired by this example. We can in fact prove that the story ascribed to Schaub in Frank's memoirs has no truth to it. The proof is Frank's diaries. Selected passages of the 38 original diaries were published as *Hans Franks Tagebuch* in 1963.[85] In the foreword to the book we are told that Frank kept a diary from the very beginning of his official duties as general governor in occupied Poland in Lodz on 25 October 1939 until his escape to Krakow on 17 January 1945.[86] Since Heim did not start to make his notes until the summer of 1941, Frank cannot possibly have been inspired by Bormann's deci-sion to take down Hitler's utterances.

That Frank's diaries really were written in shorthand has been decisively proven, not only by the stenographers themselves, who were called as witnesses during the trial in Nuremberg, but also by an entry in the diary from 1942 by Frank himself (also signed by him) testifying to this fact. According to this note by Frank, he kept the diary so as to be able to show that he had faithfully performed everything that had been asked of him. The stenographers were almost always present at the meet-ings where the notes were made (only on a few occasions did they receive already written stenographic notes), although they sometimes made notes from Frank's dictations. The stenographers then, in turn, dictated their notes to a typist. When the typed notes had been proofread and given the necessary corrections, they were sent to the chief of Frank's staff HQ, where they were put in a safe and later put in binding. Frank took his diaries with him when he escaped from Poland to the small town of Neuhaus in Bavaria, where he kept making entries. There they were discovered by the Americans who then brought them out during the Nuremberg trials as evidence of Frank's crimes.[87] Needless to say, we could only wish that the evidence of the history of Picker's and Heim's notes were anywhere near as well attested for.

In late April 1980 the court in Munich ruled in favour of Heim and against Picker when judging to whom the copyright of Heim's notes actually belonged. But in their verdict, they inadvertently offered perhaps the clearest source-critical disqualification of *Monologe* as a faithful record of Hitler's words thus far. The court fully believed in Heim's testimony and therefore concluded:

> According to the testimony of the witness Heim, the court considered it at least possible that he at most noted down supporting words of Hitler's statements, but that he later wrote them down from memory. Considering the length of the individual conversations or monologues and the limitations of human memory, it must therefore be assumed that the formulations in their concrete form come largely from the witness Heim.[88]

The court thus considered Heim's notes to be so far from Hitler's own words that he should be viewed as the independent author of them. While Heim in this case could be argued to have had legal reason to portray his notes as corresponding as little as possible to Hitler's actual words, perhaps minimizing the degree to which he made supporting notes, and perhaps overemphasizing the degree to which he re-created the conversations afterwards, the quotation is still the conclusion the court arrived at after careful evaluation and after hearing *all* the evidence. The court hence reached the very reasonable conclusion that considering the length of the conversations in question, and the limitations of the human memory to remember such a huge amount of discourse accurately, what Heim's notes, and therefore by implication *Monologe*, contained was to a considerable degree Heim's formulations – not Hitler's. Also, Heim's statements in front of the court match those in other sources too. Jochmann, obviously, did not share the court's conclusion with his readers. This is therefore the first time that that this conclusion has been made publicly available.

The table talks are thus *not at all* records that in an exact way replicates Hitler's words as they were once spoken in the FHQ. Still, historians have used them exactly as such ever since they were first published. The fact that Jochmann's *Monologe* has been used like this too is certainly a testimony to the insufficient discussion about the source-critical consequences of his findings in his introduction. Privately, Jochmann showed the reason for why he perhaps was not as critical towards his source as he would otherwise have been. In a letter to Genoud, Jochmman stressed to the owner of the manuscript that he was introducing that he had made sure to point out in his introduction "that only the now published text is authentic, and that Picker's version should thus not be cited."[89] Since Heim's notes were only a summary of what Hitler had spoken about, and one retrieved from memory at that, the word "authentic" does not really have a meaningful place here. It would be like saying that e.g. Werner Koeppen's notes are not to be quoted because they are not identical to Heim's notes. This illustrates how Heim's notes, and thus both *Table Talk* and *Monologe*, have in effect become a standard against which all other notes are measured. As if they were somehow more trustworthy. This is also why most historians choose to quote *Monologe* in cases where, for example, Koeppen's notes overlap with Heim's. Just as the *Table Talk* has become a standard for how to translate the German texts into English, even though no translation can ever be considered to be authoritative in this sense and – even more importantly – *Table Talk* was translated from the French, *Monologe* has been successfully promoted as the only reliable version of the table talks.

The fact that Heim's notes were not an exact record of Hitler's words could, of course, be seen as a considerable weakness by any other publisher. Knaus, however, discovered that this could actually be turned into a strong support for the publisher's case in the conflict with Picker's publisher Seewald. In early 1980, the CEO of Knaus Verlag, Albrecht Knaus, wrote to his counterpart at Seewald Verlag, Sixt A. Seewald. When trying to prohibit Knaus from publishing the Heim notes already published by Picker in *Tischgespräche* Seewald had used the argument that Paula Hitler had transferred the rights to Hitler's *Nachlaß* to Picker in 1960 (which she in fact had). However, Knaus pointed out, first, that since Hitler's sister had already concluded such an agreement with Genoud prior to that point in time, the rights were then no longer hers to give away. Second, Knaus pointed to the fact that the notes, constantly referred to as "stenographic notes" (*Stenogramme*) by Seewald, were in fact not stenographic notes at all.[90] Knaus wrote:

> It is demonstrable that Mr. Heim's records, as well as Dr Picker's records, are not stenographic records, but are subsequently made from memory. These minutes were written down on the basis of keywords that Mr. Heim recorded during the monologues or reconstructed from memory [afterwards].[91]

It is certainly not without a sense of wonder one watches how Knaus and Seewald found themselves arguing in private about who had the least exact notes; Seewald and Picker argued the same with regard to Picker's own notes. The weakness of the table talk notes from a source-critical perspective, i.e. that they were speech re-created from memory after the fact, became a strength from a copyright perspective. Picker and Seewald argued, effectively, that Heim's notes were much better from a source-critical perspective than Picker's own notes because Heim had allegedly used stenography, while Knaus and Genoud (and Heim) countered this claim by showing that Heim's notes were essentially just as bad as Picker's in this respect. Despite this fact, and at the same time, both sides were trying to retain the credibility of their product in public by arguing that their version was the most accurate record of Hitler's words. Picker, concluded the court, had copyright to his own notes, and Heim had copyright to his notes. Therefore Picker could stop Knaus from publishing his own notes but not Heim's.

The aftermath

In the end then, *Monologe* was thus published without Picker's notes (since he retained the copyright for these) but with all of Heim's notes. It was perhaps not the most optimal solution for Knaus, Genoud, and Jochmann, but it was the best possible one that could legally be had. Interestingly, the community of historians has thus far not seemed particularly bothered by the fact that *Monologe* is missing all of Picker's notes, nor by the fact that no one has had the possibility to compare the text in *Tischgespräche* with that in Genoud's manuscript. Instead, historians have simply quoted *Monologe* when referencing Heim's notes and *Tischgespräche* when referencing Picker's.

The lack of source-critical evaluation in Jochmann's introduction was actually commented upon by at least one early reviewer. In 1981 Georg Franz-Willing wrote a review of *Monologe* in the German academic historical journal *Klüter Blätter* in which he pointed to the fact that even though Jochmann included a long preface, the destiny of the original and the editor's treatment of it remained shrouded in uncertainty.[92] The publication of *Monologe* was a good thing for Jochmann, too, not only from an academic point of view but also financially. For the publication of *Monologe* by the Bertelsmann book club, Jochmann stood to gain DM 24,000 and another DM 50,000 would be the result of a planned paperback edition by Wilhelm Heyne Verlag. On top of these guaranteed amounts Jochmann received 6 percent on the sale price for each book up to a guaranteed amount of sold books and 8 percent per sold book thereafter.[93] The paperback edition was apparently never actually published.

As already mentioned, *Monologe* turned out to be a considerable success in so far as it has undoubtedly become the standard edition for historians who cite the table talk texts. It is almost universally assumed to be the best and most faithful record of Hitler's rantings in the wartime FHQs. It is long since out of print, and the only way to purchase a copy today is via used bookstores. It is not clear why this is. Perhaps Genoud at some point refused to let Knaus print new editions of the book; perhaps Knaus did not consider it worthwhile to publish a new edition. Many years later, however, in the early 2000s an effort was made by an American publisher called Enigma to publish an English translation of *Monologe*. This turned into an astonishing display of inability to appreciate and accept the source-critical findings regarding the reliability of the table talks.

The Enigma re-print of *Table Talk:* a bizarre affair

In late October 2003, just after his article had been published in the *German Studies Review*, Richard Carrier was contacted by the head of the American book publisher Enigma Books, Robert Miller, who told him that he had read the "fascinating article" and now had a business proposal for Carrier. Miller said that he had re-printed *Table Talk* in the United States "to some success" and he was now interested in trying to acquire the rights to *Monologe*, which he referred to as "the Jochmann version of 1980." After having asked Carrier if he considered *Monologe* to be "the 'definitive' edition of the Table Talk" he asked whether Carrier would consider "editing and writing a preface to a new English language edition."[94]

Carrier's response was long and detailed, but in summary he told Miller that he would be prepared to edit the text but not to translate it, since he had "neither the time nor the competence" to do so. Having learned "Trevor-Roper's lesson" while writing his article, Carrier also said that he would certainly randomly double-check any translation that he was to put his name to. Carrier warned Miller, however, that German history and Hitler studies was not his field of expertise and that Miller might want to consider somebody else for the job, such as Gerhard Weinberg. However, if Miller, despite this caveat, was still willing to employ him, Carrier was willing to agree to undertake the job under the circumstances he had mentioned.[95] Carrier then offered the following critical advice regarding such a volume:

> If you get the rights to translate Jochmann, you will definitely want to translate his own introduction in its entirety, as well as all his notes – everything. And I would recommend you arrange to have the translators also translate, at least in the rough, Picker's introduction and notes – even if you can't get the rights to use them, we should be able to cull useful information from those materials to supplement our own preface and notes. And if you can get the rights, the Picker intro might make a nice appendix. . . . As I conclude in my article, I do think someone needs to create a proper critical edition of the German, collating all three available versions (really only two – the "third" amounts to just a few dozen pages [Carrier is here referring to Heim's proof pages, M.N.]) with a critical apparatus noting variants where they appear. Ideally such an edition would also collate the French of Genoud, simply because that would be historically interesting, but it would not be necessary for establishing the original text, since Genoud is derivative and flawed, as my paper aimed to show. However, a straight translation from Jochmann would be historically valuable – and certainly a substantial improvement on the Trevor-Roper edition. If you were to do such a thing, it would certainly have to be noted in the introduction that a critical edition collating the three texts in the German is still needed, even from the original mss. themselves, since they don't all agree, and there are many signs of editing that don't appear in any printed editions. A "middle" solution would be to ask your translators to also follow the other two editions and note in their ★translation★ where any significant deviations occur. That will be misleading if they don't make an effort to be sure they include every significant variant.[96]

Carrier thus took a very professional approach to the endeavour right from the start and was determined not to make the same mistakes that Trevor-Roper had once done, and he was careful to point to the major problems concerning the translation process by weighing in all the various relevant versions of the text.

A month later Miller replied that his company was "in the midst of finalizing our agreement to translate the Jochmann book." He considered Carrier's proposals "an interesting exercise" but could not say anything more about his stance on the matter until the project was closer to being realized. The book would probably be translated in Europe, he said, and would "definitely" include not only Jochmann's, but also "any other available preface", as well as a "general introduction" in English. At the end of his email, Miller wondered if Carrier perhaps had copies of Heim's proof pages that Enigma could receive copies of in order "to save us some time", which was something that Carrier agreed to as long as he was reimbursed for his expenses.[97] However, it then occurred to Carrier that *Monologe* did not contain Picker's notes, and thus any translation of Jochmann's edition would not be "complete," because "over a year of material is missing."[98] Obviously, this was a mistake, since Picker's notes only covered the period between March and August 1942. He then noted:

> But this creates a minor problem for you: Ideally you should do what is necessary to legally acquire the Genoud pages from Jochmann that Jochmann could not print (if you are already in negotiation with Jochmann, make sure this is part of the deal). This may still require working some deal out with the owners of Picker, since doing precisely what you have in mind was the focus of the suit, but I got the impression this was a vendetta between Picker and Genoud and thus might no longer present a substantial obstacle. Note that this means the Genoud pages matching Picker have never been printed in the original German (unless Jochmann plans to release a new edition that contains them – you should ask him), so a translation of those pages should take especial care to note where significant deviations occur between that and Picker, since otherwise no scholar would ever know, being unable to compare them at present.[99]

The points made by Carrier were indeed poignant ones; this delicate matter did present a major problem for Enigma if the company wanted to be able to claim with any degree of credibility that its new translation was in any sense a "definite" one. Already the next day Miller emailed to tell Carrier that Jochmann had passed away but that Miller was now "negotiating with his sisters."[100] Miller was also wondering whether Picker's text, as well as Genoud's, might by now be in "the public domain", i.e. could be used without negotiating and paying for the copyright.[101]

In his reply, Carrier corrected his mistake by specifying exactly which dates were missing in *Monologe*, and also pointed out that he had noted this in his article. He also noted that not only did Jochmann address this issue in his introduction but "any comparison" between Jochmann's and Picker's texts would make this plain as well.[102] By December 11 Miller had received the copies of Heim's proof pages, and on 14 December he wrote to tell Carrier that he would get back to him as soon as the there was "an agreement with the Jochmann and Picker estates."[103] In late January Miller contacted Carrier again. At this time he had realized that the missing Picker notes consisted of some 400 pages and if these were to be included in the same volume as the Jochmann text, the book would run over 1,000 pages long. He thus wanted Carrier to confirm whether this was what he had referred to in order to "complete our feasibility study of the project."[104] Carrier replied that this sounded correct to him, although he pointed out that the number of pages certainly depended upon how they were typeset. Once more, he underlined that any new translation should certainly make an effort to repair the "loss" that the copyright squabble between Picker and Genoud had resulted in when *Monologe* was published.[105] The idea that Picker's missing notes consisted of over 400 pages was also a mistake; Miller must here have confused the missing Picker notes in *Monologe* with all of the notes included in *Tischgespräche*, which also contained many of Heim's notes.

It was not until the summer of 2004 that Miller contacted Carrier again. He and Enigma had thus far not been able to find anyone else who could handle the job of editing the text and writing an introduction, and he thus inquired whether Carrier would be interested in "being the editor and translator" of such a book. The publisher was prepared to dedicate 12 to 15 months to this job, Miller stated.[106] Considering that Carrier had already explained that he did not have the expertise necessary to translate the text, we will have to assume that this was a "slip of the tongue" on Miller's part. Naturally, Carrier also pointed this out to Miller in his reply. He was prepared to accept the role as editor, but he strongly urged Miller to find an experienced translator of German who was used to working with documents from the relevant place and time period. After all, Carrier had had help from a native German speaker when writing his article (as he had also clearly mentioned in it), and although he would perhaps not make the same mistakes as Trevor-Roper had done, he was sure that he would inadvertently commit others instead. Then Carrier made clear that he considered it to be "irresponsible to produce a new English text before producing a collated critical edition of the German text", and he stressed that he would refuse to put his name to anything that did not emanate from such an edition. An expert in German that could apply "fixed principles of textual analysis" to the various manuscripts in order to generate "an authoritative text" along with an "apparatus identifying variants and explaining the editor's decision for favouring one variant over another." Such an authoritative text would of course also have to take the handwritten additions in Heim's proof pages into consideration, said Carrier. He would, however, consider accepting something "less ambitious than that" as long as it was "suitably responsible." Carrier explained that for "an industry-standard advance and royalties" he would be prepared to shoulder the responsibilities of being the editor "arranging and producing" the text, writing the introduction, and he recommended that more than one should be used in order to guarantee the quality of the translation.[107] However, he had an important precondition, namely that he would have to be guaranteed the right:

> to state anything I want in the introduction regarding the limitations of the text thus produced, including the remaining need for a proper critical edition of the German. I must also be allowed [to] state, of course, whatever methods were used, if any, to decide between variants, and also which manuscripts or printed editions were actually used for which portions of the English translation (and you will have to use more than one, since no single edition or ms. is complete). . . . With an even larger advance, I will also be willing to undertake an informal collation of printed editions of Jochmann and Picker, and make sure the translators translate every relevant variant – this will not be a substitute for a proper critical edition, but it will at least allow your text

to include mention of where the two most recent ★printed★ editions differ and how, and to translate both variants in each case. That alone would make your translation of great value to the scholarly community. Alternatively, such an informal collation can be undertaken by the individual translators themselves, for the portions of the text they are assigned to. Those are my terms, if you are interested.[108]

Carrier thus showed a lot of integrity here, as he made clear to Miller that he was not prepared to compromise on scholarly professionalism or historical critical methodology. Miller replied the next day stating: "Ok got your point" and said that he agreed with Carrier's judgement regarding the necessity of a "complete German edition." He would keep Carrier posted on "our progress in Germany" although he expected it to be "rather slow in coming at this time."[109] This was the last the Carrier heard from Miller. Apparently, Miller had decided that the scholarly standards demanded by Carrier were too high for him to meet.

In 2007 Enigma published a new edition of *Table Talk* that was simply a re-print of the old editions; however, it contained a new preface by none other than Gerhard Weinberg, whom, as we remember, Carrier had initially suggested to Miller. Carrier noted to me in 2013 that Enigma "obviously gave up their plan to do a new trs. [translation] for some reason", and he never found out why.[110] This is where I took up the investigation in an effort to try and find out the reason for why Miller had given up on the scholarly significant project that Carrier had suggested to him. In September 2013 I contacted Claudia Vidoni of the Editorial Department at Knaus Verlag in Germany and asked her whether Enigma had ever contacted them back in 2004 or later regarding the translation rights for *Mono-loge*.[111] Vidoni, however, could not give me any information regarding this matter, but she suggested that I contact Enigma directly. If I could get a name of the person that they had negotiated with back in 2004, she told me, she promised she would follow this up.[112]

As suggested by Vidoni, I contacted Robert Miller that very same day and quickly received a reply from him. He started out by explaining that he and Enigma had worked on the *Table Talk* since 1999 and had re-published the Trevor-Roper edition "with a few corrections by him to his preface just before his passing." Later on, referring to the edition of 2007, Enigma had re-published a new edition "for the History Book Club." This edition, he said, contained an added preface by Weinberg "that raised the issue of the origins of the manuscript and particularly that it was the translation of a translation." A few years later, he told me, an Italian publisher had come out with a new edition of *Conversazioni segrete* from 1954. According to him it had not been possible to come to a satisfactory agreement with Jochmann's sisters, so the whole project had been dropped.[113]

This was another huge misunderstanding on Miller's part because Werner Jochmann did not have any sisters; his royalty and copyrights had been left to his *daughters* after his death (more on this later). However, Miller also stated something that made this whole affair take a turn that I certainly had not expected. Miller, who was unaware of the fact that I had access to all of the correspondence between him and Carrier, told me that:

> I have . . . seen the French, English and Italian versions. The truth is that the English version is NOT a translation of the French and Richard Carrier is wrong. The history of the English manuscript is detailed in a biography of Francois Genoud by Pierre Pean [sic] published in France. I can send you a few pages from Pean's book that explain why and how it all happened. I also spoke to Richard Carrier who by the way told me that he was not a historian by [sic] a Latinist and therefore could not consider himself a specialist in contemporary history. My conclusion is that Pean is correct and that Genoud told him the truth as to how the two translations were done. By the way the Italian translation was also done from the German directly.[114]

As we have seen from the correspondence related earlier, what Miller says about Carrier is a misrepresentation, and as far as the statements about Carrier being wrong about *Table Talk* being a translation from the French, our investigation has shown that Miller is just telling a brazen lie. Not only had he been completely fascinated by Carrier's article back in October 2003, but Péan does not address the translation into English at all. Moreover, to simply trust Péan's account, which was completely dependent upon Genoud retold in a book without references to sources, over a peer-reviewed scholarly article based on primary sources seems facile to say the least. Carrier had of course never told Miller that he was not a historian or that he was a "Latinist", and the fact that Carrier was not a specialist in contemporary history has nothing to do with his (well-justified and correct) claim that *Table Talk* had been translated from *Libres propos*. Not only that, Miller also relates the false information that the Italian edition was originally translated from directly from the German, when it, too, in fact, was a direct translation of Genoud's French text. Even the shallowest comparison proves that. Miller was clearly attempting a sort of character assassination of Carrier in his email to me. It was clear that Miller did not want me to listen to anything that Carrier had to say about the history of the *Table Talk*, the translation process, or the source-critical problems relating to it.

Shocked to have received such a reply from Miller, I informed him that I knew that the contract between Weidenfeld and Genoud in fact stipulated that the text *had* to be translated from the French and that even a cursory comparison revealed that Carrier was correct. I even explained that Genoud's mistranslations in *Libres propos* appear unchanged in *Table Talk*. Furthermore, I told Miller that I had documents that prove that Péan was wrong about some things in his book and that Genoud lied about how he got hold of the manuscript and that *all* second-hand sources regarding the history of the *Bormann-Vermerke* are, in the end, dependent on the same source, namely Genoud.[115] These facts, however, were not something that Miller was prepared to even entertain as possibilities. Instead of showing a professional attitude he simply stated:

> Ok we disagree: I think Genoud told Pean the truth: Stevens was present in Montreux and did his translation in parallel. Genoud wanted to own the translation so he could have a clear copyright situation not just because of Picker but because he suspected correctly, that Germany would eventually recover ownership of Hitler's writings and possibly restrict their use. This situation exists for Hitler's Second Book (which I have also published and own the translation and notes by G. Weinberg) as you may know owned by the State of Bavaria and subjected to the whims of the local parliament! Anyway the Italian edition is proof that Pean is correct it was done from the German and contains the same flow as the English edition.[116]

Now, there are a lot of mistakes and falsehoods in this paragraph. First, the idea that Genoud published a French edition in order to gain a clear copyright is, as we have seen, a red herring. It had no bearing on the copyright battle, and the issue does not address the translation into English at all. Second, the suggestion that Germany would eventually recover ownership of Hitler's books (and that Genoud was correct in suspecting this) is incorrect – thrice. He is wrong twice because the "government" already held copyright to Hitler's works (since 1948 in fact), and it was the Bavarian, and not the German, government that held it. In addition, he was wrong because Genoud never "suspected" such a thing, nor did he use it as an argument for publishing a French edition, and it is unknown where Miller got this idea. That means four major falsehoods in the second sentence alone.

The argument concerning *Hitlers zweites Buch* requires that we go into some detail, although it can immediately be said that Miller does not know what he is talking about. Even on the face of it the assertion is absurd. This book had been openly published in German in Germany in 1961 with the participation of the IfZ (this was not only announced in Hans Rothfels's introduction to the book but also on the cover),[117] and to state that it was being hindered by the state of Bavaria is ludicrous – obviously it had not been stopped. In fact, it had been published twice because it was also included as a separate volume in 1995 in the series called *Hitler. Reden, Schriften, Anordnungen* published by the IfZ.[118] In reality the Bavarian government had no way of stopping this publication because it did not possess the copyright to it, since it had not been published before 1948. What the Bavarian court had repossessed in October 1948 was the "Adolf Hitler's archive present in the state of Bavaria", i.e. only the part of Hitler's estate that was physically located in Bavaria.[119] The Bavarian government was also the owner of the estate of the NSDAP publishing house Eher Verlag that had published *Mein Kampf*.[120] That was why the Bavarian authorities could stop new editions of *Mein Kampf* before the copyright ended in 2015. This could explain why Genoud had been hiding his table talks documents in a bank vault in Switzerland for so long before going public with them; if he thought that the Bavarian state would try to confiscate the material. The publication of Picker's book by the IfZ proved that the Bavarian authorities could not stop the publication of material that had left Bavaria, and Genoud could therefore afford to go public with the fact that he had the material. Perhaps it also contributed to his unwillingness to publish it in German.

The matter concerning the Bavarian government's rights, and what it could do to stop publications, preoccupied the West German Ministry of Justice (*Bundesministerium der Justiz*, BMJ) from time to time. In late 1978 the BMJ had concluded that as long it concerned publications that had been agreed to by the heirs and as long as the publication was not against the law, there was nothing that the government could do to stop it even if it violated the Bavarian government's copyright. This certainly sounds odd, but the explanation for this rather strange situation was that a state government could not use its copyright "positively", i.e. for commercial purposes. Firstly, the Bavarian government was indeed the domestic holder of both the copyright and publication rights to Hitler's *Mein Kampf*. Secondly, though, it was still legally unable to prevent any publications of this work that had received the prior consent from the heirs (in this case, Hitler's sister Paula), or from the heir of these rights in turn and could thereby not prevent these persons from collecting the royalties of the sales of these works [this would explain why Genoud was careful enough to negotiate permission from Paula Hitler and from Schmitz, M.N.]. What the Bavarian government *could*, and *did*, do, however, was to prevent any publication emanating from a third party which had not received permission from the heir (or until such time as a proof of permission from the heir in question had been produced), including all income from the sales of the work. The BMJ at the same time concluded that the Bavarian government had no legal basis for preventing publications abroad. However, the Bavarian government did not agree with the second point and had declared to the BMJ that it was determined to continue its efforts to prevent the publication of Hitler's (and other top Nazis') works, even if these had the permission of the heirs. But the BMJ concluded that in practice the Bavarian state had not actively pursued such a course with regard to "the other works of Hitler. . . (explicit permission for the publication of 'Hitler's second book'; no objection to the publication of Hitler's table talks)." However, even though the Bavarian government had thus expressly agreed to the publication of *Hitlers zweites Buch* the publisher (Deutsche Verlags-Anstalt in Stuttgart) had nonetheless acquired a permission from Hitler's sister before publication.[121]

Most likely, Miller had no idea about any of this, but his claims were nonetheless incorrect. I told Miller that this matter was not something that we could really disagree about; it was a fact that *Table Talk* had been translated from the French, and I made sure to underline to him that Péan in fact was the first one to write about the contract stipulating this. I also detailed many other examples showing that what Miller was saying could not be correct (although at the time I had not yet seen the Italian edition and thus could not say anything about it, which I told Miller). I even provided a reference to Ron Rosenbaum's book *Explaining Hitler* to this effect, noting that the French word "confus" had been carried over to the

English edition as "confused" when no such word was to be found in the German text.[122] I then posed the following questions:

> I thought that this (i.e. the fact that he had discovered this fraud) was why you had contacted Carrier in the first place and asked if he could edit and write a preface to a new "definite" version of the Table Talk? Have you changed your mind since then about his article and in that case why? And how do you explain the findings in his article if the English translation was made only from the German original? It seems to me that the findings that Carrier presents must be impossible if what you (based on Péan, who in turn is based on Genoud,) say is correct.[123]

By this time Miller must have understood that I was pretty well informed about his correspondence with Carrier. Nonetheless, Miller continued to stubbornly, and quite disingenuously, defend his initial position, i.e. that I and Carrier were wrong, and he was right. Miller wrote:

> Sorry but you are wrong and so is Carrier who admitted to me that he was not an historian and had no other knowledge of the Hitler documents other than his personal and amateur curiosity about certain linguistic discrepancies. I also do not consider Ron Rosenbaum a serious historian: he found a few things about Hitler here and there and wanted to draw a portrait of sorts but anyone will tell you that they would not use Rosenbaum as a text to 'explain' Hitler.[124]

Note that once again Miller starts building strawmen only to immediately cut them down again in an effort to come off as if his argument actually had defeated mine. He also continued to lie about what Carrier had told him, as well as carried on the attempt at character assassination. What he says about Rosenbaum is not only wrong but also completely irrelevant, since I had never used Rosenbaum's book to explain Hitler. In fact, that is not even what his book is about; it is a book that goes through how *other* historians have explained Hitler over the years. But Miller was not done yet, so he continued:

> To base things on one word 'confused' and to mistake it for 'confus' is also absurd: no way can I accept such an easy and short cut explanation. I was told by Weinberg to read Carrier's article but I found it very lacking in larger picture ramifications. Then I called Carrier and understood that he was not a WWII historian or anything close to it, just a curious person finishing a doctoral dissertation in the classics! Basically he didn't seem firm in his understanding and did it as an amateur. I told this to Weinberg who kept on agreeing with Carrier and refused to modify his introduction which I published as he wrote it. I then read Pean [sic] and the story finally made sense. Even if Genoud was a despicable character he had no reason to lie about the way the translation took place. He had to register the copyright in France of a French translation to prevent German authorities or heirs from claiming

ownership: a very clever decision that sheltered Table Talk from censorship early after WWII when sentiments were still understandably raw about Nazi Germany and it's [sic] former leader.[125]

The matter now acquired an almost comical tone. It may be that Miller was telling the truth that he received the recommendation to read Carrier's article from Weinberg (whom Carrier, incidentally, recommended Miller to contact), but he certainly did *not* find it "very lacking." If he had, then why on earth did he contact Carrier telling him that he liked his article very much and then ask him to edit a new edition of *Table Talk*? Why did he keep this correspondence up for more than half a year in that case? No, Miller was simply lying to me here, making things up as he went along. Once again, the German authorities had not stopped Picker's *Tischgespräche* from being published, so why would Genoud have worried about this happening *after Tischgespräche* was already on the market? This was of course not the true reason, and it is incredible that Miller could think so.

Moreover, his quite scandalous misrepresentation of what Carrier had told him in their correspondence now reached new heights. Carrier had shown great care and understanding for the source-critical problems, and he had exhibited scholarly integrity in insisting upon keeping the quality high all the way through the translation and publication process. The really ironic part, of course, is his inability to understand why Weinberg would not change his preface and keep agreeing with Carrier's conclusions from his article. Obviously, Miller did not see that his critique of Carrier's alleged lack of qualifications also implicated Weinberg, whom he of course could not claim was not a historian or a scholar with expertise in the area. Miller then came back to the issue of the translation process and wrote:

> as Pean tells it Stevens went to Montreux and saw the original German [sic] Genoud was translating from and agreed to shut [sic] and do the job from the German. I also had contact with Weidenfeld through my editor some years ago. I didn't speak with him directly but he confirmed the story and said he would have to deny it publicly if asked to avoid any problems with the Federal Republic of Germany on Hitler's intellectual property. That statement ended apparently with a laugh! So Carrier is nitpicking and dead wrong, in my view and Pean got it right. . . . I am convinced of this.[126]

Miller thus simply continued to produce false and confused absurdities. What did Stevens agree to stop doing when he saw the German text in Montreux, and from what text was he translating before that point? Obviously, Miller is here inadvertently acknowledging that Stevens was after all translating at least partly from the French. He says that he had been in contact with Weidenfeld, although he never spoke to him directly, but through his editor, which contradicts his claim that he had been in contact with Weidenfeld. In fact, he had not. Weidenfeld also, very conveniently, could never confirm to anyone else that he had confirmed the story Miller was now touting, since he had since died.[127] However, in the end, and based on all these absurdities and falsehoods, Miller could confidently assert that Carrier was "dead wrong." In actuality, the only reason that Miller had for believing this was that he was already "convinced" of it. It seems as if Miller had invested so much prestige in the re-print of *Table Talk* that he was absolutely incapable of changing his mind, no matter how strong the evidence against his position turned out to be. It was fact-resistance behaviour at its worst.

But Miller continued to produce contradicting statements and absurdities, even after his initial ones had caught up to him. In my reply I pointed out that Miller now seemed to have changed his position somewhat and implicitly agreed that Stevens had indeed been translation from the French. I explained the point about Rosenbaum's book and pointed out that he was dangerously close to going against every scholar who had actually studied this matter in depth. Furthermore, I questioned why he kept stressing that Carrier was not a contemporary historian and underlined that he could at least not use that argument with me, even though he kept refusing to accept the results of my own research too. I even expressly asked him whether there was some other reason (other than methodology, competence, and evidence-based research) that made him simply brush aside all of our (my own, Carrier's, and Weinberg's) points. Lastly, I made him aware of the fact that even Ian Kershaw thought that I was on to something, and Miller could certainly not argue that Kershaw was not a qualified historian.[128]

To this Miller did not have much new to say. He repeated his assertion that he basically "don't think Carrier was qualified or very serious in his analysis." Then he claimed that he had asked Carrier over the phone regarding "a preface with his findings" and that Carrier had then quickly told him that he was not an expert on the period and that he did not have "any interest in Nazi Germany etc." Miller thus concluded, he told me, that Carrier did this "amateurishly and somehow got it published in German Studies Review." Miller then, amazingly, plainly made clear that he trusted Genoud more than Carrier. Then he stated that a reason for this was that "Col. Stevens was employed by Weidenfeld and was told by his boss to make sure he was translating from the French even though he did it from the German."[129] The latter, of course, repeats Genoud's preposterous claim in Péan's book which makes no sense at all, although it amounted to a giant admission to the fact that Miller had known all along that the translation had been done from *Libres propos*. Miller continued his odd line of argument by bringing up Kershaw:

> Finally as you must know I also published the translation into English of Hitler's Military Conferences which Sir Ian Kershaw also praised. You will see a very dubious Hitler who sounds and acts normally and is subdued in his judgements and choices of words. Those transcripts were often taken by the same stenographers that were present for Table Talk.[130]

Clearly, this is another strawman, since it does not address anything that had to do with *my* points. Moreover, Miller makes yet another mistake when he claims that Picker and Heim was involved in the stenographic recording of the military *Lagebesprechungen*. This is completely false; as is the reverse, i.e. that any of the stenographers involved in the *Lagebesprechungen* ever noted down the texts found in the *Bormann-Vermerke*.

Carrier's reaction to all of this was a simple and down-to-earth one. In an email to me he wrote: "Wow. Off his rocker."[131] I now felt I had to tell Miller that I had access to all the correspondence between him and Carrier and also made the comment about the stenographers and the *Lagebesprechungen* quite clear to him. I questioned Miller as to the details of his story about Carrier and why he went on corresponding with Carrier for so long if he had immediately, even after the first phone call, decided that he was an amateur. The issue why it took so long between the end of their correspondence until the re-print of *Table Talk* finally came out.[132] Miller's reply is worth quoting in full:

> Once I read Pean I contacted Carrier after my first talk with him. I didn't have any preconceived ideas and as I wrote asked him to consider a preface. He was not interested and said basically that this was not his field of expertise. I then turned to Weinberg who agreed and did his excellent intro basically using Carrier's research in part. Once I read Pean I went back to Weinberg and suggested that the intro may have to be nuanced to cover the other possibility that Genoud may have been correct. Weinberg said no because it completely contradicted his view. I agreed and we went on to publish his preface. My doubts remained and when I approached the Jochmann sisters about a translation I was hoping to find something that would shed more light on the episode. The Jochmann sisters were impossible to deal with and were convinced they had at the very least a Rembrandt or a Picasso! Also the translation cost would have been very high. So I kept issuing Table Talk which still sells very well. I do regret not having insisted on the Jochmann text though.[133]

Here Miller is caught telling yet another lie. Now he changes his story and claims that he read Péan's book after his first talk with Carrier, although in a previous email (cited earlier) he stated that he only read Péan while Weinberg was refusing to change his introduction. But the latter was *after* Miller and Carrier had stopped corresponding. Miller is just making it all up as he goes along. Moreover, the first sentence makes no sense; if he contacted Carrier after his phone call with him, at which time Carrier had (according to Miller) told him that he was not a specialist and Miller had thought that he was an amateur, all the questions still remain. Why did he contact him at all? Furthermore, the statement that he did not have "any preconceived ideas" when asking Carrier to write the preface is completely absurd. No matter if he considered him an unqualified Latinist or if he was highly fascinated with Carrier's article, as he had claimed in his email to Carrier, he must have had a preconceived idea (either good or bad, according to his own prior statements) going into it all. But then Miller produces yet another absurdity and contradiction by stating that he went back to Weinberg and asked him to change *his* preface once he had read Péan. The timeline simply does not add up. Did he read

Péan just before he emailed Carrier or much later when he and Weinberg discussed the latter's preface? Both cannot be the case, and yet Miller acts as if they are.

It is worth noting that Miller appeared to implicitly claim that Jochmann's "sisters" (read: daughters) actually had the copy of the *Bormann-Vermerke* in their possession. Otherwise, they could not reasonably have negotiated about it, nor could they then have been convinced they had something corresponding to a painting by a famous artist. This naturally made me quite excited, as I now believed that I had identified the whereabouts of the illusive *Bormann-Vermerke*. Hence, I asked Miller about precisely this matter and if he had the contact information for Jochmann's sisters so I could reach them.[134] However, it turned out that this information was just as unreliable as all the rest of Miller's correspondence, because he had absolutely no idea "about the manuscript" because he "never got into that." Miller promised that he would try to find their contact information for me once he got back from a trip. Upon a request I received Weinberg's email from Miller, but I never heard back from him regarding the "sisters".[135]

I managed to find this contact information on my own, however, and I could thus check Miller's story with one of Jochmann's daughters, Renate Miron. According to her, Miller had contacted her in 2003 regarding an English translation of *Monologe*. This edition was planned for publication in 2005, Miller had told her. However, the contract proposal that Miller sent to her demanded that they should sign over the entire copyright for *Monologe* to Enigma Books, and this was very unfavourable for them financially. Thus, Miron turned it down, but suggested a number of changes to the contract, which would have made a deal acceptable to her and her sister. In May 2004 Miller told her that the costs for such an edition, including translation and so on, would be too high, and Enigma had decided to drop the whole matter. After this point Miron had not heard back from Miller again.[136]

What is interesting about this, of course, is that although Enigma had given up on the project of publishing an English edition of *Monologe* in May 2004, Miller continued to negotiate with Carrier until 14 June. Moreover, in his correspondence with me Miller states that he did not contact Miron before Weinberg's preface had been written (he said that his doubts remained after having debated the preface with Weinberg and that he hoped to find more information about the matter when he approached Miron). This is not true either. Indeed, it seems as if almost nothing that Miller has said about this affair has been the truth.

After all the conversations with Carrier, and despite Weinberg's preface that agreed with Carrier's conclusion in his article, Miller decided to ignore all of the expert comments and warnings about the source-critical problems connected to the text. When, in 2007, the Enigma edition was marketed to the public it was claimed on the cover that it was "the only complete record" of Hitler's utterances.[137] This, too, was of course not true. It is certainly a bit frustrating as a scholar to spend a considerable amount of time in archives and comparing text variants, only to have the important results completely ignored and replaced by the very myths that one has done one's best to refute by savvy publishers who only have their eyes on the number of copies that their books are expected to sell. Apparently, source criticism and serious scholarly work do not sell as many books as fairy tales do. I suspect, however, that these publishers seriously underestimate their target audience.

Conclusions

In this chapter I have laid out the history of the publishing of Genoud's German text that was made public in 1980 under the title *Monologe im Führerhauptquartier*. A number of problematic factors related to both the text itself and to the way in which German historian Werner Jochmann handled it have been covered here. The history of *Monologe* also got an unexpected addendum in the early 2000s as a translation of this German edition was being planned by an American publisher.

For sure, Jochmann could have done a much better job of pointing out to the reader of the book that Heim's notes were not a word-for-word transcript of Hitler's statements and that they were actually only summaries of what Hitler had talked about based, to a large extent, on memory only. The latter was particularly true with regard to the nightly conversations at which time Heim made perfectly clear that he could not make any supporting notes at all. More precisely, Jochmann did not expand on the consequences of these facts to the extent that ought to have done. Neither did Jochmann address the fact that there was no way for the historian to know which words or statement that built on those occasional supporting words and which did not. The effect from a source-critical perspective is obviously that the distinction between utterances based on supporting words and those that were based entirely on memory disappears.

Just as the historians who had come before him, Jochmann did not have access to Genoud's original manuscript. However, he seems to have been offered access to something that none other had thus far; namely, it appears he was provided with Xerox copies of Genoud's photocopies of the originals, documents that Genoud claimed to be of very poor quality. Jochmann never included any description of the manuscript copies that he received from Genoud; nor did he share all the pertinent information related to this text with his readers. In a sense then, Jochmann behaved almost as Trevor-Roper had done in his dealings with Genoud, and it is hard to escape the conclusion that Genoud had a bad influence on the historians that he chose to work with. Jochmann was otherwise a very diligent and prudent historian with a good reputation, and the way in which he handled *Monologe* does not seem to be representative of his legacy as a historian.

I have also shown that Jochmann made a very odd decision when choosing which pages to include as facsimiles in *Monologe*. It turns out that one out of the three pages is actually *not* a facsimile of a page from Genoud's photocopied manuscript, but instead of a copy of Heim's proof page taken from the LoC. This decision makes absolutely no sense on the assumption that Jochmann had ready access to Genoud's manuscript and has to be explained in some other way. The page in question comes from a note dated 16–17 January 1942. The inescapable conclusion from this finding must be that Jochmann did not have access to this page via Genoud's copies. This way of going about things cannot be explained by assuming that this particular page in Genoud's manuscript was of too poor quality for it to be represented legibly in *Monologe* because then the question of why Jochmann simply did not choose another page has to be asked. Indeed, it has to be asked anyway because this is a form of fraud on Jochmann's part. The reader obviously has to assume that this page comes from Genoud's manuscript, since Jochmann does not inform the reader otherwise. Jochmann did keep also other critical information about his sources from his readers.

Also, I have shown how the CEO of the American book publisher Enigma Books, Robert Miller, was extremely unwilling to understand and accept the findings of both Richard Carrier's and my own research into the table talk texts. Even though Miller was presented with incontrovertible evidence that his assumptions about this source were incorrect, he refused to accept these facts. Instead, he chose to dig in his heels and insist that Carrier and I were both wrong in our assessments. He even denied the obvious fact that *Table Talk* had been translated from the French rather than from the German text eventually published as *Monologe*. The Enigma edition was not a successful one, however, and it is basically never cited by historians. By the time it came out, it had long since been made redundant by the publication of *Monologe* in 1980, and since it was not a re-translation or re-evaluation of the German text, there was no other reason for anyone to use it. Any historian who had the poor judgement to quote *Table Talk* could just as well go to the original Weidenfeld & Nicolson edition from 1953.

Notes

1 Letter from Jochmann to Eberhard Jäckel, 20 October 1977; WJN; Binder: "Schrift-wechsel A – K 1977".
2 Letter from Jochmann to Genoud, 10 July 1978, p. 2; WJN; Binder: "Schriftwechsel A – K 1977".
3 Letter from Knaus to Jochmann, 26 January 1978; WJN; Binder: "Schriftwechsel A – K 1977".
4 Letter from Genoud to Knaus, 26 February 1978; WJN; Binder: "Schriftwechsel A – K 1977".
5 Ibid.
6 Letter from Knaus to Jochmann, 2 March 1978; WJN; Binder: "Schriftwechsel A – K 1977".
7 Letter from Genoud to Jochmann, 2 March 1978; WJN; Binder: "Schriftwechsel A – K 1977".
8 Letter from Jochmann to Genoud, 28 March 1978; WJN; Binder: "Schriftwechsel A – K 1977".
9 Draft for contract between Jochmann and Albrecht Knaus Verlag, 6 June 1978; WJN; Binder: "Schriftwechsel A – K 1977".
10 Letter from Jutta Petersen (at Knaus Verlag) to Jochmann, 21 July 1978; WJN; Binder: "Schriftwechsel A – K 1977".
11 Letter from Jochmann to Genoud, 10 July 1978, p. 1; WJN; Binder: "Schriftwechsel A – K 1977".
12 Letter from Jochmann to Genoud, 31 July 1978; letter from Jochmann to Genoud, 9 January 1979, p. 1; letter from Genoud to Jochmann, 5 June 1979; letter from Genoud

to Knaus, 5 June 1979; WJN; Binder: "Schriftwechsel A – K 1977". All these letters talk about photocopies. Originals are never mentioned.

13 Letter from Genoud to Jochmann, 23 July 1978; letter from Genoud to Jochmann, 28 July 1978; WJN; Binder: "Schriftwechsel A – K 1977".

14 Letter from Genoud to Jochmann, 20 December 1978; WJN; Binder: "Schriftwechsel A – K 1977".

15 Letter from Jochmann to Genoud, 9 January 1979, pp. 1–2; WJN; Binder: "Schrift-wechsel A – K 1977".

16 Letter from Knaus to Genoud, 3 May 1979; WJN; Binder: "Schriftwechsel: A – K 1977".

17 Letter from Genoud to Knaus, 5 June 1979; letter from Genoud to Jochmann, 5 June 1979; WJN; Binder: "Schriftwechsel: A – K 1977".

18 Maser, W., *Adolf Hitler: Legende . . .*, pp. 66, 72.

19 Ibid., pp. 275, 576.

20 Ibid., pp. 315, 580.

21 Typed notes from an interview with Heim by Dr. Freiherr von Siegler in Munich 1 July 1952 for the IfZ (dated 2 July 1952), pp. 2–3; www.ifz-muenchen.de/archiv/zs/zs-0243_1.pdf, accessed: 2013–08–10. Typed notes from a conversation between Heim and the director of IfZ Dr. Mau, 17 July 1952, p. 6; www.ifz-muenchen.de/archiv/zs/zs-0243_1.pdf, accessed: 2013–08–10.

22 Toland, J., *Adolf Hitler* (Vol. II), p. 782 (p. 682 in the one-volume edition).

23 *Monologe . . .*, p. 16.

24 This same point is in fact made by "the publisher" in a footnote to the introduction in *Hitlers politisches Testament* where it says that "it is not easy to imagine that Hitler for weeks, months, and, in the end, years had not noticed that one of the participants in this round of talks had regularly taken notes." For this, see: *Hitlers politisches Testament . . .*, p. 21. It then just so happened that the publisher made a more reasonable estimation of this source than most historians have since then.

25 C.f. Typed notes from a conversation between Heim and the director of IfZ Dr. Mau, 17 July 1952, pp. 1–3; www.ifz-muenchen.de/archiv/zs/zs-0243_1.pdf, accessed: 2013–08–10. In the same interview Heim also tries to make Bormann look like a genuinely nice fellow who was not only forever faithful to his wife but who also loved the Füh-rer so much that he did not do even the smallest thing without having gotten Hitler's approval first (ibid., pp. 4–5). However, we know that this is not true, so Heim completely lacks credibility regarding this matter. Moreover, Heim immediately contradicts himself when he on the one hand states that Bormann never did anything without Hitler's approval and on the other hand insists that Bormann ordered that notes were to be made without the knowledge of the Führer. For the information about Heim's membership in the NSDAP, see: *Monologe . . .*, p. 11.

26 Typed notes from a conversation between Heim and the director of IfZ Dr. Mau 17 July 1952, pp. 7–8; www.ifz-muenchen.de/archiv/zs/zs-0243_1.pdf, accessed: 2013–08–10. About the Kristallnacht, see: Typed notes from a conversation between Heim and Dr. Freiherr von Sigler 1 October 1952, p. 1; www.ifz-muenchen.de/archiv/zs/zs-0243_1.pdf, accessed: 2013–08–10. Heim was of the opinion that David Irving was probably right in assuming that Hitler had not meant physical extermination when he ordered the "Aussiedlung" of the Jews; see: IfZ; ED 416; Vol. 2; Letter from Heim to Walter-Gerd Bauer, 11 August 1978, p. 2. Thus, in an absurd circular chain of evidence, we see Irving basing himself on Heim's testimony and Heim referring to Irving as a proof that his own statements were reasonable.

27 "Trial Transcripts", day 5, p. 44; www.hdot.org/day05/, accessed: 2016–11–28. The possibility that such discussions would not have taken place anyway did not fit Irving's ideological purpose, and thus he was unable to entertain the idea and consider it as a possible explanation for the absence of such talks.

28 Letters from Heß to Heim, 16 June and 15 September 1924; IfZ; ED 416; Vol. 2.

29 See invitation to Heim and "Gäste des Reichsführers-SS Heinrich Himmler bei der Besichtigung der SS-Anlagen Dachau am Freitag, 8. Mai 1936 zum gemeinschaftilchen Abendessen im S.S. Gemeinschaftshaus Dachau"; IfZ; ED 416; Vol. 1.

30 *Monologe . . .*, p. 16.

31 Ibid.

32 Ibid., pp. 16–18.

33 Ibid., pp. 18–20; Longerich, P., *Hitler . . .*, p. 869.

34 Schroeder, C., *Er war mein Chef . . .*, pp. 116–119, 357. Heim's 36 notes used by Picker is still called "Originalstenogrammen" in Schroeder's book (ibid., p. 356). This fact also shows that Schroeder did not know much about Heim's notes and thus cannot be trusted on details regarding how they came about.

35 *Libres propos. . .* (Vol. I, 1952), p. xxvii.

36 Letter from Kuykendall to Heim, 25 July 1977, p. 1; Letter from Kuykendall to Heim, 20 September 1977, p. 1; UALSC; PKK MS 243; Series II; Box 2, Folder 5.

37 *Libres propos. . .* (Vol. I, 1952), p. xxvi.

38 *Hitlers Tischgespräche. . .* (1963), pp. 125, 130.

39 Koeppen, W., *Herbst 1941 im "Führerhauptquartier" . . .*, p. xxii.

40 *Monologe . . .*, pp. 14–15.

41 Ibid., pp. 21–22.

42 Ibid., pp. 16, 18.

43 von Lang, Jochen, *Der Sekretär: Der Mann der Hitler beherrschte* (Unter Mitarbeit von Claus Sibyll) (Stuttgart: Deutsche Verlags-Anstalt, 1977), p. 139; Speer, A., *Erinnerungen*, p. 109. Note, however, that Speer's testimony cannot be relied on; he cannot (considering when he is writing, i.e. a long time after the event, and the suspicious circumstances regarding how his memoirs were written) be considered an independent witness.

44 Rosenbaum, Ron, *Explaining Hitler: The Search for the Origins of His Evil* (London: Papermac, 1999), pp. 72, 75. At the same time Rosenbaum too repeats the idea that Bormann heavily edited the manuscripts and writes that Bormann took the stenographer's notes and added "editing, refining, polishing, constructing a testament." This is complete fiction because there is no source that claims this. Not even Picker had the gall to state things in this brazen manner.

45 *Monologe . . .*, pp. 7–8.

46 Ullrich, V., *Adolf Hitler. . .* (Vol. II), p. 225. Unfortunately, Ullrich's book was published before my article on *Monologe* was available; see: "Hitler redivivus: *Hitlers Tischgespräche* und *Monologe im Führerhauptquartier*" – eine kritische Untersuchung" in *Vierteljahrshefte für Zeitgeschichte*, No. 67 (January 2019), pp. 105–145.

47 "Eidstattliche Erklärung", 13 February 1980, pp. 1–2; WJN; Binder: "Schriftwechsel: A – K 1977".

48 Letter from Jochmann to Else James, 23 January 1980, p. 4; WJN; Binder: "Schriftwechsel: A – K 1977". See also note dated 12/13.1.1942 in: *Monologe . . .*, p. 194.

49 *Monologe . . .*, p. 14.

50 Ibid., pp. 14–15.

51 Letter from Heim to Jochmann, 17 January 1979, p. 1; WJN; Binder: "Schriftwechsel: A – K 1977". A week prior to this, Jochmann had written to Heim: "After all, they summarized in a few pages what Hitler spoke and discussed for several hours. In the end, therefore, only the line of thought and the quintessence of the statements have been preserved." For this, see: Letter from Jochmann to Heim, 10 January 1979, p. 2; WJN; Binder: "Schriftwechsel: A – K 1977".

52 Telephone interview with Cordula Schacht, 2013-08-07.

53 Email to me from Sir Ian Kershaw, 2013-08-20.

54 *Monologe . . .*, see facsimiles on pp. 492–493. See also: Franz-Willing, G., "Hitlers Tischgespräche" in *Klüter Blätter. Monatshefte für Kultur und Zeitgeschichte*, Jahrgang 32, Dezember 1981, Heft 12, p. 29.

55 Winkler, W., *Der Schattenmann . . .*, pp. 72–73, 76.

56 Copy of note "Führerhauptquartier, 16./17.1.1942" with handwriting; WJN; Binder: "Schriftwechsel".

57 This problem cannot be solved by assuming that this page in Genoud's manuscript perhaps was of such poor quality that it could not be reproduced legibly. If that was the case then what any reasonable person would do is choose another page, one that is of better quality (like the two others he reproduced).

58 *Monologe . . .*, p. 496.

59 *Hitlers Tischgespräche. . .* (1963), pp. 18–19. "(F)ür (d)ie (R)ichtigkeit: Picker"

60 Carbon copy of the manuscript for *Tischgespräche*, p. 1; BAK; N 1128 (Hitler Nachlaß); "Henry Picker Hitlers Tischgespräche im Führerhauptquartier 1941–1942"; Vol. 31. Percy Ernst Schramm und Andreas Hillgruber (Manuskripte der Neuausgabe)".

61 *Hitlers Tischgespräche. . .* (1951), p. 33.

62 Ibid.

63 *Hitlers Tischgespräche. . .* (1963), p. 23.

64 *Hitlers Tischgespräche. . .* (1976), p. 33.

65 Schroeder, C., *Er war mein Chef . . .*, p. 354.

66 "Streit um 'Tischgespräche' beendet" in *Deutsche Zeitung*, 23 September 1961.

67 See the court's decision, 29 April 1980, pp. 1–10, quote on page p. 9; CCLO; HTRP; Vol. Soc. Dacre 6/6/2.

68 Genoud to Trevor-Roper, 9 February 1981, p. 2; CCLO; HTRP; Vol. Soc. Dacre 6/6/2.

69 Ibid. Genoud also attached a copy of his preface with these sentences underlined to prove his point and his consistency.

70 "Protokoll" from Landesgericht München, 17 April 1980, pp. 2–4; CCLO; HTRP; Vol. Soc. Dacre 6/6/2.

71 Ibid., pp. 1–9.

72 Ibid., p. 5.

73 German transcription of interview with Heinrich Heim 25 February 1975, p. 5; FDRPL; JTP; Series II "Adolf Hitler"; Box 46. The first interview with Heim was made on 17 March 1971; this transcript is from one of three follow-up interviews made in 1975.

74 Drafts for letters in stenographic shorthand by Heim to Dr. Hans Grimm, 6 May 1958; 1 June 1958; 1 May 1960; WJN; Binder: "Schriftwechsel: A – K 1977". See also: stenographic note, 5 January 1945; IfZ; ED 416; Vol. 1.

75 Toland, J., *Adolf Hitler* (Vol. II), p. 780 (p. 682 in the one-volume edition).

76 Email from FDRPL archivist Virginia Lewick to the author, 2016–10–05.

77 "Protokoll" from Landesgericht München, 17 April1980, p. 6; CCLO; HTRP; Vol. Soc. Dacre 6/6/2. Engel was used by Picker (together with several others) to authenticate his notes and to confirm that Picker's book corresponded well to the Hitler Engel had known (*Hitlers Tischgespräche. . .* (1983), pp. 55–56).

78 Letter from Heim to Werner Maser, 1 November 1972, p. 2; WJN; Binder: "Schriftwechsel: A – K 1977".

79 "Protokoll" from Landesgericht München, 17 April 1980, p. 8; CCLO; HTRP; Vol. Soc. Dacre 6/6/2.

80 Ibid., p. 9.

81 *Hitlers Tischgespräche. . .* (1963), p. 21.

82 *Hitlers Tischgespräche. . .* (1976), p. 55.

83 "Protokoll" from Landesgericht München, 17 April 1980, p. 6; CCLO; HTRP; Vol. Soc. Dacre 6/6/2.

84 Frank, H., *Im Angesicht des Galgens . . .*, p. 454. That Hitler had the tables put in a horseshoe formation during his monologues is nowhere to be found except in this statement by Schaub. Therefore, we have to regard it with great scepticism.

85 Piotrowski, Stanislaw, *Hans Franks Tagebuch* (Warszawa: Polnisher Verlag der Wissenschaften, 1963). This book was in turn a somewhat shortened version of a book in Polish by the same author. Piotrowski had been part of the Polish delegation to the Nuremberg trials between November 1945 and April 1946. Between May and October 1946, he was the only Polish delegate to the court (ibid., p. VI). It is necessary to state, as a cautionary note, that the published German text of the *Tagebuch* was translated from a Russian translation of the diaries (which, apparently, were a checked and corrected (against the original notes) version of the slightly flawed version that was used in the trial (ibid., p. 10).

86 Piotrowski, S., *Hans Franks Tagebuch*, p. 3.

87 Ibid., pp. 4–7.

88 "Urteil in dem Rechtsstreit Dr. Henry Picker gegen Firma Albrecht Knaus Verlag", 29 April 1980, p. 9; WJN; Binder: "Schriftwechsel: A – K 1977".

89 Letter from Jochmann to Genoud, 30 April 1979, p. 1; WJN; Binder: "Schriftwechsel: A – L 1979". See also: *Monologe . . .*, p. 17.

90 Letter from Seewald to Knaus, 21 January 1980, pp. 1–2; letter from Knaus to Seewald, 14 February 1980, pp. 1–2; WJN; Binder: "Schriftwechsel: A – K 1977".

91 Letter from Knaus to Seewald, 14 February 1980, p. 2; WJN; Binder: "Schriftwechsel: A – K 1977".

92 Franz-Willing, G., "Hitlers Tischgespräche", p. 22.

93 Letter from Jutta Petersen to Jochmann, 26 August 1980; WJN; Binder: "Schriftwechsel A – K 1977".

94 Email from Miller to Carrier, 20 October 2003. This correspondence was made available to me by Richard Carrier. See email from Carrier to the author, 6 September 2013.

95 Email from Carrier to Miller, 21 October 2003.

96 Ibid.

97 Email from Miller to Carrier, 24 November 2003 (7:07:38 AM PST); email from Carrier to Miller, 24 November 2003 (10:25:15 AM PST).

98 Email from Carrier to Miller, 24 November 2003 (5:19.43 PM PST).

99 Ibid.

100 Email from Miller to Carrier, 25 November 2003.

101 Email from Miller to Carrier, 26 November 2003.

102 Email from Miller to Carrier, 28 November 2003.

103 Email from Miller to Carrier, 11 December 2003; email from Miller to Carrier, 14 December 2003.

104 Email from Miller to Carrier, 29 January 2004.

105 Email from Carrier to Miller, 29 January 2004.

106 Email from Miller to Carrier, 11 June 2004.

107 Email from Carrier to Miller, 13 June 2004.

108 Ibid.

109 Email from Miller to Carrier, 14 June 2004.

110 Email from Carrier to the author, 6 September 2013.

111 Email from the author to Vidoni, 6 September 2013 (11:40 CET).

112 Email from Vidoni to the author, 6 September 2013 (11:46 CET); email from Vidoni to the author, 6 September 2013 (12:23 CET).

113 Email from the author to Miller, 6 September 2013 (5:15 AM PST); email from Miller to the author, 6 September 2013 (15:05 CET).

114 Email from Miller to the author, 6 September 2013 (15:05 CET).

115 Email from the author to Miller, 6 September 2013 (9.35 AM PST).

116 Email from Miller to the author, 6 September 2013 (15:49 CET).

117 *Hitlers zweites Buch . . .*, p. 10.

118 See: *RSA, Band II A. Außenpolitische Standortsbestimmungen nach der Reichstagswahl Juni – Juli 1928. Eingeleitet von Gerhard L. Weinberg. Herausgegeben und kommentiert von Gerhard L. Weinberg, Christian Hartmann und Klaus A. Lankheit* (Munich: K. G. Saur, 1995).

119 Decision from the Munich *Spruchkammer*, München I, 15 October 1948, p. 1; BAK; Bundesministerium der Justiz (BdJ), B 141/73827; Vol. 3602-2, Band 2.

120 Record of a Q&A in the West German parliament, the *Bundestag*, in Bonn: "Veröffentlichungen aus der schriftlichen Hinterlassenschaft ehemaliger NS-Größen", 18 October 1978, p. 2; BAK; BdJ, B 141/73827; Vol. 3602-2, Band 1.

121 "Vermerk betr. Veröffentlichungen aus der schriftlichen Hinterlassenschaft ehemaliger NS-Größen", 27 November 1978, pp. 2–4; BAK; BdJ, B 141/73827; Vol. 3602-2, Band 1. A good overview of the Bavarian government's efforts to stop *Mein Kampf* from being published both domestically and abroad can be found in: Kellerhoff, S. F., *"Mein Kampf" Die Karriere . . .*, pp. 289–308.

122 Email from the author to Miller, 6 September 2013 (10:31 AM PST).

123 Ibid.

124 Email from Miller to the author, 6 September 2013 (17:16 CET).

125 Ibid.

126 Ibid.

127 Since Miller passed away in 2016, he is now unable to further answer my critique.

128 Email from the author to Miller, 6 September 2013 (12:34 PM PST). Granted, to Miller this was at this point only me claiming Kershaw thought so, and he may well have been justified in not trusting me until he saw the actual evidence.

129 Email from Miller to the author, 7 September 2013 (00:55 CET).

130 Ibid.

131 Email from Carrier to the author, 7 September 2013 (3:30 AM CET).

132 Email from the author to Miller, 7 September 2013 (6:29 AM PST).

133 Email from Miller to the author, 7 September 2013 (16:45 CET).

134 Email from the author to Miller, 7 September 2013 (12:26 PM PST).

135 Email from Miller to the author, 7 September 2013 (18:45 CET); email from the author to Miller, 14 September 2013; email from Miller to the author, 14 September 2013.

136 Email from Miron to the author, 13 October 2016.

137 *Hitler's Table Talk, 1941–1944. New Foreword by Gerhard L. Weinberg* (Enigma Books: 2007).

8

CONCLUSIONS

The table talks have been used by almost every historian writing about Hitler, National Socialism, and Nazi Germany since 1951. Still, before this book there was no in-depth, source-critical study of these important sources. They were said to contain Hitler's honest and private statements to a small circle of confidants written down using stenography at his FHQs, and historians have cited these sources as if they contained Hitler's words *ad verbatim*. This book has shown all of this to be either factually wrong or mistaken.

The idea that the table talks contain Hitler's words as they were actually spoken to his entourage in the various military HQs during the war must, as a result, be considered to have been conclusively disproven. The table talks are not that kind of sources, since they, contrary to what has been assumed by prior research, were not the product of stenographic notes. Instead, they were (as in the case of the nightly monologues) re-constructed entirely from memory, and sometimes partly from so-called supporting words. Heim's proof pages show that they were not only edited later on – text was added, taken out, or moved around – and sometimes finished long after the date on them. Nor was Hitler more honest in these statements; the evidence is that lies from *Mein Kampf* are repeated in the table talks even though many of those present must have known that what he said was not true.

So, what does this mean for the table talks as a historical source material? Well, in fact, what we have are only *representations* and *recollections* of Hitler's utterances. This means that they are *not* Hitler's words and that they cannot, and should not, be quoted as such. We can still use them, of course, but the way in which historians have often used them thus far has been as *ad verbatim* sources. This is why they have been so frequently cited in the literature. Since we know that Hitler often misrepresented matters, either knowingly or unbeknownst to himself, as studies of, for example, *Mein Kampf* have shown, as historians we are in the position that we cannot know if what Hitler is purported as having said is true or not unless it can be verified by independent sources. Just like scholars are always aware that they are quoting Goebbels's recollection of Hitler's statements when they cite Goebbels's diaries, they should be equally aware that they are quoting Heim's or Picker's or Bormann's or Müller's recollections when they cite *Tischgespräche* and *Monologe*.

I have shown that British historian Hugh Trevor-Roper had a very central role in the publication of all of Genoud's documents and that Trevor-Roper consistently refrained from telling his readers about the many and serious source-critical problems with the sources that he validated. He benefited financially from this practice and admitted in private correspondence that he did not question Genoud's texts in public because he wished to be the one that Genoud turned to the next time he had a text for publication. The translation of *Table Talk* has furthermore been shown to be seriously flawed. *Table Talk* was translated almost entirely from Genoud's French *Libres propos*, but the translator also took large liberties with the text. Trevor-Roper knew about this but lied to his readers and said that it had been translated from the original German. *Table Talk* should therefore simply not be used by historians; instead, the German texts should be used and translated.

The publication of Picker's *Tischgespräche* in 1951 upset a lot of people, and the IfZ soon removed their involvement with the book after Genoud had shown that Picker had made many changes to his manuscript. Historian Gerhard Ritter, who edited *Tischgespräche*, also got a lot of criticism. Ritter clearly was not critical enough of Picker and his manuscript, but everything was not Ritter's fault. Picker actively opposed many of the source-critical comments that Ritter wanted to insert into the book. Ritter's choice to present the notes thematically was nonetheless a bad idea. In 1963, in the second edition, Picker re-edited his text so that it corresponded much closer to Genoud's version. However, I have shown that this manuscript also contained added material. All of this means that *Tischgespräche* has to be handled very carefully by historians referencing it. We simply often have no way of knowing how well the notes correspond to what Hitler actually said. Picker constantly lied about how his manuscript had been made in order to gain the upper hand in his constant struggles against Genoud.

Genoud too was a liar and a confidence trickster, and he spread many myths about the table talks that have been accepted as true by historians, often due to Trevor-Roper having publicly validated his claims. I have shown that Genoud lied about when he acquired the table talks. Instead of having purchased them in the summer of 1951, it is most likely that he had them as early as 1947. Why he lied about this is unknown, but Genoud spread many meaningless lies over the years. To obfuscate seems to have been his primary purpose in fact. He guarded his documents jealously and was extremely unwilling to show them to anyone. He never let anyone see other than photocopies of the so-called *Bormann-Vermerke*, and it is indeed likely that he never possessed the actual original documents but only photocopies of them. We will likely never know for sure, since the manuscript is now lost; the last person to have seen any of these copies was the editor of *Monologe*, Werner Jochmann.

Jochmann, just like Ritter, was an otherwise diligent and careful historian but in dealing with the table talk text he displayed a considerable lack of critical thinking. He often ended up acting as a validator of Genoud's claims rather than independently evaluating the source he was publishing. This no doubt had to do with his relationship with Genoud and the fact that the manuscript he was working with was in private hands. This gave Genoud enormous power; he could essentially veto access to central historical documents by denying historians access to them, and anyone allowed to see them as a consequence felt extremely privileged. They probably did not feel comfortable to repay that service by criticizing the source document and its owner. This is why public archives are so important, and it could certainly be questioned if important historical documents should be allowed to be in the hands of private collectors. The trade in Nazi documents and artefacts is not only a nuisance, it is a direct obstacle to the scientific study of history.

It is easy to understand why historians have had such a hard time remaining critical towards the table talks; they simply are such rich and fantastic sources that it is very easy to get "drawn in" by them, and to accept them as *ad verbatim* records just because they look and feel that way. In that sense they are indeed too good to be true. They also have obvious flaws, especially concerning what they do *not* divulge of Hitler's views and about his mind. Glaringly absent are all of Hitler's knowledge of the Holocaust; all we are left with are suggestive hints made by him to an entourage that of course knew full well what he was talking about, although almost all of them (Heim included) would deny that either they or Hitler had any knowledge of the full-scale extermination of Europe's Jews that was going on during the entire period covered by these sources. This fact makes the silence on this subject especially revolting.

Another related mistake that historians have continuously made when dealing with the table talk sources is that they have treated them, if not assumed them to be, as if they were the standard against which all other sources should be measured. It is as if it did not actually matter to historians whether Hitler actually used one set of words instead of another. In the cases when parallel notes exist (e.g. Koeppen) historians often choose to cite *Monologe*, and the readers are often not even told about the fact that the notes are not at all identical. There simply is no reason for historians to assume that Heim better remembered what Hitler had said than Koeppen. Yet, *Monologe* is always the source cited by historians in the cases where two (or more) of these notes coincide. Koeppen's notes are basically never used when there is a corresponding note in *Monologe*. This in and by itself is, I believe, a testimony to the fact that these collections of notes have gained an almost mythical status even among trained and professional historians.

A broader methodological point that this book has made is that the process of evaluating a document with reference to its "internal evidence" – i.e. whether the source sounds or reads 'true' – is terribly flawed. Nonetheless this method has very often been used by historians faced with questionable Hitler documents. The result has often been that forgeries have been accepted as genuine. Historians have thus far not been treating the table talks with the same source-critical attentiveness as e.g. *Mein Kampf*. Today every historian understands that what Hitler says with regards to non-ideological matters in *Mein Kampf* cannot simply be assumed to be true. However, the very same historians tend to accept what is in the table talks without any further source-critical analysis.

The results presented in this book are somewhat problematic for the history of National Socialism, Hitler, and the Third Reich in general. Historians have to a large extent simply accepted the myth about Hitler being in a private circle of close confidants where he felt free to speak the truth. This ignores, first, the important question of whether Hitler actually could still separate between truth and the fictions that he had created around his persona and the movement that he was leading. Second, it ignores the possibility of Hitler simply remembering incorrectly what had taken place 10 or even 20 years ago. Historians rarely, if ever, question the reliability of the statements in the table talks when Hitler is speaking about the *Kampfzeit* or his childhood. Third, historians must start to ask whether what we are seeing in the table talks was Hitler's true understanding of matters and events during the period of 1941–1944 and how much of it that was uttered in the spur of the moment.

Historians far too often regard matters that Hitler may very well have said off the cuff as already-decided-upon plans for the future of the Reich or for the occupied territories in the East and so on. The utterances about what was to happen to the people and the land in the East, recorded during the early months of Operation Barbarossa in the summer of 1941, have been frequently quoted by historians and presented as being Hitler's plans for the future. This is done even though the same historians otherwise show that they understand that Hitler rarely, if ever, planned *anything* so far in advance. He was a slave to his impulsiveness in politics, as in the field of military matters, and his reluctance to be nailed down on issues concerning the future is one of the best attested of his character traits in the Hitler literature. Several witnesses, including Heim, testify that Hitler was thinking out loud, and sometimes testing ideas, during these dinners and *Teestunden*. Indeed, he could not have laid out plans that he did not have yet. The notes probably tell us more about the kind of mind that would utter statements like these than they do about the actual future of the occupied territories, had Hitler won the war.

We are thus faced with the seemingly coarse conclusion that, from a source-critical perspective, the table talks cannot be used on its own to prove facts about Hitler's thoughts and life. What is in there needs to be verified by other independent sources that can be shown to portray reality correctly. This may seem a frustrating set of conclusions for most historians, but that does not make them incorrect or unreasonable. These conclusions must be evaluated according to the evidence, and that evidence has been presented in this book. They cannot simply be brushed aside because of them being inconvenient, or even perhaps to some extent (and to some observers) even offensive or disagreeable. While it is understandable that the much higher degree of uncertainty concerning what Hitler actually thought and said in his FHQs during the war may be disturbing to historians, this feeling should not be allowed to trump the facts. I believe that enough evidence has been presented in this book for it to lead to a consequential change in how historians use *Tischgespräche* and *Monologe*, not to mention *Hitlers politisches Testament*, in their research.

However, and this is *very* important, the results presented in this book should absolutely not be interpreted as meaning that the table talks are not authentic. They really are, at least for the most part, memoranda of statements that Hitler made at some point or another in his wartime HQs. They were made by either Heim, Picker, Müller, or Bormann, although there are also some notes that have no name attached to them. There are a few exceptions to this rule, however, consisting of statements that Hitler either reasonably cannot have uttered or did not utter. These statements are sometimes the product of a misunderstanding of what Hitler said; at other times the author has confused other guests' statements with Hitler's, and on an unknown number of occasions there are interpolations in the text made by Bormann. A detailed study of all statements needs to be made in order for us to know how many such examples there in fact are.

The table talks thus differ from the notes dated February and April 1945 published as *The Testament of Adolf Hitler* in 1961. This text has been shown to be, with a great amount of certainty, a forgery. Several examples of this have been given in this book, but the best piece of evidence is the note dated 6 February in which Hitler is speaking of Frederick II. This entry has been shown to copy information contained in Schwerin von Krosigk's diary as referenced in Trevor-Roper's 1947 book *The Last Days of Hitler*. Several other examples of forgery have also been provided, including false dates attached to notes and statements that Hitler reasonably cannot have made. For example, when it is said that Hitler let the British get away at Dunkirk, and when the Jews are said to be only a religion and not a race. The authenticity of *The Testament* has been questioned before, but this book has confirmed that this source should not be used by serious historians.

BIBLIOGRAPHY AND SOURCES

Unprinted primary sources

Public archives

England

Christ Church Library, Oxford University, Oxford.
Hugh Trevor-Roper Papers.

Germany

Der Bundesbeauftragte für die Unterlagen des Staatssicherheitsdienstes der ehemaligen Deutschen Demokratischen Republik; Ministerium für Staatssicherheit, Berlin.
AIM 2717/75, Band II.

Bundesarchiv in Berlin-Lichterfelde.
BD6/PK.
NS 6.
NS6–133.
R6–34a.

Bundesarchiv in Koblenz.
N 263.
N 1128
N 1166.
N 1340.

Bundeministerium der Justiz.

Diözesanarchiv Berlin.
Nachlaß Theodor Schmitz.

Institut für Zeitgeschichte (IfZ), Munich.
ED 416.
ID 34.
ID Go 02.10.
ID 101.
ID 103.
ID 103.
ID 200.
ID 507.

Staatsarchiv München.
SpkA K 659.
SpkA K 1207.

Italy

Museo Casa Rodolfo Siviero, Florence.
Personal Papers of Rodolfo Siviero.

The United States

Franklin D. Roosevelt Presidential Library, New York.
John Toland Papers.

National Gallery of Arts; Gallery Archives, Washington, D.C.
RG 28; MFAA-D Frederick Hartt Papers.

University of Arizona Library, Special Collections, Tuscon.
Papers of Karen Kuykendall.

Private archives

Private Papers of Richard Carrier, United States.
Papers of François Genoud; in the hands of Frau Cordula Schacht, Bernau am Chiemsee Germany.
Papers of François Genoud; in the hands of Pierre Péan, France.
Papers of Werner Jochmann; in the hands of Professor Ursula Büttner, Hamburg, Germany.

Printed primary sources

Works originally written and/or published before 1945

Eckart, Dietrich, *Der Bolschewismus von Moses bis Lenin. Zwiegespräch zwischen Adolf Hitler und mir* (München: Franz Eher Verlag, 1924).
Goebbels, Joseph, *Das eherne Hertz* (Munich: Zentralverlag der NSDAP, 1943).
Hitler, Adolf, *Die Südtiroler Frage und das Deutsche Bündnisproblem* (München: Franz Eher Verlag, 1926).
———, *Hitlers zweites Buch. Ein Dokument aus dem Jahr 1928. Eingeleitet und kommentiert von Gerhard L. Weinberg. Mit einem Geleitwort von Hans Rothfels* (Stuttgart: Deutsche Verlags-Anstalt, 1961).
Hitler, Mein Kampf. Eine kritische Edition, Band I. Herausgegeben von Christian Hartmann, Thomas Vordermayer, Othmar Plöckinger, Roman Töppel (München: Institut für Zeitgeschichte, 2016).

Hitler, Mein Kampf. Eine kritische Edition, Band II. Herausgegeben von Christian Hartmann, Thomas Vordermayer, Othmar Plöckinger, Roman Töppel (München: Institut für Zeitgeschichte, 2016).

Source volumes

Akten der Partei-Kanzlei der NSDAP. Rekonstruktion eines verlorengegangenen Bestandes, Band I. Hrsg. vom Institut für Zeitgeschichte. Bearb. von Helmut Heiber unter Mitw. von Hildegard von Kotze, Gerhard Weiher, Ingo Arndt und Carla Mojto [u.a.] (Oldenburg: K.G. Saur, 1983).

Akten zur Deutschen Auswärtigen Politik 1918–1945. Aus dem Archiv des Auswärtigen Amts. Serie E 1941–1945. Band I. 12. Dezember 1941 bis 28. Februar 1942 (Göttingen, 1969).

Akten zur Deutschen Auswärtigen Politik, Serie D: 1937–1941. Band XII. 2. Die Kriegsjahre. Fünfter Band. Zweiter Halbband. 6. April bis 22. Juni 1941 (Göttingen: Vandenhoeck & Ruprecht, 1969).

Akten zur Deutschen Auswärtigen Politik, Serie D: 1937–1941. Band XIII. 2. Die Kriegsjahre. Sechster Band. Zweiter Halbband. 15. September bis 11. Dezember 1941 (Göttingen: Vandenhoeck and Ruprecht, 1970).

Besymenski, Lew, *Die letzten Notizen von Martin Bormann. Ein Dokument und seine Verfasser* (Stuttgart: Deutsche Verlags-Anstalt, 1974).

Der Hitler-Prozess 1924. Wortlaut der Hauptverhandlung vor dem Volksgericht München I. Teil 4: 19. – 25. Verhandlungstag. Herausgegeben und kommentiert von Lother Gruchmann und Reinhard Weber unter Mitarbeit von Otto Gritschneder (München: K. G. Saur, 1999).

Fleischmann, Peter, *Hitler als Häftling in Landsberg am Lech 1923/24. Der Gefangenen-Personalakt Hitler nebst weiteren Quellen aus der Schutzhaft-, Untersuchungshaft-, und Festungshaftanstalt* (Neustadt: Verlag PH. C. W. Schmidt, 2015).

Generaloberst Halder. Kriegstagebuch. Band I. Vom Polenfeldzug bis zum Ende der Westoffensive (14. 8. 1939–30. 6. 1940). Bearbeitet von Hans-Adolf Jacobsen in Verbindung mit Alfred Philippi (Stuttgart: W. Kohlhammer Verlag, 1962).

Heeresadjutant bei Hitler 1938–1943. Aufzeichnungen des Major Engels. Herausgegeben und kommentiert von Hildegard von Kontze (Stuttgart: Deutsche Verlags-Anstalt, 1974).

Heiber, Helmut (ed.), *Goebbels Reden 1939–1945*, Band I & II (München: Wilhelm Heyne Verlag, 1972).

Hitler. Reden, Schriften, Anordnungen. Februar 1925 bis Januar 1933 [14 volumes with different editors] (München: K.G. Saur, 1992–2003).

"Hitlers 'grundlegende' Rede über den Antisemitismus" in *Viertelsjahrshäfte für Zeitgeschichte*, 16. Jahrgang 1968, 4. Heft, Oktober, pp. 400–420.

Hubatsch, Walther (ed.), *Hitlers Weisungen für die Kriegsführung 1939–1945. Dokumente des Oberkommando des Wehrmacht* (München: Deutscher Taschenbuch Verlag, 1965).

Jäckel, Eberhard and Axel Kuhn (eds.), *Hitler. Sämtliche Aufzeichnungen 1905–1924* (Stuttgart: Deutsch Verlags-Anstalt, 1980).

Maser, Werner, *Hitlers Briefe und Notizen. Sein Weltbild in handschriftlichen Dokumenten* (Düsseldorf: Econ Verlag, 1973).

Max, Domarus (ed.), *Hitler. Reden und Proklamationen 1932–1945. Kommentiert von einem deutschen Zeitgenossen. Band 1–4* (München Süddeutscher Verlag, 1965).

Œuvres de Frédéric le Grand, Vol. 19.

Politisches Korrespondenz Friedrichs des Großen, Vol. 14.

Weinberg, Gerhard, *Guide to Captured German Documents*, Research Memorandum No. 2, Vol. 1, December 1952 (Human Resources Research Institute, Maxwell Air Force Base, Alabama).

Whitney, M'Lisa, *M 1946. Records Concerning the Central Collection Points ("Ardelia Hall Collection"): Munich Central Collecting Point, 1945–1951* (Washington, DC: National Archives and Records Administration, 2009).

Wissenschaftsfreiheit und ihre rechtlichen Schranken. Ein Colloquium. Herausgegeben vom Institut für Zeitgeschichte (München: R. Oldenbourg Verlag, 1978).

Diaries, notes, letters et cetera

Davenport-Hines, Richard (ed.), *Letters from Oxford: Hugh Trevor-Roper to Bernard Berenson* (London: Weidenfeld & Nicolson, 2006).

Gilbert, Gustave M., *Nürnberger Tagebuch. Gespräche der Angeklagten mit dem Gerichtspsychologen* (Frankfurt am Main: Fischer Taschenbuch Verlag, (15th ed.), 2010 (first published in 1962).

Goebbels, Joseph, *Vom Kaiserhof zur Reichskanzlei. Eine historische Darstellung in Tagebuchblättern (vom 1. Januar 1932 bis zum 1. Mai 1933)* (Munich: Zentralverlag der NSDAP, 1935).

———, *Joseph Goebbels, Tagebücher 1945: Die Letzten Aufzeichnungen* (Hamburg: Hoffman and Campe Verlag, 1977).

———, *The Goebbels Diaries. Edited and Introduced by Hugh Trevor-Roper* (London: Book Club Associates, 1978).

———, *Die Tagebücher von Joseph Goebbels 1924–1945. Im Auftrag des Instituts für Zeitgeschichte und mit Unterstützung des Staatlichen Archivdienstes Rußlands. Herausgegeben von Elke Frölich. Band 1–4 & 1–15* (München: K.G. Saur, 1987–1995).

Henrik, Eberle (ed.), *Briefe an Hitler. Ein Volk schreibt seinem Führer. Unbekannte Dokumente aus Moskauer Archiven – zum ersten Mal veröffentlicht* (Bergisch Gladbach: Gustav Lübbe Verlag, 2007).

Koeppen, Werner, *Herbst 1941 im "Führerhauptquartier". Berichte Werner Koeppens an seinen Minister Alfred Rosenberg. Herausgegeben und kommentiert von Martin Vogt* (Koblenz: Materialen aus dem Bundesarchiv Heft 10, 2002).

Matthäus, Jürgen and Frank Bajohr (Hg.), *Alfred Rosenberg. Die Tagebücher von 1934 bis 1944* (Munich: S. Fischer Verlag, 2015).

Piotrowski, Stanislaw, *Hans Franks Tagebuch* (Warszawa: Polnisher Verlag der Wissenschaften, 1963).

Rudolf Heß. Briefe 1908–1933. Herausgegeben von Wolf Rüdiger Heß. Mit einer Einführung und Kommentaren von Dirk Bavendamm (München: Georg Müller Verlag, 1987).

The Bormann Letters: The Private Correspondence between Martin Bormann and his Wife from January 1943 to April 1945. Edited with an Introduction and Notes by H. R. Trevor-Roper (London: Weidenfeld and Nicholson, 1954).

Newspaper articles

von Barmettler, Stefan, "Kniefall vor dem obersten Lügner" in *Rheinischer Merkur*, 24 July, 1992.

Brown, Mick, "You Couldn't Make It Up" in *The Telegraph*, 28 July 2007.

"Edilio Rusconi vendette lettere di Bormann" in *Le Idee*, 6 June 1997.

"Hitler-Dokumente. Frei erfunden" in *Der Spiegel*, 3 July 1972.

"Hitler-Dokumente: Vom Wege ab" in *Der Spiegel* 3/1966, 10 January 1966.

"Hitler-Erbe: Zwanzig Millionen" in *Der Spiegel* 28/1952.

"Hitler-Film: Wie ihn keiner sah" in *Der Spiegel* 1/1953.

"Hitler's Table-talk" in *The Times* [London, England], 23 March 1961.

"Hitler-Testament: Lateinisches Gift" in *Der Spiegel* 3/1962.

"Italiener in größte Kunstschieberei des Jahrhunderts verwickelt. Hitlers 'Geheimmagazin in die Schweiz verkauft. Erste Spuren der aus Italien Verschwundenen 600 Kostbarkeiten" in *Kölner Stadt-Anzeiger*, 22 June 1961.

Janßen, Karl-Heinz, "Geschichte aus der Dunkelkammer" in *Sonderdruck* from *Die Zeit* 38–41/1979 (Hamburg, 1979).

"La publication en France de Propos familiers de Hitler donne naissance à un procès de propriété littéraire au cours duquel risqué d'être évoquée la disparition de Martin Bormann" in *Le Monde*, 2 July 1952.

"Lt.-Col. R. H. Stevens" in *The Times* [London, England], 14 February 1967.

Malanowski, Wolfgang, "Zitat, Zitat, Zitat und nichts weiter" in *Der Spiegel* 37/1985.

"Millionen-Streit um Hitlers Tischgespräche" in *Abendzeitung*, 3 July 1952.

Posner, Gerald, "Interpol's Nazi Affiliations Continued After War" in *The New York Times*, 6 March 1990.

"Prozeß um Hitlers 'Tischgespräche'" in *Westfälisches Volksblatt*, 13 August 1952.

"Reich's Hoard of Gold, Cash Is 'Legitimate Prize of War'" in *The Stars and Stripes* (Paris Edition), 9 April 1945.

Sereny, Gitta, "The Truth Is, I Loved Hitler" in *The Observer*, 28 April 1996.

"Sitzen die Bilderdiebe im eigenen Land? Italiener soll Gemälde aus Hitlers Bozener Geheimmagazin verschachert haben" in *Süddeutsche Zeitung*, Nr. 149, 23 June 1961.

Stehle, Hans Jakob, "Martin Bormann in west-östlichen Zweilicht" in *Die Zeit* 24/1997, 6 June 1997.

"Streit um Hitlers Tischgespräche" in *Fränkische Nachrichten*, 10 April 1953.

"Streit um 'Tischgespräche' beendet" in *Deutsche Zeitung*, 23 September 1961.

"Teure Tischgespräche" in *Die Welt*, 2 July 1952.

"The Woman from Hitler' Bunker" in *Evening News*, 30 March 1979.

Trevor-Roper, Hugh, "Paula Hitler fordert ihr Erbe. Großer Streit um den persönlichen Nachlaß des braunen Diktators" in *Westfalen-Post*, 18 October 1952.

"Wem gehören Hitlers Tischgespräche?" in *Neustädter Tageblatt*, 3 August 1952.

Printed secondary sources

Conversazioni segreti. Ordinate e annotate da Martin Bormann durante il periode piú dramatico della Seconda Guerra Mondiale (5 luglio 1941–30 novembre 1944).

Hitlers politisches Testament. Die Bormann Diktate vom Februar und April 1945. Mit einem Essay von Hugh R. Trevor-Roper und einem Nachwort von André François-Poncet (Hamburg: Albrecht Knaus Verlag, 1981).

Hitler's Table Talk 1941–1944. With an Introductory Essay on The Mind of Adolf Hitler by H. R. Trevor-Roper (London: Weidenfeld and Nicolson, 1953).

Hitler's Secret Conversations 1941–1944. With an Introductory Essay on The Mind of Adolf Hitler by H. R. Trevor – Roper (New York: Farrar, Straus and Young, 1953).

Hitler's Table Talk 1941–1944. His Private Conversations. Introduced & With A New Preface by H. R. Trevor-Roper (London: Weidenfeld and Nicolson, 1973).

Hitler's Table Talk, 1941–1944. New Foreword by Gerhard L. Weinberg (Enigma Books, 2007).

Hitlers Tischgespräche im Führerhauptquartier 1941–1942. Im Auftrage des Deutschen Instituts für Zeitgeschichte der nationalsozialistischen Zeit geordnet, eingeleitet und veröffentlicht von Gerhard Ritter, Professor der Geschichte a. d. Universität Freiburg (Bonn: Athenäum-Verlag, 1951).

Hitlers Tischgespräche im Führerhauptquartier 1941–1942. Neu herausgegeben von Percy Ernst Schramm in Zusammenarbeit mit Andreas Hillgruber und Martin Vogt (Stuttgart: Seewald Verlag, 1963).

Le testament politique de Hitler. Notes receuillies par Martin Bormann. Commentaires de André François-Poncet; version française et présentation de François Genoud (Paris: Fayard, 1959).

Libres propos sur la Guerre et la Paix. Recueillis sur l'ordre de Martin Bormann. Préface de Robert d'Harcourt de l'Academie française. Version française de François Genoud, Vol. I (Paris: Flammarion, 1952).

Libres propos sur la Guerre et la Paix. Recueillis sur l'ordre de Martin Bormann. Préface de Robert d'Harcourt de l'Academie française. Version française de François Genoud, Vol. II (Paris: Flammarion, 1954).

Monologe im Führerhauptquartier 1941–1944. Die Aufzeichnungen Heinrich Heims herausgegeben von Werner Jochmann (Hamburg: Albrecht Knaus Verlag, 1980).

The Testament of Adolf Hitler: The Hitler – Bormann Documents, February – April 1945. Edited by François Genoud; with an Introduction by Hugh R. Trevor-Roper; Translated from the German by R. H. Stevens (London: Cassell, 1961).

The Testament of Adolf Hitler: The Hitler-Bormann Document, February – April 1945. With an Introduction by L. Craig Fraser (Noontide Press, 1978).

Zoller, Albert, *Hitler privat. Erlebnisbericht seiner Geheimsekretärin* (Düsseldorf: Droste Verlag, 1949).

Memoirs

von Below, Nicolaus, *Als Hitlers Adjutant 1937–45* (Mainz: v. Hase and Koehler Verlag, 1980).

Dietrich, Otto, *12 Jahre mit Hitler* (München: Isar Verlag, 1955).

Frank, Hans, *Im Angesicht des Galgens. Deutung Hitlers und seiner Zeit auf Grund eigener Erlebnisse und Erkenntnisse* (München: Friedrich Alfred Beck Verlag, 1953).

Kubizek, August, *Adolf Hitler. Mein Jugendfreund* (Graz und Göttingen: Leopold Stocker Verlag, 1953).

Misch, Rochus, *Der Letzte Zeuge. "Ich war Hitlers Telefonist, Kurier und Leibwächter". Mit einem Vorwort von Ralph Giordano* (München: Pendo Verlag, 2008).

Price, Ward, *I Know These Dictators* (London: Harrap, 1937).

Reitsch, Hanna, *Höhen und Tiefen 1945 bis zur Gegenwart* (München: Herbig Verlag, 1978).

Rose, Olaf (ed.), *Julius Schaub – In Hitlers Schatten. Erinnerungen und Aufzeichnungen des persönlichen Adjutanten und Vertrauten Julius Schaub 1925–1945* (Stegen and Ammersee: Druffel and Vowinckel Verlag, 2005).

Schroeder, Christa, *Er war mein Chef. Aus dem Nachlaß der Sekretärin von Adolf Hitler. Herausgegeben von Anton Joachimsthaler* (München: Herbig, 1985).

Siviero, Rudolfo, *Sulle opere d'arte italiane recuperate in Germania* (Rome: Accademia nazionale dei Lincei, 1948).

———, *La difesa delle opere d'arte. Testimonianza su Bruno Becchi* (Florence: Accademia delle Arti di Deisegno, 1976).

Smyth, Craig Hugh, *Repatriations of Art from the Collecting Point in Munich after World War II* (The Hague: Maarssen, 1988).

Speer, Albert, *Erinnerungen* (Berlin: Propyläen Verlag, 1969).

———, *Spandauer Tagebücher* (Berlin: Propyläen, 1975).

Straßer, Otto, *Hitler et moi* (Paris: Éditions Bernard Grasset, 1940).

Warlimont, Walter, *Im Führerhauptquartier der deutschen Wehrmacht 1939–1945. Grundlagen, Formen, Gestalten* (Frankfurt am Main: Bernard and Graefe für Wehrwesen, 1962).

Weidenfeld, George, *Remembering Good Friends: An Autobiography* (London: HarperCollins, 1995).

Literature

Books (monographs & chapters in edited volumes)

Backes, Uwe, *Politischer Extremismus in demokratischen Verfassungsstaaten* (Wiesbaden: Springer Fachmedien, 1989).

Bavendamm, Dirk, *Der junge Hitler. Korrekturen einer Biographie 1889–1914* (Graz: Ares Verlag, 2009).

Berg, Nicolas, *Der Holocaust und die westdeutschen Historiker. Erforschung und Erinnerung* (Göttingen: Wallstein Verlag, 2003).

Bergen, Doris L., *Twisted Cross: The German Christian Movement in the Third Reich* (Chapel Hill: The University of North Carolina Press, 1996).

Bird, K. Eugene, *Heß. Der "Stellvertreter des Führers" Englandflug und britische Gefangenschaft Nürnberg und Spandau* (Herrsching: Manfred Pawlak Verlagsgesellschaft, 1974).

Brechtken, Magnus, " 'Ein Kriminalroman könnte nicht spannender erfunden werden' – Albert Speer und die Historiker" in M. Brechtken (ed.), *Life Writing and Political Memoir – Lebenszeugnisse und Politische Memoiren* (Göttingen: V&R Unipress, 2012), pp. 35–78.

———, *Albert Speer. Eine deutsche Karriere* (Munich: Siedler, 2017).

Bullock, A., *Hitler: A Study in Tyranny* (London: Odhams Press, 1952).

———, *Hitler: A Study in Tyranny* (Harmondsworth: Penguin Books, (Completely revised edition), 1962).

Calic, Edouard, *Ohne Maske. Hitler – Breiting Geheimgespräche 1931* (Frankfurt am Main: Societäts-Verlag, 1968).

Carlyle, Thomas, *History of Frederick II of Prussia, Vol. XVIII. Frederick the Great – Seven-Years War Rises to A Height – 1757–1759.*

———, *History of Frederick II of Prussia, Vol. XX. Frederick the Great – Friedrich is not to be Overwhelmed: The Seven-Years War Gradually Ends – 25 April, 1760–15th February 1763.*

Carr, William, *Hitler: A Study in Personality and Politics* (London: Edward Arnold, 1978).

Chapoutot, Johann, *La loi du sang. Penser et agir en nazi* (Paris: Gallimard, 2014).

———, *La révolution culturelle nazie* (Paris: Gallimard, 2016).

———, *Le nazisme et l'Antiquité* (Paris: Quadrige, 2016).

Chaussy, Ulrich and Christoph Püschner, *Nachbar Hitler. Führerkult und Heimatzerstörung am Obersalzberg* (8., aktualisierte Auflage) (Berlin: Ch. Links Verlag, 2017).

Colletti, Enzo and Mariani Riccardo, *The Water Colours of Hitler: Recovered Art Works. Homage to Rudolfo Siviero* (Alinari: Florence, 1984).

Conley Nelson, David, *Moroni and the Swastika: Mormons in Nazi Germany* (Norman: University of Oklahoma Press, 2015).

Cornelißen, Christoph, *Gerhard Ritter: Geschichtswissenschaft und Politik im 20. Jahrhundert* (Düsseldorf: Droste Verlag, 2001).

Delblanco, Werner, " 'Wer wie ich den Führer persönlich kennt, kann das Glück ermessen. . . ' Ein biographischer Abriss und ein Skandalon" in Bernd Kasten, Matthias Manke and Johann Peter Wurm (eds.), *Leder ist Brot. Beiträge zur norddeutschen Landes- und Archivgeschichte. Festschrift für Andreas Röpcke* (Schwerin: Thomas Helms Verlag, 2011).

Dülffer, Jost, "Kolonialismus ohne Kolonien. Deutsche Kolonialplaene 1938" in Franz Knipping and Klaus-Jürgen Müller (eds.), *Machtbewußtsein in Deutschland am Vorabend des Zweiten Weltkrieges* (Paderborn: Ferdinand Schöningh,1984).

Eberle, Henrik and Matthias Uhl (eds.), *Das Buch Hitler. Geheimdossier des NKWD für Josef W. Stalin, zusammengestellt aufgrund der Verhörprotokolle des Persönlichen Adjutanten Hitlers, Otto Günsche, und des Kammerdieners Heinz Linge, Moskau 1948/49* (Bergisch Gladbach: Gustav Lübbe Verlag, 2005).

Eckert, Astrid M., *The Struggle for the Files: The Western Allies and the Return of the German Archives after the Second World War* (Cambridge: Cambridge University Press, 2012).

Ericksen, Robert P., *Theologians under Hitler: Gerhard Kittel, Paul Althaus, and Emanuel Hirsch* (New Haven: Yale University Press, 1985).

Evans, Richard J., *Lying About Hitler: History, Holocaust, and the David Irving Trial* (New York: Basic Books, 2001).

————, *The Coming of the Third Reich: How the Nazis Destroyed Democracy and Seized Power in Germany* (London: Penguin Books, 2004).

————, *The Third Reich in Power* (London: Penguin Books, 2006).

————, *The Third Reich at War 1939–1945* (London: Penguin Books, 2008).

Faulkner Rossi, Lauren, *Wehrmacht Priests: Catholicism and the Nazi War of Annihalation* (Cambridge, MA: Harvard University Press, 2015).

Fest, Joachim, *Hitler. Eine Biographie* (Berlin: Propyläen, 1973).

Frieser, Karl-Heinz, *Bliztkrieg-Legende. Der Westfeldzug 1940* (Munich: R. Oldenburg Verlag, 1995).

Gieseke, Jens, *Die Stasi 1945–1990* (München: Pantheon, 2011).

Glover, Jonathan, *Humanity: A Moral History of the Twentieth Century* (London: Jonathan Cape, 1999).

Goeschel, Christian, *Mussolini and Hitler: The Forging of the Fascist Alliance* (New Haven: Yale University Press, 2018).

Grande, Dieter and Bernd Schäfer, *Kirche im Visier. SED Staatssicherheit und katolische Kirche in der DDR* (Leipzig: Benno Verlag, 1998).

Guttenplan, D. D., *The Holocaust on Trial: History, Justice, and the David Irving Libel Case* (London: Granta Books, 2001).

Gutteridge, Richard, *Open Thy Mouth for the Dumb! The German Evangelical Church and the Jews, 1879–1950* (Oxford: Basil Blackwell, 1976).

Haffner, Sebastian, *Anmerkungen zu Hitler* (Munich: Kindler Verlag, 1978).

Hamann, Brigitte, *Hitlers Wien. Lehrjahre eines Diktators* (München: Piper Verlag, 1996).

Hänel, Wolfgang, *Hermann Rauschnings "Gespräche mit Hitler": Eine Geschichtsfälschung* (Ingolstadt: Veröffentlichung der Zeitgeschichtlichen Forschungsstelle, 7. Band, 1984).

Harris, Robert, *Selling Hitler* (London: Arrow Books, 2009 (1st edition by Faber & Faber Ltd, 1986)).

Hastings, Derek, *Catholicism & the Roots of Nazism: Religious Identity & National Socialism* (Oxford: Oxford University Press, 2010).

Herbst, Ludolf, *Hitlers Charisma. Die eines deutschen Messias* (Frankfurt am Main: S. Fischer Verlag, 2010).

Heschel, Susannah, *The Aryan Jesus: Christian Theologians and the Bible in Nazi Germany* (Princeton: Princeton University Press, 2008).

Hett, Benjamin Carter, *Burning the Reichstag: An Investigation Into the Third Reich's Enduring Mystery* (Oxford: Oxford University Press, 2014).

Höhne, Heinz, *Der Orden unter dem Totenkopf. Die Geschichte der SS* (Augsburg: Weltbild Verlag, 1992).

Horne, Alistair, *To Lose a Battle: France 1940* (Basingstoke: Papermac, (1969) 1990).

Irving, David, *Hitler und seine Feldherren* (Frankfurt am Main: Verlag Ullstein, 1975).

———— , *Hitler's War* (London: Hodder & Stoughton, 1977).

Jäckel, Eberhard, *Hitler in History* (Hanover, NH: University Press of New England, 1984).

Jetzinger, Franz, *Hitlers Jugend. Phantasien, Lügen – und die Wahrheit* (Wien: Europa Verlag, 1956).

Joachimsthaler, Anton, *Hitlers Weg begann in München 1913–1923* (München: Herbig, 2000).

Jones, Michael, *After Hitler: The Last Days of the Second World War in Europe* (London: John Murray, 2015).

Kandel, Eric R., *In Search of Memory: The Emergent New Science of the Mind* (New York: W. W. Norton & Company, 2007).

Kellerhof, Sven Felix, *'Mein Kampf'. Die Karriere eines deutschen Buches* (Stuttgart: Klett-Cotta, 2015).

———, *The Reichstag Fire: The Case Against the Nazi Conspiracy* (Stroud: The History Press, 2016).

———, *Die NSDAP. Eine Partei und ihre Mitglieder* (Stuttgart: Klett-Cotta, 2017).

Kelley, Shawn, *Racializing Jesus: Race, Ideology and the Formation of Modern Biblical Scholarship* (London: Routledge, 2002).

Kershaw, Ian, *Hitler 1889–1936: Hubris* (London: Allen Lane, 1998).

———, *Hitler 1936–45: Nemesis* (London: Allen Lane, 2000).

Klee, Ernst, *'Die SA Jesu Christi'. Die Kirche im Banne Hitlers* (Frankfurt am Main: Fischer Taschenbuch Verlag, 1989).

Lambert, Marc, *Un peintre nommé Hitler* (Paris: Éditions France-Empire – ECS, 1986).

von Lang, Jochen, *Der Sekretär: Der Mann der Hitler beherrschte* (Unter Mitarbeit von Claus Sibyll) (Stuttgart: Deutsche Verlags-Anstalt, 1977).

Laske, Karl, *Ein Leben zwischen Hitler und Carlos: François Genoud* (Zürich: Limmat, 1996).

Linne, Karsten, *Deutschland jenseits des Äquators. Die NS-Kolonialplanungen für Afrika* (Berlin: Ch. Links Verlag, 2008).

Liulevicius, Vejas Gabriel, *The German Myth of the East: 1800 to the Present* (Oxford: Oxford University Press, 2009).

Longerich, Peter, *Hitlers Stellvertreter: Führung der Partei und Kontrolle des Staatsapparates durch den Stab Heß und die Partei-Kanzlei Bormann* (München: K. G. Saur Verlag, 1992).

Lukacs, John, *The Hitler of History* (New York: Vintage Books, 1997).

Maser, Werner, *Adolf Hitler: Legende, Mythos, Wirklichkeit* (München: Bechtle Verlag, (12th ed.), 1989).

McDonough, Frank, *The Hitler Years: Triumph 1933–1039* (London: Head of Zeus, 2019).

Miskolczy, Ambrus, *Hitler's Library* (Budapest: Central European University Press, 2003).

Missalla, Heinrich, *Für Gott, Führer und Vaterland. Die Verstrickung der katholischen Seelsorge in Hitlers Krieg* (Munich: Kösel, 1999).

Möller, Horst, "Das Institut für Zeitgeschichte und die Entwicklung der Zeitgeschichts-chreibung in Deutschland" in Horst Möller (ed.), *och Udo Wengst, 50 Jahre Institut für Zeitgeschichte. Eine Bilanz* (München: Institut für Zeitgeschichte, 1999).

Moritz, Stefan, *Grüß Gott und Heil Hitler: Katholische Kirche und Nationalsozialismus in Öster-reich* (Wien: Picus Verlag, 2002).

Péan, Pierre, *L'extrémiste: François Genoud de Hitler à Carlos* (Paris: Fayard, 1996).

Picker, Henry, *Johannes XXIII: Der Papst der christlichen Einheit und des 2. vaticanischen Konzils* (Kettweg: Blick und Bild, 1963).

Plöckinger, Othmar, *Geschichte eines Buches: Adolf Hitlers "Mein Kampf" 1922–1945. Eine Veröffentlichung des Institut für Zeitgeschichte. 2., aktualisierte Auflage* (München: Oldenburg Verlag, 2011).

von Preradovich, Nikolaus and Josef Stingl, *'Gott segne den Führer'. Die Kirchen im Dritten Reich. Eine Dokumentation von Bekenntnissen und Selbstzeugnissen* (Leoni am Starnberger See: Druffel-Verlag, 1985).

Price, Ward, *I Know These Dictators* (London: Harrap, 1937).

Pyta, Wolfram, *Hitler. Der Künstler als Politiker und Feldherr. Eine Herrschaftsanalyse* (München: Siedler, 2015).

Rankin, Nicholas, *Churchill's Wizards: The British Genius for Deception, 1919–1945* (London: Faber and Faber, 2005).

Rosenbaum, Ron, *Explaining Hitler: The Search for the Origins of His Evil* (London: Papermac, 1999).

Ryback, Timothy W., *Hitler' Private Library: The Books That Shaped His Life* (New York: Vintage Books, 2010).

Schacter, Daniel L., "Memory Distortion: History and Current Status" in Daniel L. Schacter (ed.), *Memory Distortion: How Minds, Brains, and Societies Reconstruct the Past* (Cambridge, MA: Harvard University Press, 1995).

Schieder, Theodor, *Hermann Rauschnings 'Gespräche mit Hitler' als Geschichtsquelle* (Opladen: Westdeutscher Verlag, 1972).

Schwarz, Birgit, *Geniewahn: Hitler und die Kunst* (Vienna: Böhlau Verlag, 2009).

Seebold, Gustav Hermann, *Die Hitler-Breiting-Geheimsepräche als historische Quelle* (Bochum: Master thesis, 1975).

Sereny, Gitta, *Albert Speer: His Battle with the Truth* (New York: Alfred A. Knopf, 1995).

Simms, Brian, *Hitler: Only the World was Enough* (London: Allen Lane, 2019).

Snyder, Timothy, *Black Earth: The Holocaust as History and Warning* (London: The Bodley Head, 2015).

Spicer, Kevin P., *Hitler's Priests: Catholic Clergy and National Socialism* (DeKalb: Northern Illinois University Press, 2008).

Steigmann-Gall, Richard, *The Holy Reich: Nazi Conceptions of Christianity, 1919–1945* (Cambridge: Cambridge University Press, 2003).

Stratigakos, Despina, *Hitler at Home* (New Haven: Yale University Press, 2015).

Taylor, Cory, *How Hitler Was Made: Germany and the Rise of the Perfect Nazi* (Amherst: Prometheus Books, 2018).

Toland, John, *Adolf Hitler* (New York: Doubleday & Company, 1976).

———, *Adolf Hitler*, Vols. I & II (New York: Doubleday & Company, 1976).

Trevor-Roper, H. R., *The Last Days of Hitler* (London: Macmillan & Co., 1947).

Tyrell, Albrecht, *Vom 'Trommler' zum 'Führer'. Der Wandel von Hitlers Selbstverständnis zwischen 1919 und 1924 und die Entwicklung der NSDAP* (München: Wilhelm Fink Verlag, 1975).

Ullrich, Volker, *Adolf Hitler. Biographie. Band I: Die Jahre des Aufstiegs* (Frankfurt am Main: S. Fischer, 2013).

———, *Adolf Hitler. Biographie. Band II: Die Jahre des Untergangs* (Frankfurt am Main: S. Fischer, 2018).

Voegelin, Eric, "Descent into the Ecclesiastical Abyss: The Catholic Church" in *The Collected Works of Eric Voegelin, Vol. 31, Hitler and the Germans*. Translated, Edited, and with an Introduction by Detlev Clemens and Brendan Purcell (Columbia: Universtiy of Missouri Press, 1999), pp. 110–154.

Weber, Thomas, *Hitler's First War* (Oxford: Oxford University Press, 2010).

———, *Wie Adolf Hitler zum Nazi wurde. Vom unpolitischen Soldaten zum Autor von 'Mein Kampf'* (Berlin: Propyläen, 2016).

———, *Becoming Hitler: The Making of a Nazi* (Oxford: Oxford University Press, 2018).

Weikart, Richard, *Hitler's Religion: The Twisted Beliefs that Drove the Third Reich* (Washington, DC: Regnery History, 2016).

Winkler, Willi, *Der Schattenmann. Von Goebbels zu Carlos: Das gewissenlose Leben des François Genoud* (Berlin: Rowohlt, 2011).

Wulf, Joseph, *Martin Bormann – Hitlers Schatten* (Gütersloh: Sigbert Mohn Verlag, 1962).

Zitelmann, Rainer, *Hitler: Selbstverständnis eines Revolutionärs* (Hamburg: Berg, 1987).
————, *Adolf Hitler. Eine politische Biographie* (Göttingen: Muster-Schmidt Verlag, 1998).

Journal articles

Carrier, Richard, "Hitler's Table Talk: Troubling Finds" in *German Studies Review*, Vol. 26, No. 3 (October 2003), pp. 561–576.

Eaton, Vincent L. and Frederick R. Goff, "Other Rare Acquisitions" in *Library of Congress Quarterly Journal of Current Acquisitions*, Vol. 5, No. 3 (May 1948).

Franz-Willing, Georg, "Hitlers Tischgespräche" in *Klüter Blätter. Monatshefte für Kultur und Zeitgeschichte*, Jahrgang 32, Dezember 1981, Heft 12.

Goeschel, Christian, "Suicide at the End of the Third Reich" in *Journal of Contemporary History*, Vol. 41, No. 1 (January 2006), pp. 153–173.

Griffin, Miriam, "Philosophy, Cato, and Roman Suicide: II" in *Greece & Rome*, Vol. 33, No. 2, (October 1986), pp. 192–202.

Harrison, David and John Merritt, "Agent of Hitler Cashes in on Press War" in *The Observer*, Vol. 12 (July 1992).

von Hehl, Ulrich, "Die Kontroverse um die Reichstagsbrand" in *Vierteljahr für Zeitgeschichte* Vol. 36 (1988), Heft 2, pp. 259–280.

Hübner, Stefan, "Hitler und Ostasien. 1904 bis 1933. Die Entwicklung von Hitlers Japan- und Chinabild vom Russisch-Japanischen Krieg bis zur 'Machtergreifung'" in *OAG Notizen*, No. 9 (2009).

Krausnick, Hemlut, "Legenden um Hitlers Aussenpolitik" in *Vierteljahrshefte für Zeitgeschichte*, 2. Jahrgang 1954, 3. Heft/Juli, pp. 217–239.

"Manuscripts" in *Library of Congress Quarterly Journal of Current Acquisitions*, Vol. 9, No. 3 (May 1952).

Nilsson, Mikael, "Hugh Trevor-Roper and the English Editions of *Hitler's Table Talk* and *Testament*" in *Journal of Contemporary History*, Vol. 51, No. 4 (2016), pp. 788–812.

————, "Constructing a Pseudo-Hitler? The Question of the Authenticity of *Hitlers politisches Testament*" in *European Review of History – Revue Européenne d'historie*, Vol. 26, No. 5, pp. 871–891.

————, "Hitler Redivivus: '*Hitlers Tischgespräche* und *Monologe im Führerhauptquartier*' – eine kritische Untersuchung" in *Vierteljahrshefte für Zeitgeschichte*, No. 67 (January 2019), pp. 105–145.

Phelps, Reginald H., "Die Hitler-Bibliothek" in *Deutsche Rundschau*, (September 1954), pp. 923–931.

Rovati, Frederica, "Italia 1945: il recupero delle opere d'arte trafugate dai tedeschi" in *ACME – Annali della Facoltà di Lettere e Filosofia dell'Università degli Studi di Milano*, Vol. LVII, (Settembre – dicembre 2005); Fascicolo III.

Sisman, Adam, *Hugh Trevor-Roper: The Biography* (London: Weidenfeld and Nicolson).

Stuurman, Douwe, "The Nazi Collection: A Preliminary Note" in *Library of Congress Quarterly Journal of Current Acquisitions*, Vol. 6, No. 1 (November 1948).

Wallach, Jehuda L., "Adolf Hitlers Privatbibliothek" in *Zeitgeschichte*, No. 1–2 (1992).

Wareing, E. B., "Hitlers Tischgespräche im Führerhauptquartier 1941–2" in Henry Picker and Gerard Ritter (eds.), *International Affairs (Royal Institute of International Affairs 1944)*, Vol. 28, No. 2 (April 1952).

Wiskemann, Elizabeth, "Hitler's Table Talk 1941–1944" in *International Affairs (Royal Institute of International Affairs 1944)*, Vol. 29, No. 4 (October 1953), pp. 493–494.

Wittman, Robert K. and David Kinney, *The Devil's Diary: Alfred Rosenberg and the Stolen Secrets of the Third Reich* (New York: HarperCollins, 2016).

Online sources (documents, blogs & websites)

www.archives.gov

Blog post by Dr. Greg Bradsher on the National Archive website; https://text-message.blogs.archives.gov/2016/01/19/the-search-for-hitlers-political-testament-personal-will-and-marriage-certificate-part-iii/, accessed: 2019–10–29.

www.forum-der-wehrmacht.de

www.friedrich.uni-trier.de

www.fpp.co.uk

www.hdot.org

www.hermann-historica.de

www.ifz-muenchen.de

Iken, Katja, "Nazi-Starpilotin Hanna Reitsch: Für Hitler flog sie durch die Hölle" in *Die Zeit*-Online, 29 March 2012; www.spiegel.de/einestages/nazi-starpilotin-hanna-reitsch-a-947526.html, accessed: 2016–08–03.

www.monumentsmenfoundation.org

www.museocasasiviero.it

www.mythoselser.de

www.n-tv.de

www.nytimes.com

Online-Datenbank. De Gruyter.

Schwerin von Krosigk's diary, "The Beginning and the End", 15 April 1945, p. 16; www.ifz-muenchen.de/archiv/zsa/ZS_A_0020_04a.pdf, accessed: 2019–10–27.

www.telegraph.co.uk

The Times Digital Archive.

www.venlo-zwischenfall.de.

www.wartimepress.com

de.wikipedia.org

Wood, Alan (blog post), "A District Attorney in Georgia Wrote an Introduction in a Book Praising Hitler", 10 April 2015; http://gwmac.com/a-district-attorney-in-georgia-wrote-an-introduction-in-a-book-praising-hitler/, accessed: 2019–10–29.

Email correspondence

Tim Blanning.

Magnus Brechtken.

Richard Carrier (including correspondence between Carrier & Robert Miller made available to me by Carrier).

Patrick Kerwin.

Virginia Lewick.

Robert Miller.

Dr. Klaus-Dieter Mulley.

Matthias Röth.

Gerhard L. Weinberg.

Interviews & conversations

Magnus Brechtken.

Attilio Tori.

Gina Thomson.

APPENDIX

Dates, authors, and parallel notes in various table talk sources[1]

	Monologe	Tischgespräche	Koeppen's notes	Goebbels' diary
Date				
Wolfssch. 5.7.41	H			
5–6.7.41	H			
11–12.7.41	H			
21–22.7.41	H	H		
22–23.7.41	H	H		
24–25.7.41	x			
25.7.41 (mittags)	x			
25.7.41 (abends)	x			
26.7.41 (nachts)	x			
27.7.41	x			
27–28.7.41	x^2			
1–2.8.41	H	H		
2.8.41 (mittags)	H	H		
2.8.41 (abends)	H			
2.8.41 (abends)	H			
5.9.41			K	
6.9.41			K	
7.9.41			K	
8–9.8.41	H	H		
9.8.41		H	K	
9–10.8.41	H	H		
10.8.41 (mittags)	H			
10.8.41 (abends)	H	H		
10–11.8.41	H	H		
19–20.8.41	H	H		
14–15.9.41	H			

(*Continued*)

	Monologe	*Tischgespräche*	*Koeppen's notes*	*Goebbels' diary*
17–18.9.41	H		K	
19.9.41			K	
20.9.41			K	
21.9.41	H		K	
22.9.41			K	
22–23.9.41	H			
23.9.41	H		K	
25.9.41 (mittags)	H			
25.9.41 (abends)	H			
25–26.9.41	H			
27–28.9.41	H			
28.9.41	H			
1.10.41	H		K	
2.10.41			K	
4.10.41			K	
5.10.41			K	
6.10.41			K	
7.10.41			K	
8.10.41			K	
27–28.9 & 9.10.41				
9–10.10.41	H			
10.10.41	H			
25–26.9 & 9–10.10.41	H			
10–11.10.41	H			
13.10.41 (mittags)	H			
13.10.41 (abends)	H			
13.10.41 (nachts)	H			
14.10.41 (früh)	H			
14.10.41 (mittags)	H			
14–15.10.41	H			
15.10.41	H			
16.10.41	H			
17.10.41 (mittags)			K	
17.10.41 (abends)	H		K	
17–18.10.41	H		K	
18.10.41	H			
19.10.41	H		K	
21.1041	H		K	
22.10.41	B		K	
23.10.41			K	
21–22.10.41			K	
24.10.41	H			
25.10.41	H	H	K	
26.10.41	H		K	
26 & 27.10.41			K	
27.10.41	H			
28.10.41			K	

	Monologe	*Tischgespräche*	*Koeppen's notes*	*Goebbels' diary*
29.10.41	H			
30.10.41 (mittags)	H			
30.10.41 (abends)	x			
1.11.41	H			
1–2.11.41	H			
2.11.41 (mittags)	H			
2.11.41 (abends)	H			
2–3.11.41	H			
5.11.41 (mittags)	H			
5.11.41 (abends)	H		K	
6.11.41	H		K	
10–11.11.41			K	
11.11.41 (mittags)	H			
11.11.41 (abends)	H			
12.11.41 (mittags)	H	H		
12.11.41 (abends)	H			
16.11.41 (mittags)	H			
16.11.41 (abends)	H			
19.11.41	H			
20.11.41	B			
30.11.41	B			
1–2.12.41	H			
13.12.41	H			
14.12.41	H	H		
17.12.41	H			G
17–18.12.41	H			
18.12.41	H			G
23–24.12.41	H			G
28–29.12.41	H			
29.12.41	H			
30.12.41	H			
31.12–1.1.1942	H			
1.1.42 (mittags)	H			
1.1.42 (abends)	x			
1–2.1.42	x			
2–3.1.42	H			
3.1.42	H			
3–4.1.42	H			
4.1.42 (mittags)	H			
4.1.42 (abends)	x			
4–5.15.1.42	H			
5–6.1.42	H			
6.1.42 (mittags)	H			
6.1.42 (abends)	H			
6–7.1.42	H			
7.1.42	H			
8–9.1.42	H			
9–10.1.42	H★			

(Continued)

	Monologe	Tischgespräche	Koeppen's notes	Goebbels' diary
9.1.42 (abends)	H			
10.1.42	x			
12.1.42	H			
12–13.1.42	x			
13.1.42	H			
13–14.1.42	H			
15.1.42	H			
15–16.1.42	H			
16–17.1.42	H			
17–18.1.42	H★			
18.1.42 (abends)	H★			
18–19.1.42	H★	H		
19.1.42 (abends)	x★	x		
20.1.42 (mittags)	H★	H		
22.1.42 (mittags)	x★	x		
22.1.42 (abends)	x★	x		
22–23.1.42	x			
24.1.42 (abends)	x			
24.1.42 (abends)	x★	x		
24–25.1.42	H			
24–25.1.42	H			
25.1.42	H			
25–26.1.42	x			
25–26.1.42	H			
26.1.42	H			
27.1.42 (mittags)	H			
27.1.42 (abends)	H	H		
28.1.42	x			
28–29.1.42	x	x		
30.1.42	x	x		
31.1.42	x			
1.2.42	H			
2.2.42 (mittags)	x			
2.2.42 (abends)	H			
3.2.42	x			
3–4.2.42	x			
4.2.42 (abends)	x			
5.2.42 (mittags)	x	x		
5.2.42 (abends)	x			
6.2.42	x			
7.2.42	x			
8.2.42 (mittags)	x	x		
8.2.42 (abends)	x	x		
9.2.42 (mittags)	x			
9.2.42 (abends)	x			
10.2.42	x			
17.2.42 (mittags)	x			
17.2.42 (abends)	x	x		

	Monologe	*Tischgespräche*	*Koeppen's notes*	*Goebbels' diary*
18.2.42	x			
19.2.42	x			
19–20.2.42	x			
20–21.2.42	x	x		
21.2.42	x			
22.2.42 (abends)	x			
22.2.42 (abends)	x			
22–23.2.42	x			
24.2.42	x	x		
24–25.2.42	x	x		
26.2.42 (mittags)	x			
26.2.42 (abends)	x			
26–27.2.42	x	x		
27.2.42 (mittags)	x			
27.2.42 (abends)	x			
27–28.2.42	x			
28.2.42	x			
28.2–1.3.42	x			
1.3.42 (mittags)	x	x		
1.3.42 (abends)	x			
3.3.42	x	x		
7.3.42	x	x		
10–11.3.42	x	x		
11–12.3.42	x	x		
21.3.42	x	x		
22.3.42		P		
23.3.42		P		
23.3.42		P		
24.3.42		P		
25.3.42		P		
26.3.42		P		
27.3.42		P		
28.3.42		P		
29.3.42		P		
30.3.42 Wolfsburg		P		
31.3.42		P		
1.4.42		P		
2.4.42		P		
3.4.42		P		
4.4.42		P		
5.4.42		P		
6.4.42		P		
7.4.42		P		
8.4.42		P		
9.4.42		P		
10.4.42		P		
11.4.42		P		
12.4.42		P		

(Continued)

	Monologe	*Tischgespräche*	*Koeppen's notes*	*Goebbels' diary*
13.4.42		P		
17.4.42		P		
18.4.42		P		
19.4.42		P		
20.4.42		P		
22.4.42		P		
23.4.42		P		
24.4.42		P		
Berlin 25.4.42		P		
Berlin 26.4.42		P		
26.4.42 (abends)		P		G
München 27.4.42		P		G
Berghof 29.4.42		P		
Berghof 30.4.42		P		
Berghof 1.5.42		P		
3.5.42		P		
4.5.42		P		
5.5.42		P		
6.5.42		P		
7.5.42		P		
8.5.42		P		
9.5.42		P		
10.5.42		P		
11.5.42		P		
12.5.42		P		
13.5.42		P		
14.5.42		P		
15.5.42		P		
16.5.42		P		
17.5.42		P		
18.5.42		P		
19.5.42		P		
20.5.42		P		
21.5.42		P		
Berlin 22.5.42		P		
Berlin 27.5.42		P		
Wolfssch. 28.5.42		P		G
Berlin 29.5.42		P		
Berlin 30.5.42		P		
31.5.42		P		G
1.6.42		P		G
2.6.42		P		
3.6.42		P		
4.6.42		P		
4.6.42		P		
5.6.42		P		
7.6.42		P		
8.6.42		P		

	Monologe	*Tischgespräche*	*Koeppen's notes*	*Goebbels' diary*
Berlin 9.6.42		P		
München 10.6.42		P		
Berlin 22.6.42		P		
Berlin 23.6.42		P		
24.6.42		P		
25.6.42		P		
26.6.42		P		
27.6.42		P		
28.6.42		P		
29.6.42		P		
30.6.42		P		
1.7.42		P		
2.7.42		P		
3.7.42		P		
4.7.42		P		
5.7.42		P		
6.7.42		P		
7.7.42		P		
8.7.42		P		
9.7.42		P		
16.7.42 Werwolf		P		
17.7.42		P		
18.7.42		P		
19.7.42		P		
20.7.42		P		
21.7.42		P		
22.7.42		P		
24.7.42		P		
25.7.42		P		
26.7.42		P		
27.7. .42 (Tisch)		P		
27.7.42 (abends)		P		
28.7.42		P		
29.7.42		P		
31.7.42		P		
1.8.42		P		
3.8.42		P		
4.8.42 (mittags)	H			
4.8.42 (abends)	H			
5.8.42 (mittags)	H			
5.8.42 (abends)	H			
6.8.42 (mittags)	H			
6.8.42 (abends)	H			
7.8.42	H			
8.8.42	H			
9.8.42 (mittags)	H			
9.8.42 (abends)	H			

(*Continued*)

	Monologe	*Tischgespräche*	*Koeppen's notes*	*Goebbels' diary*
11.8.42	H			
12.8.42 (mittags)	H			
12.8.42	H			
16.8.42 (mittags)	H			
16.8.42 (abends)	H			
16.8.42	H			
20.8.42 (mittags)	H			
20.8.42 (abends)	x			
21.8.42 (mittags)	H			
21.8.42 (abends)	H			
22.8.42	H			
24.8.42	H			
25.8.42	H			
26.8.42	H			
26.8.42	H			
27.8.42	H			
28.8.42 (mittags)	H			
28.8.42 (abends)	H			
29.8.42	H			
30.8.42	H			
31.8.42	H			
1.9.42	H			
2.9.42 (mittags)	H			
2.9.42 (abends)	H			
3.9.42 (mittags)	H			
3.9.42 (abends)	H			
4.9.42	H			
5.9.42	H			
5.9.42	H			
6.9.42 (mittags)	H			
6.9.42 (abends)	H			
7.9.42	H			
13.6.43 (mittags)	H			
13.6.43 (abends)	H			
14.6.43	x			
19.6.43	x			
19.6.43	Mü			
25.6.43	Mü			
13.3.44	Mü			
23.3.44	Mü			
17.5.44	x			
19.5.44	Mü			
31.11.44	Mü			
	Mü			
	B			

Notes

1 The dates in the far-right column are based on the dates in *Monologe, Tischgespräche* and Werner Koeppen's notes. *Nota bene*: some entries are divided into several notes with the same date, but the division sometimes differs between the various editions; when that is the case, I have followed *Monologe*. These dates are supplemented by Goebbels' diaries when there is an overlap of themes (usually very small overlap). Note also that Koeppen's notes and Goebbels' diary entries are dated the day they were written down, i.e. *the day after* the conversations they record, but I have chosen to list them here under the date that the conversations took place so that they match up with the notes in *Monologe* and *Tischgespräche*. Letters representing the author of each note are included in the table – H: Heim. **P**: Picker. **Mü**: Müller **B**: Bormann. **K**: Koeppen. **G**. Goebbels. **x**: author not stated/unknown. One can suspect that Heim has made at least some these x-notes too, but it is noteworthy that they have no initials attached to them in *Monologe*; this seems to indicate that they were not signed. Picker, however, state that the ones that he has copied were made by Heim, but this may simply be an assumption on his part. Therefore, when Picker has used an unsigned note that appear also in *Monologe* I have chosen to mark also this one with an x.

2 This note is included as facsimile at the end of *Monologe*; Heim's signature does not appear on this page, but it is signed by Bormann "30.7", i.e. on 30 July.

The asterisk ★ symbolizes notes that appear in the collection of Heim's proof pages found after the war.

INDEX

Africa 166n143, 253–254, 306

Albrecht Knaus Verlag (German book publisher; published *Monologe* in 1980) 323–324, 327, 333n81, 341, 342, 344, 355, 357, 363–364, 368, 378n9

American Military Government (in Italy) 157–158

anti-Semitism 33, 43–44, 57n243, 98, 102, 233

Athenäum Verlag (German book publisher; published *Tischgespräche* in 1951) xi, 58, 61, 68, 71–85, 118–119, 121–122, 125, 145, 176, 180, 189

Auschwitz-Birkenau (Nazi slave labor and death camp in occupied Poland) xivn4, 311

Baumgarten, Eduard 234, 268, 280, 282, 284, 286–297, 300, 307, 321–324, 327, 330n18, 330n19, 330n21, 330n22, 331n27, 334n105, 335n142

BBC (British Broadcasting Corporation) 6, 90, 92, 133, 195, 353

Bekennende Kirche/Confessing Church 86

Below, Nicolaus von (Hitler's *Luftwaffe* adjutant) 63–67, 104n30, 104n32, 302, 315, 337n189

Berghof (Hitler's residence in the Bavarian Alps) 99, 193, 247

Berlin xi, xiii, 10, 18, 23, 26, 34, 57n243, 93, 96, 113–114, 120, 144, 151–152, 155, 193–195, 204, 239–240, 275n109, 279, 282, 297–300, 305, 306, 308,

309, 314, 319, 325, 327, 328, 331n45, 336n155

Besymenski, Lev (historian; editor of *Die letzten Notizen von Martin Bormann*) 67, 335n150

Bolshevism 17, 34, 41–42, 70, 250

Bolzano (city in northern Italy) 113–114, 156–158, 162n17

Bormann, Albert (Chief of Main Office I: Personal Affairs of the Führer) 114, 154

Bormann, Gerda xii, 65, 112–117, 144, 152–154, 156, 158, 161, 161n10, 171n235, 193, 233, 236, 279

Bormann Letters, The (1954) 17, 152, 155, 270, 284, 303, 328

Bormann, Martin (Reichsleiter) xi, xii–xiii, xivn4, 2, 5–10, 12–13, 18, 45–46, 49n70, 62–67, 85, 91–92, 94–98, 102, 105n33, 110n188, 112–125, 130–135, 137–156, 158–161, 147–148, 150–154, 159, 161, 168n184, 169n194, 170n232, 181, 186–193, 202, 231, 256, 259, 279, 287, 307, 321, 330n21, 349

Bormann, Martin, Jr. (son of Martin and Gerda Bormann) 114

Bormann-Vermerke xi, 91, 186, 220, 237, 268, 269, 283n73, 274n102, 280, 290, 302, 342, 343, 369, 375, 376, 385

Brechtken, Magnus (historian) 85, 108n132, 337n189

Britain 37, 51n115, 123–124, 236, 247, 253, 254, 261, 275n117, 303, 306

Broszat, Martin (historian) 321, 322, 339n223

Brown House (Braunes Haus, NSDAP Party HQ in Munich) 193–195, 197, 202–203, 224n95

Buchheim, Karl (historian at the IfZ) 85, 112–113, 117–118, 125, 130, 134, 146

Bullock, Alan (historian) 14–15, 230, 316

Bürgerbräukeller (beer hall and NSDAP meeting venue in Munich) 214, 239, 255

Cameron, Norman (translator of *Hitler's Table Talk*) 237, 238

Cameroon 252–253, 275n106

Carlyle, Thomas (historian; biographer of Frederick the Great) 313, 314, 316–319, 321, 328, 337n193, 337n198, 338n202, 338n207

Carrier, Richard (historian) xvii, 2–5, 238, 239, 251, 256, 258, 271n1, 326, 364, 369, 378, 382n94

Catholic Church 3, 41–43, 64, 94–95, 97, 150–151, 169n203, 178, 215, 223n48, 244

CCP (U.S. Army Central Collection Point in Munich) 58, 157, 172, 174, 193, 194, 203, 221, 222n2, 224n95

Christian, Gerda (one of Hitler's former secretaries) 300, 327

Christianity 2–4, 10, 41–43, 56n231, 86–87, 95–98, 154, 250

churches (in Germany; in general) 55n231, 86, 97, 109n164, 186, 204

Churchill, Winston (Prime Minister of Britain) 94, 181, 183–193, 303, 312

concentration camps/KZ xiii, 239, 311

Conversazioni segreti (Italian edition of *Hitler's Table Talk*, 1954) 137, 368

copyright (issue of, to the table talk notes) xi, 5, 59, 73, 114, 122, 125–126, 128, 130–131, 134–137, 160–161, 176, 192, 233–236, 271n18, 296, 321, 326, 356–358, 363, 366, 368, 370, 371

Dachau (Nazi KZ) 239, 346

DAP (Deutsche Arbeiterpartei) 44, 54n202, 212–213

Das eherne Hertz (book by Joseph Goebbels from 1943) 276n157

Der Bolshevismus von Moses bis Lenin (book by Dietrich Eckart from 1924) 42, 86, 96

Der Spiegel 19–20, 93, 145, 147, 154, 168n184, 284, 286, 290, 291, 293, 322

Deutsche Christen/German Christians 43, 86

Dickopf, Paul (former Nazi and spy) 153, 260

Dunkirk (1940) 303–306, 328, 388

Eastern Europe/front xiv, 40, 254, 275n106, 345

Eckart, Dietrich (Hitler's friend and ideological inspirator) 37, 42, 96, 207

Ehrnsberger, Joseph (CCP gallery assistant I Munich who found Heim's proof pages) 172–173, 203, 221, 221n1, 222n2

Elisabeth of Russia (Tsarina) 312, 315–320, 328, 337n181

Elser, Georg (tried to assassinate Hitler in 1939) 239–240

Engel, Gerhard (Hitler's Army Adjutant) 8, 60–62, 66, 76, 141, 177, 304, 323, 335n127, 360, 381n77

Evans, Richard J. 1–2, 251, 337n189

Fechner, Max (forger of Goebbels diaries) 277n157, 280

Feder, Gottfried (Nazi ideologue) 217

Federal Republic of German (FRG [BRD]; democratic West Germany) 120

Fest, Joachim (historian) 15, 37, 57n250, 88, 108nn132–133, 281, 316

FHQ (Führerhauptquartir; Hitler's military headquarters during the war) i, xiii, 8, 13, 27–28, 45, 55n214, 59, 62–64, 66, 69–70, 76, 116, 132–134, 136–139, 143, 153, 177, 201–204, 208, 220, 221, 277, 304, 323, 346, 362, 364, 384, 387, 387

First World War xii, 7, 23, 35, 43, 94, 231, 247, 254, 263, 305, 306, 314

Flammarion (French book publisher; published *Libres propos*) 126, 131, 147, 149, 154, 235, 237

Florence 155–159, 171n248

France 51n115, 131, 160, 168n184, 231, 232, 234, 237, 245, 246, 251, 253–255, 263, 274n102, 276n151, 277n157, 280, 286, 304–306, 314, 325, 333n86, 334n120, 369, 372

France Soir 234–235

Franco, Fransisco (General and dictator of Spain) 251, 253, 263

François-Poincet, André (former French Ambassador to Nazi Germany) 306, 325

Frank, Hans (Head of the General Government in Nazi occupied Poland) 41, 231, 315, 360–361

Frederick the Great 133, 312–319, 325, 337n198, 338n202

Frieser, Karl-Heinz (historian) 303–304

Fugger, *first name unknown* (Bormann's secretary; wrote down many table talk notes) 125, 202, 226n14, 352

Führerbau (Nazi administrative building in Munich) 58, 138–139, 192–193, 202–203, 221–222

Funk, Walter (former Reich Minister of Economics) 282, 284, 286–288, 290–292, 297–300, 327, 331n21, 331n49

Genoud, François iii, viii, ix, xii, xv, xviii, 2–7, 10, 17, 24–26, 33, 40, 47, 49–50, 64–65, 76, 90, 92–98, 112–161, 162n10, 167n168, 169n192, 172–173, 176–182, 184–193, 195, 197, 204, 210–212, 217–221, 224n73, 227n160, 232–237, 241–245, 247, 251, 255–260, 265–266, 268, 270, 272n31, 274n105, 276n144, 277n157, 279, 280–282, 284–303, 309, 311, 314, 317–319, 320–324, 327, 330n14, 340–349, 350–354, 356–358, 360, 362–366, 369–378, 385–386

German Democratic Republic (GDR [DDR]; Communist East Germany) 145, 147, 148–150, 168n184

Glover, Jonathan (philosopher) 3, 47n12

Goebbels, Joseph 24, 26–27, 40–41, 45, 94, 97, 116, 146, 169n192, 171n245, 215, 226n125, 229n204, 230, 247, 276n157, 277, 280, 289, 297, 313, 315–319, 321, 328, 329n6, 333n90, 338n207, 341, 342, 345, 385, 390

Goethe, Johan Wolfgang von (philosopher) 242

Göring, Hermann (top Nazi; Head of the *Luftwaffe*) 60, 304, 318

Günsche, Otto (Hitler's personal adjutant) 299, 318

Hanssen, K. W. (Bormann's personal assistant at the NSDAP Party HQ in Munich) 132, 138–139, 203–204, 221

Hasselbach, Hanskarl (Hitler's physician) 110n174

Hartt, Frederick (Head of MFAA in Italy) 157–159

Heß, Rudolf (top Nazi; Hitler's official successor until May 1941) xii–xxiv, 97, 193, 213–215, 297, 346

Heim, Heinrich xi–xvi, 2, 5–10, 12, 16, 18, 21, 23, 28–29, 31–34, 36–45,

48n32, 49n70, 49n74, 53n160, 54n195, 59–60, 63–67, 69–72, 80, 87, 89–96, 98–99, 113, 116–119, 121–123, 125, 128–134, 136–143, 145–149, 154, 157, 159–161, 166n143, 172, 174–205, 207–213, 216–218, 220–221, 235, 243–244, 247–248, 252, 253, 265–268, 274n86, 276n153, 290, 293, 307–311, 323–324, 332n70, 343–367, 374, 377, 379n25, 379n26, 380n29, 384–388

Heim's proof pages xii, 124, 157, 172–177, 181, 189, 191, 193, 194, 199, 200, 204, 207, 211, 212, 218, 220, 221, 266, 267, 344, 353, 365, 377, 384

Himmler, Heinrich (Head of the SS) 114, 240, 242, 273n70, 346

Hitler, Paula 115, 126–127, 130, 160, 163n72, 233, 272n23, 356, 363, 371

Hitlers politisches Testament (1981) 13, 17–19, 21, 24, 232, 244, 266, 270, 279, 284–285, 288, 291–292, 293, 294, 296, 298, 302, 303, 306–310, 321–329, 379n24, 388

Hitler's Secret Conversations (American title of *Hitler's Table Talk* published 1953) 5, 17, 47n22

Hitler's Table Talk (1953) iii, xi, 3–6, 14–17, 24–26, 33, 40, 91–92, 94–97, 99–102, 114, 123, 125, 127–128, 134, 137, 142, 149, 162n10, 179, 183, 187, 201, 208, 210, 211, 219–220, 221, 225n111, 230–232, 234, 236, 237, 240–246, 248–249, 251–252, 254–258, 261–262, 264–271, 279–282, 284–285, 295, 322, 326, 340–343, 351, 356, 358, 362–364, 368–369, 371, 385

Hitler's Table Talk (1973) 251, 267, 271–275, 281

Hitler's Table Talk (Enigma edition) 364–377

Hitler's testament (29 April 1945) 126, 137, 210, 303, 313

Hitlers Tischgespräche (1951) xi, xiii–xiv, 1–6, 9, 13–18, 21, 23–32, 48n32, 49n70, 50n97, 58, 62–66, 69–72, 75–82, 84–90, 93–94, 99–103, 112, 116, 118–119, 121, 123, 126–131, 134–137, 145, 154, 160, 173, 175–176, 178–179, 180–187, 189–190, 199, 201, 208, 209–211, 217, 219, 221, 224n73, 230–231, 234, 242, 252, 255, 257–258, 268, 271, 308, 341, 343, 345–347, 355–357, 363–364, 367, 373, 385, 388

Hitlers Tischgespräche (1963) xii, xiii, 98–103, 120, 124, 129, 144, 183, 187, 189, 209–210, 211, 268, 355–357, 367

Hitler's War (book by David Irving) 256, 258, 325

Hitlers zweites Buch (Hitler's second, unpublished, book) 26, 192, 208, 211, 370–371

Hoßbach Protocol 254

Hofer, Franz (*Gau*-leader of Tirol) 114–117, 152–153

Holocaust xiv, 16–17, 62, 98, 143, 256, 310–311, 322, 346, 386

Hummel, Helmut von (Bormann's Chief of Staff) 116, 145, 149–150, 153

Institut für Zeitgeschichte (IfZ) xi, 6, 58–63, 68, 73–78, 80–85, 90, 93–94, 103, 106n69, 109n147, 112–113, 117–123, 125, 127–131, 133–134, 137, 145–146, 160, 173–182, 184–185, 190, 192, 1945, 220, 225n107, 291, 296, 310, 321–322, 339n234, 341, 354, 371, 385

International Red Cross 149, 173

Irving, Clifford (forger of Howard Hughes interviews/documents) 329–330n8

Irving, David (writer & Holocaust denier) 1, 159, 172–173, 219, 251–252, 254–257, 267–269, 275n106, 275n123, 275n132, 285–286, 322–325, 339n227, 345–346, 379n26, 379n27

Italy xii, 113–115, 132, 139, 144–148, 153–157, 159, 162n17, 162n22, 170n231, 180, 202–203, 264

James, Ilse (one of Hitler's former secretaries) 138–139, 143–144, 167n165, 193

Japan 34–36, 100, 208–211, 306–307, 338n219

Jesus/Christ (Biblical figure) 42–43, 56n235, 64, 95–96, 110n174, 234, 336n160

Jews xiv, 17, 23, 35, 41–42, 44–45, 54n182, 95, 116, 123, 143, 166n143, 180, 210–211, 234, 256–257, 308, 310–311, 322, 318, 346, 379n26, 386, 388

Jochmann, Werner xi–xii, xviii, 4, 6, 8–9, 16–17, 23, 48n32, 57n245, 92–93, 129, 138, 148, 150, 169n201, 191–192, 200, 207, 210–211, 219, 224n89, 240–242, 243, 246, 252, 255–256, 261–262, 265–266, 272n30, 275n130, 276n153, 277n157, 307, 310, 323–325, 335n143, 340–354, 360, 362–368, 375–378, 383, 385

Juan in America (book by Eric Linklater) 261, 277n157

Junge, Traudl (one of Hitler's former secretaries) 45, 107n112, 279, 320

Junker, Paul W. (Head of the publishing house Athenäum Verlag) 58–61, 68–71, 74–84, 119–120, 145, 176–177, 180, 188

Kempner, Robert (American head prosecutor at the International Military Tribunal) 159

Kershaw, Ian (historian) 8, 13, 16, 22, 32, 49n70, 281, 316, 318, 330n10 374, 383n128

Knaus, Albrecht (Head of German book publisher Albrecht Knaus Verlag) 341–344, 346, 368

Koeppen, Werner (Alfred Rosenberg's representative in Hitler's FHQs) 8, 16–17, 21, 35–37, 40, 44–45, 48n32, 49n70, 55n214, 57n251, 64, 67, 258, 268, 362, 380n39

Krausnick, Helmut (historian) 127–128, 137

Krosigk, von Count Schwering (Nazi official) 316–321, 328–329, 337n193, 338n217, 388

Kubizek, August (Hitler's friend from adolescence) 35, 53n175, 90

Kujau, Konrad (forger of the "Hitler diaries" and other Hitler documents) 280, 314, 324–325, 337n185

Kuykendall, Karen 139–143, 166n143, 202–203, 226n125, 309, 348

Lammers, Hans Heinrich (Chief of the Reich Chancellery) 288–289, 292, 298, 300, 309, 323

Laske, Karl (journalist; biographer of François Genoud) 116, 147, 149

Last Days of Hitler, The (book by Trevor-Roper from 1947) 230–231, 233, 310, 316–320, 328, 337n189, 388

Lausanne (Genoud's hometown in Switzerland) 112–113, 125, 159, 190, 232, 236

Lebensraum (concept and policy) 37, 254

Leipold, Karl (German painter) 142, 202, 226n125

Lenin, Vladimir 37, 232

Leningrad/Saint Petersburg 40, 100

Le testament politique (1959) 15, 270, 279, 283, 289, 293, 302, 306, 315, 322, 327–328

Libres propos (Vol. I 1952) xi, xii, 2–3, 4–7, 15, 17, 24, 40, 49n71, 65, 91, 120, 130–131, 134–135, 147, 149, 179, 183, 208, 210–211, 218–219, 234, 238–240,

255, 265–266, 268, 270, 273n56, 273n77, 340, 342–343, 349, 357–358, 369, 374, 385

Libres propos (Vol. II 1954) xi, xii, 2–3, 25–26, 40, 49n71, 65, 102, 120, 130, 187, 210–211, 238–246, 249, 255, 261, 262–263, 265–266, 268, 270, 273n71, 273n79, 273n82, 340, 342–343, 349, 358, 369, 374, 385

Linklater, Eric (Scottish author) 262, 276n157

Lipstadt, Deborah (historian) 173, 251, 256, 346

LoC (Library of Congress) xii, 130, 174–176, 178, 191, 194, 220, 268, 314, 319, 359, 377

Longerich, Peter 9–10, 31, 33–35, 48n43, 55n231, 57n250, 97, 215, 303, 305, 334n118

Ludendorff, Erich (German General in the First World War & Hitler co-conspirator 1923) 214

Lukacs, John (historian) xi–xii, 17

Maranz, George (journalist) 148

Maser, Werner (historian) 17, 49n81, 56n233, 57n243, 129, 344, 360

Mau, Hermann (historian and first chief of the IfZ) 74–76, 78–85, 113, 118–125, 130–132, 134, 152, 160, 173–176, 178–179, 185, 189–190, 194, 220, 354

May, Karl (German author of adventure novels for children; favorite author of Hitler) 24, 44–45, 57n250

McDonough, Frank (historian) 281

Mein Kampf 8, 13–14, 17, 21, 26–46, 48n57, 52n141, 53n173, 53nn179–180, 57n243, 85–86, 200, 206–211, 217, 221, 225n118, 232, 253, 274n98, 275n106, 307–308, 313, 370–371, 383n121, 384, 387

Merano (city in northern Italy) 113–114, 117, 156, 158, 297

Miller, Robert (head of American book publisher Enigma Books) 364–378

Monologe im Führerhauptquartier (published by Knaus in 1980) xi, 1–4, 6, 9, 13, 15–17, 21, 23–26, 28–32, 34–41, 43–45, 48n32, 49n71, 53n181, 54n202, 57n251, 64–65, 70, 89, 91–95, 98, 120, 125, 131, 134, 142, 149–150, 169n192, 182, 184, 187, 197–201, 204, 206–211, 217–219, 221, 223n61, 224n93, 231, 235, 238–249, 251–252, 256–257,

261–266, 271, 273n56, 276n153, 290, 308, 324, 326, 340–348, 350–358, 360, 362–364, 366–368, 376–378, 385–386, 388

Monuments, Fine Arts and Archives (MFAA) 157

Moses (Biblical character) 4

Ms. 63 (Picker's manuscript for his 1963 edition) 211

Müller, Hans (Bormann's adjutant, and one of the authors of the table talks) xi–xii, xiv, 2, 8, 16, 40, 49n70, 49n74, 125, 160, 188, 204, 221, 231, 308, 351,359, 385, 388

Munich xi–xiv, 5, 27, 29, 35, 37, 41, 57n243, 58, 83, 92, 106n69, 115, 117, 124, 126, 129–130, 132–133, 139, 145, 148, 153, 157, 172–174, 180, 182, 185, 188, 191–195, 197, 201–204, 208, 212–213, 214–215, 220–221, 222n2, 235, 239, 255, 281, 313, 319, 324, 326, 329, 344n115, 342, 357, 360, 361

National Socialism iii, 12, 14–15, 20, 45–46, 55n231, 59, 61, 68, 87, 97, 106n74, 154, 182, 216, 232–234, 238, 250, 307, 333n99, 335n150, 384, 387

Niemöller, Martin 181, 224n73

NSDAP (Nationalsozialistische Deutsche Arbeiterpartei) xii–xiv, xivn4, 22, 27, 41, 43, 52n137, 58, 76, 92, 96, 106n69, 106n74, 132–133, 139, 172–173, 193, 203, 212–219, 220–221, 227nn166–167, 228n167, 250, 253, 260, 277n157, 311, 314, 330n21, 345, 346, 348, 356, 360, 370, 379n25

NSDAP Party program 211–214, 216–217, 250, 253

Obersalzberg 114, 145, 153, 193, 206–207

OKH (Oberkommando des Heeres) 304, 305

OKW (Oberkommando der Wehrmacht) 8, 99–100, 193

Oshima, Hiroshi (former Japanese Ambassador to Nazi Germany) 100–101, 306–307

Papen, Franz von 97, 106n74, 181

Paris (capital of France) 5–6, 148, 152, 154, 235–239, 282–285, 289, 292, 312, 322, 327

Péan, Pierre (French journalist; biographer of Genoud) 138, 144–146, 148–150,

168n184, 232, 258, 271n17, 346, 369, 370–376

photocopies (purported or real; of Genoud's document) 6, 88, 96, 112, 118–119, 123, 133–134, 137, 148, 159, 168n184, 177–179, 185, 189, 243, 285–287, 288–289, 294, 300, 323, 327, 343, 377, 379n12, 385

Picker, Henry xi–xiv, 1–6, 8–9, 12–15, 17–18, 21, 23, 25, 27, 31–32, 45, 48n31, 49n70, 51n127, 58–76, 78–90, 93–103, 104n13, 107n112, 109n148, 110n168, 112–113, 117–126, 128–139, 141, 144–145, 147, 154–155, 160–161, 175–193, 197, 200, 202–204, 209–212, 217–221, 224n93, 230, 234–235, 239–243, 252, 254–256, 258, 267–268, 274n105, 275n123, 276n152, 286, 323, 341–357, 350–351, 355–361 363–366, 380n33, 382n82, 385, 388

Pius XI (former Pope; author of *Mit brennender Sorge* of 1937) 42

Pyta, Wolfram (historian) xv, 7–10, 12–14, 33, 38–39, 45, 47n27, 47n29, 48n32, 54–55n206, 57n251, 57n254, 264–265, 313, 330n9, 339n232

Quick (German feature magazine) 75–85, 103, 107n112, 129, 235

Ramcke, Hermann-Bernard 148, 168n184

Rauschning, Hermann 14–15, 18–22, 24, 50n102, 50n104, 51n116, 230–232

Rechenberg, Hans (collaborator of François Genoud) 126–127, 282, 284, 286, 287, 288, 289–297, 299, 300, 303, 311, 313, 320, 326, 328, 331n22, 344

Reitsch, Hanna (test pilot and Hitler devotee) 309, 335n155

Rheindorf, Kurt (historian) 62–67, 104n18, 105n32, 323

Ribbentrop, Joachim von (top Nazi; Foreign Minister) 76, 99–100, 253, 306, 315

Ritter, Gerhard (historian; editor of *Tischgespräche* of 1951) xi, 17, 32, 58–65, 68–87, 93–94, 98–99, 101–103, 106nn74–75, 106n77, 109n164, 119–124, 135, 152, 172–182, 184, 188–190, 194, 211, 240, 243, 385–386

Rome (capital of Italy) 114–115, 132, 151–152, 156, 158, 167n168, 202

Roosevelt, Franklin Delano (POTUS) 315–316, 320

Rosenberg, Alfred (Nazi ideologue and Chief of *Ostministerium*) 2, 8, 10, 37, 41, 43–45, 64, 110n189, 159, 249

Rundstedt, Gerd von (German General) 304, 306

Rusconi, Edilio 115, 144–145, 155–156, 158, 161, 168n179

Russia 25, 34–37, 45, 53n179, 89, 137, 140, 239, 257, 312–313, 325, 328, 335n150

Russian POWs 89

Ryback, Timothy (historian) 23, 51n118, 314, 318

Sachsenhausen (Nazi KZ) 239

Schacht, Cordula (Genoud's lawyer; daughter of Nazi Hjalmar Schacht) xviii, 96–97, 148, 159, 168n179, 169n192, 352

Schacht, Hjalmar (former Chief of the Reich bank) 69, 72–75, 96, 181

Schaub, Julius (Hitler's personal adjutant) 41, 80, 135, 145, 231, 300, 360–361, 381n84

Schmier, Louis 259–260

Schmitz, Theodor (Catholic priest and legal guardian of the Bormann children after the war) 113–118, 120, 144, 146, 149–154, 156, 161, 162n28, 169n203, 234

Schopenhauer, Artur (philosopher) 41, 231

Schramm, Percy Ernst (historian and editor of the 2nd edition of *Tischgespräche*) xi, 69–70, 90, 98–103, 110n174, 129, 144, 181–183, 209, 211, 223n53, 223n56, 227n160, 267, 273n23, 286, 355–356, 360

Schroeder, Christa (one of Hitler's former secretaries) 7, 45, 91, 109n152, 210, 227n157, 299–300, 303, 320, 327, 334n113, 338n209, 338n219, 348, 380n34

Second World War 231, 315

Seewald, Sixt A. (Head of Seewald Verlag) 363

Seewald Verlag (German book publisher; published *Tischgespräche* in 1963) 363

Seidl, Alfred (Paula Hitler's lawyer) 115–116, 126–127

Sereny, Gitta (journalist) 146, 193

Sheridan, Eugene R. 220

Simms, Brendan (historian) 281, 307

Siviero, Rudolfo 115, 144, 150, 155–161, 170n231, 170n233, 171n235, 171n248, 172

Smyth, Craig H. (head of the CCP in Munich) 194, 222n2, 224n96

Soviet Union xi–xii, 17, 39–40, 68, 70, 94, 154, 308
Spandauer Tagebücher (book by Albert Speer) 57n250, 87–89, 108n138
Speer, Albert 22, 87–89, 108n132, 109n148, 110n188, 166n143, 193, 280, 287, 291, 315, 337n194, 351, 380n43
Spögler, Franz (*SS-Obersturmbannführer*) 153
Stasi (Ministerium für Staatssicherheit, East German security service) 113, 149–153, 161, 169n203
Stehle, Hansjakob (historian and journalist) 150, 153–154, 170n222, 170n232
Stenography/stenographer (the table talks as stenographic records) xi–xii, xivn3, 5–6, 8–10, 12, 18, 20–21, 23, 46, 50n97, 60, 63–64, 86, 91, 93–94, 98, 109n152, 125, 128, 135–136, 138, 147, 160–161, 180, 185, 191–192, 227n157 271n18, 303, 316, 355, 356, 360–361, 380
Stevens, Richard Henry (translator of e.g. *Hitler's Table Talk*) 237–240, 242–244, 246, 246, 249, 258, 262 264–266, 269, 270, 271, 281, 294–295, 312, 343, 373, 374
Straßer, Otto (rival to Hitler in the early NSDAP) 106n74, 217, 311
Streicher, Julius (Nazi editor of the anti-Semitic newspaper *Der Stürmer*) 2, 228n167

Testament of Adolf Hitler, The (1961) iii, xi–xii, xiv, 14–17, 232, 270, 279, 310, 329n4, 330n17, 330n19, 331n25, 332n74, 336n164, 336n168, 336n170, 337n197, 338n219, 388
Testament of Adolf Hitler, The (US edition 1978) 329n4
Third Reich/Nazi Germany iii, 1, 14, 17, 22, 37, 46, 50n104, 56n238, 69, 93, 97, 101, 123–124, 133, 144, 153, 155, 160, 193, 226n125, 239, 247, 253–254, 258, 270 281, 325, 335n155, 353, 387
Toland, John (historian) 6, 17–18, 67, 95, 105n33, 129–130, 132–133, 139, 141, 164n94, 165n116, 166n143, 305–306, 315–316, 345, 359–360
Treblinka (Nazi death camp in Poland) 311
Trevor-Roper, Hugh R. (historian; instrumental in the publication of all of Genoud's documents) xi, 2–3, 6, 15, 92, 96, 98, 113–115, 127–128, 131, 144, 151–152, 161n10, 172, 212, 217, 219, 230–238, 250–252, 258, 259–260, 267, 268–272, 272n40, 277n174, 281,

282–298, 300, 301–302, 310, 312, 316–317, 322–328, 331n49, 332n73, 332n81, 333n82, 337n192, 337n196, 337n197, 339n239, 343, 357, 360, 364, 365–368, 377, 385, 388
Troost, Paul (architect) 194
Tsushima (battle of) 34–36
Tyrell, Albrecht (historian) 217

Ullrich, Volker (historian) 24, 33, 45, 54n202, 55n231, 110n174, 247, 303, 333n99, 352, 380n496
United States 37, 75–76, 78, 80–82, 85, 160, 171–175, 236, 261, 277n157, 306–307, 314, 329n4, 364
United States Holocaust Memorial Museum (USHMM) 160

Vatican 87, 215
Vienna (capital of Austria) 22, 29, 32–33, 35, 53n175, 218, 225n115
Voegelin, Eric (political scientist) 182

Walkenhorst, Heinrich (Nazi official) 308, 356, 360
Walter, Horst 286, 287–288
Washington, D.C. (capital of the United States) xii, 75, 81–82, 172, 189
Weber, Thomas (historian) 22, 36–37, 55n206, 105n33, 207
Weidenfeld & Nicolson (British book publisher; published *Hitler's Table Talk* 1953) 3, 266, 267, 378
Weinberg, Gerhard (historian) 191–192, 194–195, 208–211, 337n181, 365, 368, 370, 372, 376
Werwolf (FHQ near Winniza in the Ukraine) 66, 277n157
Winkler, Willi (journalist; biographer of François Genoud) 76, 85, 90, 93–94, 109n147, 144–146, 149–150, 153, 156, 168n184, 259, 276n144, 77n173, 285, 353
Wolff, Karl (general in the Waffen-SS) 114–117, 162n17
Wolfsschanze (FHQ near Kertzyn [previously Rastenburg] in Poland) 94, 99, 138, 193, 355
World War I *see* First World War
World War II *see* Second World War

Zitelmann, Rainer (historian) 15, 18–23, 50n97, 50n102, 215–216, 229n198
Zoller, Albert (pseudonymous author) 109n152, 210, 320, 338n219

Printed in Great Britain
by Amazon